Lecture Notes in Computer Science   13740

More information about this series at https://link.springer.com/bookseries/558

Javier Troya · Brahim Medjahed ·
Mario Piattini · Lina Yao ·
Pablo Fernández · Antonio Ruiz-Cortés (Eds.)

Service-Oriented Computing

20th International Conference, ICSOC 2022
Seville, Spain, November 29 – December 2, 2022
Proceedings

 Springer

Editors
Javier Troya (iD)
University of Malaga
Málaga, Spain

Brahim Medjahed
University of Michigan-Dearborn
Dearborn, MI, USA

Mario Piattini (iD)
University of Castilla-La Mancha
Ciudad Real, Spain

Lina Yao
The University of New South Wales
Sydney, NSW, Australia

Pablo Fernández (iD)
University of Seville
Seville, Spain

Antonio Ruiz-Cortés
University of Seville
Seville, Spain

ISSN 0302-9743   ISSN 1611-3349   (electronic)
Lecture Notes in Computer Science
ISBN 978-3-031-20983-3   ISBN 978-3-031-20984-0   (eBook)
https://doi.org/10.1007/978-3-031-20984-0

This Springer imprint is published by the registered company Springer Nature Switzerland AG
The registered company address is: Gewerbestrasse 11, 6330 Cham, Switzerland

Preface

We were pleased to hold the 20th International Conference on Service-Oriented Computing (ICSOC 2022) back in person after organizing it virtually for two consecutive years due to the COVID-19 pandemic. The present edition took place in the beautiful city of Sevilla (Spain) from November 29 to December 2, 2022. The conference is the premier international forum for academics, industry researchers, developers, and practitioners to report and share groundbreaking work in service-oriented computing. It provides a high-quality forum for presenting results and discussing ideas that further our knowledge and understanding of the various aspects (e.g. application and system aspects) related to service computing with a particular focus on artificial intelligence, machine learning, big data analytics, the Internet of Things (IoT), and emerging technologies, including quantum computing, blockchain, chatbots, and green IT. This edition of ICSOC built upon a history of successful series of previous editions in Toulouse (France), Hangzhou (China), Malaga (Spain), Banff (Canada), Goa (India), Paris (France), Berlin (Germany), Shanghai (China), Paphos (Cyprus), San Francisco (USA), Stockholm (Sweden), Sydney (Australia), Vienna (Austria), Chicago (USA), Amsterdam (the Netherlands), New York (USA), Trento (Italy), Dubai (United Arab Emirates, virtual), and last year's online edition.

ICSOC 2022 followed the two-round submission and reviewing process introduced in the previous edition. It was organized in five tracks as they relate to service computing research: (1) Service-Oriented Technology Trends, (2) Machine Learning and Artificial Intelligence, (3) Big Data Analytics, (4) Internet of Things (IoT), and (5) Emerging Technologies. Each track was managed by a track chair, hence enhancing the quality and rigor of the paper review process. The conference attracted 221 paper submissions (31 received in the first round) co-authored by researchers, practitioners, and academics from different countries across all continents. Each paper submission was carefully reviewed by at least three members of the Program Committee (PC); the reviews were followed by discussions moderated by a senior PC member who made a recommendation in the form of a meta-review to the track chairs and PC co-chairs. The PC consisted of 218 world-class experts in service-oriented computing and related areas (196 PC members and 22 senior PC members) from different countries across all continents. Based on the recommendations, and the discussions, 29 papers (13.2%) were accepted as full papers. We also selected 15 short papers (6%). In total, 16 of the 31 papers submitted in the first round were recommended for resubmission with minor or major revisions, and 12 of the 16 papers were accepted as full or short papers. Additionally, ICSOC 2022 included four invited vision papers from prominent researchers; these papers underwent a simplified review process aimed at judging visionary ideas that can drive future research efforts.

The conference program also included two keynotes from distinguished researchers:

- Quantum Service-Oriented Computing: Challenges and Research Directions for Quantum and Hybrid Software System, given by Juan M. Murillo (University of Extremadura, Spain)
- Securing Data Pipelines Along the Cloud Continuum: The MUSA Approach, given by Ernesto Damiani (University of Milan, Italy)

Finally, tutorials, a PhD symposium, a demo session, and the following four workshops were organized to broaden the scope of ICSOC 2022:

- The 6th Workshop on Adaptive Service-oriented and Cloud Applications (ASOCA 2022).
- The 3rd International Workshop on AI-enabled Process Automation (AI-PA 2022).
- The 3rd International Workshop on Architectures for Future Mobile Computing and Internet of Things (FMCIoT 2022).
- The 18th International Workshop on Engineering Service-Oriented Applications and Cloud Services (WESOACS 202).

We would like to express our gratitude to all individuals, institutions, and sponsors that supported ICSOC 2022. We would like to thank all authors and participants for their insightful work and discussions. We are grateful to the members of the Senior Program Committee, the international Program Committee, and the external reviewers for a rigorous and robust reviewing process. ICSOC 2022 paper management was performed through the Conftool Conference Management System. We are grateful to the professional technical support provided by Conftool system administrators.

We would like to thank the ICSOC Steering Committee for entrusting us with organizing the 20th edition of this prestigious conference. We are grateful to all the members of the Organizing Committee and all who contributed to make ICSOC 2022 a successful event. We are indebted to the local arrangements team from the University of Seville for the successful organization of all conference, social, and co-located events. We also acknowledge the prompt and professional support from Springer, who published these proceedings as part of the Lecture Notes in Computer Science series.

November 2022

Pablo Fernández
Brahim Medjahed
Mario Piattini
Antonio Ruiz Cortés
Lina Yao

Organization

General Chairs

Pablo Fernandez   University of Seville, Spain
Antonio Ruiz Cortés   University of Seville, Spain

Program Committee Chairs

Brahim Medjahed   University of Michigan-Dearborn, USA
Mario Piattini   University of Castilla-La Mancha, Spain
Lina Yao   UNSW, Australia

Local Organization Committee Chair

Jose Maria Garcia   University of Seville, Spain

Infrastructure Co-chairs

Octavio Martín-Díaz   University of Seville, Spain
Julio Barbancho   University of Seville, Spain

Social Events Chair

Cristina Cabanillas   University of Seville, Spain

Social Media and Multimedia Co-chairs

Joaquín Peña   University of Seville, Spain
Alfonso Bravo   University of Seville, Spain

Volunteers Co-chairs

Carlos Müller   University of Seville, Spain
Bedilia Estrada   University of Seville, Spain

Communications Chair

Alfonso Marquez   University of Seville, Spain

Finance Chair

Bernd Krämer   University of Hagen, Germany

Focus Area 1: Service-Oriented Technology Trends Chair

Marco Aiello   University of Stuttgart, Germany

Focus Area 2: Machine Learning/Artificial Intelligence Chair

Xianzhi Wang   University of Technology Sydney, Australia

Focus Area 3: Big Data Analytics Chair

Qi Yu   Rochester Institute of Technology, USA

Focus Area 4: Internet of Things (IoT) Chair

Azadeh Ghari Neiat   Deakin University, Australia

Focus Area 5: Emerging Technologies Chair

Manuel Resinas   University of Seville, Spain

Demo Co-chairs

Guadalupe Ortiz   University of Cádiz, Spain
Cesare Pautasso   University of Lugano, Switzerland
Christian Zirpins   Karlsruhe University of Applied Sciences, Germany

Workshop Co-chairs

Raffaela Mirandola   Politecnico di Milano, Italy
Elena Navarro   University of Castilla-La Mancha, Spain

Ph.D. Symposium Chair

Andrea Delgado   Universidad de la República, Uruguay

Publicity Co-chairs

Juan Boubeta-Puig   University of Cádiz, Spain
Zheng Song   University of Michigan – Dearborn, USA
Wei Zhang   University of Adelaide, Australia

Publication Chair

Javier Troya   University of Malaga, Spain

Sponsorhip Chair

José Antonio Parejo   University of Seville, Spain

Web Co-chairs

Javier Berrocal   University of Extremadura, Spain
José Manuel García   University of Extremadura, Spain

Steering Committee

Boualem Benatallah   UNSW, Australia
Athman Bouguettaya   University of Sydney, Australia
Fabio Casati   University of Trento, Italy
Bernd J. Krämer   University of Hagen, Germany
Winfried Lamersdorf   University of Hamburg, Germany
Heiko Ludwig   IBM, USA
Mike Papazoglou   Tilburg University, The Netherlands
Jian Yang   Macquarie University, Australia

Senior Program Committee

Boualem Benatallah   UNSW, Australia
Athman Bouguettaya   University of Sydney, Australia
Carlos Canal   University of Malaga, Spain
Fabio Casati   University of Trento, Italy
Flavio De Paoli   Univerità di Milano-Bicocca, Italy
Schahram Dustdar   TU Wien, Austria
Aditya Ghose   University of Wollongong, Australia
Hakim Hacid   Zayed University, United Arab Emirates
Mohand Said Hacid   University of Lyon, France
Zakaria Maamar   Zayed University, United Arab Emirates
Cesare Pautasso   University of Lugano, Switzerland
Barbara Pernice   Politecnico di Milano, Italy
Gustavo Rossi   UNLP, Argentina
Michael Q. Sheng   Macquarie University, Australia
Stefan Tai   TU Berlin, Germany
Farouk Toumani   LIMOS, France
Mathias Weske   University of Potsdam, Germany
Jian Yang   Macquarie University, Australia
Liang Zhanf   Fudan University, China

Program Committee

Marco Aiello   University of Stuttgart, Germany
Alessandro Aldini   University of Urbino, Italy

Mohammad Allahbakhsh	Macquarie University, Australia
Moayad M. Alshangiti	University of Jeddah, Saudi Arabia
Yacine Atif	University of Skövde, Sweden
Marcos Baez	Bielefeld University of Applied Sciences, Germany
Mohammed Bahutair	CSIRO, Australia
Dilum Bandara	CSIRO, Australia
Luciano Baresi	Politecnico di Milano, Italy
Thais Batista	UFRN, Brazil
Amin Beheshti	Macquarie University, Australia
Khalid Belhajjame	Université Paris Dauphine, France
Moez Ben Haj Hmida	National Engineering School of Tunis (ENIT), Tunisia
Salima Benbernou	Université de Paris, France
Nadia Bennani	INSA Lyon, LIRIS, France
Djamal Benslimane	University of Lyon, France
Javier Berrocal	University of Extremadura, Spain
Sami Bhiri	Telecom SudParis, France
Walter Binder	University of Lugano, Switzerland
Juan Boubeta-Puig	University of Cádiz, Spain
Omar Boucelma	Aix-Marseille University, France
Lars Braubach	Hochschule Bremen, Germany
Uwe Breitenbücher	University of Stuttgart, Germany
Antonio Brogi	University of Pisa, Italy
Antonio Bucchiarone	Fondazione Bruno Kessler, Italy
Christoph Bussler	Robert Bosch LLC, USA
Cristina Cabanillas	University of Seville, Spain
Wing-Kwong Chan	City University of Hong Kong, Hong Kong
Francois Charoy	University of Lorraine, France
Faouzi Ben Charrada	University of Tunis El Manar, Tunisia
Sanjay Chaudhary	Ahmedabad University, India
Feifei Chen	Deakin University, Australia
Liang Chen	Sun Yat-sen University, China
Shiping Chen	CSIRO, Australia
Lin Chen (Liana)	LinkedIn, USA
Lawrence Chung	University of Texas at Dallas, USA
Marco Comuzzi	UNIST, South Korea
Gianpiero Costantino	IIT-CNR, Italy
Hoa Khanh Dam	University of Wollongong, Australia
Valeria de Castro	Universidad Rey Juan Carlos, Spain
Martina De Sanctis	Gran Sasso Science Institute, Italy
Bruno Defude	Telecom SudParis, France
Andrea Delgado	Universidad de la República, Uruguay
Adela del-Río-Ortega	Universidad de Sevilla, Spain
Shuiguang Deng	Zhejiang University, China
Francesco Di Cerbo	SAP, France
Claudio Di Ciccio	Sapienza University of Rome, Italy
Gregorio Diaz Descalzo	Universidad de Castilla - La Mancha, Spain

Chen Ding	Toronto Metropolitan University, Canada
Hai Dong	RMIT University, Australia
Khalil Drira	LAAS-CNRS, France
Yucong Duan	Hainan University, China
Joyce El Haddad	Université Paris-Dauphine, France
Abdelkarim Erradi	Qatar University, Qatar
Rik Eshuis	Eindhoven University of Technology, The Netherlands
Onyeka Ezenwoye	Augusta University, USA
Noura Faci	Université Lyon 1, CNRS, France
Xiu Susie Fang	Donghua University, China
Marcelo Fantinato	University of São Paulo, Brazil
Sheik Mohammad Mostakim Fattah	University of Adelaide, Australia
Zhiyong Feng	Tianjin University, China
Afonso Ferreira	CNRS, France
Joao E. Ferreira	University of Sao Paulo, Brazil
George Feuerlicht	University of Technology Sydney, Australia
Marios-Eleftherios Fokaefs	École Polytechnique Montréal, Canada
Luca Foschini	University of Bologna, Italy
Xiang Fu	Hofstra, USA
Walid Gaaloul	Telecom SudParis, France
N. D. Gangadhar	M S Ramaiah University of Applied Sciences, India
G. R. Gangadharan	NIT Tiruchirappalli, India
Felix Garcia	University of Castilla-La Mancha, Spain
José María García	Universidad de Sevilla, Spain
Ilche Georgievski	University of Stuttgart, Germany
Mohamed Graiet	ISIMM, Tunisia
Daniela Grigori	Université Paris-Dauphine, France
Georg Grossmann	University of South Australia, Australia
Nawal Guermouche	Université de Toulouse, France
Jun Han	Swinburne University of Technology, Australia
Chihab Hanachi	IRIT, University of Toulouse, France
Qiang He	Swinburne University of Technology, Australia
Richard Hull	Unaffiliated, USA
Fuyuki Ishikawa	National Institute of Informatics, Japan
Pooyan Jamshidi	University of South Carolina, USA
Hai Jin	HUST, China
Ejub Kajan	State University of Novi Pazar, Serbia
Anup Kumar Kalia	IBM T. J. Watson Research Center, USA
Dimka Karastoyanova	University of Groningen, The Netherlands
Sokratis Katsikas	Norwegian University of Science and Technology, Norway
Marouane Kessentini	University of Michigan, USA
Hamamache Kheddouci	LIRIS, Lyon 1 University, France
Kais Klai	University of Paris 13, France

Igor Kotenko	St. Petersburg Institute for Informatics and Automation of the Russian Academy of Sciences (SPIIRAS), Russia
Gerald Kotonya	Lancaster University, UK
Hemza Labbaci	University of Tours, France
Ladjel Bellatreche	ISAE-ENSMA, France
Philippe Lalanda	UGA, France
Manuel Lama	University of Santiago de Compostela, Spain
Alexander Lazovik	University of Groningen, The Netherlands
Weiping Li	Peking University, China
Ying Li	Zhejiang University, China
Marin Litoiu	York University, Canada
Xiao Liu	Deakin University, Australia
Xuanzhe Liu	Peking University, China
Xumin Liu	Rochester Institute of Technology, USA
Heiko Ludwig	IBM, USA
Yutao Ma	Wuhan University, China
Khalid Mahmood Malik	Oakland University, USA
Maude Manouvrier	University of Paris Dauphine, France
Esperanza Marcos	Universidad Rey Juan Carlos, Spain
Philippe Massonet	CETIC, Belgium
Massimo Mecella	Sapienza Università di Roma, Italy
Nizar Messai	University of Tours, France
Tommi Mikkonen	University of Helsinki, Finland
Sumaira Sultan Minhas	Fatima Jinnah Women University, Pakistan
Raffaela Mirandola	Politecnico di Milano, Italy
Sajib Mistry	Curtin University, Australia
Mohamed Wiem Mkaouer	Rochester Institute of Technology, USA
Lars Moench	University of Hagen, Germany
Hamid Reza Motahari-Nezhad	EY AI Lab, USA
Michael Mrissa	University of Primorska, Slovenia
Juan Manuel Murillo	University of Extremadura, Spain
Adel Nadjaran Toosi	Monash University, Australia
Nanjangud C. Narendra	Ericsson Research, India
Azadeh Neiat	Deakin University, Australia
Anne Ngu	Texas State University, USA
Lanshun Nie	Harbin Institute of Technology, China
Talal H. Noor	Taibah University, Saudi Arabia
Alex Norta	Tallinn University, Estonia
Guadalupe Ortiz	University of Cádiz, Spain
Ali Ouni	ETS Montreal, University of Quebec, Canada
Helen Paik	UNSW, Australia
Li Pan	Shandong University, China
Óscar Pedreira Fernández	Universidade da Coruña, Spain
Ricardo Perez-Castillo	University of Castilla-La Mancha, Spain

Qi Yu	Rochester Institute of Technology, USA
Dong Yuan	University of Sydney, China
Gianluigi Zavattaro	University of Bologna, Italy
Uwe Zdun	University of Vienna, Austria
Wei Zhang	University of Adelaide, Australia
Xuyun Zhang	Macquarie University, Australia
Weiliang Zhao	Macquarie University, Australia
Zhangbing Zhou	China University of Geosciences, China
Floriano Zini	Free University of Bozen-Bolzano, Italy
Christian Zirpins	Karlsruhe University of Applied Sciences, Germany

Additional Reviewers

Imen Abdennadher	University of Sfax, Tunisia
Nasiru Aboki	University of Stuttgart, Germany
Mohammad Abu-Lebdeh	Concordia University, Canada
Ali Akoglu	University of Arizona, USA
Faiza Belala	Constantine 2 University, Algeria
Cheima Ben Njima	University of Sousse, Tunisia
Lamia Ben Amor	University of Sfax, Tunisia
Mohamed Reda Bouadjenek	Deakin University, Australia
Ismael Bouassida Rodriguez	University of Sfax, Tunisia
Khouloud Boukadi	Université de Sfax, Tunisia
Josue Castaneda	CNRS-LAAS, France
Saoussen Cheikhrouhou	University of Sfax, Tunisia
Vincenzo Ciancia	National Research Council, Italy
Umberto Costa	UFRN, Brazil
Javier A. Espinosa Oviedo	University of Lyon, France
Michela Fazzolari	National Research Council, Italy
Amal Gassara	CRNS, Tunisia
Carmem Hara	Universidade Federal do Parana, Brazil
Slim Kallel	University of Sfax, Tunisia
Nesrine Khabou	University of Sfax, Tunisia
Faten Kharbat	Al Ain University, United Arab Emirates
Somayeh Kianpisheh	Concordia University, Canada
Imen Lahyani	ENIS, Tunisia
Andrew Leonce	Zayed University, United Arab Emirates
Faiza Loukil	Université Jean Moulin Lyon 3, France
Abderrahmane Maaradji	ECE Paris, France
Ilaria Matteucci	IIT-CNR, Italy
Emna Mezghani	Orange Labs, France
Naouel Moha	UQAM, Canada
Riad Mokadem	IRIT, France
Amira Mouakher	University of Burgundy Franche-Comté, France
Fatma Outay	Zayed University, United Arab Emirates
Alex Palesandro	Politecnico di Torino, Italy

Deep Pandey	Rochester Institute of Technology, USA
Francesco Pierri	Politecnico di Milano, Italy
Xiaofan Que	Rochester Institute of Technology, USA
Sana Sellami	Université d'Aix-Marseille, France
Brian Setz	University of Stuttgart, Germany
Plácido A. Souza Neto	Instituto Federal do Rio Grande do Norte, Brazil
George Spanoudakis	City University London, UK
Angelo Spognardi	Sapienza University of Rome, Italy
Nicolas Travers	De Vinci Research Centre, France
Genoveva Vargas-Solar	CNRS, France
José Luis Zechinelli Martini	Universidad de las Américas Puebla, Mexico
Ervine Zheng	Rochester Institute of Technology, USA
Yuansheng Zhu	Rochester Institute of Technology, USA

Keynotes Talks

Quantum Service-Oriented Computing: Challenges and Research Directions for Quantum and Hybrid Software System

Juan Manuel Murillo

University of Extremadura, Spain

Quantum Computing is raising more interest day by day. The basis provided by Quantum Mechanics enabled the development of the Quantum Information Theory and the first Quantum Computers. From the hardware side, the advances are undeniable. Recently, the first 1000 qubit computer has been announced to be released next 2023.

Nevertheless, from the point of view of Software Engineering, advances in Quantum Computing are having less visibility. Part of the research community is still conservative and thinks that it is still early to tackle the development of quantum software engineering techniques. The reason is that how the quantum computers of the future will look like is still unknown. However, regardless of how they will be, there are some facts that we can affirm today. The first is that quantum and classical computers will coexist, each dedicated to the tasks at which they are most efficient. The second is that quantum computers will be part of the cloud infrastructure and will be, indeed already are, accessible through the Internet. Third, as is the case today, complex software systems will be made up of smaller pieces that will collaborate with each other. Fourth, some of those pieces will be quantum, therefore the systems of the future will be hybrid. Finally, the coexistence and interaction between the components of said hybrid systems will be supported by service composition and the development of quantum services will be governed by the current general criteria of Service Engineering (composability, reusability, maintainability, etc.).

Bearing all of the above in mind, this talk analyzes the challenges that the integration of quantum services poses to Service-Oriented Computing. It determines what are the current technologies that can be used for creating and operating quantum services, the limitations they present for doing that and those technologies that do not exist today but can already begin to be designed.

Securing Data Pipelines Along the Cloud Continuum: The MUSA Approach

Ernesto Damiani

Khalifa University, United Arab Emirates

In the past decade, many organizations have re-designed their operation by migrating their key business processes (to name but a few, procurement, supply chains, Human Resources management) to global public clouds, where scalability and cost flexibility could be achieved. Today, a new wave of Digital Transformation is changing again how people live, consume and work. Processes in key domains like transportation, supply chain management and healthcare need to provide low latency, high throughput and distributed access. Furthermore, their execution needs to take place within well-specified perimeters supporting traffic segregation, in order to guarantee data protection, security and resilience. The 5G architecture promises to fulfill these new requirements, supporting a "Cloud Continuum" that allows for the deployment of micro-services on the 5G operators core networks (edge-on-network) as a complement to classic edge-on-premises and cloud options. Based on the approach of the MUSA project to delivering open science research pipelines over 5G, the talk discusses the open challenges that need to be tackled to keep this promise, from the instrumentation of the 5G infrastructure to support for securing services and process orchestrations along the continuum.

Contents

Service Personalization, Recommendation, and Crowdsourcing

Blockchain

IoT and Green Computing

Vision Papers

Service Modeling and Mining

Optimization of BPMN Processes
via Automated Refactoring

Francisco Durán[1]($\boxtimes$) and Gwen Salaün[2]

[1] ITIS Software, University of Málaga, Málaga, Spain
fdm@uma.es
[2] Univ. Grenoble Alpes, CNRS, Grenoble INP, Inria, LIG, 38000 Grenoble, France

Abstract. Business process optimization has become a strategic aspect of companies' management due to the potential of cost reduction and throughput improvement. There are several ways to achieve process optimization, depending on the level of expressiveness of the processes at hand. In this paper, we focus on processes described using BPMN, but also including an explicit description of execution time and resources associated with tasks. We propose a refactoring procedure whose final goal is to reduce the total execution time of the process given as input. Such a procedure relies on refactoring operations that reorganize the tasks in the process by taking into account the resources used by those tasks. This process refactoring technique is fully automated by a tool that we implemented and applied on several examples for validation purposes.

1 Introduction

Context. Business process optimization is a strategic activity in organizations because of its potential to increase profit margins and reduce operational costs. Optimization is however a difficult task to be achieved manually since several parameters should be taken into account (execution times, resources, costs, etc.). These parameters are not systematically included in existing languages used for modelling and managing business processes. Moreover, optimization requires a high level of expertise that not all users have. Automated techniques are thus required to optimize a given process for certain criteria of interest.

In this work, we assume that a description of a business process is given using the standardized workflow modelling language BPMN. This language allows us to define the set of tasks involved in a process and the order in which they should be executed. This behavioural description of the model can be extended with information on the time each task takes to execute and an explicit description of the resources required for executing each task. As a consequence, the resulting model of the process does not only take into account behavioural aspects but also quantitative aspects.

Motivations. Processes are not built once and for all in a monolithic way. During their life time, processes have to be changed or updated for several possible reasons: addition or suppression of some specific task, improvement of the process with respect to a given criterion (e.g., overall execution time), adjustment of the process to consider a new regulation or internal directive, etc. When writing a process or when updating it as suggested before, the quality or correctness of the process has to be preserved. This might not be the case if process writing or reengineering/refactoring is achieved manually by human beings. Moreover, refactoring steps may be very difficult to apply when BPMN models also take into account quantitative aspects and when some criteria, such as resource usage or execution time, are used to guide the refactoring steps so as to generate an optimal process (e.g., the process must execute as quickly as possible). Therefore, there is a need for automated refactoring techniques in order to generate an optimal version of a process during its writing or update.

Proposal. Given a process model, we propose some optimization techniques that rely on the refactoring of the given process. By changing the structure, we aim at generating a different process whose overall execution time is reduced compared to the original process. The main idea is to increase the level of parallelism of the tasks involved in the process. The refactoring steps should however be applied with care. For instance, it is not helpful to put in parallel two tasks using a same resource since they will compete for such a resource and a resource cannot be involved in two different tasks at the same time. Moreover, it does not always make sense to put two tasks in parallel, and in some cases such causal dependencies must be preserved (e.g., some product must be packaged before its delivery).

More precisely, we propose in this paper optimization techniques based on process refactoring. Our approach takes as input a BPMN process extended with time and resources associated with tasks, and generates as output a new version of this process. To do so, we first analyze the process to identify tasks that could be executed earlier because the resources that one of these tasks requires for its execution are available before its execution begins. Alternative processes are generated by moving these tasks backwards (closer to the initial node). Our approach works using an iterative approach. Each newly generated process is similarly analyzed, and new alternative processes are generated in the same way. Since many processes can be synthesized by our approach, there are different ways to generate and handle these new processes. We have implemented and carried out experiments with two strategies: (i) an exhaustive exploration of all possible processes generated by refactoring, and (ii) a guided exploration of the new processes by using some heuristic. All these techniques are fully automated in a tool that we implemented and which has been validated on many examples.

Organization. The rest of this paper is organized as follows. Section 2 introduces the considered subset of the BPMN notation and its extension with time and resources. Section 3 provides an overview of the different steps of our approach. Section 4 focuses on the refactoring process to change the structure of the process. Section 5 presents the tool support and some experimental results to assess the accuracy and performance of our approach. Section 6 compares our solution to related work and Sect. 7 concludes.

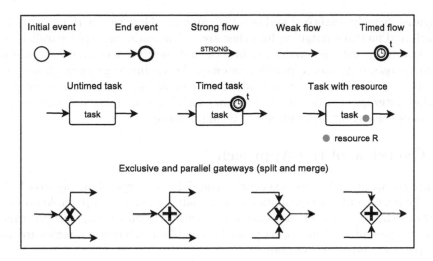

Fig. 1. Supported BPMN syntax

2   BPMN with Time and Resources

BPMN 2.0 (BPMN, as a shorthand, in the rest of this paper) was published as an ISO/IEC standard [10] in 2013 and is nowadays extensively used for modeling and developing business processes. In this paper, we focus on activity diagrams including the BPMN constructs related to control-flow modeling and behavioural aspects. Beyond those constructs, execution time and resources are also associated with tasks. Figure 1 summarizes the BPMN constructs supported in this work.

Specifically, the node types *event*, *task*, and *gateway*, and the edge type *sequence flow* are considered. Start and end events are used, respectively, to initialize and terminate processes. A task represents an atomic activity that has exactly one incoming and one outgoing flow. A sequence flow describes two nodes executed one after the other in a specific execution order. A task and a flow may have a duration or delay. The timing information associated to tasks and flows is described as a literal value (a non-negative real number, possibly 0). Resources are explicitly defined at the task level. A task that requires resources can include, as part of its specification, the required resources. Information about time and resources can be used jointly for a given task. In such a case, it means that the task needs those resources to be able to execute, and once the resources are acquired, the task is going to execute for the specified duration.

Sequence flows can be of two possible types, to explicitly specify flows that must be preserved during the refactoring process. A *strong* flow corresponds to a causal dependency between two nodes that cannot be changed (e.g., some product must be packaged before its delivery). A *weak* flow corresponds to a loose connection between two nodes that may be preserved or not (e.g., the product could be delivered before the client pays for it).

Gateways are used to control the divergence and convergence of the execution flow. We consider in this work the two main kinds of gateways used in activity diagrams, namely, *exclusive* and *parallel* gateways. Gateways with one incoming branch and multiple outgoing branches are called *splits*, e.g., split parallel gateway. Gateways with one outgoing branch and multiple incoming branches are called *merges*, e.g., merge parallel gateway. An exclusive gateway chooses one out of a set of mutually exclusive alternative incoming or outgoing branches. A parallel gateway creates concurrent flows for all its outgoing branches or synchronizes concurrent flows for all its incoming branches.

3   Overview of the Approach

In this section, we give an overview of the different steps of our approach. We start by introducing the simulation-based analysis with which possible improvements in the structure of the process in terms of resource usage are identified. Then, we present the refactoring procedure and how different strategies are used to explore the possible solutions.

3.1   Simulation-Based Analysis

In this work, the main idea of the refactoring approach is to change the structure of the process in order to reduce its total execution time. Since optimization mostly targets process execution time, we need to compute this time for a given process. To do so, we rely on simulation-based techniques which turn out to simplify the computation of execution times in the presence of resources. Indeed, a task needs to acquire the required resources to be able to execute, and if the resources are not available the task cannot execute. The competition for resources may thus induce delays, and these delays are not easy to identify. To analize the process, we simulate it a certain number of times (this is a parameter of the approach). During these executions, some information about the execution of tasks (pending, executing, completed) and the usage of resources is stored. At the end of each execution, we store the time taken for completing the process. The average of those times allows us to compute the average execution time of the process.

After completion of the simulation, there is an analysis step which explores the simulation log for retrieving specific information. In particular, we look for specific timestamps during the simulation at which a task is in a pending state (meaning that this task is still waiting to be able to execute), and all resources required for executing this task are available. This means that this specific task could execute earlier in a process, and we will use this information to change the structure of the process by trying to move this task backwards in the process. This analysis step returns as output a set of tasks that could be executed earlier. Each task in this set verifies the aforementioned constraints (pending task but with required resources available) during a period of time of the simulation.

3.2   Refactoring Procedure

A refactoring step takes as input a BPMN process and a task that can be executed earlier in that process. Then, depending on the type of the preceding node,

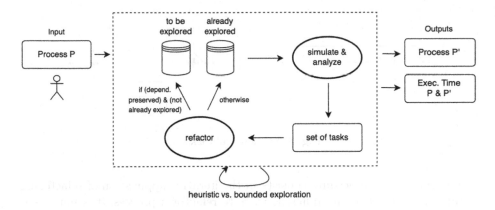

Fig. 2. Overview of the approach

a specific refactoring operation is applied. Such refactorings represent changes in fragments of the process, and multiple refactoring operations may be applied consecutively. To do so, the refactoring procedure relies on the generation and exploration of possible solutions and keeps track of the visited processes to avoid recomputations.

The refactoring operations are presented in Sect. 4. A refactoring operation can be seen as a model transformation $L \Rightarrow R \ if \ C$, with L and R subprocess patterns and C a condition on them. Each refactoring operation results in the transformation of a process (or model) into another. Thus, a refactoring operation can be applied if its left-hand side L matches a subprocess (or submodel) of the current process P, that is, $P|_p = L\sigma$, for some match σ and position p, and the condition C is satisfied for that match, that is, if $C\sigma$ is evaluated to true. The application of such a refactoring rule results in the replacement of the matched subprocess $P|_p$ by the right-hand side $R\sigma$. By repeatedly applying the available refactoring transformations on different parts of a process, new processes are generated. Strategies are thus necessary to explore all these new processes, and eventually return the optimal one.

Figure 2 depicts the input and outputs as well as the main steps of the refactoring process from a global perspective. The approach takes as input a BPMN process that includes a description of time and resources as shown in Sect. 2. This process is moved to the queue of processes to be explored. One process is then extracted from this queue (the original one in the first iteration) and the simulation-based analysis is carried out to identify the tasks that could be executed earlier. For each of these tasks, the corresponding refactoring operation is applied, generating a new process. Since the refactoring operation just moves the given task one step backwards, the resulting process may require additional changes. Therefore, if the resulting process has not been explored yet, and if the resulting process respects the strong dependencies defined in the original process (causal dependencies corresponding to strong flows must be maintained by the refactoring process), this new process is moved to the queue of processes to be explored. Otherwise, it is moved to the queue of processes already explored.

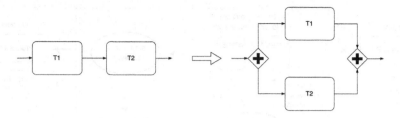

Fig. 3. Sequence of tasks

The refactoring procedure consists in the iterative application of refactoring operations. Since there are different ways to refactor a process, it is not possible to know at the beginning of the approach which refactoring step will lead to the best result (process with the minimal execution time). The exhaustive exploration of the search space, achieved by repeatedly attempting each possible refactoring operation on the tasks that may be moved backwards, may be time-consuming. To reduce the exploration space, we propose two different strategies:

- The first strategy consists in a *bounded breadth-first search*. It carries on an exhaustive exploration of all processes to be explored up to a certain bound given as parameter. For each possible task to be moved earlier in the process, the corresponding refactoring operation is applied. If the resulting process has not been analyzed before, it is placed in the to-be-explored queue. The procedure continues while there are processes in such a queue and the bound has not been reached.
- The second strategy, instead of exploring the search graph by applying refactoring operations on all tasks that can be moved earlier, only expands by applying refactoring on the task closer to the start event in the BPMN process. The intuition is that by moving this task backwards, it will be placed closer to the initial event, thus reducing the number of times it may be moved in the future. In other words, we try to move first the tasks closer to their final positions in the process. This strategy is referred as *heuristic-based* in the rest of this paper.

Several experiments showing the behaviour of the following exploration algorithms, including the use of these two strategies are presented in Sect. 5.

4 Refactoring Operations

This section presents a set of refactoring operations. In each of these refactoring operations, given as input a process and a task that has to be moved earlier in the process, a new process is returned as output. The refactoring operation to be applied depends on what type of node precedes the task to be moved backwards. There are actually three main cases: this node can be another task, a merge node, or a split node. Therefore, we will organize the rest of this section tackling successively these three cases. For each case, the proposed refactoring

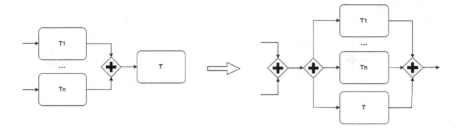

Fig. 4. Merge parallel gateway with preceding tasks (no shared resources)

operations are presented. Before starting, we also recall that this refactoring step focuses on the process structure and on the usage of resources by tasks, but does not take into account strong flows, which is handled at another level (as explained in Sect. 3.2).

4.1 Task

This first case is rather straightforward. If a task can be executed earlier, and that task is preceded by another task, we check whether these two tasks are sharing some resources. If they do not share any resources, the process is transformed to execute these two tasks within a common parallel gateway, as illustrated in Fig. 3.

4.2 Merge Node

If the task T to be moved earlier is preceded by a merge node, there are several possible (sub)cases. First of all, this node can be an exclusive or a parallel gateway. Second, before that merge, there may be only tasks, only other merge nodes, or a combination of both. We have specific operations for each of these cases. We will introduce these operations in the rest of this subsection.

Let us first consider the case in which the merge parallel gateway is preceded by a set of tasks T1...Tn, and none of these tasks share resources with the task T (left-hand side of Fig. 4). In that case, all tasks are gathered in parallel just before the merge parallel gateway (right-hand side of Fig. 4). Note that a split parallel gateway is added before these tasks in order to avoid that T executes before the tasks preceding the tasks before the merge. The preceding tasks might be using the same resources.

Assume now that the tasks preceding the merge parallel gateway share some resources with task T. If they all share resources, no refactoring is possible (since adding an additional task in parallel, competing for the same resources, would not improve the process execution time). If only one task shares resources with T, then T is moved after that task but before the merge as shown in Fig. 5. If there are several tasks sharing resources with T (but not all), then T is moved before the merge and right after an additional merge parallel gateway for this subset

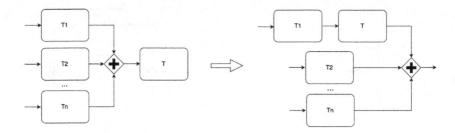

Fig. 5. Merge parallel gateway with preceding tasks (shared resources with one task)

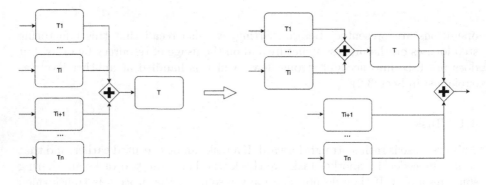

Fig. 6. Merge parallel gateway with preceding tasks (shared resources with several tasks)

of resources. Figure 6 shows such a case where T1...Ti share some resources with T. Therefore, after the refactoring operation, T appears after T1...Ti whereas Ti+1...Tn keep executing in parallel.

If what precedes the task to be moved is an exclusive gateway, and if there are only tasks before the merge, there are two cases. For each task before the merge, if task T shares some resource with that task, T is moved before the merge but after that task. If task T does not share any resource with that task, T is put in parallel with that task. Figure 7 illustrates this operation, showing that in the case of T1...Ti (shared resources), T is moved after each of them, whereas in the case of Ti+1...Tn (no shared resources), they all appear in parallel in the resulting process. Note that T appears multiple times in the resulting process, because by including T in an exclusive pattern, it has to be executed once by each existing branch to maintain the intended behaviour.

As far as cascading merges are concerned, we support cascading merge exclusive gateways (possibly finishing with a merge parallel gateway), by applying several times the patterns introduced above. However, if there are cascading merge parallel gateways or a merge parallel gateway followed by a merge exclusive gateway, refactoring is too complicated and is not applied. Let us take the example of two merge parallel gateways. If we move a task within the first one, this is ok as presented earlier. However, if there are other merge parallel gate-

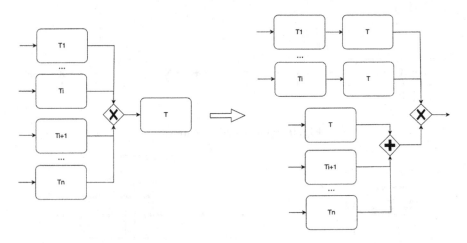

Fig. 7. Merge exclusive gateway with preceding tasks

Fig. 8. Split parallel gateway

ways inside the first one, we do not know where to move that task since we do not want to execute it multiple times.

4.3 Split Node

If the task T to be moved earlier is preceded by a split parallel gateway, then T is moved before the split, whatever precedes the split (task, split or merge). Figure 8 illustrates this pattern by moving the task before the split parallel gateway.

If the task T is preceded by a split exclusive gateway, we apply refactoring only if the split is preceded with a task (T1 for instance). In that case, we need to analyze the process to look for a merge gateway corresponding to the aforementioned split gateway. If the subprocess is balanced and the corresponding merge gateway is found, we still need to look at the resources used in that part of the process. If all tasks between the split and the merge do not share any resources with T1, then the whole block is moved in parallel with T1, as illustrated in Fig. 9, because we cannot dissociate the contents (tasks for instance) appearing in the same branch of an exclusive structure. If the task T is preceded by a split exclusive gateway, and the preceding node is not a task (it is another split for instance), there is no simple refactoring and we keep it as is. Note that if the exclusive split preceding T is not balanced or some task in that block uses any of the resources of T, then the refactoring operation is not applied because optimization is not possible.

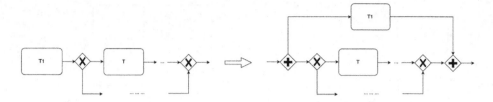

Fig. 9. Split exclusive gateway

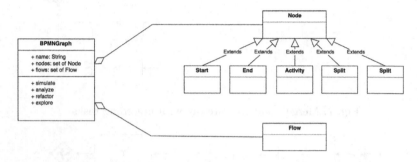

Fig. 10. Simplified class diagram

5   Implementation and Experiments

This section presents the tool support, a case study, and some experiments. Additional details about the tool and dataset used for the experiments are available online [1].

5.1   Tool

A tool implementing the above refactoring operations and their systematic application following the described procedures has been developed in Python. It works as presented in Fig. 2: the user provides as input a BPMN process and obtains as output an optimal version of that process with the gain in terms of process execution time. The implementation consists of several classes as illustrated in Fig. 10. The core of the approach is implemented in several methods dedicated to process simulation and analysis (of the simulation), refactoring operations, and exploration of the refactored processes by using different strategies. Processes to be explored and already explored are stored into dictionaries. Hash values for processes are used as keys and are computed using the number of nodes at distance 1, 2, 3, etc. from the start event. These numbers are then concatenated to form a key. Since we may have collisions, for each hash value, we store a list of processes in the dictionary. As for the transformation from BPMN XML to our encoding of BPMN into Python (in both directions), we take advantage of the transformation capabilities available in VBPMN [12,13].

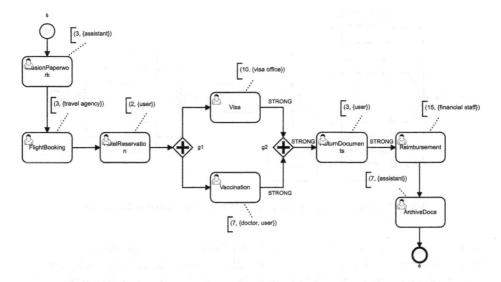

Fig. 11. Example of "Trip Organization" process in BPMN

5.2 Case Study

We illustrate our approach with a process describing the business trip organization given in Fig. 11. Each task has an annotation with a pair of values where the first value is the duration of the task (in days for instance) and the second value is the set of resources required to execute that task. Let us introduce the process with more details. First, the assistant fills in the required documents. Then, the travel agency is in charge of booking flight tickets, followed by the reservation of accommodation by the user in that case. Visa is then prepared and, in parallel, the user has to be vaccinated. The final part of the process is executed when the user is back from the trip. All necessary documents for reimbursement are returned by the user. Reimbursement is then completed by the financial staff. Finally, all documents are archived by the assistant. It is worth noting that there are several strong flows in the original process, before and after **g2**, and between task `ReturnDocuments` and task `Reimbursement`. This means that the causal dependency between these tasks is important and must be preserved by the refactoring process.

To compute the refactored version of this process, we use a bounded exploration (with 300 as bound). The resulting process is given in Fig. 12, and was obtained after about 130 iterations. It takes about 20 s to compute the resulting process. The execution time of all the tasks of the original process is 43 d whereas the new version executes in 28 d.

Let us now comment on this new version of the process. We can see that causal dependencies defined by strong flows are preserved in this process: tasks `Visa` and `Vaccination` are executed before task `ReturnDocuments`, and task `ReturnDocuments` is executed before task `Reimbursement`. In the first part of

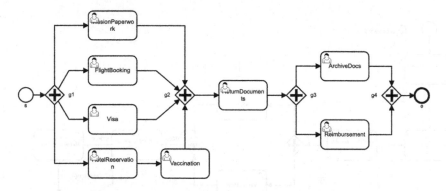

Fig. 12. Trip Organization process after automated refactoring

the process, we can see that several tasks can be executed in parallel because they all use different resources. However, tasks `HotelReservation` and `Vaccination` cannot be executed in parallel because they use the same resource `user`. After task `ReturnDocuments`, we can see that the two final tasks are executed in parallel because they use different resources.

5.3   Experiments

In this section, we show some experimental results obtained when applying our tool to different BPMN processes. The main goal of this section is to evaluate our tool in terms of performance and accuracy of the results, particularly comparing both strategies (bounded and heuristic-based exploration).

Table 1 shows some experiments on ten processes, mostly taken from the literature, e.g., BPMN processes introduced in [4–6], and from the VBPMN database of examples [12, 13]. The table first characterizes each process in terms of number of tasks, flows, gateways, and strong flows (SF). Then, the table gives the current Average Execution Time of the process (AET_c) and the Average Execution Time corresponding to the optimal process (AET_b). The optimal process corresponds to the process with the shortest execution time. This optimal process and the corresponding execution time were built and computed manually by the authors of this paper. Then, we show the results for the bounded exploration (bound fixed to 300) and for the heuristic-based approach. For each option, we give the execution time of the final process and the computation time to obtain the result.

Let us now comment on the results shown in this table. First of all, we can see that the bounded exploration succeeds in most cases to find the optimal solution, that is, the process with the shortest execution time. For larger examples (e.g., processes 7, 9 and 10 in the table), the best solution is not found because the bound (300) was too small to explore enough processes and find the best solution. However, if we increase the bound, the best solution is eventually found. As an example, for row 7, the best solution (with 18 as execution time) is found after about 750 iterations.

Table 1. Experimental results

BPMN	Characteristics						Bounded Explo.		Heuristic	
Proc.	Tasks	Flows	Gateways	SF	AET_c	AET_b	AET	Time	AET	Time
1	5	13	4⬦+	0	70	50	50	1 s	50	1 s
2	5	15	6⬦✖	0	40	25	25	2 s	25	2 s
3	6	13	2⬦+ 2⬦✖	0	19	6	6	2s	9	1 s
4	8	12	2⬦+	4	43	28	28	21 s	35	1 s
5	8	12	2⬦+	2	21	14	14	23 s	16	1 s
6	9	10	0	6	90	50	50	31s	90	1 s
7	10	20	6⬦+	0	24	18	19	38 s	20	1 s
8	10	20	2⬦+ 4⬦✖	3	23	13	13	67 s	17	1 s
9	12	29	8⬦+	0	200	120	140	50 s	120	1 s
10	15	36	10⬦+	0	260	180	220	103 s	260	3 s

As for the heuristic-based strategy, there are several cases for which the best solution is not found, but in very specific cases (e.g., process 9), it may give better results. Regarding computation time, the heuristic-based strategy is much faster (a few seconds) whereas the bounded exploration takes more time because it explores possibly many solutions (300 at most here). Regarding the computation time for the bounded exploration, we can see that this time increases with the size of the process (it takes more time to simulate, analyze and refactor a larger process than a simpler one). The number of refactorings does not really impact the computation time, since a bound is used to stop the exploration of potential solutions. Finally, the number of strong flows tends to reduce the number of possible refactorings thus the computation time, because strong flows can be seen as additional constraints on the process.

6 Related Work

This section starts with a short overview of extensions of BPMN with time and resource features, before presenting and comparing our approach with existing solutions for BPMN refactoring. Several works propose extensions of BPMN with time constructs, see, e.g., [2,9]. In [9], the authors present Time-BPMN, an extension of BPMN that allows the specification of temporal constraints and dependencies within a BPMN diagram. In [2], a metamodel-based approach to integrate temporal constraints and dependencies is introduced. The time aspects are specified using rules and OCL constraints capture the semantics of these rules. Our solution shares similarities with the approach proposed in [9].

As far as resource allocation is concerned, several solutions have been proposed by the research community in the business process domain. Schömig and

Rau [18] use colored stochastic Petri nets to specify and analyze business processes in the presence of dynamic routing, simultaneous resource allocation, forking/joining of process-control threads, and priority-based queueing. Li *et al.* [15] introduce *multidimensional workflow nets* to model and analyze resource availability and workload. Oliveira *et al.* [16] use generalized stochastic Petri nets for correctness verification and performance evaluation of business processes. In this work, we propose to associate resources to tasks, which is a flexible solution for modelling many different situations and scenarios. Moreover, our approach does not focus on the computation of metrics but changes the process structure to actually optimize some of these metrics.

Let us now focus on existing works on process refactoring. [19] presents six common mistakes made by developers when modelling with BPMN: inconsistent naming, large process diagrams, inconsistent use of gateways, inconsistent use of events, inconsistent use of loops, poor diagram layout. For each problem, the authors present best practices for avoiding these issues. As an example, the authors propose to use explicit gateways instead of using multiple incoming/outgoing sequence flows. [3] presents a technique for detecting refactoring opportunities in process model repositories. The technique works by first computing activity similarity and then computing three similarity scores for fragment pairs of process models. Using these similarity scores, four different kinds of refactoring opportunities can be systematically identified. As a result, the approach proposes to rename activities or to introduce subprocesses. IBUPROFEN, a business process refactoring approach based on graphs, is presented in [8,17]. IBUPROFEN defines a set of 10 refactoring algorithms grouped into three categories: maximization of relevant elements, fine-grained granularity reduction, and completeness. All these works mostly focus on syntactic issues and propose synctatic improvements of the process by, for instance, removing unreachable nodes or by merging consecutive gateways of the same type. They do not aim at providing any kind of optimization regarding the process being designed as we do.

In [14], the authors present an approach for optimizing the redesign of process models. It is based on capturing process improvement strategies as constraints in a structural-temporal model. Each improvement strategy is represented by a binary variable. An objective function that represents a net benefit function of cost and quality is then maximized to find the best combination of process improvements that can be made to maximize the objective. The BPMN subset used in [14] is very similar to the one we use in this paper. However, the approach is rather different since they compute optimal redesigns with respect to some constraints, whereas we propose refactoring patterns with respect to process execution times.

Last but not least, it is worth mentioning recent works providing support for building (optimal) processes. [7] proposes a semi-automated approach for helping non-experts in BPMN to model business processes using this notation. Alternatively, [11] presents an approach which combines notes taking in constrained natural language with process mining to automatically produce BPMN diagrams in real-time as interview participants describe them with stories. In this work, we tackle this issue from a different angle since we assume that an existing description of the process exists and that we want to automatically optimize it by updating its structure.

7 Concluding Remarks

In this paper, we have focused on a version of BPMN including task durations and an explicit description of resources. We have then proposed a simulation-based approach that allows us to identify some specific tasks which are waiting for being executed but for which the required resources are available. This means that, from the point of view of the process structure, these tasks could be executed earlier in the process. We then apply some refactoring transformations to move those tasks backwards in the process structure. This approach works by successively applying these refactorings and by thus exploring the possible solutions to find the optimal one. Several strategies have been implemented and vary in their way to apply these iterations. In any case, the refactoring process completes and returns as result a process whose average execution time is lower (or equal) than the one of the original process. Note that if the original process is already optimal, that process and its corresponding execution time are returned as output. All the steps of the refactoring approach are fully automated by a tool we implemented and applied on many examples of processes for validation purposes.

Acknowledgments.. F. Durán has been partially supported by projects PGC2018-094905-B-100 and UMA18-FEDERJA-180, and by Universidad de Málaga, Campus de Excelencia Internacional Andalucía Tech. This work was also supported by the Région Auvergne-Rhône-Alpes within the *"Pack Ambition Recherche"* programme.

References

1. Workflow refactoring tool and examples - (Blinded) Github repository (2022). https://github.com/afjdm/workflow-refactoring
2. Arévalo, C., Cuaresma, M.J.E., Ramos, I.M., Domínguez-Muñoz. M.: A metamodel to integrate business processes time perspective in BPMN 2.0. Inf. Softw. Technol. **77**, 17–33 (2016)
3. Dijkman, R.M., Gfeller, B., Küster, J.M., Völzer, H.: identifying refactoring opportunities in process model repositories. Inf. Softw. Technol. **53**(9), 937–948 (2011)
4. Durán, F., Rocha, C., Salaün, G.: Stochastic analysis of BPMN with time in rewriting logic. Sci. Comput. Program. **168**, 1–17 (2018)
5. Durán, F., Rocha, C., Salaün, G.: A rewriting logic approach to resource allocation analysis in business process models. Sci. Comput. Program. **183**, 102303 (2019)
6. Durán, F., Salaün, G.: Verifying timed BPMN processes using Maude. In: Jacquet, J.-M., Massink, M. (eds.) COORDINATION 2017. LNCS, vol. 10319, pp. 219–236. Springer, Cham (2017). https://doi.org/10.1007/978-3-319-59746-1_12
7. Falcone, Y., Salaün, G., Zuo, A.: Semi-automated modelling of optimized BPMN processes. In Proceedings of SCC 2021, pp. 425–430. IEEE (2021)

8. Fernández-Ropero, M., Pérez-Castillo, R., Piattini, M.: Graph-based business process model refactoring. In: Proceedings of the 3rd International Symposium on Data-driven Process Discovery and Analysis, volume 1027 of CEUR Workshop Proceedings, pp. 16–30 (2013)

9. Gagné, D., Trudel, A.: Time-BPMN. In: Proceedings of CEC 2009, pp. 361–367. IEEE Computer Society (2009)

10. ISO/IEC. International Standard 19510, Information technology - Business Process Model and Notation (2013)

11. Ivanchikj, A., Serbout, S., Pautasso, C.: From text to visual BPMN process models: design and evaluation. In: Proceedings of MoDELS 2020, pp. 229–239. ACM (2020)

12. Krishna, A., Poizat, P., Salaün, G.: VBPMN: automated verification of BPMN processes (Tool Paper). In: Polikarpova, N., Schneider, S. (eds.) IFM 2017. LNCS, vol. 10510, pp. 323–331. Springer, Cham (2017). https://doi.org/10.1007/978-3-319-66845-1_21

13. Krishna, A., Poizat, P., Salaün, G.: Checking business process evolution. Sci. Comput. Program. **170**, 1–26 (2019)

14. Kumar, A., Indradat, P.: Optimizing process model redesign. In: Sheng, Q.Z., Stroulia, E., Tata, S., Bhiri, S. (eds.) ICSOC 2016. LNCS, vol. 9936, pp. 39–54. Springer, Cham (2016). https://doi.org/10.1007/978-3-319-46295-0_3

15. Li, J., Fan, Y., Zhou, M.: Performance modeling and analysis of workflow. IEEE Trans. Syst. Man Cybern. **34**(2), 229–242 (2004). Mar

16. Oliveira, C., Lima, R., Reijers, H., Ribeiro, J.: Quantitative analysis of resource-constrained business processes. Trans. Syst. Man Cybern. **42**(3), 669–684 (2012)

17. Pérez-Castillo, R., Fernández-Ropero, M., Piattini, M.: Business process model refactoring applying IBUPROFEN. Ind. Eval. J. Syst. Softw. **147**, 86–103 (2019)

18. Schömig, A.K., Rau, H.: A petri net approach for the performance analysis of business processes. Technical Report 116, Universität Würzburg, Germany, May 1995

19. Silingas, D., Mileviciene, E.: Refactoring BPMN Models: from 'Bad Smells' to best practices and patterns. In: BPMN 2.0 Handbook, pp. 125–134 (2012)

Control-Flow-Based Querying of Process Executions from Partially Ordered Event Data

Daniel Schuster[1,2](✉)(iD), Michael Martini[1](iD), Sebastiaan J. van Zelst[1,2](iD),
and Wil M. P. van der Aalst[1,2](iD)

[1] Fraunhofer Institute for Applied Information Technology FIT,
Sankt Augustin, Germany
{daniel.schuster,michael.martini,sebastiaan.van.zelst}@fit.fraunhofer.de
[2] RWTH Aachen University, Aachen, Germany
wvdaalst@pads.rwth-aachen.de

Abstract. Event logs, as viewed in process mining, contain event data describing the execution of operational processes. Most process mining techniques take an event log as input and generate insights about the underlying process by analyzing the data provided. Consequently, handling large volumes of event data is essential to apply process mining successfully. Traditionally, individual process executions are considered sequentially ordered process activities. However, process executions are increasingly viewed as partially ordered activities to more accurately reflect process behavior observed in reality, such as simultaneous execution of activities. Process executions comprising partially ordered activities may contain more complex activity patterns than sequence-based process executions. This paper presents a novel query language to call up process executions from event logs containing partially ordered activities. The query language allows users to specify complex ordering relations over activities, i.e., control flow constraints. Evaluating a query for a given log returns process executions satisfying the specified constraints. We demonstrate the implementation of the query language in a process mining tool and evaluate its performance on real-life event logs.

Keywords: Process mining · Process querying · Partial orders

1 Introduction

Executing operational processes generates large amounts of event data in enterprise information systems. Analyzing these data provides great opportunities for operational improvements, for example, reduced cycle times and increased conformity with reference process models. Therefore, *process mining* [17] comprises data-driven techniques to analyze event data to gain insights into the underlying processes; for example, automatically discovered process models, conformance statistics, and performance analysis information. Since service-oriented computing is concerned with orchestrating services to form dynamic business

J. Troya et al. (Eds.): ICSOC 2022, LNCS 13740, pp. 19–35, 2022.
https://doi.org/10.1007/978-3-031-20984-0_2

processes [6], process mining can provide valuable insights into the actual execution of processes within organizations [16]. These insights can then be used, for example, to define services and ultimately construct service-oriented architectures. Further, process mining provides valuable tools for service monitoring.

Most process mining techniques [17] define process executions, termed *traces*, as a sequence, i.e., a *strict total order*, of executed activities. In reality, however, processes can exhibit parallel behavior, i.e., several branches of a process are executed simultaneously. Consequently, the execution of individual activities may overlap within a single trace. Thus, traces are defined by *partially ordered* executed activities. Considering traces as partial orders, the complexity of observed control flow patterns, i.e., relations among executed activities, increases compared to sequential traces. Thus, tools are needed that facilitate the handling, filtering, and exploring of traces containing partially ordered process activities.

This paper introduces a novel query language for querying traces from an event log containing partially ordered activities. The proposed language allows the specification of six essential control flow constraints, which can be further restricted via cardinality constraints and arbitrarily combined via Boolean operators. The language design is based on standardized terms for control flow patterns in process mining. We provide a formal specification of the language's syntax and semantics to facilitate reuse in other tools. Further, we present its implementation in the process mining software tool Cortado [14], which supports partially ordered event data. Query results are visualized by Cortado using a novel trace variant visualization [13]. Finally, we evaluate the performance of the query evaluation on real-life, publicly available event logs.

The remainder of this paper is structured as follows. Section 2 presents related work. Section 3 introduces preliminaries. In Sect. 4, we introduce the proposed query language. We present an exemplary application use case of the query language in Sect. 5. In Sect. 6, we present an evaluation focusing on performance aspects of the proposed query language. Finally, Sect. 7 concludes this paper.

2   Related Work

A framework for *process querying* methods is presented in [10]. In short, process query methods differ in the input used, for instance, event logs (e.g., [3,20]) or process model repositories (e.g., [2,5]), and the goal or capabilities of the query method. Overviews of process querying languages can be found in [8–10,19]; the majority of existing methods focuses on querying process model repositories. Subsequently, we focus on methods that operate on event logs.

Celonis PQL [18] is a multi-purpose, textual query language that works on event logs and process models and provides a variety of query options. However, traces are considered sequentially ordered activities compared to the proposed query language in this paper. In [3], a query language is proposed that operates on a single graph, i.e., a RDF, connecting all events in an event log by user-defined correlations among events. The query language allows to partition the events by specified constraints and to query paths that start and end with events fulfilling certain requirements. Compared to our approach, we do not initially transform the entire event log into a graph structure; instead, we operate on individual traces composed of partially ordered event data.

In [4], the authors propose a natural language interface for querying event data. Similar to [3], a graph based search is used. The approach allows specifying arbitrary queries like "Who was involved in processing case x" and "For which cases is the case attribute y greater than z." However, control flow constraints over partially ordered event data are not supported, unlike the query language proposed in this paper, which is designed exclusively for control flow constraints. In [11], the authors propose an LTL-based query language to query traces, consisting of sequentially aligned process activities, fulfilling specified constraints from an event log. In [20], the authors propose an approach to query trace fragments from various event logs that are similar to a trace fragment surrounding a selected activity from a process model using a notion of neighborhood context. Traces are, in this approach, considered sequentially ordered activities.

In summary, various process querying methods exist, most of them operating over process model repositories rather than event logs, cf. [8–10,19]. In short, the proposed query language differs in three main points from existing work.

1. First process querying language focusing on traces containing partially ordered activities (to the best of our knowledge)
2. Focus on traces rather than event data as a whole, i.e., executing a query returns traces satisfying the specified constraints
3. Specific focus on control flow patterns, i.e., extensive options for specifying a wide range of control flow patterns

3 Preliminaries

This section introduces notations and concepts used throughout this paper.

We denote the natural numbers by $\mathbb{N}$ and the natural numbers including 0 by $\mathbb{N}_0$. We simplify by representing timestamps by positive real numbers denoted by $\mathbb{R}^+$. We denote the universe of activity labels by $\mathcal{L}$, activity instance identifier by $\mathcal{I}^A$, and case identifier by $\mathcal{I}^C$. Further, we denote a missing value by $\bot$.

Definition 1 (Activity instances). *An activity instance $a = (i, c, l, t_s, t_c) \in \mathcal{I}^A \times \mathcal{I}^C \times \mathcal{L} \times (\mathbb{R}^+ \cup \{\bot\}) \times \mathbb{R}^+$ uniquely identified by $i \in \mathcal{I}^A$ represents the execution of an activity $l \in \mathcal{L}$ that was executed for the process instance identified by $c \in \mathcal{I}^C$. The activity instance's temporal information is given by the optional start timestamp $t_s \in \mathbb{R}^+ \cup \{\bot\}$ and the complete timestamp $t_c \in \mathbb{R}^+$. If $t_s \neq \bot \Rightarrow t_s \leq t_c$. We denote the universe of activity instances by $\mathcal{A}$.*

Let $a=(i, c, l, t_s, t_c) \in \mathcal{A}$ be an activity instance, we use short forms to assess the different components of a; we write a^i, a^c, a^l, a^{t_s}, and a^{t_c}.

An event log can be seen as a set of activity instances describing the same process; Table 1 shows an example. Each row corresponds to an activity instance describing the execution of an activity. For instance, the first row describes the execution of the activity "credit request received" executed on 16.06.21 at

Table 1. Example of an event log with partially ordered event data

| ID | | Activity label | Timestamp | | ... |
Activity instance	Case		Start	Completion	
1	1	Credit request received (CRR)	$\perp$	16.06.21 12:43:35	...
2	1	Document check (DC)	17.06.21 08:32:23	18.06.21 12:01:11	...
3	1	Request info. from applicant (RIP)	19.06.21 09:34:00	22.06.21 09:12:00	...
4	1	Request info. from third parties (RIT)	19.06.21 14:54:00	25.06.21 08:57:12	...
5	1	Document check (DC)	$\perp$	28.06.21 14:23:59	...
6	1	Credit assessment (CA)	30.06.21 13:02:11	04.07.21 08:11:32	...
7	1	Security risk assessment (SRA)	01.07.21 17:23:11	06.07.21 18:51:43	...
8	1	Property inspection (PI)	$\perp$	05.07.21 00:00:00	...
9	1	Loan-to-value ratio determined (LTV)	$\perp$	05.07.21 00:00:00	...
10	1	Decision made (DM)	$\perp$	08.07.21 14:13:18	...
11	2	Credit request received (CRR)	$\perp$	17.06.21 23:21:31	...
...	...	...		...	...	...

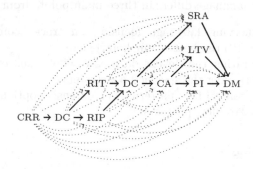

Fig. 1. Ordering of the activity instances within the trace describing case 1. Solid arcs depict the transitive reduction; solid and dotted arcs the transitive closure.

12:43:35 for the process instance identified by case-id 1. Individual process executions within an event log are termed *traces*. Next, we formally define traces as a partially ordered set of activity instances belonging to the same case.

Definition 2 (Trace). *Let $T \subseteq \mathcal{A}$. We call $(T, \prec)$ a trace if:*

1. *$\forall a_i, a_j \in T (a_i^c = a_j^c)$ and*
2. *$\prec \subseteq T \times T$ and for arbitrary $a_i, a_j \in T$ holds that $a_i \prec a_j$ iff:*
   - *$a_i^{t_c} < a_j^{t_s}$ given that $a_i^{t_c}, a_j^{t_s} \in \mathbb{R}^+$, or*
   - *$a_i^{t_c} < a_j^{t_c}$ given that $a_i^{t_c} \in \mathbb{R}^+$ and $a_j^{t_s} = \perp$.*

We denote the universe of traces by $\mathcal{T}$.

For a trace $(T, \prec) \in \mathcal{T}$, note that the relation $\prec$ (cf. Definition 2) is the *transitive closure*. We denote the *transitive reduction* of $\prec$ by $\prec^R$. For $\prec^R$ it holds that $\forall a, b \in T \left[a \prec^R b \leftrightarrow \left(a \prec b \wedge \left(\nexists \tilde{a} \in T (a \prec^R \tilde{a} \wedge \tilde{a} \prec^R b) \right) \right) \right]$. Figure 1 visualizes the ordering relations of the activity instances of the trace describing case 1 (cf. Table 1). Solid arcs show direct relationships among activity instances. Thus, the solid arcs represent the transitive reduction. Solid and dotted arcs represent all relations among activity instances and thus, represent the transitive closure.

Finally, we define notation conventions regarding the existential quantifier. Let $k \in \mathbb{N}$ and X be an arbitrary set, we write $\exists^{=k}$, $\exists^{\geq k}$, and $\exists^{\leq k}$ to denote that there exist *exactly*, *at least*, and *at most* k distinct elements in set X satisfying a given formula $P(\dots)$. Below we formally define the three existential quantifier.

- $\exists^{=k} x_1, \dots, x_k \in X \ \left(\forall_{1 \leq i \leq k} \ P(x_i)\right) \equiv \exists x_1, \dots, x_k \in X \left[\left(\forall_{1 \leq i < j \leq k} \ x_i \neq x_j\right) \wedge \left(\forall_{1 \leq i \leq k} \ P(x_i)\right) \wedge \left(\forall_{x \in X \setminus \{x_1, \dots, x_k\}} \ \neg P(x_i)\right)\right]$
- $\exists^{\geq k} x_1, \dots, x_k \in X \ \left(\forall_{1 \leq i \leq k} \ P(x_i)\right) \equiv \exists x_1, \dots, x_k \in X \left[\left(\forall_{1 \leq i < j \leq k} \ x_i \neq x_j\right) \wedge \left(\forall_{1 \leq i \leq k} \ P(x_i)\right)\right]$
- $\exists^{\leq k} x_1, \dots, x_k \in X \ \left(\forall_{1 \leq i \leq k} \ P(x_i)\right) \equiv \exists x_1, \dots, x_k \in X \left[\left(\forall_{1 \leq i \leq k} \ P(x_i)\right) \wedge \left(\forall_{x \in X \setminus \{x_1, \dots, x_k\}} \ \neg P(x)\right)\right]$

Note that $x_1, \dots, x_k$ must not be *different* elements in the formula above; it specifies that at most k distinct elements in X exist satisfying $P(\dots)$.

4 Query Language

This section introduces the proposed query language. Section 4.1 introduces its syntax, while Sect. 4.2 defines its semantics. Section 4.3 covers the evaluation of queries. Finally, Sect. 4.4 presents the implementation in a process mining tool.

4.1 Syntax

This section introduces the syntax of the proposed query language. In total, six operators exist, allowing to specify control flow constraints. Table 2 provides an overview of these six operators, three binary, (i.e., isContained (isC), isStart (isS), and isEnd (isE)), and three unary operators (i.e., isDirectlyFollowed (isDF), isEventuallyFollowed (isEF), and isParallel (isP)). Next to each operator, we list query examples, including the corresponding operator, and present its semantics in natural language. As the examples show, each operator can be additionally constrained by a cardinality. We call a query a leaf query if only one operator is used, for instance, all examples shown in Table 2 are query leaves. Query leaves can be arbitrarily combined via Boolean operators, for instance, see Fig. 2. Next, we formally define the query language's syntax.

$$\Big(('DC' \ isC \ =2) \ OR \ (('DC' \ isC \ =1) \ AND \ ('CRR' \ isDF \ 'DC')) \Big) \ AND \ \Big(NOT('DC' \ isDF \ 'DM') \Big)$$

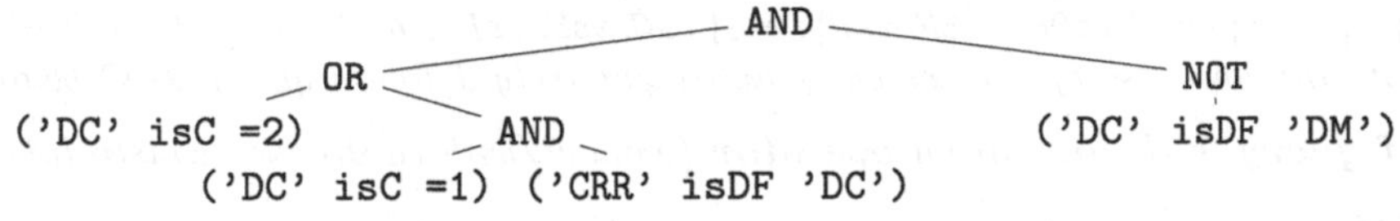

Fig. 2. Example of a query. Leaves represent individual control flow constraints (cf. Table 2) that are combined via Boolean operators.

Table 2. Overview of the six control flow constraints and corresponding examples

Type	Syntax	Example		
		Nr.	Query	Description of semantics
unary	isContained (isC)	E1	'A' isC	activity A is contained in the trace
		E2	'A' isC $\geq$ 6	activity A is contained at least 6 times in the trace
		E3	ALL{'A','B'} isS $\geq$ 6	activity A and B are both contained at least 6 times each in the trace
	isStart (isS)	E4	'A' isS	there exists a start activity A
		E5	'A' isS = 1	exactly one start activity of the trace is an A activity
		E6	ANY{'A','B'} isC = 1	trace starts with exactly one A activity or/and with exactly one B activity
	isEnd (isE)	E7	'A' isE	there exists an end activity A
		E8	'A' isE $\geq$ 2	at least two end activities of the trace are an A activity
		E9	ALL{'A','B'} isE	trace ends with at least one A and one B activity
binary	isDirectly Followed (isDF)	E10	'A' isDF 'B'	a B activity directly follows *each* A activity in the trace
		E11	'A' isDF 'B' = 1	trace contains exactly one A activity that is directly followed by B
		E12	'A' isDF ALL{'B','C'}	every A activity is directly followed by a B and C activity
	isEventually Followed (isEF)	E13	'A' isEF 'B'	after *each* A activity in the trace a B activity eventually follows
		E14	'A' isEF 'B' $\geq$ 1	trace contains at least one A activity that is eventually followed by B
		E15	ALL{'A','B'} isEF 'C'	all A and B activities are eventually followed by a C activity
	isParallel (isP)	E16	'A' isP 'B'	each A activity in the trace is in parallel to some B activity
		E17	'A' isP 'B' $\leq$ 4	trace contains at most four A activities that are in parallel to some B activity
		E18	'A' isP ANY{'B','C'} $\leq$ 2	trace contains at most two A activities that are parallel to a B or C activity

(a) Trace may contain arbitrary further start respectively end activities.

Definition 3 (Query Syntax). *Let* $l_1,\ldots,l_{n-1},l_n \in \mathcal{L}$ *be activity labels,* $k \in \mathbb{N}_0$, $\Box \in \{\leq, \geq, =\}$, $\circ \in \{isDF, isEF, isP\}$, $\bullet \in \{isC, isS, isE\}$, *and* $\triangle \in \{ALL, ANY\}$. *We denote the universe of queries by* $\mathcal{Q}$ *and recursively define a query* $Q \in \mathcal{Q}$ *below.*

Leaf query with an unary operator *(without/with cardinality constraint)*

– $Q = 'l_1' \bullet$ $\qquad\qquad\qquad$ $Q = 'l_1' \bullet \Box k$
– $Q = \triangle\{'l_1',\ldots,'l_{n-1}'\} \bullet$ $\qquad$ $Q = \triangle\{'l_1',\ldots,'l_{n-1}'\} \bullet \Box k$

Leaf query with a binary operator *(without/with cardinality constraint)*

- $Q= \, 'l_1 \, ' \circ \, 'l_n \, '$
- $Q=\triangle\{ \, 'l_1 \, ', \dots, \, 'l_{n-1}\} \, ' \circ \, 'l_n \, '$
- $Q= \, 'l_n \, ' \circ \triangle\{ \, 'l_1 \, ', \dots, \, 'l_{n-1}\} \, '$

- $Q= \, 'l_1 \, ' \circ \, 'l_n \, ' \, \square k$
- $Q=\triangle\{ \, 'l_1 \, ', \dots, \, 'l_{n-1}\} \, ' \circ \, 'l_n \, ' \, \square k$
- $Q= \, 'l_n \, ' \circ \triangle\{ \, 'l_1 \, ', \dots, \, 'l_{n-1}\} \, ' \, \square k$

Composed query using Boolean operators

- If $Q_1, Q_2 \in \mathcal{Q}$ are two queries and $\blacksquare \in \{$AND, OR$\}$, then $Q= (Q_1 \blacksquare Q_2)$ is a query
- If $Q_1 \in \mathcal{Q}$ is a query, then $Q=$NOT(Q_1) is a query

4.2   Semantics

This section introduces the query language's semantics. Table 2 presents query examples with corresponding semantics. In short, the unary operators allow to specify the existence of individual activities within a trace, for example, is contained (isC), is a start activity (isS), or is an end activity (isE). Optionally, operators can have cardinality constraints that extend the existential semantics of unary operators by quantification constraints. Binary operators allow to specify relationships between activities; for example, two activities are parallel (isP), directly follow each other (isDF), or eventually follow each other (isEF). In contrast to unary operators, binary operators always have to hold globally when no cardinality constraint is given. For example, E10 (cf. Table 2) specifies that a B activity must directly follow each A activity, i.e., there is an arc in the transitive reduction from each A activity to a B activity. In comparison, E11 specifies that the trace contains precisely one A activity that is directly followed by a B activity. ALL sets specify that a constraint must be fulfilled for all activity labels within the set. Analogously, ANY sets specify that the constraint must be fulfilled at least for one activity. Next, we formally define the semantics.

Definition 4 (Query Semantics). *Let $Q, Q_1, Q_2 \in \mathcal{Q}$ be queries, $T^{\prec}=(T, \prec) \in \mathcal{T}$ be a trace, and $l_1, \dots, l_n \in \mathcal{L}$ be activity labels. We recursively define the function eval : $\mathcal{Q} \times \mathcal{T} \to \{true, false\}$ assigning a Boolean value, i.e., $eval(Q, T^{\prec})$, to query Q and trace $T^{\prec}$.*

Unary Operators

- *If* $Q= \, 'l_1 \, '$ isC $\square k$ *, then* $eval(Q, T^{\prec}) \Leftrightarrow$
  $\exists^{\square k} a_1, \dots, a_k \in T \left[\forall_{1 \leq i \leq k}(a_i^l = l_1) \right]$
- *If* $Q= \, 'l_1 \, '$ isS $\square k$ *, then* $eval(Q, T^{\prec}) \Leftrightarrow$
  $\exists^{\square k} a_1, \dots, a_k \in T \left[\forall_{1 \leq i \leq k}\left(a_i^l = l_1 \land \neg \exists \tilde{a} \in T(\tilde{a} \prec a_i) \right) \right]$
- *If* $Q= \, 'l_1 \, '$ isE $\square k$ *, then* $eval(Q, T^{\prec}) \Leftrightarrow$
  $\exists^{\square k} a_1, \dots, a_k \in T \left[\forall_{1 \leq i \leq k}\left(a_i^l = l_1 \land \neg \exists \tilde{a} \in T(a_i \prec \tilde{a}) \right) \right]$

Binary Operators

- If $Q=$ 'l_1' *isDF* 'l_2' , then $eval(Q,T^{\prec}) \Leftrightarrow$
  $$\forall a{\in}T\left[a^l{=}l_1 \rightarrow \exists\tilde{a}{\in}T\left(\tilde{a}^l{=}l_2 \wedge a{\prec}^R\tilde{a}\right)\right]$$

- If $Q=$ 'l_1' *isDF* 'l_2' $\Box k$, then $eval(Q,T^{\prec}) \Leftrightarrow$
  $$\exists^{\Box k}a_1,\ldots,a_k{\in}T\left[\forall_{1\leq i\leq k}\left(a_i^l{=}l_1 \wedge \exists\tilde{a}{\in}T\left(\tilde{a}^l{=}l_2 \wedge a_i{\prec}^R\tilde{a}\right)\right)\right]$$

- If $Q=$ 'l_1' *isDF ANY*{ 'l_2' , $\ldots$, 'l_n' } , then $eval(Q,T^{\prec}) \Leftrightarrow$
  $$\forall a{\in}T\left[a^l{=}l_1 \rightarrow \exists\tilde{a}{\in}T\left(a{\prec}^R\tilde{a} \wedge \left(\bigvee_{j=2}^{n}\tilde{a}^l = l_j\right)\right)\right]$$

- If $Q=$ 'l_1' *isDF ANY*{ 'l_2' , $\ldots$, 'l_n' } $\Box k$, then $eval(Q,T^{\prec}) \Leftrightarrow$
  $$\exists^{\Box k}a_1,\ldots,a_k{\in}T\left[\forall_{1\leq i\leq k}\left(a_i^l{=}l_1 \wedge \exists\tilde{a}{\in}T(a_i{\prec}^R\tilde{a} \wedge \bigvee_{j=2}^{n}(\tilde{a}^l{=}l_j))\right)\right]$$

- If $Q=$ 'l_1' *isDF ALL*{ 'l_2' , $\ldots$, 'l_n' } $\Box k$, then $eval(Q,T^{\prec}) \Leftrightarrow$
  $$\exists^{\Box k}a_1,\ldots,a_k{\in}T\left[\forall_{1\leq i\leq k}\left(a_i^l{=}l_1 \wedge \exists\tilde{a}_2,\ldots,\tilde{a}_n{\in}T\left(\bigwedge_{j=2}^{n}\left(a_i{\prec}^R\tilde{a}_j \wedge \tilde{a}_j^l{=}l_j\right)\right)\right)\right]$$

- If $Q=$ 'l_1' *isEF* 'l_2' , then $eval(Q,T^{\prec}) \Leftrightarrow$
  $$\forall a{\in}T\left[a^l{=}l_1 \rightarrow \exists\tilde{a}{\in}T\left(\tilde{a}^l{=}l_2 \wedge a{\prec}\tilde{a}\right)\right]$$

- If $Q=$ 'l_1' *iEF* 'l_2' $\Box k$, then $eval(Q,T^{\prec}) \Leftrightarrow$
  $$\exists^{\Box k}a_1,\ldots,a_k{\in}T\left[\forall_{1\leq i\leq k}\left(a_i^l{=}l_1 \wedge \exists\tilde{a}{\in}T\left(\tilde{a}^l{=}l_2 \wedge a_i{\prec}\tilde{a}\right)\right)\right]$$

- If $Q=$ 'l_1' *isEF ANY*{ 'l_2' , $\ldots$, 'l_n' } , then $eval(Q,T^{\prec}) \Leftrightarrow$
  $$\forall a{\in}T\left[a^l{=}l_1 \rightarrow \exists\tilde{a}{\in}T\left(a{\prec}\tilde{a} \wedge \left(\bigvee_{i=2}^{n}\tilde{a}^l = l_i\right)\right)\right]$$

- If $Q=$ 'l_1' *isEF ANY*{ 'l_2' , $\ldots$, 'l_n' } $\Box k$, then $eval(Q,T^{\prec}) \Leftrightarrow$
  $$\exists^{\Box k}a_1,\ldots,a_k{\in}T\left[\forall_{1\leq i\leq k}\left(a_i^l{=}l_1 \wedge \exists\tilde{a}{\in}T\left(a_i{\prec}\tilde{a} \wedge \left(\bigvee_{j=2}^{n}\tilde{a}^l{=}l_j\right)\right)\right)\right]$$

- If $Q=$ 'l_1' *isEF ALL*{ 'l_2' , $\ldots$, 'l_n' } $\Box k$, then $eval(Q,T^{\prec}) \Leftrightarrow$
  $$\exists^{\Box k}a_1,\ldots,a_k{\in}T\left[\forall_{1\leq i\leq k}\left(a_i^l{=}l_1 \wedge \exists\tilde{a}_2,\ldots,\tilde{a}_n{\in}T\left(\bigwedge_{j=2}^{n}(a_i{\prec}\tilde{a}_j \wedge \tilde{a}_j^l{=}l_j)\right)\right)\right]$$

- If $Q=$ 'l_1' *isP* 'l_2' , then $eval(Q,T^{\prec}) \Leftrightarrow$
  $$\forall a{\in}T\left[a^l{=}l_1 \rightarrow \exists\tilde{a}{\in}T\left(\tilde{a}^l{=}l_2 \wedge a{\not\prec}\tilde{a} \wedge \tilde{a}{\not\prec}a\right)\right]$$

- If $Q=$ 'l_1' *isP* 'l_2' $\Box k$, then $eval(Q,T^{\prec}) \Leftrightarrow$
  $$\exists^{\Box k}a_1,\ldots,a_k{\in}T\left[\forall_{1\leq i\leq k}\left(a_i^l{=}l_1 \wedge \exists\tilde{a}{\in}T\left(\tilde{a}^l{=}l_2 \wedge a_i{\not\prec}\tilde{a} \wedge \tilde{a}{\not\prec}a_i\right)\right)\right]$$

- If $Q=$ 'l_1' *isP ANY*{ 'l_2' , $\ldots$, 'l_n' } , then $eval(Q,T^{\prec}) \Leftrightarrow$
  $$\forall a{\in}T\left[a^l{=}l_1 \rightarrow \exists\tilde{a}{\in}T\left(a{\not\prec}\tilde{a} \wedge \tilde{a}{\not\prec}a \wedge \left(\bigvee_{j=2}^{n}\tilde{a}^l = l_j\right)\right)\right]$$

- If $Q=$ 'l_1' *isP ANY*{ 'l_2' , $\ldots$, 'l_n' } $\Box k$, then $eval(Q,T^{\prec}) \Leftrightarrow$
  $$\exists^{\Box k}a_1,\ldots,a_k{\in}T\left[\forall_{1\leq i\leq k}\left(a_i^l{=}l_1 \wedge \exists\tilde{a}{\in}T\left(a_i{\not\prec}\tilde{a} \wedge \tilde{a}{\not\prec}a_i \wedge \left(\bigvee_{j=2}^{n}\tilde{a}^l{=}l_j\right)\right)\right)\right]$$

- If $Q = {'l_1'}$ isP ALL$\{'l_2', \ldots, 'l_n'\}$ $\square k$, then $eval(Q, T^{\prec}) \Leftrightarrow$
$\exists^{\square k} a_1, \ldots, a_k \in T \left[\forall_{1 \leq i \leq k} \left(a_i^l = l_1 \wedge \exists \tilde{a}_2, \ldots, \tilde{a}_n \in T \left(\bigwedge_{j=2}^n (a_i \not\prec \tilde{a}_j \wedge \tilde{a}_j \not\prec a_i \wedge \right. \right. \right.$
$\left. \left. \left. \tilde{a}_j^l = l_j) \right) \right) \right]$

Boolean Operators

- If $Q = NOT(Q_1)$, then $eval(Q, T^{\prec}) \Leftrightarrow \neg eval(Q_1, T^{\prec})$
- If $Q = (Q_1$ OR $Q_2)$, then $eval(Q, T^{\prec}) \Leftrightarrow eval(Q_1, T^{\prec}) \vee eval(Q_2, T^{\prec})$
- If $Q = (Q_1$ AND $Q_2)$, then $eval(Q, T^{\prec}) \Leftrightarrow eval(Q_1, T^{\prec}) \wedge eval(Q_2, T^{\prec})$

Note that Definition 4 does not cover all queries constructible using the syntax in Definition 3. However, any query can be rewritten into a *logically equivalent* one covered by Definition 3. We call queries $Q_1, Q_2 \in \mathcal{Q}$ logically equivalent, denoted $Q_1 \equiv Q_2$, iff $\forall T^{\prec} \in \mathcal{A}^* \big(eval(Q_1, T^{\prec}) \Leftrightarrow eval(Q_2, T^{\prec}) \big)$. Below, we list query rewriting rules.

- $'l_1' \bullet \equiv 'l_1' \bullet \geq 1$
- ANY$\{'l_1', \ldots, 'l_n'\} \bullet \equiv ('l_1' \bullet)$ OR $\ldots$ OR $('l_n' \bullet)$
- ALL$\{'l_1', \ldots, 'l_n'\} \bullet \equiv ('l_1' \bullet)$ AND $\ldots$ AND $('l_n' \bullet)$
- ANY$\{'l_1', \ldots, 'l_n'\} \bullet \square k \equiv ('l_1' \bullet \square k)$ OR $\ldots$ OR $('l_n' \bullet \square k)$
- ALL$\{'l_1', \ldots, 'l_n'\} \bullet \square k \equiv ('l_1' \bullet \square k)$ AND $\ldots$ AND $('l_n' \bullet \square k)$
- ANY$\{'l_1', \ldots, 'l_{n-1}'\} \circ 'l_n' \equiv ('l_1' \circ 'l_n')$ OR $\ldots$ OR $('l_{n-1}' \circ 'l_n')$
- ALL$\{'l_1', \ldots, 'l_{n-1}'\} \circ 'l_n' \equiv ('l_1' \circ 'l_n')$ AND $\ldots$ AND $('l_{n-1}' \circ 'l_n')$
- ANY$\{'l_1', \ldots, 'l_{n-1}'\} \circ 'l_n' \square k \equiv ('l_1' \circ 'l_n' \square k)$ OR $\ldots$ OR $('l_{n-1}' \circ 'l_n' \square k)$
- ALL$\{'l_1', \ldots, 'l_{n-1}'\} \circ 'l_n' \square k \equiv ('l_1' \circ 'l_n' \square k)$ AND $\ldots$ AND $('l_{n-1}' \circ 'l_n' \square k)$
- $'l_1' \circ$ ALL$\{'l_2', \ldots, 'l_n'\} \equiv ('l_1' \circ 'l_2')$ AND $\ldots$ AND $('l_1' \circ 'l_n')$

Note that according to Definition 4, the following queries are *not* logically equivalent. Thus, ANY and ALL sets are not syntactic sugar.

- $'l_1' \circ$ ANY$\{'l_2', \ldots, 'l_n'\} \not\equiv ('l_1' \circ 'l_2')$ OR $\ldots$ OR $('l_1' \circ 'l_n')$
- $'l_1' \circ$ ANY$\{'l_2', \ldots, 'l_n'\} \square k \not\equiv ('l_1' \circ 'l_2' \square k)$ OR $\ldots$ OR $('l_1' \circ 'l_n' \square k)$
- $'l_1' \circ$ ALL$\{'l_2', \ldots, 'l_n'\} \square k \not\equiv ('l_1' \circ 'l_2' \square k)$ AND $\ldots$ AND $('l_1' \circ 'l_n' \square k)$

For example, consider E18 in Table 2. The query states that there exist at most two A activities that are in parallel to B or C activities. Thus, a trace containing four A activities, two parallel to an arbitrary number (greater than zero) of B activities, and two parallel to C activities, does not fulfill query E18. However, the described trace fulfills the query $Q = ('A'$ isP $'B' \leq 2)$ OR $('A'$ isP $'C' \leq 2)$; hence, $E18 = 'A'$ isP ANY$\{'B', 'C'\} \leq 2 \not\equiv Q$.

4.3   Evaluating Queries

This section briefly discusses our approach to query evaluation. As shown in Fig. 2, queries represent trees. Since each leaf represents a query, we evaluate the queries composed of Boolean operators bottom-up. First, the leaves are evaluated on a given trace, resulting in Boolean values per leaf. Then, bottom-up, the given Boolean operators are applied recursively.

In many cases, however, a complete query evaluation is not needed to determine its overall Boolean value for a given trace. For instance, if one leaf of a logical AND parent evaluates to false, the other leaves do not need to be further evaluated for the given trace. Similar applies to the logical OR. Reconsider the query given in Fig. 2 and the trace depicted in Fig. 1. The query consists of four leaves; however, only two must be evaluated. Following a depth-first traversing strategy, we first evaluate the leaf ('DC' isC =2) satisfied by the given trace. Thus, we do not need to evaluate the right subtree of the OR, i.e., leaves ('DC' isC =1) and ('CRR' isDF 'DC'). Finally, we evaluate the leave ('DC' isDF 'DM'). In short, by evaluating only two leaves, we can evaluate the entire query.

4.4 Implementation

This section briefly demonstrates the implementation of the proposed query language in the process mining tool Cortado [14][1]. We refer to [14] for an introduction to Cortado's architecture and a feature overview.

Figure 3 depicts a screenshot of Cortado. The shown chevron-based visualizations represent *trace variants*[2] from the loaded event log that satisfies the

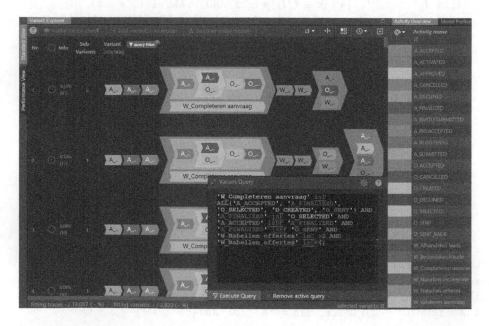

Fig. 3. Excerpt from a screenshot of Cortado showing a query editor (bottom right), a trace variant explorer visualizing the matching trace variants of the query, and a tabular overview of activities from the event log

---

[1] Available at https://cortado.fit.fraunhofer.de/.

[2] A trace variant summarizes traces that share identical ordering relationships among the contained activities.

displayed query. We refer to [13] for an introduction to the trace variant visualization. As shown in Fig. 3, the query editor offers syntax highlighting; colors of the activity labels in the query editor correspond to the colors used in the variant explorer to improve usability. Executing a query results in an updated list of trace variants satisfying the query. In Fig. 3, the numbers at the top next to the blue filter icon indicate that 109 out of 3,830 trace variants satisfy the displayed query. In the backend, we use ANTLR [7] for generating a parser for the query language. The language's design ensures that every valid query, when parsed with ANTLR, corresponds to a single parse tree that can be transformed into a unique query tree (cf. Fig. 2).

5   Application Scenario Example

This section presents an exemplary application scenario of the proposed query language. *Process discovery* is concerned with learning a process model from an event log. Conventional discovery approaches [1] are fully automated, i.e., an event log is provided as input and the discovery algorithm returns a process model describing the event data provided. Since automated process discovery algorithms often return process models of low quality, *incremental/interactive process discovery* approaches have emerged [15] to additionally utilize domain knowledge next to event data. Incremental process discovery allows users to gradually add selected traces to a process model that is considered under construction. By building a process model gradually, users can control the discovery phase and intervene as needed, for example, by selecting different traces or making manual changes to the model. In short, gradually selecting traces from event data is the major form of interaction in incremental process discovery, cf. Fig. 4.

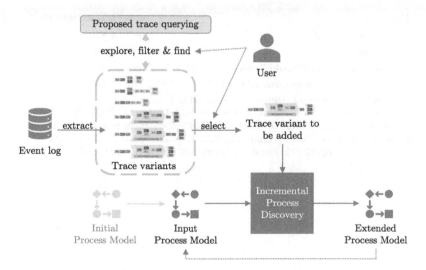

Fig. 4. Example of an application scenario of the proposed query language, i.e., trace variant selection in the context of incremental process discovery

With event logs containing numerous trace variants, user assistance in exploring, finding, and selecting trace variants is critical for the success of incremental process discovery. For instance, the log used in Fig. 3 contains 3,830 trace variants. Manual visual evaluation of all these variants is inappropriate. In such a scenario, the proposed query language is a valuable tool for users to cope with the variety, complexity, and amount of trace variants. As most process discovery approaches [1], including incremental ones, focus on learning the control flow of activities, a specialized query language focusing on control flow constraints is a valuable tool. To this end, we implemented the query language in Cortado, a tool for incremental process discovery, cf. Fig. 4.

6   Evaluation

This section presents an evaluation focusing on performance aspects of the query language. Section 6.1 presents the experimental setup and Sect. 6.2 the results.

6.1   Experimental Setup

We used four publicly available, real-life event logs, cf. Table 3. For each log, we automatically generated queries from which we pre-selected 1,000 such that no finally selected query is satisfied by all or by no trace in the corresponding log. With this approach, we have attempted to filter out trivial queries to evaluate. We measured performance-related statistics given the 1,000 queries per log.

Table 3. Statistics about the event logs used

Event log	#Traces	#Trace variants[a]
BPI challenge 2012[b]	13,087	3,830
BPI challenge 2017[c]	31,509	5,937
BPI challenge 2020, Prepaid Travel Cost log[d]	2,099	213
Road traffic fine management (RTFM)[e]	150,370	350

(a) Based on the variant definition presented in [13].
(b) https://doi.org/10.4121/uuid:3926db30-f712-4394-aebc-75976070e91f.
(c) https://doi.org/10.4121/uuid:5f3067df-f10b-45da-b98b-86ae4c7a310b.
(d) https://doi.org/10.4121/uuid:52fb97d4-4588-43c9-9d04-3604d4613b51.
(e) https://doi.org/10.4121/uuid:270fd440-1057-4fb9-89a9-b699b47990f5.

6.2   Results

Each query is applied to all traces from the given event log. Since not all leaves of a query have to be evaluated, cf. Sect. 4.3, the number of leaves evaluated may differ per trace. Thus, the actual trace determines how many leaves of a given query must be evaluated. Figure 5 shows the runtime (in seconds) of the queries per event log for the median number of leaf nodes that were evaluated. Thus, each boxplot is made up of 1,000 data points, i.e., 1,000 queries each evaluated on all traces from the given log. Across all four event logs, we clearly observe a linear trend of increasing runtime the more query leaves are evaluated.

Figure 6 depicts the distribution of queries according to their evaluation time. Further, we can see the proportion of leaves evaluated at the median. As before,

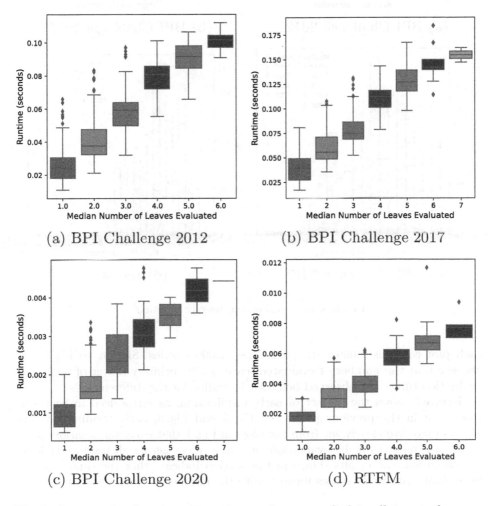

Fig. 5. Query evaluation time. Since the queries are applied to all traces, they are ordered by the median number of leaves evaluated per trace

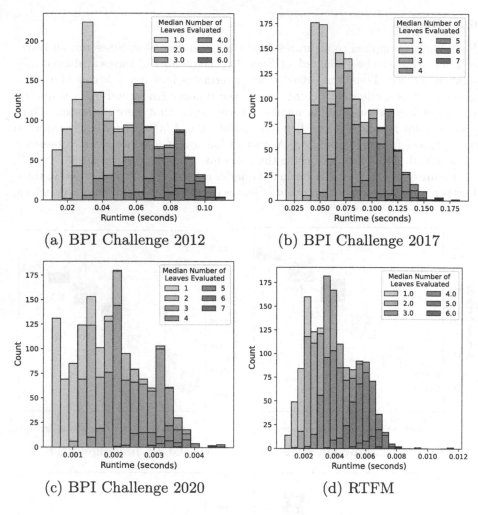

(a) BPI Challenge 2012

(b) BPI Challenge 2017

(c) BPI Challenge 2020

(d) RTFM

Fig. 6. Query evaluation time distribution

each plot contains 1,000 data points, i.e., 1,000 queries. Similar to Fig. 5, we observe that the number of evaluated leaves is the primary driver of increased evaluation time. The observed behavior is similar for the different logs.

Figure 7 shows the impact of early termination, as introduced in Sect. 4.3. Note that in the previous plots, i.e., Fig. 5 and Fig. 6, early termination was always used. We clearly see from the plots in Fig. 7 that early termination has a significant impact on the evaluation time of a query across all used event logs. In conclusion, the results shown in this section indicate that the time required to evaluate queries increases linearly with the number of leaves evaluated.

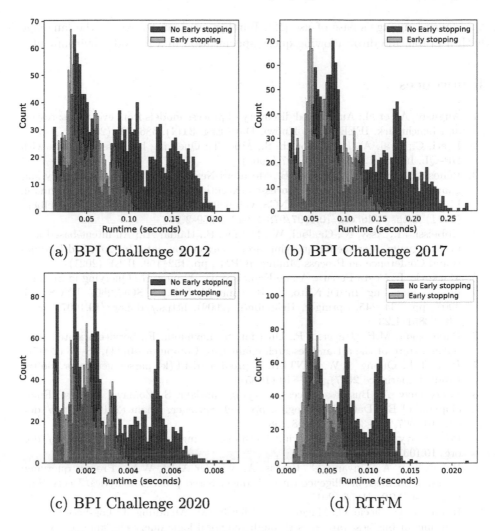

Fig. 7. Impact of early termination on the query evaluation time

7   Conclusion

We proposed a novel query language that can call up traces from event logs containing partially ordered event data. The core of the language is the control flow constraints, allowing users to specify complex ordering relationships over executed activities. We formally defined the query language's syntax and semantics. Further, we showed its implementation in the tool Cortado. We presented one potential application scenario of the language, i.e., the trace selection within incremental process discovery. In short, the proposed query language facilitates handling large event logs containing numerous traces consisting of partially ordered activities. For future work, we plan to conduct user studies exploring the query language's ease of use [12]. Further, we plan to extend the language with a graphical editor allowing query specification in a no-code environment.

References

1. Augusto, A., et al.: Automated discovery of process models from event logs: review and benchmark. IEEE Trans. Knowl. Data Eng. **31**(4), 686–705 (2019)
2. Beeri, C., Eyal, A., Kamenkovich, S., Milo, T.: Querying business processes with BP-QL. Inf. Syst. **33**(6), 477–507 (2008)
3. Beheshti, S.-M.-R., Benatallah, B., Motahari-Nezhad, H.R., Sakr, S.: A query language for analyzing business processes execution. In: Rinderle-Ma, S., Toumani, F., Wolf, K. (eds.) BPM 2011. LNCS, vol. 6896, pp. 281–297. Springer, Heidelberg (2011). https://doi.org/10.1007/978-3-642-23059-2_22
4. Kobeissi, M., Assy, N., Gaaloul, W., Defude, B., Haidar, B.: An intent-based natural language interface for querying process execution data. In: 2021 3rd International Conference on Process Mining (ICPM), pp. 152–159. IEEE (2021)
5. Markovic, I., Costa Pereira, A., de Francisco, D., Muñoz, H.: Querying in business process modeling. In: Di Nitto, E., Ripeanu, M. (eds.) ICSOC 2007. LNCS, vol. 4907, pp. 234–245. Springer, Heidelberg (2009). https://doi.org/10.1007/978-3-540-93851-4_23
6. Papazoglou, M.P., Traverso, P., Dustdar, S., Leymann, F.: Service-oriented computing: state of the art and research challenges. Computer **40**(11), 38–45 (2007)
7. Parr, T.J., Quong, R.W.: ANTLR: a predicated-LL(k) parser generator. Softw. Pract. Experience **25**(7), 789–810 (1995)
8. Polyvyanyy, A.: Business process querying. In: Sakr, S., Zomaya, A. (eds.) Encyclopedia of Big Data Technologies, pp. 1–9. Springer, Cham (2019). https://doi.org/10.1007/978-3-319-63962-8_108-1
9. Polyvyanyy, A.: Process Querying Methods. Springer, Cham (2022). https://doi.org/10.1007/978-3-030-92875-9
10. Polyvyanyy, A., Ouyang, C., Barros, A., van der Aalst, W.M.: Process querying: enabling business intelligence through query-based process analytics. Decis. Support Syst. **100**, 41–56 (2017)
11. Räim, M., Di Ciccio, C., Maggi, F.M., Mecella, M., Mendling, J.: Log-based understanding of business processes through temporal logic query checking. In: Meersman, R., et al. (eds.) OTM 2014. LNCS, vol. 8841, pp. 75–92. Springer, Heidelberg (2014). https://doi.org/10.1007/978-3-662-45563-0_5
12. Reisner, P.: Human factors studies of database query languages: a survey and assessment. ACM Comput. Surv. **13**(1), 13–31 (1981)
13. Schuster, D., Schade, L., van Zelst, S.J., van der Aalst, W.M.P.: Visualizing trace variants from partially ordered event data. In: Munoz-Gama, J., Lu, X. (eds.) ICPM 2021. LNBIP, vol. 433, pp. 34–46. Springer, Cham (2022). https://doi.org/10.1007/978-3-030-98581-3_3
14. Schuster, D., van Zelst, S.J., van der Aalst, W.M.P.: Cortado—an interactive tool for data-driven process discovery and modeling. In: Buchs, D., Carmona, J. (eds.) PETRI NETS 2021. LNCS, vol. 12734, pp. 465–475. Springer, Cham (2021). https://doi.org/10.1007/978-3-030-76983-3_23
15. Schuster, D., van Zelst, S.J., van der Aalst, W.M.P.: Utilizing domain knowledge in data-driven process discovery: a literature review. Comput. Ind. **137**, 103612 (2022). https://doi.org/10.1016/j.compind.2022.103612

16. van der Aalst, W.M.P.: Service mining: using process mining to discover, check, and improve service behavior. IEEE Trans. Serv. Comput. **6**(4), 525–535 (2013)
17. van der Aalst, W.M.P.: Process Mining: Data Science in Action. Springer, Berlin (2016). https://doi.org/10.1007/978-3-662-49851-4
18. Vogelgesang, T., Ambrosy, J., Becher, D., Seilbeck, R., Geyer-Klingeberg, J., Klenk, M.: Celonis PQL: a query language for process Mining. In: Polyvyanyy, A. (eds.) Process Querying Methods, pp. 377–408. Springer, Cham (2022). https://doi.org/10.1007/978-3-030-92875-9_13
19. Wang, J., Jin, T., Wong, R.K., Wen, L.: Querying business process model repositories. World Wide Web **17**(3), 427–454 (2014)
20. Yongsiriwit, K., Chan, N.N., Gaaloul, W.: Log-based process fragment querying to support process design. In: 2015 48th Hawaii International Conference on System Sciences, pp. 4109–4119. IEEE (2015)

A Framework for Extracting and Encoding Features from Object-Centric Event Data

Jan Niklas Adams[1]([⊠]) [iD], Gyunam Park[1] [iD], Sergej Levich[3],
Daniel Schuster[1,2] [iD], and Wil M. P. van der Aalst[1,2] [iD]

[1] Process and Data Science, RWTH Aachen University, Aachen, Germany
{niklas.adams,gnpark,schuster,wvdaalst}@pads.rwth-aachen.de
[2] Fraunhofer Institute for Applied Information Technology, Sankt Augustin,
Germany
[3] Information Systems Research, University of Freiburg, Freiburg, Germany
sergej.levich@is.uni-freiburg.de

Abstract. Traditional process mining techniques take event data as
input where each event is associated with exactly one object. An object
represents the instantiation of a process. Object-centric event data contain events associated with multiple objects expressing the interaction
of multiple processes. As traditional process mining techniques assume
events associated with exactly one object, these techniques cannot be
applied to object-centric event data. To use traditional process mining
techniques, object-centric event data are flattened by removing all object
references but one. The flattening process is lossy, leading to inaccurate
features extracted from flattened data. Furthermore, the graph-like structure of object-centric event data is lost when flattening. In this paper,
we introduce a general framework for extracting and encoding features
from object-centric event data. We calculate features natively on the
object-centric event data, leading to accurate measures. Furthermore,
we provide three encodings for these features: *tabular*, *sequential*, and
graph-based. While tabular and sequential encodings have been heavily
used in process mining, the graph-based encoding is a new technique
preserving the structure of the object-centric event data. We provide six
use cases: a visualization and a prediction use case for each of the three
encodings. We use explainable AI in the prediction use cases to show
the utility of both the object-centric features and the structure of the
sequential and graph-based encoding for a predictive model.

Keywords: Object-centric process mining · Machine learning ·
Explainable AI

1 Introduction

Process mining [1] is a branch of computer science producing data-driven insights
and actions from event data generated by processes. These insights are typically grouped into three categories: process discovery, conformance checking, and

J. Troya et al. (Eds.): ICSOC 2022, LNCS 13740, pp. 36–53, 2022.
https://doi.org/10.1007/978-3-031-20984-0_3

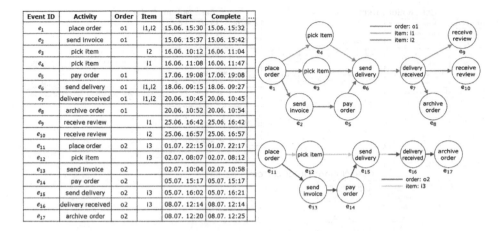

Event ID	Activity	Order	Item	Start	Complete	...
e_1	place order	o1	i1,i2	15.06. 15:30	15.06. 15:32	
e_2	send invoice	o1		15.06. 15:37	15.06. 15:42	
e_3	pick item		i2	16.06. 10:12	16.06. 11:04	
e_4	pick item		i1	16.06. 11:08	16.06. 11:47	
e_5	pay order	o1		17.06. 19:08	17.06. 19:08	
e_6	send delivery	o1	i1,i2	18.06. 09:15	18.06. 09:27	
e_7	delivery received	o1	i1,i2	20.06. 10:45	20.06. 10:45	
e_8	archive order	o1		20.06. 10:52	20.06. 10:54	
e_9	receive review		i1	25.06. 16:42	25.06. 16:42	
e_{10}	receive review		i2	25.06. 16:57	25.06. 16:57	
e_{11}	place order	o2	i3	01.07. 22:15	01.07. 22:17	
e_{12}	pick item		i3	02.07. 08:07	02.07. 08:12	
e_{13}	send invoice	o2		02.07. 10:04	02.07. 10:58	
e_{14}	pay order	o2		05.07. 15:17	05.07. 15:17	
e_{15}	send delivery	o2	i3	05.07. 16:02	05.07. 16:21	
e_{16}	delivery received	o2	i3	08.07. 12:14	08.07. 12:14	
e_{17}	archive order	o2		08.07. 12:20	08.07. 12:25	

Fig. 1. An object-centric event log and the underlying structure of events. The left-hand side depicts the event log. Events may be associated with multiple objects of different object types (here: Order and Item). The right-hand side shows the graph of directly-follows relationships for the events given by the objects. An event with multiple objects may have multiple predecessor events.

enhancement. Process discovery techniques create process models describing the possible paths of actions in a process. Conformance checking techniques quantify and qualify the correspondence between a process model and event data. Process enhancement techniques take an encoding of features of the event data as input and deliver insights, predictions, or actions as output. Such enhancement techniques include process performance analysis [20,24], prediction [10,26,29] or clustering of similar process executions [25].

Generally, process enhancement techniques encode features of event data in either of two ways: as a table [9,18] or as a set of sequences [12,19,26]. In a tabular encoding, each row corresponds to feature values for, e.g., an event. This tabular encoding is used, for example, for regression, decision trees, and feed-forward neural networks. However, each process execution (also: case) is a timely ordered sequence of events. Therefore, summarizing event data to tabular encoding removes the sequential structure of the event data. Since this structure itself is meaningful, sequential encodings were developed [19]. These encodings represent each process execution as a sequence of feature values and are used for predictive models considering sequentially encoded data, such as LSTMs [26], or to visualize the variant of the process execution.

Traditional process mining builds on two central assumptions: Each event is associated with exactly one *object* (the case) and each object is of the same type. Each object is associated with a sequence of events. A traditional *event log*, therefore, describes a collection of homogeneously typed, isolated event sequences. This is a valid assumption when analyzing, e.g., the handling of insurance claims. In this example, each object describes an instantiation of the same type: an insurance claim. Events are associated to exactly one insurance claim. However, real-life information systems often paint another picture: Events may be related

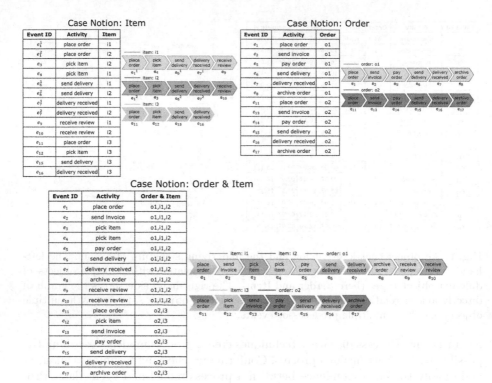

Fig. 2. Flattening an object-centric event log (cf. Fig. 1) such that it can be used for traditional process enhancement techniques. The event log is transformed into sequences of a chosen case notion. Due to deficiency, convergence and divergence, the features calculated on a flattened log might be misleading, e.g., through missing events. Furthermore, the graph-like structure of the original event log is lost.

to multiple objects of different types [3,4,11,28]. The most prominent example of information systems generating event data with multiple associated objects are ERP systems. Objects in such systems would correspond to, e.g., an order, different items of this order, and invoices in an order-to-cash process. Consider the simplified example of an order handling process depicted in Fig. 1. An event may be related to objects of type order, item, or both. An event with multiple objects may have multiple predecessor events. Therefore, the structure of an *Object-Centric Event Log (OCEL)* resembles a graph, not a sequential structure as is assumed in traditional process mining.

This gap between OCELs and traditional process enhancement techniques is currently bridged by *flattening* an event log [2], i.e., mapping an OCEL into traditional event log format by enforcing a homogeneous, sequential structure. This involves two steps: Choosing a *case notion* and duplicating events with multiple objects of that notion. All objects not included in this case notion are discarded. Flattening the event log of Fig. 1 is depicted in Fig. 2 for three different case notions. The first two are case notions of a single object type [2]. The third

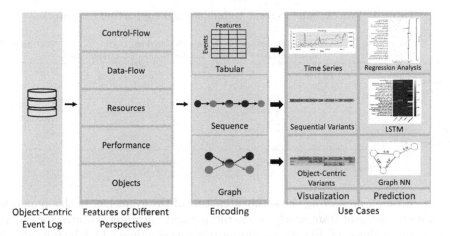

Fig. 3. Our framework enables accurate feature extraction for object-centric event data. Furthermore, we provide three encodings for object-centric features: tabular, sequential, and graph-based. We present a visualization and prediction use case for each encoding.

case notion is a composite case notion of co-appearing orders and items, i.e., an order and all corresponding items. The flattened event data may be used as input for traditional process enhancement techniques.

However, flattening manipulates the information of the object-centric event log. The problems related to flattening are *deficiency* (disappearing events) [3], *convergence* (duplicated events) [2] and *divergence* (misleading directly-follows relations) [2,28]. We showcase divergence using an example. One might use a composite case notion of order and item to flatten the event log (cf. Fig. 2 Case Notion: Order & Item). All orders and items related through events form one composite object, i.e., o1,i1,i2, and o2,i3. The events of these objects are flattened to one sequence, introducing inaccurate precedence constraints. E.g., events e_3 and e_4, which describe an item being picked, are now sequentially ordered, indicating some order between them. However, the original event data show that these two picking events are independent. The same holds for the relationship of pick item and pay order: The object-centric event data do not indicate any precedence constraint. However, the sequential representation enforces one.

The three problems of flattening have major consequences on the quality of the calculated features of the flattened OCEL: Due to missing events, duplicated events, or wrong precedence constraints, many features deliver incorrect results (cf. Sect. 4). Furthermore, the tabular or sequential encoding constructed from these features does not preserve the graph-like structure of the event data, removing important structural information. Therefore, features for OCELs can not accurately be extracted and encoded.

To solve the previously mentioned problem, an approach is necessary that calculates features natively on the object-centric event data and enables a graph-

Table 1. Process enhancement techniques and supporting frameworks.

		Feature extraction		Feature encoding			Existing work
		Object-centric	Flattened	Tabular	Sequential	Graph-based	
(a) Process enhancement techniques	P1		✓	✓			[9,13]
	P2		✓		✓		[12,19,26]
	P3		✓			✓	[16,23,27]
(b) Frameworks	F1		✓	✓			[18]
	F2		✓		✓		[7,14]
	This paper	✓		✓	✓	✓	

based encoding preserving the actual structure of the event log. In this paper, we introduce a general framework for extracting and encoding features for object-centric event data (cf. Fig. 3), providing two contributions: **1)** We translate the computation of the features introduced in the framework of de Leoni et. al [18] to the object-centric setting, providing accurate measures. **2)** We provide three different encodings to represent the extracted features for different algorithms and methods: tabular, sequential, and graph-based. Using features and encoding, we provide six use cases. These use cases showcase the generalizability of our framework to a plethora of different tasks. We use one visualization and one prediction use case for each encoding. In the prediction use cases, we depict how the different features and the structure of the encodings are utilized by predictive models, leveraging on explainable AI and SHAP values [21]. These contributions may be used as a foundation for new algorithms, new visualizations, new machine learning models, more accurate predictions, and more.

This paper is structured as follows. First, we discuss related work on feature extraction and encoding in Sect. 2. We introduce object-centric event data and process executions in Sect. 3. In Sect. 4, we provide an overview of native feature calculation for object-centric event data. In Sect. 5, we define three encodings for object-centric features. Sect. 6 depicts our six use cases for features and their encodings. We conclude this paper in Sect. 7.

2 Related Work

A plethora of process enhancement techniques exist in the literature, including process performance analysis, predictive process monitoring, and trace clustering [1]. Such techniques use encoded features extracted from an event log as input. Table 1(a) shows three categories of techniques using different feature extraction (i.e., feature extractions using 1. OCELs and 2. flattened event logs) and encoding (i.e., 1. tabular, 2. sequential, and 3. graph encoding) approaches with representative examples. First, *P1* represents the techniques using features extracted from flattened event logs and encoded as tabular formats. For instance, van Dongen et al. [9] use tabular encoding by transforming an event log into feature-outcome pairs to predict remaining times using non-parametric regression. Also, in [13], an event log is encoded into a tabular format with additional features on context, e.g., resource availability, to predict processing times. Second, techniques in *P2* also use features based on flattened event logs but encoded as sequential formats. Leontjeva et al. [19] propose *complex sequence encoding* to encode an event log to sequences to predict the outcome of an ongoing case. To predict the next activity of an ongoing case, Evermann et al. [12] encode control-flow features using *embedding* techniques, whereas Tax et al. [26] use *one-hot encoding*. Finally, *P3* consists of techniques using features extracted from flattened event logs and encoded as graph formats. Philipp et al. [23] encode an event log to a graph where each node represents an activity, and each edge indicates the relationship between activities. The graph is used to learn a *Graph Neural Network (GNN)* to predict process outcomes. Venugopal et al. [27] extend [23] by annotating nodes with temporal features. They use GNNs to predict the next activity and next timestamp of an event. Instead of representing a node as an activity, Harl et al. [16] uses one-hot encoding of an activity to represent a node to deploy *gated graph neural network* that provides the explainability based on *relevance score*.

Furthermore, to support the development of process enhancement techniques using different feature extraction and encoding, several frameworks have been proposed (cf. Table 1(b)). First, De Leoni [18] in *F1* suggest a framework to compute features using flattened event logs and encode them to tables. Second, Becker et al. [7] and Di Francescomarino et al. [14] in *F2* propose frameworks for techniques for sequentially encoding extracted features. To the best of our knowledge, no framework supporting graph encoding exists.

Despite the limitations of flattened event logs to extract misleading features, no study has been conducted to develop process enhancement techniques using features based on OCELs. In this work, we provide a framework for extracting and encoding features based on OCELs, with the goal of facilitating the development of object-centric process enhancement approaches. Our proposed framework supports all existing encoding formats, i.e., tabular, sequential, and graph, to be used for different algorithms and methods.

3 Object-Centric Event Data

Given a set X, the powerset $\mathcal{P}(X)$ denotes the set of all possible subsets. A sequence $\sigma : \{1, \ldots, n\} \to X$ of length $len(\sigma) = n$ assigns order to elements of X. We denote a sequence with $\sigma = \langle x_1, \ldots, x_n \rangle$ and the set of all sequences over X with X^*. We overload the notion $x \in \sigma$ to express $x \in range(\sigma)$.

A graph is a tuple $G = (V, E)$ of nodes V and edges $E \subseteq V \times V$. The set of all subgraphs of G is given by $sub(G) = \{(V', (V' \times V') \cap E) \mid V' \subseteq V\}$. A path connects two distinct nodes through edges. The set of paths between two nodes $v, v' \in V, v \neq v'$ is defined by $path_G(v, v') = \{\langle (v, v_1), (v_1, v_2), \ldots, (v_k, v') \rangle \in E^*\}$. Two distinct nodes are connected if the set of paths between them is not empty $path_G(v, v') \neq \emptyset$. The distance between two nodes is the length of the shortest path $dist_G(v, v') = len(\sigma_d)$ such that $\sigma_d \in path_G(v, v') \wedge \neg \exists_{\sigma'_d \in path_G(v, v')} len(\sigma_d) > len(\sigma'_d)$. A graph $G = (V, E)$ is connected iff a path exists between all edges $\forall_{v, v' \in V} v \neq v' \wedge path_G(v, v') \neq \emptyset$. The set of connected subgraphs of $G = (V, E)$ is defined as follows $consub(G) = \{G' \in sub(G) \mid G'$ is connected$\}$.

An event log is a collection of events associated with objects. Each event contains an activity, describing the executed action, a start and complete timestamp and additional attributes. Each object is associated to a sequence of events.

Definition 1 *(Event Log). Let $\mathcal{E}$ be the universe of events, $\mathcal{O}$ be the universe of objects, $\mathcal{OT}$ be the universe of object types, $\mathcal{A}$ be the universe of activities, $\mathcal{C}$ be the universe of attributes and $\mathcal{V}$ be the universe of attribute values. Let $A \subseteq \mathcal{A}$ be a set of activities and $C \subseteq \mathcal{C}$ be a set of attributes. Each object is mapped to exactly one object type $\pi_{type} : \mathcal{O} \to \mathcal{OT}$. An event log $L = (E, O, OT, \pi_{ct}, \pi_{st}, \pi_{trace}, \pi_{act}, \pi_{att})$ is a tuple composed of*

- *events $E \subseteq \mathcal{E}$, objects $O \subseteq \mathcal{O}$, and object types $OT \subseteq \mathcal{OT}$,*
- *two time mappings for the completion $\pi_{ct} : E \to \mathbb{R}$ and the start $\pi_{st} : E \to \mathbb{R}$ of an event such that $\pi_{st}(e) \leq \pi_{ct}(e)$ for any $e \in E$,*
- *a mapping $\pi_{trace} : O \to E^*$ mapping each object to a sequence of events such that $\forall_{o \in O} \, \pi_{trace}(o) = \langle e_1, \dots, e_n \rangle \wedge \forall_{i \in \{1, \dots n-1\}} \, \pi_{ct}(e_i) \leq \pi_{ct}(e_{i+1})$,*
- *an activity mapping $\pi_{act} : E \to A$ and,*
- *an attribute mapping $\pi_{att} : E \times C \nrightarrow V$.*

The table in Fig. 1 depicts an example of an OCEL. A row corresponds to one event. Sorting the events of an object in timely order, we retrieve the event sequence for the object, e.g., $\pi_{trace}(i3) = \langle$place order, pick item, send delivery, delivery received$\rangle$. The relationships between objects can be expressed in the form of a graph, connecting objects that share events.

Definition 2 (Object Graph). *Let $L = (E, O, OT, \pi_{ct}, \pi_{st}, \pi_{trace}, \pi_{act}, \pi_{att})$ be an event log. We denote the objects of an event $e \in E$ with $\pi_{obj}(e) = \{o \in O \mid e \in \pi_{trace}(o)\}$. The object graph $OG_L = (O, I)$ is an undirected graph of nodes O and edges of object interactions $I = \{\{o, o'\} \subseteq O \mid o \neq o' \wedge \exists_{e \in E} \, \{o, o'\} \subseteq \pi_{obj}(e)\}$.*

Objects which are directly or transitively connected in the object graph depend on each other by sharing events. In traditional process mining, a process execution (case) is the event sequence of one object. We use the definitions of process executions [6] and generalize this notion such that a process execution is the set of events for multiple, connected objects.

Definition 3 *(Process Execution). Let $L = (E, O, OT, \pi_{ct}, \pi_{st}, \pi_{trace}, \pi_{act}, \pi_{att})$ be an event log and $OG_L = (O, I)$ be the corresponding object graph. A process execution $p = (O', E')$ is a tuple of objects $O' \subseteq O$ and events $E' \subseteq E$ such that $e' \in E' \Leftrightarrow \pi_{obj}(e') \subseteq O'$ and O' forms a connected subgraph in OG_L.*

We define two techniques to extract process executions from an OCEL. These two techniques are two out of many possible process execution extraction techniques. The first technique extracts process executions based on the connected components of the object graph. All transitively connected objects form one process execution. This might lead to large executions for entangled event logs. Therefore, we introduce the leading type extraction. A process execution is constructed for each object of a chosen leading object type. Connected objects are added to this process execution unless a connected object of the same type has a lower distance to the leading object. This limits executions in size but also removes dependencies.

Definition 4 (Execution Extraction). *Let* $L=(E, O, OT, \pi_{ct}, \pi_{st}, \pi_{trace}, \pi_{act}, \pi_{att})$ *be an event log. An execution extraction* $EX \subseteq consub(OG_L)$ *retrieves connected subgraphs from the object graph. A subgraph* $ex = (O', I') \in EX$ *is mapped to a process execution* $f^{extract}(ex, L) = (O', E')$ *with* $E' = \{e \in E \mid O' \cap obj(e) \neq \emptyset\}$. *We define two extraction techniques:*

- $EX_{comp}(L) = \{G \in consub(OG_L) \mid \neg\exists_{G' \in consub(OG_L)} G \in sub(G')\}$, *and*
- $EX_{lead}(L, ot) = \{G \in lead\_graphs = \{G' = (O', I') \in consub(OG_L) \mid \exists_{o \in O'} \pi_{type}(o) = ot \wedge \forall_{o' \in O'} \neg\exists_{o'' \in O'} o'' \neq o' \wedge \pi_{type}(o'') = \pi_{type}(o') \wedge dist_{G'}(o, o') > dist_{G'}(o, o'')\} \mid \neg\exists_{G'' \in lead\_graphs} G \in sub(G'')\}$ *for* $ot \in OT$.

When looking at the example of Fig. 1, the process executions retrieved by applying EX_{comp} would be based on the connected components of the object graph, i.e., $\{o1, i1, i2\}$ and $\{o2, i3\}$. Using the leading type order, we would retrieve the same executions. Using item as the leading type, we would retrieve $\{i1, o1\}$, $\{i2, o1\}$ and $\{i3, o2\}$.

4   Object-Centric Features

This section deals with the problem resulting from flattening OCELs to apply process enhancement techniques: Features are calculated on the manipulated, flattened event data. Therefore, they might be inaccurate. We propose an object-centric adaptation of the features introduced by the seminal machine learning framework of de Leoni et al. [18]. We calculate them natively on the OCEL. Furthermore, we provide several new features recently introduced in the literature on object-centric process mining. A feature is, generally, calculated for an event. It might describe a measure for the single event, in relationship to its process executions, or the whole system.

Definition 5 (Features). *Let* $L = (E, O, OT, \pi_{ct}, \pi_{st}, \pi_{trace}, \pi_{act}, \pi_{att})$ *be an event log and* $EX \subseteq consub(OG_L)$ *be a set of extracted process executions. A feature* $f_L : E \times EX \nrightarrow \mathbb{R}$ *maps an event and a process execution onto a real number.*

The primary need for adapting traditional feature calculation arises from two main differentiations between object-centric and traditional event data: First, each event can have multiple predeccesors/successors, one for each object. Second, each event might have multiple objects of different types. The computation of features that are depended on previous and following behavior has to be adapted to the graph structure. The most obvious example are preceding activities: In traditional feature extraction, there is only one preceding activity for each event. In object-centric feature extraction, there are multiple preceding activities, one for each object. The graph-structure as well as the multiplicity of objects also enables the definition of new features leveraging on the graph

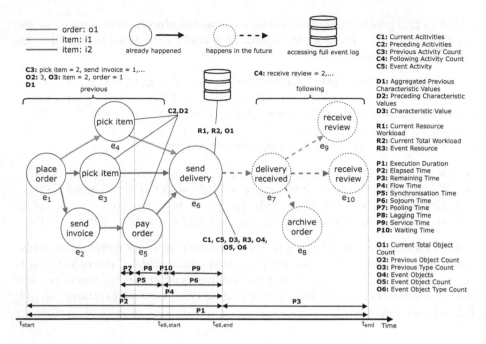

Fig. 4. Overview of the features that can be extracted for event e_6. These features are the object-centric adaptations of [18].

structure and object (type) associations. Previous (i.e., all events that happened before the considered event in an execution) and following events can be adapted in two ways: time-based (using the event's timestamp) and path-based (using path information of the graph). We use a simple time-based adaptation. However, the graph-based adaptation might give interesting new research directions.

An overview of the features collected from an object-centric adaptation of de Leoni et al.'s framework [18] and features recently introduced in the literature [3,22] is depicted in Fig. 4. Similar to de Leoni et al., we group features according to different perspectives: Control-Flow, Data-Flow, Resource, Performance and Objects. We, now, discuss the different perspectives and the adaptations that are necessary to apply them to the object-centric setting. Table 2 provides a qualitative evaluation of the impact of flattening on the resulting feature value: Features can be equal, they can be misleading/incorrect after flattening, and not be available for flat event data.

The main adaptations of the control-flow perspectives are concerned with the switch from sequential to graph-like control-flow. Multiple preceding activities (**C2**) as well as multiple current activities (**C1**) (endpoints of the current execution graph) are possible. For previous and following activities (**C3**, **C4**), we use a simple time-based adaptation.

The data-flow perspective needs slight adaptations for preceding characteristic values (**D2**). Since there might be multiple preceding values, these need to

Table 2. Impact of flattening on calculated feature values. Calculating a feature for an event on object-centric vs. flattened data can lead to correct or misleading results. Some features only exist on object-centric event data. Most features are misleading due to the graph structure and object multiplicity.

Features		Impact of flattening		Only available for OCEL
		Correct	Misleading	
Control-Flow	C1, C2, C3, C4		✓	
	C5	✓		
Data	D1, D2		✓	
	D3	✓		
Resource	R1		✓	
	R2, R3	✓		
Performance	P1, P2, P3, P6, P10		✓	
	P4, P5, P7, P8			✓
	P9	✓		
Objects	O1, O2, O3, O4, O5			✓

be aggregated. Previous characteristic values (**D1**) are adapted on a time basis, and the characteristic value (**D3**) needs no adaptation.

The resources perspective's features are mainly concerned with system-wide measurements, such as the workload of the current resource (**C1**) or the total system workload (**C2**). Therefore, this perspective remains mostly unaffected by a move to object-centricity. Future research might investigate new features derived from resource multiplicity per event.

The performance perspective has recently been studied for new object-centric features [22]. Due to an event having multiple predecessors, the established performance measures can be extended by several features expressing the time for synchronization between objects (**P5**), the pooling time of an object type (**P7**), or the lag between object types before the event (**P8**).

Finally, a new feature perspective concerning objects opens up. The paper introducing the discovery of object-centric Petri nets [3] introduces some basic features of the object perspective. For example, an event's number of objects (**O5**), the event's number of objects of a specific type (**O6**), or the current system's total object count (**O1**). Investigations of additional features in this perspective, e.g., quantifying the relationships between objects through graph metrics on the object graph, might also be an interesting research direction.

5 Feature Encodings

In this section, we tackle the absence of feature encodings that represent the graph-like structure of object-centric event data. We extend the currently used tabular and sequential encodings with a graph-based one and introduce all three encodings formally. Together with the formal definition of each encoding, we provide some common use cases, advantages, disadvantages and a continuation of our running example from Fig. 1. As an example of extracted features we choose the number of previous objects (**O2**), the synchronization time (**P5**) and the remaining time (**P3**). The execution extraction for our example is the connected components extraction EX_{comp}. A tabular encoding is a common representation of data points used for many use cases, such as regression analysis, clustering, different data mining tasks, etc.

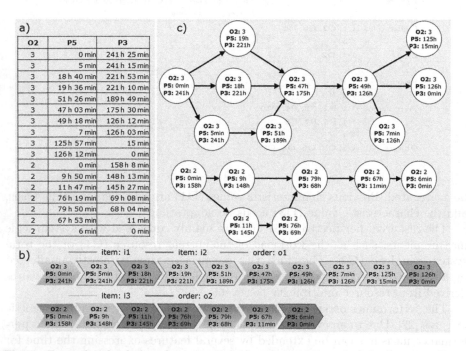

Fig. 5. Example of tabular a), sequential b) and graph-based c) feature encodings for the running example in Fig. 1. The graph-based encoding preserves the structural information from the OCEL.

Definition 6 (Tabular Encoding). *Let* $L = (E, O, OT, \pi_{ct}, \pi_{st}, \pi_{trace}, \pi_{act},$ $\pi_{att})$ *be an event log and* $EX \subseteq consub(OG_L)$ *be a set of process executions. Let* $F_L \subseteq E \times EX \nrightarrow \mathbb{R}$ *be a set of features. The event feature table is defined by* $tab(e, f_L) = f_L(e, ex)$ *for all* $e \in E$, $ex \in EX$ *(rows) and all* $f_L \in F_L$ *(columns).*

We depict an example of tabular encoding in Fig. 5 a). Such an encoding is easily readable and versatile usable, however, the structural order information of the event log is lost in the process of tabular encoding. A sequential encoding is commonly used in sequence visualization, clustering, classification or next value predictions (cf. Sec. 2).

Definition 7 (Sequential Encoding). *Let* $L = (E, O, OT, \pi_{ct}, \pi_{st}, \pi_{trace},$ $\pi_{act}, \pi_{att})$ *be an event log and* $EX \subseteq consub(OG_L)$ *be a set of extracted process executions. Let* $F_L = \{f_{L,1}, \dots, f_{L,m}\} \subseteq E \times EX \nrightarrow \mathbb{R}$ *be a set of features. The sequential encoding of an execution* $ex \in EX$ *is defined by* $seq(ex, F_L) =$

Table 3. Results for the different models based on different encodings.

	Regression	LSTM	GNN
Baseline MAE		0.7598	
Train MAE	0.5101	0.4717	0.4460
Validation MAE	NA	0.4625	0.4534
Test MAE	0.5087	0.4568	0.4497

$\langle (f_{L,1}(e_1, ex), \ldots, f_{L,m}(e_1, ex)), \ldots, (f_{L,1}(e_n, ex), \ldots, f_{L,m}(e_n, ex)) \rangle$ *with with* $(O', \{e_1, \ldots, e_n\}) = f^{extract}(ex, L)$ *and* $\pi_{ct}(e_1) \leq \cdots \leq \pi_{ct}(e_n)$.

We depict a sequential encoding of the running example in Fig. 5 b). The events for process executions are ordered according to the complete timestamp of the event. The resulting sequence is attributed with the different feature values for each event. This encoding respects the timely order of events. *However, it does not respect the true precedence constraints of the event log*: By merging all events into one sequence, some event pairs are forced into a precedence relationships they did not exhibit in the event log (cf. Sec. 1). A graph encoding of features may be used for extensive visualization, applying graph algorithms or for utilizing graph neural networks [30].

Definition 8 *(Graph Encoding).* *Let* $L=(E, O, OT, \pi_{ct}, \pi_{st}, \pi_{trace}, \pi_{act}, \pi_{att})$ *be an event log* $EX \subseteq consub(OG_L)$ *be a set of extracted process executions. Let* $F_L = \{f_{L,1}, \ldots, f_{L,m}\} \subseteq E \times EX \nrightarrow \mathbb{R}$ *be a set of features. For an extracted execution* $ex \in EX$, *the graph of the corresponding process execution* $p = (O', E') = f^{extract}(ex, L)$ *is defined by* $G_p = (E', K)$ *with edges* $K = \{(e, e') \in E' \times E' \mid e \neq e' \wedge o \in O' \wedge \langle e_1, \ldots, e_n \rangle \in \pi_{trace}(o) \wedge e = e_i \wedge e' = e_{i+1} \wedge i \in \{1, \ldots, n-1\}\})$. *The graph encoding is defined by* $G_{feat}(p, F_L) = (E', K, l)$ *with a node labeling function* $l(e) = \{f_L(e, ex) \mid f_L \in F_L\}$ *for any* $e \in E'$.

An example of the graph-based feature encoding for our running example is depicted in Fig. 5 c). Each process execution is associated with a graph. Each node of the graph represents the feature values of an event.

6 Use Cases

In this section, we evaluate our framework by providing six use cases. We pursue two evaluation goals with this approach: First, we aim to showcase the generalizability of the framework by providing a collection of common process mining tasks the framework can be applied to. Second, we aim to showcase the feature's and encoding's effectiveness in the use cases. Over the last years, explainable AI has been increasingly employed to make predictive process monitoring transparent [15,17]. Through the use of SHAP [21] values, we are able to quantify feature importance as well as structural importance of sequential and graph-based encoding.

48   J. N. Adams et al.

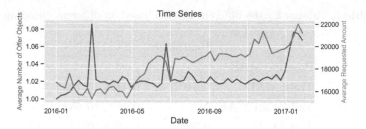

Fig. 6. Time series describing two features over time: the weekly average number of loan offers per event and the weekly average requested amount for each application. Using this evaluation some initial insights can be generated, e.g., the gradual increase in requested amount over time.

The use cases are split into two parts: three visualization and three prediction use cases. We use a real-life loan application event log [8] as an OCEL. An event can be related to an application and multiple loan offers as objects. We use tabular, sequential, and graph-based encoding to gain insights into the process through the visualization use cases. The prediction use cases aim at predicting the remaining time of an event's process execution (**P3**) using three different techniques for the different encodings: regression (tabular), LSTM neural networks (sequential), and GNNs (graph-based). We use the same features for each encoding: Preceding activities (**C2**), average previous requested amount (**D1**), the elapsed time (**P2**), and the previous number of offers (**O3**). We use a 0.7/0.3 train/test split of the same events for each model for comparability reasons. We set aside 20% of the training set as a validation set. The performance is assessed using the *Mean Absolute Error (MAE)* of the normalized target variable. Furthermore, we provide a baseline MAE achieved by predicting the training set's average remaining time. The summarized results are depicted in Table 3.

We provide an open-source python implementation of our framework[1]. Our experiments can ge reproduced through a GitHub repository[2]. The framework can be extended with new features and adapted algorithms.

6.1 Tabular Encoding

Visualization. We split the event log into subsequent sublogs containing the events of one week each. For each sublog, we extract the average requested amount (**D3**) and the number of offers per event (**O6**). The resulting time series is depicted in Fig. 6. We can observe the dynamics of the process over time, e.g., the increase in the requested amount over time. Furthermore, we can observe that the number of offers is stable, except for a few short spikes.

Prediction. We use a linear regression model to predict the remaining time based on the tabular encoding (cf. Table 3). This is an object-centric adaption of use

---
[1] https://github.com/ocpm/ocpa.
[2] https://github.com/niklasadams/OCELFeatureExtractionExperiments.

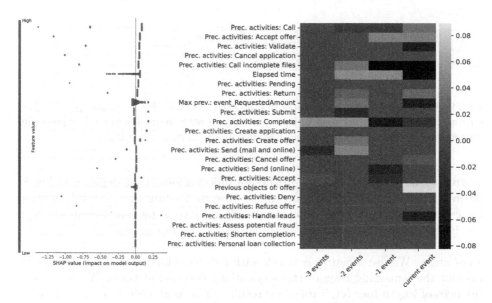

Fig. 7. Left: Bee swarm plot of SHAP values for the regression model, showing the aggregated importance of different features to the predictions. Right: SHAP values of one LSTM prediction, visualized for the different positions of the input sequence.

Fig. 8. Sequential variant visualization of a process execution enriched with the object information (blue = application, orange = first and second offer). (Color figure online)

cases [9,13]. We generate the SHAP values, i.e., the impact of different features on the individual model prediction, for 1000 predictions of the test set. The resulting bee swarm plot is depicted in Fig. 7 (left side). Red points indicate a high feature value. The more they are positioned to the left, the more the feature value reduces the model's prediction. Therefore, the combination of color and position gives insights into the feature value's impact on the model output. We can, e.g., observe a high decreasing impact of the existence of the *Call* activity in the preceding activities to the predicted remaining time. One can also observe an impact of the new object-centric feature of the number of previous objects of type offer on the predicted remaining time: the more offers were previously recorded in a case, the lower the predicted remaining time. In conclusion, the selected set of object-centric feature adaptations yields valuable information for a predictive model.

6.2   Sequential Encoding

Visualization. We choose one specific process execution and extract the sequential encoding for the current event's activity (**C5**) and the event's objects (**O4**)

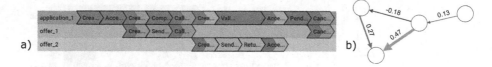

a)   b)

Fig. 9. Use cases for the graph encoding: a) activities and objects of one process execution. Shared events between objects are colored with multiple colors. b) shows the importance of different edges of one instance graph when predicting.

features. The result is a variant enriched by object information, depicted in Fig. 8. Even though such a visualization might have misleading causality information for events between objects, one can already retrieve some valuable insight into the intra-object order and the overall activities of an execution.

Prediction. We use a neural network with two 10-hidden-node LSTM layers to predict the remaining time of the sequentially encoded features. We use subsequences of length four (cf. Table 3 for results). This is an object-centric adaption of use cases [19,26]. The regression use case already covered the importance of features for the prediction. Therefore, we focus on the importance of the sequential encoding in this use case. We use SHAP values for each feature of the four positions in the sequential encoding. The calculated feature impacts for an individual prediction are depicted in Fig. 7 (right side). The more the value diverges from zero, the higher the feature's impact on the model's output. We observe features with high importance among all four positions of the sequence. Therefore, the model utilizes the sequential encoding of the features, showcasing its usefulness.

6.3   Graph Encoding

Visualization. Fig. 9 a) depicts the graph-based variant visualization retrieved from OCπ [5] of the same process execution as Fig. 8. Using the graph, one can place concurrent events in two different lanes according to their objects, not indicating any precedence between them. One can intuitively determine the concurrent paths in the variant and the interaction of different objects. For large process executions, this provides structured access to the control-flow of the underlying process.

Prediction. We use the graph-based feature encoding as an input for a GNN. The GNN contains two graph convolution layers. Each node in both layers has a size of 24. Input graphs are constrained to four nodes (cf. LSTM use case). We read the graphs out by averaging over the convoluted values, summarizing to one predicted remaining time (cf. Table 3 for results). This is an object-centric adaptation of use cases [23,27]. We adapt SHAP values to determine the importance of graph edges to the predicted remaining time. Fig. 9 b) depicts the calculated values for one graph instance. The more the value of an edge diverges from zero, the higher its existence impacts the model's prediction. We observe substantially different values for all edges: While some edges have a relatively low negative or positive impact on the model's output, the presence of other edges heavily impacts the predicted remaining time. Therefore, the graph structure itself yields important information for predicting the remaining time.

7 Conclusion

We introduced a general framework to extract and encode features from OCELs. Currently, object-centric event data needs to be flattened to apply process enhancement techniques to the data. This leads to inaccurate features. Additionally, no feature encoding is available to express the graph-like structure of object-centric event data. Our framework calculates features natively on the object-centric event data, leading to accurate features. Furthermore, we provide a graph-based encoding of the features, preserving the underlying structure of an OCEL. We show the utility of the features and encodings in six use cases, a visualization and prediction use case for each of the three encodings. This framework lays a foundation for future machine learning approaches utilizing object-centric event data and new algorithms using our encodings as a basis.

We provide a collection of use cases showing the applicability of our framework for extracting and encoding features. For each of our framework steps, interesting future research directions are present: Which feature work well with which encoding? What are the best prediction techniques for which encoding? How to optimize existing network architectures to achieve maximum results? Furthermore, investigations of new features derived from the graph structure and object-multiplicity as well as further traditional features not included in de Leoni et al.'s framework [18] is an interesting direction for future research.

References

1. van der Aalst, W.M.P.: Process Mining: Data Science in Action. Springer, Berlin (2016). https://doi.org/10.1007/978-3-662-49851-4
2. Ölveczky, P.C., Salaün, G. (eds.): SEFM 2019. LNCS, vol. 11724. Springer, Cham (2019). https://doi.org/10.1007/978-3-030-30446-1
3. van der Aalst, W.M.P., Berti, A.: Discovering object-centric petri nets. Fundam. Informaticae **175**(1–4), 1–40 (2020). https://doi.org/10.3233/FI-2020-1946
4. Adams, J.N., van der Aalst, W.M.P.: Precision and fitness in object-centric process mining. In: ICPM, pp. 128–135. IEEE (2021). https://doi.org/10.1109/ICPM53251.2021.9576886
5. Adams, J.N., van der Aalst, W.M.P.: Ocπ: object-centric process insights. In: Bernardinello, L., Petrucci, L. (eds.) Application and Theory of Petri Nets and Concurrency. PETRI NETS 2022. Lecture Notes in Computer Science, vol. 13288, pp. 139–150. Springer, Cham (2022). https://doi.org/10.1007/978-3-031-06653-5_8
6. Adams, J.N., Schuster, D., Schmitz, S., Schuh, G., van der Aalst, W.M.P.: Defining cases and variants for object-centric event data. CoRR abs/2208.03235, 10.48550/arXiv.2208.03235 (2022)

7. Becker, J., Breuker, D., Delfmann, P., Matzner, M.: Designing and implementing a framework for event-based predictive modelling of business processes. In: EMISA, pp. 71–84. GI (2014)
8. van Dongen, B.: BPI challenge 2017 (2017). https://doi.org/10.4121/uuid: 5f3067df-f10b-45da-b98b-86ae4c7a310b
9. van Dongen, B.F., Crooy, R.A., van der Aalst, W.M.P.: Cycle time prediction: when will this case finally be finished? In: Meersman, R., Tari, Z. (eds.) OTM 2008. LNCS, vol. 5331, pp. 319–336. Springer, Heidelberg (2008). https://doi.org/ 10.1007/978-3-540-88871-0_22
10. Ehrendorfer, M., Mangler, J., Rinderle-Ma, S.: Assessing the impact of context data on process outcomes during runtime. In: Hacid, H., Kao, O., Mecella, M., Moha, N., Paik, H. (eds.) ICSOC 2021. LNCS, vol. 13121, pp. 3–18. Springer, Cham (2021). https://doi.org/10.1007/978-3-030-91431-8_1
11. Esser, S., Fahland, D.: Multi-dimensional event data in graph databases. J. Data Semant. **10**(1–2), 109–141 (2021). https://doi.org/10.1007/s13740-021-00122-1
12. Evermann, J., Rehse, J., Fettke, P.: Predicting process behaviour using deep learning. Decis. Support Syst. **100**, 129–140 (2017). https://doi.org/10.1016/j.dss.2017. 04.003
13. Folino, F., Guarascio, M., Pontieri, L.: Discovering context-aware models for predicting business process performances. In: Meersman, R., et al. (eds.) OTM 2012. LNCS, vol. 7565, pp. 287–304. Springer, Heidelberg (2012). https://doi.org/10. 1007/978-3-642-33606-5_18
14. Di Francescomarino, C., Dumas, M., Federici, M., Ghidini, C., Maggi, F.M., Rizzi, W.: Predictive business process monitoring framework with hyperparameter optimization. In: Nurcan, S., Soffer, P., Bajec, M., Eder, J. (eds.) CAiSE 2016. LNCS, vol. 9694, pp. 361–376. Springer, Cham (2016). https://doi.org/10.1007/978-3-319-39696-5_22
15. Galanti, R., Coma-Puig, B., de Leoni, M., Carmona, J., Navarin, N.: Explainable predictive process monitoring. In: ICPM, pp. 1–8. IEEE (2020). https://doi.org/ 10.1109/ICPM49681.2020.00012
16. Harl, M., Weinzierl, S., Stierle, M., Matzner, M.: Explainable predictive business process monitoring using gated graph neural networks. J. Decis. Syst. **29**(sup1), 312–327 (2020). https://doi.org/10.1080/12460125.2020.1780780
17. Huang, T.H., Metzger, A., Pohl, K.: Counterfactual explanations for predictive business process monitoring. In: Themistocleous, M., Papadaki, M. (eds.) Information Systems. EMCIS 2021. Lecture Notes in Business Information Processing, vol. 437, pp. 399–413. Springer, Cham (2022). https://doi.org/10.1007/978-3-030-95947-0_28
18. de Leoni, M., van der Aalst, W.M.P., Dees, M.: A general process mining framework for correlating, predicting and clustering dynamic behavior based on event logs. Inf. Syst. **56**, 235–257 (2016). https://doi.org/10.1016/j.is.2015.07.003
19. Leontjeva, A., Conforti, R., Di Francescomarino, C., Dumas, M., Maggi, F.M.: Complex symbolic sequence encodings for predictive monitoring of business processes. In: Motahari-Nezhad, H.R., Recker, J., Weidlich, M. (eds.) BPM 2015. LNCS, vol. 9253, pp. 297–313. Springer, Cham (2015). https://doi.org/10.1007/ 978-3-319-23063-4_21
20. Li, C.-Y., van Zelst, S.J., van der Aalst, W.M.P.: Stage-based process performance analysis. In: Hacid, H., et al. (eds.) ICSOC 2020. LNCS, vol. 12632, pp. 349–364. Springer, Cham (2021). https://doi.org/10.1007/978-3-030-76352-7_34
21. Lundberg, S.M., Lee, S.: A unified approach to interpreting model predictions. In: NeurIPS, pp. 4765–4774 (2017)

22. Park, G., Adams, J.N., van der Aalst, W.M.P.: OPerA: object-centric performance analysis. In: Ralyté, J., Chakravarthy, S., Mohania, M., Jeusfeld, M.A., Karla-palem, K. (eds.) Conceptual Modeling. ER 2022. LNCS, vol. 13607, pp. 281–292. Springer, Cham (2022). https://doi.org/10.1007/978-3-031-17995-2_20
23. Philipp, P., et al.: Analysis of control flow graphs using graph convolutional neural networks. In: ISCMI, pp. 73–77 (2019). https://doi.org/10.1109/ISCMI47871.2019.9004296
24. Rogge-Solti, A., Weske, M.: Prediction of remaining service execution time using stochastic petri nets with arbitrary firing delays. In: Basu, S., Pautasso, C., Zhang, L., Fu, X. (eds.) ICSOC 2013. LNCS, vol. 8274, pp. 389–403. Springer, Heidelberg (2013). https://doi.org/10.1007/978-3-642-45005-1_27
25. Sun, Y., Bauer, B., Weidlich, M.: Compound trace clustering to generate accurate and simple sub-process models. In: Maximilien, M., Vallecillo, A., Wang, J., Oriol, M. (eds.) ICSOC 2017. LNCS, vol. 10601, pp. 175–190. Springer, Cham (2017). https://doi.org/10.1007/978-3-319-69035-3_12
26. Tax, N., Verenich, I., La Rosa, M., Dumas, M.: Predictive business process monitoring with LSTM neural networks. In: Dubois, E., Pohl, K. (eds.) CAiSE 2017. LNCS, vol. 10253, pp. 477–492. Springer, Cham (2017). https://doi.org/10.1007/978-3-319-59536-8_30
27. Venugopal, I., Töllich, J., Fairbank, M., Scherp, A.: A comparison of deep-learning methods for analysing and predicting business processes. In: IJCNN, pp. 1–8 (2021). https://doi.org/10.1109/IJCNN52387.2021.9533742
28. Waibel, P., Pfahlsberger, L., Revoredo, K., Mendling, J.: Causal process mining from relational databases with domain knowledge. CoRR abs/2202.08314 (2022)
29. Wang, C., Cao, J.: Interval-based remaining time prediction for business processes. In: Hacid, H., Kao, O., Mecella, M., Moha, N., Paik, H. (eds.) ICSOC 2021. LNCS, vol. 13121, pp. 34–48. Springer, Cham (2021). https://doi.org/10.1007/978-3-030-91431-8_3
30. Wu, Z., et al.: A comprehensive survey on graph neural networks. IEEE Trans. Neural Networks Learn. Syst. 32(1), 4–24 (2021). https://doi.org/10.1109/TNNLS.2020.2978386

Automated RESTful API Service Discovery with Various Interface Features

Shuaijun Wang, Yuanyuan Zhou, and Zhijun Ding[✉]

Department of Computer Science and Technology, Tongji University, Shanghai, China
{wangsj,yuanyuan_zhouTJ,dingzj}@tongji.edu.cn

Abstract. In recent years, the rapid increase in the number of RESTful API services has made it more difficult for developers to select functionally suitable and callable ones from massive service information, which brings new challenges for service discovery. Most existing RESTful API discovery methods only use the function description texts, ignoring the information contained in the input and output interfaces, making the callability of the discovery results unguaranteed. This paper proposes an automated RESTful API service discovery framework considering both the description texts and interfaces. Based on the three newly-noticed RESTful API features of interface design and parameter matching, this paper presents an interface preprocessing and matching strategy. Interface preprocessing consists of interface transformation and identifier expansion to deal with parameter abbreviations. About the matching strategy, required and optional input parameters are matched with different importance, and one-to-many parameter matching relationships are allowed in this scheme. Experiments show that the proposed method is more suitable for automated RESTful API service discovery with various interface features. Better results are reflected in three metrics.

Keywords: Automated service discovery · Interface matching · Identifier expansion · Rapid API

1 Introduction

With the introduction of service-oriented architectures and development of Internet technology, more services can be published, searched, and invoked through the Internet. More developers choose to reuse existing services instead of redevelopment. Service registries such as UDDI were established and Web Service Description Language(WSDL) became the commonly used description language for SOAP-based services. After the REST architecture style was brought up, web services gradually turn to be designed as RESTful APIs because the new style is lighter and easier to understand. The platforms for service registry and discovery have also moved from UDDI to some mainstream API markets such as Programmable Web[1] and Rapid API[2]. The explosive growth of the number

---

[1] https://www.programmableweb.com/.
[2] https://rapidapi.com/hub.

© The Author(s), under exclusive license to Springer Nature Switzerland AG 2022
J. Troya et al. (Eds.): ICSOC 2022, LNCS 13740, pp. 54–70, 2022.
https://doi.org/10.1007/978-3-031-20984-0_4

of services brings more choices to the users, while at the same time the challenge about how to efficiently find the services meeting the user's requirements arrives.

The change of service form leads to the change of service discovery research object from SOAP-based services to RESTful APIs and mashups [1,14]. However, most of the WSDL-based service discovery methods adopt keyword-matching technologies which cannot assure the discovery accuracy [18]. Ontology based semantic service description languages are then introduced to help with the understanding of parameters. However, RESTful APIs do not provide corresponding semantic annotations, which makes it difficult for the SOAP-based methods to be migrated to the API scenario. In the meantime, most of the API discovery research [12] focus on improving natural language processing technologies to understand the description better, which ignores the service callability. Therefore, it is necessary to propose a RESTful API-oriented service discovery method considering both the function description and interfaces.

To achieve this, we turn to the world's largest API hub, Rapid API [22]. On this platform, besides the functional description text of APIs, the interface and performance information can also be automatically collected. Based on Rapid API, we notice three new features of RESTful API interfaces in aspects of interface design and parameter matching. Firstly, many abbreviations can be noticed in parameters. Due to the lack of semantic annotations, these abbreviations can greatly affect the accuracy of interface matching. Secondly, input parameters can have different necessities as required or optional, which affects their importance during matching. The third one is about matching relationships. There may have one-to-many matches between parameters. For example, when a weather forecast service needs *coordinate* as input, the data provided by the user may be two separate parameters, *latitude* and *longitude*. We all know that *coordinate* refers to the combination of *latitude* and *longitude*. In this case, both provided data should be assigned to *coordinate*. These features can affect the discovery accuracy to a certain extent. However, most existing work ignores their existence.

According to the problems, the main contributions are as follows:

- A framework for automatically RESTful API service preprocessing and discovery is proposed. Based on the description texts and interfaces of large-scale APIs, this framework provides more accurate discovery results considering both the functional similarity and interface callability.
- Due to the features of RESTful APIs in the aspect of interface design and parameter matching, an interface processing and matching method is proposed. The interface processing includes the interface transformation and identifier expansion, which is based on domain experience base and parameter context. The one-to-many parameter matching with similarity threshold is allowed, and the difference between required and optional input parameters is considered, which can better fit with various user requirements.
- A new API dataset covering multi-angle information is collected from Rapid API. Experiments are carried out based on this dataset. The discovery platform based on the proposed work is now accessible[3].

---

[3] https://www.scafe.net.cn/.

2   Related Work

According to the service forms during development, we introduce the existing service discovery work based on SOAP-based web services and APIs respectively.

Keyword matchmaking mechanism is mainly used for WSDL-based service discovery, such as the implementation in UDDI [3,8]. Although this kind of strategy can achieve higher efficiency, the limited semantics contained in keywords leads to poor discovery accuracy. With the appearance of semantic web, ontology technologies help with more accurate solution. Improved semantic languages with annotations are designed and introduced to help with parameter matching. Paolucci et al. [19] adopt DAML-S as service description language. They take advantages of DAML ontologies and match a request and a service advertisement based on four discrete matching degrees. Plebani et al. [20] calculate parameter similarities depending mainly on domain-specific ontology. They also provide a solution when the services are described by SAWSDL.

Ontology annotation certainly helps a lot with service discovery. However, it is impractical to expect all new web services to have semantic tagged descriptions [5]. Although there exists research on semantic annotation for syntactic API specifications [13,24], these methods are semi-automatic, requiring manual adjustment of the annotations, and the correctness has not been verified. The obstacles encountered in obtaining semantic annotations in RESTful APIs make it difficult for ontology-based methods to be migrated to API interface matching.

Most of the existing RESTful API discovery methods are based on data from Programmable Web and they often focus on improving natural language processing technologies to obtain accurate discovery results using API description texts. Neural networks and deep learning methods are commonly used for behaving well in mining the latent semantics features of texts. For example, Liu et al. [12] propose a two-step transfer learning method to support endpoint-level web API search. However, these methods can hardly assure the callability of discovered APIs for not considering the interfaces.

TASSIC [14] takes interface matching into consideration. However, we find it ignoring the three API interface features as we mentioned before. Firstly, it simplifies the interface formalization by ignoring the path parameters in JSON, parameter necessity and abbreviations. The Hungarian algorithm used for interface matching also limits the parameters' matching relationship to be one-to-one. These problems can also be found in some WSDL-based work like [4].

3   Preliminaries

Involved definitions are introduced in this section. An API service is often composed of multiple functionally related endpoints [12], and the atomic unit of selection and invocation is a single endpoint. Therefore, the proposed work is based on the endpoint level. Unless otherwise specified, every "service" mentioned in this paper refers to an endpoint. The formalization of this problem is mainly composed of user request and endpoint service information.

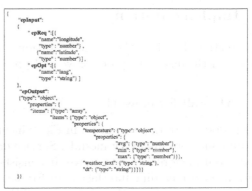

(a) Example of request interfaces   (b) Example of endpoint interfaces

Fig. 1. A weather forecast running example

Definition 1: Endpoint. $ep=\langle epName, epGroup, epDesc, epInput, epOutput, apiInfo\rangle$

$epName$ refers to the endpoint name. $epGroup$ is the name of the group that joined in by the endpoint, which can be null. $epDesc$ refers to the functional description text. The input and output parameters are represented by $epInput$ and $epOutput$, separately. $epInput$ consists of $epReq$ and $epOpt$, where $epReq$ refers to parameters necessarily required for invocation and $epOpt$ are those can be optionally filled. $apiInfo$ is the information of API that this endpoint belongs to, where $apiName$ refers to the API's name and $apiDesc$ refers to the API function description text.

Definition 2: Request. $r = \langle rDesc, rInput, rOutput, rDomain\rangle$

$rDesc$ is the description text of the function required. $rInput$ are the input parameters provided and the required output parameters are represented by $rOutput$. $rDomain$ refers to the domain of the targeted service that user required. When a request arrives, based on the $rDomain$, we firstly pick the corresponding endpoints as the initial candidate set $EP = \{ep_i\}$.

Definition3: Parameter. $p = \langle pName, pType\rangle$

$pName$ refers to the transformed parameter name phrase and $pType$ refers to the data type of the leaf node parameter.

JSON is a common data exchange format between RESTful APIs. This paper introduces the parameters in terms of "root node" and "leaf node" from tree structures [5]. During invocation of a service, the parameter assignment finally focuses on the matching of the leaf parameters [21]. Still, to retain more path information, this paper turns the JSON Schema[4] format interfaces into sets of parameters which are phrases concatenating all identifiers on the path from the root node to the leaf node. The conversion will be introduced in Sect. 4.2.

Figure 1 presents our running example. We create a request and an endpoint based on real interfaces in Rapid API. The request interface here is designed to be JSON example data and the endpoint interface is in JSON Schema format.

---

[4] http://json-schema.org/.

4   Implementation

This section describes the implementation. After briefly introducing the framework and the discovery process, we will present the details of each module.

4.1   Overall Framework

The proposed framework shown in Fig. 2 includes the service data preprocessing module and core discovery module. Service data preprocessing module prepares service data before requests arrive. It consists of Rapid API data collecting and pretreatment including interface transformation and parameter processing, after which a service information database will be built. The core discovery module describes the whole discovery process, which mainly includes three phases: function similarity calculation phase (Phase1), interface matching phase (Phase2), and the comprehensive phase(Phase3). When a user request comes, the candidate services will go through the three phases in turn to measure their similarities with the user request in terms of function description and interfaces. During the first two phases, some services may be filtered out. Finally, for each remained candidate, its total score will be calculated in phase 3. According to the total scores, the user will be provided with the sorted discovered endpoints.

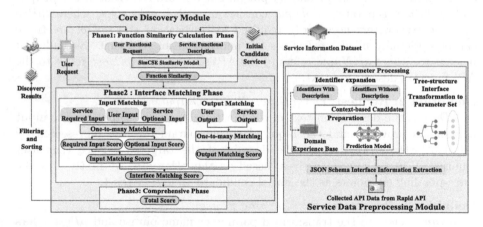

Fig. 2. Service discovery framework

4.2   Service Data Preprocessing Module

Preprocessing Framework. The foundation of API discovery is the service information base. The preprocessing framework is in Fig. 2. We collect the service data from Rapid API and preprocess the service interface information in terms of transformation and identifier expansion.

First we introduce the transformation process. According to the interfaces in Rapid API, JSON is mostly used as interface format and interface information is often provided by body or schema. The body refers to the interface sample data provided, and schema is interface template. JSON Schema is more suitable for the matching task for giving explicit interface template including parameter data types. Therefore, in preprocessing, for those services that do not provide their interface schemas, this paper first converts the body data to the corresponding JSON Schema template by recursively identifying the keywords and data types in the sample data. After unifying the interface format, this paper recursively transforms the JSON Schema formatted interfaces to the parameter sets defined in Sect. 3. In the end, the user request and each service will obtain two parameter sets as input and output separately. In the process of the transformation, the identifier expansion is performed.

Identifier Expansion in Service Discovery Scenario. Interface matching is based on the obtained similarities between parameters. Most existing work directly use common tools as Wordnet [16] for parameter similarity calculation. However, in this case, naming conventions of identifiers such as abbreviations can greatly affect the accuracy for the following two reasons. First, Wordnet does not contain all the possible abbreviations, which may cause that some terms in identifiers cannot be retrieved. It also does not specifically identify abbreviations which may cause the misunderstanding of a certain term. For example, the definition of *temp* in Word-Net is "a worker hired on a temporary basis", but in the context of weather forecast, it is often the abbreviation of *temperature*.

Current work on identifier expansion is mainly in the software maintenance field [10,17]. The sources of candidate words used in the software scenario are rich and targeted because the abbreviations in function parameters can often be directly expanded [17] from the source code. For example, a formal parameter can be expanded using its actual parameters as references and vice versa [10]. In service discovery scenarios, however, most of the information contained are descriptions of the whole service which is less targeted for a single parameter. The parameter identifiers in Rapid API mainly have the following features:

- Some providers attach description to each identifier to introduce the parameter's meaning and format. In this case, an abbreviation inside the identifier can often find its corresponding expansion directly from the description.
- Although the information of a single service is limited, there are commonly used abbreviated specifications for services in the same domain. For example, in weather services, *lat* usually means *latitude*.
- The same set of parameters often appear together for services in the same domain. For example, in weather services, *wind*, *cloud*, and *temperature* often occur together at the same level in the interfaces of several services to describe weather conditions.

Based on the above information, this paper proposes an identifier expansion method based on RESTful APIs. It is composed of two phases: preparation and the expansion algorithm. Identifier expansion algorithm is used in the service interface preprocessing and whenever a user request arrives. It includes two steps: separation and term expansion [11]. This paper uses Spiral [9] for separation. As for term expansion, the identifiers with or without description are processed in two different ways, which will be introduced later.

Preparation Work.

– Domain expansion experience base

Because parameter descriptions are targeted information, first we try to expand parameters with description and use it for experience base construction. The construction process is as follows: for each identifier with description, segment its description texts to obtain the candidate word set. For each term after separation, decide whether there is a word or phrase in the candidates that has an abbreviation relationship with it in turn. If there is, it is regarded as a successful expansion. The identifier itself won't be changed during preparation, only the result will be recorded. So how to decide a term's expansion from candidates? We consider all possible abbreviation formats to be acronym, prefix, or dropped letter [10], and decide one by one to find whether there exists a candidate that has one of the above three relationships with the term processed. If there find several possible expansions, select the shortest one as the most likely result to return. It should be noted that for the acronyms, this paper finds the candidate terms from combined initials of the terms in the description in case of combined acronyms being ignored, such as *tz* for *timezone*.

– Domain word set and prediction model

Domain word set refers to the valid words appearing in all services under the domain and is used as a reference when expanding the terms without description and those who are not in the experience base. It is challenging to select the most likely expansion from the large-scale domain word set. In the existing work, they often choose the expansion according to word frequency or transformation cost [2,6]. However, with these methods, the same terms tend to choose the same expansion all the time, while the expansion should be the most likely appeared one according to the context. Therefore, this paper uses the Continuous Bag-of-Words Model (CBOW) [15] as the context-based word occurrence probability prediction model. We collect the sentences in all APIs from the same domain together with those composed of parameter identifiers at the same JSON level in all interfaces to constitute a training dataset.

The training task of CBOW is to predict the current word based on the context words. The trained model will be used in the expansion algorithm to obtain the occurrence probability of each domain word according to the term's context. And the sorted domain words can be obtained as the candidates.

Identifier Expansion Algorithm. Algorithm 1 provides the algorithm pseudo-code. The inputs are the *identifier* to be processed, *description* of the *identifier*(if there is), the *context* terms from other parameter identifiers from the same JSON level and the domain experience base $dict_{record}$, and the output is the expanded phrase $identifier_{exp}$. First, the *identifier* will be separated into terms (line 1), and *context* will be put into the trained CBOW model. The obtained sorted words will be used as context referenced candidates named $cans_{context}$(line 2). Then we start to try to expand every segmented term. If the identifier has a description text, the expansion will firstly be selected from the description. If it is successfully expanded, the result will be added to the final expansion result (line 4-10). If not, first turn to check the $dict_{record}$. If there exists a record of this term, choose the shortest record as the expansion and add to the final result (line 12–15). If not, first check if this term is actually an abbreviation. If it's not an abbreviation, this term will be directly added to the result; otherwise the $cans_{context}$ will be used to locate the possibly correct expansion. Because the $cans_{context}$ are already sorted by occurrence possibility, once a candidate is found to be a possible expansion, it will be returned immediately instead of choosing the shortest one (line 17–21). If this expansion still fails, the abbreviation will be directly added to the result.

Algorithm 1. Identifier Expansion

Input: $identifier, context, dict_{record}, description$
Output: $identifier_{exp}$
1: $termList \leftarrow segment(identifier)$
2: $cans_{context} \leftarrow sortedWordsByCBOW(context)$
3: **for** $term$ in $termList$ **do**
4:     **if** $description$ not null **then**
5:         $cans_{description} \leftarrow segment(description)$
6:         $exp \leftarrow expand(term, cans_{description})$
7:     **end if**
8:     **if** exp not null **then**
9:         $identifier_{exp} \leftarrow identifier_{exp} + exp$
10:        continue
11:    **end if**
12:    **if** $term$ in $dict_{record}$ **then**
13:        $exp \leftarrow shortest(dict_{record}[term])$
14:        $identifier_{exp} \leftarrow identifier_{exp} + exp$
15:        continue
16:    **else**
17:        **if** isAbbr($term$) **then**
18:            $exp \leftarrow expandByContext(term, cans_{context})$
19:            **if** exp not null **then**
20:                $identifier_{exp} \leftarrow identifier_{exp} + exp$
21:                continue
22:            **end if**
23:        **end if**
24:        $identifier_{exp} \leftarrow identifier_{exp} + term$
25:    **end if**
26: **end for**
27: **return** $identifier_{exp}$

4.3   Core Discovery Module

Function Similarity Calculation Phase. This paper uses the sentence embedding model SimCSE [7], which is proved to be suitable for semantic textual similarity tasks, and calculate the cosine similarities as the function similarity.

We concatenate the texts related to the description of endpoint functional information into a single paragraph as (1) and use SimCSE with cosine distance to calculate its similarity with the $rDesc$, which is $score_{text}(r, ep_i) = sim_{text}(rDesc, epText_i)$, between [0,1].

$$epText_i = epName_i . epDesc_i . epGroup_i . apiName_i . apiDesc_i \qquad (1)$$

where . represents sentence concatenation.

After phase1, those whose score is lower than the function similarity threshold μ will be filtered out, and the remained candidates in $EP_{text} = \{ep_j\}$ will enter the next phase.

Interface Matching Phase. This section describes how to measure the interface matching degree. After converting the interfaces of the request and service into parameter sets, a bipartite graph model can be built. Due to the different representation of input and output, this section first takes two non specific sets P and Q as example, where $P = \{p_1, p_2, ..., p_N\}, Q = \{q_1, q_2, ..., q_M\}$.

For each ep_j in EP_{text}, the matching degree between its and the request r's input/output interface parameter sets will be calculated and synthesized. Similarity calculation between parameter sets depends on similarity calculation between each pair of parameters. Therefore, this section first introduces the similarity calculation between two single parameters.

Similarity Calculation between Parameters. The similarity between two parameters can be measured from two aspects: semantics and data type.

For the semantic similarity, this paper uses $pName$ for calculation and the similarity $sim_{sem}(p_n, q_m)$ is gained using the same SimCSE model as Sect. 4.3. Data type similarity $sim_{type}(p_n, q_m)$ can be obtained by looking up the Table 1, which is designed according to [23] and expanded considering the format specification of JSON and the type options of Rapid API.

Table 1. Similarities between types

	Integer	Number	String	Boolean	Date	Time	Geopoint	Enum	Object	Array
Integer	1	0.5	0.3	0.1	0.1	0	0	0.8	0	0
Number	1	1	0.1	0.1	0	0	0	0.8	0	0
String	0.7	0.7	1	0.3	0.8	0.8	0.8	0.8	0.5	0.5
Boolean	0.1	0	0.1	1	0	0	0	0	0	0
Date	0.1	0	0.1	0	1	0	0	0	0	0
Time	0	0	0.1	0	0	1	0	0	0	0
Geopoint	0	0	0.1	0	0	0	1	0	0	0
Enum	0.5	0.1	0.1	0	0	0	0	1	0	0
Object	0	0	0.1	0	0	0	0	0	1	0
Array	0	0	0.1	0	0	0	0	0	0	1

The semantic and data type similarities between parameters are weighted and synthesized to obtain the total similarity $sim_{param}(p_n, q_m)$. w_{sem} is the weight of semantic similarity.

$$sim_{param}(p_n, q_m) = sim_{sem}(p_n, q_m) * w_{sem} + sim_{type}(p_n, q_m) * (1 - w_{sem}) \qquad (2)$$

The existing interface matching often directly uses the calculated similarities. In this way, the gained matching score can be higher than it should be, because with the existing method, two parameters can still be matched as long as their similarity is higher than others, even if it only values 0.05. So this paper set the threshold η to bring out a higher demand for two parameters to match. According to (3), if the similarity is lower than η, its value will be set to 0. As:

$$sim(p_n, q_m) = \begin{cases} sim_{param}(p_n, q_m), sim_{param} \gg \eta \\ 0, else \end{cases} \qquad (3)$$

Interface Matching Degree between ep_j and r. Due to the asymmetry of the proposed one-to-many matching, this section still first takes P and Q as an example to show how to calculate the matching degree when using Q to fill P. In this situation, "one-to-many" means that one parameter in Q may be selected and matched by several parameters in P.

When using Q to fill P, for each p_i in P, select the parameter in Q that has the highest similarity with p_i to match as in (5). Add all the matching scores and then normalize it to [0,1] as the final score between the two sets. As:

$$match(p_i, Q) = \max\{sim(p_i, q_1), ..., sim(p_i, q_M)\} \qquad (4)$$

$$matched(P, Q) = \bigcup_{i=1}^{N} \arg\max_{q_j \in Q} \{sim(p_i, q_j)\} \qquad (5)$$

$$score_{match}(P, Q) = \frac{\sum_{i=1}^{N} match(p_i, Q)}{N} \qquad (6)$$

Back to service discovery. First, about input matching, the required and optional input parameters are discussed separately. The required parameters directly affect the service invocation, so they must be completely covered. The optional parameters are often auxiliary parameters such as *language* and *filter*. When the required parameters are equally met, the satisfaction of optional parameters to user's input data means how much the service gives extra consideration of user needs. Therefore, this paper sets "basic-bonus" scoring mechanism to measure the input matching degree.

– Step1: Service required parameters matching

First, fill the endpoint's required parameters with the user's input as (7).

$$score_{basic}(r, ep_j) = score_{match}(epReq, rInput) \qquad (7)$$

Due to the setting of the parameter similarity threshold, the matching scores of parameter pairs can be 0. When the matching score of any service required parameter is 0, the service is considered to be not callable. In this case, this service will not be returned in the final result.

– Step2: Service optional parameters matching

Then fill in the remaining user's input parameters *unmatched* after the first step with the *epOpt*.

$$unmatched = rInput - matched(epReq, rInput) \tag{8}$$

$$score_{bonus} = score_{match}(unmatched, epOpt) \tag{9}$$

Add the basic and bonus scores to obtain the input matching score:

$$score_{in}(r, ep_j) = score_{basic}(r, ep_j) + score_{bonus}(r, ep_j) \tag{10}$$

For the outputs, directly use the service output parameter set to fill the user request output parameter set as (11). Similarly, if the matching score of any of the output parameters required by the user is 0, the service will not return.

$$score_{out}(r, ep_j) = score_{match}(rOutput, epOutput) \tag{11}$$

Taking w_{in} as the weight of input matching degree, the synthesized interface matching score is:

$$score_{interface}(r, ep_j) = score_{in}(r, ep_j) * w_{in} + score_{out}(r, ep_j) * (1 - w_{in}) \tag{12}$$

We use our example as Fig. 1 to show the process. First, we calculate the input matching degree. We begin with the matching of required parameters. Based on the principle of one-to-many matching and the setting of parameter threshold, both *longitude* and *latitude* of the endpoint are matched with *coordinates* provided by user. So the $score_{basic}$ is $(0.77442 + 0.73651)/2 = 0.75547$. The parameter *language* from request is then matched with the expanded optional parameter *lang*. Therefore the $score_{bonus}$ equals 1.0 and the $score_{in}$ equals 1.75547. The bonus score shows that the endpoint can better fit the user request with being able to provide weather information in various languages. Similarly, we can obtain the output matching result in Table 2. The output matching degree is $(0.75309 + 0.83990 + 0.85277 + 0.79706 + 0.76471)/5 = 0.80150$. Therefore, the overall interface matching degree is $1.75547 * 0.2 + 0.80150 * 0.8 = 0.99230$.

Table 2. Output parameters similarity

	Items temperature average	Items temperature minimum	Items temperature maximum	Items weather text	Items date
List date	0.41998	0.32875	0.39211	0.53297	**0.75309**
List main temperature minimum	0.75512	**0.83990**	0.75185	0.35799	0.24199
List main temperature maximum	0.78571	0.71710	**0.85277**	0.35444	0.28260
List main temperature average	**0.79706**	0.64821	0.72287	0.39970	0.29178
List main weather description	0.58043	0.49227	0.52341	**0.76471**	0.47978

Comprehensive Phase. This phase synthesizes the scoring results of the previous two phases, with w_{text} as the weight of function similarity to obtain the total $score(r, ep_j)$. The total score threshold λ is set and the filtered service set EP_{result} will be sorted and returned.

$$score(r, ep_j) = score_{text}(r, ep_j) * w_{text} + score_{interface}(r, ep_j) * (1 - w_{text}) \quad (13)$$

5 Experiments

5.1 Dataset

Rapid API Dataset. Experiments are carried out on the Rapid API dataset, in which 7881 APIs are collected, including 37,037 endpoints, involving 46 domains.

Interface Information Statistics. According to our statistics, 90.03% of the APIs provide interface information, and 96.93% of the output information are provided in JSON, as shown in Fig. 3.

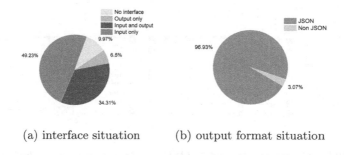

(a) interface situation   (b) output format situation

Fig. 3. Statistical result of interface situation in Rapid API

This paper also calculates the proportion of optional parameters and abbreviations in the dataset. The proportion of optional input parameters is about 48.52%. As for abbreviations, we first separate the parameters, remove the stop words and non-English words, and regard the terms that do not exist in WordNet as abbreviations. All the single characters are also thought to be abbreviations. In this way, 349,552 terms are obtained from the whole dataset, of which 44,301 are abbreviations, accounting for about 12.67%. The above data shows that the analyzed interface features account for a considerable proportion of the real dataset, which can easily affect the service discovery results.

5.2 Experimental Settings

Evaluation Metrics. The metrics are Top-k precision, recall and F1-score which are commonly used in service discovery. The formulas are as follows:

$$Precision_k(r) = \frac{|result_k(r) \bigcap truth(r)|}{k} \quad (14)$$

$$Recall_k(r) = \frac{|result_k(r) \bigcap truth(r)|}{|truth(r)|} \tag{15}$$

$$F1 - score_k(r) = \frac{2 * Precision_k(r) * Recall_k(r)}{Precision_k(r) + Recall_k(r)} \tag{16}$$

Among them, $result_k(r)$ represents the top k services returned, and $truth(r)$ represents the accurate reference result corresponding to r. $Precision_k(r)$ is used to measure the accuracy of the top k results; $Recall_k(r)$ is used to measure the comprehensiveness of the top k results. $F1 - score_k(r)$, as the harmonic mean of precision and recall, is used to measure the performance comprehensively.

Requests Design. This paper designs 10 different requests involving 10 categories for experimental verification: Monitoring, Weather, Visual Recognition, Location, Translation, Movies, Text Analysis, Social, Food, News&Media. For each category, this paper prepares a request that can be used to discover more than one accurate result. The corresponding accurate services are manually collected in the meantime.

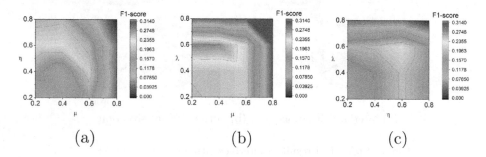

Fig. 4. Thresholds impact on API discovery result

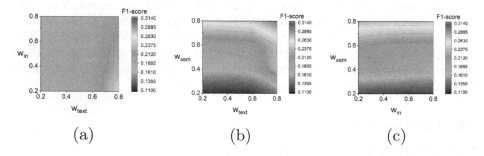

Fig. 5. Weights impact on API discovery result

Parameters. Six parameters are involved in the method. We discuss the influence of different parameter combinations on discovery results to decide the best group. We set each parameter to be 0.2,0.4,0.6,0.8 and try different combinations in grid. F1-score in (16) is chosen to show the discovery performance, with k being set to $|result(r)|$. The obtained optimal combination is $\mu = 0.4, \eta = 0.6, \lambda = 0.6; w_{text} = 0.8, w_{in} = 0.2, w_{sem} = 0.8$.

We can see from Fig. 4c that when η is set to 0.6, the performance has an obvious improvement. After η is decided, Fig. 4a shows that better discovery results can be obtained when μ is below 0.6 because when μ is higher than 0.6, most endpoints will be filtered out at phase 1. In general, it can be seen from Fig. 4a and Fig. 4b that the discovery performance shows a central decline around (0.4, 0.6, 0.6). As for the weights, it can be seen from both Fig. 5b and Fig. 5c that as the w_{sem} increases, the performance keeps improving. This shows the importance of parameter semantics to the discovery result. In the meantime, better result still appears when they are set to be 0.2 and 0.8, respectively.

5.3   Comparison Methods

The comparative experiment consists of three groups to reflect the effect of identifier expansion, the consideration of interface, and the impact of one-to-many matching. Due to the lack of semantic annotation in RESTful APIs, we mainly compare with the latest API discovery methods, which include:

noAbbr. The framework of this method is the same as the proposed work, only the interfaces are transformed without identifiers being expanded. It is used to verify the impact of the proposed identifier expansion phase.

textOnly. This method is designed as the representative of the API discovery methods that consider only the function description of APIs to verify the effect of considering interface. It only retains the phase 1 with μ. The discovery results are returned after filtering and sorting according to the function similarity.

TASSIC. [14] Due to different dataset scenarios and formalization, this method is adjusted according to the scenario of this paper. The framework is consistent with our work, only the interface matching is replaced by the idea of TASSIC. Firstly, the number of interface parameters is preliminarily screened. Then, the Hungarian algorithm is adopted. To ensure the experiment's validity, the proposed interface preprocessing is used in this comparison method. This design compares the discovery results to verify the effectiveness of the proposed interface matching scheme.

5.4 Results

Effect of Identifier Expansion. Figure 6 shows the comparison of the service discovery results obtained by the method noAbbr and the proposed work. The result is the average of 10 requests. It can be seen that better results are achieved in all three metrics after identifier expansion, indicating that the discovery result returned by the proposed work is more accurate and comprehensive. It is effective to add the identifier expansion based data preprocessing module in this scheme.

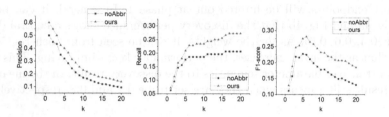

Fig. 6. Comparison of service discovery with or without identifier expansion

Effect of Interface Matching Phase. Both of the two comparison experiments with the methods textOnly and TASSIC are shown in Fig. 7. As can be seen, compared with the textOnly method, TASSIC and the proposed work have significantly improved the effect of service discovery, indicating that the interface matching phase plays an important role in improving the service discovery result. And when compared with the modified TASSIC method, the proposed scheme still shows advantages in all three metrics. Also, most of the returned results of our work are fewer than those returned by TASSIC, which means that we can return more accurate results in more advanced positions and save the users from further selection.

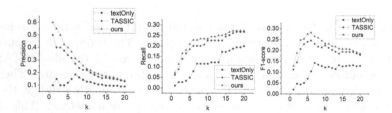

Fig. 7. Comparison of service discovery with different interface matching scheme

6   Conclusion and Future Work

This paper proposes an automated service discovery framework for RESTful API services considering the features of RESTful API interfaces. Firstly, this paper proposes an API discovery framework that comprehensively scores the similarity between user requests and candidate services to provide callable discovery results with user-required function. Then, considering the three interface features of RESTful APIs that are sorted out based on Rapid API, this paper provides a new endpoint formalization and designs new interface matching strategy. The identifier expansion phase based on context and experience base is introduced to solve the abbreviated parameter problem. This paper also provides comprehensive solutions for required and optional parameter matching and set the matching algorithm into one-to-many mode with parameter similarity threshold. Comparison experiments show the discovery performance improvement of the proposed method. In the future, the adaptive tuning of the six parameters used in our method will be discussed. And deep learning methods will be considered to further improve the accuracy and response time of service discovery.

Acknowledgements. This work is supported by the National Key Research and Development Program of China under Grant 2019YFB1704102.

References

1. Azmy, M.R., Muhamad, W., et al.: Advanced technologies to support service discovery in service-oriented systems. In: 2020 International Conference on Information Technology Systems and Innovation (ICITSI), pp. 300–305. IEEE (2020)
2. Carvalho, N.R., Almeida, J.J., Henriques, P.R., Varanda, M.J.: From source code identifiers to natural language terms. J. Syst. Softw. **100**, 117–128 (2015)
3. Chen, F., Lu, C., Wu, H., Li, M.: A semantic similarity measure integrating multiple conceptual relationships for web service discovery. Exp. Syst. Appl. **67**, 19–31 (2017)
4. Chen, K., Kuang, C.: Web service discovery based on maximum weighted bipartite graphs. Comput. Commun. **171**, 54–60 (2021)
5. Cheng, B., Li, C., Zhao, S., Chen, J.: Semantics mining & indexing-based rapid web services discovery framework. IEEE Trans. Serv. Comput. **14**(3), 864–875 (2018)
6. Corazza, A., Di Martino, S., Maggio, V.: Linsen: an efficient approach to split identifiers and expand abbreviations. In: 2012 28th IEEE International Conference on Software Maintenance (ICSM), pp. 233–242. IEEE (2012)
7. Gao, T., Yao, X., Chen, D.: Simcse: simple contrastive learning of sentence embeddings. In: Proceedings of the 2021 Conference on Empirical Methods in Natural Language Processing, pp. 6894–6910 (2021)
8. He, Q., et al.: Keyword search for building service-based systems. IEEE Trans. Softw. Eng. **43**(7), 658–674 (2016)
9. Hucka, M.: Spiral: splitters for identifiers in source code files. J. Open Source Softw. **3**(24), 653 (2018)
10. Jiang, Y., Liu, H., Zhu, J., Zhang, L.: Automatic and accurate expansion of abbreviations in parameters. IEEE Trans. Softw. Eng. **46**(7), 732–747 (2018)

11. Lawrie, D., Binkley, D.: Expanding identifiers to normalize source code vocabulary. In: 2011 27th IEEE International Conference on Software Maintenance (ICSM), pp. 113–122. IEEE (2011)
12. Liu, L., Bahrami, M., Park, J., Chen, W.-P.: Web API search: discover web API and its endpoint with natural language queries. In: Ku, W.-S., Kanemasa, Y., Serhani, M.A., Zhang, L.-J. (eds.) ICWS 2020. LNCS, vol. 12406, pp. 96–113. Springer, Cham (2020). https://doi.org/10.1007/978-3-030-59618-7_7
13. Lucky, M.N., Cremaschi, M., Lodigiani, B., Menolascina, A., De Paoli, F.: Enriching API descriptions by adding API profiles through semantic annotation. In: Sheng, Q.Z., Stroulia, E., Tata, S., Bhiri, S. (eds.) ICSOC 2016. LNCS, vol. 9936, pp. 780–794. Springer, Cham (2016). https://doi.org/10.1007/978-3-319-46295-0_55
14. Ma, S.P., Chen, Y.J., Syu, Y., Lin, H.J., Fanjiang, Y.Y.: Test-oriented restful service discovery with semantic interface compatibility. IEEE Trans. Serv. Comput. 14(5), 1571–1584 (2018)
15. Mikolov, T., Chen, K., Corrado, G., Dean, J.: Efficient estimation of word representations in vector space. arXiv preprint arXiv:1301.3781 (2013)
16. Miller, G.A.: Wordnet: a lexical database for English. Commun. ACM 38(11), 39–41 (1995)
17. Newman, C.D., Decker, M.J., Alsuhaibani, R.S., Peruma, A., Kaushik, D., Hill, E.: An empirical study of abbreviations and expansions in software artifacts. In: 2019 IEEE International Conference on Software Maintenance and Evolution (ICSME), pp. 269–279. IEEE (2019)
18. Paliwal, A.V., Shafiq, B., Vaidya, J., Xiong, H., Adam, N.: Semantics-based automated service discovery. IEEE Trans. Serv. Comput. 5(2), 260–275 (2011)
19. Paolucci, M., Kawamura, T., Payne, T.R., Sycara, K.: Semantic matching of web services capabilities. In: Horrocks, I., Hendler, J. (eds.) ISWC 2002. LNCS, vol. 2342, pp. 333–347. Springer, Heidelberg (2002). https://doi.org/10.1007/3-540-48005-6_26
20. Plebani, P., Pernici, B.: Urbe: Web service retrieval based on similarity evaluation. IEEE Trans. Knowl. Data Eng. 21(11), 1629–1642 (2009)
21. Rachad, T., Boutahar, J., et al.: A new efficient method for calculating similarity between web services. arXiv preprint arXiv:1501.05940 (2015)
22. RapidAPI: What is rapidapi? https://docs.rapidapi.com/docs/what-is-rapidapi/
23. Sara, R., Fatima, A., Lakhdar, L.: A new approach for grouping similar operations extracted from WSDLs files using k-means algorithm. Int. J. Adv. Comput. Sci. Appl. 8(12), 84–91 (2017)
24. Schwichtenberg, S., Gerth, C., Engels, G.: From open API to semantic specifications and code adapters. In: 2017 IEEE International Conference on Web Services (ICWS), pp. 484–491. IEEE (2017)

Enhancing Performance Modeling of Serverless Functions via Static Analysis

Runan Wang[(✉)][iD], Giuliano Casale[iD], and Antonio Filieri[iD]

Department of Computing, Imperial College London, London, UK
{runan.wang19,g.casale,a.filieri}@imperial.ac.uk

Abstract. Serverless computing leverages the design of complex applications as the composition of small, individual functions to simplify development and operations. However, this flexibility complicates reasoning about the trade-off between performance and costs, requiring accurate models to support prediction and configuration decisions. Established performance model inference from execution traces is typically more expensive for serverless applications due to the significantly larger topologies and numbers of parameters resulting from the higher fragmentation into small functions. On the other hand, individual functions tend to embed simpler logic than larger services, which enables inferring some structural information by reasoning directly from their source code. In this paper, we use static control and data flow analysis to extract topological and parametric dependencies among interacting functions from their source code. To enhance the accuracy of model parameterization, we devise an instrumentation strategy to infer performance profiles driven by code analysis. We then build a compact layered queueing network (LQN) model of the serverless workflow based on the static analysis and code profiling data. We evaluated our method on serverless workflows with several common composition patterns deployed on Azure Functions, showing it can accurately predict the performance of the application under different resource provisioning strategies and workloads with a mean error under 7.3%.

Keywords: Serverless computing · Performance modeling · Layered queueing networks · Static analysis · Code profiling

1 Introduction

Serverless computing is a novel cloud computing paradigm that aims at making operations concerns transparent to developers and cloud users [9,13]. It has recently gained increasing attention in industry due to the potential for significant cost savings and on-demand billing modes. Function-as-a-Service (FaaS) is a cloud computing execution model introduced within serverless computing that allows developers to deploy single functions as basic building blocks [9]. Compared to monolithic applications and microservice-based architectures, FaaS-based applications can be triggered and served by events (e.g., HTTP requests) and executed on-demand. There are several cloud vendors providing FaaS capabilities like AWS Lambda, Google Cloud Functions and Microsoft Azure Functions, as well as open-source alternatives such as OpenFaaS or KNative.

J. Troya et al. (Eds.): ICSOC 2022, LNCS 13740, pp. 71–88, 2022.
https://doi.org/10.1007/978-3-031-20984-0_5

Developers can write individual serverless functions and compose them in complex workflows deployed on the FaaS platforms. FaaS platforms enable automatic management, scaling, and billing of the execution of FaaS-based workflows to take over most operational efforts from developers and users. However, maintaining Quality-of-Service (QoS) requirements and meeting service-level agreements (SLAs) of FaaS applications remains an outstanding concern [26].

Performance models provide analytical prediction and simulation results to help to reason about and improve the quality of FaaS-based applications. Accurate and efficient performance modeling benefits not only the developers and operators, but also FaaS providers. On the one hand, with performance models, the developers have a better understanding and prediction capabilities of the quality of the application under different workloads and deployment configurations, which may also help direct development decisions. On the other hand, FaaS providers can take advantage of accurate cost prediction and resource management, inferring related metrics from performance models. There are well-established stochastic models such as queueing networks [16], layered queueing networks (LQNs) [14], Petri nets [22] that can describe the system with a simplified abstraction. Among them, LQNs are particularly suitable for capturing the dependencies and interactions between different FaaS functions.

Building performance models for FaaS applications accurately and efficiently is a non-trivial problem. However, differently from monolithic or service-based applications that aggregate larger functionalities behind each endpoint, the source code of individual serverless functions is usually more focused and succinct, rendering it amenable to static code analysis to infer additional information about the internals of FaaS applications. Our insight is to exploit established control and data flow analysis methods [23] to improve the granularity of performance models for FaaS-based applications, ultimately improving the accuracy of models and performance predictions. However, building LQN models for FaaS functions and workflows is still challenging due to the information gap between modeling and monitoring granularity compared to the classical performance modeling for web applications and microservice-based applications.

The first challenge in building LQN models for FaaS applications is learning the topological graph representing the application behavior on both inter- and intra-function levels. Attempting to accurately and completely reconstruct this structure only from traces or monitoring data may be difficult because it relies on the test inputs capable of covering all the relevant execution traces. However, when functions are observed as black-boxes, i.e., without knowing which parts of their code have been exercised, there is no reliable way to ascertain whether any behavior has remained uncovered. In turn, the LQN model inferred from such partial traces may itself be incomplete.

Additionally, appropriate model parameterization is critical to define effective and efficient parameter estimation methods. Estimating service demand for individual endpoints from system monitoring measurements, like utilization or response time, is particularly challenging, with most methods typically resorting to regression algorithms to combine different measurements [25]. However, these methods estimate service demand based on queueing theory and may lead to inaccurate results due to the uncertainty introduced by the approximation based on the queueing theory.

This paper proposes to build performance models for FaaS workflows combining static analysis and code profiling. We assume that the source code and configuration metadata of FaaS functions and workflows are accessible. To learn the topology of the model, we apply static analysis on the source code to obtain the inter-procedural call graph of the orchestrator defining the workflow composing the individual functions, and the intra-procedural control flows for each function. To more accurately characterize the model parameterization, we propose to inject code to hook system function calls during the profiling stage and capture the distribution of the service demand based on profiling data instead of estimating based on system measurement. The profiling data, being measured within the process executing the function, depends only on the function inputs, while it is largely workload-independent since queueing time does not affect the measures. Then, we derive the LQN models for serverless workflows by mapping the static graphs and code profiling data. In the experiments, we implement FaaS-based workflows representing different function compositing patterns to evaluate our proposed method. We compare the results by solving LQN to the data collected from the workflow execution. The experimental results yield model predictions with a mean error under 7.3% in all the evaluated scenarios.

The remainder of the paper is structured as follows. In Sect. 2, we give background on static analysis and LQN. In Sect. 3, we discuss the methodology of building LQN model based on static analysis and code profiling. In Sect. 4, we conduct experiments with different FaaS workflows to evaluate the effectiveness and efficiency of our proposed modeling method. In Sects. 5 and 6, respectively, we discuss related work and draw conclusions.

2   Background

Static Analysis of Source Code. Static analysis is widely used to infer information about a program by reasoning on the structure and features of its source code, or convenient intermediate representations, without actually executing the program [23] (as opposed to dynamic analyses that require executing the program). For example, it can infer which statements in a program affect the value of a variable at a specific line. Two widely used representations that can be statically extracted are control and data flow graph. A control flow graph (CFG) captures (a superset of) all the possible paths that can be executed at runtime. A CFG represents how the evaluation of conditional statements (e.g., branches and loops) determines the next code block to be executed. At intra-procedural level, CFGs represent the dependencies between code blocks and all the possible execution orderings, subject to the decisions at conditional nodes. Intra-procedural CFGs can be related to one another via the program call graph. A call graph (CG) captures for each caller function all the callee functions it can invoke, providing an inter-procedural representation of the dependencies and interactions among functions. Instead, a data flow graph represents the propagation

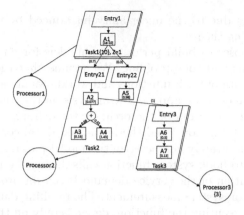

Fig. 1. An example LQN model

of information throughout program statements and variables [18]. Static data flow analysis, for example, can compute execution paths that propagate values of interests from their sources to sinks. Data can flow through dependent nodes of a CFG, e.g., through the arguments of a function invocation or the decision at a conditional node. Taint analysis is a data flow analysis that can track which program variables at which code locations are affected by the values of a function's inputs. While typically used for security purposes [27], taint analysis can capture what input information can flow to other function invocations.

Layered Queuing Networks. LQNs are an extended queuing network formalism that has been widely used to abstract web applications [17]. The main components of LQN models covered in this paper are shown with an example in Fig. 1. The large parallelograms, denoted as *Task*, represent software and hardware entities. There are mainly two types of tasks: a task representing the clients, and tasks representing the servers processing incoming requests. Tasks are hosted on resources that are denoted as processors in the circle, and multiprocessor hosts can be specified with a multiplicity figure. Smaller parallelograms inside a task are called *Entry* and represent different service classes provided by a task (e.g., different endpoints). The detailed operations inside each entry can be described with a set of *Activity* specified with their execution order (rectangular nodes for activities and circular "+" nodes representing probabilistic choices). Each activity is parameterized with service demand, for example, specifying the mean value of the exponential demand distribution. Activities can make requests to different entries by sending synchronous or asynchronous calls. For instance, in the top task, 10 concurrent clients are sending synchronous requests to $E21$ and $E22$ and the arcs are labelled with the value of the mean number of requests.

3   Methodology

Our methodology for modeling serverless applications combining static analysis and code profiling includes three main phases: a static analysis to learn the

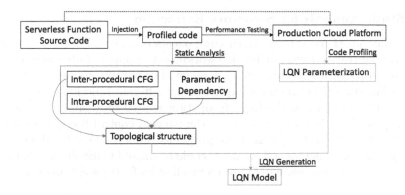

Fig. 2. The overview of the proposed methodology

topology for LQN structure modeling, a dynamic analysis with code profiling to collect data for model parameterization, and LQN model generation.

Overview. The overview of the proposed methodology is shown in Fig. 2. Assume that after the development of individual serverless functions or FaaS-based workflows, we are able to access and instrument the source code and configuration metadata either from developers or cloud providers. (Black-box functions whose performance models have been constructed with alternative methods can in principle be included in the LQN model as well, with possible increase of the overall uncertainty of the model. However, in this paper, we focus on modeling functions whose source code is accessible.) First, to define the topological structure of the workflow, we apply static analysis to extract the intra-procedural and inter-procedural control flow graphs from the source code of FaaS-based workflows, including individual functions and orchestration code composing them. Besides, we try to infer the dependencies between the input parameters of each individual serverless function and which function calls they affect; this can help to reduce the number of nodes in the topological graph. We then inject profiling instructions into the source code to enable code-level profiling during performance testing (we will refer to the instrumented code as *profiled code*). Next, the profiled code can be deployed on the production platform as required for performance testing and data collection. After exercising the test inputs, the service demand distribution is captured with the profiling data. The availability of the static graph also allows inspecting if any static execution path has not been covered, enabling the developer to decide whether 1) the static path is effectively not executable (e.g., the FaaS application does not require all the features of a library function, thus using only some of its possible behaviors), 2) the static path implements features not relevant to ensure the SLAs thus it was deliberately not exercised during performance testing, or 3) the performance test suite needs improvement to cover more missing relevant application behaviors. Finally, we can generate LQN models using the topological graph for components specification, and accurately characterize the model parameters with code-profiling data.

In the remainder of this section, we will detail each of the three phases.

3.1 Static Analysis for Structure Extraction

We assume that there are two major components in a given FaaS-based application: an orchestration function defining workflows to compose individual serverless functions with suitable patterns (e.g., sequential or parallel execution), and a set of individual serverless functions implementing different functionalities. We first construct the topology of the LQN from static source code analysis. The static analysis provides a fast way to capture the internal control flows by identifying (a superset of) all feasible paths of the programs. This can help build a complete topological graph, whereas certain parts could be missed in monitoring data if the inputs used to test the system do not cover all of its features extensively.

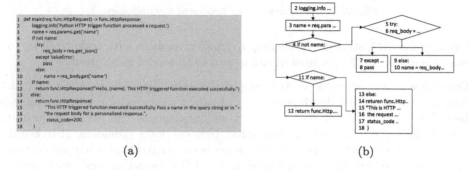

(a)   (b)

Fig. 3. An exampled source code in Python from Azure Functions (a) and the corresponding control flow graph (b).

Static Graph Generation. In this paper, we use both inter- and intra-procedural static graphs to derive the topological structure of the LQN models. A call graph (CG) is mainly responsible for extracting the calling relationships on the workflow, which is extracted from the orchestration function. While intra-procedural information can be obtained by generating a control flow graph (CFG) for each serverless function. Both CG and CFG are constructed by traversing nodes in the abstract syntax tree (AST) on the profiled code, resulting in a collection of code blocks and control nodes representing conditional execution [23]. Combining both CG and CFG of the serverless workflow, we obtain an inter-procedural static description of the system that we call the static graph (SG) as $SG = \{CG, CFG\}$.

Given the control graph of an individual serverless function as $CFG = (\boldsymbol{N}, \boldsymbol{E})$, the control flow is formalized by conditions, loops, function calls, and sequential code blocks. In CFG, $\boldsymbol{N}$ and $\boldsymbol{E}$ denote the nodes and edges, respectively. In order to enable further analysis of the CFG, we then define each node N_i as a tuple (i, l_s, l_e), where l_s and l_e are the starting and end lines of the ith code block. A directed edge in $\boldsymbol{E} = \{(N_i, N_j), \dots\}$ describes the relationship between nodes N_i and N_j. The example source code in Fig. 3a is available at [1], and Fig. 3b shows the control flow for the example serverless function. The resulting CFG is represented with $\boldsymbol{N} = \{N_1, N_2, \dots, N_9\}$,

$E = \{(1,2),(2,3),(3,4),(4,5),(4,6),(4,7),(3,7),(7,8),(7,9)\}$ and, for example, $N_9 = (9,13,18)$.

Data Flow Analysis for Parameter Dependency Inference. The static graph of serverless applications could be large due to redundant nodes representing the statements whose execution times are not influenced by a function's input parameters (e.g., constant time initialization). Thus, from a performance perspective, these statements could be aggregated into single blocks to reduce the size and fragmentation of the static graph. We apply a static data flow analysis to the profiled code to infer the potential parametric dependencies between input parameters and function calls using taint analysis. This can help reduce the number of nodes in a static graph by aggregating input independent nodes, in turn lowering the computation complexity of solving the inferred LQN models. Taint analysis in this phase works by marking a statement in the source code as tainted if its execution or assigned value is affected by function input values. The parametric dependency inference can be formulated as detecting any existing tainted statement in the nodes of the CFG. If there are input parameters used by the statement of any node, we then deduce that the execution times of the detected node N_i are potentially dependent on such input parameters. Formally, potential parametric dependencies can be described as a set of $PD_i = (source, sink, lineno)$, where $source$ and $sink$ are the identifiers of a function input parameter and a function call whose arguments are affected by the input parameter, while $lineno$ is the line number identifying the call site of the sink function to distinguish possible multiple calls.

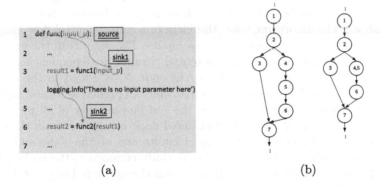

(a)   (b)

Fig. 4. An example excerpt of code with taint analysis results highlighted (a), and the control flow graph reduction process (b).

If there is no potential parametric dependency detected in N_j, we can infer that the demand for executing N_j is not impacted by function inputs, resulting in a reduction of N_j by aggregating it with its predecessor. Figure 4a shows an example source code with the taint analysis results highlighted. Let the left graph in Fig. 4b be the original CFG of the example code, with $N_4 = (4,3,3)$

Algorithm 1. Control flow graph reduction with potential parametric dependencies

---

Input: $CFG \leftarrow$ Control flow graph of the source code $CFG = (\boldsymbol{N}, \boldsymbol{E})$
  $\boldsymbol{PD} \leftarrow$ Set of potential parametric dependencies $[PD_1, PD_2, \ldots, PD_n]$
Output: $CFG_r \leftarrow$ Optimized CFG with reduction on nodes
1: Initialize $\boldsymbol{r_N} = \emptyset$, $\boldsymbol{E_r} = \emptyset$
2: **for** N_i in CFG **do**
3:   **for** PD_i in $\boldsymbol{PD}$ **do**
4:     **if** $lineno$ is not in the range of $[l_s, l_e]$ **then**
5:       $\boldsymbol{r_N} \leftarrow \boldsymbol{r_N} \cup N_i$
6:       $\boldsymbol{succ} \leftarrow$ all successors of N_i, $\boldsymbol{pred} \leftarrow$ all predecessors of N_i
7:       update l_e of $\boldsymbol{pred}$ to include N_i
8:     **end if**
9:   **end for**
10:   $\boldsymbol{N_r} \leftarrow \boldsymbol{N} \setminus \boldsymbol{r_N}$
11:   **for** $succ_i$ in $\boldsymbol{succ}$ **do**
12:     **for** $pred_i$ in $\boldsymbol{pred}$ **do**
13:       $\boldsymbol{E_r} \leftarrow \boldsymbol{E} \setminus (pred_i, N_i)$, $\boldsymbol{E_r} \leftarrow \boldsymbol{E} \cup (pred_i, succ_i)$
14:     **end for**
15:     $\boldsymbol{E_r} \leftarrow \boldsymbol{E} \setminus (N_i, succ_i)$
16:   **end for**
17: **end for**
18: **return** $CFG_r \leftarrow (\boldsymbol{N_r}, \boldsymbol{E_r})$

---

and $N_5 = (5, 4, 4)$. The right graph in Fig. 4b shows the reduction of node N_5 into node $N_{4,5}$ due to no detected parametric dependencies in node N_5.

Algorithm 1 formulates the control flow graph reduction process based on taint analysis. The algorithm takes the intra-procedural control flow graph and the detected parametric dependencies as inputs. The algorithm traverses N_i in the original CFG and checks if any potential parametric dependencies occurred at N_i. If no dependency exists, the current node N_i is added to the untainted set $\boldsymbol{r_N}$. At Line 6 and 7, the algorithm first finds all predecessors and successors of the untainted node and then revises the end line number of all predecessors with l_e of N_i. Then at Line 10, the untainted node is removed from the original graph. From Line 11 to Line 16, the algorithm iterates on the nodes and removes the edges containing the affected nodes. By fully connecting the nodes in $\boldsymbol{succ}$ and $\boldsymbol{pred}$, the new edges are generated to form the untainted edge set $\boldsymbol{E_r}$. After iterating on all the nodes in the original graph, the reduced graph $CFG_r = (\boldsymbol{N_r}, \boldsymbol{E_r})$ is generated by combining nodes in which there are no function calls or parametric dependencies.

It can be noticed that the parametric dependency inference is only capable of detecting potential relationship between function calls and input parameters from the code syntax. For example, consider y = 0*x; f(y); most taint analyses would conclude that the invocation of f may depend on the input parameter x. This may lead to a conservative over-approximation, with possibly only a subset of the statically detected dependencies satisfied during runtime. In this case, the static graph could have been further reduced, realizing that 0*x is identically 0. Nonetheless, even when non-optimal, taint analysis may still help to reduce the size of the static graph.

3.2   Code Profiling for Model Parameterization

Application-level monitoring data may be too coarse-grained to accurately infer service demand parameters of LQN activities, representing the operations inside individual serverless functions. We instead propose instrumenting the code of a function to obtain fine-grained measurements that can bridge the information gap between the granularity of the topology extracted via static analysis and the data used for model parameter inference.

Code-Level Profiling. To avoid changing any functionality of the source code and try to instrument the code as less as possible, we only wrap the *MAIN* function block into a wrapper function and inject a decorator to record the execution times with a standard line-level profiler [2] (while we refer mainly to Python code in this work, similar profiler utilities exist for all mainstream programming languages). Here, we take the assumption that the performance test inputs are representative of all relevant production behaviors. If executable paths in the static graph are not covered by the current test inputs, while they may affect the application's SLAs, the developer has the opportunity to identify the gap and produce additional performance tests.

We denote a sample from the collected profiling data as $s = (lineno, dt, iter)$, where dt is the execution duration of the statement at line $lineno$ and $iter$ is the iteration counter to distinguish different iterations in a loop. We can then map the profiling data into the static graph according to line numbers $lineno$ in s and (l_s, l_e) of nodes in CFG_r to extend the static graph with profiling data; we will refer to this extended structure as profiled static graph.

Besides obtaining the execution times of nodes in the graph, we also need to learn the probabilities of branches and the number of iterations for loops to infer the remaining parameters of an LQN model. For the branch probabilities, we define the executed path of each test input request eP. Each $eP_i \in eP$ represents one of the feasible paths in the static graph that has been executed according to the profiling data s. Therefore, the probability of a given selection path[i] on each conditional statement can be derived as the fraction of eP_i taking each branch over the number of eP_i evaluating the corresponding condition. For loop iterations, we represent the body of *for* or *while* loop as an entire activity and infer the expected number of iterations from the profiling data, which is consistent with the typical specification of LQNs. This can be further optimized by considering the branch probabilities inside loops to indicate a probabilistic loop, however, this is out of the scope of our current modeling method. In our proposed method, the number of iterations of loops in each execution can be directly extracted from the profiled data with $iter$.

LQN Activity Service Demand Distribution. Service demands are critical parameters for the specification of activities, as they represent the cumulative computation time the activity requires to run. To capture the demand of the activities in LQN, we model the service demand distribution with acyclic phase-type (APH) distributions and Erlang distributions by moment matching. Based on the execution duration dt in the profiling data, we first try to fit an APH distribution by matching the first three moments of dt. If there is no solution for APH distribution with the current data, we then fit an Erlang distribution with mean value and squared coefficient of variation (scv). In this way, the service demand of each activity can be directly characterized by the profiling data.

3.3   LQN Model Generation

To construct an LQN model from the profiled static graph, we first define a reference task to represent the incoming workload and an orchestration task to abstract the workflow logic composing individual serverless functions. Then, each individual serverless function can be modeled with a single task hosted on a separate processor, since it can be deployed with different configurations of resources and even to different platforms.

The entry node of the LQN is then specified according to the entry point of each function. We further assume that the sequential or parallel (fork-join) composition of the functions is specified in the orchestration function, e.g., using Azure Functions code constructs. The degree of concurrency allowed to each function is specified in the configuration metadata. The scheduling policy of the processor can be specified as either First-come-first-serve (FCFS), if the source code is with single-thread implementation, or Processor-sharing (PS) if function invocations can be interleaved on the same processor. Both scheduling policies are supported in LQN modeling [15].

LQN Activity Graph Characterization. The static graphs and profiling information collected so far allows for a systematic construction of the LQN model. First, we consider that the orchestration function is allowed to specify the workflow patterns with HTTP calls to invoke the individual serverless functions. Each activity inside the orchestration entry can be defined according to the nodes in the call graph and takes the role of sending synchronous and asynchronous calls for parallel execution to the entries of individual functions in the lower layers of the LQN. Whereas, the skeleton of the activity graph for an individual function can be directly derived from the reduced CFG. The activity graph representing the set of activities act is defined as $AG = \{act, sd, prec\}$, where sd presents the service demand and the precedence relation among activities is denoted as $prec$.

Now we discuss the procedure of activity graph specification for the serverless function f following the approach in [14]. For each activity representing N_i', all the successors and predecessors of N_i' are computed. There are mainly 4 types of activity precedence included in our method: (1) If the current node is included in its predecessors, it indicates that loops are occurring at N_i' which can be extracted with the number of iterations $iter_i$ derived from profiled data. (2) If the current node only has one successor and one or fewer predecessors, it means that N_i' is sequentially connected to its successor. (3) When there is more than one successor of N_i', there are branches with *IF* or *SWITCH* statements for jumping to different nodes, whose branching probabilities have previously been computed from profiling data. (4) If there is more than one predecessor, different conditional blocks can be merged at N_i'. From the orchestration function, we also capture parallelism and synchronization among the execution of different serverless functions. Combining all the listed cases, our method can describe the operator precedence in the activity graph including sequential interactions, conditioning and merging on branch nodes, as well as fork-join synchronization.

4 Evaluation

In this section, we first introduce the experimental setup and metrics to evaluate the accuracy of performance models constructed with our method. The comparison of LQN model predictions against execution monitoring traces for serverless workflows with different composition patterns is presented afterwards.

4.1 Experimental Setup

To evaluate the proposed method for automatically building LQN models based on static analysis and code profiling, we first implement 4 serverless workflows including sequential, branching, parallel and complex execution scenarios. The source code of the serverless workflow implementation is available at [1].

We create 13 serverless functions and 4 orchestration functions to define a collection of common workflow patterns on Azure Functions Service. The individual serverless functions are adapted from public examples that use TensorFlow with Azure functions [3] and models from Onnx Model Zoo [4]. The functionality of different workflows includes preprocessing of input images and classification based on machine learning algorithms or pre-trained models. Some metrics for the composition workflows implemented by the 4 orchestration functions are shown in Table 1, where c^2 is the squared coefficient of variation of the execution times.

Table 1. FaaS-based workflow patterns

	$wf1$	$wf2$	$wf3$	$wf4$
Number of functions	8	9	8	14
c^2 of execution times	0.26	5.71	0.84	7.44

To evaluate the accuracy of our modeling method, we conduct several experiments with different workloads and compare the performance predictions from the LQN models against the application-level monitoring data of the serverless workflows. The experimental environment is as follows. All the individual serverless functions are developed with Python 3.7 and deployed with Azure Functions 3.0. We take the response times of requests from the real traces as ground truth to evaluate our model-based predictions. To collect the real traces, we use Azure Application Insights as the monitoring tool and expose the code profiling data on the same service. As workload-independent execution times can be profiled in isolation, we can perform offline profiling on the production platform as required to collect profiling data, and then deploy the non-instrumented functions to the target cloud service (without the profiling instructions) to collect application-level runtime monitoring data.

The static analysis is built on top of the *ast module* in Python 3.7. For the taint analysis on the static data flow, we use the open-source tool Pyre shipped with Pysa [6] to infer the potential parametric dependencies. To obtain the analytical results, we use LQNS via LINE to solve the generated LQN models [11]. For performance testing, we generate closed workloads with different intensities using Locust [5].

We compare the model prediction accuracy of mean response times to the collected traces, using mean relative error (MRE) as our comparison metric, where $MRE = |m - m'|/m$ is computed with the mean response times m of the monitored execution traces and m' for LQN predicted response times.

4.2   Experimental Result

We first evaluate the static graph reduction based on inferring static parametric dependencies. Next, to evaluate the accuracy of parameterization for LQN models, we conduct extensive experiments with different settings of the number of processors and the dynamic auto-scaling to simulate two resource provision scenarios. Here, we regard these two experimental settings as limited resources and sufficient resources in the following discussion.

LQN Model Node Reduction. In Sect. 3.2, we introduced Algorithm 1 to reduce the size of the static graph by aggregating code blocks independent of input parameters, with the ultimate goal of further reducing the size and complexity of the generated LQN models. We here compare the accuracy and efficiency of the original LQN models to the reduced LQN models. From Table 2, we can observe that after node reduction, for example, the number of activities of $wf2$ is reduced to 69, which indicates that nearly 30% of nodes have been merged according to the static parametric dependencies. Besides, it can be noticed from

Table 2. The comparison results of based on LQN node reduction

	Number of activities		Execution times (s)		MRE	
	Original	Reduced	Original	Reduced	Original	Reduced
$wf1$	91	67	2.793	2.092	0.044	0.030
$wf2$	96	69	2.804	2.133	0.029	0.038
$wf3$	27	21	1.545	1.542	0.222	0.236
$wf4$	122	89	3.682	3.257	0.103	0.117

the table that the execution times of solving model are decreased by up to 25% for $wf2$, while the MRE increases only to a small degree for all the subjects, which is likely an acceptable trade-off between prediction accuracy and model complexity in most situations. We can conclude that the reduction of nodes in static graphs can directly help to reduce the number of activities in the LQN model, thus saving analysis costs. The savings come with a marginal increase in the MRE for three out of four subjects, while the MRE marginally decreased for $wf1$. Overall, the impact of reduction on the MRE appears marginal.

Sufficient Resource. In the following experiments with sufficient resources, we assume that dynamic auto-scaling is enabled for each FaaS function and there is no need to operate on the configuration of the resources. In LQN models, we set the multiplicities of each processor to 100 to simulate sufficient resource provision not to limit the scaling out of the individual functions.

We evaluate the above 4 different workflow patterns and take $wf1$ as an example under different workloads. The comparison of LQN model predictions against the real traces is shown in Fig. 5, and the details of model accuracy evaluation are in Table 3. It can be seen from Fig. 5a that the mean response times among different workflow patterns vary in a range of 0 to 15 s, while all prediction results are close to the measurements. Figure 5b, which zooms on $wf1$, shows that there is no obvious increase in response times as the number of clients grows. This is because under sufficient provision, all required resources can be allocated and there are no significant queueing times for each request. Therefore, the LQN modeling results capture the correct trend of response times changing with workloads. Besides, it can be observed from Table 3 that the prediction of the LQN model yields good accuracy with an average MRE over the four workflows of 5.5% (min=2.9% for $wf2$, max = 10.3% for $wf4$), indicating a fairly accurate characterization of the performance of the FaaS workflows.

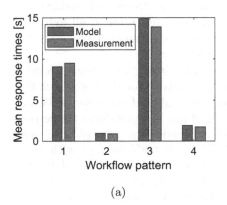
(a)

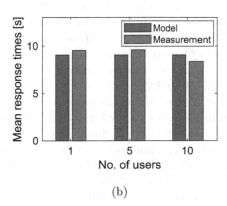
(b)

Fig. 5. Mean response times of different workflow patterns (a) and of $wf1$ under different workloads (b), comparing model prediction and real trace measurements.

84   R. Wang et al.

Table 3. MRE of compared results in Fig. 5

| | Workflow pattern | | | | Workload | | |
	$wf1$	$wf2$	$wf3$	$wf4$	1	5	10
Model	9.081	0.927	10.144	1.923	9.081	9.081	9.081
Measurement	9.501	0.901	9.737	1.744	9.501	9.613	8.390
MRE	0.044	0.029	0.042	0.103	0.044	0.055	0.082

Limited Resource. For the limited resources experiments, we tune the configuration of each serverless function to variate the number of cores for the processor. Practically, we first identify the most resource-demanding serverless function as the bottleneck function and then study the accuracy of our model for different values of the maximum number of instances on Azure and, coherently, of the multiplicity parameter of the corresponding LQN activity.

However, when a single processor is allowed, Azure Function Consumption plan limits the allocated memory to 1.5Gb, which in the case of $wf3$ and $wf4$ is not sufficient to serve 10 users without scaling strategies for the most resource-demanding serverless function. Therefore, we selected the second most resource-demanding serverless function as the bottleneck function for $wf3$ and $wf4$. The comparison of results on LQN model prediction and monitoring traces measurements is shown in Tables 4 and 5.

First, we investigate the model performance with increasing concurrent users between $N = 1$ to 10 with only one processor ($P = 1$) available for the bottleneck function. It can be seen from Table 4 that, with increased workload intensity, the mean response time grows with different trends. For example, in $wf1$, the response time with 10 users is nearly 5 times higher than with 1 user due to the contention on the bottleneck function that forces the users to wait. Nevertheless, regardless of the variation trends in the response time, the model predicts accurately the performance measurements from monitoring traces in all four workflows, with average MRE across all the experiments of about 6.2% (min=0.8% for $wf1$ with $N = 10$, max=12.2% for $wf4$ with $N = 10$).

Next, we evaluate model prediction accuracy using an intense workload (N=10) and varying the number of processors available for the bottleneck function. Table 5 shows the comparative data for the number of processors P between 1 and 10. As expected, increasing the number of processors reduces the response time for all the workflows, albeit with different trends. The average MRE across all the experiments is in this case about 9.5% (min=0.8% for $wf1$ with $P = 1$, max=22.2% for $wf1$ with $P = 5$). While average MRE remained under 10%, we observed a performance deterioration for $P = 5$. By observing the execution traces, we conjecture this deterioration may be caused of some implicit optimization or automation happening on the serverless platform around $P = 5$ which is not accurately captured by our models and may require additional investigation.

Summary. The evaluation of our LQN modeling strategy for serverless functions based on static analysis and code profiling may be summarized with the

Table 4. Comparison results on different number of processors on 4 workflow patterns with limited resource $P = 1$

	$wf1$			$wf2$		
	$N = 1$	$N = 5$	$N = 10$	$N = 1$	$N = 5$	$N = 10$
Model	9.081	22.718	49.016	0.927	1.454	3.085
Measurement	9.501	24.397	48.606	0.901	1.394	2.952
MRE	0.044	0.069	0.008	0.029	0.043	0.045
	$wf3$			$wf4$		
	$N = 1$	$N = 5$	$N = 10$	$N = 1$	$N = 5$	$N = 10$
Model	10.144	10.664	12.545	1.923	2.229	3.215
Measurement	9.737	12.125	13.626	1.744	2.3	3.655
MRE	0.042	0.120	0.079	0.103	0.031	0.122

Table 5. Comparison results on different workloads on 4 workflow patterns with limited resource $N = 10$

	$wf1$			$wf2$		
	$P = 1$	$P = 5$	$P = 10$	$P = 1$	$P = 5$	$P = 10$
Model	49.016	10.325	9.083	3.085	0.928	0.927
Measurement	48.606	13.27	8.018	2.952	1.149	0.879
MRE	0.008	0.222	0.133	0.045	0.192	0.054
	$wf3$			$wf4$		
	$P = 1$	$P = 5$	$P = 10$	$P = 1$	$P = 5$	$P = 10$
Model	12.545	10.144	10.144	3.215	1.923	1.923
Measurement	13.626	8.600	10.489	3.655	2.031	1.895
MRE	0.089	0.180	0.033	0.120	0.053	0.015

following two observations. First, node reduction on the static graph leads to smaller LQN models, saving computation time for both LQN model generation and model-based performance prediction, with negligible impact on prediction accuracy. Second, model-based performance prediction achieved a close fit to the measurements from monitoring traces (average MRE=7.3%), under different workload intensity and in both sufficient and limited resources. Finally, we remark that the availability of the static graph also allows assessing the coverage of the performance test inputs, highlighting possible execution paths relevant to the satisfaction of the application's SLAs that are not exercised (enough), thus driving the refinement of the performance test suite.

5   Related Work

The question of how to predict the performance of serverless functions is closely followed by researchers. However, fine-grained analytical performance modeling for serverless functions still lacks investigations to our knowledge. Eismann et al. [12] propose to use mixture density networks to predict the response time distribution of a single serverless function and then estimate the cost of serverless workflow execution by Monte-Carlo simulation. In [7], the authors develop a framework called COSE for serverless function configuration with a trace-based performance model. Based on the performance model, they apply Bayesian Optimization into obtaining the optimal serverless function configuration. These works can be identified as data-driven performance predictions for serverless functions, which cannot give an explicit, interpretable abstraction of a serverless application.

On the other hand, model-driven performance prediction can help developers and providers to better understand different performance prediction and reason about performance issues or design alternatives. Boza et al. [10] propose to use $M(t)/M/\infty$ queues to model serverless functions, enabling the calculation of performance and cost. Mahmoudi et al. [20,21] propose an analytical performance model by using a continuous-time semi-Markov process to accurately predict the performance metrics. However, this work mainly focuses on modeling aspects of the computing platform to support tuning its configuration, and does not directly relate to the internals of serverless functions. Lin et al. [19] use probabilistic directed acyclic graph abstractions to predict the end-to-end response times of serverless applications. The smallest representable unit in this work is a whole serverless function, which may limit the performance prediction accuracy due to the coarse modeling granularity.

Finally, the generation of LQN models for software performance prediction have also been investigated starting from higher-level, architectural specifications, e.g., from UML [24] or Palladio Component Models (PCM) [8]. Recently, TOSCA specifications have been extended to specify several concerns of serverless applications [28] and can be used to generate LQN performance models. However, most of these approaches require expert knowledge to define accurate architectural models in the first place. This is typically expensive and error-prone due to the need to keep the models consistent with the actual implementation, which also requires manual instrumentation and adequate performance test suite to measure the implementation's performance.

6   Conclusion and Future Work

We presented a new method to build LQN performance models for serverless applications using information from static analysis to enhance model-based prediction accuracy. We exploit the relatively smaller size of serverless function implementations, together with advances in static analysis methods for modern programming languages, to extract intra- and inter-procedural control and data dependencies among functions and their invocation parameters at different call sites. The topological structures identified by these dependencies then drives both code-level performance profiling and the automatic generation of a succinct LQN model to reason about the performance of the application. Experimental results indicate that our method can accurately capture the characterization of FaaS workflows and yield accurate prediction results under different workloads and resource provisions.

Among the possible future research directions, we aim to explore the integration of performance modeling of FaaS-based applications with performance issues diagnosis. Intra- and inter-function LQN models can help to relate performance bottlenecks to code artifacts, potentially helping to locate the root causes of SAL violations.

References

1. https://anonymous.4open.science/r/Enhancing-Performance-Modeling-of-Serverless-Functions-via-Static-Analysis-828D
2. https://github.com/pyutils/line_profiler
3. https://github.com/Azure-Samples/functions-python-tensorflow-tutorial
4. https://github.com/onnx/models
5. https://locust.io/
6. Pyre. https://pyre-check.org/
7. Akhtar, N., Raza, A., Ishakian, V., Matta, I.: Cose: configuring serverless functions using statistical learning. In: IEEE INFOCOM 2020-IEEE Conference on Computer Communications, pp. 129–138. IEEE (2020)
8. Altamimi, T., Petriu, D.C.: Incremental change propagation from UML software models to LQN performance models. In: CASCON, pp. 120–131 (2017)
9. Baldini, I., et al.: Serverless computing: current trends and open problems. In: Chaudhary, S., Somani, G., Buyya, R. (eds.) Res. Adv. Cloud Comput., pp. 1–20. Springer, Singapore (2017). https://doi.org/10.1007/978-981-10-5026-8_1
10. Boza, E.F., Abad, C.L., Villavicencio, M., Quimba, S., Plaza, J.A.: Reserved, on demand or serverless: model-based simulations for cloud budget planning. In: 2017 IEEE Second Ecuador Technical Chapters Meeting (ETCM), pp. 1–6 (2017)
11. Casale, G.: Integrated performance evaluation of extended queueing network models with line. In: Winter Simulation Conference (WSC), pp. 2377–2388. IEEE (2020)
12. Eismann, S., Grohmann, J., Van Eyk, E., Herbst, N., Kounev, S.: Predicting the costs of serverless workflows. In: Proceedings of the ACM/SPEC International Conference on Performance Engineering, pp. 265–276 (2020)
13. Eismann, S., et al.: Serverless applications: why, when, and how? IEEE Softw. **38**(1), 32–39 (2020)
14. Franks, G., Al-Omari, T., Woodside, M., Das, O., Derisavi, S.: Enhanced modeling and solution of layered queueing networks. IEEE Trans. Softw. Eng. **35**(2), 148–161 (2008)
15. Franks, G., Maly, P., Woodside, M., Petriu, D.C., Hubbard, A., Mroz, M.: Layered queueing network solver and simulator user manual. Department of Systems and Computer Engineering, Carleton University (December 2005), pp. 15–69 (2005)

16. Garetto, M., Cigno, R.L., Meo, M., Marsan, M.A.: A detailed and accurate closed queueing network model of many interacting TCP flows. In: Proceedings IEEE INFOCOM 2001, vol. 3, pp. 1706–1715. IEEE (2001)
17. Israr, T.A., Lau, D.H., Franks, G., Woodside, M.: Automatic generation of layered queuing software performance models from commonly available traces. In: Proceedings of the 5th international Workshop on Software and Performance, pp. 147–158 (2005)
18. Khedker, U.P., Sanyal, A., Karkare, B.: Data Flow Analysis: Theory and Practice. CRC Press, Boca Raton (2017)
19. Lin, C., Khazaei, H.: Modeling and optimization of performance and cost of serverless applications. IEEE Trans. Parallel Distrib. Syst. **32**(3), 615–632 (2020)
20. Mahmoudi, N., Khazaei, H.: Performance modeling of serverless computing platforms. IEEE Trans. Cloud Comput. (2020)
21. Mahmoudi, N., Khazaei, H.: Temporal performance modelling of serverless computing platforms. In: Proceedings of the 2020 Sixth International Workshop on Serverless Computing, pp. 1–6 (2020)
22. Marsan, M.A., Balbo, G., Conte, G., Donatelli, S., Franceschinis, G.: Modelling with generalized stochastic Petri nets, vol. 292. Wiley, New York (1995)
23. Nielson, F., Nielson, H., Hankin, C.: Principles of Program Analysis. Springer, Berlin (2015). https://doi.org/10.1007/978-3-662-03811-6
24. Petriu, D.C., Shen, H.: Applying the UML performance profile: graph grammar-based derivation of LQN models from UML specifications. In: Field, T., Harrison, P.G., Bradley, J., Harder, U. (eds.) TOOLS 2002. LNCS, vol. 2324, pp. 159–177. Springer, Heidelberg (2002). https://doi.org/10.1007/3-540-46029-2_10
25. Spinner, S., Casale, G., Brosig, F., Kounev, S.: Evaluating approaches to resource demand estimation. Perform. Eval. **92**, 51–71 (2015)
26. Tariq, A., Pahl, A., Nimmagadda, S., Rozner, E., Lanka, S.: Sequoia: enabling quality-of-service in serverless computing. In: Proceedings of the 11th ACM Symposium on Cloud Computing, SoCC 2020, pp. 311–327. Association for Computing Machinery (2020)
27. Tripp, O., Pistoia, M., Fink, S.J., Sridharan, M., Weisman, O.: Taj: effective taint analysis of web applications. ACM Sigplan Notices **44**(6), 87–97 (2009)
28. Zhu, L., Giotis, G., Tountopoulos, V., Casale, G.: Rdof: deployment optimization for function as a service. In: 2021 IEEE 14th International Conference on Cloud Computing (CLOUD), pp. 508–514. IEEE (2021)

Service Regulation: Modeling and Recognition

Jintao Chen[1], Jianwei Yin[1], Shuiguang Deng[1], Tiancheng Zhao[2], and Meng Xi[1(✉)]

[1] Zhejiang University, Hangzhou, China
{chenjintao,mengxi}@zju.edu.cn, {zjuyjw,dengsg}@cs.zju.edu.cn
[2] Binjiang Institute of Zhejiang University, Hangzhou, China
tianchez@zju-bj.com

Abstract. Service regulation applies modern management theory and information technology to provide intelligent, efficient and in-depth regulation of service quality and compliance operation. The Modern Service Industry with rapid innovation and evolution of services is confronted with many challenges such as compliance operation, yet traditional regulation methods rely heavily on manual labour and are less efficient. Therefore it is urgent to research efficient and intelligent methods of regulation in order to promote the healthy development of Modern Service Industry. As for process compliance in service regulation, this paper proposes a conceptual model of service regulation that includes service organization domain, business process domain and service regulation domain. Furthermore, a modeling language based on π calculus is introduced to formalize regulation issues. We have summarised six categories of general regulation rules based on regulation source materials from different service domains. To the best of our knowledge, there is currently no dataset available for service process violation recognition. Therefore, we construct a labelled process dataset for violation recognition (LPD4VR) of Internet healthcare service and propose a baseline method to detect the violation issue which achieves a recognition accuracy of 83.33%.

Keywords: Service regulation · Service regulation model · Violation recognition

1 Introduction

Advances in information technology have promoted the prosperity of the Modern Service Industry. In the process of vigorous development, many innovative services with new service delivery methods, represented by Internet healthcare services, have emerged. Changing the traditional offline delivery methods of service to online interaction greatly facilitates the lives of consumers. However, rapid development and innovation lead to many hidden risks. Various non-compliance and low-quality services occur frequently, which seriously affects the user experience of the service and the sustainable development of the modern service industry.

© The Author(s), under exclusive license to Springer Nature Switzerland AG 2022
J. Troya et al. (Eds.): ICSOC 2022, LNCS 13740, pp. 89–104, 2022.
https://doi.org/10.1007/978-3-031-20984-0_6

Take Internet healthcare service for example, it is undertaken via Internet, which has a distinctly non-contact nature compared to traditional service delivery methods. With the help of information technologies, Internet healthcare services have redistributed medical resources, thereby reconstructed relevant processes, improved service efficiency as well as promoted fairness across the industry. Healthcare organizations, including hospitals of different types and sizes, outpatient clinics for primary and secondary care, and even some Internet companies which involved in the medical field, provide public with a variety of online healthcare services. Internet healthcare services offer not only the traditional ones such as remote consultation and chronic disease management, but also some new-styles, for instance, health education and nursing school. A typical Internet healthcare service is clarified in Fig. 1. Although Internet healthcare services have gained rapid growth in the past decade or so, many irregularities and quality issues have been identified. Take the qualifications of medical institutions for example: the "hospital concept" was arbitrarily applied; medical service areas were arbitrarily expanded; the scope of specialties and grades were not strictly audited; etc. According to the Ponemon Institute, breaches affecting healthcare providers are the most costly to deal with and take the longest to recover from. Building intelligent methods for compliance management can help improve regulatory efficiency and reduce regulatory cost. Therefore, intelligent and efficient regulation methods will play an extremely important role in the future of compliance management.

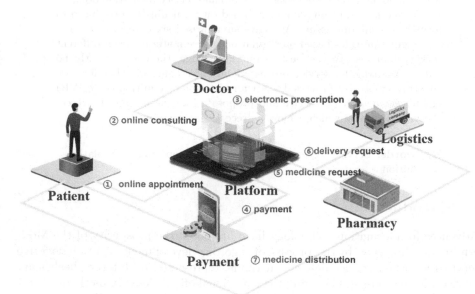

Fig. 1. Online treatment service: a typical service of Internet healthcare service

Service regulation is now more maturely studied in the financial sector and has resulted in systematic regulation technology (RegTech). RegTech is a branch of FinTech (financial technology). The UK Financial Conduct Authority (FCA) first introduced the concept of RegTech in 2015: innovative applications of technology that efficiently and cost-effectively address regulatory and compliance requirements, primarily for financial institutions, with a focus on those technologies that can facilitate regulation more effectively than existing instruments. Due to compliance needs, other service areas are also beginning to look into RegTech. Hence Wikipedia's definition of regulatory technology expands on the FCA's definition which defined as a new technology that uses information technology to enhance regulation. Current research on RegTech is focused on the financial sector, with less research on models and methods to support general regulation of Modern Services Industry. Service regulation can be divided into three stages: beforehand, halfway and afterward. In stage of beforehand, modelling of service and regulation rules is the focus. Therefore, we propose a conceptual model of service regulation satisfying the requirements of business process and service regulation. It contains three domains including service organization domain, business process domain and service regulation domain. Furthermore we construct a regulation language based on π calculus and conceptual model. We also built a dataset and develop a baseline method for violation recognition. Our major contributions in this paper are summarized as follows:

- propose a conceptual model of service regulation with three dimensions: service organization domain, business process domain and service regulation domain;
- present the service regulation language based on π calculus which includes six categories of general regulation rules;
- construct a labelled process dataset for violation recognition (LPD4VR) and a baseline for violation recognition.

The rest of this paper is organized as follows. Section 2 reviews the previous research. We introduce the conceptual model and modeling language for service regulation in Sect. 3. Section 4 is an introduction to the dataset including construction strategies and analysis. We present the service regulation baseline method in Sect. 5. The case study in the field of Internet healthcare services is carried out in Sect. 6. Finally we conclude this work in Sect. 7.

2   Related Work

Business process compliance focuses on the consistency of regulatory rules with the design, verification and validation of business processes [8].

Conformance Checking. Conformance checking is a key function of process mining. It is significant for providers and regulators to confirm whether regulations are being met or where and why there are deviations so that they can manage their processes accordingly. Conformance checking compares process instances with a given process model to identify deviations between the process instances' actual behaviour and its modelled behaviour [6]. It allows to check the relation between a process model and process data collected by IT systems, and to identify as well as analyze deviations between them [15]. As a kind of modeling language, the Petri net is widely used for conformance checking [2,5]. In addition, BPMN is also used for conformance checking in [9]. As for perspectives of conformance checking, multi-perspectives are taken into consideration such as time, roles, and contextual data [2,10]. In [7], Felli et al. adopted data Petri nets (DPNs) as the underlying reference formalism and introduced the CoCoMoT (Computing Conformance Modulo Theories) framework for conformance checking with multi-perspective processes. Berti et al. proposed an improved token-based replay approach to avoid known problems (e.g., "token flooding") which is much faster and scalable [4]. In [17], Valencia-Parra et al. introduced an architecture that supports the creation and distribution of alignment subproblems based on an innovative horizontal acyclic model decomposition to empower conformance checking. A taxonomy of uncertain event logs and models was defined in [14] in response to uncertain event data. In literature [3], a method for evaluating temporal compliance rules in sublinear time by pre-computing data structures was proposed, which summarises the temporal relationships between activities in the log.

Compliance Regulation in Different Service Domains. A number of studies of compliance have emerged in specific service areas. For E-commerce, Siek et al. analyzed event log data from the web databases of an e-commerce company to check their conformance with the standardized processes [16]. Wang et al. [18] proposed a model called Extended Data Petri net (DPNE) based on the conformance checking algorithm [1]. For healthcare, the review in [11]systematically assess the criteria used to measure adherence to clinical guidelines and explore the suitability of using process mining techniques.

3   Service Regulation Modeling

The traditional service relationship model, which includes service provider, service consumer and service objectives, represents the relationship between the subject and the object in the service delivery process. However, the model is missing the important role of the regulator, which makes it difficult to meet the needs of service regulation modelling. The regulator has taken on the role of ensuring that services are developed in compliance. Therefore we propose a conceptual model and introduce the regulation language to satisfy the requirements of service regulation.

3.1   Conceptual Model of Service Regulation

Figure 2 gives an overview of the key components in the regulation modeling. As modern service industries are often complex services characterised by a diversity of participants and a variety of services, internal synergies are more complex while service delivery methods are more convenient. Therefore, the modelling of service regulation is divided into three main domains:

- Service Organization Domain: describes the organizational relationships and collaborative mechanisms in complex services and define the qualifications of service provider;
- Business Process Domain: assumes that business processes are designed as a collection of process; elements [12].
- Service Regulation Domain: defines the core components of service regulation and the relationships between them.

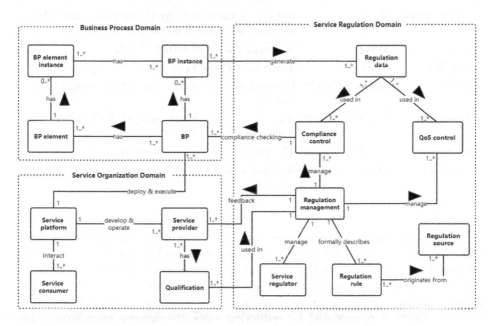

Fig. 2. Conceptual model of service regulation

The service organization domain includes service platform, service provider, service consumer and qualification. It is primarily aimed at modelling the top level of service design. The business process domain follows the BPMN2.0 specification. The service regulation domain covers the three stages: beforehand, halfway and afterward. As the basis for regulation management, regulation rules are formal representations of regulation source. And the regulation management includes compliance control and QoS control. Both controls need to receive the regulation data generated by the business process instances.

3.2 Service Regulation Language Based on Π Calculus

Preliminary. The π-calculus is a mathematical model of processes whose interconnections change as they interact [13]. Due to space constraints and its complexity, we briefly introduce the basic concepts in this subsection. Table 1 shows the basic syntax of the π-calculus.

Table 1. The syntax of the π-calculus.

Agents	Symbol	Definition
Empty agent	**0**	The empty agent can not perform any actions
Output prefix	$\bar{a}x \cdot P$	After the name x is sent along the name a, the agent P continues
Input prefix	$a(x) \cdot P$	After the name a receives the name x, the agent P continues
Silent prefix	τ	Refers to invisible actions, i.e. internal actions that are not observable from outside the system
Sum	P+Q	An agent can enact either P or Q
Parallel	P| Q	The agents P and Q are executed in parallel
Match	if x = y then P	If names of x and y are same, then the agent P continues
Mismatch	if x $\neq$ y then P	If names of x and y are same, then the agent P continues
Restriction	(vx)P	The name x can only be used inside P
Identifier	$A(y_1, ..., y_n)$	Behaves as agent P with y_i replacing x_i for each i

The π-calculus is based on the paradigm of synchronous communication. The simplest entities of π-calculus are names (denoted by lowercase) and agents (denoted by uppercase). There are various representations of the operational semantics of the π-calculus, of which the two main ones are the labelled transition system, which is represented by transition rules, and the unlabelled transition system, which is represented by reduction rules. To achieve asynchrony, this can be done by a sub-calculus: asynchronous π-calculus. Alternatively, this can be achieved by adding an agent representing an asynchronous communication medium between sender and receiver.

Since the Internet and the applications running on it are mostly dynamically coupled systems, π-calculus is well suited as a model for dynamically coupled systems, so we choose π-calculus as the formal method to formalize services.

Business Process Domain. In business process domain, BP and BP element are in design-time. The BP is a set of participants, tasks, data objects and flows, which can be designed as:

$$BP = (Participants, Tasks, DataObjects, Flows, Gateways) \tag{1}$$

The participants are divided into service providers and service consumers. The tasks, data objects and flows which follow the BPMN2.0 specification. The definition of data objects, tasks, flows and gateways are defined as:

$$DataObjects = (log\_data, resource\_data, flows\_data, provider\_data,$$
$$service\_content\_data, consumer\_data) \tag{2}$$

$$Flows = (sequence\_flow, message\_flow) \tag{3}$$

$$Gateways = (exclusive\_gateway, parallel\_gateway, join\_gateway) \tag{4}$$

For data objects, the specific data categories are explained below:

- log_data: system execution data, includes timestamp, user, event and etc.
- resource_data: the record of the resources on which service delivery depends;
- flows_data: the messages required for the π-calculus to pass through flows;
- service_content_data: data on the content of the services received by the consumer;
- consumer_data and provider_data: contains provider and consumer profiles, qualifications and other information.

In our dataset, flows contain both sequential and message streams, and gateways are divided into parallel gateway, exclusive gateway and join gateway. The definitions of gateways are as follows:

$$parallel\_gateway = f_{in}(m).\tau.\bar{f}_{out}(m_{task1}, m_{task2}) \tag{5}$$

$$join\_gateway = f_{in}(m_{task1}, m_{task2}).\tau.\bar{f}_{out}(m) \tag{6}$$

$$exclusive\_gateway = f_{in}(m).\tau.(if m = m_1 \ then \ \bar{f}_{out}(m_{task1}) + if \ m = m_2 \\ then \ \bar{f}_{out}(m_{task2})) \tag{7}$$

The f_{in} and f_{out} represent the flow of inputs and outputs, the m represents the message delivered by flow.

$$startEvent = \tau_s.(vm_s)\bar{f}_{out}m_s \tag{8}$$

$$endEvent = f_{in}(m_e).\tau_e \tag{9}$$

$$Task = f_{in}(m_{in}, m_{data1}).T.\bar{f}_{out}(m_{out}, m_{data2}) \tag{10}$$

The *startEvent* and *endEvent* are special tasks at the beginning and end of the business process. The m_s and m_e represent the start/end message, m_{in} and m_{out} are the input and output messages in the task.

Service Regulation Domain. In service regulation domain of Fig. 2, the regulation management includes compliance control and QoS control, which cover the whole chain of regulation. The regulation rules originate from regulation source which contains laws, industry standards and etc. The regulatory rules are the key basis for regulation management. The ground rules for service regulation can be defined in the following six categories:

* **Rule 1:**

$$d_{required} = (d_1, d_2, ..., d_n);$$
$$f(m).(if \; m \; == d_{required} \; then \; P_{compliance} \; else \; P_{violation})$$
(11)

* **Rule 2:**

$$d_{standard} = (m_1, m_2);$$
$$f(m).(if \; m \notin d_{standard} \; then \; P_{violation} \; else \; P_{compliance})$$
(12)

* **Rule 3:**

$$m_{specific} = (m_1, m_2);$$
$$f(m).(if \; m \notin m_{specific} \; then \; P_{violation} \; else \; P_{compliance})$$
(13)

* **Rule 4:**

$$m_{violation} = (m_{task1}, m_{task2}, ..., m_{taskn});$$
$$f(m).(if \; m \; subseteqm_{violation} \; then \; P_{violation} \; else \; P_{compliance})$$
(14)

* **Rule 5:**

$$m_{required} = (m_{task1}, m_{task2}, ..., m_{taskn});$$
$$f(m).(if \; m_{required} \notin m \; then \; P_{violation} \; else \; P_{compliance})$$
(15)

* **Rule 6:**

$$m_{finished} = (m_{task1}, m_{task2}, ..., m_{taskn});$$
$$f(m).(if \; m \subset m_{finished} \; then \; Task2).P_{compliance} \; else \; P_{violation})$$
(16)

The $d_{required}$ represents the data required by regulation and the $d_{standard}$ are scope of compliance. $P_{compliance}$ and $P_{violation}$ refer to the activation of the corresponding compliance agent or violation agent. The $Rule1$ and $Rule2$ are formal definitions of data compliance. The remaining four rules are formal definitions of behavioural compliance. The $Rule1$ represents the required content of regulation source, such as the various types of qualifications required in the access approval tasks. The $Rule2$ defines the scope of compliance with the data. $m_{violation}$, $m_{specific}$, $m_{required}$ and $m_{finished}$ correspond to violation tasks, special tasks, normative tasks and completed tasks respectively. The $Rule3$ indicates that certain tasks can only be executed under certain circumstances. The $Rule4$ is a formal expression of the prohibited conduct in the regulation source. Correspondingly, the $Rule5$ describes the tasks that must be performed. The $Rule6$ defines the order of execution of tasks which corresponds to the case where certain tasks have to be executed after the end of some specific tasks.

In conjunction with the regulation tasks mentioned in Sect. 4, service regulation is carried out in three stages: design time, running time and post-execution time. In design time, access approval and business process compliance checking are major tasks, which can be described as:

$$P_{access} = f_{provider}(m_{required}).P_{accessCheck}.\bar{f}_{manage}(m_{result})$$
(17)

The $f_{provider}$ means the inputs submitted by the provider, $f_{\overline{manage}}$ means the output of regulation management.

$$P_{accessCheck} = f(m).(if m == Qualification_{data} \ then \ P_{compliance} \ else \ P_{violation})$$
(18)

$Qualification_{data}$ refers to the necessary qualifications for service approval.

$$P_{complianceCheck} = f(m).P_{ruleCheck}.\bar{f}(m_{res})$$
(19)

$P_{complianceCheck}$ and $P_{ruleCheck}$ correspond to the compliance checking process and the specific rule checking process. m_{res} is the result of compliance checking. The running time requires monitoring of the operation of business processes, timely recognition of irregularities and real-time alerts which are defined as:

$$P_{alert} = f(m).(\bar{m}|pass.0 + fail.warning)$$
(20)

The $pass$ and $fail$ are the possible values of input. The $warning$ refers to the activation of the alert agent.

$$P_{monitorCheck} = f(m).P_{ruleCheck}.\bar{f}(m_{res}).P_{alert}$$
(21)

The $P_{monitorCheck}$ is a real-time checking agent.

$$P_{monitor} = !P_{monitorCheck}$$
(22)

The afterward regulation is carried out mainly by means of audits:

$$P_{audit} = f(q).P_{ruleCheck}.\bar{f}(m_{result}).P$$
(23)

4 LPD4VR: A Labelled Process Dataset for Violation Recognition

To the best of our knowledge, there are currently no process datasets available for service violation recognition. To further facilitate research into the intelligence of service regulation, a labelled process dataset (LPD4VR) has been constructed.

The processes in the area of Internet healthcare services covers the main businesses of Internet healthcare services. This dataset contains mainly 40 compliant processes, 9 violation processes, and 17 unknown processes. The process files in XML format follow the BPMN2.0 standard. In the build process, we first built 16 compliant business processes manually based on existing Internet healthcare services. Based on these 16 compliance processes, the dataset was constructed through the following strategies:

– The back-translation method which is currently the most effective enhancement method for text data enhancement is used to implement existing process data for text enhancement. We use the Google Translate interface to augment the manually built compliance process with an "English-French-English" back translation.

- Randomly removing some of the task nodes. We select 10% of the processes to randomly delete task nodes from them, destroying the topological integrity of the process, as part of the violation processes.
- Targeted change of some compliance processes to violation processes, e.g. removal of some data objects required for compliance.

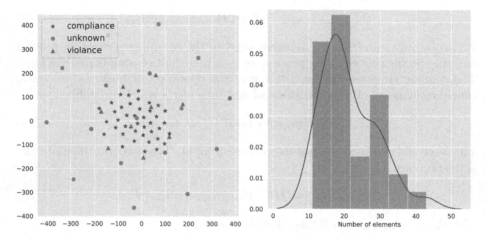

Fig. 3. Semantic distribution of processes in the LPD4VR

Fig. 4. Distribution of the number of BPMN elements in the LPD4VR

Based on the above construction strategies, there are two main types of violation processes: one is an incomplete process that is obtained by randomly deleting nodes, and the other is a process that has undergone targeted modifications. The former is a violation process that does not meet the general service rules, and the latter is a violation process that does not meet the business domain rules. Unknown processes are mainly processes that are difficult to judge under existing rules. We collected 17 processes from other service areas as the unknown processes section, such as the e-commerce service area and the insurance service area. Figure 3 reveals the semantic distribution of compliance processes, non-compliance processes and unknown processes. Both the compliance and violation processes are in the area of Internet healthcare services, and thus the semantics of these two categories are relatively close, while the unknown processes are in other business areas, as the semantic distribution is more dispersed. Figure 4 shows statistics on the length of processes (number of elements, containing data objects, task nodes) in the LPD4VR, which mainly concentrated in the interval [10, 30].

5   A Baseline for Violation Recognition

Violation recognition of service processes can help service providers and regulators to identify violation issues in a timely manner and reduce the cost of breaches. In order to effectively regulate the active service ecosystems of the modern service industry, we propose a framework for identifying violations as shown in Fig. 5.

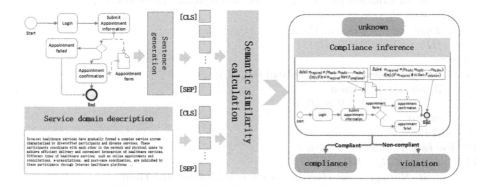

Fig. 5. The violation recognition framework

In the course of business development, crossover service is an important form for innovation which involves new service domains. However, regulation rules have a limited scope of action and thus lack the ability to regulate new service domains. Therefore, we first perform a service domain determination on the input service process. For processes that do not belong to the known service domains, the violation recognition method directly marks them as 'unknown'. Service domain determination is carried out mainly through semantic analysis. With the help of text generation techniques in NLP, we generate service process descriptions by using the names of participants and tasks in the service process as prompt words. At the same time, a business description text needs to be prepared for the service domains that are in the scope of regulation. The semantic similarity is calculated for the two texts and a threshold θ is used to determine whether the process is within the regulation range. The value of θ is determined according to the specific semantic distribution of regulation dataset.

Processes that fall within the scope of regulation are subject to compliance inference based on regulation rules. The regulation rules consist of two main categories: general service regulation rules and domain-related regulation rules. As for the inference, rules first need to be bound with BPMN process elements based on the semantics. The violation is then recognized according to the rules. The recognition method is described in algorithm 1. In this algorithm, the two thresholds are semantic similarity thresholds, determined in conjunction with domain semantic analysis. Regulation rules are formal representations of regulation source texts, but regulation source texts are relatively easier to understand semantically. Therefore, both the regulation source text and the regulation rules are used as input to the algorithm. The algorithm 1 consists of two main steps: rule binding and recognition of the violation BPMN elements, which returns the

---

Algorithm 1. Compliance inference

Input: BPMN process: BP; Regulation source text: R_t;
       $Regulation rule : R_r; Threshold_1 : \alpha; Threshold_2 : \beta$

Output: BPMN process with binding regulation rules: BP_r;
       Set of violation processes: P_v; Set of compliance processes, P_c;

1: $BP_r \leftarrow \emptyset, P_v \leftarrow \emptyset, P_c \leftarrow \emptyset$
2: **if** $Type(R_t) == general$ **then**
3:    $BP_r = \text{Bind}(BP, R_t, R_r)$
4: **else**
5:    $Sim_{p\&r} = similarityCalculation(BP, R_t)$
6:    **if** $Sim_{p\&r} \geq \alpha$ **then**
7:       $BP_r = \text{Bind}(BP, R_t, R_r)$
8:    **end if**
9: **end if**
10: **for** each $Element \in BP_r$ **do**
11:    **for** each $R_t \in BP_r$ **do**
12:       **if** $Sim_{e\&r} = similarityCalculation(Element, R_t)$ **then**
13:         $Element = Bind(Element, R_t, R_r); BP_r.Element \leftarrow Element$
14:       **end if**
15:    **end for**
16: **end for**
17: **for** each BP in BP_r **do**
18:    **for** each $Element$ in BP **do**
19:       $rule.m \leftarrow Element_{input}$
20:       $result = rule.expressions(rule.m, \ rule.required)$
21:       **if** $result == P_{violation}$ **then**
22:         $BP.label \leftarrow violation; P_v.append(BP)$
23:       **else**
24:         $BP.label \leftarrow compliance; P_c.append(BP)$
25:       **end if**
26:    **end for**
27: **end for**
28: **return** P_v; P_c

---

set of compliance processes P_c and the set of violation processes P_v. In the binding phase, general regulation rules are bound directly to the process, and service domain regulation rules are bound where the semantic similarity is greater than the threshold α. After completing the process-level rule binding, the element-level binding is carried out in the same way. The violation recognition is based on regulation rule expressions. The label for that process is then returned based on the result of the expression.

6   Case Study

To verify the effectiveness of the regulatory language and methodology proposed in this paper, we select Internet healthcare service, an innovative service of medical service, for analysis.

Unified Concept Base. The construction of a unified concept base is a necessary step before formal modelling of the Internet healthcare services domain can be carried out. Incorporate existing ISO international standards related to healthcare services, the unified concept base contains nine categories:

- Medication concepts: includes prescription and over-the-counter medicines and vaccines, etc.
- Workflow concepts: the concepts involved in automating parts or the whole of a healthcare service process in a computer application environment
- Clinical concepts: the concepts involved in the clinical diagnostic process, including surgery, disease, etc.
- Financial concepts: financial practices such as payment and health insurance settlement involved in the process of medical services
- Participants concepts: the concept of participants involved in the process of Internet health services
- Qualification concepts: the concept of qualifications required of Internet healthcare participants
- Equipment concepts: the concept of medical devices, the concept of Internet service devices and other necessary equipment involved in Internet health services
- Data concepts: the concept of data required and generated by the whole process of Internet health services, including electronic health records, electronic prescriptions, etc.
- QoS concepts: the concepts of indicators needed to assess the quality of Internet health services

Regulation Rule Base. Regulation rules are the basis for compliance determinations. The regulatory rule base is divided into two parts, one for generic rules and the other for domain rules. The generic rule base is mainly topology-constrained rules for the processes and some business-independent rules. For example, compliance processes must first meet the requirement of process integrity. Business-independent rules refer to service rules that are common to the modern service industry. For example, customer service staff must not use abusive language in after-sales service. The domain rule base is based on a certain amount of domain knowledge. Combined with the unified concept base, we extract regulation rules from regulation sources such as laws and industry standards related to the Internet healthcare services sector to build a formal regulation rule base. According to rule types proposed above, the regulation rule base contains six categories of species atomic rules as well as one category of compound rules. Compound rules are used where two or more atomic rules are required to express the specification. As different regulation sources have different binding effects, each rule will be prioritised accordingly when constructing the regulation rule base. The priorities consist of two main categories, the first being rules that must be followed and the second being norms that are recommended to be followed. The first category is more binding than the second.

Table 2. The results of experiment.

	Compliance	Violance	Unknown	Overall
Numbers in dataset	40	9	17	66
Numbers of accurate recognition	33	6	16	55
Accuracy of recognition	82.5%	66.7%	94.12%	83.33%

Experiment of Violation Recognition. After the unified concept base and regulation rule base were constructed, we conduct violation recognition experiment on LPD4VR. In the experiments, we set the threshold α to 0.3, and the threshold β to 0.5. The specific experimental results are shown in the following Table 2. We found that the 'unknown' class to be the most accurate, with 94.12% accuracy. This accuracy result is also broadly consistent with the results of the semantic analysis of the dataset. The least accurate process recognition rate is 66.7% for 'violation' class. This may be due to the weak semantics of the task phrase, which makes it difficult to accomplish a highly relevant binding to the rule. The overall recognition accuracy achieved is 83.33%. To improve overall recognition accuracy, future work will be to improve compliance process recognition accuracy and violation identification accuracy.

7   Conclusion

The rapid development of the modern service industry is accompanied by many irregularities. Traditional methods of regulation rely heavily on manual labour, which is inefficient and costly. Research into intelligent and efficient methods of service regulation has therefore become an important aspect of ensuring the healthy development of modern service industries. This paper proposes a conceptual model of service regulation for service process compliance management. Furthermore we present a formal modelling approach based on the π calculus. In terms of violation recognition, to our best knowledge, there are no widely used datasets. Therefore we construct the LPD4VR dataset in the field of Internet healthcare services. Our proposed violation recognition method has also been experimented on this dataset. As for future works, we will focus on real-time regulation, especially for service processes that generate multi-modal data including video, picture, audio and text.

Acknowledgements. This work was supported in part by National Natural Science Foundation of China under Grant 61825205, in part by the Key Research and Development Program of Zhejiang Provence under grant 2021C01017, in part by the Key Research Project of Zhejiang Province under Grant 2022C01145 and in part by the National Natural Science Foundation of China under Grants U20A20173 and 62125206.

References

1. Van der Aalst, W., Adriansyah, A., van Dongen, B.: Replaying history on process models for conformance checking and performance analysis. Wiley Interdisc. Rev. Data Min. Knowl. Disc. **2**(2), 182–192 (2012)
2. Alizadeh, M., Lu, X., Fahland, D., Zannone, N., van der Aalst, W.M.: Linking data and process perspectives for conformance analysis. Comput. Secur. **73**, 172–193 (2018)
3. Augusto, A., Awad, A., Dumas, M.: Efficient checking of temporal compliance rules over business process event logs. arXiv preprint arXiv:2112.04623 (2021)
4. Berti, A., van der Aalst, W.M.P.: A novel token-based replay technique to speed up conformance checking and process enhancement. In: Koutny, M., Kordon, F., Pomello, L. (eds.) Transactions on Petri Nets and Other Models of Concurrency XV. LNCS, vol. 12530, pp. 1–26. Springer, Heidelberg (2021). https://doi.org/10.1007/978-3-662-63079-2_1
5. Burattin, A., van Zelst, S.J., Armas-Cervantes, A., van Dongen, B.F., Carmona, J.: online conformance checking using behavioural patterns. In: Weske, M., Montali, M., Weber, I., vom Brocke, J. (eds.) BPM 2018. LNCS, vol. 11080, pp. 250–267. Springer, Cham (2018). https://doi.org/10.1007/978-3-319-98648-7_15
6. Dunzer, S., Stierle, M., Matzner, M., Baier, S.: Conformance checking: a state-of-the-art literature review. In: Proceedings of the 11th International Conference on Subject-Oriented Business Process Management, pp. 1–10 (2019)
7. Felli, P., Gianola, A., Montali, M., Rivkin, A., Winkler, S.: CoCoMoT: conformance checking of multi-perspective processes via SMT. In: Polyvyanyy, A., Wynn, M.T., Van Looy, A., Reichert, M. (eds.) BPM 2021. LNCS, vol. 12875, pp. 217–234. Springer, Cham (2021). https://doi.org/10.1007/978-3-030-85469-0_15
8. Hashmi, M., Governatori, G., Lam, H.P., Wynn, M.T.: Are we done with business process compliance: state of the art and challenges ahead. Knowl. Inf. Syst. **57**(1), 79–133 (2018)
9. de Leoni, M., van der Aalst, W.M.P., van Dongen, B.F.: Data- and resource-aware conformance checking of business processes. In: Abramowicz, W., Kriksciuniene, D., Sakalauskas, V. (eds.) BIS 2012. LNBIP, vol. 117, pp. 48–59. Springer, Heidelberg (2012). https://doi.org/10.1007/978-3-642-30359-3_5
10. Mannhardt, F., De Leoni, M., Reijers, H.A., Van Der Aalst, W.M.: Balanced multi-perspective checking of process conformance. Computing **98**(4), 407–437 (2016)
11. Oliart, E., Rojas, E., Capurro, D.: Are we ready for conformance checking in healthcare? measuring adherence to clinical guidelines: a scoping systematic literature review. J. Biomed. Inf. **130**, 104076 (2022)
12. Papazoglou, M.P.: Making business processes compliant to standards and regulations. In: 2011 IEEE 15th International Enterprise Distributed Object Computing Conference, pp. 3–13. IEEE (2011)
13. Parrow, J.: An introduction to the π-calculus. In: Handbook of Process algebra, pp. 479–543. Elsevier (2001)
14. Pegoraro, M., Uysal, M.S., van der Aalst, W.M.: Conformance checking over uncertain event data. Inf. Syst. **102**, 101810 (2021)
15. Pufahl, L., Rehse, J.R.: Conformance checking with regulations-a research agenda. In: EMISA, pp. 24–29 (2021)
16. Siek, M., Mukti, R.: Business process mining from e-commerce event web logs: conformance checking and bottleneck identification. In: IOP Conference Series: Earth and Environmental Science, vol. 729, p. 012133. IOP Publishing (2021)

17. Valencia-Parra, Á., Varela-Vaca, Á.J., Gómez-López, M.T., Carmona, J., Bergen-
    thum, R.: Empowering conformance checking using big data through horizontal
    decomposition. Inf. Syst. **99**, 101731 (2021)
18. Wang, Y., Yu, W., Teng, P., Liu, G., Xiang, D.: A detection method for abnormal
    transactions in e-commerce based on extended data flow conformance checking.
    Wireless Commun. Mob. Comput. **2022** (2022)

Quality of Service

WebQMon.ai: Gateway-Based Web QoE Assessment Using Lightweight Neural Networks

Enge Song[1], Tian Pan[1,2]([✉]), Qiang Fu[3]([✉]), Chenhao Jia[1], Jiao Zhang[1,2], Tao Huang[1,2], and Yunjie Liu[1,2]

[1] State Key Laboratory of Networking and Switching Technology, BUPT, Beijing, China
[2] Purple Mountain Laboratories, Nanjing, China
pan@bupt.edu.cn
[3] Royal Melbourne Institute of Technology, Melbourne, Australia
qiang.fu@rmit.edu.au

Abstract. Users' perception of their experience accessing web pages greatly affects users' willingness to continue browsing the website. However, it is difficult to assess user perception through a generic Quality of Experience (QoE) model. Web content consists of a large variety of static as well as dynamic objects, with some of them coming from the remote sites. This makes QoE assessment a challenge for the traditional methods. To build a generic QoE model, we introduce WebQMon.ai, a lightweight Web QoE assessment architecture using machine learning methods without setting any specific formula or threshold. WebQMon.ai can evaluate web-browsing QoE using mostly network-layer data with only one piece of application-layer information, the *referer* in the HTTP header, which is used to aggregate the packets associated with the same web page. The distribution of the arriving packets requested by the web page is used to construct WebQMon.ai. WebQMon.ai requires little storage space (80KB~6MB). More importantly it can be deployed directly at edge routers/gateways, due to the weak dependence on the application-layer payload. We further improved our algorithm by *ensemble learning* combining multiple orthogonal features, to generate a stronger classifier. We evaluated WebQMon.ai on three popular websites. It shows that the QoE assessment results for *4,800* unknown samples can be obtained within just *0.07s* and reach an average accuracy of *97%*.

Keywords: Web-browsing QoE · Neural networks

1 Introduction

The web-based Internet activities produce a large amount of HTTP traffic [15]. Internet users often visit a variety of websites to search for information, watch

This work was supported by National Key Research and Development Program of China (2019YFB1802600).

video clips or socialise with someone. The page loading latency is critical to user experience (UE). A study shows that there is a strong correlation between the performance of e-commerce websites and online shoppers' behavior [1]. The observation from the experiment with 1,048 online shoppers indicates that *two seconds* is the critical threshold for page loading latency, after which consumers may become impatient if the page is still not loaded, and 40% of the consumers will abandon the site if it goes beyond three seconds. Research also shows that slow page loading damages consumers' loyalty to an e-commerce site, especially for high spenders [3]. Up to 79% of online shoppers who experienced a dissatisfying visit would never visit the site again while 27% of them would not visit its physical store either. QoS has been widely used to measure network performance. But, it is not a direct reflection of QoE [5]. ISPs and equipment vendors can however leverage their knowledge of the traffic going through their networks and create hypothetical QoE prediction models to estimate UE or QoE anywhere in the network. They can then refine the network settings or give feedback and recommendations to website owners to improve QoE.

However, real-time QoE assessment is a challenge. Casas et al. [4] propose YOUQMON, which can predict in real-time the stalling events of YouTube videos with network-layer data. Unfortunately, it is not a generic QoE assessment tool, as the thresholds and formulas are made specific to YouTube. The web-browsing QoE is mostly affected by the loading time of the last visible object shown on the screen, that is, above-the-fold (ATF) time. The study in [7] shows that among a variety of QoE metrics including page load time (PLT), ATF is most correlated to user experience. Many studies use ATF or its variants to capture how users perceive web-browsing experience [7,9,11,12,14]. Although predicting QoE by ATF works well, it is not a trivial task to obtain ATF. Most of the existing methods obtain ATF or its variants with client-side support by analyzing the video recordings of the web page rendering process [9,11,17] or tracing loading time of different resource types [6,7,12,14,16]. However, these analysis methods have a common issue: relying on client-side support to install software or hardware plugins and thus obtain or infer ATF or its variants. In contrast, we use machine learning methods to predict ATF.

To this end, we design WebQMon.ai, a generic real-time tool for assessing web-browsing QoE without requiring client-side support. It uses network-layer data and a single piece of application-layer data (the *referer* field in HTTP header) to predict ATF. As the *referer* is in the first few bytes of the HTTP request packet, no packet reassembly is needed. The *referer* is not even required, if the content from the third-party web site is not a concern. Hence, WebQMon.ai can be deployed at access routers or gateways without additional security or privacy concerns, which may be an issue for those requiring client-side support.

As ATF increases QoE deteriorates. We can classify ATF into multiple categories. Each category corresponds to a certain level of QoE, *e.g.*, an ATF below two seconds indicating good user experience [1]. We gather TCP traffic generated from web browsing, and then characterize the traffic by the two proposed traffic metrics: *Traffic Volume per Second* (TVS) and *Cumulative Traffic Volume* (CTV). TVS and CTV in time series exhibit different patterns under different network conditions, which is a good indication of distinct QoE. WebQMon.ai can predict QoE by distinguishing these patterns. Based on this architecture, we propose five supervised learning-based models to classify the patterns. The collected samples of the traffic metrics in time series are labeled by the estimated ATF. The labeled data is then used as training data to train the machine learning model. The trained model takes up a small amount of storage space, from tens of KBs to a few MBs. WebQMon.ai is capable of real-time and accurate prediction. For instance, more than four thousand samples can be predicted within *0.07* seconds, with an average accuracy of *97%*.

Our major contributions are summarized as follows:

- We propose WebQMon.ai, a generic web-browsing QoE assessment system, capable of real-time prediction with high accuracy. It can be deployed on gateways instead of end hosts, with little storage space required. WebQMon.ai is powered by a data-driven model. It can be easily updated with new data to adapt to new types of web content in a timely manner, without the complexity of mathematical formulations or threshold settings (Sect. 3).
- To realize the data-driven model, we develop five models based on machine learning algorithms and the WebQMon.ai architecture to predict ATF. These methods are lightweight, easy to train and enable real-time and accurate prediction without being limited to a certain type of content (Sect. 4).
- We implement the five models with 1,876 lines of code, available at our github repository [2] (Sect. 5). The extensive evaluation shows that WebQMon.ai works very well on QoE prediction (Sect. 6).

2   Related Work

The current work requires client-side support for web QoE assessment. Some of the approaches rely on models specifically designed for a particular web site such as YouTube. WebQMon.ai is a generic architecture that can be easily applied to different types of web content. The other adopt generic models using formulas or machine learning models. These solutions acquire ATF and/or its variants with client-side support, and then perform QoE mapping through formulas or machine learning models. These solution are conceptually different to WebQMon.ai, which aims to estimate ATF without client-side support.

Non-generic Models. The solutions in [4,10] predict QoE through mathematical formulations and empirical threshold settings. This is a complex procedure, and more importantly, limits its applicability to other types of web content. For example in [4], YouTube stalling events are predicted using two thresholds α_{sta} and α_{play}, which are estimated from large measurement campaigns. This is a complex procedure, and more importantly, limits its applicability to other types of web content [4]. For a different application, it may require to re-estimate the threshold from another large measurement campaign. WebQMon.ai is data-driven, which does not require threshold settings or mathematical formulations.

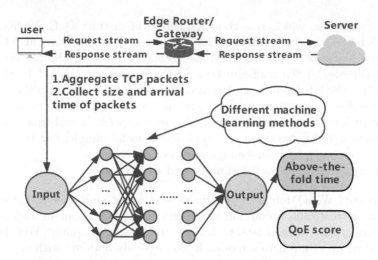

Fig. 1. WebQMon.ai architecture.

Formula-Based QoE Mapping. Given the user-perceived metrics, the solutions in [11,14] uses formulas for QoE mapping. For example, the work in [11] analyzes the video frames of the recorded web page rendering process and then obtains ATF related metrics such as SpeedIndex. The work in [14] has a customized application embedded into the user devices to get the relevant information for QoE mapping. These systems rely on client-side plugins to obtain relevant metrics to do QoE mapping and have to be deployed on the client-side.

Machine Learning-Based QoE Mapping. Some solutions use machine learning models for fine-grained QoE mapping, after acquiring ATF or relevant metrics from the client-side [7,9,12,13]. The studies in [7,12,13] get the metrics through the browser's API. Similar to [11], the work in [9] obtains ATF through analyzing the recorded web page rendering process. These solutions are conceptually different to our approach, as WebQMon.ai uses machine learning models to estimate ATF based on traffic characteristics. However, we did get inspired by these studies and adopted the machine learning-based approach.

3   WebQMon.ai Architecture

3.1   System Architecture

ATF determines user's web-browsing experience. We propose WebQMon.ai to predict ATF and thus user experience. We collect network-level data from the Gateway and transform raw data into a useful format (Fig. 1). Then, our model is trained with the processed data. After that, WebQMon.ai can predict ATF when the user visits the web pages. In Sect. 4, based on the architecture, we propose five models using different input metrics and machine learning algorithms. These models can be trained and/or updated with the diverse types of content or web sites, giving it the ability to learn and adapt to the new context.

The access routers or gateways all perform DPI (Deep Packet Inspection) for a variety of reasons. Raw data is readily available without needing additional resources. No packet reassembly is even needed as packets are processed as they need to be. We only need to get the statistics and construct the proposed traffic metrics. As to be discussed in Sect. 3.2, the overhead can be managed by following vendor's restrictions on sampling intervals. The test time of the models is instant as shown in Sect. 6, predicting over 4,000 samples within 0.07 s. The storage requirement is in the order of tens of KBs to a few MBs. All these indicate that WebQMon.ai can be conveniently deployed at gateways.

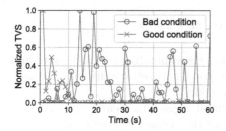

Fig. 2. Traffic Volume per Second.

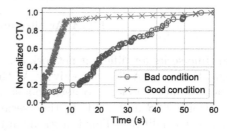

Fig. 3. Cumulative Traffic Volume.

3.2 Dataset and Data Preprocessing

The training and test dataset are derived from the TCP streams appearing when the user visits a web page. In Fig. 1, we can easily get all TCP traffic at the Edge Router or Gateway. The *referer*, a field in HTTP header, is used to identify and aggregate the traffic requested by the visited web page from other sources such as a third-party website. The arrival pattern of TCP packets is highly correlated to network conditions. The arriving packets are from different TCP flows. We will first need to aggregate the packets into their individual flows to establish the correlation. To extract meaningful flow features that can reflect network dynamics, we propose two *traffic metrics* to be defined below.

Traffic Volume per Second (*TVS*) measures the instantaneous throughput of a flow. The challenge is the sampling granularity. A fine granularity may cause a high-level of measurement overhead, which the gateway may struggle to handle. A coarse granularity may result in the loss of detailed flow features, which will decrease classification accuracy. The sampling interval is set to one second, the finest sampling granularity limited by the switch without overloading the gateway. Figure 2 shows the normalized *TVS* in time series with good and bad network conditions, respectively. Good network conditions result in satisfactory ATF while bad network conditions result in unsatisfactory ATF, as defined in Eq. (1). We will elaborate on this in Sect. 5. It shows that when the network condition is good, a large amount of content arrives quickly and the peak rate appears at the early stage of the transmission. In contrast, when the network condition is bad, the content is loaded slowly and there is no clear peak rate.

Cumulative Traffic Volume (*CTV*) measures the total amount of traffic received over a flow at a time point. Figure 3 illustrates the normalized *CTV*

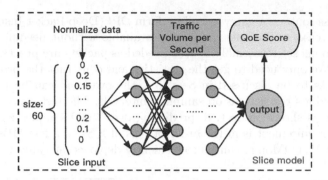

Fig. 4. Architecture of the Slice model.

in time series for different network conditions, corresponding to satisfactory and unsatisfactory ATF, respectively. With the good network condition, the curve shows a steep slope, or otherwise a shallow slope.

Both *TVS* and *CTV* in time series exhibit a pattern clearly correlated to network conditions. This is a strong indication that these two traffic metrics may be used to reflect web-browsing QoE.

3.3   Training and Prediction

The raw TCP data is processed to generate the proposed traffic metrics. Each of them is marked with a unique label for supervised learning and the ATF can be predicted by exploring the time series patterns of the metrics. When using machine learning methods, *TVS* and *CTV* need to be processed to generate input variables. We will elaborate on this in a later section. In the training stage, the difference between the predicted value and the label is reduced iteration by iteration. In order to get the prediction results (*i.e.*, ATF), we conduct simple matrix calculations. The ATF can then be mapped to the QoE score by a mapping function [7]. This enables real-time QoE assessment.

4   WebQMon.ai Algorithm

To explore *TVS* and *CTV* for QoE assessment, we design five classification models based on machine learning methods, namely, Slice, NN, LSTM, R-LSTM and Combine. All the models use the WebQMon.ai architecture, with selected machine learning algorithms and feature variables, to be discussed in Sect 4.3. Slice classifies *TVS* using the fully connected neural networks. NN is based on the maximum slope and time domain features of *CTV*. LSTM relies on the *linear interpolation* data of *CTV*. R-LSTM improves LSTM by reversing the input variables. The fifth method, Combine, uses the idea of *ensemble learning*, which can subtly combine the predictions from multiple learning models to achieve more accurate, stable, and robust results. It is particularly suitable in our case as the features of Slice, NN and R-LSTM are distinct to each other.

4.1 Basic Classification Models

The packets that arrive within 60 s after the HTTP request are collected and preprocessed. We calculate and normalize *TVS* and *CTV*, which are then used as the input of the first four models. The output is the label of ATF or QoE score, which is determined by the probability of the estimated ATF, for example, being below or above 2 s.

Slice takes *TVS* as input. The different forms of *TVS* correspond to different ATF. Slice uses fully connected neural networks for fast training and testing and good performance. Since packets are collected for 60 s, the data format of *TVS* is a 60-dimensional vector as shown in Fig. 4. The input variable is the normalized data.

NN takes *CTV* as input and uses fully connected neural networks. Figure 3 shows that the *maximum slope* of *CTV* can reflect the network condition — the deeper the slope is, the better the condition is. This makes *maximum slope* one of the classification features. The time when *CTV* reaches x% is denoted as $t_{x\%}$. It makes sense to use $t_{25\%}$, $t_{50\%}$, $t_{75\%}$ and $t_{90\%}$ as inputs, to capture *CTV* in time domain while making them relatively independent. Together with *maximum slope*, we have a five-dimensional input, that is, $t_{25\%}$, $t_{50\%}$, $t_{75\%}$, $t_{90\%}$, *maximum slope*. Note that the time domain inputs $t_{x\%}$ do have some correlation. This violates the assumption to use NN and explains its less impressive performance on ternary classification in Sect. 6. LSTM is more suitable to use *CTV*.

LSTM. (*Long Short-Term Memory Neural Networks*), a variant of *Recurrent Neural Networks* (RNN), is often used to process the time series data. Compared to the simple RNN, LSTM can keep the *Long-Term Memory* feature of the

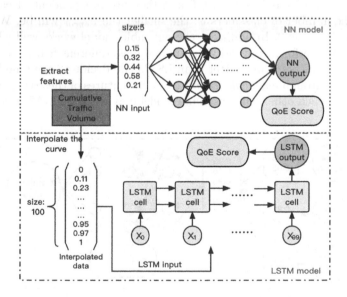

Fig. 5. Architecture of the NN model and the LSTM model.

sequence. Therefore, LSTM is particularly suitable to address the long delays of *CTV* and capture the dependency between data points. As shown in Fig. 5, to construct the input, *linear interpolation* is used to create approximate 100 points of *CTV* for curve fitting.

R-LSTM. The packets that arrive earlier within the 60 s represent the initial response of the loading process, and thus may have a greater impact on user experience. However, in LSTM the early input has less impact on the output. This is not desirable. Therefore, we *reverse* the interpolated data, that is, the early data points of *CTV* are processed last, giving them more influence on the output. We call this model R-LSTM. Note that LSTM and R-LSTM differ only in the input vector. We shall demonstrate in Sect. 6 that R-LSTM indeed performs better than LSTM.

4.2   Combine Classification Model

Combine Leverages *Ensemble Learning.* The idea is to first generate multiple learners, then combine them with some integration strategies, and finally generate the output. The theoretical basis of *ensemble learning* is that strong learners and weak learners are equivalent, so we can find ways to convert weak learners into strong learners instead of having to directly search for strong learners that are hard to find. Take the binary classification problem as an example. Assume that there are N independent classifiers with an error rate of p. Using a simple voting method to combine all the classifiers, the error rate of the integrated classifier is $P_{error} = \sum_{k=0}^{N/2} C_N^k (1-p)^k p^{N-k}$. It can be seen from the equation that when $p < 0.5$, the error rate P_{error} decreases as N increases. If the error rate of each classifier is less than 0.5 and they are independent of each other, the more the number of classifiers is, the smaller the P_{error} will be. When N is infinite, the P_{error} is 0. In addition, the ensemble model works well when these weak classifiers perform well individually and have different features.

Since R-LSTM performs better than LSTM, we decide to combine R-LSTM, Slice, and NN through *ensemble learning.* As the features of these three classifiers are distinct to each other, the ensemble model may work well. After completing

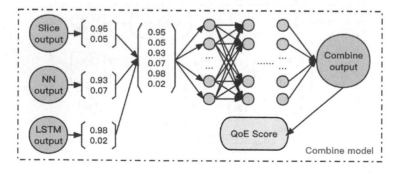

Fig. 6. Architecture of the combine model.

the training of the three basic models, we combine them using fully connected neural networks. As shown in Fig. 6, based on binary classification, the predicted values of the three models are combined into a six-dimensional vector as the input variable of the fully connected neural networks.

4.3 Feature and Algorithm Selection

For the fully connected neural networks, we assume that all inputs are relatively independent of each other. In contrast, the idea behind LSTM neural networks is to make use of sequential correlated information. The models are designed to take advantage of the different input variables. For example, *TVS* is used for Slice while *CTV* is used for NN. The input variables for LSTM and R-LSTM are derived from *CTV*, with the earlier input related to the latter input. The other three models does not have this property and thus can take a simple approach using the fully connected neural networks. Combine aims to take advantage of the other models for better performance.

All these models are data-driven methods, which means that we can update our models with new data in a timely manner on a regular basis. The real-time ability of these methods allows ISPs and equipment vendors to assess user experience on the fly and take actions if necessary.

5 Implementation and Experimental Settings

5.1 Dataset Collection

Data Collection. Our experiments took place from September 2020 to February 2021 in a laboratory. The hardware was equipped with i5-8600K CPU and GTX 1070Ti. We selected three websites to visit, that is, "amazon.com", "sina.com.cn", ranked the eighth and the nineteenth, respectively, in Alexa Traffic Rank, and "youku.com.cn," which represent widely used *shopping*, *news* and *video* sites. For simplicity, we will use Amazon, Sina and Youku to refer to these websites. Our data was obtained by visiting the homepage of the website. Note that the homepage is the most popular, diverse and dynamic page and its content changes over the months of the sampling period. Being able to classify the homepage of the three different types of websites is a challenge. We collected the packets arriving within 60 s after the user visited the website. Then, we got the *TVS* and the *CTV* from these packets and labeled this sample of *TVS* or *CTV* in time series according to the estimated ATF. We used *Dummynet* to create a bottleneck to control the network condition and construct samples with different labels accordingly. There were already mature plugins for the aggregation of packets belonging to the same visit. Traffic aggregation was implemented by the Firefox browser.

Data Labeling. We evaluate the performance of Slice, NN, LSTM, R-LSTM and Combine to predict ATF using the collected dataset. Our experiments have two parts: binary classification and ternary classification. We adjust the network condition through *Dummynet* to ensure that the ATF meets our requirements, measured by the chrome plugins released in [6]. We then label the data according to the estimated ATF using the following rules based on Akamai's research on customer behaviours, 2 s being the psychological threshold [1]:

$$Binary : label = \begin{cases} 0, ATF \leq 2\,s \\ 1, ATF > 2\,s \end{cases}; \quad Ternary : label = \begin{cases} 0, ATF \leq 2\,s \\ 1, 2\,s < ATF \leq 5\,s \\ 2, ATF > 5\,s \end{cases}$$

(1)

We use a simple one-to-one correspondence to map ATF to QoE, which could be implemented through a mapping function [7]. For binary classification, "0" represents good UE, and "1" represents poor UE. For ternary classification, "0" means good UE, "1" means poor UE, and "2" means terrible UE.

Dataset. For binary classification, we collected about *16,000, 16,000, 8,000* samples from Sina, Amazon and Youku, respectively, of which the proportion of positive and negative samples was 1:1. This balanced split is for the purpose of learning, to ensure that the models learn both positive and negative cases. In reality the occurrence of positive cases is much less common than that of negative cases. However, only positive cases are of interest to ISPs and vendors. For ternary classification, we only got extra 6,000 samples from Sina due to being blocked later on. The proportion of "0", "1" and "2" samples was 4:4:3. 70% of the samples are used as the training dataset with the rest as the test dataset. Since most websites have a mechanism against crawling, this prevents us from frequently refreshing the same web page. For example, when we collected data from Amazon, it always required to provide a verification code. This made it extremely difficult to create a larger dataset. We believe that the amount of available data can demonstrate the feasibility of the model to a certain extent, and the three websites represent the typical scenarios of web browsing activities. For a certain website, different models share the same training and test dataset, ensuring that the results are not affected by how the dataset is split. We use the training dataset to train each model separately, that is, we train five models for each of the test websites, for a total of 15 models.

5.2   Model Parameters

Parameter Setting. The parameters common to all models are: *number of iterations = 100,000, learning rate = 0.003*, and *batch size =128*. These param-

Table 1. Other model parameters.

	No. of input units	No. of hidden units	No. of hidden layers
Slice	60	480	2
NN	5	40	2
R-/LSTM	100	256	1
Combine	6	48	2

Table 2. Dropout effect.

	No Dropout	P_{keep} of 80%
Accuracy	0.9425	0.9495
Precision	0.9569	0.97
Recall	0.9512	0.9489
F1 score	0.954	0.9593

eters were chosen to achieve the highest accuracy on the validation set. Other parameters are shown in the Table 1. The *Number of input units* is the dimension of the input variable, while the *Number of hidden units* is the number of neurons in the hidden layer. The *Number of hidden layers* is the number of the network layers between input and output layers. The classic "trial-and-error" method was used for creating neural network layers. It was a simple process with several iterations. There was no need to readjust the parameters and it worked well across all the three web sites, indicating the ease of parameter selection. It also shows that all the five models have a simple lightweight architecture.

Overfitting and Dropout. In machine learning, overfitting may occur when a model corresponds too closely or exactly to the training data and thus may fail to fit the test data or predict reliably. Dropout regularization is one of the popular techniques to avoid overfitting, which helps make the model globally fit. As shown in Sect. 6, the Slice model is overfitting. Dropout is applied by deactivating a portion of neurons at the training time. P_{keep} represents the portion of active neurons. After tests on the validation set, we found that the Slice model had the best performance with P_{keep} set to 80%.

6   Experimental Results

Accuracy, precision, recall and *F1 score* are commonly used performance metrics. In a real-world scenario, the chance to have an unsatisfactory ATF (positive) is small. *Accuracy* can be misleading for imbalanced data sets, *e.g.*, small portion of positives vs large portion of negatives. *Precision* represents true positives per predicted positive while *recall* represents true positives per real positive. As *recall* increases, *precision* may drop, and vice versa. *F1 score* is the harmonic mean of *precision* and *recall*. A high *F1 score* indicates a good balance between the two. As we have a focus on positive cases and the number of negatives is unknown and large, this makes the latter three metrics particularly suitable in our evaluation. Equation (1) shows the label of our data. For binary classification, label with "1" is the positive instance and label with "0" is the negative instance. For ternary classification, each category is treated as a positive class for calculating the values of the metrics. The test dataset is used to predict labels. The predicted label is compared to the actual label, which serves as the ground truth.

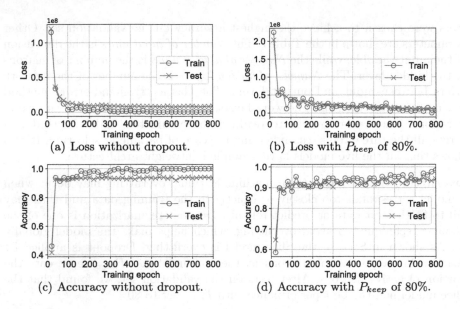

(a) Loss without dropout.

(b) Loss with P_{keep} of 80%.

(c) Accuracy without dropout.

(d) Accuracy with P_{keep} of 80%.

Fig. 7. Without dropout regularization vs. P_{keep} of 80%.

6.1 Basic Models

Dropout Effect on Slice. Figure 7 compares the results with and without dropout regularization (P_{keep} set to 80%). It shows that the Slice model is indeed overfitting. Figures 7(a) and 7(b) show the loss functions measuring the inconsistency between the predicted value and the actual label against the number of training epochs. The loss functions decrease as the number of epochs increases. Without dropout (Fig. 7(a)), the loss function of the test dataset is not as small as that of the training dataset, and this gap does not decrease as the number of epochs increases. This is an indication of overfitting. With dropout (Fig. 7(b)), the loss function of the training and test datasets matches each other very well. Similarly, Fig. 7(c) and 7(d) show the accuracy performance of the model against the number of epochs. The accuracy improves as the number of epochs increases.

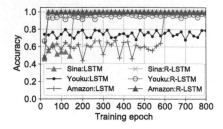

Fig. 8. Accuracy comparison (LSTM vs R-LSTM).

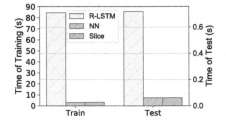

Fig. 9. Training and test time comparison (Amazon).

Without dropout (Fig. 7(c)), the accuracy of the test dataset does not match the accuracy of the training dataset, which reaches 100%, and the gap is not narrowed as the number of epochs increases. The model fits the training dataset well but fails to fit the test dataset. This indicates that the Slice model is indeed overfitting. With dropout (Fig. 7(d)), the accuracy of the training and the test datasets matches each other closely. Although dropout reduces the accuracy of the training dataset, it helps improve the accuracy of the test dataset.

Table 2 shows that, with dropout regularization, the accuracy, precision and F1 score of the model slightly increase but the recall decreases a little bit. Note that precision and recall are mutually influential (true positives per predicted positive vs per real positive). True positives are usually achieved at the cost of false positives. A high recall may come with a low precision, and vice versa [8]. Ideally, we want to keep both precision and recall high, to ensure that the positives are true positives without any missing positives. A high F1 score (as shown in Table 2) indicates a good balance between the two. Based on these results, we can conclude that dropout regularization improves the performance of Slice. Dropout is applied to Slice in the later experiments.

LSTM vs R-LSTM. We will now demonstrate that the improved LSTM model, R-LSTM, has better performance. Figure 8 shows the prediction accuracy by LSTM and R-LSTM against the number of training epochs for the three test websites. It shows that the model converges much faster with R-LSTM at roughly epoch 50 for both Sina and Amazon. With LSTM, the model converges at roughly epochs 150 and 600, for Sina and Amazon, respectively. For Youku, R-LSTM has much higher accuracy than LSTM, roughly 97% vs. 75%. Based on these results, we believe that reversing the input variables can significantly improve convergence time as well as accuracy, depending on the type of web content. In later experiments, we will use R-LSTM instead of LSTM.

Performance. Table 3 shows the performance of the models for binary classification on accuracy, precision, recall, and F1 score. The data volumes of the test datasets for Amazon, Sina, and Youku are approximately 4,800, 4,800, 2,400 samples (30% of the dataset), respectively. The results suggest that for Amazon and Sina, the three models work remarkably well on ATF prediction. The performance on all the metrics is close to 1. There are fewer than five prediction errors for Amazon and Sina. For Youku, the performance is less impressive. The

Table 3. ATF prediction performance comparison.

	Amazon			Sina			Youku		
	Slice	NN	R-LSTM	Slice	NN	R-LSTM	Slice	NN	R-LSTM
Accuracy	0.9991	0.9991	**0.9995**	**0.9988**	0.9986	0.9983	0.9466	0.9536	**0.9684**
Precision	1	0.9996	1	**0.9992**	0.9987	0.9987	0.9642	0.9674	**0.9789**
Recall	0.9984	0.9988	**0.9992**	**0.9983**	**0.9983**	0.9979	0.9501	0.9583	**0.9690**
F1 score	0.9992	0.9992	**0.9996**	**0.9987**	0.9985	0.9983	0.9571	0.9628	**0.9739**

Table 4. Performance comparison with combine on Youku.

	R-LSTM	Slice	NN	Combine
Accuracy	0.9546	0.9546	0.9546	**0.9693**
Precision	**0.9899**	0.9728	0.9765	0.9826
Recall	0.939	0.9561	0.9523	**0.9695**
F1 score	0.9638	0.9644	0.9643	**0.976**

Table 5. Performance for ternary classification.

	R-LSTM	Slice	NN	Combine
...	0.9439	0.9109	0.8607	**0.9518**
...	**0.941**	0.891	0.828	**0.941**
...	0.9192	0.8907	0.8299	**0.9452**
...	0.9281	0.8908	0.8289	**0.943**

values of the performance metrics vary between 0.94 and 0.98. Since Youku is a video site, there are a lot of dynamically loaded content on its home page. Therefore, regardless of the network conditions, the diversity of the content (or the dataset) on its home page is a challenge to classification and thus reduces the accuracy. Within the 2,400 samples, there are about 100 prediction errors, an error rate roughly between 2% to 6%. Among the three models, R-LSTM appears to be the best performer on Youku.

Training and Test Time. Figure 9 shows the training and test time of the three models on Amazon. The data volume of the training and test datasets are about 11,200 and 4,800 samples, respectively. It shows that the training time of R-LSTM is much higher than that of the other two models. The training time of LSTM depends on the number of iterations, which is 100 in our model. Therefore, *backpropagation* of LSTM needs to be performed 100 times per training batch. In contrast, Slice and NN use fully connected neural networks as the classifier, which requires only one *backpropagation* per training batch. As a result, the training time of LSTM is much longer than that of Slice and NN. For test time, it is a similar situation. The *forward propagation* of LSTM requires 100 executions to generate an output, but the *forward propagation* of the fully connected neural network only needs to be performed once to generate an output. The time it takes R-LSTM to complete 4,800 predictions is much longer than it takes Slice and NN. However, as *backpropagation* is only needed for training, not for prediction, the gap between LSTM and NN/Slice on test time is much smaller than on training time. The time required for the three models to predict 4,800 samples is about 0.7 s, 0.08 s, and 0.07 s, respectively. It confirms the possibility of using our model to assess the user's QoE in real-time.

6.2   Combine

Ensemble Learning. We combine the trained Slice, NN, and R-LSTM through a fully connected neural network to generate a new model, Combine. The three basic models were trained using the 70% of the total dataset as the training dataset and were able to predict with few errors. If we reuse the 70% for Combine, the inputs and the labels are likely to be the same or similar, making the training no longer meaningful. Therefore, Combine uses the remaining 30% as its training and test datasets. We still use 70:30 split of the dataset for training and testing. It is observed that all models perform very well on Amazon and Sina with no much difference, although Combine performs the best with no prediction errors at all. The advantage of Combine is getting clearer on Youku. Table 4 shows Combine's performance on Youku in comparison with the other models. The performance of all models is not as great, because of the highly dynamic content on Youku's home page. However, Combine still performs the best on accuracy, recall and F1 score, and only behind R-LSTM on precision. This motivates us to further explore the effectiveness of ensemble learning on ternary classification.

Ternary Classification. Table 5 shows the performance on the test dataset. The precision, recall, and F1 score here are established as follows: an initial value of the metrics is obtained for each of the three QoE categories as a binary classification problem, and then a weighted average across the three QoE categories is calculated, which becomes the value of the metrics shown in Table 5. It shows that the performance of the models is substantially degraded for ternary classification. This is expected because of the finer granularity of the QoE. R-LSTM is the best performer among the three basic models, with the values of the metrics ranging from 0.919 to 0.941. NN is the worst, with F1 score of only 0.8289. The features used by NN do not describe well the differences between categories "1" and "2". Also as stated in Sect. 4, NN's inputs are not as independent as assumed. In contrast, R-LSTM performs well because the accumulated data makes the input statistically significant, which facilitates classification. Slice sits in the middle, with the values of the metrics varying slightly around 0.90.

Combine performs the best across all the metrics, with their values all greater than 0.94. Through ensemble learning, we use three weak classifiers to form a strong classifier, making the model well suited for ternary classification.

6.3   Summary

WebQMon.ai can predict ATF well when users visit the websites, whether it is a binary or ternary classification problem. R-LSTM performs the best among the three basic models, but it takes the longest time to train and predict. Slice is more balanced, having a reasonable performance with the shortest training and prediction time. NN requires a short time to train and predict but has the worst performance. Combine performs the best through ensemble learning. However, since the model needs to use the results of the three basic models, it has the longest training and prediction time. Furthermore, we collected data for four months, during which the content of the websites changed greatly. Nonetheless, our model still predicts ATF well, which proves that the model can be updated by new data to accommodate changes in website content. It would be difficult to do this through threshold settings or mathematical formulations. In addition, the trained model takes up very little storage space, a minimum of *80KB* and a maximum of *6MB*. WebQMon.ai only requires the *referer* from the application layer, making it possible to deploy on edge routers.

7   Discussion

HTTP vs HTTPS. In contrast to current work, WebQMon.ai minimizes the use of application layer data — it only needs the *referer* to aggregate the traffic associated with a page. This is under the assumption that the content associated with a page may be sourced from other sites. Nevertheless, if we are only interested in the content from a particular site, WebQMon.ai does not need access to application data at all. The limitation is that WebQMon.ai would not be able to predict page-based QoE, as the objects of the page may be from different sites. However, it can still provide a QoE assessment for the content from a particular site. This is of great value to content providers as well as ISPs.

Placement. Predicting web-browsing QoE on the client-side usually occupies user network bandwidth and needs the user to cooperate and install specific software. It may provide the best possible prediction accuracy, but it is also the most costly choice. If deployed on the server-side, it may work for the websites who have the budget to do so. However, from the client's point of view, this may result in the least accurate prediction, and the prediction is limited to a specific site. In contrast, WebQMon.ai can be deployed on edge routers/gateways, and thus is transparent to the server and the client. In some scenarios, WebQMon.ai may not be able to achieve the prediction as accurate as some client-based solutions. But it can still achieve a high level of accuracy, and more importantly, without the client-side constraints. WebQMon.ai has access to all the websites that ISP's clients are interested in. This enables close collaboration between ISPs and content providers to serve their clients.

Versatility and Real-time. WebQMon.ai is powered by a data-driven model, which is easy to update and apply for all websites with different types of content. It can be updated on a regular basis as long as there is new data, that is, WebQMon.ai has the ability to learn and adjust to the new context. Current solutions that rely on empirical threshold settings or mathematical formulations are usually designed specifically to a certain site, limiting their applicability for other sites. In addition, WebQMon.ai only needs to use lightweight neural networks to achieve a high level of accuracy. This demonstrates not only that WeQMon.ai can get updated quickly and work in a real-time fashion, but also the practical applicability of machine learning in this field.

Fine-Grained ATF Prediction. WebQMon.ai can handle very well binary and ternary classifications, which are common cases for QoE prediction. However, as the granularity of QoE classification increases, the performance of WebQMon.ai deteriorates. At some stage, finer-grained ATF prediction may be required, which can be done through addressing the regression problem. The mapping from ATF to QoE can then be done through Mean Opinion Score (MOS) [7]. We can imagine this would improve the performance at the cost of training and test latency, due to the complexity of the model.

8   Conclusion

In this paper, we present WebQMon.ai to predict web-browsing QoE. WebQMon.ai relies on packet-level measurements without deeply parsing the packet payload, and thus can be deployed on edge routers/gateways instead of end hosts. WebQMon.ai is data-driven, empowered by lightweight supervised learning methods, which enables the system to learn and adapt to new contents in a timely manner. WebQMon.ai works very well for binary and ternary classification based QoE prediction, achieving a high level of accuracy in real-time. Furthermore, we demonstrate the potential and feasibility of machine learning methods in web-browsing QoE assessment.

References

1. Akamai research. https://www.akamai.com/us/en/about/news/press/2009-press/akamai-reveals-2-seconds-as-the-new-threshold-of-acceptability-for-ecommerce-web-page-response-times.jsp/. Accessed 2020
2. Webqmon.ai. https://github.com/songng/WebQMon.ai/. Accessed 2022
3. Caruana, A.: Service loyalty: the effects of service quality and the mediating role of customer satisfaction. Eur. J. Mark. **36**(7/8), 811–828 (2002)
4. Casas, P., Seufert, M., Schatz, R.: Youqmon: a system for on-line monitoring of YouTube QoE in operational 3g networks. ACM SIGMETRICS Perform. Eval. Rev. **41**(2), 44–46 (2013)
5. Chen, X., et al.: Reinforcement learning based QoS/QoE-aware service function chaining in software-driven 5g slices. Trans. Emerg. Telecommun. Technol. **29**, e3477- (2018)
6. Da Hora, D., Rossi, D., Christophides, V., Teixeira, R.: A practical method for measuring web above-the-fold time. In: Proceedings of the ACM SIGCOMM 2018 Conference on Posters and Demos, pp. 105–107. ACM (2018)
7. Da Hora, D.N., Asrese, A.S., Christophides, V., Teixeira, R., Rossi, D.: Narrowing the gap between QoS Metrics and Web QoE using above-the-fold metrics. In: Beverly, R., Smaragdakis, G., Feldmann, A. (eds.) PAM 2018. LNCS, vol. 10771, pp. 31–43. Springer, Cham (2018). https://doi.org/10.1007/978-3-319-76481-8_3
8. Davis, J., Goadrich, M.: The relationship between precision-recall and roc curves. In: Proceedings of the ICML 2006, pp. 233–240. ACM (2006)
9. Dey, P., Ahammad, P., et al.: Perceived performance of top retail webpages in the wild. ACM SIGCOMM Comput. Commun. Rev. **47**(5), 42–47 (2017)
10. Gutterman, C., et al.: ReqUet: real-time QoE detection for encrypted YouTube traffic. In: Proceedings of the 10th ACM Multimedia Systems Conference, pp. 48–59 (2019)
11. Hoßfeld, T., Metzger, F., Rossi, D.: Speed index: Relating the industrial standard for user perceived web performance to web QoE. In: 2018 Tenth International Conference on Quality of Multimedia Experience (QoMEX), pp. 1–6. IEEE (2018)
12. Huet, A., Houidi, Z.B., Mathieu, B., Rossi, D.: Detecting degradation of web browsing quality of experience. In: CNSM 2020, pp. 1–7. IEEE (2020)
13. Saverimoutou, A., Mathieu, B., Vaton, S.: A 6-month analysis of factors impacting web browsing quality for QoE prediction. Comput. Netw. **164**, 106905 (2019)
14. Seufert, M., Wehner, N., Wieser, V., Casas, P., Capdehourat, G.: Mind the (QoE) gap: On the incompatibility of web and video QoE models in the wild. In: CNSM 2020, pp. 1–5. IEEE (2020)
15. Singh, V., Bharti, S., Pathak, V., Sengar, A., Singh, T., Goswami, M.: On dominant characteristics of residential broadband internet traffic. In: ACM SIGCOMM Conference on Internet Measurement (2009)

16. Subramanian, M., Ye, E., Korlipara, R., Smith, F.: Techniques for measuring above-the-fold page rendering, US Patent 8,812,648, 19 Aug 2014
17. Varvello, M., Blackburn, J., Naylor, D., Papagiannaki, K.: EYEORG: a platform for crowdsourcing web quality of experience measurements. In: Proceedings of the CoNEXT 2016, pp. 399–412. ACM (2016)

Temporal-Aware QoS Prediction via Dynamic Graph Neural Collaborative Learning

Shengxiang Hu[1], Guobing Zou[1(✉)], Bofeng Zhang[2,3], Shaogang Wu[1], Shiyi Lin[1], Yanglan Gan[4], and Yixin Chen[5]

[1] School of Computer Engineering and Science, Shanghai University, Shanghai, China
{shengxianghu,gbzou}@shu.edu.cn
[2] School of Computer and Information Engineering, Shanghai Polytechnic University, Shanghai, China
bfzhang@sspu.edu.cn
[3] School of Computer Science and Technology, Kashi University, Xinjiang, China
[4] School of Computer Science and Technology, Donghua University, Shanghai, China
ylgan@dhu.edu.cn
[5] Department of Computer Science and Engineering, Washington University in St. Louis, St. Louis, MO 63130, USA
chen@cse.wustl.edu

Abstract. How to effectively predict missing QoS has become a fundamental research issue for service-oriented downstream tasks. However, most QoS prediction approaches omit high-order implicit invocation correlations and collaborative relationships among users and services. Thus, they are incapable of effectively learning the temporally evolutionary characteristics of user-service invocations from historical QoS records, which significantly affects the performance of QoS prediction. To address the issue, we propose a novel framework for temporal-aware QoS prediction by dynamic graph neural collaborative learning. Dynamic user-service invocation graph and graph convolutional network are combined to model user-service historical temporal interactions and extract latent features of users and services at each time slice, while a multi-layer GRU is applied for mining temporal feature evolution pattern across multiple time slices, leading to temporal-aware QoS prediction. The experimental results indicate that our proposed approach for temporal-aware QoS prediction significantly outperforms state-of-the-art competing methods.

Keywords: Web service · Temporal-aware QoS prediction · Dynamic user-service invocation graph · Graph convolutional network · Latent feature extraction

1 Introduction

With the rapid advancements of Internet technology, service-oriented architecture (SOA) has been widely used in real-world applications. As one of the

J. Troya et al. (Eds.): ICSOC 2022, LNCS 13740, pp. 125–133, 2022.
https://doi.org/10.1007/978-3-031-20984-0_8

key implementation techniques of SOA, web services have extremely promoted interoperatable machine-to-machine interactions. However, many services supply users with analogous functionalities. Quality of Service (QoS) [11] is applied to represent the non-functional characteristics of web services and differentiate those functionally equivalent ones. Because of the enormous number of users and services, it is impractical and time-consuming for users to invoke all web services and record the corresponding QoS values in the constantly changing network environment. Thus, it is of vital importance to precisely perform temporal-aware QoS prediction, which has become a challenging issue due to the sparsity of historical user-service invocations across multiple time slices in real scenarios.

Some recent investigations concentrate on collaborative filtering (CF) and neural network-based approaches for temporal-aware QoS prediction. They generally compose a sequence of QoS invocation matrices from different consecutive time slices, and extract the features of users and services at each time slice, then apply deep learning techniques, such as gate recurrent unit (GRU) [3] and long short-term memory (LSTM) [7], to learn the evolution pattern of QoS across multiple time slices. However, they mainly characterize a user in terms of those directly invoked services or a service in terms of those users who have directly invoked the service, without the consideration of high-order implicit invocation correlations between users and services through indirect interactions as well as the high-order collaborative relationships between similar users or services. Due to the lack of the extraction of high-order latent features that are hidden in the user-service interactions, it is still difficult in effectively encoding latent features of users and services, yielding to low accuracy of temporal-aware QoS prediction.

To address the issues, inspired by the developments of graph and Graph Convolutional Networks (GCNs) [2], we propose a novel framework for temporal-aware QoS prediction by dynamic graph neural collaborative learning. First, we formulate user-service historical QoS interactions as a temporal-aware service ecosystem, which is transformed into a dynamic user-service invocation graph across multiple time slices. Then, a GCN-based [2] graph neural collaborative feature extractor is learned to extract high-order latent features of users and services at each time slice, taking into account both indirect user-service invocation correlations and collaborative relationships by similar users or services. Finally, a multi-layer GRU [3] is applied for mining temporal feature evolution pattern across multiple time slices, leading to temporal-aware QoS prediction. To evaluate the effectiveness of our proposed approach for temporal-aware QoS prediction, extensive experiments are conducted on a large-scale real-world dataset. By comparing with several state-of-the-art baselines, experimental results demonstrate that our proposed approach receives the best prediction performance in multiple evaluation metrics. The main contributions of this paper are summarized as follows:

– We propose a novel dynamic graph neural collaborative learning framework for temporal-aware QoS prediction. It can more effectively reveal user-service invocation features at each time slice and mine temporal feature evolution pattern across multiple time slices for better QoS prediction.

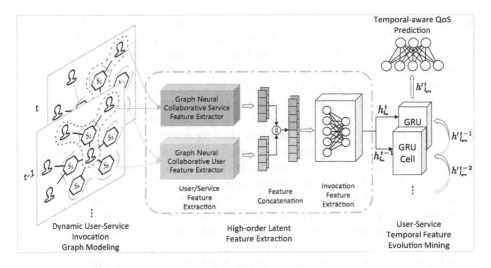

Fig. 1. The overall framework of our proposed approach.

- We propose a novel approach for extracting high-order latent features of a user and service by dynamic user-service invocation graph modeling and graph convolutional network learning. Compared to the existing approaches, the advantage is that we can more deeply reveal the latent features of users and services, with the consideration of both high-order user-service invocation correlations and collaborative relationships by similar neighborhoods.
- Extensive experiments are conducted on a large-scale real-world QoS dataset, and the results indicate that our approach receives superior performance for temporal-aware QoS prediction compared with baseline approaches.

The remainder of this paper is structured as follows. Section 2 elaborates the proposed approach. Section 3 shows and analyzes experimental results. Finally, Sect. 4 concludes the paper and discusses future work.

2   Approach

The overall framework of our proposed approach is illustrated in Fig. 1. It mainly consists of four stages, including dynamic user-service invocation graph modeling, high-order latent feature extraction, user-service temporal feature evolution mining, and temporal-aware QoS prediction.

2.1   Dynamic User-Service Invocation Graph Modeling

A temporal-aware service ecosystem can be formulated as $\xi = < U, S, T, R >$, where there are n users $U = \{u_i\}_{i=1}^{n}$, m web services $S = \{s_i\}_{i=1}^{m}$, t time slices $T = \{1, 2, \ldots, t\}$, and a sequence of corresponding historical QoS matrix $R = \{R^i \in \Re^{n \times m}\}_{i=1}^t$, $r_{ij}^t \in R^t$ indicates the corresponding QoS value when a user $u_i \in U$ invokes a service $s_j \in S$ at time t. To model the high-order implicit invocation correlations and collaborative relationships among users and services, we transform ξ into a dynamic user-service invocation graph $\mathcal{G} = \{\mathcal{G}^i\}_{i=1}^t$. Each snapshot $\mathcal{G}^t = < V_u, V_s, E^t, W^t >$ is transformed from $\xi^t = < U, S, t, R^t >$ at time slice t. Here, $V_u = \{u_i\}_{i=1}^n$ is a set of n user vertices; $V_s = \{s_i\}_{i=1}^m$ is a set of m service vertices; E^t is a set of edges that represents user-service invocation relationships. If $r_{ij}^t \in R^t$, there exists an edge $e_{ij}^t = e_{ji}^t \in E^t$ between $u_i \in V_u$ and $s_j \in V_s$; W^t is a set of edge weights. If $e_{ij}^t \in E^t$, there exists a corresponding weight $w_{ij}^t \in W^t$, which can be converted from $r_{ij}^t \in R^t$.

The edge weight $w^t \in W^t$ measures the strength of the connection, i.e. the invocation relationship, between a user vertex and a service vertex at time slice t. Generally, a lower value implies a higher QoS under a negative QoS criteria, such as response time. It is observed that most of real QoS values are clustered around a certain value for a QoS criterion, but there are also a small number of outliers that may influence model training deviating from expectations. In order to ensure robustness of our proposed model, we further convert the original QoS value r_{ij}^t to a normalized range as the corresponding edge weight w_{ij}^t. By taking into account both the distribution characteristics of QoS values and practical observations, a heuristic conversion function is designed to project r_{ij}^t to w_{ij}^t under a negative QoS criterion. It is expressed as follows:

$$w_{ij}^t = \begin{cases} \frac{exp(r_{ij}^t) - exp(-1/r_{ij}^t)}{exp(1/r_{ij}^t) + exp(-1/r_{ij}^t)} & \text{if } r_{ij}^t > 1 \\ \frac{1}{exp(r_{ij}^t)} - \frac{1}{e} + \frac{exp(2)-1}{exp(2)+1} & otherwise \end{cases} \tag{1}$$

where w_{ij}^t denotes the associated weight for edge $e_{ij}^t \in E^t$. By using the conversion function, we project all of the QoS values to their corresponding edge weights for each time slice $t \in T$. Thus, the dynamic user-service invocation graph $\mathcal{G}$ can be generated, which is used to extract high-order latent features of users and services at each time slice.

2.2   High-Order Latent Feature Extraction of Users and Services

Based on $\mathcal{G}$, we extract the high-order latent feature of a target user u and service s at each time slice. We initially represent u and s with a randomized feature vector $x_u \in \Re^d$ and $x_s \in \Re^d$, respectively, where d specifies the dimension of the feature vector. It is intuitive that a user's feature can be partially reflected by the directly invoked services and indirectly characterized by the non-adjacent user and service neighbors. It can be performed by a multi-layer recursive way in a user-service invocation graph $\mathcal{G}^t$ at each time slice t. Analogously, we can also extract a service's latent feature with the consideration of user-service invocation correlations and collaborative relationships among services.

Here, we leverage the GCN's [2] message passing mechanism to capture high-order latent features of users (services) along the structure of $\mathcal{G}^t$. The procedure

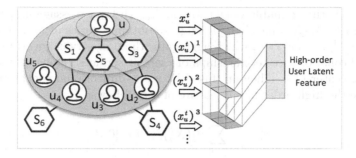

Fig. 2. High-order user latent feature extraction by graph neural collaborative feature extractor.

of high-order user latent feature extraction by graph neural collaborative feature extractor is illustrated in Fig. 2. which applies a recursive way of message propagation and aggregation. More specifically, $\mathcal{N}_u^t \subseteq V_s$ denotes the set of adjacent service vertices that are directly connected to u in $\mathcal{G}^t$, i.e., the first-hop service neighbors of u at time slice t. In such case, for each service $s' \in \mathcal{N}_u^t$, the message $m_{u \leftarrow s'}^t$ propagated from s' to u is calculated as follows:

$$m_{u \leftarrow s'}^t = \frac{exp(w_{us'}^t)}{\sum_{i \in \mathcal{N}_u^t} exp(w_{ui}^t)} W^1 x_{s'} \tag{2}$$

where $W^1 \in \Re^{d \times d}$ is a trainable weight matrix, and $w_{us'}^t$ denotes the weight associated with edge $e_{us'}^t$. With a larger $w_{us'}^t$, more messages are retained and s' contributes more to u's high-order latent feature. Following that, we aggregate messages from all of the u's first-hop neighbors in message aggregation:

$$x_u^t = x_u \tag{3}$$

$$(x_u^t)^1 = \alpha(x_u^t + \sum_{s' \in \mathcal{N}_u^t} m_{u \leftarrow s'}^t) \tag{4}$$

where $(x_u^t)^1$ signifies the representation of u that aggregates first-order messages, which implies the behavioral features embodied by the directly invoked services, α is the activation function. By stacking l_{gcn} message-passing procedures, we can aggregate messages from l_{gcn}-hop user and service neighbors, leading to the high-order connectivity characteristics of u. These heuristic information can strengthen the feature representation of a user by the latent invocation correlations between u and non-invoked services, as well as the latent collaborative relationships of the user neighbors who are structurally nearby vertices of u. The recursive aggregation of user representation can be expressed as:

$$(m_{u \leftarrow s'}^t)^{l_{gcn}-1} = \frac{exp(w_{us'}^t)}{\sum_{i \in \mathcal{N}_u^t} exp(w_{ui}^t)} W^{l_{gcn}} (x_{s'}^t)^{l_{gcn}-1} \tag{5}$$

$$(x_u^t)^{l_{gcn}} = \alpha(x_u^t + \sum_{s' \in \mathcal{N}_u^t} (m_{u \leftarrow s'}^t)^{l_{gcn}-1}) \tag{6}$$

where $W^{l_{gcn}}$ is the trainable weight for the l_{gcn}-th layer message propagation.

Through l_{gcn}-layers message passing, we obtain a series of user representations $x_u^t, (x_u^t)^1, \ldots, (x_u^t)^{l_{gcn}}$, which aggregates the user-service invocation correlations and collaborative relationships of users or services among different hops around the center of u. They are fused by a one-dimensional convolution layer to generate the high-order latent feature of u as follows:

$$(x_u^t)_i^* = \sum_{j=0}^{l_{gcn}} \omega_j (X_u^t)_{i,j}, \; i \in [0, d) \tag{7}$$

where $(x_u^t)^* \in \Re^d$ is the extracted high-order latent feature of u, $\omega \in \Re^{l_{gcn}+1}$ denotes the convolution kernel, $X_u^t \in \Re^{d \times (l_{gcn}+1)}$ is the matrix of combining $(l_{gcn} + 1)$ user representations $x_u^t, (x_u^t)^1, \ldots, (x_u^t)^{l_{gcn}}$. It is important to note that the procedure for extracting the high-order latent feature $(x_s^t)^*$ of a target service s is identical to the one of u.

Based on the high-order latent features of $(x_u^t)^*$ and $(x_s^t)^*$, they are concatenated as a whole that is fed into a l_m-layer multi-layer perceptron (MLP) to obtain the invocation feature $h_{l_m}^t$ of u and s at time slice t. Consequently, $h_{l_m}^t$ is used for mining temporal feature evolution between u and s.

2.3   User-Service Temporal Feature Evolution Mining

To reveal the evolution pattern of the user-service invocation features across multiple time slices, we mine the hidden temporal nonlinear relationship by a multi-layer GRU [3]. Given a set of extracted invocation features $H_k = \{h_{l_m}^{t-k+1}, h_{l_m}^{t-k+2}, \ldots, h_{l_m}^t\}$ of a current u and a target service s across k consecutive time slices, the hidden state of GRU layer can be calculated as follows:

$$z^t = \sigma(W_z \cdot [h'^{t-1} || h_{l_m}^t]) \tag{8}$$

$$r^t = \sigma(W_r \cdot [h'^{t-1} || h_{l_m}^t]) \tag{9}$$

$$\hat{s}^t = \tanh(W \cdot [(r^t \odot h'^{t-1}) || h_{l_m}^t]) \tag{10}$$

$$h'^t = (1 - z^t) \odot h'^{t-1} + z^t \odot \hat{s}^t \tag{11}$$

where W_z, W_r, W are the trainable weight matrices, d' is the dimension of the GRU layer's output, and $\odot$ represents element-wise product. Due to traditional GRU is a shallow model with limited capacity to extract deep implicit features, we stack l_{gru} GRU layers. The hidden output of last GRU layer $h'^t_{l_{gru}} \in \Re^{d'}$ is used as the evolutionary invocation feature for temporal-aware QoS prediction.

2.4   Temporal-Aware QoS Prediction

Based on the evolutionary invocation feature of a current user u and target service s, we can predict the missing QoS $\hat{r}_{us}^{t+1}$ at time slice $t + 1$, by a fully-connected neural network. The output layer is calculated as:

$$\hat{r}_{us}^{t+1} = ReLU(W_o h'^t_{l_{gru}} + b_o) \tag{12}$$

where W_o is a trainable weight matrix, b_o is a offset item, and $\hat{r}_{us}^{t+1}$ is the predicted QoS when a current user u invokes a target service s at time slice $t + 1$. To train and optimize the model parameters, we take Mean Square Error as the loss that is defined as:

$$Loss = \frac{\sum_{u \in U} \sum_{s \in S} (\hat{r}_{us}^{t+1} - r_{us}^{t+1})^2}{n \times m} + \lambda \|\Theta\|_2^2 \qquad (13)$$

where U, S represent the user and service set, respectively, and $|U| = n, |S| = m$. Θ is all the trainable parameters of our proposed model, λ controls the $L2$ regularization strength to prevent overfitting. We adopt mini-batch AdamW [4] to update and optimize the parameters.

Table 1. Results of temporal-aware QoS prediction among competing approaches.

Density	MAE				RMSE			
	0.05	0.1	0.15	0.2	0.05	0.1	0.15	0.2
UPCC	0.946	1.209	1.107	1.006	1.908	1.778	1.720	1.683
IPCC	1.135	1.041	0.994	0.989	2.255	1.867	1.795	1.795
WSRec	0.807	0.578	0.967	0.758	1.917	1.328	2.407	1.733
WSPred	0.781	0.689	0.673	0.663	1.707	1.633	1.608	1.593
PNCF	1.165	1.089	1.043	1.013	1.836	1.722	1.653	1.617
RNCF	1.048	1.010	0.974	0.958	1.616	1.546	1.503	1.470
TUIPCC	0.731	0.576	0.819	0.697	1.776	1.207	2.059	1.635
Ours	**0.574**	**0.526**	**0.489**	**0.462**	**1.284**	**1.193**	**1.158**	**1.123**
Gains	**22.5%**	**8.7%**	**27.4%**	**30.4%**	**20.6%**	**1.2%**	**23.6%**	**23.5%**

3 Experiments

3.1 Dataset

To validate the effectiveness of the proposed approach, we conduct extensive experiments on a large-scale real-world web service QoS dataset called WS-DREAM[1], which has been widely used in service computing for QoS prediction. WS-DREAM employed 142 distributed PlanetLab computers (i.e. users) located across 22 countries, to monitor a total of 4,500 publicly accessible real-world web services from 57 countries continuously in 64 different time slices at 15-minute interval. And a total of 27,392,643 detailed response-time values ranging from 0 s to 20 s are collected as the sub-dataset *rtdata* [11], on which our experiments are extensively conducted to demonstrate the superiority performance of the proposed temporal-aware QoS prediction approach. The overall data sparsity is approximately 66.98%.

---

[1] http://wsdream.github.io/dataset.

3.2   Experimental Results and Analyses

We evaluate the temporal-aware QoS prediction results by two widely adopted evaluation metrics: MAE (Mean Absolute Error) and RMSE (Root Mean Squared Error). In addition, we compare our proposed approach with 7 state-of-the-art methods: UPCC [8], IPCC [5], WSRec [10], WSPred [9], PNCF [1], RNCF [3] and TUIPCC [6]. To thoroughly validate the effectiveness of our proposed approach for temporal-aware QoS prediction, we conduct extensive experiments on temporal QoS dataset with four different densities: 5%, 10%, 15%, and 20%, and report the MAE and RMSE, respectively. For all baseline approaches, we follow the optimal parameter settings specified in the corresponding papers.

The results are summarized in Table 1, with the best performance among baseline approaches highlighted in dark and the overall best results bolded. It is obvious from the results that our proposed approach outperforms all of the competing approaches at different QoS densities, with the relative improvements ranging from 8.7% to 30.4% on MAE and 1.2% to 23.6% on RMSE, respectively. In terms of MAE, TUIPCC receives superior performance among baseline approaches at QoS densities of 0.05 and 0.1, whereas WSPred achieves the best among baseline approaches at QoS densities of 0.15 and 0.2. As for RMSE, RNCF is better than the other baseline approaches for the densities of 0.05, 0.1, and 0.2, respectively. As can be seen from the above results, the baseline approaches suffer from instability for QoS prediction at different densities. For example, while TUIPCC achieves a lower MAE, it cannot perform very well on RMSE, indicating that it is unable to fit certain outliers when predicting the missing QoS. Therefore, compared to the baseline approaches, our proposed prediction model consistently achieves the lowest MAE and RMSE across all different QoS densities, revealing that it can predict QoS values more precisely with better robustness.

It concludes that two aspects may potentially contribute to the best performance of our proposed approach. First, an optimized dynamic neural graph collaborative learning model is designed to encode the high-order latent features of users and services, that overcomes the constraint of sparse historical QoS invocations across multiple time slices, leading to more precisely user-service invocation feature. Second, a multi-layer GRU is applied to boost the accuracy of QoS prediction by effectively mining the implicit temporal evolution patterns of user-service invocation features across multiple time slices.

4   Conclusion and Future Work

This paper proposes a novel framework for temporal-aware QoS prediction by dynamic graph neural collaborative learning. It first models a temporal-aware service ecosystem as a dynamic user-service invocation graph, which is then fed into a graph neural collaborative feature extractor for extracting high-order latent features of users and services at each time slice, considering both indirect user-service invocation correlations and collaborative relationships by similar users or services. Finally, a multi-layer GRU is employed to mine temporal feature evolution patterns across multiple time slices, leading to vacant QoS prediction. Extensive experiments are conducted based on a large-scale QoS dataset in service computing to validate the superior prediction accuracy of our proposed approach, compared to state-of-the-art competing baselines on MAE and RMSE. In the future work, we are devoted to deeply investigating on how to effectively leverage the contextual information and graph structural properties of users and services to further strengthen the capability of temporal-aware QoS prediction.

Acknowledgements. This work was supported by National Natural Science Foundation of China (No. 62272290, 62172088), and Shanghai Natural Science Foundation (No. 21ZR1400400).

References

1. Chen, L., Zheng, A., Feng, Y., Xie, F., Zheng, Z.: Software service recommendation base on collaborative filtering neural network model. In: Pahl, C., Vukovic, M., Yin, J., Yu, Q. (eds.) ICSOC 2018. LNCS, vol. 11236, pp. 388–403. Springer, Cham (2018). https://doi.org/10.1007/978-3-030-03596-9_28
2. Kipf, T.N., Welling, M.: Semi-supervised classification with graph convolutional networks. arXiv preprint arXiv:1609.02907 (2016)
3. Liang, T., Chen, M., Yin, Y., Zhou, L., Ying, H.: Recurrent neural network based collaborative filtering for QoS prediction in IoV. IEEE Trans. Intell. Transp. Syst. **23**(3), 2400–2410 (2022)
4. Loshchilov, I., Hutter, F.: Decoupled weight decay regularization. arXiv preprint arXiv:1711.05101 (2017)
5. Sarwar, B., Karypis, G., Konstan, J., Riedl, J.: Item-based collaborative filtering recommendation algorithms. In: International Conference on World Wide Web (WWW), pp. 285–295 (2001)
6. Tong, E., Niu, W., Liu, J.: A missing QoS prediction approach via time-aware collaborative filtering. IEEE Trans. Serv. Comput. (2021). https://doi.org/10.1109/TSC.2021.3103769
7. Wu, X., Fan, Y., Zhang, J., Lin, H., Zhang, J.: QF-RNN: QI-matrix factorization based RNN for time-aware service recommendation. In: IEEE International Conference on Services Computing (SCC), pp. 202–209. IEEE (2019)
8. Xue, G.R., et al.: Scalable collaborative filtering using cluster-based smoothing. In: International ACM SIGIR Conference on Research and Development in Information Retrieval (SIGIR), pp. 114–121 (2005)
9. Zhang, Y., Zheng, Z., Lyu, M.R.: WSPred: a time-aware personalized QoS prediction framework for web services. In: IEEE International Symposium on Software Reliability Engineering, pp. 210–219. IEEE (2011)
10. Zheng, Z., Ma, H., Lyu, M.R., King, I.: WSRec: a collaborative filtering based web service recommender system. In: IEEE International Conference on Web Services (ICWS), pp. 437–444. IEEE (2009)
11. Zheng, Z., Zhang, Y., Lyu, M.R.: Investigating QoS of real-world web services. IEEE Trans. Serv. Comput. **7**(1), 32–39 (2014)

Mobility-Aware Proactive QoS Monitoring for Mobile Edge Computing

Ting Wei[1], Pengcheng Zhang[1(✉)], Hai Dong[2], Huiying Jin[1],
and Athman Bouguettaya[3]

[1] College of Computing and Information, Hohai University, Nanjing 211100, China
`pchzhang@hhu.edu.cn`
[2] School of Computing Technologies, RMIT University, Melbourne, Australia
`hai.dong@rmit.edu.au`
[3] School of Computer Science, The University of Sydney, Sydney, NSW, Australia
`athman.bouguettaya@sydney.edu.au`

Abstract. This article presents a novel probabilistic QoS (Quality of Service) monitoring approach called LSTM-BSPM (DonLSTM-Den based BayeSian Runtime Proactive Monitoring), which is based on the DouLSTM-Den model and Gaussian Hidden Bayesian Classifier for mobile edge environments. A DouLSTM-Den model is designed to predict a user's trajectory in mobile edge environments. The predicted trajectory is leveraged to obtain the mobility-aware QoS and capture its spatio-temporal dependency. Next, a parent attribute is constructed for each QoS attribute to reduce the influence of dependence between QoS attributes on monitoring accuracy. A Gaussian hidden Bayes classifier is trained for each edge server to proactively monitor the user's mobility-aware QoS. We conduct a set of experiments respectively upon a public data set and a real-world data set demonstrate the feasibility and effectiveness of the proposed approach.

Keywords: Mobile/Multi-access edge computing · Quality of service · Monitoring · Bayesian classifier · LSTM model

1 Introduction

Mobile (or Multi-Access) edge computing is a new distributed computing paradigm that transfers the computing power from cloud data centers to the edge of a network [1]. Mobile edge services refer to the services provisioned in mobile edge environments [2]. Users' requirements on mobile edge services have gradually shifted from functional requirements to non-functional requirements, i.e. QoS (Quality of Service) [3,4]. There has been a stronger focus recently on selecting a service that meets a user's QoS requirements among many services with similar functions [5]. Monitoring the runtime QoS is a key means to ensure the accurate service selection.

© The Author(s), under exclusive license to Springer Nature Switzerland AG 2022
J. Troya et al. (Eds.): ICSOC 2022, LNCS 13740, pp. 134–142, 2022.
https://doi.org/10.1007/978-3-031-20984-0_9

A variety of monitoring methods have been devised for probabilistic quality attributes. These include QoS monitoring methods based on traditional probability statistics [3], hypothesis testing [4,6] and Bayes' theorem [7,8]. Those methods aim to perform continuous QoS monitoring based on user-defined standards in addition to computation overhead reduction. However, these methods encounter the following problems in the mobile edge environment:

Traditional QoS Monitoring Approaches Lack a Proactive Mechanism. Service providers usually deploy a large number of services in the network environment. It is impractical for sensors to monitor and record in real-time the QoS generated by different users due to time, financial and resource constraints. In addition, monitoring the current status of a service cannot fully prevent the service from failure. In this regard, the monitoring results received by a user at present can only reflect the service status in the past due to the network latency. Therefore, it is essential to develop proactive service monitoring solutions to detect service failure in advance.

The Current QoS Monitoring Approaches Ignore the Temporal and Spatial Characteristics of QoS. Our literature survey reveals that existing QoS monitoring approaches overlook the spatio-temporal dependency of QoS. This defect may lead to deviation of monitoring results from the real situation. The QoS of a service (observed from the client side) relies on the state of the service (on the server side) and the network environment. The service state is impacted by the server capacity and workload, the allocated computing resources, etc. The network environment is influenced by users and servers' locations, network bandwidth and traffic, the number of clients, etc. Both of them are highly dynamic over time and space.

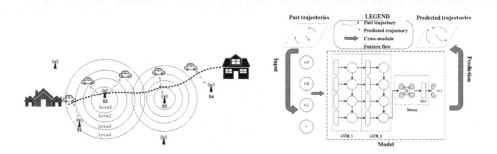

Fig. 1. Motivation scenario   **Fig. 2.** Architecture of model

2   Related Work

Many probabilistic QoS monitoring techniques based on Bayesian classifiers were proposed to address the limitation of the aforementioned methods on variable user requirements. A new mobility and dependency-based QoS monitoring method named ghBSRM-MEC was presented in [9]. This method assumes that the QoS attribute value of an edge server obeys Gaussian distribution. A parent attribute is constructed for each attribute, thereby reducing the dependence between attributes. A Gaussian implicit Bayes classifier is constructed for each edge server to realize QoS monitoring in the mobile edge environment.

Proactive monitoring techniques have also been applied into other fields. A QoS monitoring algorithm that can quickly detect broken or congested links was depicted in [10]. This algorithm takes advantage of a multithreaded design based on lock-free data structures. It improve the performance by avoiding synchronization among threads. Their work specifically focuses on real-time streaming. It does not realize proactive QoS monitoring. A proactive solution was introduced in [11]. It migrates the virtual machines before violating the actual delay threshold. The authors proposed a delay-aware resource allocation method that considers an adaptive delay warning threshold for various users. Their work focuses on dynamic resource allocation for hosting delay-sensitive vehicular services in a federated cloud. It cannot realize proactive QoS monitoring.

All the above monitoring methods do not take into account the proactive selection of servers by capturing the mobility of users in mobile edge environments. They also ignore the temporal and spatial dependency of QoS monitoring. These defects would lead to their failure to address the problems of lagging monitoring and long monitoring delay. This inspires us to devise a context-dependent proactive QoS monitoring method to fully cater to mobile edge environments.

3   The LSTM-BSPM Approach

As shown in Fig. 1, we use a mobile edge service scenario to illustrate our motivation. And its main framework is shown in Fig. 3. It mainly includes three steps.

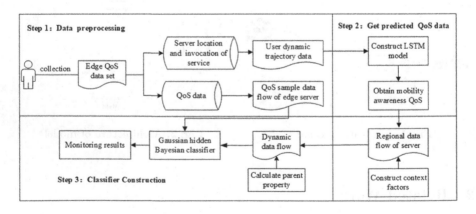

Fig. 3. Structure of proactive QoS monitoring

3.1 Data Preprocessing

First, we partition the spatial QoS data according to the locations of their belonged edge servers. The monitoring process in a mobile edge environment needs to consider user's historical trajectory data and information of service calls. The existing data sets do not meet such requirements. Hence, we need to construct a data set for mobile edge servers and users. The second major mission of the data preprocessing is to filter invalid data, such as the sample data with response time of –1 and 0. It makes the experimental data more in line with the real situation.

3.2 Mobility-Aware QoS Acquisition Based on DouLSTM-Den

The primary purposes of this step is to construct and train the DouLSTM-Den model to obtain the user's mobility-aware QoS. Here we propose a model named DouLSTM-Den to predict a user's future location. As shown in Fig. 2, DouLSTM-Den comprises an LSTM layer with 3 units, a hidden LSTM layer with 2 units, and a normal dense layer with 2 hidden outputs for 2 columns. The details how this structure is determined is explained in the evaluation part.

The original trajectory data of the moving user is converted into a sequence of h positions $H_i = \{Y_1, Y_2, ..., Y_h\}$, where H_i represents the movement trajectory of $user_i$, $Y_i = \{lng_m, lat_m\}$ represents the mth longitude and latitude of $user_i$ based on time series. The current location is $Y' = \{lat_t, lng_t\}$. In practice, we continuously update the trajectory by combining the current location of the user for trajectory prediction.

We predict the $t+1$th location Y_{t+1} of the $user_i$ through the DouLSTM-Den model. A high-level definition of the DouLSTM-Den model can be expressed as:

$$Y_{t+1} = f(\{Y_1, Y_2, ..., Y_h, Y_t\}) \tag{1}$$

Its technical details can be referenced from Sect. 3.2.

The network conditions in different coverage areas of an edge server are odd. In this regard, the network loads in different locations are diverse. This would cause distinct QoS values among different coverage areas of an edge server. The coverage area of a sever is usually circular. We accordingly divide the coverage area of a server into several circular rings and monitor QoS in each circular ring.

We set the coverage of each edge sever to 2 km by analyzing the users' locations under each server's coverage. The coverage of each edge server is divided into 5 circular areas through the analysis of user distributions. The circular areas are $[1, 400)$, $[400, 800)$, $[800, 1200)$, $[1200, 1600)$, and $[1600, 2000]$ based on their distance to an edge server.

We choose the server closest to a user as the edge server that the user is most likely to access. We then determine the exact circular area of the server. The historical QoS data of the service to be invoked by the user is extracted from all the users in the same circular area of the predicted edge server. It is denoted by $T_{area_{t+1}} = \{T_{u_1}, T_{u_2}, ..., T_{u_n}\}$, where T_{u_i} represents the QoS of the service invoked by the user i. The average value of the historical QoS data is calculated to obtain the mobility-aware QoS of the service. It is denoted by $QoS_{t+1} = \sum_n^1 T_{area_{t+1}}/n$, where n is the number of the users in this area.

3.3   QoS Monitoring Based on Gaussian Hidden Bayesian Classifier

The main purpose of this step is to train a Gaussian Hidden Bayes classifier based on historical data. The classifier will proactively monitor the mobility-aware QoS acquired from the last step. A Naive Bayes classifier assumes that the attribute values are independent of each other. However, tt ignores the fact that there might be dependence between QoS attribute values, leading to inaccurate classification results. Here we define a parent attribute $\pi(x_i)$ to reduce the dependence between QoS attributes. Each parent attribute represents the influence of the other attributes to each independent attribute. The value of the parent attribute $\pi(x_i)$ is the mean value of $x_1 \sim x_{k-1}$. The improved Bayesian classifier formula can be expressed as:

$$C(X) = \arg\max_{c_j \in C} \left\{ P(c_j) \prod_{i=1}^n P(x_i|\pi(x_i), c_j) \right\} \tag{2}$$

The Gaussian distribution is generally used to represent the class conditional probability distribution of continuous attributes. We apply Gaussian distribution to the probability distribution of continuous variables in Bayesian classifier. The assumption of the Gaussian distribution is expressed as follows:

$$P(x_i|\pi(x_i), c_j) = N_{c_j} \left(\begin{array}{c} u_{x_i} + \rho \frac{\sigma_{x_i}}{\sigma_{\pi(x_i)}}(\pi(x_i) - u_{\pi(x_i)}), \\ \sigma_{x_i}^2(1 - \rho^2) \end{array} \right) \tag{3}$$

where N_{c_j} represents the Gaussian distribution of the corresponding category c_j, u_{x_i} and $\sigma_{x_i}^2$ are the mean and variance of the sample attributes, and $u_{\pi(x_i)}$ and $\sigma_{\pi(x_i)}$ are the mean and variance of the parent attributes corresponding to the sample. The correlation coefficient between x_i and $\pi(x_i)$ is denoted by $\rho = \frac{conv(x_i, \pi(x_i))}{\sigma_{x_i}\sigma_{\pi(x_i)}}$.

In the training phase, a Gaussian hidden Bayesian classifier is constructed upon its parent attributes for each sample, i.e., the mobility-aware QoS value of the user. The classifier is trained based on the historical data of each edge server. The spatio-temporal QoS data (i.e., the QoS data in the same circular area of a sever within the same time period) is used as the input in the classifier. Every time a new QoS value is obtained, whether or not the QoS value satisfies with the pre-defined probabilistic requirements can be determined. We assume that the QoS attribute value follows the Gaussian distribution. Therefore, the determination can be implemented by the probability density integral formula:

$$P(X < Qos\_Value) = \int_{-\infty}^{Qos\_Value} \frac{1}{\sqrt{2\pi}\sigma} e^{-\frac{(x-u)^2}{2\sigma^2}} \tag{4}$$

where μ and σ represent the mean and standard deviation of the QoS value. For example, if a QoS requirement is that the probability that the service response time is less than 2 s is greater than 85%, the value of QoS_Value is 2.

In the QoS monitoring process, users pre-define a set of QoS requirement vectors as $T_{QoS} = [X_1, X_2, \cdots, X_n]$, where $X_n = [x_1, x_2, \cdots, x_n]^T$ refers to the set of required QoS values of all the services called by the user n when accessing a server. The category set is $C = \{c_0, c_1\}$, where c_0 refers to a satisfactory grade and c_1 refers to a unsatisfactory grade. The posterior probabilities of c_0 and c_1 are calculated via the aforementioned process. The category with a higher posterior probability is regarded as the final monitoring result.

4 Experiment

4.1 Experimental Environment Configuration

Experiment Setup. The TensorFlow 2.4.0 deep learning framework[1] is used to implement the proposed DouLSTM-Den model. The model is trained with a computer with Nvidia GTX1080Ti GPU. The model is trained 30 epochs with a batch size of 128. The initial learning rate is set to 0.001. All these parameters are optimal settings according to our experimental observation.

Data Sets. This experiment involves three data sets in the experiment.

- Data Set 1 bases on the Shanghai Telecom data set[2]. This data set includes the geographic location information of 3,233 base stations and 611,507 service calling records.
- Data Set 2 bases on a real-world Web service quality data set released by Chinese University of Hong Kong[3]. This data set includes the response time of 4,500 Web services called by 142 users in 64 different time slices.
- Data Set 3 is a simulated verification data set. The verification data set is generated according to users' QoS requirements in the experiment. The verification data is used to verify the effectiveness of the proposed method. For example, if the QoS requirement is that the probability that the response time of the service is less than 3.6s is greater than 80%, we inject more than 20% exceptional response time (i.e. greater than 3.6 s) samples in a certain range of the original samples as the verification data.

Comparison Method. We compare LSTM-BSPM with the following state-of-the-art service quality monitoring methods to verify the superiority of LSTM-BSPM. These include ghBSRM [9], wBSRMM [8] and IgS-wBSRM [12].

---

[1] https://github.com/tensorflow/tensorflow/tree/v2.4.0.
[2] http://sguangwang.com/TelecomDataset.html.
[3] http://wsdream.github.io/dataset/wsdream_dataset2.html.

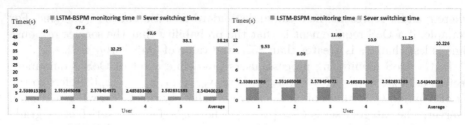

(a) When driving cars   (b) When taking high-speed trains

Fig. 4. Time consumption comparison between proactive service monitoring ($t_{LSTM-BSPM}$) and server switching (t_{tra})

4.2 Feasibility Verification of Proactive Monitoring

We set up an experiment to assess the feasibility of the proposed method. We verify whether our approach can detect abnormal service states before users access new edge servers. The experiment assumes that a group of 160 users call services when driving a car and taking a high-speed train respectively. We assume that the speed of the vehicle is 72 km/h and the speed of the train is 300 km/h. The monitoring time $t_{LSTM-BSPM}$ mainly contains two parts: the time t_{LSTM} to obtain the mobility-aware QoS attribute value based on the DouLSTM-Den model, and the time t_{mon} to monitor the QoS using the Bayesian classifier. The estimated time t_{tra} required for a user to access a new edge server is obtained by calculating the distance between two edge servers divided by the speed.

Figure 4a and Fig. 4b respectively show the time needed for proactive monitoring and connecting to a new edge server for 5 randomly selected users and all the users when driving and taking high-speed trains respectively. We can draw a conclusion that our approach can efficiently complete the proactive service monitoring before users access new edge servers. This would provide more time for servers to make decisions if service anomalies occur.

4.3 Effectiveness Verification of Positive Monitoring

We establish an experiment to verify whether the proposed proactive monitoring method can more quickly and accurately detect service exceptions before users calling the services. The proposed method is compared with the three aforementioned baseline methods. Data Set 3 is used for the experiment. First, we extract the QoS values of 2000 services to train a Gaussian hidden Bayes classifier. We then inject 200 exceptional samples with response time of 3 s in the ranges of [200, 400] and [400, 600] of 1000 test samples (i.e. services).

Figure 5a and Fig. 5b respectively show the monitoring results of the exceptional samples injected in different intervals. The abscissa represents the number of samples that a monitoring method can obtain based on the test set The ordinate represents the monitoring result, where 1 represents normal, and –1 represents abnormal. The number of samples required for each method to monitor

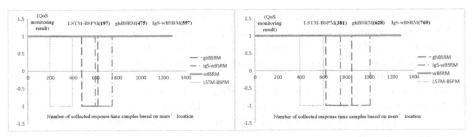

(a) Exceptional samples injected in [200,400]

(b) Exceptional samples injected in [400,600]

Fig. 5. Result of response time monitoring

the abnormality of the service status is marked on the top of the diagram. It can be seen that the proposed proactive monitoring method (i.e. LSTM-BSPM) needs the lowest numbers of samples to detect the service exceptions. In general, it can be seen that the prediction results of LSTM-BSPM are more consistent with the injected exceptions. The experimental results verify the effectiveness of the proposed proactive monitoring method in the mobile edge environment.

5   Conclusion

This paper presents a proactive QoS monitoring method in the mobile edge environment based on DouLSTM-Den model and a Gaussian hidden Bayes classifier. Experiments are conducted on both simulated and real data sets. The experimental results show the effectiveness and feasibility of the proposed method.

For the future work, the following tasks will be considered: i) we will design solutions to accurately predict users' multi-lag moving paths; ii) we will improve this method to adapt to multivariate QoS monitoring; iii) we will consider user privacy protection when designing future proactive QoS monitoring methods.

Acknowledgements. This work is funded by the National Natural Science Foundation of China under Grant (No. 62272145, No. U21B2016), the Natural Science Foundation of Jiangsu Province under grant No. BK20191297, the Fundamental Research Funds for the Central Universities under grant No. B210202075. This research was also partially supported by the Australian Government through the Australian Research Council's Discovery Projects funding scheme (project DP220101823).

References

1. Wang, S., Zhang, X., Zhang, Y., Wang, L., Yang, J., Wang, W.: A survey on mobile edge networks: convergence of computing, caching and communications. Access **5**, 6757–6779 (2017)
2. Wang, S., Xu, J., Zhang, N., Liu, Y.: A survey on service migration in mobile edge computing. Access **6**, 23511–23528 (2018)

3. Chan, K., Poernomo, I., Schmidt, H., Jayaputera, J.: A Model-oriented framework for runtime monitoring of nonfunctional properties. In: Reussner, R., Mayer, J., Stafford, J.A., Overhage, S., Becker, S., Schroeder, P.J. (eds.) QoSA/SOQUA - 2005. LNCS, vol. 3712, pp. 38–52. Springer, Heidelberg (2005). https://doi.org/10.1007/11558569_5

4. Sammapun, U., Lee, I., Sokolsky, O., Regehr, J.: Statistical Runtime checking of probabilistic properties. In: Sokolsky, O., Taşıran, S. (eds.) RV 2007. LNCS, vol. 4839, pp. 164–175. Springer, Heidelberg (2007). https://doi.org/10.1007/978-3-540-77395-5_14

5. Billhardt, H., Hermoso, R., Ossowski, S., Centeno, R.: Trust-based service provider selection in open environments. In: SAC, pp. 1375–1380 (2007)

6. Grunske, L.: An effective sequential statistical test for probabilistic monitoring. Inf. Softw. Technol. **53**(3), 190–199 (2011)

7. Zhu, Y., Xu, M., Zhang, P., Li, W., Leung, H.: Bayesian probabilistic monitor: a new and efficient probabilistic monitoring approach based on Bayesian statistics. In: QSIC-13, pp. 45–54, IEEE (2013)

8. Zhang, P., Zhuang, Y., Leung, H., Song, W., Zhou, Y.: A novel QoS monitoring approach sensitive to environmental factors. In: ICWS, pp. 145–152, IEEE (2015)

9. Zhang, P., Zhang, Y., Dong, H., Jin, H.: Mobility and dependence-aware QoS monitoring in mobile edge computing. IEEE Trans. Cloud. Comput. **9**(3), 1143–1157 (2021)

10. Tommasi, F., De Luca, V., Melle, C.: QoS monitoring in real-time streaming overlays based on lock-free data structures. Multim. Tools Appl. **80**(14), 20929–20970 (2021)

11. Najm, M., Patra, M., Tamarapalli, V.: An adaptive and dynamic allocation of delay-sensitive vehicular services in federated cloud. In: 2021 COMSNETS, pp. 97–100, IEEE (2021)

12. Zhang, P., Jin, H., He, Z., Leung, H., Song, W., Jiang, Y.: IGS-WBSRM: a time-aware web service QoS monitoring approach in dynamic environments. Inf. Softw. Technol. **96**, 14–26 (2018)

TRQP: Trust-Aware Real-Time QoS Prediction Framework Using Graph-Based Learning

Suraj Kumar and Soumi Chattopadhyay[✉]

Indian Institute of Information Technology Guwahati, Guwahati, India
{suraj.kumar,soumi}@iiitg.ac.in

Abstract. QoS prediction algorithm requires to be real-time to be integrated with most real-time service recommendation or composition algorithms. However, real-time algorithms are prone to compromise on the solution quality to improve their responsiveness, which we aim to address in this paper. The collaborative filtering (CF) technique, the most widely used QoS prediction method, consider the influences of all users/services while predicting the QoS value for a given target user-service pair. However, the presence of untrustworthy users/services, whose QoS invocation patterns are different from the rest, may lead to degradation in prediction accuracy. Moreover, in many cases, the quality of the prediction algorithms often deteriorates to ensure faster responsiveness due to their inability to capture non-linear, higher-order, and complex relationships among user-service QoS data. This paper proposes a trust-aware QoS prediction framework leveraging a novel graph-based learning approach. Our framework (TRQP) is competent enough to identify trustworthy users and services while learning effective feature representation for finding a rich collaborative signal in an end-to-end fashion. Our experiments on the publicly available WS-DREAM-1 dataset show that TRQP is not only eligible as a real-time algorithm but also is well capable of handling various challenges associated with QoS prediction problems (e.g., extracting complex non-linear relationships among QoS data) and outperformed major state-of-the-art methods.

1 Introduction

Recommending suitable service for a target user comes under commercial and personal interest. However, it is a challenge in a decentralized environment, where the functionally equivalent web services are increasing rapidly. Due to the frequent addition of new functionally redundant services, obtaining the QoS profile for each service for every user is practically infeasible and time/resource-consuming. Therefore, QoS prediction [6] of services across different users appears as a fundamental problem to solve.

This work is supported by the Science and Engineering Research Board, Department of Science and Technology, Government of India, under Grant SRG/2020/001454.

Recent studies reveal that collaborative filtering (CF)-based methods are most effective for QoS prediction [24]. CF-based methods exploit the QoS log for predicting the QoS value. The memory-based CFs [18,22] are the most simplistic methods by design for QoS prediction. However, they fail to achieve a desirable prediction accuracy due to many challenges, including the data sparsity, scalability, cold-start, etc. Model-based CFs (e.g., matrix factorization [11], factorization machines [14], deep-learning-based [21] approaches) and a few hybrid methods [2,4] combining memory-based and model-based CF have been introduced to address the above challenges. Although these methods are able to achieve satisfactory performance, however, most of them are not suitable for the real-time system due to their slower responsiveness [2,4]. On the other hand, the methods with faster responsiveness have significantly low prediction accuracy [18]. A clear trade-off between the prediction time and prediction accuracy has been observed in the literature [6]. Some recent papers attempted to address this issue [3]. However, due to the absence of quantitative measurement of prediction time to designate an algorithm to be a real-time one, these works are yet to be faster enough to be chosen as a real-time algorithm.

Another important observation is that most of the conventional CF-based methods consider the influence of every user/service to predict the QoS of a target user-service pair. However, all the users/services present in the QoS log are not trustworthy because they may have very different QoS invocation patterns compared to the rest. These users/services are generally referred to as grey-sheep [8]. The influence of grey-sheep users/services in the computation of the QoS of non-grey-sheep users/services lead to highly inaccurate results. Avoiding untrustworthy users/services could improve the QoS prediction accuracy. Li et al. [10] proposed a reputation algorithm for detecting trustworthy users based on geographical location, which could result in the inappropriate set of untrustworthy users since geographical distance may not be equivalent to network-wise distance. The authors in [17] proposed a two-phase K-means clustering-based credibility-aware QoS prediction method, where a cluster with a minimum number of users is considered untrustworthy. However, the clusters with minimum number of users can still be large set. The authors in [12,15] provided a similar approach for detecting grey-sheep using 3σ rule. Although these methods were proposed to detect the untrustworthy users/services, the notion of trustworthiness, however, is yet to be standardized.

In this paper, we propose a real-time, trust-aware QoS prediction algorithm using graph-based learning that can achieve reasonably high prediction accuracy. The graph has been established as a functional data structure that can explore higher-order connectivity (i.e., depth of relationship) in the non-euclidean data space, which helps the graph exploit every possible relationship from nodes and edges. In recent years, graph neural network (GNN) [9] has attracted vast research attention. However, to the best of our knowledge, QoS prediction using graph-based learning is mostly unexplored in the literature. We now summarize the major **contributions** of our paper:

(i) We propose a novel framework for real-time QoS prediction (TRQP) utilizing a graph convolution network that captures the multi-hop collaborative signal by the node message passing and aggregating them over the users/services. The comparative experimental analysis with ablation study shows the efficiency of TRQP in terms of prediction accuracy and prediction time.

(ii) We propose an effective method for identifying trustworthy users/services. Our analysis shows that TRQP improved the accuracy for the non-gray-sheep users/services.

(iii) We performed extensive experiments on publicly available WS-DREAM-1 dataset [23] to validate the performance of TRQP.

In subsequent sections, we formulate the problem and discuss our solution.

2   Formulation of QoS Prediction Problem

Given a set of n users $\mathcal{U} = \{u_1, u_2, \ldots, u_n\}$ with their contextual data (consisting of latitude, longitude, country, and autonomous systems), a set of m services $\mathcal{S} = \{s_1, s_2, \ldots, s_m\}$ with the set of contextual data (includes latitude, longitude, country, service provider), and their partial interactions in terms of a QoS parameter q given in the form of a sparse QoS log matrix $\mathcal{Q}$, the objective of the QoS prediction problem is to predict the value of the QoS parameter for a target user-service pair, where each valid entry of $\mathcal{Q}$ (say, q_{ij}) represents the value of q of $s_j \in \mathcal{S}$ when invoked by $u_i \in \mathcal{U}$.

The conventional collaborative filtering (CF) based approaches fail to achieve high accuracy due to the presence of grey-sheep users/services [8]. Since grey users/services have their unique QoS invocation patterns, predicting the QoS for the non-grey-sheep users/services with the help of the QoS patterns of grey-sheep users/services results in a high prediction error.

The main objective of this paper is to identify the grey-sheep users/services from the given set of users and services and come up with a prediction framework that not only provides a high prediction accuracy but also has a lower prediction time to make the framework compatible with a real-time system.

3   Proposed QoS Prediction Framework

In this section, we discuss different modules of our solution framework (namely, TRQP) for trust-aware QoS prediction problem.

3.1   Identification of Trustworthy Users and Services

The first component of TRQP focuses on identifying the grey-sheep users/services. We first compute an abnormality score of each user u_i and a service s_j (say, $\mathscr{A}(u_i)/\mathscr{A}(s_j)$) as described in [8]. A user u_i (or service s_i) is considered to be more trustworthy as compared to another user u_j (or service s_j) if $\mathscr{A}(u_i)$ is less than $\mathscr{A}(u_j)$ (or, $\mathscr{A}(s_i) < \mathscr{A}(s_j)$). A user $u_i \in \mathcal{U}$ (service $s_j \in \mathcal{S}$) is called grey-sheep, if $\mathscr{A}(u_i)$ ($\mathscr{A}(s_j)$) is more than a given threshold $\mathcal{T}^u_{\mathscr{A}}$ ($\mathcal{T}^s_{\mathscr{A}}$). $\mathcal{T}^u_{\mathscr{A}}$ and $\mathcal{T}^s_{\mathscr{A}}$ are hyper-parameters, required to be set externally. In this

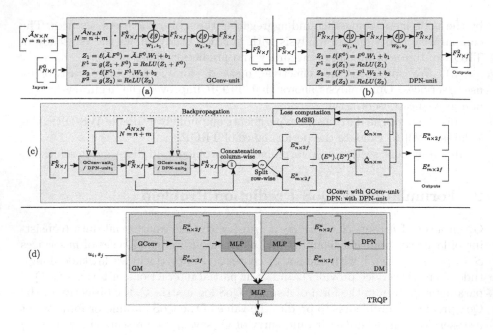

Fig. 1. Model architecture for TRQP

paper, we consider $\mathcal{T}_{\mathscr{A}}^{u} = \mu_{\mathscr{A}}^{u} + c*\sigma_{\mathscr{A}}^{u}$ ($\mathcal{T}_{\mathscr{A}}^{s} = \mu_{\mathscr{A}}^{s} + c*\sigma_{\mathscr{A}}^{s}$), where $\mu_{\mathscr{A}}^{u}$ and $\sigma_{\mathscr{A}}^{u}$ ($\mu_{\mathscr{A}}^{s}$ and $\sigma_{\mathscr{A}}^{s}$) are the mean and standard deviation of the abnormality scores of users (services), respectively. c is a hyper-parameter, which can be tuned externally. Once the grey-sheep users and services are identified, we remove them from the given list of users and services to train our model for prediction. In the next subsection, we present the details of our model.

3.2   Design of the Learning Framework for TRQP

In this subsection, we discuss our proposed architecture (designated as, TRQP) for QoS prediction. TRQP is an ensemble learning model combining two networks (i.e., GM and DM), as shown in Fig. 1. Each of these networks includes two separate modules. The first module is accountable for computing user/service feature embedding, the second module is responsible for QoS prediction.

GM consists of a graph convolution network [9] (say, GConv) for obtaining user/service feature embedding followed by a multi-layer perceptron (MLP) for QoS prediction, where DM comprises a deep prediction framework (say, DPN) for generating user/service feature embedding followed by an MLP for prediction. A final MLP is used in TRQP to aggregate the outputs of GM and DM for the final prediction. We now elaborate each of these modules below.

3.2.1   Architecture of GM.   Here, we introduce the graph modeling for the prediction problem. We begin with defining the QoS prediction graph.

Definition 1 (QoS Prediction Graph (QPG)). A QoS prediction graph $G = (V_1 \cup V_2, E)$ is a bipartite graph, where the vertices V_1 and V_2 represent the set of users $\mathcal{U}$ and the set of services $\mathcal{S}$, respectively. An edge $e_{ij} = (v_i^1, v_j^2) \in E$ exists between two vertices $v_i^1 \in V_1$ and $v_j^2 \in V_2$ if the QoS log $\mathcal{Q}$ includes a valid QoS entry for the service s_j corresponding to v_j^2 invoked by the user u_i corresponding to v_i^1. ∎

We represent the QPG in terms of an adjacency matrix $\mathcal{A}^{(n+m)\times(n+m)}$, which is used in graph convolutional network to obtain user/service feature embedding. However, instead of using $\mathcal{A}$ by itself, we normalize $\mathcal{A}$, so that more influence of the higher degree nodes can be avoided during learning [9]. Moreover, normalization helps in scaling. The normalized matrix is denoted by $\bar{A} = \mathcal{D}^{-\frac{1}{2}} \mathcal{A} \mathcal{D}^{-\frac{1}{2}}$, where $\mathcal{D}$ is a diagonal matrix representing the degree of each node of the QPG G by its diagonal elements. It may be noted, each non-zero element of $\bar{A}$, i.e., $\bar{A}(i,j)$, is normalized by the square root of the number of invocations of the corresponding user u_i and service s_j as recorded in $\mathcal{Q}$, i.e., $\bar{A}(i,j) = \frac{\mathcal{A}(i,j)}{\sqrt{d_{ii}} \cdot \sqrt{d_{jj}}}$. Each node of QPG is associated with an embedding representing the features of that node (i.e., initial user/service feature embedding consisting of the latent representation of QoS profile and contextual data of user/service of length f).

3.2.2 Description of GConv: We now discuss the architecture of GConv, as shown in Fig. 1(c). We begin with illustrating the primary component of GConv, i.e., GConv-unit, as presented in Fig. 1(a). GConv-unit takes the normalized adjacency matrix $\bar{A}_{N\times N}$ and an input feature matrix F^i with dimension $N \times f$, where $N = (n+m)$. The objective of a GConv-unit is to accumulate the input feature embedding of each node $v_i^k \in (V_1 \cup V_2), k \in \{1,2\}$ of G with the feature embedding of its subsequent hop (i.e., the node directly connected to v_i^k through an edge in E of G), as modeled by the four equations of Fig. 1(a). Therefore, the output of the GConv-unit is another feature matrix of the same dimension.

The user/service embedding matrix $\mathcal{E}$ serves as the input feature embedding matrix for GConv, i.e., $F^0 = \mathcal{E}$. The initial node embedding for each node $v_i^k \in (V_1 \cup V_2), k \in \{1,2\}$ of G is refined while propagated through multiple GConv-units by accumulating the features of other nodes directly/indirectly connected to v_i^k via a path in G. Therefore, in a GConv network with L number of GConv-units, the final embedding for each node in QPG is able to aggregate the feature embedding of all neighbors reachable through L-hops.

3.2.3 Description of MLP of GM: An MLP is used for QoS prediction in GM. The network is trained with a sample for each $u_i \in \mathcal{U}$ and $s_j \in \mathcal{S}$ such that $q_{ij} \neq 0$ in $\mathcal{Q}$. The concatenation of the features of u_i and s_j obtained from GConv is used as the feature to train the MLP, while q_{ij} is served as the target value. It may be noted, the MLP is trained before the deployment of TRQP.

3.2.4 Architecture of DM: The architecture of DM is similar to GM. Here, instead of GConv, a deep prediction network (DPN) comprising DPN-unit (refers to Fig. 1(b)) is used to generate the user/service embedding, while a following MLP is used for QoS prediction. The architecture of DPN is similar to GConv. The only difference in DPN is that the adjacency matrix is not used in DPN.

3.2.5   Architecture of TRQP: As discussed earlier, TRQP comprises GM, DM, and an additional MLP to combine the outputs of GM and DM (Refer to Fig. 1(d)). The MLP is trained before the deployment of TRQP as well. Each training sample of MLP consists of a feature vector of size 2, the outputs of GM and DM, for each $u_i \in \mathcal{U}$ and $s_j \in \mathcal{S}$ such that $q_{ij} \neq 0$ in $\mathcal{Q}$. q_{ij} is again served as the target value. The output of the MLP is considered the final output of TRQP.

Finally, we employ an outlier detection algorithm [3] for detecting outliers from the dataset, which are removed to measure the performance of TRQP. The next section presents the performance of TRQP through experiments.

4   Experimental Analysis

We have implemented our proposed method in TensorFlow with Python. The training of TRQP was done on NVIDIA's Quadro RTX 3000/PCIe/SSE2 GPU with 1920 cores, and 6 GB memory. For testing, we used i9-10885H @ 2.40 GHz×16 processor with x86_64 CPU with 128 GB RAM.

To validate the performance of TRQP, we performed extensive experiments on WS-DREAM-1 dataset [23]. Table 1 shows the description of the dataset used for our experiment.

Table 1. WS-Dream-1 dataset description

QoS	(# user, # service)	Min	Max	Mean	Median	Std. Dev
Response time (RT)	(339×4998)	0.001	19.999	0.915	0.319	2.000
Throughput (TP)	(339×5004)	0.017	1000.0	46.786	14.018	108.918

The configuration of TRQP, used for our experiments, is as follows. For identifying grey-sheep users/services, we used $c = 2$ throughout our experiments. We reported our results by eliminating 3% outliers. The size of initial user/service feature embedding is 255. Our GConv and DPN includes 2 GConv-units and 2 DPN-units, respectively. In our experiment, we have used ADAM optimizer and mean squared error as the loss function [7].

4.1   Experimental Analysis

We compared the performance of TRQP with 14 major state-of-the-art (SoA) methods with and without trustworthiness taken into consideration. Tables 2(a) and (b) show the comparative analysis of TRQP in terms of the prediction accuracy, measured by mean absolute error (MAE) [3]. Figure 2(a) shows the comparative study of TRQP in terms of the prediction time. Below we summarize our observations from Tables 2(a), (b) and Fig. 2(a).

(i) In all cases other than OffDQ, TRQP outperformed the SoA for both training percentages for both datasets. The improvement of TRQP over the second-best value for each of the 4 cases is shown in the final row of Table 2(b).

(ii) Although OffDQ performed better than TRQP in terms of the prediction accuracy, the results of the OffDQ was presented by removing 5% to 15% outliers. However, in our case, we removed 3% outliers and about 10% entries due to grey-sheep analysis. Moreover, TRQP performed better than OffDQ in terms of the prediction time (refer to Fig. 2(a)). While the prediction time for OffDQ is in the order of 10^{-1} s, the same for the TRQP is in the order of 10^{-5} s.

Table 2. Comparison of TRQP with SoA on prediction accuracy (MAE)

Without Trust-aware Prediction

Methods	Response time		Throughput	
	10%	20%	10%	20%
WSRec [22]	0.6394	0.5024	19.9754	16.0762
NRCF [16]	0.5312	0.4607	-	-
RACF [18]	0.4937	0.4208	-	-
GMF [1]	0.4737	0.4233	-	-
DAFR [21]	0.3461	0.3404	16.9020	15.5670
LBFM [20]	0.3750	0.3421	-	11.9291
CNCF [5]	0.3380	0.3140	18.189	16.826
OffDQ [3]	0.2000	0.1800	9.1600	8.6700
TRQP	**0.2540**	**0.2520**	**10.5760**	**9.5660**

(a)

With Trust-aware Prediction

Methods	Response time		Throughput	
	10%	20%	10%	20%
TAP [15]	0.5502	-	-	-
RAP [13]	0.5250	0.4400	19.4333	16.4104
CAP [17]	0.5030	0.4394	15.1148	13.8192
RMF [19]	0.4877	0.4414	-	-
LRMF [10]	0.4719	0.4384	-	-
S-RAP [12]	0.4833	-	-	-
TRQP	**0.2540**	**0.2520**	**10.5760**	**9.5660**
Improvement	24.85%	19.75%	30.03%	19.81%

(b)

(iii) One of the crucial characteristics of a real-time QoS prediction algorithm is that it is supposed to have negligible prediction time compared to the service's response time. This makes the prediction framework compatible with a real-time recommendation system, where a service is first recommended based on its predicted QoS, before its execution. Therefore, one preliminary criterion of a real-time prediction algorithm is to have a much lesser prediction time compared to the response time of services. As observed in Table 1, the minimum response time of service is in order of 10^{-3} s. In comparison to the response time of services, our framework has an insignificant prediction time (i.e., in the order of 10^{-5} s), which makes TRQP a real-time algorithm.

(iv) Furthermore, TRQP outperformed the SoA methods that are known to have less prediction time.

Ablation Study: From this analysis onwards we have used the RT dataset with 10% training data. Figures 2(b) and (c) present the results for our ablation study. Our observations from Figs. 2(b) and (c) are listed below:

(i) Figure 2(b) shows the model ablation study, where we reported the performance of the individual components of TRQP. As evident from Fig. 2(b), TRQP performed the best in the presence of all its components.

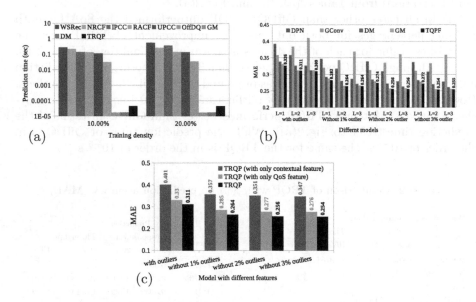

(a)

(b)

(c)

Fig. 2. (a) Comparison of TRQP with respect to SoA on prediction time; Ablation study (b) Model ablation; (c) Feature ablation

(ii) As observed in Fig. 2(a), GM and DM have better prediction times as compared to TRQP. However, TRQP performed better than GM and DM in terms of prediction accuracy.

(iii) We reported the performance of all the networks for $L = 1, 2, 3$ (i.e., GConv/DPN with 1/2/3 GConv-units/DPN-units). For $L = 2$ and $L = 3$, the performance of TRQP is almost the same and better than the performance for $L = 1$. This may be due to the over-smoothing problem in graph convolution network [9]. GConv with more number of GConv-units cannot improve its performance, and it often leads to severe degradation in the feature extraction since it may end up obtaining similar embedding for all the nodes in QPG. In our experiment, we used 2 GConv-units.

(iv) Figure 2(c) shows the feature ablation study. We reported the performance of TRQP with only contextual features, only QoS features, and their combinations. As it turned out, TRQP, with the combination of the contextual and QoS features, performed the best as compared to the others. The performance of TRQP with only the contextual feature was not good. TRQP achieved a 25.6% improvement on average over TRQP with only contextual features. However, in the absence of contextual features, we can still use TRQP with only QoS features for the prediction, as TRQP achieved only a 7.1% improvement on average over TRQP with only QoS features.

(v) Furthermore, we observed the overall MAE for the non-grey-sheep users or services obtained from TRQP is 0.254, which is less than the one obtained from TRQP with grey-sheep users or services (which is 0.261 as reported). This, in turn, shows the effectiveness of our trustworthiness analysis.

In summary, TRQP without grey-sheep users and services achieved reasonably high prediction accuracy while being suitable for a real-time system.

5   Conclusion

This paper proposes a trust-aware, real-time QoS prediction framework. To the best of our knowledge, TRQP is one of the first methods in the QoS prediction literature to leverage the graph-based feature embedding exploiting the graph convolution for QoS prediction. The graph convolution over bipartite representation of QoS data helps exploit the non-linear, deep/higher-order, and complex relationship among user/service QoS data that enhances the collaborative signal for better QoS prediction. We also propose a means to determine trustworthy users/services. Focusing on the trustworthiness problem, identifying the grey-sheep users/services, and removing them to achieve better prediction accuracy proves the usefulness of our framework for trust-aware QoS prediction. The experimental analysis in the paper shows that TRQP outperformed major SoA methods in terms of prediction accuracy and/or prediction time.

As a future endeavor, we wish to develop more sophisticated algorithms for predicting the QoS for untrustworthy users/services. We also aim to explore a Spatio-temporal graph convolution for time-aware QoS prediction.

References

1. Chang, Z., Ding, D., Xia, Y.: A graph-based QoS prediction approach for web service recommendation. Appl. Intell. **51**(10), 6728–6742 (2021)
2. Chattopadhyay, S., Banerjee, A.: QoS value prediction using a combination of filtering method and neural network regression. In: ICSOC, pp. 135–150 (2019)
3. Chattopadhyay, S., et al.: OffDQ: an offline deep learning framework for QoS prediction. In: ACM the Web Conference, pp. 1987–1996. WWW (2022)
4. Chowdhury, R.R., et al.: CAHPHF: context-aware hierarchical Qos prediction with hybrid filtering. IEEE Trans. Serv. Comput. **15**(4), 2232–2247 (2022)
5. Gao, H.: Xothers: context-aware QoS prediction with neural collaborative filtering for internet-of-things services. IEEE IoT J. **7**(5), 4532–4542 (2019)
6. Ghafouri, S.H., et al.: A survey on web service QoS prediction methods. IEEE TSC (2020). https://doi.org/10.1109/TSC.2020.2980793
7. Goodfellow, I.J., Bengio, Y., Courville, A.C.: Deep Learning. Adaptive Computation and Machine Learning. MIT Press, London (2016)
8. Gras, B., et al.: Identifying grey sheep users in collaborative filtering: a distribution-based technique. In: ACM UMAP, pp. 17–26 (2016)
9. Kipf, T.N., Welling, M.: Semi-supervised classification with graph convolutional networks. In: ICLR 2017 (2017)

10. Li, S., Wen, J., Wang, X.: From reputation perspective: A hybrid matrix factorization for QoS prediction in location-aware mobile service recommendation system. Mob. Inf. Syst. **2019**(8950508), 1–12 (2019)
11. Lo, W., et al.: An extended matrix factorization approach for QoS prediction in service selection. In: IEEE SCC, pp. 162–169 (2012)
12. Muslim, H.S.M., et al.: S-RAP: relevance-aware QoS prediction in web-services and user contexts. Knowl. Inf. Syst. **64**, 1997–2022 (2022)
13. Qiu, W., et al.: Reputation-aware QoS Value prediction of web services. In: IEEE SCC, pp. 41–48 (2013)
14. Shen, L., et al.: Contexts Enhance accuracy: on modeling context aware deep factorization machine for web API QoS prediction. IEEE Access **8**, 165551–165569 (2020)
15. Su, K., et al.: TAP: a personalized trust-aware QoS prediction approach for web service recommendation. Knowl.-Based Syst. **115**, 55–65 (2017)
16. Sun, H., et al.: Personalized web service recommendation via normal recovery collaborative filtering. IEEE TSC **6**(4), 573–579 (2013)
17. Wu, C., et al.: QoS prediction of web services based on two-phase k-means clustering. In: IEEE ICWS. pp. 161–168 (2015)
18. Wu, X., et al.: Collaborative Filtering Service Recommendation based on a Novel Similarity Computation Method. IEEE Trans. Serv. Comput. **10**(3), 352–365 (2017)
19. Xu, J., et al.: Web service personalized quality of service prediction via reputation-based matrix factorization. IEEE Trans. Reliab. **65**(1), 28–37 (2016)
20. Yang, Y., et al.: A location-based factorization machine model for web service QoS prediction. IEEE Trans. Serv. Comput. **14**(5), 1264–1277 (2021)
21. Yin, Y., et al.: QoS prediction for service recommendation with features learning in mobile edge computing environment. IEEE Trans. Cogn. Commun. Netw. **6**(4), 1136–1145 (2020)
22. Zheng, Z., et al.: QoS-aware web service recommendation by collaborative filtering. IEEE Trans. Serv. Comput. **4**(2), 140–152 (2011)
23. Zheng, Z., et al.: Investigating QoS of Real-World Web Services. IEEE Trans. Serv. Comput. **7**(1), 32–39 (2014)
24. Zheng, Z., et al.: Web service QoS prediction via collaborative filtering: a survey. IEEE Trans. Serv. Comput. (2020). https://doi.org/10.1109/TSC.2020.2995571

Microservices

Misty: Microservice-Based Streaming Trajectory Similarity Search

Jiachun Tao, Zhicheng Pan, Junhua Fang$^{(\boxtimes)}$, Pingfu Chao, Pengpeng Zhao, and Jiajie Xu

Department of Computer Science and Technology, Soochow University, Suzhou, China
{jctao31,zcpan28}@stu.suda.edu.cn,
{jhfang,pfchao,ppzhao,xujj}@suda.edu.cn

Abstract. As a fundamental operation in various LBS (Location Based Service) applications, the trajectory similarity search has long been a performance bottleneck in applications like (e.g., traffic optimization and contact tracing). When handling streaming trajectory data, the variable workload and stateful compute requirement are two crucial challenges that further complicate the problem. Distributed microservice, a mainstream industrial software design architecture, is the preferred way to address such issues. However, the trajectory instance will inevitably be split under the parallel framework. Therefore, how to distribute trajectory data among the parallel processing tasks in a real-time and lightweight manner is the crux. In this paper, we propose a Microservice-based real-time processing framework for streaming trajectory similarity search, called **Misty**, which effectively reduces the update cost of the secondary index and supports high scalability. Moreover, on top of Misty, we can build resilient and stateful cloud-native applications. Misty is composed of the assembler, index, coordinator, and executor. Specifically, the assembler and the index module ensure retrieval performance, while the coordinator and executor module enable the system with elastic scaling. Extensive experimental studies on real-world data demonstrate higher query throughput and lower latency over traditional approaches.

Keywords: Real-time data processing · Trajectory similarity · Microservice · Distributed processing · Streaming spatio-temporal data

1 Introduction

A trajectory is an ordered arrangement of latitude and longitude of the moving object in the time dimension, which contains the movement trend and pattern of the moving object. Trajectory similarity is a measure that describes the degree of correlation between pair-wise trajectories [9], which is an infrastructural operation in LBS and can be extended to various fields, such as contact tracing during COVID-19, ride-sharing [5] and route planning [8].

J. Troya et al. (Eds.): ICSOC 2022, LNCS 13740, pp. 155–170, 2022.
https://doi.org/10.1007/978-3-031-20984-0_11

Most existing related schemes [1,4,6,7] focus on solving the trajectory similarity query problem on a single machine. However, when processing similarity queries for massive data, such schemes will face inconceivable storage and process capability. Moreover, it is difficult to directly extend these schemes to the distributed environment. The fundamental reason is that the trajectory needs to be split under the parallel processing architecture. No matter whether the partitioner divides the trajectories into parallel processing by the trajectory ID or by the trajectory segments, the computational state of the similarity processing will be destroyed. Specifically, by using the hash function, two trajectories (T_1 and T_2) will be dispatched into two different partitions, respectively. As a result, the system cannot get their similarity result directly. By using range partition, the first two points named T_{11} of T_1 and the first three points named T_{21} of T_2 will be distributed to partition P_1. The rest of the points, named T_{12} and T_{22} accordingly, will be distributed into partition P_2. In effect, the system can only compute a partial similarity.

Nowadays, some works focusing on parallel trajectory similarity processing have been proposed. However, the current mainstream trajectory similarity processing platform is all based on generic big data processing frameworks, such as Spark and Flink. In general, these frameworks cannot adjust the architecture at runtime in a lightweight manner, so the retrieval efficiency and flexibility cannot reach the ideal state. The detailed description is as follows:

- **Retrieval efficiency:** Distributed spatial indexing is a key technology to improve the retrieval efficiency of trajectory similarity. This technology has been widely studied in offline scenarios and greatly improves retrieval efficiency. However, in the face of real-time scenarios, frequent and heavy-weight updates of indexes will lead to a sharp drop in system performance. We believe that the bottleneck of this problem lies in the following two aspects: *At the logical level*, the update mode of the secondary index is synchronized, which makes the update of the global index and the local index extremely time-consuming. *At the physical level*, the update of the index relies on the APIs of big data processing frameworks (e.g., Spark or Flink), so our development is limited by the programming mode of these frameworks.
- **Runtime scalability:** Although existing works [8,9,11,12] can improve high-performance queries, their architecture is rigid at runtime. This is because they are usually based on big data processing frameworks such as Spark, which have development issues with runtime parallelism scaling. In conclusion, these frameworks do not have lightweight elastic scaling capabilities, and scalability is not comprehensive. In addition, the slave node itself isn't able to scale actively, and design patterns such as JVM and DAG have a large resource overhead. In short, it cannot provide lightweight runtime scalability.

As shown in Fig. 1(a), when the existing secondary index mode encounters a need to adjust (such as inserting new data), it will first update the local index, then adjust the global index, and finally, redistribute the data. Needless to say, such an operation consumes a lot of performance and resources. Such a scheduling method based on workload reshuffling will inevitably reduce the retrieval

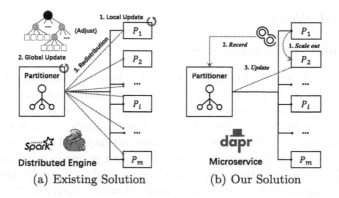

Fig. 1. Existing solution v.s. Our solution

efficiency and hinder the flexibility of the system. The recent emergence of the micro-services architecture effectively addresses the maintenance and scalability demands of online service providers. Moreover, such architectures intend to overcome the shortcomings of monolithic architectures where all of the application's logic and data are managed in one deployable unit. Inspired by it, we design a lightweight processing solution based on the micro-services architecture (such as Dapr) for trajectory stream similarity processing by updating the index and scaling out a task on demand (as shown in Fig. 1(b)).

To ensure the retrieval efficiency and scalability of our system **Misty**, we propose a novel trajectory similarity search framework for continuous trajectory similarity search. Firstly, we design a hierarchy tree-like distributed spatial index structure. This is a hybrid index that uses a grid index in partition and a tree index inside a single machine. Secondly, to address the huge overlapping problems for wide-span trajectories, we split trajectories into segments before inserting them into our index. To summarize, the main contributions of our work are:

- We propose the full-fledged microservice-based distributed framework called Misty. It leverages a hierarchy tree-like distributed spatial index to answer continuous similarity search queries over massive streaming trajectory data.
- Misty utilizes a segment-based data model with several optimizations for storing, indexing and pruning to ensure efficient querying capability.
- We conduct a comprehensive empirical evaluation for Misty using large synthetic and real-world trajectory data streams to measure its scalability, throughput and latency. The experimental results demonstrate the superior performance that our framework achieves against possible alternatives.

The rest of the paper is organized as the following. Section 2 surveys existing spatial indexes, trajectory similarity measures and distributed processing frameworks. Section 3 formalizes the continuous trajectory similarity search. We describe the proposed framework in Sect. 4. Section 5 presents the results of our experimental study and Sect. 6 concludes the paper with remarks on future work.

2   Related Work

2.1   Distributed Similarity Search

DFT [9], DITA [8] and REPOSE [12] are state-of-the-art distributed trajectory similarity search frameworks. DFT [9] is the first distributed framework that leverages segment-based partitioning and indexing to answer similarity search queries over large trajectory data. DFT speeds up queries with a two-level R-Tree and compresses index items with roaring bitmaps. DITA [8] selects pivot points to represent a trajectory and stores close pivot points in the same MBR. In addition, DITA considers the connections when calculating similarities and uses the bipartite graph model to enhance the load balancing capability. REPOSE [12] is a distributed in-memory framework for the processing of Top-k trajectory similarity queries on Spark. REPOSE uses a trie-tree to index trajectories.

Although these frameworks can achieve satisfactory performance in offline scenarios, they still have retrieval performance and runtime scalability issues. Therefore, these frameworks cannot process trajectory streaming data well in real-time with a distributed architecture.

2.2   Distributed Spatial Indexing

Generally speaking, the distributed spatial indexes are processed in two steps, in line with a *filtering-and-refinement* framework. In particular, DITIR [2] is a distributed index for indexing and querying trajectory data in real-time. It supports the ingestion and indexing of trajectory data at high rates. Xie et al. [9, 10] used the Sort-Tile-Recursive packing algorithm at the master node to determine the sub-region responsible for each slave node, which is a partitioning method with a fixed spatial region. After determining the sub-regions for each slave node, they use an STR-tree [7] to build a local index on each slave node, thus completing the construction of a distributed spatial index. Shang et al. [8] use the Sort-Tile-Recursive packing algorithm twice with the first and last sample points of each trajectory in the trajectory set to form two rectangular sets MBR_f and MBR_l and created two R-trees on the master node with MBR_f and MBR_l respectively to partition the query trajectories, and then created a local index on each slave node.

2.3   Spatio-temporal Data Analytics Systems

Simba [10] extends Spark SQL and DataFrame API to make spatial support for Spark. It improves the query performance by introducing multi-level (global and local) R-tree indexing on RDDs, and spatial-aware (logical and cost-based) query planning. Moreover, the STR partitioner [7] mitigates the data partitioning skew significantly. Later, Simba extended its support for spatial partitioning and indexing. However, Simba only supports spatial operations over point and rectangle objects. Zeyuan et al. [8] developed DITA, which supports both SQL and Dataframe API for trajectory analysis. DITA adopts the STR [7] partitioning strategy to create balanced partitions of trajectory points. Like TrajSpark, it also uses multi-level indexing to expedite query performance. Besides, DITA has developed a cost model to reduce inter-worker transmission costs and balance the workload. Dragoon is a multi-purpose system capable of processing both offline and online trajectory data. Dragoon [3] designs a mutable RDD so that data can be updated.

3   Preliminaries

Misty focuses on the flexibility and efficiency of the real-time trajectory processing framework. In this section, we first introduce the relevant definitions of Misty, and then we give an overview of Misty's framework and core components.

3.1   Definitions

Definition 1. *A **trajectory** is a sequence of consecutive line segments, denoted as $T = (l_1, l_2, ..., l_i)$. The notation l_i means a line segment in $\mathbb{R}^2$. The end point of l_i is denoted as s_{i+1} and it is the starting point of l_{i+1}.*

Trajectory T in our system is assumed as unbounded, which means when doing similarity calculation, we refer to the snapshot of T at time t. After a new point arrives in the system, one particular trajectory should be updated and distance needs to be recalculated.

Definition 2. *Given two trajectory segments $l_1 = (s_1, e_1)$, $l_2 = (s_2, e_2)$ and distance criteria $d()$ their distance is*

$$d(l_1, l_2) = max(d(s_1, l_2), d(e_1, l_2), d(s_2, l_1), d(e_2, l_1))$$

where the distance between a point p and a segment l is defined as: $d(p, l) = min_{q \in l} \|p - q\|$

The above definition for the distance between two segments l_1 and l_2 is equivalent to the well-known Hausdorff distance. This is because a line segment l is a convex object, thus the point on l with the maximum distance to another line segment must be one of the two end points of l.

We decide to use the classical Hausdorff distance as the distance measure of our framework due to its capability for parallel computing. Since we choose trajectory segment as the most basic data structure, we use discrete segment Hausdorff distance designed by [9]. Here we represent it again using our notation.

Definition 3. *For query trajectory $Q = (g_1, g_2, ..., g_k)$ and $T = (l_1, l_2, ..., l_i) \in \tau$ their discrete segment Hausdorff distance is defined as:*

$$D_H = max \left\{ \begin{array}{l} max_{g_i \in Q} min_{l_j \in T} d(g_i, l_j) \\ max_{l_j \in T} min_{g_i \in Q} d(g_i, l_j) \end{array} \right\}$$

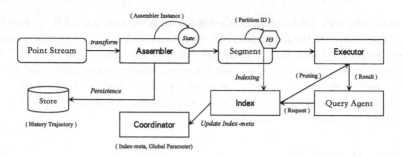

Fig. 2. Overview of Misty

The above definitions describe the distance between trajectory segments and the distance between trajectories. The query on the real-time trajectory stream revolves around the trajectory similarity, including but not limited to the range, top-k and threshold queries. We define a continuous trajectory similarity query problem with top-k queries as primers:

Definition 4. *Given a trajectory stream* $\tau = [T_1, T_2, ..., T_N]$, *a query trajectory* Q, *a distance measure* D, *a max distance* ε, *and an integer* k; *A **continuous trajectory similarity search** continuously returns the set* $S(Q, \tau, D, k) \subset \tau$ *where* $|S(Q, \tau, D, k)| = k$ *and for any* $T, T' \in \tau$:

$$If \ \ T \in S(Q, \tau, D, k) \qquad And \ \ T' \notin S(Q, \tau, D, k)$$
$$Then \ \ D(Q, T) < D(Q, T') \qquad And \ \ D(Q, T) < \varepsilon$$

It should be noted that other queries on the trajectory stream are also in the above-mentioned pattern, and they replace the parameter k with a certain range or a maximum tolerated similarity value.

3.2 Overview of Misty

The overall architecture of Misty is shown in Fig. 2. We first briefly introduce the four core components as follows:

1. **Assembler** converts the received stream of trajectory points into segments and stores the entire trajectory as a state, simplifying the semantics of the query. Historical trajectory will be persisted to disk, identified as "Store" in the figure.
2. **Index** partitions the data entering the system, specifically according to the Uber H3 hexagonal grid partition. After data partitioning, the data will be distributed to shared-nothing nodes. In them, Misty builds local indexes (R-Tree) to provide efficient local search capabilities.
3. **Coordinator** stores the *index-meta*, which is an improved R-tree structure whose leaf nodes contain MBR of H3 addresses. When the index is updated, the coordinator will also update the index-meta synchronously. In addition, the coordinator is responsible for the parallelism, scheduling, etc. of distributed tasks.

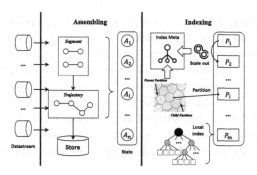

Fig. 3. Assembling and Indexing

4. **Executor** collects candidate data through the index and performs distributed incremental similarity calculation. Since indexing will greatly reduce the amount of candidate data, this specific operation will consume less time. We will detail the execution flow of the executor and how it interacts with high concurrency queries.

The integration of the above core components forms our continuous query framework for processing trajectory similarity with high efficiency and scalability. We will introduce all components of Misty in Sect. 4.

4 Framework

4.1 Assembler

The assembler first converts the point stream data into segments and then assembles them into assembler instances. We introduce the trajectory segment and assembly process separately below.

Trajectory Segment. The real trajectory of a moving object is always a continuous curve in space, but trajectories collected and stored in the database are not. Because only discrete samples are taken by the sensing devices. For example, a taxi equipped with GPS will report its location every 1 min. Discrete samples from one moving object form an ordered sequence of segments. When the sample rate is high enough, these segments will be able to approximate the real trajectory of a moving object fairly accurately.

The trajectory segment is defined in Definition 1. In a nutshell, the trajectory segment is a structure composed of the current point and the predecessor point. These segments have two downstream processing directions. On the one hand, they will be the input to the assembling process and output as assembler instances. Then, such instances will be cached in the state store, contributing to the final result while waiting for the query to execute. On the other hand, it will be stored incrementally and persistently as historical trajectory data.

Assembling Process. This process will assemble segments into state instances for final result computation. As shown in Fig. 3, Misty assembles a start point s and endpoint e into a segment, then integrates the segments into a trajectory at the state store. Simultaneously, the assembler will assemble and cache the sequence of trajectory segments as a state, for example, T_1 (a set of segments) will be assembled as A_1, which provides convenience for subsequent queries.

For a new trajectory point without a predecessor point, we will initialize a new structure to store it. For new trajectory points with predecessor points, we assemble them into segments and update the state incrementally.

4.2 Index

The Index aims to find candidate trajectories. The computational complexity of meeting query requirements based on candidate trajectory sets will be greatly reduced. As shown in Fig. 3, each H3 partition has a local R-Tree index. The local R-Tree has a maximum size of K, insertion ratio R and a buffer with a maximum size of M. These properties will affect how the native R-Tree responds differently in case of inserts, splits, etc. The following will first introduce the R-tree insertion process when new data (segments with H3 partitions) arrive.

Algorithm 1 presents how a new trajectory segment is formed. When receiving a new segment, Misty needs to determine whether the partition it belongs to has expired. After such a judgment, Algorithm 1 adds the trajectory segment to the buffer.

Algorithm 2 presents how new trajectory segments are added to the index. Trajectory segments from the assembler will be inserted into the buffer first. When the buffer size reaches M or meets the condition of $\frac{c.size()}{I.size()} > R$, the partition will insert the data in the buffer into the R-Tree all at once. Misty build an R-Tree of trajectory segments in each partition as its local index. The local index has an additional input buffer. New-coming segments will firstly be stored in a hash table. When the number of data in the buffer reaches the dynamic insertion threshold R, the index will stop responding to new requests and commit the hash table to R-Tree.

Algorithm 3 shows the process of partition splitting checking. When a partition reaches capacity threshold K this will trigger a partition split. This partition will temporarily stop responding to new requests and divide itself into several smaller partitions. After new partitions are set and ready to serve, the old big partition will still exist for a while acting as a router, directing traffic to new smaller partitions until there is no more possible traffic.

4.3 Coordinator

The coordinator is the Master node in the Master-slave architecture, and there is only one. The coordinator maintains meta information of index nodes called index-meta and coordinates distributed jobs (such as the number of nodes for specific computing tasks and the upper limit of parallelism).

Algorithm 1. Accept New Segment

Input: Segment s, Buffer C
Output: New segment buffer C
1: **if** $isExpired()$ **then**
        return $self.resolution$
2: **end if**
3: $C.add(s)$
4: $checkInsertion()$
5: **return** C

Algorithm 2. Check Insertion

Input: Segment buffer C, Index I,
    Buffer size M, Insertion ratio R,
    Splitting threshold K
Output: New Index I
1: **if** $C.size() > M, \frac{c.size()}{K} > R$ **then**
2:    $I.add(C)$
3:    $C \leftarrow \varnothing$ $\triangleright$ clear the buffer
4: **end if**
5: $checkSplitting()$
6: **return** I

Algorithm 3. Check Splitting

Input: Index I, Splitting threshold K
Output: New Index I
1: **if** $I.size() > K \wedge self.resulotion < 15$ **then**
2:    $childRes \leftarrow self.res + 1$
3:    $childRegions \leftarrow split\_reg(childRes)$
4:    **for** s in I **do**
5:      $new\_s\_reg \leftarrow getRegion(s.start())$
6:      $new\_end\_reg \leftarrow getRegion(s.end())$
7:      **if** $new\_start\_reg \in child\_regs$ **then**
8:        $sendToRegion(s, region)$
9:      **end if.**
10:     **if** $new\_end\_reg \in child\_regs$ **then**
11:       $sendToRegion(s, region)$
12:     **end if**
13:    **end for**
14:    $self.isExpired \leftarrow True$
15:    $informRegionSplit(regions)$
16: **return** 0
17: **end if**
18: **return** 1

Index-meta is an improved R-tree structure whose leaf nodes contain MBR of H3 hexagons. Index-meta collects the information of each partition. When an index partition expires, if some data wants to enter it, the data will be rejected. Misty updates the index-meta when a partition expires by adding new child partitions and deleting the old parent partition. Index-meta is similar to the global index structure in traditional secondary indexes.

4.4 Query Agent

The query agent is responsible for the invocation of components. Each microservice only needs to do its part to help complete the query.

Firstly, the agent calculates the candidate areas in H3 with max distance R. Then it queries the coordinator for relevant indexes. Then, it sends Q to relevant indexes to calculate overlapped candidates' *tids*. Next, the agent split the list of *tids* with batch size B and sends batches to executors. Finally, the agent sorts out top-k trajectories and answers the client. For continuity, the agent will start a new round of searches at a fixed interval.

4.5 Executor

The Executor mainly performs segment-based Hausdorff distance calculations, and it transmits the results directly to the Query Agent. The Executor reads the trajectory state from State to provide incremental computation. Misty can dynamically change the parallelism of the executors through the query Agent to meet the best resource utilization.

Example: We have two trajectories named T and Q. For every segment of T named l_i, we figure out the minimum distance from it to every segment g_j of Q. Then we get a maximum distance of all $d(l_i, g_j)$ and that's the distance from T to Q. Distance from Q to T is the same. Finally, we take the larger number of the distances between T to Q and Q to T as the distance between T and Q.

5   Experimental Evaluation

5.1   Experimental Settings

Experimental Environment. The Misty[1] is built based on *dapr*, and *Python3*. The framework is deployed on a local cluster with one twelve-core CPU (AMD Ryzen 9 3900X @ 3.80 GHz).

Datasets. T-Drive Taxi Trajectories is a sample of trajectories from the Microsoft Research T-Drive project, generated by over 10,000 taxicabs in a week in Beijing. The full dataset was used to suggest the practically fastest driving directions to normal drivers, recommend a passenger-pickup location for taxi drivers, enable dynamic taxi ride-sharing, glean the problematic design in a city's transportation network, and identify urban functional regions.

Experimental Metric. We mainly focus on evaluating the following metrics in our experiments:

- **Query Time:** Average query time of all continuous queries. In the experiments, we conduct continuous queries as repeatedly query one particular trajectory(e.g. trajectory with id 1) and takes the average time of all queries.
- **Insertion Time:** The insertion time of a new trajectory. In our experiments, due to the inconsistent length of real-world trajectories, we take the total insertion time of all trajectories as the insertion time.
- **Throughput:** Number of all trajectory points divided by insertion time.

Independent Variable. Next, we will list parameters in Misty.

- **Resolution** ρ. As mentioned in Sect. 4.2, each index partition is responsible for a particular area on the map. Its size is up to the resolution ρ. In the experiments, the minimum resolution ρ is called initial resolution. We choose 5 as the default initial resolution for balancing resource consumption and overall performance.
- **Max buffer size** M **and Insertion ratio** R. For max buffer size M and insertion ratio R, as mentioned in Sect. 4.2, these two parameters play a critical role when each partition inserts data from the buffer into the R-Tree. R should control the insertion. We choose 0.2 as the default value of R.
- **Splitting threshold** K. Lower K will lead to more frequent partition splitting causing higher system resource consumption such as CPU usage and network I/O. We choose 2000 as the default value of K.

---

[1] Source code available at https://github.com/LionTao/misty.

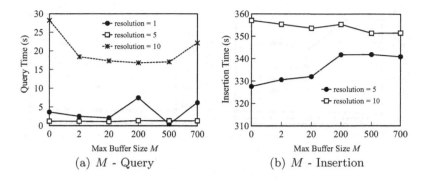

(a) M - Query   (b) M - Insertion

Fig. 4. Effect of M.

- **Query batch size b and Query threshold**. Query batch size controls distance computes batch size as described in Sect. 4.5. The query threshold controls the width of the trajectory corridor.

Baselines. We compare our solution with the naive R-Tree method and Spark. We put the R-Tree into our Dapr-based framework with K set to infinite, R set to 0, M set to 0 and initial resolution ρ set to 0. We compare the total data manipulation times and total insertion time of both methods. Comparison results are shown in Fig. 7. Due to the inflexibility of spark, we only compare query time between Spark and Misty.

5.2 Result Analysis

Effect of Max Buffer Size M. Figure 4(a) shows continuous query results during insertions as M increases. Our solution has very stable results when the initial index partition resolution is 5. Performance starts decreasing when the resolution is 10 because data distribution is too sparse. Network overhead is significantly high when the index module has a sparse data distribution.

Figure 4(b) shows the total data insertion time as M increases. We can see a significant time increment after M is above 200. This is because maintaining a big non-repeatable data set is time-consuming. With the default parameter, M larger than 400 will have no more effect on insertion time because buffer will insert into R-Tree before reaching buffer size limit. During experiments, we notice higher CPU and memory usage when the initial resolution goes higher. This is because more index partitions were created. When the initial resolution is 5, we can see a usage drop on both parts of the system when the M size is relatively larger. This is expected as a larger buffer size leads to fewer tree insertions.

Effect of Inserting Ratio R. Figure 5(a) shows continuous query results during insertions as tree insertion ratio R increases. Our solution has very stable results when the initial index partition resolution is 5 and 10 across all tests.

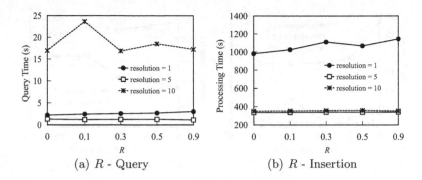

Fig. 5. Effect of R.

Performance decreases when resolution starts with 1 because partitions are busy splitting themselves.

Figure 5(b) shows the total data insertion time as R increases. Our solution has solid and stable results when the initial resolution is relatively high. When the initial resolution is 1, R starts to affect the overall performance because splitting partitions is more time-consuming and R controls buffer insertion which leads to partition splitting. When R is large, there is a large probability that the last insertion of the partition will significantly exceed the split threshold K and cause an immediate big splitting thus impacting the performance. Moreover, we can see both less CPU and memory usage when the initial resolution goes higher because when more index partitions were created, less data was inserted into each partition on average. When the initial resolution is 10, we can see a slight increase in memory because of memory overhead with a lot of active partitions. As to the CPU, more partitions at initial resolution 10 result in less splitting thus lowering the CPU usage.

Effect of Splitting Threshold K. Figure 6(c) and Fig. 6(a) show continuous query results during insertions as splitting threshold K increases with or without insertion buffer. We can see in Fig. 6(a), that having an insertion buffer has an edge over Fig. 6(c) in average query time when the initial resolution is 10. Figure 6(d) and Fig. 6(b) show total data insertion time as K increases. Comparing both figures, we can see that having an insertions buffer has a significant advantage on total insertion time when the initial resolution is 10. We can conclude that when there are plenty of index partitions, a decent amount of insertion buffer can benefit the data insertion.

Comparison with R-Tree. We compare our solution with the naive R-Tree method in terms of total insertion time and total numbers of R-Tree insertion operations. For our solution, we choose the default parameter as described in Sect. 5.1.

As shown in Fig. 7(a), our solution outperforms the R-Tree in all tests. To be specific, in larger dataset sizes such as 100 trajectories, our solution achieves up to 5× speedup in the insertion time test. This result shows the advantage

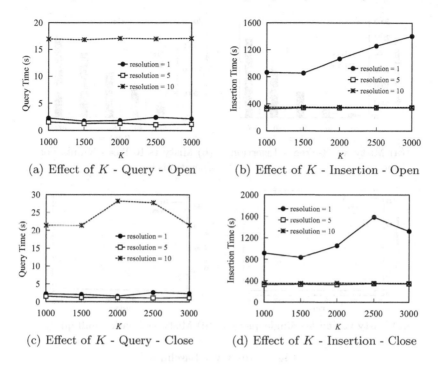

(a) Effect of K - Query - Open

(b) Effect of K - Insertion - Open

(c) Effect of K - Query - Close

(d) Effect of K - Insertion - Close

Fig. 6. Effect of K.

of using a buffer to cache incoming trajectory segments temporarily for a more efficient bulk load into the R-Tree. Also, the distributed manner of our solution gains advantages for being capable of concurrent insertion which leads to a more stable insertion time curve as the amount of data grows. Without the ability of parallel processing and the buffer, the baseline method must rebuild the entire R-Tree every time the data is updated. Benefiting from our distributed index module as discussed in Sect. 4.2, our solution has an edge over the baseline in terms of total insertion time.

Also, our solution has a clear advantage in the number of operations as shown in Fig. 7(b). With data size at 100, our solution with K set to 2000, R set to 0.2, M set to 500 and initial resolution ρ set to 5 takes only 60% of total R-Tree insertion to complete the test. This is because we use an insertion buffer while the baseline needs to rebuild R-Tree upon every data update. Thanks to a decent amount of max buffer size M and insertion ratio R as discussed in Sect. 4.2, our solution outperforms the baseline in terms of R-Tree operations.

Comparison with Spark. Figure 7(c) and Fig. 7(d) shows a comparison between the worst case of misty with default parameters and the spark implementation in terms of single trajectory query and full dataset trajectory query. For a single query, we use spark to join one dataset containing the target trajectory with another trajectory containing all trajectories. For the full query, we use spark to cross join the dataset containing all trajectories with itself.

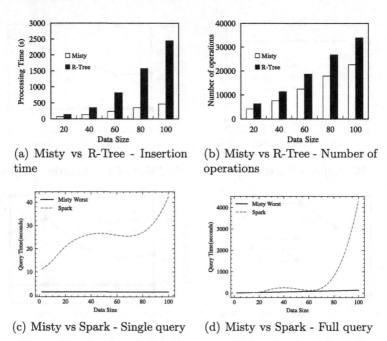

(a) Misty vs R-Tree - Insertion time

(b) Misty vs R-Tree - Number of operations

(c) Misty vs Spark - Single query

(d) Misty vs Spark - Full query

Fig. 7. Misty v.s. Baselines

As shown in Fig. 7(c), our solution shows stable performance while spark suffers performance loss as data size grows up. This result shows the advantage of Misty's distributed index. The index can help prune unnecessary trajectories thus greatly reducing the computation cost.

As shown in Fig. 7(d), our solution has a clear advantage over spark in the full query which is typically seen in high concurrency query scenarios. Without the proper pruning capability of an index, spark has to calculate the trajectory distance using brute force. As data sizes grow, spark must use drastically more time to complete the task. This result shows the advantage of the micro-service style that Misty adopts. When large amounts of data flood into the system, Misty is able to cope with it with ease.

6   Conclusions

This work presents a microservice-based real-time processing framework for streaming trajectory similarity search queries. Our framework is composed of the assembler, index, coordinator, and executor. The assembler and index enable a distributed trajectory to be ingested and indexed in our system. The coordinator and executor enable various query patterns including continuous queries. An extensive experimental study proves that Misty is quite effective for the indexing trajectories and corresponding queries compared to single node plain R-Tree and Spark. As a future direction, we are working on Misty's extension to spatial join and query plan optimization for higher throughput and more elastic index scaling.

Acknowledgment. This work was supported by National Natural Science Foundation of China under grant (No. 61802273, 62102277), Postdoctoral Science Foundation of China (No. 2020M681529), Natural Science Foundation of Jiangsu Province (BK2021070 3), China Science and Technology Plan Project of Suzhou (No. SYG202139), Postgraduate Research & Practice Innovation Program of Jiangsu Province (SJC X2_11342), Project Funded by the Priority Academic Program Development of Jiangsu Higher Education Institutions.

References

1. Beckmann, N., Kriegel, H., Schneider, R., Seeger, B.: The r*-tree: an efficient and robust access method for points and rectangles. In: Garcia-Molina, H., Jagadish, H.V. (eds.) Proceedings of the 1990 ACM SIGMOD International Conference on Management of Data, Atlantic City, NJ, USA, 23–25 May 1990, pp. 322–331 (1990). https://doi.org/10.1145/93597.98741,https://doi.org/10.1145/93597.98741
2. Cai, R., Lu, Z., Wang, L., Zhang, Z., Fur, T.Z.J., Winslett, M.: DITIR: distributed index for high throughput trajectory insertion and real-time temporal range query. Proc. VLDB Endow. **10**(12), 1865–1868 (2017). 10.14778/3137765.3137795, https://doi.org/10.14778/3137765.3137795
3. Fang, Z., Chen, L., Gao, Y., Pan, L., Jensen, C.S.: Dragoon: a hybrid and efficient big trajectory management system for offline and online analytics. VLDB J. **30**(2), 287–310 (2021)
4. Fu, A.W., Chan, P.M., Cheung, Y., Moon, Y.S.: Dynamic VP-tree indexing for n-nearest neighbor search given pair-wise distances. VLDB J. **9**(2), 154–173 (2000). https://doi.org/10.1007/PL00010672, https://doi.org/10.1007/PL00010672
5. Fu, Y.C., Hu, Z.Y., Guo, W., Zhou, D.R.: QR-tree: a hybrid spatial index structure. In: Proceedings of the 2003 International Conference on Machine Learning and Cybernetics (IEEE Cat. No.03EX693), vol. 1, pp. 459–463 (2003). https://doi.org/10.1109/ICMLC.2003.1264521
6. Kamel, I., Faloutsos, C.: Hilbert R-tree: an improved r-tree using fractals. In: Bocca, J.B., Jarke, M., Zaniolo, C. (eds.) VLDB'94, Proceedings of 20th International Conference on Very Large Data Bases, 12–15 September 1994, Santiago de Chile, Chile. pp. 500–509 (1994). https://www.vldb.org/conf/1994/P500.PDF
7. Leutenegger, S.T., Lopez, M.A., Edgington, J.: STR: a simple and efficient algorithm for R-tree packing. In: Proceedings 13th International Conference on Data Engineering, pp. 497–506. IEEE (1997)
8. Shang, Z., Li, G., Bao, Z.: DITA: distributed in-memory trajectory analytics. In: Proceedings of the 2018 International Conference on Management of Data, pp. 725–740 (2018)
9. Xie, D., Li, F., Phillips, J.M.: Distributed trajectory similarity search. Proc. VLDB Endow. **10**(11), 1478–1489 (2017)
10. Xie, D., Li, F., Yao, B., Li, G., Zhou, L., Guo, M.: Simba: efficient in-memory spatial analytics. In: Proceedings of the 2016 International Conference on Management of Data, SIGMOD 2016, pp. 1071–1085. Association for Computing Machinery, New York, NY, USA (2016). https://doi.org/10.1145/2882903.2915237,https://doi.org/10.1145/2882903.2915237

11. Yuan, H., Li, G.: Distributed in-memory trajectory similarity search and join on road network. In: 2019 IEEE 35th International Conference on Data Engineering (ICDE), pp. 1262–1273. IEEE (2019)
12. Zheng, B., Weng, L., Zhao, X., Zeng, K., Zhou, X., Jensen, C.S.: Repose: distributed top-k trajectory similarity search with local reference point tries. In: 2021 IEEE 37th International Conference on Data Engineering (ICDE), pp. 708–719. IEEE (2021)

BSDG: Anomaly Detection of Microservice Trace Based on Dual Graph Convolutional Neural Network

Kuanzhi Shi[1] , Jing Li[1(✉)] , Yuecan Liu[2], Yuzhu Chang[2], and Xuyang Li[2]

[1] College of Computer Science and Technology/College of Artificial Intelligence,
Nanjing University of Aeronautics and Astronautics, Nanjing, China
{skz16sz,lijing}@nuaa.edu.cn
[2] State Grid Information & Telecommunication Branch, Beijing, China

Abstract. Microservice architecture has been widely used by more and more developers in recent years. Accurate anomaly detection is crucial for system maintenance. Trace data can reflect the microservice dependency relationship and response time, which has been adopted for microservice anomaly detection now. However, due to the lack of unification modeling framework of response time and call path, the performance of anomaly detection degrades, and difficult to adapt to downstream tasks. To address the above issues, we propose BSDG, a trace anomaly detection method based on a dual graph convolutional neural network (dual-GCN). First, BSDG extracts the microservice call dependencies, combing the learnable node attributes generated by Bi-directional Long Short-Term Memory(BiLSTM) to build an attribute dependency graph combined response time and call path. Then, a self-attention mapping graph is constructed and we use a dualGCN with mutual attention to generate effective feature embedding representation. Finally, BSDG adopts a multilayer perceptron with a new classification loss function to train the model in an end-to-end way for anomaly detection. The experimental results on public benchmarks show that the proposed BDSG outperforms baseline methods. We also conduct experiments on our constructed microservice trace dataset to validate the robustness of BSDG. Experiments show that the BSDG outperforms existing methods in microservice trace anomaly detection.

Keywords: Microservices · Trace · dualGCN · Anomaly detection

1 Introduction

With the development of information technology, microservice have been widely used for developing large-scale applications in cloud environments due to their advantages of flexibility. Microservice systems consisting of hundreds or thousands of cooperative services perhaps lead to unstable microservice performance,

J. Troya et al. (Eds.): ICSOC 2022, LNCS 13740, pp. 171–185, 2022.
https://doi.org/10.1007/978-3-031-20984-0_12

so an accurate and robust method for microservice anomaly detection is urgently needed. Recently, anomaly detection based on trace has received more and more attention because it can better reflect the dependencies between response time and call path. Most current microservice trace anomaly detection methods are based on response time [1–3], call path [4–7], as well as response time and call path anomalies [8–12].The response time anomaly detection method [1–3] judges whether the response time of each microservice is abnormal by analyzing whether it conforms to the normal distribution. Since the response time is also affected by the microservices it invokes, this type of method is prone to cause the detection effect to be poor. The call path anomaly detection method [4–7] compares the calling sequence of each node in the trace with the entire traces to determine trace anomaly, but it can only be used to detect structural anomalies in the microservice trace. Response time and call path anomaly detection method [8–12] consider these two cases comprehensively, however, most of the existing methods mainly model them in different stages. For example, TraceAnomaly [11] starts to perform anomaly detection on the call path to find the abnormal trace, then continues to find the abnormal span according to the response time anomaly detection. Therefore, this kind of anomaly detection result mainly depends on the previous step, which will bring error accumulation. In summary, microservice anomaly detection based on response time and call path mainly face the following two challenges:

(1) How to express the relationship between response time and the call path effectively.

As shown in Fig. 1(a) and (b), the average response time and response time distribution of microservice calls under different call paths are listed in the normal operation of the microservice system. Because the calling and request resources between microservices differ, there will be large response time fluctuations when calling the same microservice. Therefore, how to provide a unified framework to model the information between them is a challenge.

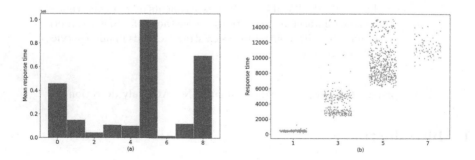

Fig. 1. The relationship between response time and call path.

(2) How to effectively deal with the problem of the missing call paths of trace.

Since the microservices cooperate to complete tasks through remote calls, when an anomaly occurs, it may occur that the span is missing, causing its sub-calls to be broken in the trace, resulting in the lack of the call paths of the trace. In this way, it is difficult for us to construct a complete trace topology graph based on the existing call relationship between spans. If we remove such samples directly and ignore the impact of missing call paths, it will lead to poor performance of the model. Therefore, how to effectively deal with the missing call paths of the trace is another challenge.

To address the above two challenges, we propose a microservice trace anomaly detection method BSDG based on dualGCN. First, it extracts the call dependency between spans in the trace, combines the node attributes based on BiLSTM, constructs the attribute dependency graph based on response time and call path, and then uses the self-attention mechanism to generate a self-attention mapping graph. Finally, the dualGCN with mutual attention is used to fuse the node attribute dependence and the self-attention node mapping.

Our contributions of this paper are summarized as follows.

(1) We propose a method for generating trace embedded representation of node attributes based on BiLSTM. By constructing attribute dependency graphs and self-attention mapping graphs, a unified modeling framework with effective integration of microservice response time and call paths is achieved.

(2) We first apply dualGCN to the microservice trace anomaly detection. Through the information propagation of the multi-layer dualGCN and the fusion mechanism based on mutual attention, the effective feature embedding representation performance of the trace is generated.

(3) Our Multi-point fault injection (MPFI) microservice trace dataset is constructed in the cloud environment, and the accuracy and robustness of the anomaly detection algorithm proposed in this paper are validated.

2   BSDG

Trace data can be used for microservice anomaly detection. Trace data consists of multiple traces. Each trace composed of span data blocks is a set of call trees. Span is used to storing information such as operation name, timestamp, span ID, response time and status code. BSDG models microservice trace anomaly detection as a multi-dimensional binary classification problem. BSDG first parses trace and generates node attributes through BiLSTM to build an attribute dependency graph. Then, uses the self-attention mechanism to construct the self-attention graph, aggregates the unified information representation by the dualCNN, and finally completes the anomaly detection through the classification module. The BSDG framework is shown in Fig. 2.

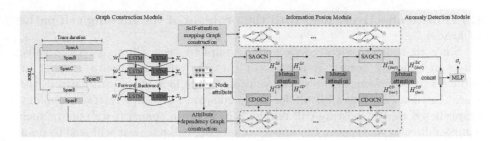

Fig. 2. The framework of the proposed BSDG.

2.1 Graph Construction Module

Trace with timestamp can be expressed as $T_i = \left[s_1^i, s_2^i, \ldots, s_N^i\right], i \in \{1, \ldots, M\}$, where T_i denotes the ith trace, s_j^i is the jth span, and N is the length of T_i. The response time is normalized by Min-max normalization as $S_{t,scaled} = \frac{S_t - \min(S)}{\max(S) - \min(S)}$ is used to process the response time, where $\max(S)$ and $\min(S)$ is the maximum and minimum values of response time in span, and S_t is the response time of span at time t. Other non-numeric fields use one-hot encoding, and the above data constitutes a node performance vector $p_j^i \in \mathbb{R}^d$. To model the relationship between the current span and its history, each trace is divided using sliding windows technique. The divided traces are represented as $T_i' = \left[w_1^i, w_2^i, \ldots, w_N^i\right]$, where $w_j^i = \left[p_{j-l}^i, p_{j-l+1}^i, \ldots, p_j^i\right]$ is a sliding window data, and l is the size of sliding window.

Node Attribute Generation. To overcome the limitations of LSTM, we use BiLSTM to capture the bidirectional features of node performance representation $P = \{p_1^i, p_2^i, \ldots p_n^i\}$, consisting of two LSTM hidden layers with opposite input directions. In this module, previous and future information can be utilized in the output layer to generate learnable node attributes. For a given input sample $T_i' = \left[w_1^i, w_2^i, \ldots, w_N^i\right]$, we use a BiLSTM to mine the important node attribute information and output the corresponding hidden layer state variables $\overrightarrow{h}(t)$ and $\overleftarrow{h}(t)$. Concatenate them to get node attributes $X = \{x_1^i, x_2^i, \ldots x_N^i\}$ as follows:

$$X = \mathrm{Concat}(\overrightarrow{h}(t), \overleftarrow{h}(t)) \tag{1}$$

Attribute Dependency Graph Construction. Combined with the span ID, the call dependencies between span and the node attributes, we construct the attribute dependency graph $\mathcal{G}_{AD} = < V, A^{dep}, X >$, where V denotes the set of vertices composed of span IDs, $A^{dep} \in \mathbb{R}^{N \times N}$ denotes an adjacency matrix, formed by the calling relationship between spans, X is the node attributes of each node in graph $\mathcal{G}_{AD}$.

Self-attention Mapping Graph Construction. We use the self-attention mechanism to calculate the node attribute similarity by inputting the node attributes into two linear layers separately, and then generate the self-attention mapping matrix $A^{sam} \in \mathbb{R}^{N \times N}$:

$$A^{sam} = \text{softmax}(\frac{(W_Q X + b_Q) \times (W_K X + b_K)^{\mathrm{T}}}{\sqrt{N}}) \tag{2}$$

where W_Q and W_K are the weights matrix of the linear layer, b_Q and b_K are the bias of the linear layer, N is the number of input nodes. Moreover, we use the span ID set, A^{sam} and X to construct the self-attention mapping graph $\mathcal{G}_{SA} =< V, A^{sam}, X >$.

We introduce an orthogonal regularization [13] to ensure the self-attention mapping matrix is as orthogonal as possible by computing the Frobenius norm of $A^{sam}(A^{sam})^T$ and unit matrix.

$$R_O = \frac{\|A^{sam}(A^{sam})^{\mathrm{T}} - I\|_F}{N} \tag{3}$$

where I is the unit matrix and $\| \bullet \|_F$ denotes the Frobenius norm.

2.2   Information Fusion Module

Given attribute graph $\mathcal{G}_{AD}$ and self-attention mapping graph $\mathcal{G}_{SA}$, we aim to generate a new embedding representation fusing above information. We address this problem using dualGCN architecture composed with self-adaptive based GCN(SAGCN), call-dependent based GCN(CDGCN) and mutual attention block. In addition, we use differential regularization [13] for A^{sam} in SAGCN to encourage the SAGCN to capture the node feature information that cannot be captured by the CDGCN.

CDGCN Block. The CDGCN uses a layer-by-layer propagation multilayer graph convolutional neural network(GCN) to aggregate global information between node attributes in the attribute dependency graph based on the true dependency relationships of A^{dep} to enhance the ability to accurately capture the dependency relationships between node attributes. Specifically, the graph convolutional layer of CDGCN is based on the following Equation:

$$H^{CD}_{(l+1)} = \sigma \left(A^{\tilde{d}ep} H^{CD}_{(l)} W_{(l)} \right) \tag{4}$$

where $\tilde{A}^{dep} = \tilde{D}^{-\frac{1}{2}}(A^{dep} + I)\tilde{D}^{-\frac{1}{2}}$ denotes the symmetrically normalized adjacency matrix with self-loops, $H^{CD}_{(l)} \in \mathbb{R}^{N \times d}$ is the node representation matrix in l^{th} layer of the CDGCN, $H^{CD}_{(0)} = X$, $W_{(l)}$ is a trainable weight matrix in l^{th} layer and σ is the ReLU activation function.

SAGCN Block. Based on the different weights of neighbor nodes in A^{sam}, SAGCN uses another GCN to capture the information between the attributes of each node in the self-attention mapping graph to capture additional information that cannot be extracted from CDGCN. Specifically, the graph convolutional layer of SAGCN is based on the following Equation:

$$H_{(l+1)}^{SA} = \sigma \left(A^{s\tilde{a}m} H_{(l)}^{SA} W_{(l)} \right) \tag{5}$$

where $\tilde{A}^{sam} = \tilde{D}^{-\frac{1}{2}}(A^{sam} + I)\tilde{D}^{-\frac{1}{2}}$ denotes the symmetrically normalized adjacency matrix with self-loops, $H_{(l)}^{SA} \in \mathbb{R}^{N \times d}$ is the node representation matrix in l^{th} layer of the SAGCN, $H_{(0)}^{SA} = X$.

Mutual Attention Block. Cross-modality information between CDGCN and SAGCN in BSDG brings richer information. However, only concatenating them for calculations will lose much complementary information, and this information perhaps has a significant effect on anomaly detection. So, we use the mutual attention block of dualGCN to improve the fusion of information.

We first define the mutual attention operator between matrix $A \in \mathbb{R}^{N \times d}$ and $B \in \mathbb{R}^{N \times N}$ as: $MutualAtt(A, B) = w^T \tanh(W_1 A + W_2 B) + soft \max(A W_3 B^T)$, and W is the weight matrix. Second, we calculate the new output $H_{(l)}^{SA'}$ and $H_{(l)}^{CD'}$ of lth dualGCN using $H_{(l)}^{SA'} = MutualAtt(H_{(l)}^{SA}, H_{(l)}^{CD})H_{(l)}^{CD}$ and $H_{(l)}^{CD'} = MutualAtt(H_{(l)}^{CD}, H_{(l)}^{SA})H_{(l)}^{SA}$ based on mutual attention operator. This mutual attention block can help achieve effective fusion between node attribute dependencies and self-attention mapping features through the exchange of node attribute features between CDGCN and SAGCN.

Finally, in order to make SAGCN and CDGCN have more differentiated feature representation, we use a differential regularizer to calculate the difference between A^{sam} and A^{dep} using the Frobenius norm, the inverse of the Frobenius norm is taken as the final differential regularization term R_D.

$$R_D = \frac{N}{\|A^{sam} - A^{dep}\|_F} \tag{6}$$

2.3   Anomaly Detection Module

The last layer output of dualGCN from CDGCN and SAGCN are concatenated to obtain the node attribute feature representation $\tilde{H} = \text{Concat}(H_{(last)}^{CD'}, H_{(last)}^{SA'})$.

Then $\tilde{H}$ is input to the multilayer perceptron (MLP) to complete anomaly detection. We use a linear mapping followed by a non-linear activation function as:

$$a_i = \sigma(w_f \tilde{H} + b_f) \tag{7}$$

where w_f and b_f are the weights and bias parameters of MLP, σ is the softmax activation function, a_i is the ith sample predicted anomaly probability. We use the cross-entropy loss function widely used defined l_C as:

$$l_c = -\frac{1}{N} \sum_i^N [y_i \cdot \log(a_i) + (1 - y_i) \cdot \log(1 - a_i)] \tag{8}$$

where y_i is the true label of span samples, and N denotes the total number of span samples. Then the combined l_C, R_O and R_D to get the total loss function:

$$l_T = l_C + \lambda_1 R_D + \lambda_2 R_O \tag{9}$$

where λ_1 and λ_2 denote the regularization coefficients.

3   Experimental Results and Analysis

3.1   Data Set Description

We conduct experiments on datasets of TTFI[1], AIOps2020[2] and MPFI. Among them, TTFI comes from TLFD [10], which collected the trace data by simulating fault injection to the Train Ticket[3] microservice application. AIOps2020 comes from the International AIOps Challenge, which provides real production data of a large service provider. MPFI is a data set constructed used for our paper by simulating multi-point failure. We summarize their characteristics in Table 1 and provide the example of microservice trace in Table 2.

TTFI consists of eight fault files according to the injected fault type, which includes container JVM failures, container CPU utilization failures, and microservice or container networking type failures. AIOps2020 monitors the calling relationship and performance metrics between microservices in the application system and divides multiple fault files by date. The types of failures include container CPU utilization failures, container memory utilization failures, database type failures, and host or container network type failures. Compared with the TTFI, the failure distribution in the AIOps2020 is more random and diverse.

During the construction of the MPFI, we first deploy the Train Ticket microservice in the cloud environment using Kubernetes[4], and use Chaosblade[5] to inject faults into the microservice and the container where it is located, mainly including increasing the communication delay between microservices, improve the random packet loss rate of microservices, accidentally delete microservices, suspend the container where the microservice is located, and exhaust the load

---

[1] https://github.com/BIGXT/TTFI.
[2] https://github.com/NetManAIOps/AIOps-Challenge-2020-Data.
[3] https://github.com/FudanSELab/train-ticket.
[4] https://Kubernetes.io/.
[5] https://github.com/chaosblade-io.

resources of the node pool where the microservice is located. Finally, the open-source distributed tracing system Jaeger[6] based on the OpenTracing[7] protocol, is used to collect trace data and save it in the Elasticsearch[8] database.

Table 1. Dataset Statistics.

Dataset	Train	Validation	Test	Dimensions	Anomalies(%)
TTFI	183682	61227	61228	12	0.410
AIOps	7482487	2494162	2494164	9	0.106
MPFI	7294	2431	2433	12	1.349

Table 2. Example of Microservice Trace.

TraceID	SpanID	ParentSpanID	Response time	ServiceName	OperationName	Kind
100f3f1c3fae86f1a	a9637b3cb377a652	None	8123	ts-ui-dashboard	ts-ui-dashboard	server
100f3f1c3fae86f1a	7aeb835cc7a7992a	a9637b3cb377a652	7581	ts-ui-dashboard	ts-order-service	client
100f3f1c3fae86f1a	22201ee383adf0ef	7aeb835cc7a7992a	6940	ts-order-service	ts-order-service	client
100f3f1c3fae86f1a	28bfc57affae0e2d	22201ee383adf0ef	2454	ts-order-service	ts-station-service	client
100f3f1c3fae86f1a	d4d1eb7f838579f0	28bfc57affae0e2d	2044	ts-station-service	ts-station-service	client

3.2 Baseline Methods for Anomaly Detection

We select the current state-of-the-art TLFD [10], Multimodal LSTM [9] and Deeplog [5] in microservice trace anomaly detection as baseline comparison methods. TLFD is a two-stage modeling method based on call path and response time. It first detects whether there is an abnormal call path by calculating the similarity between the trace and the normal trace. If there exists an anomaly, then it uses statistical methods to determine whether there is an abnormal response time. Multimodal LSTM is a typical unified modeling method of call path and response time. By using multimodal LSTM to learn the properties of response time and call path in the normal trace, and then judge whether there is an anomaly by whether the trace mode deviates from the normal mode. Deeplog is a widely used deep learning anomaly detection algorithm, which uses the LSTM model to detect call path anomalies in microservice anomaly detection.

We use Precision, Recall and the F1-score as measures of detection effectiveness. Precision represents the proportion of true anomalies among the detected anomalies, and recall represents the proportion of all true anomalies marked as anomalies by the model. The F1-Score, as shown in Equation (10), is a performance measure that combines precision and recall.

$$F1 = \frac{2 \times \text{Precision} \times \text{Recall}}{\text{Precision} + \text{Recall}} \tag{10}$$

---

[6] https://www.jaegertracing.io/.
[7] https://opentracing.io/.
[8] https://www.elastic.co/.

3.3   Experimental Setup

During training, we tune the hyperparameters of competing models and our model with grid search by early stopping on the validation set. In general, the size of the window is set to 10. The dualGCN layers are set to 4. The learning rate is 0.001. The regularized factors L1 and L2 are 0.1. The hyper-parameters are summarized in Table 3.

Table 3. Hyperparameter configurations of BSDG.

Hyperparameter	Value
Window sizes	10
dualGCN layers	4
Learning rate	0.001
L1&L2	0.1
Early Stopping epochs	10

3.4   Overall Performance

We show the overall performance empirical results of three datasets in Tables 4, 5 and 6. As can be seen in Table 4, BSDG has the average highest precision, recall and F1-score on the TTFI. The overall performance of BSDG on eight fault files is 6.6% higher than that of Multimodal LSTM, and the performance of TLFD is slightly worse, mainly because TLFD does not fully consider the relationship between the call path and response time. Multimodal LSTM also does not deeply explore this correlation. The overall performance is lower than BSDG, which validated the superiority of our method based on unified modeling in microservice anomaly detection.

Table 4. Overall performance results on TTFI. P:Precision, R: Recall, F1: F1-score.The best P,R and F1 scores are highlighted in bold.

Fault File	TLFD			BSDG			Multimodal LSTM			Deeplog		
	P	R	F1	P	R	F1	P	R	F1	P	R	F1
F1	0.907	0.888	0.887	**0.999**	0.964	**0.975**	0.951	0.957	0.954	0.554	0.913	0.700
F2	0.979	0.979	0.979	**0.987**	1.0	**0.993**	0.881	0.904	0.892	0.522	0.833	0.642
F3	0.921	**0.907**	0.906	0.933	0.902	**0.917**	**0.956**	0.792	0.866	0.527	0.878	0.659
F4	0.953	0.949	0.949	**0.990**	1.0	**0.999**	0.905	0.776	0.835	0.542	0.748	0.629
F5	0.963	0.960	0.960	**0.997**	1.0	**0.990**	0.935	0.889	0.911	0.531	0.852	0.654
F6	0.832	0.747	0.729	**0.958**	0.999	**0.979**	0.912	0.984	0.947	0.593	0.953	0.731
F7	0.914	0.906	0.906	**0.980**	1.0	**0.990**	0.920	0.992	0.955	0.593	0.953	0.731
F8	0.915	0.890	0.886	**0.959**	1.0	**0.979**	0.860	1.0	0.920	0.520	1.0	0.684
Average	0.915	0.890	0.886	**0.975**	**0.983**	**0.978**	0.915	0.912	0.910	0.546	0.891	0.679

Table 5. Overall performance results on AIOps2020.

Fault File	BSDG			Multimodal LSTM			Deeplog		
	P	R	F1	P	R	F1	P	R	F1
05_23	**0.885**	**0.990**	**0.935**	0.823	0.500	0.623	0.587	0.440	0.502
05_24	**0.973**	**0.998**	**0.986**	0.837	0.513	0.636	0.549	0.417	0.474
05_25	**0.998**	**1.0**	**0.999**	0.842	0.501	0.631	0.869	0.343	0.492
05_26	**0.960**	**0.828**	**0.889**	0.797	0.534	0.640	0.375	0.742	0.498
05_27	**0.940**	**0.972**	**0.956**	0.840	0.521	0.643	0.754	0.445	0.559
Average	**0.951**	**0.958**	**0.953**	0.828	0.5138	0.635	0.627	0.477	0.505

Table 5 shows the performance comparison of other BSDG methods on the AIOps2020 dataset. It can be seen that Multimodal LSTM and Deeplog have poor performance, while BSDG is better than them in all metrics.

To further verify the performance of BSDG, experiments are conducted on our MPFI dataset with multi-point fault. As can be seen from Table 6, BSDG still achieves the average performance of 0.856 on this complex dataset, outperforming other methods.

Table 6. Overall performance results on MPFI.

Method	P	R	F1
BSDG	**0.856**	**0.857**	**0.856**
Multimodal LSTM	0.574	0.710	0.634
Deeplog	0.671	0.464	0.548

3.5   Parameter Sensitivity Analysis

In order to test the robustness of our method to hyperparameters, we designed a parameter sensitivity analysis experiment of BSDG, the results are shown in Fig. 3.

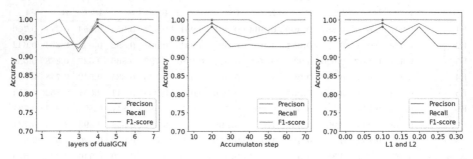

Fig. 3. Anomaly detection accuracy in terms of precision, recall, and F1-scoreon different parameter setups

It can be seen that the performance of BSDG will fluctuate as the number of layers of dualGCN increases. When the number of layers of dualGCN is 4, BSDG achieves the best performance. The change in the accumulation step will affect the model training time and the amplitude of the training oscillation. When the accumulation step is 20, BSDG has the best performance. When the regularization coefficients L1 and L2 are 0.1, the performance of BSDG is the best.

3.6   Root Cause Localization Experiment

In order to use the results of BSDG anomaly detection for the microservice fault root cause location task, we use the Pagerank algorithm [14], combined with the correlation probability model [15], to design a BSDG-based microservice root cause location algorithm. The experimental results are shown in Table 7.

Table 7. Performance of BSDG anomaly detection results on root cause localization algorithm. Top-k accuracy (Top@k) refers to the probability that the root causes are included in the top-k results.

Dataset	Top@1	Top@2	Top@3	Top@4
TTFI	0.75	0.875	1.0	1.0
AIOps	0.846	0.846	0.923	1.0
MPFI	0.727	0.818	0.909	0.909

3.7   Ablation Study

To study the relative importance of each component of BSDG, we set up two variant methods of BSDG. That is Only-BiLSTM and Only BiLSTM&CDGCN. Only-BiLSTM represents the model in BSDG using only the node attribute information of the trace. Only BiLSTM&CDGCN represents the model using only attribute dependency graphs in BSDG. As shown in Fig. 4, the experimental results show that Only-BiLSTM and BiLSTM&CDGCN will degrade the performance of BSDG, which validates the necessity of unified modeling based on call path and response time.

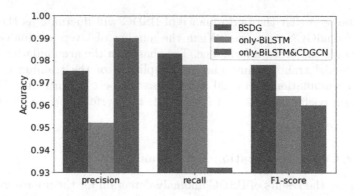

Fig. 4. Ablation study on BSDG.

4   Related Work

4.1   Microservice Trace Anomaly Detection

Most anomaly detection methods are based on response time and call path modeling in a separate way. Anomaly detection based on response time mainly judges the anomaly according to whether the response time of each microservice conforms to the normal response time distribution. Zhang [1] proposed a supervised learning-based anomaly detection method that uses a convolutional neural network combined with LSTM to predict the probability of each microservice service quality degradation. However, it only focuses on response time anomalies and does not consider call path anomalies. Nedelkoski [2] proposed an unsupervised deep Bayesian network model based on AEVB to detect the anomaly response time of trace. This method needs to train a model for each microservice, and there are problems such as high training overhead. Aiming at the fact that the response time is easily affected by the competition of system resources and fluctuates. Bogatinovsk [4] proposed a method based on self-supervised learning through training an autoencoder to reconstruct random masked events in the input trace. When detected, to predict the events that may occur at each location in the trace according to the reconstruction results, but this method can only detect structural anomalies in the microservice trace. Du [5] proposed the Deeplog method, which uses the template prediction instead of the reconstruction method for anomaly detection. The above anomaly detection methods based on separate modeling of response time and call path cannot simultaneously consider the relationship between response time and call path, resulting in performance degradation.

The other anomaly detection methods are based on unified modeling of response time and call path. To improve the performance of anomaly detection, unified modeling based on response time and call path can be used for anomaly detection of microservice trace. Nedelkoski [9] proposed a multimodal LSTM anomaly detection method, but it ignores the context of the event sequence in the trace, and the model structure cannot effectively learn the correlation between the microservice call path and response time. Chen [10] proposed TLFD as a two-stage modeling method based on the call path and response time by calculating the similarity between trace and normal trace to detect whether there is an anomaly call path, if there exits anomaly, use statistical methods to judge whether there is an anomaly response time, but this method does not consider the relationship between the response time and the call path, and unable to detect anomalies where delays in the application cause unexpected increases in response time for some requests. Liu [11] proposed an unsupervised anomaly detection method TraceAnomaly based on a deep Bayesian network and knowledge base of normal call paths, but this knowledge base type method has problems such as high computational complexity and long detection time. The above-mentioned methods based on unified modeling of response time and call path lack effective processing and deep integration of response time and call path, resulting in low model detection performance and difficulty in adapting to downstream tasks such as microservice fault location. So we propose a microservice trace anomaly detection model BSDG that can perform unified modeling and deep integration of response time and call path.

4.2   Graph Neural Networks

In recent years, graph neural networks (GNN) [16] have attracted a lot of attention when dealing with anomaly detection tasks. GNN have also been applied in microservice anomaly detection. Zhang [17] constructed a trace event graph (TEG) for trace data and log events, using a gated graph neural networks (GGNNs) to fuse the multi-source information. Recently, Xu [12] also applied GNN to anomaly detection, using a graph attention network to aggregate influence relationships between nodes, and finally judges whether a node is an anomaly by the deviation between the predicted value and actual value. However, these methods suffer from fixed graph structure and the construction method is relatively in a single form. Different from GNN, dualGCN models the global context of the input features in a single general framework. After inference, the perceptual features of the two complementary relationships are further fused to form a refined feature and can be further provided to the next layer for specific tasks, and many research results have emerged in different fields. Li [13] considered the complementary information of syntactic structure and semantic correlation in the process of sentiment analysis, and proposed a dualGCN to integrate the information. Ma [19] designed a dualGCN to predict cancer drug response models. Sun [20] designed a dual dynamic graph convolutional neural network (DDGCN) to learn the representation of dynamic events in a fine-grained way for better detection of rumors. We will take full advantage of dualGCN to achieve unified modeling of the trace response time and call path relationship.

5   Summary

We propose BSDG, a microservice trace anomaly detection method based on dualGCN in this paper. BiLSTM is used to generate node attribute representation, and a trace attribute dependency graph and self-attention mapping are constructed tounified modeling microservice response time and call path. Then, through the propagation of the multi-layer dualCNN and information fusion based on the mutual attention, the effective feature embedding representation of microservice trace is generated, and then detect the anomalies using multi-layer perceptron. Finally, extensive experiments are conducted on three datasets, TTFI, AIOps and our MPFI. Compared with the three state-of-the-art trace anomaly detection methods TLFD, MultimodalTrace and Deeplog, BSDG has superior performance in microservice trace anomaly detection.

Acknowledgements. This work was supported by the Science and Technology Program of State Grid Corporation of China under Grant 5700-202152169A-0-0-00.

References

1. Gan, Y., Zhang, Y., Hu, K., Cheng, D., He, Y., Pancholi, M., Delimitrou, C.: Seer: leveraging big data to navigate the complexity of performance debugging in cloud microservices. In: Proceedings of the Twenty-Fourth International Conference on Architectural Support for Programming Languages and Operating Systems, pp. 19–33 (2019)
2. Nedelkoski, S., Cardoso, J., Kao, O.: Anomaly detection and classification using distributed tracing and deep learning. In: 2019 19th IEEE/ACM International Symposium on Cluster, Cloud and Grid Computing (CCGRID), pp. 241–250. IEEE (2019)
3. Samir, A., Pahl, C.: DLA: detecting and localizing anomalies in containerized microservice architectures using markov models. In: 2019 7th International Conference on Future Internet of Things and Cloud (FiCloud), pp. 205–213. IEEE (2019)
4. Bogatinovski, J., Nedelkoski, S., Cardoso, J., Kao, O.: Self-supervised anomaly detection from distributed traces. In: 2020 IEEE/ACM 13th International Conference on Utility and Cloud Computing (UCC), pp. 342–347. IEEE (2020)
5. Du, M., Li, F., Zheng, G., Srikumar, V.: DeepLog: anomaly detection and diagnosis from system logs through deep learning. In: Proceedings of the 2017 ACM SIGSAC Conference on Computer and Communications Security, pp. 1285–1298 (2017)
6. Meng, L., Ji, F., Sun, Y., Wang, T.: Detecting anomalies in microservices with execution trace comparison. Future Gener. Comput. Syst. **116**, 291–301 (2021)
7. Wang, T., Zhang, W., Xu, J., Gu, Z.: Workflow-aware automatic fault diagnosis for microservice-based applications with statistics. IEEE Trans. Netw. Serv. Manag. **17**(4), 2350–2363 (2020)
8. Zhou, X., et al.: Latent error prediction and fault localization for microservice applications by learning from system trace logs. In: Proceedings of the 2019 27th ACM Joint Meeting on European Software Engineering Conference and Symposium on the Foundations of Software Engineering, pp. 683–694 (2019)

9. Nedelkoski, S., Cardoso, J., Kao, O.: Anomaly detection from system tracing data using multimodal deep learning. In: 2019 IEEE 12th International Conference on Cloud Computing (CLOUD), pp. 179–186. IEEE (2019)

10. Chen, H., Wei, K., Li, A., Wang, T., Zhang, W.: Trace-based intelligent fault diagnosis for microservices with deep learning. In: 2021 IEEE 45th Annual Computers, Software, and Applications Conference (COMPSAC), pp. 884–893. IEEE (2021)

11. Liu, P., et al.: Unsupervised detection of microservice trace anomalies through service-level deep Bayesian networks. In: 2020 IEEE 31st International Symposium on Software Reliability Engineering (ISSRE), pp. 48–58. IEEE (2020)

12. Xu, P., Gao, X., Zhang, Z.: Graph neural network-based anomaly detection for trace of microservices. Available at SSRN 4111928

13. Li, R., Chen, H., Feng, F., Ma, Z., Wang, X., Hovy, E.: Dual graph convolutional networks for aspect-based sentiment analysis. In: Proceedings of the 59th Annual Meeting of the Association for Computational Linguistics and the 11th International Joint Conference on Natural Language Processing (Volume 1: Long Papers), pp. 6319–6329 (2021)

14. Mariani, L., Monni, C., Pezzé, M., Riganelli, O., Xin, R.: Localizing faults in cloud systems. In: 2018 IEEE 11th International Conference on Software Testing, Verification and Validation (ICST), pp. 262–273. IEEE (2018)

15. Li, Z., et al.: Practical root cause localization for microservice systems via trace analysis. In: 2021 IEEE/ACM 29th International Symposium on Quality of Service (IWQOS), pp. 1–10. IEEE (2021)

16. Deng, A., Hooi, B.: Graph neural network-based anomaly detection in multivariate time series. In: Proceedings of the AAAI Conference on Artificial Intelligence, vol. 35, pp. 4027–4035 (2021)

17. Zhang, C., et al.: DeepTraLog: trace-log combined microservice anomaly detection through graph-based deep learning (2022)

18. Kipf, T.N., Welling, M.: Semi-supervised classification with graph convolutional networks. arXiv preprint arXiv:1609.02907 (2016)

19. Ma, T., Liu, Q., Li, H., Zhou, M., Jiang, R., Zhang, X.: DualGCN: a dual graph convolutional network model to predict cancer drug response. BMC Bioinform. 23(4), 1–13 (2022)

20. Sun, M., Zhang, X., Zheng, J., Ma, G.: DDGCN: dual dynamic graph convolutional networks for rumor detection on social media (2022)

SCORE: A Resource-Efficient Microservice Orchestration Model Based on Spectral Clustering in Edge Computing

Ning Li[1]([✉])[iD], Yusong Tan[1]([✉])[iD], Xiaochuan Wang[1][iD], Bao Li[1][iD], and Jun Luo[2][iD]

[1] School of Computer, National University of Defense Technology, Changsha 410073, China
lining20@nudt.edu.cn
[2] Tianjin Institute of Advanced Technology, Tianjin 300450, China

Abstract. Microservices architecture has an essential characteristic of loose coupling compared to traditional monolithic applications, allowing applications to be created, updated, and extended independently. With lightweight virtualization technologies, such as container, microservices-based applications can be widely deployed to the edge of the network. However, challenges of deploying microservice in edge come from the contradiction between the latency sensitivity of applications and limited node resources. We propose a microservice orchestration model(SCORE) for edge scenarios that enable microservice scheduling based on spectrum clustering(MSSC) and dynamic resource allocation under multi-dimension constraints based on the sliding window(SW) mechanism. MSSC significantly reduces the cross-node communication traffic between microservices by portraying the dependencies between microservices through a graph and then using spectral clustering to map microservices to edge nodes. At the same time, the process of cluster scaling under multi-dimension provides more fine-grained resource allocation for microservices and improves resource utilization while ensuring service-level performance objectives(SLOs). The experimental results indicate that our approach reduces the inter-node communication traffic by 17.7% compared to baseline, and the overall average memory requested for processing a single request is 19.4% and 45.8% of baseline, respectively.

Keywords: Microservice · Resource allocation · Edge computing · Scheduling · Spectral clustering

1 Introduction

With the large-scale deployment of 5G cellular networks and the widespread use of intelligent devices at the edge, more and more computing tasks are being sunk to the network's edge. Edge devices have also shifted from a single role as data consumers to a dual role as producers and consumers of data.

© The Author(s), under exclusive license to Springer Nature Switzerland AG 2022
J. Troya et al. (Eds.): ICSOC 2022, LNCS 13740, pp. 186–202, 2022.
https://doi.org/10.1007/978-3-031-20984-0_13

Performing tasks on edge devices save bandwidth resources and protect privacy, and reduces response time [15, 24, 30]. However, edge environments are often characterized by constrained resources, dynamic network changes, and frequent application iterations. Traditional SOA architecture-based applications have been unable to bridge the gap between application requirements and environmental characteristics. In this case, microservices architecture-based applications are widely deployed in edge computing. It decouples monolithic applications into independent microservice components [12, 18], and through container technology, the entire lifecycle of microservices can be independently managed and rapidly iterated with minimal resource consumption. With the dramatic increase in microservices, orchestrating and managing containers has become more complex. There are a variety of mature container orchestration tools, such as Google's open-source project Kubernetes [1], Docker Swarm [2] and Open-Shift [3], etc. Kubernetes, the most mature container orchestration engine, is widely deployed in data centers. Its default scheduling algorithm includes two phases, *Predicates*, and *Priorities*, where nodes that do not meet the requirements can be filtered out in the *Predicates* phase, and then the remaining nodes are scored and ranked in the *Priorities* stage to select the best. The default algorithm is competent for container scheduling in general, but there are still two main challenges in edge scenarios. The first is that a distinctive feature of edge computing is the requirement for low latency, which is directly related to user experience [27], and frequent cross-node communication in edge environments can significantly increase application response time, which is not taken into account by the default algorithm. The second is that although Kubernetes' Horizontal Pod Autoscaler (HPA) mechanism can adapt to changes in load by changing the number of container replicas, there is over-provisioning in resource allocation based on multi-dimension constraints (see Sect. 3.2) [20], which is unfriendly to edge environments.

In allusion to the shortage of the default scheduling algorithm, we design a microservice scheduling and resource allocation model that is more adaptable to the characteristics of edge scenarios. In summary, the main contributions of the paper are as follows.

- **Microservice scheduling based on spectral clustering.** MSSC significantly reduces the cross-node communication traffic between microservices by portraying the dependencies through a graph and then using spectral clustering to map microservices to edge nodes.
- **Dynamic resource allocation under multi-dimension constraint based on sliding window mechanism.** We address the problem of over-provisioning resources in cluster scaling under multi-dimension constraints by adopting a more accurate resource allocation algorithm while combining the sliding window mechanism to avoid drastic changes in the cluster and improve resource utilization while ensuring the quality of service.
- **Simulation experiments under real production environment.** We built a simulated cluster using Raspberry Pi and virtual machines. To verify the model's performance in the production environment, we analyzed

the cluster-trace-microservices-v2021 dataset [4] from Alibaba's open-source Alibaba Cluster Trace Program to simulate the traffic characteristics of the production environment for stress testing.

The experimental results show that compared with the baseline, the proportion of intra-node traffic increases to 2.7 times, the inter-node traffic decreases by 17.7%, and the minimum, average and maximum application response times decrease by 37.8%, 10.7%, and 26.6%, respectively. During cluster scaling, the average memory value requested for processing a single request on two high-load microservice applications is equivalent to 19.4% and 45.8% of baseline, respectively. In contrast, the total number of requests and response time remains unchanged.

The rest of this paper is structured as follows. In Sect. 2, related works about microservice scheduling in edge computing are discussed. System architecture and proposed microservice scheduling and resource allocation algorithm are discussed in Sect. 3. In Sect. 4, we evaluate the proposed algorithm on a cloud-edge continuum. Section 5 concludes the paper and highlights future directions.

2 Related Works

In this section, we introduce the work on microservice scheduling and resource allocation.

Microservice Scheduling. Previous work [11] uses multiple clustering algorithms to classify hosts and then uses principal component analysis(PCA) to extract key metrics of containers and decide which containers need to be scheduled. [9,13,14,21,28], etc. map microservices or hosts into a graph, convert the scheduling problem into a problem of finding the least-cost graph, and then use the shortest path algorithm, maximum flow algorithm, etc. to obtain the final scheduling policy. The graph provides convenience for handling microservices-based scheduling. However, when the number of nodes increases, the performance of these algorithms will become the bottleneck of the system, and they can only adopt approximate methods to compromise. They cannot cope with the dynamic edge environment. [25] introduces a way combining deep learning and Q-learning algorithm to model container migration strategy as a multi-dimension Markov decision problem (MDP). However, this approach requires learning features in different application scenarios and lacks generality. [17,19,27,29] constructs a task scheduling model from the perspective of improving resource utilization by collecting multiple metrics for scheduling at different stages, including node metrics, container metrics, and application layer metrics. Although the above methods optimize the scheduling of microservices from different perspectives, they lack the analysis of the dependencies between microservices. They cannot solve the problem of latency caused by cross-node communication.

Resource Allocation. To improve the foresight of resource allocation, [9,13, 16,22,26] adopt the methods of reinforcement learning, deep learning, Gaussian regression, and statistical analysis to forecast the resource demand of the application. First, use a pre-trained model to interact with the environment. Dynamically collect data to update the model, predict the future state of the environment, and allocate resources based on the anticipated results. This method needs to learn the characteristics of different application scenarios, the inference and training of the model are resource-intensive tasks, it cannot adapt to the features of the edge environment, and the model also lacks a certain degree of versatility. [9,10] designed a closed-loop feedback control model from the cybernetics perspective and then used a proportional-integral-derivative(PID) algorithm to realize the control of microservices. However, the parameters of the cybernetics-based algorithm are highly coupled with the application scenario, requiring iterative testing and precise parameter tuning, which lacks versatility. [9,12,23,29] introduces multi-level metrics to monitor the application for resource allocation. However, these approaches have a coarse granularity in coping with the resource allocation problem under multiple resource constraints, resulting in poor resource utilization.

Table 1. System parameters

Parameter	Description
G	The graph abstracted from a microservice application
W	The adjacency matrix of graph
D	The degree matrix of a graph
L	The Laplace matrix of the graph
V	An n-dimensional real vector
G_i	The i'th subgraph of G
$W(G_i, G_j)$	The sum of weights of all edges between subgraphs G_i and G_j
E	Average resource usage per request processed by microservices
w_{ij}	The weight of the edge between nodes i and j
d_i	The diagonal element of a degree matrix
v_i	The components of the real vector V
λ	The eigenvalues of the Laplace matrix
N_k	The k'th node of the graph
T_i	The target resource utilization rate specified by the user for the i'th resource
U_i	Actual resource utilization of the i'th resource for microservice
C	The current number of replicates
R_i	The i'th resource required by the microservice in the new state
r_i	The i'th resource required by the microservice in the initial state
c_i	The number of replicates calculated from the i'th resource
u_{ij}^t	The current resource utilization of the i'th resource on the j'th node at time t for microservice
t_k	The duration of the k'th resource allocation

3   System Design

In this section, we present the system architecture (see Fig. 1) and discuss how it works. First, *Locust* [5] is used to generate the traffic, then *Cilium* and

Hubble are used to analyze the dependencies between microservices, and finally, microservices are mapped to nodes by spectral clustering. At the foundation of Cilium is a new Linux kernel technology called eBPF, which enables the dynamic insertion of powerful security visibility and control logic within Linux itself. Hubble is built on top of Cilium and eBPF to enable deep visibility into the communication and behavior of services [6]. Then, accurate resource allocation is accomplished through the monitoring unit, mapping unit, resource allocation unit, and execution unit, $InfluxDB$ [7] is used to store the monitoring metrics. See Sects. 3.1 and 3.2 for detailed description of each unit of the system.

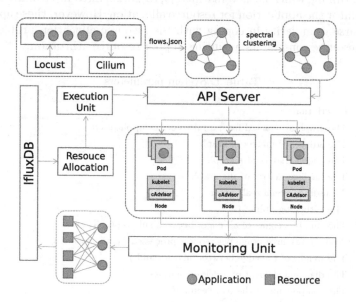

Fig. 1. System architecture.

3.1   Microservice Scheduling Based on Spectral Clustering

With the continuous expansion of the application scale, the number of microservices increases sharply, and the invocation relationship between services becomes more complex. The traditional scheduling mechanism usually makes decisions based on the status of the target node, including the usage of resources such as CPU, memory, and port. However, in the edge computing scenario where microservices architecture is widely used, the constraint relationship between microservices is the critical factor affecting user experience. The graph is used to portray the dependencies between microservices and then uses a clustering algorithm to complete the mapping of microservices to nodes so that microservices with strong dependencies are deployed to the same nodes, thus reducing the response time (see Fig. 2).

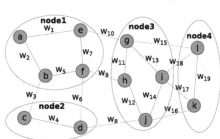
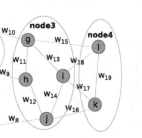
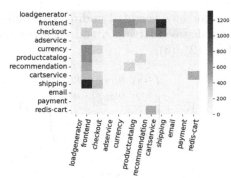

Fig. 2. Service mapping.   **Fig. 3.** Traffic between microservices.

Spectral clustering is performed by cutting the graph to make the sum of weights between the subgraphs as large as possible and the sum of weights within the subgraphs as small as possible, which is a minimum cut problem. There have been many related types of research on this problem in graph theory, such as $Ford - Fulkerson$ algorithm, $RatioCut$ algorithm, and $NormalizedCut$ algorithm, etc., which can prove that the minimum cut problem and the maximum flow problem are equivalent. The $Ford - Fulkerson$ algorithm is to get the solution of the minimum cut problem by solving the maximum flow problem, which is a circular, iterative algorithm with high time complexity when the graph is large [13]. It does not meet the latency requirements of edge applications. This paper solves the minimum cut problem based on the $RatioCut$ algorithm, which maps the application to a directed acyclic graph (DAG), where the vertices represent individual microservices and the edges define the invocation relationships between microservices. We derived the invocation frequencies among different microservices by analyzing 30,000 historical access data (see Fig. 3) and quantified them as the weights of edges. The invocation frequency reflects the closeness between microservices. Then a weighted undirected graph is used to portray a microservice architecture-based application, whose objective function for the minimum cut problem can be expressed as Eq. (1). The parameters are explained in Table 1.

$$
\begin{aligned}
\min_{G_i \in G} RationCut(G_1, ..., G_k) &= \min_{G_i \in G} \frac{1}{2} \sum_{i=1}^{k} \frac{W(G_i, \overline{G_i})}{|G_i|} \\
&= \min_{G_i \in G} \sum_{i=1}^{k} \frac{cut(G_i, \overline{G_i})}{|G_i|}
\end{aligned}
\tag{1}
$$

where G_i denotes the i'th subgraph, $W(G_i, \overline{G_i})$ denotes the weight between G_i and other subgraphs, and to prevent the granularity of the division from being too fine, $|G_i|$ is introduced in the denominator for correction, $|G_i|$ denotes the number of nodes in the subgraph G_i.

For any weighted undirected graph, we can obtain its adjacency matrix W and degree matrix D, and then compute its Laplacian matrix L, as shown in Eqs. (2), (3).

$$W = \begin{pmatrix} w_{11} & w_{12} & \cdots & w_{1n} \\ w_{21} & w_{22} & \cdots & w_{2n} \\ \vdots & \vdots & \ddots & \vdots \\ w_{n1} & w_{n2} & \cdots & w_{nn} \end{pmatrix} \quad D = \begin{pmatrix} d_1 & & & \\ & d_2 & & \\ & & \ddots & \\ & & & d_n \end{pmatrix} \quad d_i = \sum_{j=1, j\neq i}^{n} w_{i,j} \quad (2)$$

$$L = D - W = \begin{pmatrix} \sum_{j=2}^{n} w_{1,j} & -w_{12} & \cdots & -w_{1i} & \cdots & -w_{1n} \\ -w_{21} & \sum_{j=1, j\neq 2}^{n} w_{2,j} & \cdots & -w_{2i} & \cdots & -w_{2n} \\ \vdots & \vdots & \ddots & \vdots & \ddots & \vdots \\ -w_{i1} & -w_{i2} & \cdots & \sum_{j=1, j\neq i}^{n} w_{i,j} & \cdots & -w_{in} \\ \vdots & \vdots & \ddots & \vdots & \ddots & \vdots \\ -w_{n1} & -w_{n2} & \cdots & -w_{ni} & \cdots & \sum_{j=1}^{n-1} w_{n,j} \end{pmatrix}$$

$$(3)$$

For an undirected weighted graph, it is evident that the Laplacian matrix is symmetric, and there exists an eigenvalue of 0, whose corresponding eigenvector is $(1, \cdots, 1) \in R^n$. It can be proved that there exists an n-dimensional real vector V,

$$V^T \cdot L \cdot V = \frac{1}{2} \sum_{i,j=1}^{n} w_{i,j} \cdot (v_i - v_j)^2$$
$$= |G| \cdot RationCut(G, \overline{G}) \quad (4)$$
$$= \lambda \cdot n$$

So the problem of minimizing the objective function can be transformed into finding the minimum eigenvalues and eigenvectors of the Laplacian matrix. First, the graph's adjacency matrix is derived by analyzing the cluster trace, based on which we can obtain the degree matrix and the Laplace matrix and then calculate the eigenvalues and eigenvectors of the Laplace matrix. By arranging the eigenvectors corresponding to the first k smallest eigenvalues of the Laplacian matrix except 0 into an $n * k$-dimensional matrix, an n-dimensional classification vector is finally obtained using k-means clustering, which represents the nodes corresponding to each microservice. Finally, the deployment of the service is realized by calling $APIServer$, as shown in Algorithm 1.

3.2   Dynamic Resource Allocation Under Multi-dimension Constraint Based on Sliding Window Mechanism

After the microservices are deployed to the nodes, multiple resources are required to ensure their regular operation. On the one hand, the over-allocation of resources will lead to resource competition on the same node. Once the resource

---

Algorithm 1: MSSC algorithm

Input: Cluster Trace(30000)
Output: Results of spectral clustering: *clustermap*.
1 **Initialize:** Analyzing application Data $\Rightarrow w\_matrix$;
2 $w\_matrix \Rightarrow d\_matrix$;
3 $l\_matrix = d\_matrix - w\_matrix$;
   // Calculate eigenvalues and eigenvectors
4 $eigenlist, vectorlist = Matrix(l\_matrix)$;
   // Sort the eigenvectors
5 $sort\_vectorlist = Sort(eigenlist, vectorlist)$;
6 **for** $i = 1; i < k + 1; i + +$ **do**
7 $\quad | \quad sub\_matrix = Append(sub\_matrix, sort\_vectorlist[i])$
8 **end**
9 $cluster\_map = kmeans(sub\_matrix, k)$;
10 $cluster\_map \Rightarrow APIServer$

---

limit of the node is exceeded, the node may crash. On the other hand, if the resource allocation is insufficient, the application performance will be degraded or even unable to provide services normally. Therefore, reasonable resource allocation is the premise to ensure the normal operation of the cluster. The upper limit of resources is set to prevent node crashes caused by an application's unlimited use of resources. The overall resource utilization of the cluster can be represented by a matrix as follows (see Eq. 5). Each row of the matrix represents a resource, each column represents a node, and each element represents the usage of a resource on the corresponding node.

$$
\begin{pmatrix}
u_{11} & u_{12} & \cdots & u_{1k} \\
u_{21} & u_{22} & \cdots & u_{2k} \\
\vdots & \vdots & \ddots & \vdots \\
u_{n1} & u_{n2} & \cdots & u_{nk}
\end{pmatrix}
\tag{5}
$$

The original HPA mechanism expands and shrinks the capacity based on static configuration templates. Each replicate applies for the same and a fixed amount of resources. In the process of cluster scale expansion based on multiple indicators, the controller calculates the optimal number of replicates for each resource and then selects the maximum value as the final number of replicates for this round of scheduling, as shown in Eqs. (6), (7).

$$
\begin{cases}
c_i = \frac{\sum_{j=1}^{k} u_{ij}}{T_i}, & i \in 1, 2, 3 \ldots \\
C = Max\left(c_1, c_2, c_3, \ldots, c_n\right)
\end{cases}
\tag{6}
$$

$$
U_i = \frac{\sum_{j=1}^{k} u_{ij}}{C}, \qquad i \in 1, 2, 3 \ldots
\tag{7}
$$

according to (6), (7), for $C \neq c_i$, it can be derived that $U_i < T_i$.

In this case, the resource corresponding to the small number of replicates is over-provisioning, especially when the application resource request is not balanced, the phenomenon will be more noticeable and even affect the overall load capacity of the node. This situation is not friendly to the edge computing scenario.

The number of resources allocated and the actual demand of the application should be matched dynamically so that the quality of service can be satisfied while avoiding resource over-provisioning as much as possible. To solve this problem, we propose a dynamic resource allocation method based on a sliding window, consisting mainly of a monitoring unit, a mapping unit, a resource allocation unit, and an execution unit. The monitoring unit consists of node daemons *cAdvisor* and *metrics − server*, mainly responsible for collecting resource metrics from each node and pod in the cluster. The mapping unit completes the binding of metrics and microservices and stores the metrics for each microservice in *InfluxDB*. The resource allocation unit analyzes historical data based on a sliding window mechanism, i.e., it calculates the resource allocation not only based on the current requests but takes into account the resource usage in the most recent window (see Fig. 4). When the system detects that a new resource allocation process is triggered, it will build the new window with the current slot as the endpoint, push forward the *winlen* length as the starting point, and calculate the new resource allocation scheme with the average value within the window. This is mainly to prevent drastic fluctuations in the cluster state, affecting service quality. The latest allocated resources are shown in Eq. (8),

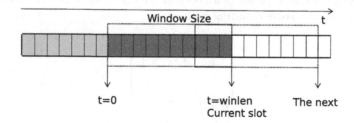

Fig. 4. Sliding window mechanism.

$$R_i = \frac{\sum_{t=1}^{winlen} \sum_{j=1}^{k} u_{ij}^t \cdot r_i}{winlen \cdot C \cdot T_i} \tag{8}$$

The numerator indicates the total resource usage of all replicas of the same application on different nodes, reflecting the current load level of the application, and *winlen* is the size of the sliding window. The minimum resource usage can be calculated while satisfying the user requirements based on the final number of replicas and the target resource usage. The execution unit is responsible for communicating with *APIServer* to update the cluster status, as shown in Algorithm 2. The time complexity of the algorithm is $O\left(s^2 \cdot r \cdot i + s \cdot w\right)$, s represents the number of microservices, r represents the number of replicas, i represents the resource type, and w represents the window length.

Algorithm 2: Resource allocation algorithm

Input: The length of sliding window, $winlen$;
The initial resource requests, $Initlist$;
List of microservices, $servicelist$;
The target resource utilization, T.

```
1  while True do
2  |   for service in servicelist do
       |     // Calculate the number of replicates
3  |   |   averagelist = getwinvalue(service, winlen)
4  |   |   for i = 1; i < n; i + + do
5  |   |   |   c[i] = averagelist[i]/Initlist[i] · T[i]
6  |   |   end
7  |   |   new_C = Max(c[i])
8  |   end
       |   // Reallocate resources
9  |   for i = 1; i < n; i + + do
10 |   |   if c[i] < new_C then
11 |   |   |   newlist[i] = averagelist[i]/new_C · T[i]
12 |   |   end
13 |   end
14 |   if old_C ≠ new_C then
15 |   |   update(new_C, newlist)
16 |   |   old_C = new_C
17 |   end
18 end
```

For each microservice, we first calculate the average value of each type of resource in the new window and the corresponding number of replicas and take the maximum value new_C as the new final number of replicas. Then we reallocate all kinds of resources according to the new replicas and the SLAs target T. Finally, it triggers a new round of updates when the new number of replicas is different from the old. The owner's SLOs are the target for adjustment. For containers, the over-provisioning of resources will lead to the poor utilization of the device, and conversely, there is a risk of SLOs violations. The algorithm is to perform accurate resource allocation while satisfying the SLOs.

4 Evaluation

In this section, we present the performance comparison between our proposed approach and the default scheduler of Kubernetes, which mainly covers two aspects, 1) the performance of clustering-based microservice scheduling and 2) the performance of dynamic resource allocation.

Cluster Setup: We evaluated the system in a simulated environment consisting of seven nodes, including a master node and six working nodes, where the Raspberry Pi was connected to the cluster through a wireless channel. The hardware configuration is shown in Table 2.

Software Setup: Kubernetes version v1.19.3, container runtime is Docker 20.10.7, database version is InfluxDB v2.3.0.

Load Generation: We use Alibaba dataset cluster-trace-microservices-v2021 as our primary workload, which reflects user access characteristics in the real world. Locust is used as a load generator deployed outside the cluster to avoid interference.

Benchmark: Using Kubernetes scheduler as well as HPA as the baseline, MSSC and SW were evaluated using Google's open-source online application *Online Boutique* [8], which consists of a total of 12 microservices including front-end web service, shopping cart, checkout center, back-end database, etc., covering the main application scenarios.

Table 2. Hardware Configuration.

Name	CPU	Memory	Disk	ISA	OS
Master	2/2.8GHz	4G	50G	x86	Ubuntu 21.04 LTS
Edge1	2/2.8GHz	4G	50G	x86	Ubuntu 21.04 LTS
Edge2	2/2.8GHz	4G	50G	x86	Ubuntu 21.04 LTS
Edge3	2/2.8GHz	4G	50G	x86	Ubuntu 21.04 LTS
Raspberrypi1	4/1.5GHz	8G	120G	ARM	Ubuntu Server 20.04.2 LTS
Raspberrypi2	4/1.5GHz	8G	120G	ARM	Ubuntu Server 20.04.2 LTS
Raspberrypi3	4/1.5GHz	8G	120G	ARM	Ubuntu Server 20.04.2 LTS

4.1 Performance of Cluster-Based Microservice Scheduling

To verify the performance of the clustering algorithm in reducing the cross-node communication of microservices, we deployed Cilium and Hubble in the cluster. First, when the application is deployed to the cluster, the Kubernetes default scheduler deploys the microservices to different nodes. After stress testing, we discovered the dependencies between the microservices by analyzing 30,000 access records. Figure 5) and Fig. 6) respectively depict the traffic distribution under the action of baseline and MSSC during a round of testing. It can be seen that the former has a general cross-node flow, while the latter decreases significantly after clustering. We conducted ten rounds of tests to eliminate the effect of randomness. The results show that 90.1% of the traffic in the cluster belong to cross-node communication, while only 9.9% of the traffic belongs to intra-node communication (see Fig. 7).

Secondly, a spectral clustering analysis was performed based on the access records collected in the previous step, and the microservices were mapped to different nodes based on the clustering results.

Finally, the same number of application access records are recaptured for analysis under the current scheduling decision, and 72.4% of the traffic is inter-node communication, and 27.6% of the traffic is intra-node communication. Compared with the baseline, the proportion of intra-node traffic increased to 2.7 times, and the traffic of inter-node communication decreased by 17.7% (see Fig. 8). The response time of the application is also evaluated, the MSSC is reduced in all intervals of the cumulative distribution function (CDF) compared to baseline (see Fig. 9). Under MSSC, the minimum, average and maximum values of response time are reduced by 37.8%, 10.7%, and 26.6%, respectively (see Fig. 10), and the overall fluctuation range decreased by 26.3%, mainly benefits from the reduction of cross-node communication.

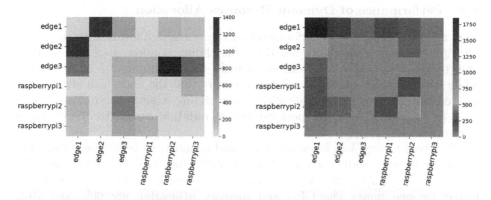

Fig. 5. Traffic distribution(Kubernetes-1).   **Fig. 6.** Traffic distribution(MSSC-1).

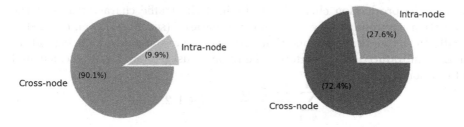

Fig. 7. Traffic distribution(Kubernetes-2).   **Fig. 8.** Traffic distribution(MSSC-2).

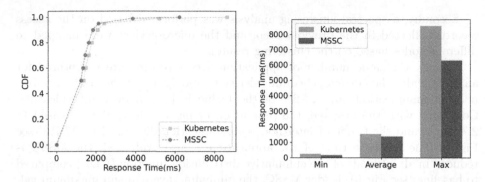

Fig. 9. Distribution of response time(a).   **Fig. 10.** Distribution of response time(b).

4.2 Performance of Dynamic Resource Allocation

This section validates the performance of the resource allocation model under multiple resource constraints based on the sliding window mechanism (SW). Our target is to conserve resources as much as possible in the edge scenario while satisfying the application SLOs to ensure that the nodes can allocate the limited resources to more applications. The sliding window mechanism is also used to suppress the cluster performance degradation caused by the dramatic fluctuations in a short period.

We chose two typical resources, CPU and memory, to verify the algorithm's performance with sliding window lengths of 5s, 30s, and 60s, respectively. To eliminate uncertainty, we had the same SLOs for each round of testing, which lasted for one hour. The CPU and memory utilization are 60% and 70%, respectively. To simulate real-world traffic characteristics, we used cluster-trace-microservices-v2021 from the Alibaba Cluster Trace Program, which contains 20000+ microservices in 12 h, and introduced the runtime metrics of microservices in the production cluster. We obtained the traffic characteristics of the production environment by analyzing the dataset (see Fig. 11), and scaled it equally to fit the local test conditions. An average resource consumption indicator E_i is introduced to characterize the resource usage, and it can be calculated in Equation 9.

$$E_i = \sum_{k=1}^{n} \frac{c_i^k \cdot r_i^k \cdot t_k}{n}, \qquad i \in 1, 2, 3 \ldots \tag{9}$$

Where c_i^k represents the number of replicas in the k-th stage, r_i^k represents the number of i-th dimension resources requested by the copy in the k-th stage, t_k represents the duration of the k-th stage, and n represents the number of requests processed in the entire process.

When using the dynamic resource allocation method, the percentage of memory resources requested by the two high-load microservices *currencyservice* and *frontend* to complete a single request relative to HPA is shown in Fig. 12, where

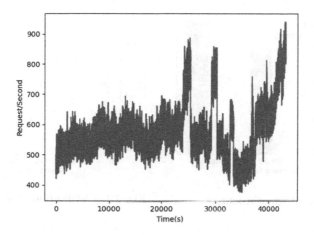

Fig. 11. Alibaba Cluster Trace.

E for $frontend$ is 37%, 9%, and 12.2% of HPA in three different windows, respectively. 9% and 12.2% of HPA, and the indicator for $currencyservice$ is 42.8%, 41.5% and 53.2%, respectively. The results show that the performance of the algorithm based on dynamic resource allocation is better than its competitors under different window sizes, and it can be found that the performance is better than the other two conditions when the $winlen$ is 30s. This indicates that there is no simple linear relationship between the size of the window and the performance, which aligns with our intuitive impression. The window size reflects the strategy's sensitivity and represents the system's inertia. When the window size increases, on the one hand, it avoids frequent fluctuations, but on the other hand, it makes the system not reflect the actual situation accurately. A smaller window has the opposite effect. It shows that the hyperparameter $winlen$ needs to be chosen reasonably according to the system's characteristics.

Figure 13 depicts that the response time of microservices does not show a significant decrease due to the compression of resources. Instead, Our approach's latency is more diminutive than HPA in all intervals of the CDF for SW-30, and the indicator is 80% for SW-60. It is mainly due to the more accurate resource allocation based on real-time load analysis, balancing performance and efficiency. The introduction of the sliding window mechanism also effectively suppresses system fluctuations and improves the cluster's performance.

Figure 14 depicts the total number of requests completed by the system and the average response time. From the results, HPA is better than SW-5 and SW-60, but worse than SW-30, indicating that the performance of HPA can be fully achieved or even exceeded by setting the appropriate $winlen$. Figure 15 depicts the request failures. Our approach introduces a failure rate of 0.1%, but we consider these losses acceptable compared to the increase in resource utilization.

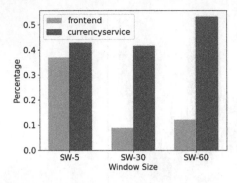

Fig. 12. Percentage of resources.

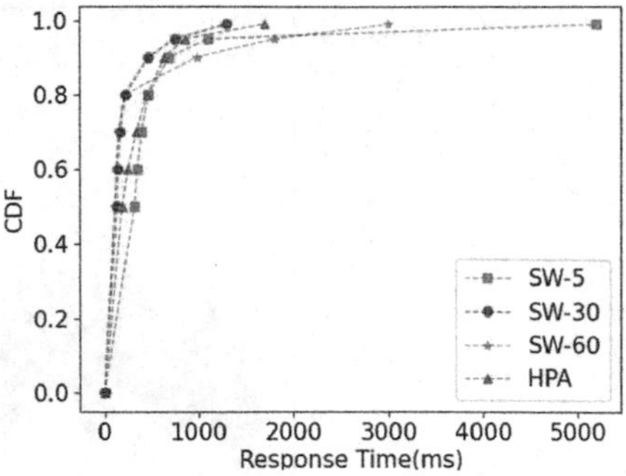

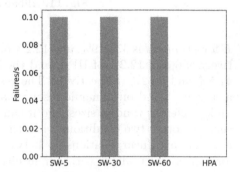

Fig. 13. Distribution of response time.

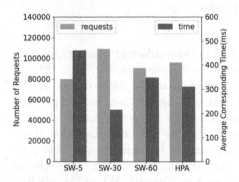

Fig. 14. Request and response time.

Fig. 15. Failures statistics.

5   Conclusions

We propose a model for microservice scheduling and resource allocation in edge scenarios. It significantly reduces the cross-node communication traffic between microservices by portraying the dependencies between microservices through a graph and then using spectral clustering to map microservices to edge nodes. We adopt precise resource allocation algorithms during cluster scaling under multi-dimension constraints to improve resource utilization of edge devices while ensuring SLOs. The experimental results show that compared with the baseline, the inter-node traffic decreases by 17.7%, and the minimum, average and maximum application response time decrease by 37.8%, 10.7%, and 26.6%, respectively. During cluster scaling, the average value of memory requested for processing a single request on two high-load microservice applications is overall equivalent to 19.4% and 45.8% of baseline, respectively. In contrast, the total number of requests and response time remain essentially unchanged.

The model itself is platform bound, mainly considering the fact that Kubernetes is widely deployed in the field of microservice orchestration, and the algorithm needs to be reimplemented for the new API when it is transplanted to other platforms. In the future, we will optimize the model for the characteristics of device hardware heterogeneity and network mode heterogeneity in the edge environment and use real-time application dependency analysis and graph generation algorithms to improve the autonomy and adaptability of the model.

References

1. Kubernetes documentation, https://kubernetes.io/. Accessed 30 Jun 2022
2. Swarm mode overview, https://docs.docker.com/engine/swarm/. Accessed 30 Jun 2022
3. OpenShift container platform 4.10 documentation, https://docs.openshift.com/container-platform/4.10/welcome/index.html. Accessed 30 Jun 2022
4. Overview of microservices traces, https://github.com/alibaba/clusterdata/tree/master/cluster-trace-microservices-v2021. Accessed 30 Jun 2022
5. An open source load testing tool, https://locust.io/. Accessed 30 Jun 2022
6. eBPF-based networking, observability, security, https://docs.cilium.io/en/stable/. Accessed 30 Jun 2022
7. The time series data platform where developers build IoT, analytics, and cloud applications, https://www.influxdata.com/. Accessed 30 Jun 2022
8. Microservices demo application., https://github.com/GoogleCloudPlatform/microservices-demo. Accessed 30 Jun 2022
9. Baarzi, A.F., Kesidis, G.: SHOWAR: right-sizing and efficient scheduling of microservices. In: Proceedings of the ACM Symposium on Cloud Computing, pp. 427–441 (2021)
10. Baresi, L., Guinea, S., Leva, A., Quattrocchi, G.: A discrete-time feedback controller for containerized cloud applications. In: Proceedings of the 2016 24th ACM SIGSOFT International Symposium on Foundations of Software Engineering, pp. 217–228 (2016)
11. Chhikara, P., Tekchandani, R., Kumar, N., Obaidat, M.S.: An efficient container management scheme for resource-constrained intelligent IoT devices. IEEE Internet Things J. 8(16), 12597–12609 (2021). https://doi.org/10.1109/JIOT.2020.3037181
12. Fourati, M.H., Marzouk, S., Jmaiel, M.: EPMA: elastic platform for microservices-based applications: towards optimal resource elasticity. J. Grid Comput. 20(1), 1–21 (2022)
13. Fu, K., et al.: QoS-aware and resource efficient microservice deployment in cloud-edge continuum. In: 2021 IEEE International Parallel and Distributed Processing Symposium (IPDPS). pp. 932–941 (2021). https://doi.org/10.1109/IPDPS49936.2021.00102
14. Hu, Y., Zhou, H., de Laat, C., Zhao, Z.: Concurrent container scheduling on heterogeneous clusters with multi-resource constraints. Future Gener. Comput. Syst. 102, 562–573 (2020)
15. Jiang, C., Cheng, X., Gao, H., Zhou, X., Wan, J.: Toward computation offloading in edge computing: a survey. IEEE Access 7, 131543–131558 (2019). https://doi.org/10.1109/ACCESS.2019.2938660

16. Kang, P., Lama, P.: Robust resource scaling of containerized microservices with probabilistic machine learning. In: 2020 IEEE/ACM 13th International Conference on Utility and Cloud Computing (UCC), pp. 122–131. IEEE (2020)
17. Li, X., Li, X., Tan, Y., Zhu, H., Tan, S.: Multi-resource workload mapping with minimum cost in cloud environment. Concurr. Comput.: Pract. Exper. **31**(15), e5167 (2019)
18. Luo, S., et al.: Characterizing microservice dependency and performance: Alibaba trace analysis. In: Proceedings of the ACM Symposium on Cloud Computing, p. 412–426. SoCC '21, Association for Computing Machinery, New York, NY, USA (2021). https://doi.org/10.1145/3472883.3487003
19. Mao, Y., Oak, J., Pompili, A., Beer, D., Han, T., Hu, P.: DRAPS: dynamic and resource-aware placement scheme for docker containers in a heterogeneous cluster. In: 2017 IEEE 36th International Performance Computing and Communications Conference (IPCCC), pp. 1–8. IEEE (2017)
20. Marko, L.: Qiniu: Kubernetes in Action. Publishing House of Electronics Industry, Beijing (2021)
21. Rausch, T., Rashed, A., Dustdar, S.: Optimized container scheduling for data-intensive serverless edge computing. Future Gener. Comput. Syst. **114**, 259–271 (2021)
22. Rossi, F., Nardelli, M., Cardellini, V.: Horizontal and vertical scaling of container-based applications using reinforcement learning. In: 2019 IEEE 12th International Conference on Cloud Computing (CLOUD), pp. 329–338. IEEE (2019)
23. Taherizadeh, S., Stankovski, V.: Dynamic multi-level auto-scaling rules for containerized applications. Comput. J. **62**(2), 174–197 (2019)
24. Tan, Y., Wu, F., Wu, Q., Liao, X.: Resource stealing: a resource multiplexing method for mix workloads in cloud system. J. Supercomput. **75**(1), 33–49 (2019)
25. Tang, Z., Zhou, X., Zhang, F., Jia, W., Zhao, W.: Migration modeling and learning algorithms for containers in fog computing. IEEE Trans. Serv. Comput. **12**(5), 712–725 (2019). https://doi.org/10.1109/TSC.2018.2827070
26. Yang, Z., Nguyen, P., Jin, H., Nahrstedt, K.: MIRAS: model-based reinforcement learning for microservice resource allocation over scientific workflows. In: 2019 IEEE 39th International Conference on Distributed Computing Systems (ICDCS), pp. 122–132. IEEE (2019)
27. Yin, L., Luo, J., Luo, H.: Tasks scheduling and resource allocation in fog computing based on containers for smart manufacturing. IEEE Trans. Industr. Inform. **14**(10), 4712–4721 (2018)
28. Zhang, J., Zhou, X., Ge, T., Wang, X., Hwang, T.: Joint task scheduling and containerizing for efficient edge computing. IEEE Trans. Parallel Distrib. Syst. **32**(8), 2086–2100 (2021)
29. Zhong, Z., Buyya, R.: A cost-efficient container orchestration strategy in kubernetes-based cloud computing infrastructures with heterogeneous resources. ACM Trans. Internet Technol. (TOIT) **20**(2), 1–24 (2020)
30. Zhou, Z., Chen, X., Li, E., Zeng, L., Luo, K., Zhang, J.: Edge intelligence: paving the last mile of artificial intelligence with edge computing. Proc. IEEE **107**(8), 1738–1762 (2019). https://doi.org/10.1109/JPROC.2019.2918951

Combining Static and Dynamic Analysis to Decompose Monolithic Application into Microservices

Khaled Sellami[1], Mohamed Aymen Saied[1(✉)], Ali Ouni[2],
and Rabe Abdalkareem[3]

[1] Laval University, Quebec, QC, Canada
mohamed-aymen.saied@ift.ulaval.ca
[2] ETS Montreal, University of Quebec, Montreal, QC, Canada
[3] Carleton University, Ottawa, ON, Canada

Abstract. In order to benefit from the advantages offered by the microservices architectural design, many companies have started migrating their monolithic application to this newer design. However, due to the high cost and development time associated to this task, automated approaches need to be developed to solve these issues.

Solutions that tackle this problem can be classified based on the information available for the monolithic application which are often based on source code or runtime traces. The latter provides a more accurate representation of the interactions between the classes within the application however it often fails to cover all of the classes. On the other hand, the source code of the application is more readily available and can be used to extract additional information like semantic meaning of the classes.

The objective of this paper is to provide a hybrid solution that combines both of these approaches in order to take advantage of their strengths while covering their weaknesses. The proposed solution performs static and dynamic analysis on the monolithic application based on the available information and the user's input. Afterwards, an iterative clustering process is applied on the processed data in order to generate the microservices decomposition. We compare different strategies for combining the static and dynamic approaches and we evaluate the performance of the hybrid approach compared to each of the separate approaches on 4 monolith applications. We provide as well a comparison with state-of-the-art solutions.

Keywords: Microservices · Clustering · Legacy decomposition · Static analysis · Dynamic analysis

1 Introduction

Monolithic architectural styles implemented in the legacy applications often lead to maintainability issues as these applications evolve and as such fail to meet user demands or provide their services adequately [4]. Service Oriented Architectures (SOA) have emerged as an alternative when building new software which tries to answer the problems found in monolithic applications. The microservices architecture [1,13] builds upon the philosophy used in SOAs to utilize a

© The Author(s), under exclusive license to Springer Nature Switzerland AG 2022
J. Troya et al. (Eds.): ICSOC 2022, LNCS 13740, pp. 203–218, 2022.
https://doi.org/10.1007/978-3-031-20984-0_14

Domain Driven Design (DDD) [8] to build autonomous, fine-grained and scalable components (microservices) that can function independently. A large number of developers have sought to adopt this style and migrate their legacy applications. However, this migration process proved to be costly, lengthy and complex in many cases, requiring a large amount of time and monetary investment from these developers and as such served as a barrier to improve their software [10]. Approaches that try to tackle this issue attempt at automating this part of the process by proposing the set of potential microservices which is called a decomposition. Each approach tackles this issue in a different way mostly based on the type of input it utilizes and how it analyzes it. One of the most commonly used approach relies on the information found within the run-time traces of the monolithic application [3,6,7] since it provides a more accurate view of the interactions of the components within this application. However, this approach, called Dynamic Analysis, requires the availability of enough execution traces to provide this advantage and, as such, methods that employ it often fail to cover all of the components within the application. The other most common approach uses the source code of the legacy application [11,15,16] since it is rare that this information would be unavailable for a developer that is trying to migrate his application. In addition, this analysis approach, called Static Analysis, can cover all of the components within the legacy software and include them in the decomposition.

In this research, we present a solution that merges Static Analysis and Dynamic Analysis approaches in order to complement each other by providing more robust decompositions which take advantage of the run-time traces while covering the whole application by supplementing the inference phase with the information extracted from the source code. Our solution analyzes the run-time traces and the source code independently in order to extract semantic, structural and dynamic representations of the monolithic application. Afterwards, we apply an iterative clustering approach that combines representations from different domains in order to generate a single result in a hierarchical structure that represents the microservices.

In this paper, we compare different strategies for combining the analysis approaches and we evaluate our approach in comparison with other baselines in the literature that tackle problems similar to the microservices decomposition issue. The results obtained show that our approach improved the coverage of our proposed decompositions while maintaining Structural Modularity, Conceptual Modular Quality and Inter Call Percentage metrics that are better or similar to most of the baselines.

The paper is organized as follows. In Sect. 2, we present the related work to our research. Afterwards, we showcase a formal formulation of the problem and the details of our proposed approach in Sect. 3. Then, in the 4th section, we specify and describe the empirical evaluation of our approach. Subsequently, we move on to discussing the threats to the validity of this work in Sect. 5. Finally, we provide a conclusion to the paper, and we outline our future work in Sect. 6.

2   Related Work

Recent research in the migration process from a monolithic architecture to a microservices architecture has focused mainly on the decomposition phase where given a monolithic application, an approach proposes a set of potential microservices. There has been numerous attempts to automate this task. These approaches can be categorized by how they process the monolithic application and how they analyze it.

Some solutions focused on the use of execution traces to represent the legacy systems. Mono2micro [7] associates execution traces with use cases and then analyzes them to calculate a shared similarity metric between the classes. Then, it uses a hierarchical clustering algorithm to suggest the microservices. FoSCI [6] addresses this problem by proposing a solution that relies on execution traces and a search-based algorithm to group together the classes of the monolithic application. The approach CoGCN [3] is based on a graph neural network that provides the proposed decomposition while outputting the list of outliers. This approach builds its neural network using the structural data in the source code and trains the model using the execution traces.

Most other solutions that tackle this problem rely on the source code for their analysis. hierDecomp [16] analyzes the source code in order to extract the structural and semantic information within it which is used in conjunction with a hierarchical DBSCAN algorithm variant to generate the decomposition options. Bunch [11] is a tool designed to provide an architectural-level view of a software system by decomposing it and clustering its components using search algorithms and using only the source code of the application.

Some approaches have tried to represent the monolithic applications using different sources of information. MEM [9], for example, relies on the source code and the version control history of the application to generate a graph. It proposes its microservices by applying a clustering algorithm on this graph. ServiceCutter [5] takes as input a JSON format of the design documents of the monolithic application. Using this input, ServiceCutter generates scores for 16 coupling criteria and generates a weighted graph. The developers can use this graph to generate a service oriented architecture.

3   Proposed Approach

In this section, we present the details of our solution. We start by defining the problem we are trying to solve. Afterwards, we showcase an overview of the proposed approach. Then, we explain in detail the different components used in this approach.

3.1   Problem Formulation

Given a legacy monolithic application, our approach needs to generate a set of candidate microservices which is called in this case a decomposition. This task is achieved by analyzing the source code and execution traces. Even though this solution can be applied on each one of these inputs individually, we will assume that both types of information are available for the rest of the paper.

The legacy application is represented as a set of classes $C = \{c_1, c_2, ..., c_N\}$ where c_i is the class's id and N is the total number of classes. In addition, given that dynamic analysis rarely covers all of the classes within the code base, we define $C_d = \{c'_1, c'_2, ..., c'_{N_d}\}$ as the set of classes mentioned within the execution traces where $c'_i \in C$ and $N_d \leq N$.

The result of our approach is a hierarchical representation of the suggested decomposition. It is defined as a list of layers, each representing a level of the hierarchy. The ith layer is defined as $L_i = \{M_{i,1}, M_{i,2}, ..., M_{i,N_i}\}$ where $M_{i,j} = \{c_{i,j,1}, c_{i,j,,2}, ..., c_{i,j,N_{i,j}}\}$ is a microservice containing $N_{i,j}$ classes and $c_{i,j,k} \in C$. If a microservice contains only one class, that class is defined as an outlier. In addition, for each microservice $M_{i,j}$ in the ith layer, there exists a microservice $M_{i+1,j'}$ in the $(i+1)^{th}$ layer where $M_{i,j} \subseteq M_{i+1,j'}$.

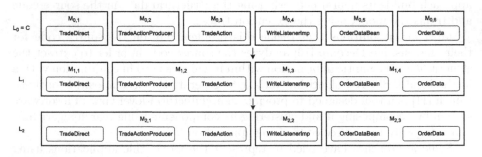

Fig. 1. An example showcasing the result of a microservice decomposition.

Figure 1 showcases an example of a decomposition results for a small subset of classes within an open-source monolithic Java application called *DayTrader*[1]. The initial layer is defined as a set of microservices each having exactly one class. The second layer contains 4 microservices since the couple of classes *TradeAction* and *TradeActionProducer* as well as *OrderData* and *OrderDataBean* have been merged into a single microservice each. Since the microservices $M_{1,1}$ and $M_{1,3}$ have only the classes *TradeDirect* and *WtiteListenerImp* respectively, both of these classes are categorized as outliers within this layer. For the final layer, the microservices $M_{1,1}$ and $M_{1,2}$ have merged to create the 3-class microservice $M_{2,1}$. As such, the suggested decomposition contains 2 microservices and *WriteListenerImp* as the only outlier.

Having defined the input and output of our solution, the following subsection explains the details of our approach as well as the theoretical reasoning behind it.

---

[1] https://github.com/WASdev/sample.daytrader7.

3.2   Approach Overview

Our approach takes as input the source code and execution traces of a given monolithic application. Afterwards, three separate and distinct analysis approaches are executed on this input in order to generate a dataset for each approach. The three datasets are then fed to the clustering component which combines them in order to output the decomposition layers. Nonetheless, any combination of the analysis approaches is possible including having a single one.

The Fig. 2 showcases the different steps taken in order to generate a decomposition for a given monolithic application. The smaller rectangles within the figure represent the task done by our solution while the ellipses represent inputs and outputs.

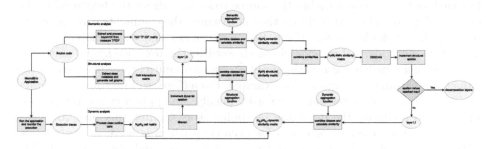

Fig. 2. An overview of the process used to output the microservices decomposition.

3.3   Extracting the Datasets for Each Approach

Dynamic Calls Matrix. This phase requires as input a list of execution traces recording the dynamic interactions of the classes. These traces represent the execution logs. Each trace should represent a call path from the first class until the last called class. Branches in the call path create another trace. For example, if during an execution, *TradeActionProducer* called *TradeAction* which then called *TradeDirect* this would create the first trace: [*TradeActionProducer, TradeAction, TradeDirect*]. If *TradeDirect* finished its task and returned, and afterwards *TradeAction* called *OrderData*, we would create a second trace: [*TradeActionProducer, TradeAction, OrderData*]. All circular dependencies within the traces and all duplicates are removed in a pre-processing step. Using these traces, we generate the dynamic calls matrix. We define the dynamic calls matrix M_{dyn} as a $N_d \mathrm{x} N_d$ matrix where each cell is equal to the sum of direct calls and indirect calls between every couple of classes within the execution traces. For example, given the following traces: [*TradeActionProducer, TradeAction, TradeDirect*] and [*TradeActionProducer, TradeDirect*] and the order of classes is [*TradeActionPro-*

ducer, TradeAction, TradeDirect], the call matrix would be equal to : $\begin{bmatrix} 0 & 1 & 2 \\ 0 & 0 & 1 \\ 0 & 0 & 0 \end{bmatrix}$

Structural Interactions Matrix. We define an interaction between a class A and a class B when within class A, class B was declared, used as a type for a method's parameter, inherited or had one of its methods called. In addition, all classes acquire the interactions of the class they inherit from.

As such, we start by extracting the metadata within the source code. Any static analysis tool that can analyze the Abstract Syntax Trees of the application's programming language can be used to extract this information. Afterwards, for each couple of classes, we measure the number of interactions between them in order to create the structural interactions matrix M_{str} which is a NxN matrix.

Term Frequency - Inverse Document Frequency (TF-IDF) Matrix. For each of the N classes within the source code, we extract the text used in the class' definition. The text includes the class' name, the comments, the members' names, the methods' names, the parameters' names and the variables' names within its methods. Afterwards, for each word in the text, we apply camelcase case splitting which separates the input string into multiple words based on the camelcase naming convention. For example, *CamelCase* will be split into *Camel* and *Case*. Then, we filter out stopwords. Finally, we apply a stemming process in order to facilitate the detection of similar words. After this pre-processing step, we acquire a vector of words for each class which is used, in conjunction with the vocabulary V to measure the TF-IDF values and obtain the TF-IDF matrix M_{sem}. The final result would be a NxD_V matrix where D_V represents the number of words in the vocabulary.

3.4   The Hybrid Clustering Process

The objective of this task is to combine the different matrices generated in the previous task in order to provide a better decomposition than each of the approaches separately. Both structural and semantic analysis can utilize similarity functions that generate $N \times N$ matrices whose values are in the range *[0,1]* where N refers to the total number of classes within the monolithic application. For this reason, an intuitive and simple solution would be to calculate the weighted sum of structural and semantic similarity matrices using a weight value called alpha in the range *[0,1]*. For the rest of the paper, we will call this matrix the static analysis matrix since it's based on a couple of approaches that employ static analysis.

On the other hand, the dynamic calls matrix can't be used to generate a NxN matrix since it lacks information regarding some of the classes. As such, a simple weighted sum is not sufficient. In this case, we use a clustering strategy that combines 2 datasets from different domains in order to generate a single clustering result introduced in [14]. This approach builds upon a modified DBSCAN algorithm [12,16].

This algorithm, which we call hierarchical-DBSCAN, executes DBSCAN in multiple iterations and slowly increments the epsilon hyper-parameter in order to loosen the restriction on the condition for grouping together the classes until a maximum epsilon value, defined by the user, is reached. Each iteration takes as input additionally the clustering of the previous iteration. As such, the final result is a list of layers describing the hierarchy of the clusters since each cluster with a layer contains at least one of the clusters of the previous layer similarly to the example shown in Fig. 1.

Combination Strategy. The algorithm introduced in [14] proposed two different strategies to combine the datasets. The first strategy involves running the hierarchical-DBSCAN processes separately and in a sequential manner.

As shown in Fig. 3, we start with one of the datasets, which in our case is the dynamic call matrix and we execute all of the iterations of the hierarchical clustering algorithm. At each iteration, we take as input the previous iteration's result and the original dataset. Then, for each cluster in the previous layer, we generate a new sample that represents the cluster depending on an aggregation function. Afterwards, we calculate a similarity matrix based on the newly created samples. Using the similarity matrix, we run the DBSCAN algorithm in order to acquire the new clusters. After incrementing the epsilon parameter, we verify if it exceeds a maximum threshold called Max epsilon and that is defined by the user. If it does not, we feed the clustering result to the next iteration. Otherwise, we feed it as input into the second phase which applies the same process on the second dataset, its corresponding aggregation function and its Max epsilon hyper-parameter. Finally, when the second epsilon reaches its maximum, the acquired clustering layers are returned as the output of the algorithm.

The Fig. 4 showcases the second strategy. In this case, we alternate between the datasets. We start by running an iteration for the first dataset. Afterwards, we update the first epsilon value and we feed the result to an iteration of the second dataset. Similarly, we update the second epsilon value and use the result as the input of the second iteration of the first dataset. We keep alternating between both datasets until both epsilon values have reached their respective maximum values. Finally, we output the clustering layers.

Given the assumption that dynamic analysis data are a better representation of the application at the cost of a lower class coverage, we always start the clustering process with the dynamic call matrix as the first dataset.

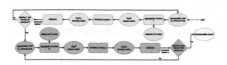

Fig. 3. A showcase of the sequential strategy.

Fig. 4. A showcase of the alternating strategy.

Aggregation Functions. During each iteration and for each different type of analysis, we take as input the previous clusters and the original dataset. We define a function capable of aggregating each cluster into a single point. The newly generated vectors replace the vectors of the clusters' components within the dataset. The resulting dataset is then used in the next steps of the current iteration

For semantic analysis, each cluster is transformed into a normalized vector representing the mean of the TF-IDF vectors of its classes. Given a cluster C, we generate the new vector as:

$$\vec{c_C} = \frac{\sum_{c_i \in C} M_{sem}\vec{[c_i]}}{|C|} \tag{1}$$

where $M_{sem}\vec{[c_i]}$ is the vector encoding the class i in the TF-IDF Matrix M_{sem}

As for both structural and dynamic analysis, we use the same aggregation function which measures the sum of the vectors representing its classes. Given a cluster C and the label a in $\{dyn, str\}$, we generate the new vector as:

$$\vec{c_C} = \sum_{c_i \in C} M_a\vec{[c_i]} \tag{2}$$

4   Evaluation

In this section, we conduct experiments in order to evaluate the performance of our approach in identifying the optimal decomposition.

4.1   Research Questions

We developed our experimental setups in order to answer the following research questions:

- **Q1:** What is the best approach for combining different representations and interpretations of the monolithic application?
- **Q2:** How does our approach perform when compared to state-of-the-art microservices decomposition baselines?

4.2   Experimental Setup

Evaluation Metrics. In order to properly evaluate our solution and compare it with other approaches, we need to define metrics that can quantify the quality of the generated microservices. However, since we are dealing with a problem that does not contain true values we can compare with, we will need to evaluate the quality of the decomposition based on defined criteria that theoretically represent an acceptable microservices architecture [10]. As such, for this evaluation, we will compare the proposed decompositions based on how much the decomposition respects the Domain Driven Design (DDD) philosophy [8], how coherent the microservices are, how much coupling exists between them and the granularity of the microservices

For these reasons, we selected the following evaluation metrics from the literature that encode in different ways the selected criteria:

- **Structural Modularity (SM):** [6] is an evaluation metric that can be associated with both the cohesion and coupling criteria since it defines a way to quantify the structural coherence of the microservices as well as the coupling between then combines them into a single metric. It is defined as follows:

$$SM = \frac{1}{K} \sum_{i=1}^{K} \frac{\mu_i}{m_i^2} - \frac{1}{(K(K-1))/2} \sum_{i \neq j}^{K} \frac{\sigma_{i,j}}{2\,m_i\,m_j} \tag{3}$$

Where K is the number of the extracted microservices, μ_i is the number of unique calls between the classes in microservice i, m_i is the number of classes in microservice i and $\sigma_{i,j}$ is the number of unique calls between classes of microservice i and classes of microservice j. Decompositions with higher cohesiveness and lower coupling result in higher SM values and as such reflect a higher structural quality.

- **Conceptual Modular Quality(CMQ):** [6], quantifies the conceptual quality of the decomposition. The cohesion and coupling components within this metric are based on the common textual terms between the classes. As such, this metric evaluates how focused the contexts represented by the microservices are. Thus, it can be categorized as a metric for evaluating the DDD aspects.

$$CMQ = \frac{1}{K} \sum_{i=1}^{K} \frac{\mu_i'}{m_i^2} - \frac{1}{(K(K-1))/2} \sum_{i \neq j}^{K} \frac{\sigma_{i,j}'}{2\,m_i\,m_j} \tag{4}$$

Where K is the number of the extracted microservices, μ_i' is the number of common terms between the classes in microservice i, m_i is the number of classes in microservice i and $\sigma_{i,j}'$ is the number of common terms between classes of microservice i and classes of microservice j. Higher CMQ values reflect better decompositions.

- **Non-Extreme Distribution (NED):** [3] This metric corresponds to the granularity criteria and introduces a way to quantify this aspect by measuring the percentage of classes with extremely small or extremely large microservices. It is defined in detail in the following equation:

$$NED = 1 - \frac{|\{m_i \; ; \; 5 < |m_i| < 20, i \in [1, K]\}|}{K} \tag{5}$$

Where K is the number of the extracted microservices and $|m_i|$ is the size of microservice m_i. In our evaluation, we selected the values 5 and 20 as the thresholds for the definition of extreme sizes for all sample applications in order to be consistent with the literature [2,3,7]. Having high NED often corresponds to worse results.

- **Inter Call Percentage (ICP)**: [7] is based on the percentage of static calls between two microservices. This metric quantifies the dependencies between the microservices and as such can represent the coupling criteria.

$$ICP = \frac{\sum_{i=1,j=1,i\neq j}^{K} \sum_{c_k \in M_i} \sum_{c_l \in M_j} (log(calls(c_k, c_l)) + 1))}{\sum_{i=1,j=1}^{K} \sum_{c_k \in M_i} \sum_{c_l \in M_j} (log(calls(c_k, c_l)) + 1)} \tag{6}$$

Where K is the number of microservices, M_i is the set of classes in microservice i, $calls(c_k, c_l)$ is the number of calls from class c_k to class c_l. Lower values of ICP correspond to fewer interactions and as such lower coupling and a better decomposition.

- **Coverage (COV)**: is simply defined as the percentage of classes from the monolithic application that were included in the proposed decomposition. For our approach, we won't consider outlier classes as part of the proposed decomposition. If we measure this metric for the decomposition example shown if Fig. 1 which has 5 classes and detected 1 outlier, the result would be equal to 0.8. On the other hand, if the used approach is only based on run-time execution trace analysis and only 3 classes were detected, the result for this approach would 0.6.

Evaluation Applications. We selected 4 monolithic Open-source Java applications that we evaluate our approach on. The selected applications have varying scales in order to evaluate how scalable our approach is. The metadata of these applications are described in the Table 1 where we specify the number of classes detected using static analysis (SA) and dynamic analysis (DA) separately and the number of unique interactions found using static analysis.

Table 1. Monolithic applications metadata.

Project	Version	SLOC	# of SA classes	# of DA classes	# of unique interactions
Plants	1.0	7,347	40	20	123
JPetStore	1.0	3,341	73	37	209
AcmeAir	1.2	8,899	86	23	242
DayTrader(see footnote 1)	1.4	18,224	118	73	378

[1] https://github.com/WASdev/sample.mono-to-ms.pbw-monolith.
[2] https://github.com/KimJongSung/jPetStore.
[3] https://github.com/acmeair/acmeair.

Experimental Process. For each research question, we propose different alternatives that we compare their results. However, hyper-parameter choices can significantly impact the quality of the output. As such, we applied a grid-search like approach where we select intervals of possible values for each hyper-parameter that is not under evaluation and then we generate the decompositions for each hyper-parameter combination and we measure their evaluation metrics. Afterwards, we filter out the decompositions that have a NED score equal to 1. Since NED is calculated by the percentage of microservices with extreme sizes, having a NED score equal to 1 signifies that all the microservices within this decomposition can be considered invalid and as such this solution should be excluded. Additionally, we exclude the decompositions that have a coverage lower than a defined threshold. In this process, we used 0.5 as the threshold.

4.3   Experimental Setup and Results for RQ1

In this research question, we evaluate which combination strategy as described in the section Combination strategy performs better. Therefore, we start by comparing the performance of the sequential strategy and the alternating strategy.

After applying the experimental process and excluding the extreme cases, we evaluate the influence of the chosen strategy independently from the hyper-parameters based on the analysis of over 40000 potential decompositions. The Table 2 shows the median result for each evaluation metric, sample application and strategy.

Table 2. Comparison of median evaluation results for approach combination strategies.

	SM ↗		CMQ ↗		ICP ↘		NED ↘		COV ↗	
	Alternating	Sequential	Alternating	Sequential	Alternating	Sequential	Alternating	Sequential	Alternating	Sequential
Plants	0.4037	0.4042	0.0385	0.0246	0.1776	0.1752	0.3077	0.3478	0.675	0.65
JPetStore	0.0767	0.0789	0.1647	0.1539	0.3378	0.4641	0.5968	0.5082	0.863	0.8493
AcmeAir	0.093	0.1031	0.3127	0.2757	0.3885	0.5799	0.7229	0.6125	0.8652	0.7753
DayTrader	0.2219	0.227	0.2047	0.1991	0.2425	0.347	0.7103	0.6848	0.8305	0.7627

As we can observe in the table, both methods had very close median results for the metric SM with the largest difference being around 0.004 for the project AcmeAir. However, we can see that using the alternating strategy achieved higher results for all projects. As for ICP, the alternating strategy managed to lower its values and achieve a worse but very close median score compared to the sequential strategy. On the other hand, when comparing the scores for NED, we can see that the alternating had more extreme microservices in all projects except for Plants. Finally, the coverage it achieved was better in all applications.

We hypothesize that the increased performance observed in this case is due to the feedback loop between the clustering processes that exists in the alternating strategy compared to the sequential approach. In the first case, the results of the dynamic analysis clustering process feed into the static analysis clustering process at each iteration which should improve the quality of this process and vice versa. As for the sequential strategy, the results of the dynamic analysis clustering process are only used as the input for the first iteration of the static analysis clustering process.

For the following experiments, we will exclusively use the alternating strategy.

> Using the alternating strategy when combining the static and dynamic analysis results generated decompositions that had better metrics, in general, than those achieved by the sequential strategy decompositions.

4.4 Experimental Setup and Results for RQ2

In order to answer this research question, we selected the six approaches that tackle the monolithic to microservices decomposition problem or a similar problem using different methods and views of the monolithic applications. These approaches are **Bunch** [11], **CoGCN** [3], **Hierarchical DBSCAN (HierDec)** [16], **FoSCI** [6], **MEM** [9] and **Mono2micro (M2M)** [7].

For each one of the baselines we compare with as well as our approach (HyDec), we use different ranges of hyper-parameters in order to generate multiple decompositions. Then we calculate all five of the evaluation metrics. Similarly to the previous research questions, we eliminate all decompositions that have a NED score equal to 1.

Figure 5 showcases the results of each baseline for each metric and each sample application in boxplot figures. Our solution is highlighted in red.

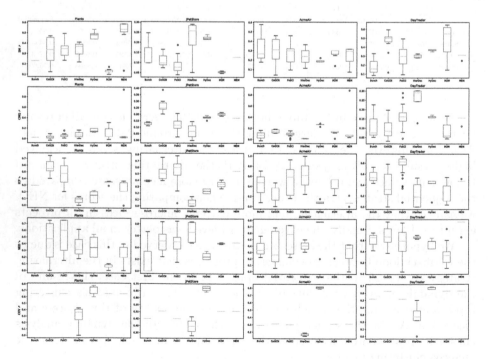

Fig. 5. Boxplots of the evaluation results for each baseline. (Color figure online)

For the sample application Plants, we can observe in the Figure that our approach achieved the highest CMQ median score while managing to have the second highest SM median score and second best ICP score. Only MEM and HierDec managed to have a better score than our approach respectively in SM and ICP. As for NED, our solution had a better score than MEM, FoSCI and CoGCN while M2M achieved the lowest NED. Finally, Our approach had the highest coverage while HierDec had the lowest.

As for JPetStore, our approach managed to achieve the second-best score in both SM and ICP in which HierDec had the best score. However, our approach had significantly better NED and coverage score than the rest of the baselines with only Bunch as an exception for the NED metric. Although HyDec did not reach the best score for CMQ like in the case of Plants, its score managed nonetheless to be the third best and is very close to M2M's score.

When comparing our approach with the rest of the baselines in the AcmeAir project, we can see that it achieved much better coverage than the rest where the median is at least twice as much as the second highest coverage. In addition, it had the highest CMQ and a similar median score to the highest result in ICP which was acquired by MEM. However, these scores came at the cost of lower SM values and higher NED values.

Finally, by comparing the results generated for the application DayTrader using our approach to those created by the other baselines, we can see that HyDec had the highest coverage, the second highest CMQ score, the second-best NED score and the third-highest SM score. As for ICP, our approach managed to have a better score than 3 out of the 7 baselines.

HyDec had the best median COV in all of the sample applications since our approach does not rely too heavily on the run-time execution traces but instead combines it with the source in order to improve the results while having enough information to place as many classes as possible into their adequate microservices. In addition, HyDec managed to be within the 3 best approaches for all sample applications for the metrics SM, CMQ and ICP with the exception of a couple of cases: SM for AcmeAir and ICP for DayTrader. These results showcase that even with the higher coverage, which serves as a disadvantage when calculating these metrics, our approach still managed to improve over the baselines for some cases and remain competitive for the rest. As for NED, the results varied from one application to another. For example, even though HyDec had a significantly higher coverage than the baselines, it did not negatively affect the NED score unlike what happened with AcmeAir. As for the other applications, HyDec's NED score was close to the average of the baselines.

Our approach, HyDec, managed to increase the coverage of the decomposition and to achieve better conceptual and static cohesion and coupling than the other baselines in most cases.

5   Threats to Validity

For internal threats to validity, the biggest threat lies within the selection evaluation metrics and the hyper-parameters for our approach. For the former, we
tried to use five metrics that differ in the criteria that they represent and that
use different inputs, except for the proposed decomposition, to calculate. As for
the latter, we tried to mitigate this threat by varying these hyper-parameters in
order to generate multiple decompositions for the comparison. Particularly for
the comparison with the baselines, we applied the same process and the same
conditions on all of the approaches. The implementation of the approaches could
be a threat to the validity of this research as well. We attempted to mitigate
this issue by extensively testing the code and verifying the obtained results.

In this paper, we evaluated our approach on only four monolithic applications. Although we tried to select a set of applications that have varying numbers
of classes and interactions, it would be beneficial to our research to evaluate its
performance on additional sample monolithic applications. Our approach uses
the classes of the monolithic application as the granularity level of its representation. There is a debate within the literature on which granularity level would be
more suitable for the decomposition task [6]. In our case, we decided on the class
level since this research focused mainly on Object-Oriented Languages for which
the classes represent a core concept when coding. Having a more fine-grained
level, like for example at the procedural level, can lead to more coupling issues
and as such more refactoring would be required.

6   Conclusion and Future Work

We presented a microservices decomposition solution that takes as input the
source code of a monolithic application as well as run-time traces of its execution. The proposed approach analyzes each of the sources individually extracting
semantic and structural information of the classes within the monolithic application from the source code and dynamic interactions between the classes from
the execution traces. Then, an iterative clustering process starts which groups
together the classes based on the current analysis type, the results of the previous layer and the current constraints. The final result is a hierarchical view of
the proposed microservices. The evaluation results showcase that this approach
improves over individual applications of each analysis approach and a comparison with state-of-the-art approaches shows that our solution managed to surpass
the coverage of the rest of the baselines while providing decompositions that have
competitive structural and conceptual cohesion and coupling.

In the future, we would like to work on improving the analysis phase of our
approach, and particularly the semantic analysis approach in order to extract
more accurate information from the source code of the monolithic applications.
We would like to investigate as well if we can combine information extracted from

other sources like the version control history or the documentation. Finally, it would be interesting to study the impact of prioritizing the domain relationship between the classes over the structural and dynamic interactions and find a way to evaluate whether these solutions would be more beneficial.

References

1. Benomar, O., Abdeen, H., Sahraoui, H., Poulin, P., Saied, M.A.: Detection of software evolution phases based on development activities. In: 2015 IEEE 23rd International Conference on Program Comprehension (2016)
2. Bittencourt, R.A., Guerrero, D.D.S.: Comparison of graph clustering algorithms for recovering software architecture module views. In: Proceedings of the European Conference on Software Maintenance and Reengineering, CSMR (2009)
3. Desai, U., Bandyopadhyay, S., Tamilselvam, S.: Graph neural network to dilute outliers for refactoring monolith application (2021)
4. Fritzsch, J., Bogner, J., Wagner, S., Zimmermann, A.: Microservices migration in industry: Intentions, strategies, and challenges. In: 2019 IEEE International Conference on Software Maintenance and Evolution (ICSME) (2019)
5. Gysel, M., Kölbener, L., Giersche, W., Zimmermann, O.: Service cutter: a systematic approach to service decomposition. In: Aiello, M., Johnsen, E.B., Dustdar, S., Georgievski, I. (eds.) ESOCC 2016. LNCS, vol. 9846, pp. 185–200. Springer, Cham (2016). https://doi.org/10.1007/978-3-319-44482-6_12
6. Jin, W., Liu, T., Cai, Y., Kazman, R., Mo, R., Zheng, Q.: Service candidate identification from monolithic systems based on execution traces. IEEE Trans. Softw. Eng. **47**(5), 987–1007 (2019)
7. Kalia, A.K., Xiao, J., Krishna, R., Sinha, S., Vukovic, M., Banerjee, D.: Mono2micro: a practical and effective tool for decomposing monolithic java applications to microservices. In: ESEC/FSE 2021. Association for Computing Machinery Inc (2021)
8. Lewis, J., Fowler, M.: Microservices: a definition of this new architectural term (2017)
9. Mazlami, G., Cito, J., Leitner, P.: Extraction of microservices from monolithic software architectures. In: Proceedings - ICWS 2017. Institute of Electrical and Electronics Engineers Inc (2017)
10. Mazzara, M., Dragoni, N., Bucchiarone, A., Giaretta, A., Larsen, S.T., Dustdar, S.: Microservices: migration of a mission critical system. IEEE Trans. Serv. Comput. **14**(5), 1464–1477
11. Mitchell, B.S., Mancoridis, S.: On the automatic modularization of software systems using the bunch tool. IEEE Trans. Softw. Eng. **32**(3), 193–208 (2006)
12. Saied, M.A., Ouni, A., Sahraoui, H., Kula, R.G., Inoue, K., Lo, D.: Improving reusability of software libraries through usage pattern mining. J. Syst. Softw. **145**, 164–179 (2018)
13. Saied, M.A., Raelijohn, E., Batot, E., Famelis, M., Sahraoui, H.: Towards assisting developers in API usage by automated recovery of complex temporal patterns. Inf. Softw. Technol. **119**, 106213 (2020)
14. Saied, M.A., Sahraoui, H.: A cooperative approach for combining client-based and library-based API usage pattern mining. In: 2016 IEEE 24th International Conference on Program Comprehension (ICPC) (2016)

218   K. Sellami et al.

15. Sellami, K., Ouni, A., Saied, M.A., Bouktif, S., Mkaouer, M.W.: Improving microservices extraction using evolutionary search. Inf. Softw. Technol. **151**, 106996 (2022)
16. Sellami, K., Saied, M.A., Ouni, A.: A hierarchical dbscan method for extracting microservices from monolithic applications. In: The International Conference on Evaluation and Assessment in Software Engineering 2022. Association for Computing Machinery (2022)

MicroSketch: Lightweight and Adaptive Sketch Based Performance Issue Detection and Localization in Microservice Systems

Yufeng Li[1], Guangba Yu[2], Pengfei Chen[2(✉)], Chuanfu Zhang[1], and Zibin Zheng[2]

[1] School of Systems Science and Engineering, Sun Yat-Sen University, Guangzhou, China
liyf323@mail2.sysu.edu.cn, zhangchf9@mail.sysu.edu.cn
[2] School of Computer Science and Engineering, Sun Yat-Sen University, Guangzhou, China
yugb5@mail2.sysu.edu.cn, {chenpf7,zhzibin}@mail.sysu.edu.cn

Abstract. With the rapid growth of microservice systems in cloud-native environments, end-to-end traces have become essential data to help diagnose performance issues. However, existing trace-based anomaly detection and root cause analysis (RCA) still suffer from practical issues due to either the massive volume or frequent system changes. In this study, we propose a lightweight and adaptive trace-based anomaly detection and RCA approach, named *MicroSketch*, which leverages Sketch based features and Robust Random Cut Forest (RRCForest) to render trace analysis more effective and efficient. In addition, *MicroSketch* is an unsupervised approach that is able to adapt to changes in microservice systems without any human intervention. We evaluated *MicroSketch* on a widely-used open-source system and a production system. The results demonstrate the efficiency and effectiveness of *MicroSketch*. *MicroSketch* significantly outperforms start-of-the-art approaches, with an average of 40.9% improvement in F1 score on anomaly detection and 25.0% improvement in Recall of Top-1 on RCA. In particular, *MicroSketch* is at least 60x faster than other methods in terms of diagnosis time.

Keywords: Microservice · Anomaly detection · Root cause analysis · Sketch

1 Introduction

Over the years, more and more enterprises (e.g., Amazon, Netflix, and Twitter) have gradually replaced monolithic applications with loosely-coupled and lightweight microservices [2,16]. The loosely-coupled paradigm of microservice applications enables independent refactoring and dynamic scaling for each service [19,20]. Despite various resilience strategies in modern microservice architecture (e.g., load balancing and circuit breaking), system-wide issues of microservice

© The Author(s), under exclusive license to Springer Nature Switzerland AG 2022
J. Troya et al. (Eds.): ICSOC 2022, LNCS 13740, pp. 219–236, 2022.
https://doi.org/10.1007/978-3-031-20984-0_15

applications are still pervasive due to resource exhaustion, network jam, etc. Performance issues that manifest themselves as high latency are easier to happen but more difficult to diagnose than availability issues [4].

Distributed tracing [14] becomes a mainstream tool for troubleshooting in microservice systems. Distributed tracing records the detailed executions of completing a user request, including the invocation paths of service instances and latency information of these invocations between service instances. Because distributed tracing has an irreplaceable advantage in capturing interactions between service instances, it is becoming an indispensable infrastructure for monitoring, profiling, analyzing and diagnosing in modern distributed software systems, especially in large microservice applications. However, current tracing tools (e.g., Jaeger[1] and Zipkin[2] are primarily designed to collect and present traces rather than automatically diagnose performance issues.

It is an error-prone and labor-intensive process to manually detect performance issues and localize root causes based on current tracing tools. Therefore, some automated trace analysis approaches have been proposed in microservice systems [6,10,18]. However, state-of-the-art studies with traces for performance analysis encounter practical issues due to the massive volume of traces or frequent system changes. As shown in Table 1, tprof [6] takes over 600 s and MicroRank [18] needs over 100 s to infer root causes by analyzing 10,000 traces when one fault occurs. This is because tprof [6] hierarchically groups traces by request types and trace structures, and calculates increasingly detailed aggregated statistics, which consumes a great deal of time. MicroRank introduces PageRank to calculate the weights of traces, which needs a long time to get the converged results when meeting a larger scale of traces. The inference time will be further exacerbated when a larger-scale microservice system is encountered. TraceAnomaly [10] takes less time to infer root causes than MicroRank, but it needs to retrain the deep Bayesian network after microservice updates. In addition, this training process is extremely time-consuming, resulting in poor adaptability.

Table 1. Resource overhead and inference time for some state-of-the-art trace analysis systems. (The experiment platform is shown in Subsect. 4.1)

System	Method	CPU utilization (%)	Memory usage (MB)	Time(s)
tprof [6]	Hierarchical analysis	12 ± 2 single core	800 ± 50	600 ± 30
TraceAnomaly [10]	Deep Bayesian network	75 ± 5 single core	550 ± 50	65 ± 10
MicroRank [18]	PageRank+Spectrum	12 ± 2 single core	430 ± 50	105 ± 10

To address the above drawbacks of existing work, we propose *MicroSketch*, which leverages Sketch [11] based features and Robust Random Cut Forest (RRCForest) [5] to detect performance issues and localize root causes using distributed traces in a lightweight and adaptive way, with a low time and space com-

---

[1] Jaeger, https://jaegertracing.io/.
[2] Zipkin, https://zipkin.io/.

plexity. It consists of three main procedures including *Status Encoder*, *Anomaly Detector*, and *Fault Locator*. *Status Encoder* collects trace data and encodes these data into a status vector in order to conduct *Anomaly Detector*. Then *Anomaly Detector* determines whether it is an anomaly. Once an anomaly is detected, *Fault Locator* is triggered and generates a ranking list containing possible root causes for the anomaly. We evaluated *MicroSketch* on a widely-used open-source system and a production system. The results demonstrate the efficiency and effectiveness of *MicroSketch*. Moreover, *MicroSketch* significantly outperforms start-of-the-art approaches, with an average of 40.9% improvement in F1 score on anomaly detection and 25.0% improvement in Recall of Top-1 on root cause analysis (RCA). In particular, *MicroSketch* is at least 60x faster than other methods in terms of diagnosis time. Besides, *MicroSketch* has the ability to automatically adapt to the changes of microservice systems and continually work without any manual intervention.

Overall, the contribution of this paper is three-fold summarized as follows.

- We improve the DDSketch, state-of-the-art sketch technology, so that it keeps all the original features while reducing storage space to calculate the quantiles with sublinear space and linear time complexity.
- We propose a novel anomaly detection and RCA approach in microservice environments based on the adaptive RRCForest, which automatically adapts to variable-length input vector and renders our model appropriate for dynamic microservice systems.
- We implement *MicroSketch* to detect performance issues and localize root causes in a lightweight and adaptive way. We conduct extensive experiments based on a widely-used microservice benchmark and a production microservice system. Experimental results demonstrate that *MicroSketch* achieves good results both on anomaly detection and RCA. In addition, *MicroSketch* is at least 60x faster than other methods in terms of diagnosis time.

2   Background

Distributed tracing is an important technique for gaining insight and observability into microservice systems [15]. In large-scale microservice systems, a request is typically handled by multiple services deployed in different nodes or even data centers. Distributed tracing provides a method to track the complete execution path of each request. A span represents a logical unit of execution, handled by an operation of a service instance in a microservice system. All spans that serve for the same request collectively form a trace, as illustrated in the left part of Fig. 1. Spans generated by the same request have the same trace ID. For each span, it records some attributes (i.e., Trace ID, Span ID, and Start time), as shown on the right part of Fig. 1.

As shown in Fig. 1, the duration of a span is the accumulated time spent by this operation and all downstream operations. Therefore, when the duration of span E increases due to a fault, all upstream spans of E (i.e., span A and D) will increase as well due to fault propagation, making it difficult to determine which span is the root cause. To overcome this problem, we transform duration into a more directional metric. For each span, we subtract the duration of its all child spans from its duration to get its real handling time. In Fig. 1, the non-shaded part is called the span's handling time.

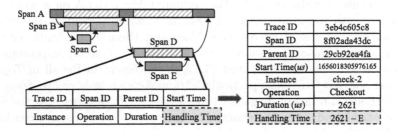

Fig. 1. An example of trace with five spans in Hipster-Shop (Hipster-Shop, https://github.com/GoogleCloudPlatform/microservices-demo).

3   System Design

3.1   System Overview

Figure 2 demonstrates the framework of *MicroSketch*. It consists of three modules, including *Status Encoder*, *Anomaly Detector* and *Fault Locator*. We use *time interval* to denote the trace analysis frequency (1 min default in this study). Firstly, given the traces in a time interval, *Status Encoder* leverages the extended DDSketch to calculate the quantile of the handling time for each invocation group and encodes them as status vector $x = (x_1, x_2, ..., x_m)$ (Subsect. 3.2). Secondly, *Anomaly Detector* analyzes the status vector based on adaptive Robust Random Cut Forest (RRCForest) and outputs the anomaly score of x (Subsect. 3.3). If the score of x is over the predefined threshold τ, *Fault Locator* is triggered to determine the root cause (Subsect. 3.4).

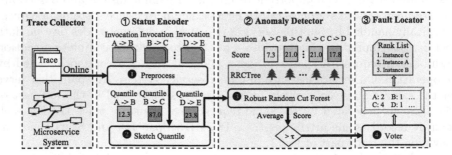

Fig. 2. The framework of *MicroSketch*

3.2   Status Encoder

At each time interval, *MicroSketch* queries all traces in the time interval and inputs them into *Status Encoder*.

Status Vector. Quantile is a splendid statistic for profiling data, especially for latency data. The quantile of the handling time, such as the 50th or the 90th percentiles, reflects the quality of service instance. As shown in Fig. 3, p90 of the operation (product-1.sql-query) rises when issue occurs. Quantile [11] can be formalized as follows. Given a multiset S of size n, the q-quantile item $x_q \in S$ is the item x whose index $R(x)$ in sorted multiset S is $\lfloor 1 + q(n-1) \rfloor$ for $0 \le q \le 1$.

After all spans are collected, we group them by the type of invocation. The invocation owning the same upstream service instance, same downstream service instance and same operation belongs to the same type. We calculate the quantile (p90 in this paper) of the handling time for each group and manage these quantiles as a vector $\boldsymbol{x} = [x_1, x_2, ..., x_m]$, where x_i means the quantile of the handling time that belongs to the invocation group i. Status vector $\boldsymbol{x}$ largely reflects the performance status of the global microservice system in this time interval.

Sketch Technology. Commonly, we sort the multi-set S first and then query by index $\lfloor 1 + q(n-1) \rfloor$ to generate an exact q-quantile, but it requires huge computing resources and time for sort. Nevertheless, it is not so necessary to get the exact quantile value in our scenarios. An estimated quantile that does not deviate too far from the exact value can also be enough to conduct anomaly detection. Therefore, we introduce Distributed Distribution Sketch (DDSketch) [11], which is able to calculate the quantile much faster and more economically with relative-error guarantees and sublinear space and linear time complexity. DDSketch keeps rigorously relative-error guarantees by dividing the data stream into fixed buckets. It means that, given a parameter α, each estimated q-quantile $\tilde{x}_q$ and the exact q-quantile x_q are satisfied to $|\tilde{x}_q - x_q| \le \alpha x_q$.

However, we do not need to satisfy the rigorous relative-error guarantees. Because we hardly focus on the head latency data (i.e., the main-body distribution of latency data). We use an equi-width histogram to extend the DDSketch, which allows us to reduce memory usage without losing the relative-error guarantees in the tail data, compared to DDSketch. To elaborate on how extended DDSketch works, the three phases, namely *initialization, insertion* and *query* are summarized.

In the phase of initialization, we define the *tail relative-error rate* α, *boundary* L and *head granularity factor* β to keep the error guarantees. Given a quantile percentage q, if $x_q < L$, the estimated quantile $\tilde{x}_q$ will be satisfied to $|\tilde{x}_q - x_q| \le \beta$ and if $x_q \ge L$, the estimated quantile $\tilde{x}_q$ will be satisfied to $|\tilde{x}_q - x_q| \le \alpha x_q$. Thus, we keep the relative-error guarantees in the *tail data* (the numbers are greater than L), and reduce the memory usage at the cost of losing the relative-error guarantees in the *head data* (the numbers are less than L). In this paper, α is set as 1%, L is set as p50 estimated by the last or 0 and β is set as $\frac{L}{100}$ or other reasonable values.

Algorithm 1. extended DDSketch Insert Algorithm

Input: the number $x \in \mathbb{R} > 0$
1: **if** $x < L$ **then**
2:     $i \leftarrow \lceil \frac{x}{\beta} \rceil$ //Find bucket index i if x belongs to the head data
3:     $H_i \leftarrow H_i + 1$ //Bucket H[i] adds 1
4: **else**
5:     $i \leftarrow \lceil \log_\gamma(x) \rceil$ //Find bucket index i if x belongs to the tail data
6:     $B_i \leftarrow B_i + 1$ //Bucket B[i] adds 1
7: **end if**

In the phase of insertion, let $\gamma := \frac{(1+\alpha)}{(1-\alpha)}$. If the input number x is less than L, bucket $H[\lceil \frac{x}{\beta} \rceil]$ adds 1. Otherwise, bucket $B[\lceil \log_\gamma(x) \rceil]$ adds 1. This is shown in Algorithm 1.

In the phase of query, given a quantile percentage q, extended DDSketch try to find the minimum index i which makes $\sum_{j=0}^{i} H_j > q(n-1)$. If we succeed in finding the index i, extended DDSketch returns the estimated quantile $\frac{2i-1}{2}\beta$. Otherwise, extended DDSketch finds the minimum index i which makes $\sum_{j=0}^{i} H_j + \sum_{j=0}^{i} B_j > q(n-1)$ and returns the estimated quantile $\frac{2\gamma^i}{\gamma+1}$. The detail is described in Algorithm 2. Finally, we update L to the estimated p50.

Algorithm 2. extended DDSketch Query Algorithm

Input: $0 \leq q \leq 1$
Output: the estimated q-quantile
1: count $\leftarrow 0$ $i \leftarrow -1$
2: **while** $i < len(H)$ && count $\leq q(n-1)$ **do**
3:     $i \leftarrow i + 1$
4:         count $\leftarrow$ count $+H_i$ //Accumulate bucket H[i] in order
5: **end while**
6: **if** count $> q(n-1)$ **then**
7:     **return** $\frac{2i-1}{2}\beta$ //The q-quantile falls in bucket H[i]
8: **end if**
9: **while** count $\leq q(n-1)$ **do**
10:     $i \leftarrow \min(\{j : B_j > 0 \wedge j > i\})$ //Accumulate non-empty bucket B[j] in order
11:     count $\leftarrow$ count $+B_i$;
12: **end while**
13: **return** $\frac{2\gamma^i}{\gamma+1}$ //The q-quantile falls in bucket B[i]

3.3 Anomaly Detector

After encoding, traces in time interval are transformed into status vector $x = [x_1, x_2, ..., x_m]$. Anomaly detection is converted to outlier detection based on the time series of status vector x. Robust Random Cut Forest (RRCForest) [5] is a streaming model and follows the mechanism of isolation forest [9]. In detail, the point set is distributed in a multidimensional space $S \subset \mathbb{R}^m$, for each case,

RRCForest randomly chooses a dimension and randomly chooses a value in this dimension to cut. This process is called *dimension cut*. After one dimension cut, the whole space is divided into two subspaces. Subsequently, two subspaces are recursively cut in the same way. A point is determined to be isolated if it occupies a subspace exclusively. The scatter chart in Fig. 3 shows an isolated point occupying the shaded left upper corner exclusively.

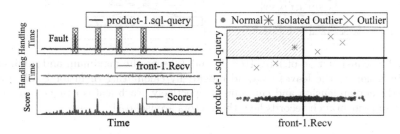

Fig. 3. The distribution of status vectors and the mechanism of RRCForest. The first and second line charts in the left part are p90 handling time of operation front-1.Recv and product-1.sql-query, respectively. The third line chart is the anomaly score given by adaptive RRCForest. The scatter chart is the distribution of status vectors and an example of the dimension cut of a two-dimensional space $S \subset \mathbb{R}^2$.

Taking two operations (front-1.Recv and product-1.sql-query) in Hipster-Shop (Subsect. 4.1) as an example, we use *Status Encoder* to transform traces in each time interval into status vector $x = [x_1, x_2]$. Both the distribution of each dimension and the distribution of the vectors are shown in Fig. 3. We intermittently injected four anomalies into service instance product-1. There are four peaks in the handling time of product-1 because of fault injection. The scatter chart in Fig. 3 presents that several vectors corresponding to the peaks are labeled as red forks. The red forks can be isolated by two or three dimension cuts and those dense normal blue dots require more cuts to be isolated.

Next, we describe how RRCForest detects anomalies. The process of dimension cut mentioned above is described by a binary tree structure, called Robust Random Cut Tree (RRCTree). As shown in Fig. 4, RRCTree owns two kinds of nodes. One is *leaf*, represented as a square rectangle, the other is **branch**, represented as a rounded rectangle. We also summarize three phases for the construction of RRCTree, namely *initialization*, *insertion* and *query*.

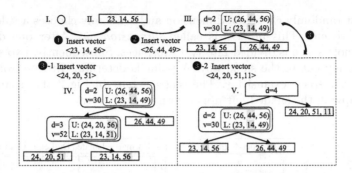

Fig. 4. The construction of RRCTree. U and L keeps the maximum and minimum of each dimension of the leaves to avoid repeatedly calculating them for Eq. 1. d and v denote the cut dimension and cut value, respectively. Each leaf is assigned to a status vector and each branch records how the vectors are isolated.

In the phase of initialization, we create an empty tree, given in Fig. 4-I.

$$w_i = \frac{max_{x \in S} x_i - min_{x \in S} x_i}{\sum_i \left(max_{x \in S} x_i - min_{x \in S} x_i \right)}. \tag{1}$$

In the phase of insertion, given a RRCTree T', we insert a vector x. Let S' as all vectors in RRCTree T' and $S = S' \cup x$. If RRCTree is empty (case 1), we directly create a leaf, assigned to this vector. Figure 4-❶ shows the case 1.

If RRCTree is non-empty (case 2), we move on to the following discussion. The case 2 is further divided into three sub-cases. We randomly select the *cut dimension d* according to the weight w_i which is calculated in the Eq. 1. After selecting cut dimension d, we randomly and uniformly choose a *cut value* $v \in [min_{x \in S} x_d, max_{x \in S} x_d]$. If $v \leq min_{x' \in S'} x'_d$ (case 2–1), we create a branch and a leaf that is assigned to the vector x. Then, we set the created leaf as the left subtree of the created branch and the RRCTree T' as the right subtree. If $v > max_{x' \in S'} x'_d$ (case 2–2), we set the RRCTree T' as the left subtree of the created branch and the created leaf as the right subtree. If neither is the case (case 2–3), we consider inserting the vector x into the left subtree of RRCTree T' or right subtree. In detail, for the cut dimension d' and cut value v' of the root branch, if $x_{d'} \leq v'$, we insert the vector x into the left subtree of RRCTree T'. Otherwise, we insert the vector x into the right subtree. Since the subtree is also a RRCTree, the insertion can run recursively until it goes back to the case 2–1 or case 2–2. In sum, Fig. 4-❷ shows the case 2–1. The case 2–2 is similar to the case 2–1. Figure 4-❸-1 shows the case 2–3.

The last case (case 3) is to insert a variable-length vector x and $len(x) > max_{x' \in S'} len(x')$. We create a branch, named *dimension branch*, which represents that a new dimension occurs. Then, we set RRCTree T' as the left subtree of the created dimension branch and the inserted vector as the right subtree. Figure 4-❸-2 shows the case 3.

Further, in order to prevent the tree from excessively expanding, we set *tree size* (128 in this paper) in advance and delete the earliest point from the tree when the number of leaves exceeds *tree size*. Deletion is similar to insertion.

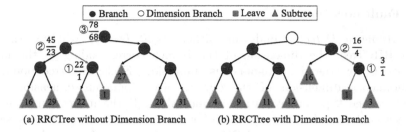

(a) RRCTree without Dimension Branch   (b) RRCTree with Dimension Branch

Fig. 5. An example of calculating the anomaly score. (a) The cut rates of red leaf are $\frac{22}{1}$, $\frac{45}{23}$ and $\frac{78}{68}$. The score of the leaf is 22. (b) The cut rates of red leaf are $\frac{3}{1}$ and $\frac{16}{4}$ and the score of the leave is 4. The higher the score, the more anomalous the vector.

In the phase of query, we obtain an anomaly score for the inserted vector. As soon as the insertion of a vector is complete, we query its score. We define the cut rate of a branch as $r = \frac{max(n_{left}, n_{right})}{min(n_{left}, n_{right})}$, where n_{left} is the number of leaves that belong to the left subtree of the branch and n_{right} is the number of leaves that belong to the right subtree of the branch. We find all ancestor branches in the path from the leaf corresponding to the vector to the root branch except dimension branch and calculate these branches' cut rates. Logically, the score of the vector is equal to the maximum in these cut rates. Figure 5 presents two examples of how to calculate the anomaly score of a leaf.

Therefore, anomaly score is closely related to *tree size*. Practically, we give a threshold $\tau = mean \times \log(tree\ size)$, where *mean* denotes the average history score. If one's score exceeds the threshold τ, we regard it as an anomaly.

The above section illustrates how a RRCTree is constructed and queried. As listed in Eq. 1, the selection of cut dimension is random and probabilistic. To make this random construction more convergent to its expectation, we generally build multiple RRCTrees simultaneously and independently. The final score is the average of all RRCTrees' scores. Therefore, in practice, we have to define a parameter *tree number* (50 in this paper by default), which determines how many RRCTrees *Anomaly Detector* maintains.

RRCForest	🌲	🌲	🌲	🌲	①
Anomalous Dimension	Invocation (A, C)	Invocation (B, C)	Invocation (A, C)	Invocation (C, D)	②
Vote	A: 2	B: 1	C: 4	D: 1	
Rank List	❶ C	❷ A	❸ B	❸ D	③

Fig. 6. The details of *Fault Locator*. Each RRCTree independently points out an anomalous invocation. The instance C is viewed as the root cause because there are four RRCTrees voting for C.

3.4   Fault Locator

Once *Anomaly Detector* finds an outlier, *Fault Locator* will be triggered. For a RRCTree, the dimension of the branch corresponding to the largest cut rate is considered an anomalous dimension. Each RRCTree points out an anomalous dimension of the outlier. An anomalous dimension represents that one type of invocation is anomalous. If the invocation is anomalous, we conclude that the upstream service instance or downstream service instance may be anomalous. RRCForest gives a set of anomalous invocations $[I(u_1, d_1), I(u_2, d_2), ..., I(u_k, d_k)]$, where u and d denote upstream service instance and downstream service instance, respectively. To further determine the most likely root cause, we propose a voting mechanism. Each anomalous invocation $I(u, d)$ votes for service instance u and service instance d. The service instance with the most votes is regarded as the root cause. Figure 6 presents that instance C is determined as the root cause after the vote of four RRCTrees.

4   Experiment Setup

4.1   Datasets

We use two datasets to validate our approach. One, named $\mathcal{A}$, is based on one of the most widely-used open-source microservice systems, Hipster-Shop. The other, named $\mathcal{B}$, is based on a production microservice system in China Mobile, the largest telecommunication company in China. Table 2 shows some details of our experimental datasets. We implement *MicroSketch* with Python 3.7. All experiments are conducted on a workstation with 4-core 2 GHz Intel Core i5-1038NG7 CPU and 16 GB memory.

Table 2. Experimental datasets

Dataset	Benchmark	Fault number	Fault type	Trace number
$\mathcal{A}$	Hipster-shop	50	Network, CPU, IO read, IO write	2,902 K
$\mathcal{B}$	Production system	8	Network, CPU	168 K

Hipster-Shop Microservice System. This system is an e-commerce website with 10 microservices that are implemented in different programming languages and intercommunicate using gRPC. We continuously run a workload generator, which can simulate real-world users. The microservice benchmark is deployed in a Kubernetes cluster that consists of 1 master node and 5 worker nodes based on virtual machines, which singly run with Ubuntu 18.04 OS. To mimic performance issues, we use two tools, Chaosblade[3] and Strace[4] to inject four types of faults into Hipster-Shop. We injected 50 faults to Hipster-shop in total. Each fault injection lasts for 30 to 60 s.

---

[3] Chaosblade, https://github.com/chaosblade-io/chaosblade.
[4] Strace, https://strace.io.

Real-World Microservice System. Dataset $\mathcal{B}$, released by the 2020 AIOps Challenge Event, is based on a real-world production microservice system in China Mobile. In particular, the workload of the system in $\mathcal{B}$ is a replica of the real-world workload. The types of faults include network fault and CPU fault. Note that since this event does not only focus on microservice applications, we only selected those faults related to microservices on May 31st, 2020.

4.2   Evaluation Metric

We use **Precision** (P), **Recall** (R) and **F1 score** ($F1$) to compare the performance of anomaly detection. Precision is computed by $\frac{TP}{TP+FP}$, while Recall is computed by $\frac{TP}{TP+FN}$, where TP, FP and FN refer to the number of anomalous time intervals that are correctly predicted to be anomalous, the number of normal time intervals that are incorrectly predicted to be anomalous, and the number of anomalous time intervals that are incorrectly predicted to be normal, respectively. F1 score is calculated by $2 \times \frac{P \times R}{P+R}$.

We employ the following two widely-used metrics by previous work [18], to evaluate the effectiveness of *Fault Locator*. **Recall of Top-k** ($R@k$) refers to the probability that root causes can be included in the top k results. Higher $R@k$ denotes more effective root cause localization. We choose $R@k$ ($k = 1, 2, 5$) in the experiment. **EXAM Score** (ES) refers to the average count of incorrect candidates that have to be excluded manually by operators before localizing the correct root cause. If ES is larger than 10, we set ES as 10.

5   Experimental Evaluation

5.1   Effectiveness Comparison

We use some state-of-the-art trace-based unsupervised approaches to validate the performance of *MicroSketch* on anomaly detection and RCA, including MicroRank [18], tprof [6] and TraceAnomaly [10]. Note that we assume that all the anomalies have been detected before RCA.

Anomaly Detection. Table 3 compares the overall performance of anomaly detection and lists the obtained result with the best F1 score. *MicroSketch,*

Table 3. Comparisons of *MicroSketch's anomaly detector* and baselines.

Dataset	Approach	F1 score	F1 score impr.	Precision	Precision impr.	Recall	Recall impr.
$\mathcal{A}$	*MicroSketch*	**0.925**	–	**0.93**	–	**0.92**	-
	MicroRank	0.834	↑ 10.9%	0.84	↑ 10.7%	0.829	↑ 11.0%
	tprof	0.413	↑ 124.0%	0.327	↑ 184.4%	0.493	↑ 86.6%
	TraceAnomaly	0.804	↑ 15.0%	0.823	↑ 13.0%	0.786	↑ 17.0%
$\mathcal{B}$	*MicroSketch*	**0.934**	–	**0.877**	–	**1.0**	–
	MicroRank	0.865	↑ 8.0%	0.90	↓ −2.6%	0.833	↑ 20.0%
	tprof	0.545	↑ 71.4%	0.48	↑ 82.7%	0.631	↑ 58.5%
	TraceAnomaly	0.804	↑ 16.2%	0.70	↑ 25.3%	0.946	↑ 5.7%

Table 4. Comparisons of *MicroSketch*'s *fault locator* and baselines

Dataset	Approach	R@1	R@1 Impr.	R@2	R@2 Impr.	R@5	R@5 Impr.	Exam Score
$\mathcal{A}$	*MicroSketch*	**0.96**	–	**0.96**	–	**1.0**	–	**0.16**
	MicroRank	0.98	↓ –2.0%	0.98	↓ –2.0%	0.98	↑ 2.0%	0.2
	tprof	0.64	↑50.0%	0 .64	↑ 50.0%	0.70	↑ 42.9%	3.12
	TraceAnomaly	0.62	↑ 54.8%	0.70	↑ 37.1%	0.86	↑ 16.3%	1.98
$\mathcal{B}$	*MicroSketch*	**1.0**	–	**1.0**	–	**1.0**	–	**0.0**
	MicroRank	1.0	0.0%	1.0	0.0%	1.0	0.0%	0.0
	tprof	0.75	↑ 33.3%	0.75	↑ 33.3%	1.0	0.0%	1.0
	TraceAnomaly	0.875	↑ 14.3%	0.875	↑ 14.3%	0.875	↑ 14.3%	1.125

MicroRank and TraceAnomaly achieve over 0.8 in F1 score. However, *MicroSketch* achieves the best result on both $\mathcal{A}$ and $\mathcal{B}$ with an average of 40.9% improvement in F1 score. The F1 score of *MicroSketch* outperforms the compared unsupervised approaches by 10.9%~124% on $\mathcal{A}$ and by 8.0%~71.4% on $\mathcal{B}$. tprof performs poorly because tprof detects anomalies using simple ratio relationships.

Root Cause Localization. Table 4 compares the overall effectiveness of RCA. The R@1 results of *MicroSketch* on $\mathcal{A}$ and $\mathcal{B}$ are 0.96 and 1, respectively. *MicroSketch* achieves an average of 25.0% improvement in R@1. The ES of *MicroSketch* achieves 0.16. MicroRank works better in RCA since MicroRank fully leverages PageRank and Spectrum technology and takes a lot of time to get a convergent result. tprof intuitively believes that the more times an operation is called and the longer time it takes, the more anomalous it is. In the operation and maintenance phase, the uncommon pattern should be more concerned rather than the time-consuming pattern. TraceAnomaly analyzes root causes by one specific anomalous trace rather than combining all available traces.

5.2   Adaption

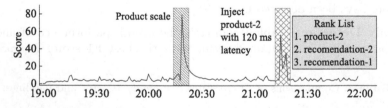

Fig. 7. The anomaly score varies from 19:00 to 22:00 about three hours in Hipster-Shop. At 20:17, product service instances increase from 2 to 3. This is shown in blue slash shadow. At 21:14, we inject product-2 instance with 120 ms latency and this is shown in the red grid shadow. (Color figure online)

Figure 7 demonstrates the adaptability of *MicroSketch* to changes in system topology. In Fig. 7, the topology of Hipster-Shop changes due to the product service's auto-scaling at 20:17. *MicroSketch* perceives that the pattern of trace data is out of the way and gives the system a high anomaly score at 20:18. Since the topology change is stable, *MicroSketch* adapts to the new pattern and the anomaly score gradually returns to normal again. At 21:14, we actively inject a latency fault to product-2, one of the instances of product service. At 21:15, *MicroSketch* successfully detects anomaly and localizes the root cause (product-2). *MicroSketch* also owns the ability to adapt to other forms of service changes, such as service update.

Table 5. The overhead of the entire *MicroSketch* and single modules of *MicroSketch*.

Module	CPU utilization (%)	Memory usage (MB)	Time(s)	Note
MicroSketch	12 ± 2	200 ± 20	1.1 ± 0.3	10000 traces
Status encoder	12 ± 2	170 ± 10	0.9 ± 0.2	10000 traces
Anomaly detector	12 ± 2	180 ± 10	0.2 ± 0.1	1 time interval
Fault locator	12 ± 2	120 ± 10	0.001	1 anomaly

5.3   Overhead

Table 5 shows the overhead of various modules of *MicroSketch*. *Status Encoder* consumes about 12% CPU utilization, 170 MB memory and 0.9 s to encode 10000 traces as status vector. *Anomaly Detector* takes about 12% CPU utilization, 180 MB memory and 0.2 s to detect whether a vector is anomalous or not. *Fault Locator* spends very little time which is smaller than 0.001 s and consumes 12% CPU utilization and 120 MB memory. The whole *MicroSketch* costs about 12% CPU utilization, 200 MB memory and 1.1 s to analyze 10000 traces. Compared to the overhead of other baselines in Table 1, *MicroSketch* reduces the memory usage by about 50% and is at least 60x faster. *MicroSketch* is more lightweight because *MicroSketch* exploits two efficient data structure DDSketch and RRCForest with a low complexity.

Status Encoder' space complexity is sublinearly related to the number of traces in the time interval, and the time complexity is linearly related to the number of traces in the time interval. *Anomaly Detector*'s space complexity is linearly related to the product of *tree size* and *tree number*, and the time complexity is sublinearly related to the product of *tree size* and *tree number*.

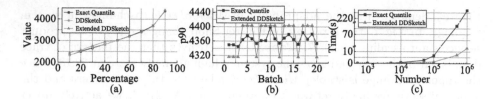

Fig. 8. Comparisons of exact quantile, DDSketch and extended DDSketch. (a) The exact quantiles vs. the values estimated by DDSketch and extended DDSketch. (b) The exact p90 vs. the estimated p90 of a data stream (20 batches of 100,000 values). (c) The consuming time of exact quantile and extended DDSketch.

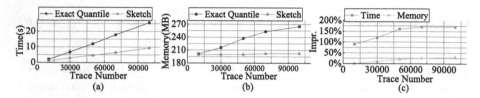

Fig. 9. Comparisons of exact quantile and sketch technology. (a) The time using exact quantile and the time using sketch. (b) The memory usage using exact quantile and the memory usage using sketch. (c) The improvements that sketch brings.

5.4 Sketch Technology

Efficiency and Error. Figure 8-a shows that extended DDSketch has the same relative-error guarantees as DDSketch on the tail data. However, extended DDS-ketch reduces bucket usage at the cost of losing the relative-error guarantees on the head data which we barely focus on. We employ extended DDSketch on 20 batches of 100000 values to calculate the p90 and the result is shown in Fig. 8-b. The estimated p90 always keeps relative-error guarantees. The relative-error guarantees ensure that the estimated quantiles can be used for the following modules. We implement quicksort to calculate exact quantiles. Figure 8-c shows the consuming time of exact quantile and extended DDSketch. The time of calculating the estimated value is much less than the exact value when the number of data increases.

Ablation. For *MicroSketch*, sketch technology is not indispensable. We remove the sketch technology from *Status Encoder* and use exact quantile instead of it. We analyze various numbers of traces in the time interval. Figure 9-a and 9-b show that the overhead of exact quantile rises dramatically as the number of traces increases, but the rise of sketch technology is relatively flat. Figure 9-c presents that the sketch technology achieves 170% improvement on time and 25.0% improvement on memory usage by analyzing 100000 traces. Thus, *MicroSketch* can scale up readily in large microservice systems.

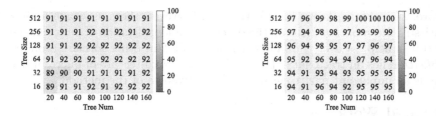

Fig. 10. F1 score using various parameters.

Fig. 11. R@1 using various parameters.

5.5 Sensitivity

Tree Size and Tree Number. *Tree size*, which determines how many vectors RRCTree maintains, is a key parameter for our model. *Tree number* means how many RRCTrees *MicroSketch* creates and also is significant. We set the different values for these two parameters and conduct experiments on $\mathcal{A}$. Figure 10 shows that the difference between the maximum and minimum values of F1 score is 3%. Figure 11 shows that larger parameters can achieve a better result on RCA. However, non-optimal parameters also work well and achieve 91%-95% in R@1. In conclusion, *MicroSketch* is not sensitive to these two parameters.

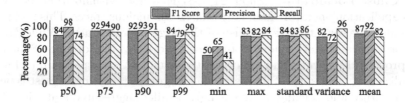

Fig. 12. The performance of our model using various statistics.

Statistical Magnitude. We replace the p90 in the status vector with other statistics. Figure 12 presents that different statistics have different effects. The maximum and minimum values do not work well because of the system jitter. Other simple statistics, such as mean, standard deviation and variance, are easily influenced by a few extremums and lack the ability to perceive issues that slightly affect only part of the requests. Therefore, quantile is a splendid statistic for profiling data. Specific quantile forms specific feature. In practice, it is essential to apply various key quantiles simultaneously in *MicroSketch*.

6 Discussion

MicroSketch forms sketch-based features for anomaly detection and combines the information provided by all anomalous invocations for root cause localization.

Therefore, *MicroSketch* keeps its effectiveness. However, there are some limitations. Firstly, *MicroSketch* focus on the detection and localization of performance issue, so it is helpless over the faults which manifest in other forms. Secondly, *MicroSketch* relies on trace data. The credible trace architecture of microservice systems is an important part to ensure the effectiveness of the method.

7   Related Work

Anomaly Detection. Both TraceAnomaly [10] and Nedelkoski [12], use deep learning method to learn normal patterns of traces offline and detect anomalous traces online. They are useful to detect trace anomalies. However, they require a long time to train the model. Further, when the microservice system changes, they have to retrain the model. Compared to them, *MicroSketch* does not need training and owns the ability to adapt to the system without any human intervention. Seer [3] leverages deep learning to learn spatial and temporal patterns with the KPIs of each service. Hora [13], based on monitored time series metrics, combines architectural knowledge with Bayesian networks to determine the occurrence of performance issues. Microscope [8] detects anomalies by comparing the KPIs with the SLOs of the application. Fully leveraging various types of KPIs, these methods can detect more comprehensive anomaly types. Instead, *MicroSketch* focuses on detecting performance anomalies and localizing root causes more efficiently and effectively.

Root Cause Localization. Zhou [21] designs a trace visualization tool, which allows application operators manually analyze anomalous traces. This tool is very practical but labor-intensive because of the large scale of traces. While *MicroSketch* provides automatic anomaly diagnosis and RCA. MicroRank [18] analyzes clues provided by normal and abnormal traces and utilizes spectrum techniques to localize root causes. tprof [6] hierarchically groups traces by request type and trace structure and calculates increasingly detailed aggregated statistics. These two methods spend a lot of time on obtaining fine-grained and convergent localization results. Compared to them, *MicroSketch* is at least 60x faster and more suitable for large-scale systems. As the number of traces grows, *MicroSketch* will be more advantageous. Many RCA methods are based on KPI, such as MonitorRank [7], Sieve [17] and CauseInfer [1]. MonitorRank [7] forms a system topology graph and uses the personalized PageRank algorithm to determine possible root causes. Sieve [17] reconstructs the system topology and infers possible root causes by representative KPIs. CauseInfer [1] builds a two-layered hierarchical causality graph and uses statistical methods to infer root causes. *MicroSketch* utilizes traces, which carry request information about invocation paths and latency of these invocations, to acquire an API-level system topology that helps to precisely localize root causes.

8   Conclusion

This paper presents *MicroSketch*, an unsupervised lightweight approach to detect performance issues and localize root causes in microservice environments via Sketch-based features and adaptive RRCForest. *MicroSketch* can adapt to changes in microservice systems. The experimental evaluation demonstrates the efficiency and effectiveness of *MicroSketch*. Moreover, *MicroSketch* is at least 60x faster than other methods in terms of diagnosis time. In practice, *MicroSketch* overcomes the challenges imposed by the large scale of traces and the dynamic of microservices, and can scale up readily in large microservice systems.

Acknowledgements. The research is supported by the National Key Research and Development Program of China (2019YFB1804002), the National Natural Science Foundation of China (No. 62272495, 61902440), the Basic and Applied Basic Research of Guangzhou (No. 202002030328), and the Natural Science Foundation of Guangdong Province (No. 2019A1515012229). The corresponding author is Pengfei Chen.

References

1. Chen, P., Qi, Y., et al.: Causeinfer: automatic and distributed performance diagnosis with hierarchical causality graph in large distributed systems. In: INFOCOM 2014, pp. 1887–1895. IEEE (2014)
2. Dragoni, N., et al.: Microservices: yesterday, today, and tomorrow. In: Present and Ulterior Software Engineering, pp. 195–216. Springer, Cham (2017). https://doi.org/10.1007/978-3-319-67425-4_12
3. Gan, Y., Zhang, Y., et al.: Seer: leveraging big data to navigate the complexity of performance debugging in cloud microservices. In: ASPLOS, pp. 19–33 (2019)
4. Gao, K., Sun, C., et al., S.W.: Buffer-based end-to-end request event monitoring in the cloud. In: NSDI 22, pp. 829–843. USENIX Association (2022)
5. Guha, S., Mishra, N., et al.: Robust random cut forest based anomaly detection on streams. In: ICML, pp. 2712–2721. PMLR (2016)
6. Huang, L., Zhu, T.: tprof: performance profiling via structural aggregation and automated analysis of distributed systems traces. In: SoCC 2021, pp. 76–91. ACM (2021)
7. Kim, M., Sumbaly, R., et al.: Root cause detection in a service-oriented architecture. ACM SIGMETRICS Perform. Eval. Rev. **41**(1), 93–104 (2013)
8. Lin, J., Chen, P., Zheng, Z.: Microscope: pinpoint performance issues with causal graphs in micro-service environments. In: Pahl, C., Vukovic, M., Yin, J., Yu, Q. (eds.) ICSOC 2018. LNCS, vol. 11236, pp. 3–20. Springer, Cham (2018). https://doi.org/10.1007/978-3-030-03596-9_1
9. Liu, F.T., Ting, K.M., et al.: Isolation-based anomaly detection. TKDD **6**(1), 1–39 (2012)
10. Liu, P., Xu, H., et al.: Unsupervised detection of microservice trace anomalies through service-level deep bayesian networks. In: ISSRE 2020, pp. 48–58. IEEE (2020)
11. Masson, C., Rim, J.E., et al.: DDSketch: a fast and fully-mergeable quantile sketch with relative-error guarantees. Proc. VLDB Endow. **12**(12), 2195–2205 (2019)
12. Nedelkoski, S., Cardoso, J., Kao, O.: Anomaly detection from system tracing data using multimodal deep learning. In: CLOUD 2019, pp. 179–186. IEEE (2019)
13. Pitakrat, T., Okanović, D., et al.: Hora: architecture-aware online failure prediction. JSE **137**, 669–685 (2018)
14. Shkuro, Y.: Mastering Distributed Tracing: Analyzing performance in Microservices and Complex Systems. Packt Publishing Ltd, Birmingham (2019)

15. Sigelman, B.H., Barroso, L.A., et al.: Dapper, a large-scale distributed systems tracing infrastructure. Google, Inc, Technical Report (2010)
16. Soldani, J., Tamburriand, et al.: The pains and gains of microservices: a systematic grey literature review. J. Syst. Softw. **146**, 215–232 (2018)
17. Thalheim, J., Bhatotia, P., et al.: Cntr: Lightweight {OS} containers. In: 2018 USENIX, pp. 199–212 (2018)
18. Yu, G., Chen, P., et al.: Microrank: end-to-end latency issue localization with extended spectrum analysis in microservice environments. In: WWW 2021, pp. 3087–3098. ACM / IW3C2 (2021)
19. Yu, G., Chen, P., Zheng, Z.: Microscaler: automatic scaling for microservices with an online learning approach. In: ICWS 2019, pp. 68–75. IEEE (2019)
20. Yu, G., Chen, P., Zheng, Z.: Microscaler: cost-effective scaling for microservice applications in the cloud with an online learning approach. IEEE TCC **10**(2), 1100–1116 (2022)
21. Zhou, X., Peng, X., et al.: Fault analysis and debugging of microservice systems: industrial survey, benchmark system, and empirical study. TSE **47**(2), 243–260 (2018)

Proactive-Reactive Global Scaling, with Analytics

Lorenzo Bacchiani[1(✉)], Mario Bravetti[1,2], Maurizio Gabbrielli[1,2], Saverio Giallorenzo[1,2], Gianluigi Zavattaro[1,2], and Stefano Pio Zingaro[1,2]

[1] Università di Bologna, Bologna, Italy
lorenzo.bacchiani2@unibo.it
[2] Focus Team, INRIA, Sophia Antipolis, France

Abstract. In this work, we focus on *by-design global scaling*, a technique that, given a functional specification of a microservice architecture, orchestrates the scaling of all its components, avoiding cascading slowdowns typical of uncoordinated, mainstream autoscaling. State-of-the-art by-design global scaling adopts a reactive approach to traffic fluctuations, undergoing inefficiencies due to the reaction overhead. Here, we tackle this problem by proposing a *proactive* version of *by-design global scaling* able to anticipate future scaling actions. We provide four contributions in this direction: i) a platform able to host both reactive and proactive global scaling; ii) a proactive implementation based on data analytics; iii) a hybrid solution that mixes reactive and proactive scaling; iv) use cases and empirical benchmarks, obtained through our platform, that compare reactive, proactive, and hybrid global scaling performance. From our comparison, proactive global scaling consistently outperforms reactive, while the hybrid solution is the best-performing one.

Keywords: Microservices · Architecture-level scaling · Predictive scaling

1 Introduction

Modern Cloud architectures use microservices as their highly modular and scalable components, which, in turn, enable effective practices such as continuous deployment [1] and horizontal (auto)scaling [2]. Although a powerful resource, scaling comes with its own challenges. As Ghandi et al. [3] put it:

> [...] it is up to the customer (application owner) to leverage the flexible platform. That is, the user must decide when and how to scale the application deployment to meet the changing workload demand.

Research partly supported by the H2020-MSCA-RISE project ID 778233 "Behavioural Application Program Interfaces (BEHAPI)".

Background. Our work focuses on *global scaling* [4–9]; which orchestrates the scaling of all microservices in a given architecture. This contrasts with *local scaling*, intended as the mainstream interpretation of (auto)scaling [2], which scales microservices in an uncoordinated way. Performance-wise, local scaling suffers from *domino effects*, also called *bottleneck shift*, where the uncoordinated scaling actions cause waves of cascading slowdowns and possibly generate outages [4,10].

Problem. Existing global scaling approaches focus on smoothing out domino effects [4,6,8] or on removing them by design [5,7,9]. This "by-design" approach performs the coordinated scaling of the microservices based on a quantification of their functional relations. However, existing work on by-design global scaling only focused on *reacting* to fluctuations of inbound traffic, wasting time to the detriment of customers, who can endure delays, downtimes, and receive a lower-than-expected level of service.

Contributions. In this paper, we challenge the existing reactive interpretation of by-design global scaling—hereinafter, we omit the "by-design" suffix. We hypothesise that global scaling might endure some performance inefficiencies due to its reaction overhead, which is the starting point of our contributions.

In Sect. 2, we *present a platform* able to host both reactive and *proactive global scaling*, e.g., it allows users to programmatically switch between the two approaches. We simulate an ideal, oracle proactive global scaler, and we show *empirical benchmarks* of the inefficiencies of reactive global scaling and of the possible gains of proactive global scaling.

In Sect. 3, we introduce a *proactive global scaling* implementation based on analytics [11]. We present a use case on email traffic from the Enron dataset [12]. We *benchmark* this implementation, which overcomes the limitations of its reactive counterpart and approximates the ideal performance of the oracle

In Sect. 4, we present an algorithm that (deployed in our platform) integrates proactive and reactive global scaling. *Benchmarks* on the Enron use case show that this hybrid approach is the best-performing one.

Our datasets, trained models, and simulations are publicly available at [13], which also contains a containerized version of the testbed.

2 Proactive Global Scaling

We introduce a platform that DevOps can use to perform proactive and reactive global scaling. In doing so, we do not start from scratch, and we build on previous work on global scaling, proposing a redesign able to capture proactive scaling on the existing reactive global scaling platform from [5,7,9]. Our new architecture is immediately useful. We use it at the end of this section to quantify the untapped potential of proactive global scaling—comparing the performance of reactive local and global scaling vs an ideal, oracle proactive global scaler. We use our platform also later, in Sects. 3 and 4, to benchmark our implementations of proactive and proactive-reactive scalers.

Global Scaling. In global scaling, the user provides a specification of the scaling constraints of each component of a given architecture, both in terms of necessary resources (such as CPU and memory) and of its dependencies on other microservices (e.g., microservice M_1 needs two copies of the microservice M_2 to run properly). Then, given one such specification, and using dedicated resolution engines [5], deployment plans can be computed such that: i) scale the whole architecture w.r.t. an expected increase/decrease of inbound traffic; ii) respect (if any) the constraints of resource allocation and dependency of the scaled microservices; iii) optimise the plan towards some set goals, e.g., minimising the cost of running the scaled architecture, i.e., using the minimal amount of virtual machines that supports the execution of the scaled architecture.

2.1 Design of a Proactive-Reactive Global Scaling Platform

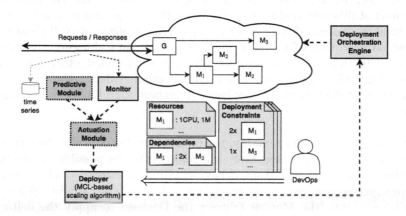

Fig. 1. Architectural view of the proactive-reactive global scaling platform.

We depict the architecture of the platform in Fig. 1, which includes two kinds of elements. The components found in the "cloud" are the microservices of a given architecture, labelled G, M_1, M_2, M_3. The global scaling platform manages the scaling of these microservices. Since the platform sees microservices as instance parameters, we abstract from their actual behaviour and use them in examples. The other elements in Fig. 1 are the components of the platform. Specifically, the elements with continuous-line borders are the ones inherited from previous work [5,7,9]. The main new elements, drawn with a dotted border, are the Predictive Module and the Actuation Module.

For completeness, we first describe the elements of the platform already present in the original proposals [5,7,9], and then dedicate to the new components for proaction, i.e. Actuation and Predictive Modules. Before doing so, we highlight the three kinds of flows in Fig. 1: continuous-line arrows → show the traffic addressed to the microservice architecture; dashed-line arrows --→ regard the runtime execution of global scaling; the thick arrow ⇐ indicates the compilation time of deployment plans.

Deployment Orchestration Engine. This component performs the actual scaling, (de)allocating replicas of microservices. It is a loosely-coupled component of the platform, taken from existing solutions (the only requirement is that it provides a programming interface for the application of deployment plans), such as Kubernetes.

Deployer. The Deployer implements the Maximum Computational Load (MCL) scaling algorithm and the deployment strategy proposed in [9], and it regards two flows. The first one, represented by $\Leftarrow$, regards the computation of the deployment plans, applied by the scaling $-\rightarrow$. As such, this process is asynchronous w.r.t. both the scaling and the traffic flow $\rightarrow$. In $\Leftarrow$, the Deployer takes the specifications given by the user (DevOps in Fig. 1) and computes the deployment plans that satisfy the Resources needed by each microservice (e.g., M_1 needs 1 CPU and 1 Memory), the Dependencies among the microservices (e.g., microservice M_1 needs two copies of M_2 to work), and the Deployment Constraints of different scaling targets. Since these deployment plans represent differential increments/decrements in microservice replicas, we call them *deltas*. The second flow, that of the runtime scaling $-\rightarrow$, runs alongside the inbound traffic $\rightarrow$. In this case, the Deployer acts as a service that other components call to trigger the application of a target, computed delta. Upon activation, the Deployer interacts with the Deployment Orchestration Engine to perform the scaling.

Monitor. In its original formulation, the monitor tracks the traffic flowing on the architecture within a prefixed time unit and checks the possible occurrence of a *workload deviation*, i.e., a discrepancy between the current, tracked workload and the expected one, correspondent to the delta currently applied. When such a condition occurs, the Monitor triggers the Deployer to apply the delta that corresponds to the current traffic load. To support proaction, we break the above, direct relation between the Monitor and the Deployer, as detailed below.

Actuation Module. This is the first component we introduce to support the coexistence of proactive and reactive global scaling. This is achieved by breaking and controlling the once-direct triggering relation between the Monitor and the Deployer, i.e., it is now the Actuation Module that decides when/whether to trigger the Deployer. This redesign allows the seamless coexistence of the previous reactive modality with the new proactive one. Indeed, to obtain the same behaviour of the original proposal, we just need to set the Actuation Module in "passive" mode and let it forward triggers from the Monitor to the Deployer. When active, the Actuation Module can choose to act independently of the traffic, e.g., choosing to ignore information coming from the Monitor and trigger the Deployer according to signals coming from other sources, e.g., from the Predictive Module, described below. As discussed in Sect. 4, the Actuation Module is where the DevOps defines algorithms that can dynamically decide when to follow the anticipated scaling from forecasts or react to the signals from the Monitor.

Predictive Module. The Predictive Module acts independently of the actual inbound traffic forwarding the prediction to the Actuation Module. For instance, the Predictive Module can use a static model, e.g., forecasting traffic peaks at pre-determined times, or sophisticated techniques to have more accurate predictions of traffic fluctuations, e.g., based on data analytics. In Fig. 1, we represent the input of the Predictive Module with the greyed-out arrow receiving information from the traffic flow and stores it into a time series dataset for further usage.

2.2 Benchmarking the Platform

To run our benchmarks, we relied on simulations. Specifically, we modelled our platform and the scaling approaches via the ABS programming language [14], compiling it into a system of Erlang programs that run the simulation. These programs and their execution environment form the test-bed of all our simulations, and we provide it as a container in the companion repository [13].

The simulation receives three kinds of inputs, which are statically defined within a simulation run: a *real inbound workload* (RIW), a *predicted inbound workload* (PIW), and the *deployment plans* (DP). The simulation combines these inputs to benchmark the performance of a target microservices architecture.

Notably, while we fix all inputs in simulations, this diverges from real executions only on the source of RIWs. Indeed, in real executions, RIWs corresponds to the traffic reaching the architecture, while, in our simulations, we generate RIWs beforehand–specifically, from samplings of actual traffic. RIW apart, also in real executions PIW and DP are normally computed before their utilisation time-window. For instance, since they tend to be time-consuming calculations, one can compute PIWs and DPs for the coming day during the preceding night.

Since our simulator is parametric to a target microservices architecture, we fix one for the benchmarks throughout this paper: the Email Pipeline Processing System from Bacchiani et al. [9], which includes twelve microservices, each with its own load balancer for distributing requests over the available replicas.

2.3 Reactive Local vs Reactive Global vs Proactive Global Scaling

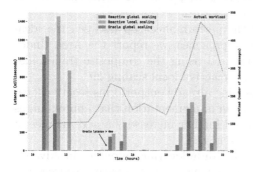

Fig. 2. Latency of proactive oracle global scaling vs reactive global and reactive local scaling.

We use our platform to empirically benchmark the gain of proactive global scaling vs both classic reactive global scaling and local scaling, in terms of latency, considered as the average time for completely processing a request that entered the system. We simulate an oracle, an ideal omniscient predictor that proactively triggers the global scaling of the architecture on forecasted traffic.

Since our benchmarks (throughout the paper) concern time, we partition the inbound traffic within discrete "time units" (e.g., we aggregate all requests received between 9 a.m. and 10 a.m. within a corresponding logical time unit). In this benchmark, we draw the traffic flow from [9].

Technically, the oracle knows the exact number of incoming requests and anticipates by one time unit the triggering of the Deployer and the related provisioning of resources. Here, we assume that a time unit is enough for the Deployer to (de)allocate the necessary resources before the traffic arrives.

As mentioned in the previous section, to run the benchmarks for the global reactive case, we disable the Predictive Module. Indeed, we obtain the same results from [9], with the only difference that we modified the Monitor to keep track of the maximum inbound workload, while Bacchiani et al. [9] use the average. We deem this choice sensible, since it provides results consistent with those of Bacchiani et al. [9], but it is less sensitive to irregular workloads. Also the implementation of the oracle is straightforward: we provide the Predictive Module with the considered traffic flow, shifted by one time unit, so that the Actuation Module anticipates the overhead of triggering the Deployer and applying the delta to handle the traffic of the next time unit. Finally, we adopt the same program (defined in ABS and run with Erlang) Bacchiani et al. [9] used to simulate reactive local scaling for that architecture.

Notably, while the traffic flow (generator) from [9] follows a fixed curve, it generates email attachments randomly. This is the only information unknown to the oracle that we expect to impact on its (otherwise non-existent) latency.

In Fig. 2, we show the comparison between oracle proactive global scaling, reactive global scaling, and local scaling. From the results, local scaling is the worse-performing one, due to both the reactive overhead and the domino effect (see Sect. 1). Reactive global scaling does not suffer from the latter phenomenon, but (confirming our hypothesis) it endures the overhead of applying deltas in response to traffic fluctuations (e.g., while the scaling takes effect, new messages arrive that are enqueued, increasing latency). As expected, the oracle performs almost perfectly and shows minimal latency at the time units between 14–16, likely due to the number of attachments in emails that exceeded the expected average considered in the deployment plans (this parameter is the same across all three modalities).

To give a quantitative intuition of the performance gap between the ideal proactive oracle and the other reactive approaches, we report the Area Under Curve for the latencies, in seconds, computed using the composite trapezoidal rule: oracle 0.1, reactive global scaling 13, reactive local scaling 29.

Summing up, while reactive global scaling already outperforms reactive local scaling (ca. 44% reduced latency), having an implementation that approximates the behaviour of the proactive oracle could further increase the performance of global-scaling system (ca. 70% reduced latency).

Notably (as illustrated later in Sect. 3) (de)allocating resources in advance does not have drawbacks from the point of view of costs, since resources are also (de)allocated earlier than in a reactive approach—indeed, by definition, the oracle does not change the scaling sequence applied also by the reactive global scaler, but rather anticipates them by one time unit.

3   Analytics-Based Proactive Global Scaling

Given the promising results from Sect. 2, we demonstrate how one can develop a realistic proactive global scaling implementation, i.e., using a state-of-the-art data analytics technique to obtain a predictor and integrating it in our Predictive Module. Here, we introduce the steps of general data analytics and we specify how these impact the workflow of Fig. 1. Next, we concentrate on the use case and how we applied data analytics to build the predictor. Finally, we compare our implementation of analytics-based proactive global scaling against oracle proactive global scaling (similar to the one presented in Sect. 2) reactive global scaling, and oracle proactive local scaling.

3.1   Data Analytics for Global Scaling

The Steps of Data Analytics. We provide a general overview of the elements of data analytics [11] (DA) and then detail how we applied these in our use case.

Using data analytics to predict the occurrence of the event in a given time unit, we aim to understand which variables influence and describe the phenomenon (*descriptive DA*). Once we selected the variables, we need to understand which attribute values are most relevant (*diagnostic DA*). Then, using the attributes and diagnostic(s) of the phenomenon, we are able to build a dataset to automatically train a model and infer the outcome of a new instance of the phenomenon, i.e., an event (of the same nature as the one being studied) not yet observed (*predictive DA*). The model created provides a description of all the observed and new events. Each of the possible outcomes relates with one or more configurations of the system. Each configuration corresponds to a response strategy to the occurrence of events similar to those already observed (*prescriptive DA*). Given a specific system configuration, we can compute its efficiency and select the one that offers the best cost-benefit trade-off (*proactive DA*). This optimal configuration, if any, is the one sent to the actuator.

The Workflow of Analytics-based Proactive Global Scaling. As mentioned in Sect. 2, we use the new modules introduced in this work in our global scaling platform (cf. Figure 1), namely the Predictive Module and the Actuation Module, to capture the steps of data analytics. Specifically, the Predictive Module implements the steps of descriptive and diagnostic (prepare the dataset) and predictive data analytics (train and inference) while the Actuation Module realises the prescriptive (define the scaling strategy) and proactive steps (triggering policies).

In pure proactive scaling, the Actuation Module computes the scaling strategy, given the outcomes of the Predictive Module and directly triggers the Deployer, disregarding any inputs coming from the Monitor.

Architecture and Dataset used in the Benchmark. After seeing the general workflow of analytics-based proactive global scaling, we introduce our use case and illustrate how each of its parts fit into said workflow.

However, instead of using the fixed traffic from [9], which provides too little information to train a data analytics model, we draw our dataset from another, renowned source—e.g., for training email schedulers and SPAM filters—from the literature, that has a compatible structure (i.e., email traffic): the Enron corpus dataset [12], made public by the Federal Energy Regulatory Commission during investigations concerning the Enron corporation (version of May 7th, 2015). The dataset contains 517,431 emails from 151 users, without attachments, distributed over a time window of about 10 years (1995–2005).

Descriptive and Diagnostic DA in Predictive Module. Leveraging the pre-processing routine from [12], we perform the cleaning procedure of the Enron dataset for classification tasks, and then we extract the attributes for predicting the number of incoming emails for a given time. First, we extract the *datetime* attribute for each email in the dataset, and then we sum the number of emails in the desired monitored time unit—i.e., one hour—for each month of the year, day of the month, and day of the week. Thus, we generate five new attributes: *month, day, weekday, hour*, and *counter*—the target—for each dataset instance. This gives us a representation of the email flow in the system at a given hour. The intuition for such a pre-processing is simple. The phenomena of increase or decrease in the flow of emails that occur in a company depend on factors such as the specific time of the working day (peak in the early hours versus the night hours), the month (monthly, bimonthly, etc. deadline), the day of the month (salary) or the day of the week (weekdays versus holidays).

Predictive DA in Predictive Module. For the predictive phase, we use off-the-shelf machine learning technique, specifically MLP (Multi-Layer Perceptron), which is capable—in contrast with purely linear models, e.g., linear regression—of exploring nonlinear patterns and increase prediction performance while containing complexity (about 7k parameters) and resource usage (about 1ms inference time). We categorise the numerical variables using the standard one-hot encoding technique, to prevent our model from attributing wrong semantics to these (e.g., month 12 is "greater than" month 1), resulting in a data representation of 70 attributes plus the *counter* target.

Then, we followed the traditional training process for machine learning. We partitioned the cleaned, processed data into three sets: one for training the neural network model, one for validating its hyperparameters (the parameters of the training process and network architecture), and one for testing the accuracy of the model. We use this last set to compute the error rate of the model.

The neural network used in the training process consists of three fully-connected layers. We applied the Rectified Linear Unit (ReLU) nonlinear activation function to the output of each layer. Each level compresses the input into a smaller representation, going from 70 to 64 attributes, in the first level, and from 64 to 32 attributes, in the second level. Finally, the 32 attributes are linearly projected into a single value, corresponding to the target of the regression. To compute the error rate, we adopt the loss function Mean Squared Error (MSE). To optimise the network parameters we use Adaptive Moment Estimation (Adam). We performed the training process with a learning rate of 0.1 and an exponential decay scheduler with gamma 0.9.

After the training, given a time slot—the tuple month (1–12), day (1–31), weekday (1–7), and hour (0–24)—the predictor forecasts the amount of emails incoming therein.

This is the third and last step of the data analytics workflow that concerns the Predictive Module. Here, we embedded the trained model to make the Predictive Module yield a prediction of the expected traffic, given a target time slot.

Prescriptive and Proactive DA in Actuation Module. The last two steps of the data analytics workflow are the prescriptive and proactive ones. We realise these in the Actuation Module. Since we implement pure predictive autoscaling, the prescriptive step is straightforward: we follow the prediction from the Predictive Module. The proactive step is the implementation of the strategy, where we forward of the expected traffic from the Predictive Module to the Deployer.

3.2   Benchmarking the Performance of Analytics-Based Global Scaling

Analytics-Based Proactive vs Reactive and Oracle Global Scaling. To give an intuition of the effectiveness of our analytics-based proactive global scaler, we test its performance against reactive global scaling [9] and an oracle similar to that seen in Sect. 2—also here, simulated by fixing a traffic flow and applying the related deltas one time-unit before the actual execution time.

Consistently with the oracle in Sect. 2, we do not fix also here the number of attachments in inbound emails but define them randomly. This comparison mainly aims at showing the performance gap between the analytics-based proactive and the oracle proactive variants (i.e., how close the former approximates the ideal proactive scaler), keeping reactive global scaling as a baseline for the comparison. To this aim, we report latency, message loss, cost, and number of deployed microservices. All benchmark tests shown in this section are performed on email traffic on a weekday in May 2001.

Considering latency, as shown in Fig. 3a, reactive scaling is the worst and presents high peaks of latency when the inbound workload grows. The oracle, similarly as in Sect. 2, is barely visible because, by construction, it knows in advance the exact amount of inbound messages, thus, it anticipates required scaling actions, with negligible latency. Performance-wise, our analytics-based global scaler closely approximates the oracle. Indeed, it mainly differs in two small spikes, imputable to inaccuracies in the workload predictions. Since latency and message loss (see Fig. 3b) are strictly related, we have similar conclusions: the oracle loses no messages, followed by the analytics-based one, while reactive scaling loses the most, at sudden peaks of workload. The number of deployed microservices and costs are also directly proportional, as seen in respectively Fig. 3c and 3d. Despite the sensible performance difference between the oracle, analytics-based, and reactive scaling, the costs/number of deployed instances are the same, although shifted by a time-unit backwards. The reason is that, since

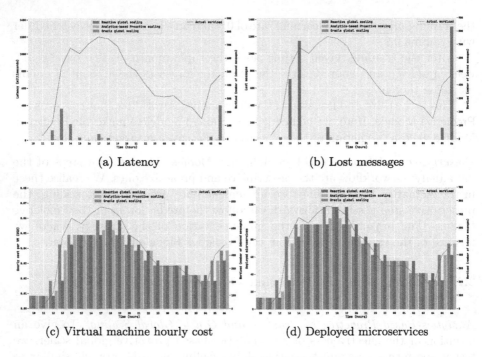

(a) Latency

(b) Lost messages

(c) Virtual machine hourly cost

(d) Deployed microservices

Fig. 3. Comparison between reactive, analytics-based proactive, and oracle-based proactive global scaling approaches.

the traffic is the same, resource (de)allocations are the same across all scalers, although these happen one time-unit in advance in the oracle and analytics-based proactive cases—divergences of the analytics-based proactive scaling derive from inaccuracies of the trained predictor.

Analytics-Based Proactive Global Scaling vs Oracle Local Scaling. We also compare our analytics-base proactive global scaler with oracle local scaling in Fig. 4a and Fig. 4b, i.e., a scaler that knows the future traffic of each microservice in an architecture and performs microservice-level scaling in advance. The purpose of this test is to give empirical evidence of the benefits of global vs local scaling, which holds in the reactive case—as proven in [9]—as well as in the proactive one (oracle and analytics-based). The rationale is that, if we show that analytics-based proactive global scaling outperforms ideal proactive local scaling, then i) the latter performs worse than the oracle global scaler and ii) the former outperforms any analytics-based local scaling.

In this experiment, we focus on the evaluation of the same performance as in the previous benchmark, but, for brevity, we only report latency and the number of deployed microservices measures, since these are proxies for the respective other two, directly-proportional measures: message loss and costs. Starting from latency, reported in Fig. 4a, analytics-based proactive global scaling outperforms ideal proactive local scaling. The former has almost 0 latency throughout the entire

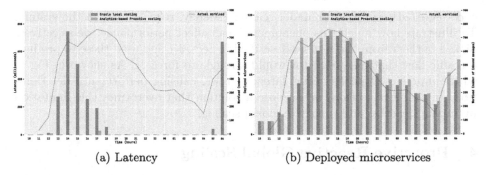

(a) Latency   (b) Deployed microservices

Fig. 4. Comparison between analytics-based proactive global scaling and oracle-based proactive local scaling.

experiment, except for little spikes within time unit 17. The latter struggles to adapt to rapid changes in inbound requests (intervals 13–18 and 5–6). The deterioration in performance of the oracle-based local scaling is caused by the so-called "domino" effect, i.e., single services scaling one after the other, causing chained slowdowns [9]. Besides worsening the performance, the domino effect also limits the predictive power of the local approach: the first microservice in a call chain is the one that anticipates the scaling, while the other ones cascade-scale only after that moment. This uncoordinated scaling leads to situations where the overheads of scaling accumulate sequentially (instead of executing in parallel, as in the global case), degrading performance. The presence of the domino effect is witnessed in particular in Fig. 4b. In analytics-based proactive global scaling, the number of deployed instances reaches the target amount to handle the inbound workload as soon as it is foreseen by the proactive module. Instead, the ideal proactive local scaler can only grow the number of deployed instances linearly over time, following the chain of scaling/forecast of the single microservices.

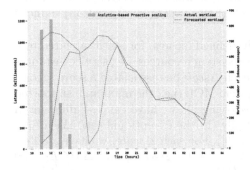

Fig. 5. Latency of the analytics-based proactive global scaling on the outliers test set.

Limitations of Analytics-Based Proactive Global Scaling: Outliers. The analytics-based proactive approach presented in this section proved to be quite effective. However, predictors are not infallible: if the traffic greatly deviates from the historical data, due to some unprecedented occurrence, the predictor can fail to provide an accurate estimation of the traffic.

This fact, considered in the context of purely analytics-based global scaling (like the one implemented above) where scaling decisions neglect actual traffic fluctuations, can result in over- (wasted resources) or under-scaling (latency, request loss) of the system. To illustrate how much this phenomenon can affect performance, we selectively picked outliers from the test set described in Sect. 3.1 and used these to produce a traffic flow that our predictor would struggle to forecast. As shown in Fig. 5, when unpredicted peaks occur, latency grows, causing performance deterioration. In the next section, we propose a solution that overcomes this limitation by mixing reactive and proactive global scaling.

4   Proactive-Reactive Global Scaling

The fact that predictors are weak against exceptional events is a well-known fact (see Sect. 5), which we concretely showed (see Sect. 3) can affect pure proactive global scaling too, resulting in the application of inappropriate deltas (either wasting resources or degrading the level of service). In this section, we propose a solution to this limitation, mixing proactive global scaling with reactive global scaling. Our global-scaling platform architecture (Sect. 2) simplifies this task: we program the Actuation Module to calculate an accuracy threshold which defines when to follow the forecasts of the Predictive Module or switch to the reactive signals of the Monitor.

Our algorithm does not rely on comparing the estimated and actual number of inbound requests in a given time unit. The reason is that the dynamic interaction between message queues and scaling times makes it difficult to reliably estimate the accuracy of the predicted scaling configuration w.r.t. traffic fluctuations. Hence, we introduce a new, stable estimation, rooted in the workload measure defined below.

Our idea is to use the Maximum Computation Load (MCL) from [9], which measures the capacity of a system configuration to handle a given workload. Using the MCL, we cast the comparison as the capacity of the system to deal with a given workload, defined by its current scaling configuration. Hence, we have a way to estimate both over- and under-scaling of proactive global scaling, given by the distance between the MCL (of the scaling configuration) induced by the actual traffic.

Our estimation considers statically-defined scores for each architectural reconfiguration increment (allocating new system resources, i.e., service instances and bindings [9]), called $\Delta scale$. Hence, each $\Delta scale$ has associated a score s, computed on the basis of the increment in system MCL (i.e., the maximum supported workload for a given inbound traffic). Following [9], we have $i \in [1, 4]$ different $\Delta scale_i$ plans, which are applied sequentially (in the exceptional case $\Delta scale_4$ is not enough, we restart from $\Delta scale_1$, see [9]). For each $\Delta scale_i$ we have a differential system MCL increment of: $\Delta MCL_1 = 60$ for $\Delta scale_1$ and $\Delta MCL_i = 90$ for $\Delta scale_i$ with $2 \leq i \leq 4$. Given ΔMCL_i, we compute $s_i = \frac{\Delta MCL_i}{\sum_{j=1}^{4} \Delta MCL_j}$. Notice that this yields $\sum_{i=1}^{4} s_i = 1$.

Then, for each time unit t, we compute our estimation following these 3 steps.

In step 1, we calculate, for each index i, the absolute value $|diff_i|$ of the difference between the $\Delta scale_i$ of the predicted workload and the observed

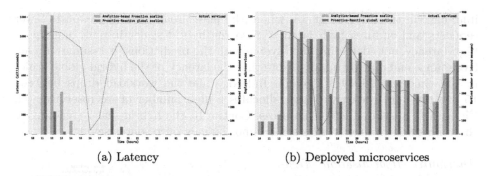

(a) Latency   (b) Deployed microservices

Fig. 6. Comparison between hybrid and pure proactive (analytics-based) global scaling, on the outliers test set.

one at time t. Then, we compute a weight $w \in [0,1]$ that we later use to combine the predicted workload and the measured one. Since $|diff_i| > 1$ only happens in exceptional cases (when $\Delta scale_4$ is not enough), we compute $w = min\left(\sum_{i=1}^{4} s_i \cdot |diff_i|, 1\right)$.

We keep track of the values w computed in the last 3 time units using function $h = \{(1, w_{t-2}), (2, w_{t-1}), (3, w_t)\}$, where w_t is the weight computed for the current time unit and w_{t-2}, w_{t-1} are the preceding ones. The pairs $(1, w_{t-2}), (2, w_{t-1})$ are included in h only if the system was already running at those times.

In step 2, we compute the overall weight $overall\_w = \frac{\sum_{(i,w) \in h} w \cdot i}{\sum_{(i,\_) \in h} i}$ of t. In particular, $w \cdot i$ means that the most recent w is the most influential one in the sum. The overall weight indicates the distance between the measured workload and the predicted one. Specifically, the closer the overall weight is to 1 the more distant the prediction is from the actual workload.

In step 3, we linearly combine the predicted and the measured workload through $overall\_w$ to estimate the workload used by the global scaler to compute the current system configuration: $workload\_estimation = (overall\_w \cdot workload\_measured) + ((1 - overall\_w) \cdot workload\_predicted)$.

Benchmarking the Performance of Proactive-Reactive Global Scaling. In the following, we benchmark our hybrid global scaler in two ways. First, we compare the hybrid scaler against the pure proactive global scaler from Sect. 3. Second, we compare our hybrid scaler with an alternative implementation from the literature [4]. In both benchmarks we re-use the same highly-volatile traffic used in Sect. 3.

Proactive-Reactive Global Scaling vs Pure Proactive Global Scaling. Similarly to what done in Sect. 3 , we report only latency (Fig. 6a) and number of deployed microservices (Fig. 6b), which are proxies for message loss and costs.

From Fig. 6a, hybrid local scaling rapidly recovers from wrong predictions, while pure proactive scaling neglects unexpected traffic fluctuations. This is visible, e.g., in the interval 11–13, where the pure proactive scaler expects fewer requests and endures high latency. Also the hybrid scaler initially undergoes high latency, but, detecting the diverge with the predictions, it assumes a reactive stance and quickly adapts. Note that the latency of the hybrid global scaler in the timespan 18–19 is "good". Indeed, while the workload drops between 15–17, the pure proactive scaler allocates a high number of microservices (cf. Figure 6b), wasting a lot of resources. Contrarily, the hybrid scaler (reacting to the unforeseen change) trades some minor latency off resource savings.

Alternative Hybridisation Techniques. Many hybrid local scaling techniques, see Sect. 5, use local metrics (CPU, memory) that cannot directly translate into global scaling ones. This is because we would need a global measure out of the local ones, however none of them provide a method to obtain this aggregate global measure (understandably, because they are interested in local scaling). Therefore, for the aim of comparison with our hybrid global scaler, we cannot

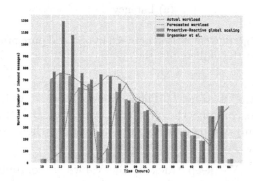

Fig. 7. Comparison of the workload obtained (in our hybrid approach and that of [4]) by mixing the actual and forecasted one.

translate the local scaling algorithm used in such techniques into a global one.

We are instead able to compare our algorithm with the global one of [4], which, like us, computes the target workload (used for scaling) in terms of received requests per time unit. We implement the algorithm proposed in [4] into an alternative hybrid global scaler and benchmark it using the outliers test set. We report in Fig. 7: the workload of the actual traffic, of the forecasted traffic, and the target workload of our hybrid scaler and that of [4].

As shown in Fig. 7, both techniques adjust underestimations, i.e., they do not let the system degrade its level of service. However, the alternative implementation is not able to adjust overestimated predictions (range 15–18), which end up wasting resources (and money)—a shortcoming reported in [4]. Besides this qualitative trait, quantitatively, our mixing approach is more accurate than that of [4]. In range 11–14 of Fig. 7 our scaler approximates the actual workload on the system. The algorithm of [4] overcompensates the innacurate prediction with the peaks at 12–13.

5   Related Work

Global Scaling. The strand of work closest to ours [5, 7, 9] introduced a kind of reactive global scaling that eliminates domino effects by design; building upon this we propose our proactive-reactive solution. More distant work on global scaling focus on smoothing, rather than removing, the domino effect (called "bottleneck shifts") as, e.g.: [6], which however only considers reactive scaling, and [4], which we already discussed in detail in Sect. 4. Besides [4], also [8] mixes reactive and proactive. The main differences of [8] with our work are: (*i*) the microservice architectures considered in [8] disregard fork-join patterns, i.e. those accomplishing a task via parallel execution of pipelines as in the use case we consider (where the analysis of an email requires analysing its subparts, i.e., attachments, text body, etc. . .); (*ii*) the global scaling algorithm of [8] suffers from the domino effect in that, when global adaptation is triggered, the maximum number of replicas for each microservice is established only from metrics obtained by its local monitoring.

Local Scaling. Reactive and proactive local-scaling proposals abound in the literature (both pure and mixed) [15,16]. Recent examples of pure reactive local scaling include Bayesian Optimisation techniques [17] and Fuzzy Logic [18]. Researchers already followed this path for the case of local scaling—due in part to how susceptible local scaling is to domino effects [19]—, also proposing ways to mix the reactive nature of local autoscaling with *proactive* elements, e.g., by forecasting the incoming workload [16]. The proactive mode involves adopting future workload prediction techniques to create early scaling mechanisms. The prediction of future system load is usually addressed with probabilistic modelling frameworks or time series analysis techniques. Mathematical modelling of processes entails the usage of techniques such as Markov chains [20], model-checking or probabilistic time automata [21,22], enabling the analysis and anticipation of system behaviours. Time series analysis is a data-oriented technique that involves extracting relevant information from the behaviour of the studied system. The most commonly used techniques include machine-learning algorithms, such as k-means [23], neural networks [24,25]—which we also use to maximize accuracy and precision of our predictor.

Previous work also presented approaches that mixed reactive-proactive scaling at the local level. However, a significant difference between our hybrid global scaling approach and the local ones is that the latter, for the most part, exploit local metrics of the virtual machine hosting services (CPU, memory). As argued in Sect. 4, looking at local metrics is fine as long as we aim at local replications, however these metrics are not enough to account for functional dependencies between system requests and local requests to single microservices (which allow us to eliminate the domino effect). Thus, we cannot directly compare with the literature on hybrid local scaling and we only draw a coarse comparison. Previous work also presented local-scaling hybrid reactive-proactive systems. These improve system behaviour and effectively deal with unexpected traffic fluctuations, while simultaneously benefiting from the analytics-based proactive and reactive power of the system [24,26]. Industry-wise, the main platforms delivering Cloud services, e.g., Amazon and Google, offer integrated solutions for reactive local scaling of resources based on user thresholds or rules for adapting to the workload [27,28]. Recently, these platforms have introduced predictive capabilities in their systems [29], exploiting gathered historical information for automatic adaptation and orchestrating between reactive and proactive modalities. Following the hybrid approach, we developed our platform to accommodate both reactive and proactive global modes and showed a possible implementation (see Sect. 4). Specifically, we favour analytics-based proactive scaling and pass control to the reactive modality when traffic fluctuations exceed some set accuracy threshold.

6 Conclusion and Future Work

We proposed a platform that can host both reactive and proactive global scaling and compared the analytics-based proactive and proactive-reactive scaling.

Low-hanging fruits from this work include both the introduction and refinement of analytics-based prediction and hybridisation techniques. For example, one can use natural language processing to extract complementary features for the representation of the regression target (in our case, the inbound requests).

Another direction towards using data analytics to help global scaling is helping DevOps in compiling the deployment constraints of the scaling plans (cf. Fig. 1). In this case, monitors would track how requests hop among the microservices of the observed architecture, and data-analytics techniques would provide hints for DevOps to quantify the multiplicative deployment factors among the microservices.

References

1. Humble, J., Farley, D.: Reliable software releases through build, test, and deployment automation, Anatomy of Deployment Pipeline (2010)
2. Lorido-Botran, T., Miguel-Alonso, J., Lozano, J.A.: A review of auto-scaling techniques for elastic applications in cloud environments. J. Grid Comput. **12**(4), 559–592 (2014)
3. Gandhi, A., Dube, P., Karve, A., et al.: Adaptive, model-driven autoscaling for cloud applications. In: 11th International Conference on Autonomic Computing (ICAC 14), pp. 57–64 (2014)
4. Urgaonkar, B., Shenoy, P.J., Chandra, A., et al.: Agile dynamic provisioning of multi-tier internet applications. ACM Trans. Auton. Adapt. Syst. **3**(1), 1–39 (2008)
5. Bravetti, M., Giallorenzo, S., Mauro, J., Talevi, I., Zavattaro, G.: Optimal and automated deployment for microservices. In: Hähnle, R., van der Aalst, W. (eds.) FASE 2019. LNCS, vol. 11424, pp. 351–368. Springer, Cham (2019). https://doi.org/10.1007/978-3-030-16722-6_21
6. Gias, A.U., Casale, G., Woodside, M.: Atom: model-driven autoscaling for microservices. In: 2019 IEEE ICDCS, pp. 1994–2004. IEEE (2019)
7. Bravetti, M., Giallorenzo, S., Mauro, J., Talevi, I., Zavattaro, G.: A formal approach to microservice architecture deployment. In: Microservices, pp. 183–208. Springer, Cham (2020). https://doi.org/10.1007/978-3-030-31646-4_8
8. Rossi, F., Cardellini, V., Presti, F.L.: Hierarchical scaling of microservices in kubernetes. In: ACSOS, pp. 28–37. IEEE (2020)

9. Bacchiani, L., Bravetti, M., Giallorenzo, S., Mauro, J., Talevi, I., Zavattaro, G.: Microservice dynamic architecture-level deployment orchestration. In: Damiani, F., Dardha, O. (eds.) COORDINATION 2021. LNCS, vol. 12717, pp. 257–275. Springer, Cham (2021). https://doi.org/10.1007/978-3-030-78142-2_16
10. Hellerstein, J.M., Faleiro, J. M., Gonzalez, J., et al.: Serverless computing: one step forward, two steps back. In: CIDR 2019 (2019). www.cidrdb.org
11. Kelleher, J.D., Mac Namee, B., D'arcy, A.: Fundamentals of Machine Learning for Predictive data Analytics: Algorithms, Worked Examples, and Case Studies. MIT Press, Cambridge (2020)
12. Klimt, B., Yang, Y.: The Enron corpus: a new dataset for email classification research. In: Boulicaut, J.-F., Esposito, F., Giannotti, F., Pedreschi, D. (eds.) ECML 2004. LNCS (LNAI), vol. 3201, pp. 217–226. Springer, Heidelberg (2004). https://doi.org/10.1007/978-3-540-30115-8_22
13. Bacchiani, L., Bravetti, M., Gabbrielli, M., Giallorenzo, S., Zingaro, S.P.: Repository of the datasets, testbed, and tests (2022). www.github.com/LBacchiani/predictive-autoscaling
14. Johnsen, E.B., Hähnle, R., Schäfer, J., Schlatte, R., Steffen, M.: ABS: a core language for abstract behavioral specification. In: Aichernig, B.K., de Boer, F.S., Bonsangue, M.M. (eds.) FMCO 2010. LNCS, vol. 6957, pp. 142–164. Springer, Heidelberg (2011). https://doi.org/10.1007/978-3-642-25271-6_8
15. Al-Dhuraibi, Y., Paraiso, F., Djarallah, N., et al.: Elasticity in cloud computing: state of the art and research challenges. IEEE Trans. Serv. Comput. 11(2), 430–447 (2017)
16. Qu, C., Calheiros, R.N., Buyya, R.: Auto-scaling web applications in clouds: a taxonomy and survey. ACM Comput. Surv. (CSUR) 51(4), 1–33 (2018)
17. Yu, G., Chen, P., Zheng, Z.: Microscaler: cost-effective scaling for microservice applications in the cloud with an online learning approach. IEEE Trans. Cloud Comp. 10, 1100–1116 (2020)
18. Liu, B., Buyya, R., Nadjaran Toosi, A.: A fuzzy-based auto-scaler for web applications in cloud computing environments. In: Pahl, C., Vukovic, M., Yin, J., Yu, Q. (eds.) ICSOC 2018. LNCS, vol. 11236, pp. 797–811. Springer, Cham (2018). https://doi.org/10.1007/978-3-030-03596-9_57
19. Roy, N., Dubey, A., Gokhale, A.: Efficient autoscaling in the cloud using predictive models for workload forecasting. IEEE CLOUD 2011, 500–507 (2011)
20. Moreno, G.A., Cámara, J., Garlan, D., et al.: Efficient decision-making under uncertainty for proactive self-adaptation. IEEE ICAC 2016, 147–156 (2016)
21. Naskos, A., Stachtiari, E., Gounaris, A., et al.: Dependable horizontal scaling based on probabilistic model checking. IEEE/ACM CCGRID 2015, 31–40 (2015)
22. Moreno, G.A., Cámara, J., Garlan, D., et al.: Proactive self-adaptation under uncertainty: a probabilistic model checking approach. ACM ESEC/FSE 2015, 1–12 (2015)
23. Dutta, S., Gera, S., Verma, A., et al.: Smartscale: automatic application scaling in enterprise clouds. In: 2012 IEEE Fifth International Conference on Cloud Computing, pp. 221–228 (2012)
24. Marie-Magdelaine, N., Ahmed, T.: Proactive autoscaling for cloud-native applications using machine learning. GLOBECOM 2020, 1–7 (2020)
25. Park, J., Choi, B., Lee, C., Han, D.: GRAF: a graph neural network based proactive resource allocation framework for SLO-oriented microservices, pp. 154–167 (2021)
26. Bauer, A., Lesch, V., Versluis, L., Ilyushkin, A., Herbst, N., Kounev, S.: Chamulteon: coordinated auto-scaling of micro-services. In: ICDCS, pp. 2015–2025. IEEE (2019)

27. Amazon, AWS Auto Scaling. aws.amazon.com/autoscaling (2022)
28. Microsoft, Overview of autoscale in Microsoft Azure. docs.microsoft.com/en-us/azure/azure-monitor/autoscale/autoscale-overview (2022)
29. Google, Scaling based on predictions. cloud.google.com/compute/docs/autoscaler/predictive-autoscaling (2022)

Semantics-Driven Learning for Microservice Annotations

Francisco Ramírez[1,2,3], Carlos Mera-Gómez[3], Shengsen Chen[4],
Rami Bahsoon[2], and Yuqun Zhang[1(✉)]

[1] Southern University of Science and Technology, Shenzhen, China
11756009@mail.sustech.edu.cn, zhangyq@sustech.edu.cn
[2] University of Birmingham, Edgbaston, UK
{fmr067,r.bahsoon}@cs.bham.ac.uk
[3] ESPOL Polytechnic University, Escuela Superior Politécnica del Litoral, ESPOL,
Facultad de Ingeniería en Electricidad y Computación, Campus Gustavo Galindo Km
30.5 Vía Perimetral, P.O. Box 09-01-5863, Guayaquil, Ecuador
{frramire,cjmera}@espol.edu.ec
[4] Cotell Inc., Shenzhen, China
ss.chen@cotell.cn

Abstract. Annotations are program metadata that generates code and
configuration files, among others. Different frameworks provide annotations to facilitate the implementation of microservice applications while
their absence can slow down the maintenance of microservices and their
misuse can lead to potential bugs. In this paper, we propose a novel
semantics-driven learning approach for capturing the relation between
code fragments and annotations, leveraging a Recurrent Neural Network (RNN) and a K-Nearest-Neighbour (KNN) classifier. The approach
locates similar pieces of code to increase the probability of suggesting
annotations of unseen fragments. We utilise PyTorch and Sci-kit Learn
to evaluate our approach with a set of Java code fragments, and we
measure how similar two code fragments are by a number between zero
(close) and one (distant). The results indicate that our semantics-driven
learning framework achieves an average of 87% of correct recommendations of annotations when the code fragments have a distance of 0.4
against the expected annotations subset.

Keywords: Microservice annotations · Semantic analysis · Static
analysis

1 Introduction

Annotations are a form of program metadata that generates code, configuration
files, and warnings, among others. Microservice frameworks provide annotations
to facilitate the implementation of cloud-based applications in terms of the reuse
of features and support for software evolution. However, the misuse of microservice annotations generates potential bugs whose detection requires the analysis

J. Troya et al. (Eds.): ICSOC 2022, LNCS 13740, pp. 255–263, 2022.
https://doi.org/10.1007/978-3-031-20984-0_17

of multiple logs and source code files. This detection effort is not trivial for developers since debugging microservices may take days or even weeks.

Developers go through a reduced amount of source code and infer the functionality of code fragments [2]. However, comprehension of programs takes around 58% of the time spent on software maintenance due to outdated or missing comments. Similarly, the wrong usage of annotations introduces errors with unexpected behaviour. Despite the significance of annotations for microservice development, only a few approaches have worked with annotations [6, 7]. Lacking static analysis on microservice annotations results in a gap between detecting warnings and correcting errors before deployment. To overcome these issues, it is essential to match source code with the usage of annotations.

In this paper, we contribute to a novel static analysis approach using semantics-driven learning of code fragments collected from open-source repositories. In particular, our approach implements a new mechanism that leverages a Recurrent Neural Network (RNN) and a K-Nearest-Neighbour (KNN) classifier to learn the semantic relation of code fragments against their annotations and predict a suitable annotation.

Moreover, our approach is the first to exploit the relation between code fragments and their annotations. We convert the Abstract Syntax Trees (ASTs) representation of Java code fragments to vectors following prior work [4,5]. We further conduct a set of experiments to identify incorrect or missing annotations by performing the approach through a simulation tool that extends PyTorch and Sci-Kit Learn Library. Our results indicate that our semantic learning of microservice annotations achieves an average of 87% of the correct recommendations of annotations.

2   Preliminaries

2.1   Tokenisation and AST Representation

Tokenisation is a common Natural Language Processing (NLP) task for separating the source code into words or tokens. Usually, such techniques take the AST representation of the source code as input. Specifically, an AST contains additional semantic information inside a tree structure with a statement denoted as a node. Note that an AST tree is usually traversed in a preorder manner.

2.2   Vector Representation of Code

Source code files can be transformed into a vector space [4] where the identification of annotations from source code can be deemed as a transformation problem as well. Such approaches are widely used in many AI-assisting software engineering tasks, such as code summarization [8], defect prediction [11], and fault localization [13].

3   Proposed Approach

We develop an approach to learn the semantic information of existing code fragments to give suggestions about the declaration of microservice annotations in a code fragment, as in Fig. 1 with Algorithm 1 describing the overall steps. The output of our approach is a set of suggestions, each composed of an action followed by an annotation name, e.g., *KEEP PostConstruct*. We illustrate our approach by using two actions: (i) *ADD* action suggests the incorporation of a missing annotation; (ii) and *KEEP* action suggests no change in the usage of an annotation.

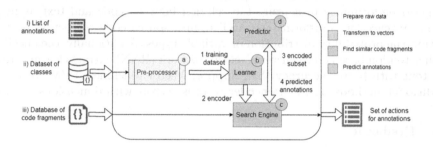

Fig. 1. Conceptual model of our semantics-diven learning approach

---

Algorithm 1. Semantics-Driven Learning Algorithm

Input: *datasets*   // contains the datasets for training, validate and testing the learning model
Input: *database*   // Java database to search similar code fragments
Input: *queries*   // List of queries to predict annotations and suggest actions
Output: *allActions*
1: *preProcessor* ← new PreProcessor()
2: *learner* ← newLearner()
3: *predictor* ← newPredictor()
4: *searchEngine* ← newSearchEngine()
5: *allActions* ← newList()
6: *trainingDataset* ← *preProcessor.prepare(datasets)*
7: *encoder* ← *learner.buildModel(trainingDataset).getEncoder()*
8: *searchEngine.setDatabase(database)*
9: *searchEngine.setEncoder(encoder)*
10: **for each** *query* ∈ *queries* **do**
11:      *encodedSubset* ← *searchEngine.getClosestCodeFragments(query)*
12:      *predictor.train(encodedSubset)*
13:      *predictedAnnotation* ← *predictor.predictAnnotation(query)*
14:      *action* ← *searchEngine.suggestAction(predictedAnnotation)*
15:      *allActions.add(action)*
16: **end for**

3.1   Pre-processor

The pre-processor transforms raw data, i.e., Java source code and the list of targeted microservice annotations, into training, validation, and testing sets. We convert each Java file into their AST representation and split it into methods with attached annotations. We also build two databases (Java and Queries) where a Java database is required to search for subsets and references for the predictor and search engine. We build the AST representation by using a Java Lang Parser which follows the language syntax by tokenising the source code to identify the types, constructors, members and expressions. We split the string representation of Java class into methods with the keyword *MethodDeclaration* and identify annotations after the keyword *Annotation*.

3.2   Learner

The goal of this component is to learn the semantic information of a code fragment. Specifically, we choose a sequence-to-sequence-based learner considering its good performance to capture the relation between code and text as in [2] where an encoder transforms the AST from a source code to vectors by predicting the probability distribution of variable types. Additionally, the encoders with attention based on Recurrent Neural Network (RNN) extracts features from the text with better accuracy than Support Vector Machines (SVM) based on traditional methods [12]. Our encoder returns vectors with dimensions $N * M$.

3.3   Predictor

This model predicts the best microservice annotations for a given source code upon a classifier. For the training process, we match each code fragment with the elements of the annotation list. The decoder of our learner provides a sequence of tokens with words of similar meaning. To enhance its accuracy, we require specific words for each annotation. Specifically, we consider that (i) every query requires a subset of limited code fragments with similar features; (ii) fast classifiers that support non-linear boundaries with sensitivity to overfitting; and (iii) classifiers based on probabilistic are unacceptable due to their demand for more training data. To this end, We choose a K-Nearest-Neighbour (KNN) classifier, which fulfils the above requirements by creating K clusters, locating the input inside the closest cluster and selecting the class of the neighbour.

3.4   Search Engine

The goal of our search engine is the suggestion of annotations. First, the engine encodes the query to get its vector representation. Then, it selects a subset of vectors from the Java database to reduce the scope and execution time of the prediction. Our search engine calls the predictor with the query and a subset and returns an annotation. Finally, it suggests actions for the query. Note that we adopt the cosine similarity as our similarity metric.

4   Evaluation

The study investigates how helpful is the semantics information of code fragments to keep or add annotations for unseen code fragments. We target more than 109,000 open-source repositories with the topic 'microservices' on GitHub. Most of those repositories (76%) adopt ten different languages. Specifically, our study chooses Java (29%) to investigate the effectiveness of our approach in terms of the number of correct annotations and the usage of classifiers to make predictions when a code fragment requires keeping or adding a single annotation. We also analyse the subsets of wrong suggestions and the distances between expected and unexpected annotations.

We calculate the following metrics: (i) *Accuracy* which is the percentage of correct values out of the total predictions; (ii) *F1-score* which is derived from the quality of positive predictions and the ability to detect positive samples; (iii) *BLEU Score* which is a measure to evaluate the quality of a candidate translation compared to one or more supposed correct translations [2]; and (iv) *Overlapping* which is the intersection between code fragments within the same distance range.

4.1 Experiment Setup

We extend PyTorch to train the learner and build vectors. The KNeighborsClassifier of the Sci-Kit Learn library allows the predictor to classify new code fragments. The search engine has a Java database of code fragments to find similar pieces of code and provides suggestions of annotations. For our dataset, we cloned a few Java methods using keywords and distributed them into 20 experiments. All our experiments can be replicated via a package[1] which includes the dataset for training, the databases and scripts to replicate and run the experiments.

4.2 Results and Discussion

We draw scatter and box-and-whisker plots to show the accuracy of queries and annotations. Besides, we plot the average BLEU score per length to show the quality of searching code fragments. We compare the distance of queries and their subset in case of correct and wrong predictions.

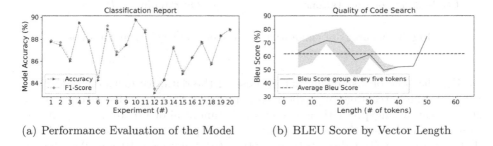

(a) Performance Evaluation of the Model   (b) BLEU Score by Vector Length

Fig. 2. Performance and quality of our approach

---

[1] https://bitbucket.org/semantics-driven-learning/replication-package/.

Our approach achieves an accuracy between 83.09% and 89.8%, with an average of 87.03%. Figure 2(a) shows that 60.00% of the experiments are above the average. The difference between F1-score and accuracy is slight, i.e., 0.13% and 0.37%. The small difference means the precision and recall are good because of low false positives and negatives. The accuracy shows the quality of our approach by counting its positive results. We elaborate the box-and-whisker plot with the percentage of correct predictions. We focus on five annotations which open-source projects widely attach in their methods. Additionally, we assess the quality of searching code fragments using the BLEU score. Figure 2(b) shows the quality of good queries with different lengths grouped every five tokens. We have got BLEU scores between 41.84% and 81.24% with an average of 63.12%, which is a good value considering that comment generation has 38% and translation language has an average of 41% [2].

The experiment results indicate that our semantics-driven learning achieves an average accuracy between 74.95% and 93.92% for annotations and a general average of 87.26%. Our results also show that the minimum accuracy of 67.11% is for *Before* annotation, while the unexpected annotations have 90.37% on average. Figure 3(a) shows that *RequestMapping* and *GetMapping* have higher accuracy with an average above 90%. *Before* and *RequestMapping* have a minimum difference of 31.64% and a maximum of 3.11%.

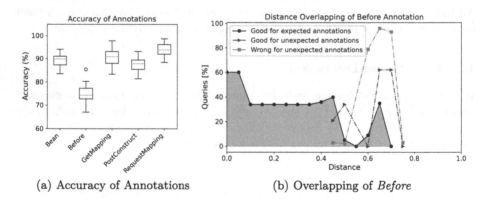

(a) Accuracy of Annotations   (b) Overlapping of *Before*

Fig. 3. Accuracy of annotations and wrong actions per annotations

For the sake of visualising and discussing the data, we focus on *Before* and calculate the percentage of predictions per every 0.05 unit of distance. Figure 3b shows that wrong predictions occur for distances above 0.40. The green area indicates the expected annotations of the good predictions are below 0.70 with distance ranges: (i) bellow 0.10 has 60%. (ii) between 0.10 and 0.45 has an average of 60%; and (iii) above 0.45 increase from 10% up to 39%. The red line refers to the unexpected annotations of the wrong predictions and shows that 80% occurs for a distance between 0.41 and 0.75. The blue line refers to the unexpected annotations of the good predictions between 40% and 60%.

Beyond the results of our experiments, our approach can reduce the misuse of annotations. We provided a quantitative way of indicating if a set of code fragments are different from a particular Java database and how different they are. Developers can thus identify which code fragments need adjustment to the usage of annotations. Additionally, they can increase the Java database to add new rules and extend them for other features such as parameters and their types. Overall, our approach suggests annotations on code fragments with specific behaviours while increasing the visibility of issues with missing annotations.

4.3   Threats to Validity

Theoretical validity: We mitigate the databases manual construction by selecting simple code fragments, introducing small changes and checking similarity against others. **Internal validity**: A noisy Java database of code fragments may increase wrong suggestions, which we reduce by cloning real-world code fragments. **External validity**: We mitigate the limited number of repositories by splitting the source code into methods that increase the records for training.

Table 1. Related work

Features	Related work										Our work
	[6]	[7]	[5]	[4]	[9]	[3]	[14]	[1]	[10]	[15]	
Microservices	✓	✓	✓	✓	✗	✗	✗	✗	✗	✗	✓
Annotations	✓	✓	✗	✗	✗	✗	✗	✗	✗	✗	✓
AST	✗	✗	✗	✓	✗	✗	✓	✓	✗	✗	✓
NLP	✗	✗	✓	✓	✓	✓	✓	✓	✓	✓	✓
RNN	✗	✗	✓	✓	✓	✗	✗	✓	✓	✗	✓
Extracting features	✗	✗	✓	✗	✓	✓	✗	✗	✗	✗	✓
Smell detection	✓	✗	✓	✗	✗	✗	✗	✗	✗	✗	✓
Defect detection	✗	✗	✗	✗	✗	✗	✓	✓	✗	✗	✓
Clone detection	✗	✗	✗	✓	✓	✗	✗	✗	✓	✓	✓
Bug detection	✗	✓	✗	✗	✗	✓	✗	✗	✗	✗	✓

5   Related Work

In this study, we focus on the misuse of annotations in the area of microservices. Table 1 shows how our work fits in the state-of-the-art techniques.

While existing works applied techniques to detect microservice smells [6] and modify the declaration of annotations [7]. Our research differs from their work in two dimensions: (i) we extract methods with microservice annotations using the AST of the source code; (ii) we create a model to learn the usage of microservice annotations, compare code fragments and suggest the best annotations.

Previous works used NLP in microservices projects for detecting architectural smells and clones of code fragments [4,5]. Unlike those works, our approach extracts terms from annotations and learns their relation with the code.

Other previous approaches applied NLP techniques for bug detection in different contexts: (i) generation of sentences from source code for summarisation of its behaviour [9]; (ii) extracting pieces of text/comments/reports and features from source code for detecting bugs and warning analysis [3]; (iii) detecting defects by using AST [1,14]; and (iv) detecting clones or similarities on code fragments [10,15].

6 Conclusion and Future Work

We are the first to propose a semantics-driven learning approach to suggest annotations according to the similarities between code fragments under an RNN and a KNN classifier to learn the semantic relation of code fragments against their annotations and predict a suitable annotation.

We conclude that using a database of rules based on code fragments with annotations is good enough to identify missing annotations, specifically for the ADD actions. Moreover, the analysis on overlapping of the subsets returns that increasing the distance between code fragments would reduce the number of wrong suggestions. In our ongoing research, we are introducing the analysis of multiple interconnected annotations for advanced features to study interdependence between annotations.

References

1. Dam, H.K., et al.: Lessons learned from using a deep tree-based model for software defect prediction in practice. In: Proceedings of the IEEE/ACM 16th International Conference on Mining Software Repositories (MSR 2019), pp. 46–57. IEEE (2019)
2. Hu, X., et al.: Deep code comment generation. In: Proceedings of the 26th Conference on Program Comprehension (ICPC 2018), pp. 200–210. ACM Press (2018)
3. Liang, G., et al.: Automatic construction of an effective training set for prioritizing static analysis warnings. In: Proceedings of the IEEE/ACM International Conference on Automated Software Engineering (ASE 2010), pp. 93–102. ACM (2010)
4. Perez, D., Chiba, S.: Cross-language clone detection by learning over abstract syntax trees. In: Proceedings of the 16th International Conference on Mining Software Repositories (MSR 2019), pp. 518–528. IEEE (2019)
5. Pigazzini, I.: Automatic detection of architectural bad smells through semantic representation of code. In: Proceedings of the 13th European Conference on Software Architecture (ECSA 2019), pp. 59–62. ACM (2019)
6. Pigazzini, I., Fontana, F.A., Lenarduzzi, V., Taibi, D.: Towards microservice smells detection. In: Proceedings of the 3rd International Conference on Technical Debt (TechDebt 2020), pp. 92–97. ACM (2020)
7. Pinheiro, P., et al.: Mutation operators for code annotations. In: Proceedings of the III Brazilian Symposium on Systematic and Automated Software Testing (SAST 2018), pp. 77–86. ACM (2018)

8. Wang, W., et al.: Reinforcement-learning-guided source code summarization using hierarchical attention. IEEE Trans. Softw. Eng. **48**(2), 102–119 (2022)
9. Yao, Z., Peddamail, J.R., Sun, H.: Coacor: code annotation for code retrieval with reinforcement learning. In: Proceedings of the the World Wide Web Conference (WWW 2019), pp. 2203–2214 (2019)
10. Yu, H., et al.: Neural detection of semantic code clones via tree-based convolution. In: Proceedings of the 27th International Conference on Program Comprehension (ICPC 2019), pp. 70–80. IEEE (2019)
11. Zeng, Z., Zhang, Y., Zhang, H., Zhang, L.: Deep just-in-time defect prediction: how far are we? In: ISSTA 2021: 30th ACM SIGSOFT International Symposium on Software Testing and Analysis, Virtual Event, Denmark, 11–17 July 2021, pp. 427–438. ACM (2021)
12. Zhang, J., et al.: A novel neural source code representation based on abstract syntax tree. In: Proceedings of the 41st International Conference on Software Engineering (ICSE 2019), pp. 783–794. IEEE (2019)
13. Zhang, M., et al.: An empirical study of boosting spectrum-based fault localization via pagerank. IEEE Trans. Softw. Eng. **47**(6), 1089–1113 (2021)
14. Zhou, Y., Gu, R., Chen, T., et al.: Analyzing APIs Documentation and Code to Detect Directive Defects. In: Proceedings of the 39th International Conference on Software Engineering (ICSE 2017). pp. 27–37. IEEE Press (2017)
15. Zilberstein, M., Yahav, E.: Leveraging a corpus of natural language descriptions for program similarity. In: Proceedings of the ACM International Symposium on New Ideas, New Paradigms, and Reflections on Programming and Software (Onward! 2016), pp. 197–211. ACM (2016)

MicroEGRCL: An Edge-Attention-Based Graph Neural Network Approach for Root Cause Localization in Microservice Systems

Ruibo Chen, Jian Ren[✉], Lingfeng Wang, Yanjun Pu, Kaiyuan Yang, and Wenjun Wu

State Key Laboratory of Software Development Environment, Beihang University, Beijing, China
{chenruibo,renjian,wlfbuaa,buaapyj,yangkaiyuan,wwj09315}@buaa.edu.cn

Abstract. Microservices architecture has become the latest trend in building modern applications due to its flexibility, scalability, and agility. However, due to the complex interdependencies between microservices, an anomaly in any one service in a microservice system has the potential to propagate along service dependencies and affect multiple services. Therefore, accurate and efficient root cause localization is a significant challenge for current microservice system operation and maintenance. Focusing on this challenge and leveraging the dynamically constructed service call graph, we propose MicroEGRCL, a root cause localization approach based on graph neural networks with an attention mechanism that includes edge feature enhancement. We conducted an experimental evaluation by injecting various types of service anomalies into two microservice benchmarks running in a Kubernetes cluster. The experimental results demonstrate that MicroEGRCL can achieve an average top1 localization accuracy of 87%, exceeding the state-of-the-art baseline approaches.

Keywords: Microservice · Root cause localization · Graph neural network · Anomaly detection

1 Introduction

The need for high availability, high maintainability, and high scalability of complex Internet applications has led to the evolution of application architectures as their scale increases. In this context, microservice architecture is the most recent trend in developing complex cloud-native applications [2,3,6]. A large-scale industrial microservice system may contain multiple services, each of which may be comprised of several hundreds of instances executing in distinct containers. There are complex invocation relationships between these services and

© The Author(s), under exclusive license to Springer Nature Switzerland AG 2022
J. Troya et al. (Eds.): ICSOC 2022, LNCS 13740, pp. 264–272, 2022.
https://doi.org/10.1007/978-3-031-20984-0_18

their instances. In such circumstances, a service anomaly may propagate through lengthy service call chains and affect other services in the chain [9]. This issue also makes it challenging for system operation staff to conduct troubleshooting and recovery. Therefore, it is essential to aid microservice system operation personnel in accurately locating service faults.

In this paper, we propose a novel root cause localization algorithm called MicroEGRCL that is based on a new graph neural network (GNN) model and incorporates a graph attention mechanism with enhanced edge features. In the event of system abnormality, this method generates the service invocation graph by dynamically obtaining the invocation relationship between services.

The contributions of this paper are threefold:

- We propose a novel approach to microservice root cause localization using a graph neural network based on a service call graph.
- We propose an edge-feature-enhanced attention mechanism for graph neural networks, upon which we implement weighted sampling for various nodes to improve the algorithm performance.
- We designed and implemented the MicroEGRCL root cause localization method and achieved excellent localization accuracy in a number of test scenarios, with a significant improvement over the baseline.

The remainder of this paper is organized as follows. Section 2 discusses related work. Section 3 presents an overview of our approach. The experimental evaluation of the method is described in Sect. 4, and Sect. 5 concludes the paper.

2   Related Work

In recent years, a great deal of research has been devoted to identifying the root of anomalies in distributed systems, clouds, and microservices. These methods can be broadly classified into the following categories according to their research subjects and approaches.

Log-Based Analysis Approaches. This type of approach is mainly proposed for traditional distributed systems and cloud systems [9]. By analyzing and clustering logs, such as LogDC [13] and Logsurfer [11], it identifies the root cause of a failure. These approaches are limited in terms of adaptability and processing time, and they necessitate frequent manual updates to the rules to accommodate various exceptions.

Trace-Based Approaches. This approach is commonly used to identify the root cause of microservices or service-based systems [9]. Commonly method to root cause localization is by comparing fault tracing with historical tracing and learning trace logs for fault prediction [4,10,14]. Typically, these approaches require the collection and analysis of a large number of traces in order to identify anomaly patterns and train predictive models. Therefore, they are inefficient for microservice systems on a large scale.

Service Call Graph-Based Approaches. This type of approach is mainly used for inferring root causes based on the call graph of microservice systems.

The first approach is based on graph similarity and was proposed by Álvaro *et al* [1]. Its dependence on the graph anomaly library is the method's most significant limitation. The methods in the second category are based on Random Walk [7,8,12]. The main problem with this approach is its inefficiency in large-scale systems. To overcome the limitations of these methods, we propose MicroEGRCL, a novel graph-based root cause localization method that employs a GNN and edge features to accurately infer the root cause of microservice call graphs. Our method improves the inference accuracy and computational efficiency of root cause analysis significantly.

3   Method

3.1   Formal Definition of the Root Cause Localization Problem

In this study, root cause localization is performed based on the service call graph. We extract the data of a microservice system's call chains in order to generate its call graph, which consists of n nodes, each with m features, and the features of node i are represented by the vector $\vec{S}_i$. All the features of the service nodes in the entire call graph can be represented by a feature matrix $\mathbb{S}^{m \times n}$.

The existence of a call relationship between nodes can be represented by the adjacency matrix $\mathbb{A}^{n \times n}$. Each element in $\mathbb{A}$ is either 1 or 0, representing the existence and non-existence of a call relationship.

For the invocation information between nodes, the edge feature matrix $\mathbb{R}$ is used for representation. If there is a call relationship between nodes i and j, then r_{ij} is its corresponding metric; otherwise, it is 0. Since communication between services generates several metrics, they are represented by d different matrices R, where d is the number of generated metrics.

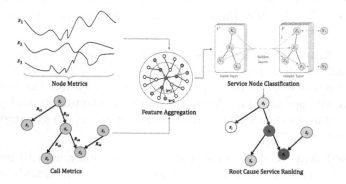

Fig. 1. Major components and root cause localization workflow of MicroEGRCL

The major component of the MicroEGRCL algorithm is a root cause classifier that can automatically infer the actual root cause. The inputs of this classifier include the adjacency matrix $\mathbb{A}$, the set of call relationship attributes $\mathbb{R}$, and the features matrix $\mathbb{S}$ of all nodes. A fault localization result vector Z of length equal to the number of service nodes is the output. Each element z_i represents the likelihood that node i will become the fault's root cause. The specific computational process of the MicroEGRCL algorithm is shown in Fig. 1.

3.2   Service Root Cause Localization Method Based on GNN

This paper formulates root cause localization as the classification of call graph nodes. Since inter-service call metrics are the most important indicator of node health. Therefore, edge characteristics are critical for accurately locating root cause services. Based on these analyses, we propose a GNN-based algorithm for root cause localization with an enhanced attention mechanism for edge features [5]. This method implements non-equal weight sampling of nodes via the attention mechanism, which mitigates the effect of local information loss on node information aggregation to some degree.

In this study, the metrics we focus on include two main categories. The first is the service node metrics, which include resource utilization (RU) and network status (NS, e.g., request time, TCP packet count). The second is inter-service call metrics (edge metrics), including response time (RT) and TCP send count (TSC).

3.3   Attention-Based Mechanism with Weighted Node Sampling

To implement weighted node feature aggregation based on the attention mechanism. In this paper, the correlation information between nodes is used directly to sample the attention of neighboring nodes. The attention vector a is calculated as Eq. (1).

$$a'_{ij} = \text{Softmax}\left(e'_{ij}\right) = \frac{\exp\left(\sum_{h^m_{ij} \in L(h_{ij})} k_m h^m_{ij}\right)}{\sum_{m \in N_i} \exp\left(e'_{im}\right)} \tag{1}$$

$L(h_{ij})$ represents the indicator set that contains all the metrics measured between node i and node j. h^m_{ij} represents the $m-th$ value in the set $L(h_{ij})$ and the pre-defined k_m determines the weight coefficient for h^m_{ij}. By a weighted summation over the indicator set $L(h_{ij})$, we can obtain e'_{ij} as the attention coefficients. Finally, we can calculate the normalized coefficients a'_{ij} using the Softmax function.

The final attention consists of two parts, the traditional attention based on node metrics and the attention calculated based on edge features, and the attention is calculated as shown in Eq. (2).

$$a_{ij} = \frac{\exp\left(\text{LeakyReLU}\left(\vec{a}^T \left[W\vec{S_i} \| W\vec{S_j}\right]\right)\right)}{\sum_{m \in N_i} \exp\left(\text{LeakyReLU}\left(\vec{a}^T \left[W\vec{S_i} \| W\vec{S_m}\right]\right)\right)} + a'_{ij} \tag{2}$$

where $\vec{a}$ represents the weight matrix of the feedforward neural network, $\vec{a} \in R^{2F'}$, F' is the feature dimension of the nodes entering the next layer of the neural network, and T indicates matrix transpose. Use the LeakyReLU nonlinear activation function (with a slope of 0.2 for negative input values). W represents the weight matrix of the graph convolution layer.

In this model, the sampling depth $k = 2$ (i.e., each node can only aggregate neighbor nodes whose distance from itself is ≤ 2). The final sampling aggregation process can be expressed as Eq. (3).

$$S_i^k \leftarrow \sigma \left(W \cdot \left(\left\{ S_i^{k-1} \right\} || MEAN \left\{ a_{ij} \cdot S_j^{k-1}, \forall j \in N(i) \right\} \right) \right) \tag{3}$$

S_i^k represents the sampling result of node i at the kth layer. The $MEAN$ function represents averaging over the node features. The node feature aggregation process of MicroEGRCL is shown in Algorithm 1. Eventually, the model will output the probability of each node being the root cause node.

Algorithm 1. Algorithm of node feature aggregation

Input:
 Call graph $G(V, E)$, Input features $x_i, \forall i \in V$
 Weight matrix $W^k, \forall k \in \{1, \cdots, K\}$
 Nonlinear function σ, Aggregation function $AGG_k, \forall k \in \{1, \cdots, K\}$
 Attention factor$\{a_{ij}, \forall i, j \in V\}$
Output:
 The new node vector represents $z_i, i \in V$
1: $S_i^0 \leftarrow x_i, \forall i \in V$
2: **for** $k \in \{1, 2\}$ **do**
3: **for** $i \in V$ **do**
4:   $S_{N(i)}^k \leftarrow AGG_k \left(\{ a_{ij} \cdot S_i^{k-1}, \forall i \in N(i) \} \right)$
5:   $S_i^k \leftarrow \sigma \left(W^k \cdot CONCAT \left(S_i^{k-1}, S_{N(i)}^k \right) \right)$
6: **end for**
7: $S_i^k \leftarrow S_i^k / \| S_i^k \|_2, \forall i \in V$
8: **end for**
9: $z_i \leftarrow S_i^K, i \in V$
10: **return** Z

---

4 Experimental Evaluation

To validate the effectiveness of the MicroEGRCL, we conducted experimental validation using two microservice applications and various failure scenarios. The first is Sock-shop, a widely used microservice benchmark that consists of 15 microservices in total. In order to evaluate the performance of our algorithm at a large scale, we extracted dependencies between services based on a real business scenario involving an online ride-hailing company. We developed the ride-hailing Mock-up microservice application, which consists of sixty distinct microservices and a more complex service invocation graph. Microservice systems are constructed within a Kubernetes[1] environment. Additionally, Prometheus[2] is utilized to monitor and collect service metrics.

In this work, we focus on three types of anomalies that cause most of the availability issues in microservice systems. **Availability Anomaly:** an anomalous increase in the number of failed service invocations is indicative of an availability anomaly, which is typically caused by defects in the service or anomalies in the operating environment. **Performance Anomaly:** performance anomaly is characterized by abnormal increases in service response times, typically resulting from resource anomalies (e.g., CPU, MEM). **Communication Anomaly:** a communication anomaly characterized by a significant increase in the number of service requests or an increase in service packet loss, which is typically caused by network anomalies between services.

We construct a service call graph using the service metrics, which indicate the source and destination services of this request, respectively. On the basis of the aforementioned information, we can generate a service call graph based on a structured set of data representing different service instances and the invocation relationships between them. In addition, we use the BIRCH clustering algorithm for anomaly detection.

4.1   Experimental Setup

We set up an experimental environment to simulate online user requests and emulate various microservice system anomalies. Chaos-mesh[3] is used to inject a variety of anomalies for the microservice systems running on Kubernetes. In our experiment, different service nodes are injected with distinct faults over a period of time, during which node metrics, call metrics, and call chain information are collected for training. For the sake of simplification, we only inject one fault per experiment run into each call chain per service node.

Table 1. Accuracy evaluation of the algorithms on the sock-shop

P@K	Method	Frontend	Orders	Payment	Catalogue	Shipping
P@1	RS	0.06	0.07	0.06	0.08	0.06
	GraphSAGE	**0.95**	0.88	0.57	0.33	0.96
	MicroEGRCL	0.94	**0.99**	**0.78**	**0.56**	**0.98**
P@3	RS	0.19	0.19	0.2	0.2	0.16
	GraphSAGE	0.99	0.99	0.96	0.71	1
	MicroEGRCL	1	1	**0.96**	**0.99**	1

To thoroughly validate the effectiveness of MicroEGRCL, we compare it to two state-of-the-art baseline methods. The first method is Random Walk, which

---

[1] Kubernetes - https://kubernetes.io.

[2] Prometheus - https://prometheus.io.

[3] Chaos-mesh - https://chaos-mesh.org.

is utilized by MonitorRank [7] and MicroRCA [12]. In this paper, we utilize one of them, MicroRCA, which is more effective, as the comparison method. The second is a classical GNN algorithm called GraphSAGE. In addition, we compared it with the case of randomly selected(RS) root causes.

As an evaluation metric, we employ $P@K$ (Precision at topK, topK accuracy) to assess the effectiveness of the MicroEGRCL method. $P@K$ denotes the probability that the first K results predicted by the algorithm are the actual cause of a given fault.

4.2   Results and Discussion

In our experiments, we injected anomalies into multiple services in two microservice applications and performed a statistical analysis of the results. It should be noted that in the dataset of this paper, we only counted the location accuracy under different anomalies for MicroRCA due to its inability to properly locate some of the service anomalies selected for this experiment.

Table 2. Accuracy evaluation of the algorithms by anomaly types on sock-shop

Anomaly type	P@K	RS	MicroRCA	GraphSAGE	MicroEGRCL
Availability	P@1	0.06	0.3	0.78	**0.88**
	P@3	0.19	0.78	0.92	**0.99**
Performance	P@1	0.07	0.3	0.72	**0.79**
	P@3	0.2	0.82	0.91	**0.97**
Communication	P@1	0.08	0.36	0.65	**0.86**
	P@3	0.17	0.83	0.95	**1**

We investigated the localization accuracy of MicroEGRCL and other baseline methods for different fault types and service faults, and the experimental results are presented in Tables 1 and 2. In both experiments, the results demonstrate that the MicroEGRCL achieves the highest localization accuracy, achieving an average of greater than 80% top1 localization accuracy and greater than 98% top3 localization accuracy in all scenarios, thereby proving that this method is effective for Sock-shop applications.

We conducted the same experiment as Sock-shop in the Ride-hailing Mockup dataset, but only the $P@1$ accuracy was counted. The experimental results are presented in Tables 3 and 4. In larger-scale applications, the results indicate that MicroEGRCL is still able to demonstrate superior localization accuracy to other methods. Comparing the accuracy changes of different methods for the two datasets reveals that the number of nodes decreases the localization accuracy of MicroRCA to some degree. In contrast, the method based on graph neural networks does not have this issue. Compared to the GraphSAGE algorithm,

Table 3. Accuracy evaluation of $P@1$ by service nodes on ride-hailing mock-up

Method	driver-gs	guard-gs	kronos-publish	ogs-gs	gz-gs	pay-gs	**trans-gs**
RS	0.02	0.01	0.03	0.02	0.02	0.02	0.02
GraphSAGE	0.78	0.69	0.91	0.62	0.87	0.88	0.69
MicroEGRCL	**0.93**	**0.76**	**0.99**	**0.76**	**0.99**	**0.98**	**0.95**

Table 4. Accuracy evaluation of $P@1$ by anomaly types on ride-hailing mock-up

Anomaly type	RS	MicroRCA	GraphSAGE	MicroEGRCL
Availability	0.02	0.31	0.85	**0.91**
Performance	0.02	0.25	0.75	**0.91**
Communication	0.02	0.27	0.72	**0.9**

the MicroEGRCL demonstrates an average level of accuracy, which represents a 6%–18% improvement.

Based on all experimental results, GNN-based localization accuracy is significantly superior to RandomWalk. More significantly, by introducing the edge features enhanced attention, we further improve the localization accuracy of the GNN-based approach. The effectiveness of the proposed method in this paper is verified.

5   Conclusion and Future Work

This paper proposes an edge-attention-based GNN root cause localization approach for microservice systems, named MicroEGRCL. The root cause localization results are improved by making full use of the invocation information between services. Specifically, we propose an attention mechanism with enhanced call information for the weighted aggregation of feature weights across different nodes. We evaluate our method by comparing it to the state-of-the-art baseline approaches and the conventional GNN method. The experimental results demonstrate that MicroEGRCL outperforms or is comparable to existing methods, and has a certain generalization ability. Future work will introduce additional domain information to enhance the model's capabilities and validate it in real-world business scenarios.

Acknowledgment. This paper was supported by National Key R&D Program of China (Funding No. 2021ZD0110601) and the State Key Laboratory of Software Development Environment (Funding No. SKLSDE-2020ZX-01).

References

1. Brandón, Á., Solé, M., Huélamo, A., Solans, D., Pérez, M.S., Muntés-Mulero, V.: Graph-based root cause analysis for service-oriented and microservice architectures. J. Syst. Softw. **159**, 110432 (2020)
2. Di Francesco, P., Malavolta, I., Lago, P.: Research on architecting microservices: Trends, focus, and potential for industrial adoption. In: 2017 IEEE International Conference on Software Architecture (ICSA), pp. 21–30. IEEE (2017)
3. Dragoni, N., Lanese, I., Larsen, S.T., Mazzara, M., Mustafin, R., Safina, L.: Microservices: How to make your application scale. In: Petrenko, A.K., Voronkov, A. (eds.) PSI 2017. LNCS, vol. 10742, pp. 95–104. Springer, Cham (2018). https://doi.org/10.1007/978-3-319-74313-4_8
4. Gan, Y., Zhang, Y., Hu, K., Cheng, D., Delimitrou, C.: Seer: Leveraging big data to navigate the complexity of performance debugging in cloud microservices. In: the Twenty-Fourth International Conference (2019)
5. Hamilton, W., Ying, Z., Leskovec, J.: Inductive representation learning on large graphs. In: 30th Proceedings of the conference on Advances in Neural Information Processing Systems (2017)
6. Khazaei, H., Barna, C., Beigi-Mohammadi, N., Litoiu, M.: Efficiency analysis of provisioning microservices. In: 2016 IEEE International Conference on Cloud Computing Technology and Science (CloudCom), pp. 261–268. IEEE (2016)
7. Kim, M., Sumbaly, R., Shah, S.: Root cause detection in a service-oriented architecture. ACM SIGMETRICS Perform. Eval. Rev. **41**(1), 93–104 (2013)
8. Lin, J., Chen, P., Zheng, Z.: Microscope: pinpoint performance issues with causal graphs in micro-service environments. In: Pahl, C., Vukovic, M., Yin, J., Yu, Q. (eds.) ICSOC 2018. LNCS, vol. 11236, pp. 3–20. Springer, Cham (2018). https://doi.org/10.1007/978-3-030-03596-9_1
9. Liu, D., et al.: Microhecl: High-efficient root cause localization in large-scale microservice systems. In: 2021 IEEE/ACM 43rd International Conference on Software Engineering: Software Engineering in Practice (ICSE-SEIP), pp. 338–347 (2021). https://doi.org/10.1109/ICSE-SEIP52600.2021.00043
10. Pham, C., et al.: Failure diagnosis for distributed systems using targeted fault injection. IEEE Trans. Parallel Distrib. Syst. **28**(2), 503–516 (2016)
11. Prewett, J.E.: Analyzing cluster log files using logsurfer. In: Proceedings of the 4th Annual Conference on Linux Clusters. Citeseer (2003)
12. Wu, L., Tordsson, J., Elmroth, E., Kao, O.: Microrca: root cause localization of performance issues in microservices. In: NOMS 2020–2020 IEEE/IFIP Network Operations and Management Symposium, pp. 1–9. IEEE (2020)
13. Xu, J., Chen, P., Yang, L., Meng, F., Wang, P.: Logdc: problem diagnosis for declartively-deployed cloud applications with log. In: 2017 IEEE 14th International Conference on e-Business Engineering (ICEBE), pp. 282–287. IEEE (2017)
14. Zhou, X., et al.: Latent error prediction and fault localization for microservice applications by learning from system trace logs. In: Proceedings of the 2019 27th ACM Joint Meeting on European Software Engineering Conference and Symposium on the Foundations of Software Engineering, pp. 683–694 (2019)

Mining the Limits of Granularity for Microservice Annotations

Francisco Ramírez[1,2,3], Carlos Mera-Gómez[3], Rami Bahsoon[2],
and Yuqun Zhang[1(✉)]

[1] Southern University of Science and Technology, Shenzhen, China
11756009@mail.sustech.edu.cn, zhangyq@sustech.edu.cn
[2] University of Birmingham, Edgbaston, UK
{fmr067,r.bahsoon}@cs.bham.ac.uk
[3] ESPOL Polytechnic University, Escuela Superior Politécnica del Litoral, ESPOL,
Facultad de Ingeniería en Electricidad y Computación, Campus Gustavo Galindo Km
30.5 Vía Perimetral, P.O. Box 09-01-5863, Guayaquil, Ecuador
{frramire,cjmera}@espol.edu.ec

Abstract. Microservice architecture style advocates the design and coupling of highly independent services. Various granularity dimensions of the constituent services have been proposed to measure the complexity and refinement levels of the service provision. Moreover, attaching annotations to operations adds granularity to the services while adding features and facilitating the implementation of applications. Microservice applications with inadequate granularity affect the system quality of service (e.g., performance), introduce issues for management, and increase the diagnosing and debugging time of microservices to days or even weeks. In this paper, we propose a semantics-driven learning approach to mining the granularity limits of operations with their annotations according to the developer community. The learning process pursues to build a vector space for clustering similar operations with their annotations that facilitate the identification of granularity. The evaluation shows that clustering annotations by operations similarity achieves significantly high accuracy when classifying unseen operations (89%).

Keywords: Granularity · Microservice annotations · Semantic analysis

1 Introduction

Microservice architecture style is a software development approach that implements a set of refined and highly cohesive services. In this context, granularity is related with the size of microservices within the application. Typical granularity measurements are the number of lines, complexity and dependencies [4].

There is no agreement on the right size of microservices because project teams interpret the size in different terms such as line of code, number of classes, entities, among others [4]. Then, an application could have microservices with

© The Author(s), under exclusive license to Springer Nature Switzerland AG 2022
J. Troya et al. (Eds.): ICSOC 2022, LNCS 13740, pp. 273–281, 2022.
https://doi.org/10.1007/978-3-031-20984-0_19

different granularity. However, tiny microservices introduce managing issues into the whole architecture, while huge microservices affect the quality attributes, especially performance which reduces the overall system quality. The detection effort to solve the above issues is time-consuming and not trivial for developers since debugging microservices may take days or weeks [12].

The novel contribution of this paper is a mechanism for mining granularity limits of operations with semantics similarity. The approach contributes to the fundamentals of microservice granularity, where, to our best knowledge, we are the first to cluster similar operations to avoid/reduce the amount of microservice invocation or time response.

The importance and methods to determine an optimal granularity have been considered in several studies [2,9,10]. However, to our knowledge, our work is the first to identify the granularity limits implemented in source code by clustering operations with similar behaviour. The results indicates that our approach achieves a high accuracy when classifying unseen operations (89%).

2   Background

2.1   Annotations by Operations

Annotations are a form of program metadata for adding features to a piece of code that facilitate the implementation of microservice applications. Developers follow coding style guidelines [1], which means one project has operations with similar syntax. Thus, similar usage of annotations appears in operations with semantics similarity.

Some annotations expose services through RESTful HTTP with attached annotations such as *GetMapping*, *GET*, *POST* and *RequestMapping*. Note that Java Parser can be used for listing the project classes with their content and searching for annotations attached to methods. The microservice applications allow the usage of multiple frameworks such as Spring, Redis and others where an operation allows more than one annotation. For instance, Spring Boot and Spring Cloud help run microservices in embedded web servers with common distributed patterns such as Circuit Breaker.

2.2   Granularity Dimensions

The most common granularity dimensions are the number and length of services calculated by aggregating the number of operations and their lines of code while others involve coupling, cohesion and complexity. Note that finding the optimal level of granularity has potential issues when finalising the level too early [3].

2.3   Learning Process

Semantics-driven learning extracts features from a text by focusing on its syntax and semantics and is applied to perform tasks such as learning the relation between two texts in terms of their plain forms or Abstract Syntax Trees (ASTs) [5]. It typically encodes the operations into vectors and keeps the inner relation between operations and annotations.

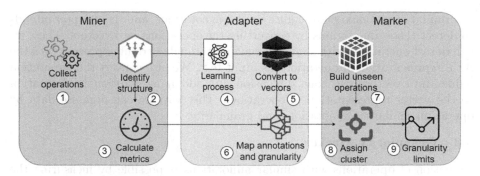

Fig. 1. The components of our approach

3 Proposed Approach

In our approach, we collect code fragments, extract their annotations, identify operations, map the operations by annotations and calculate their granularity. We analyse the granularity utilised by the developer community when attaching annotations to operations. In particular, the semantic information of operations enhances the searching for similar operations.

3.1 Operation Miner

The goal of the Operation Miner is pre-processing the raw files from the Java dataset. This component gets, organises, and formats the operations before continuing with the other components. The Miner executes three essential functions, which are: (i) collecting code fragments, (ii) inspecting their structure, and (iii) measuring their granularity.

The initial task of our miner is to collect the code fragments from open-source repositories. First, we download complete source code files from different projects. Second, we identify Java files with annotations. Third, we need to split the files into code fragments. Next, we select only code fragments that correspond to operations. Then, we map the selected operations according to their projects, packages, and classes.

3.2 Annotation Adapter

The goal of our Annotation Adapter is to map the operations, their annotations and granularity. This component gets the AST representation and converts operations into vectors. The Adapter executes three essential functions, which are: (i) parsing the operations, (ii) learning the relation between operations and annotations, and (iii) connecting the mentioned relations to their granularity metrics.

We parse the source code of operations to build their AST representation as a text. Our approach requires a Java Parser, a library that reads the source code of complete Java files and provides an AST structure to work with Java code in a programmatic way. Java Parser allows us to produce a text by reading the tree with the transversal algorithm in post-order. The result is a text where each word is a token for the next step of the learning process.

Similar operations could require similar annotations, and the Adapter intends to detect those annotations by converting the operations into vectors. Thus, we can detect operations with similar behaviour through a training process with the AST representation of operations as input text. We also convert the annotation names into vectors with one dimension and add it as additional information to the vector representation of operations. This way, we can organise data by operation similarity, annotation, and granularity.

3.3   Granularity Marker

Detection of operations with similar annotations is possible by measuring the distance between two vectors. In this paper, we adopt Cosine similarity for measuring annotation similarity following prior work [13]. In particular, we avoid excluding operations with similarities higher than a specific threshold, e.g., 0.70.

The cosine similarity reduces the searching scope by finding the nearest vectors. We form a subset using the closest vectors with similar behaviour operations. Then, we build clusters using the K-Means algorithm, which requires the number of clusters as a parameter. If one operation has more than one annotation, we could join the annotations in pairs of two.

The subset helps search the granularity limits according to the nearest annotation. The KNN algorithm predicts the clusters of annotations. Then, we filter the operations by using the prediction. The filtered options contain the granularity metrics ordered from minimum to maximum. The granularity limits for specific annotation are near the extremes.

4   Evaluation

For our evaluation, we measure the effectiveness of our approach by counting the percentage of operations inside the range of granularity limits. Our evaluations can be replicated via this package [1] which contains examples of exposed operations, the datasets, databases and scripts to run the experiments.

4.1   Experiment Design

We prepare a Java dataset by cloning the source code from GitHub open-source repositories selected with the following criteria: (i) Java projects; (ii) microservices; (iii) more than 300 stars. We search with Java Parser for RequestMapping, GetMapping and RestTemplate annotations to detect operations and connections between them. Our text parser reads the selected Java files and splits their content into operations. We choose the operations with annotations, generate their AST representation and calculate the length of operations. Additionally, our learning model needs three datasets of selected operations for training, validating and testing its encoder. Then, we add to our dataset the vector after converting the operations with the encoder.

---

[1] https://bitbucket.org/mining-granularity-limits/replication-package/.

4.2   Experiment Setup

We implement the Miner with Java and Python libraries to extract the operations. Specifically, the Java Parser Lang library helps identify connections between operations, while Python Java Parser builds the AST representation. Additionally, we implement semantics-driven learning by extending PyTorch, a Python-based library for NLP and deep neural networks. We train the learner in nodes environment for the Annotation Adapter and then build the vectors using its encoder. The experiments mainly run on a laptop (Core i7 and 16 GB).

4.3   Results and Discussion

We identify the top 20 annotations that appear near 69% of 20,540 code fragments with one, two or three annotations. We select the annotations such as *RequestMapping* and *GetMapping* which expose operations. We reduce the experimentation scope by selecting operations with more token usage.

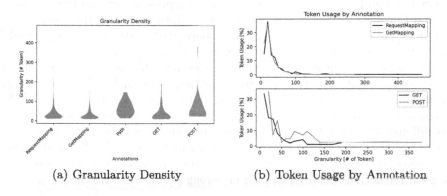

(a) Granularity Density   (b) Token Usage by Annotation

Fig. 2. Mining operations and granularity exploration

Figure 2(a) represents the probability density of different granularity values. We observe that three annotations, *RequestMapping*, *GetMapping* and *GET* have a similar density. They show that developers prefer operations with less than 75 tokens on average. After 100 tokens, the number of operations almost disappears. There are different shapes for the Path and POST annotations. Operation Granularity tends to decrease slowly between the 75 and 150 tokens in both cases. Although POST looks to disappear after 200 tokens, it slightly reappears near the 400 tokens. Thus, clusters of the operations with similar behaviour may have their own granularity density. Additionally, Fig. 2(b) shows the percentage of token usage for the top annotations. We can see decay in all cases, meaning that operations with a granularity above 80 tokens have a small usage.

We identify the granularity limits by clustering the vector representation of operations per annotation. Then, we consider 10 clusters (K10) as a base to continue the exploration. Figure 3(a) shows the granularity limits of RequestMapping. The whisker boxes present the lower and high granularity values for each

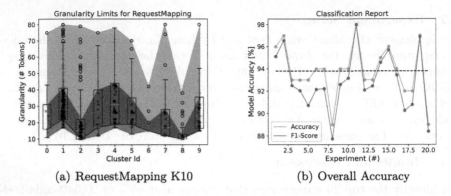

(a) RequestMapping K10   (b) Overall Accuracy

Fig. 3. Granularity limits and overall results

cluster, and each operation is a coloured data point. Thus, blue data points (below 25%) and red data points (above 75%) represent low and high granularity, and the green area contains 50% of data points, including the mean.

Our approach achieves an accuracy above 89%, with an average of 94%. Figure 3(b) shows that our approach has 55% of experiments above the average. We also notice a slight difference between the Accuracy and F1-Score. The difference of 2% means low false positives and negatives for Precision and Recall. Additionally, we group the results of good and wrong predictions by cluster. For instance, Fig. 4(a) shows the cumulative percentage of distance occurrence for two different cluster IDs. We observe subset imbalance effects. C6 is a cluster with a similar cumulative percentage but a gap between the distance of good and wrong predictions (0.04 to 0.05). C9 has a significant cumulative percentage for good predictions but overlapping on wrong predictions (above 0.11).

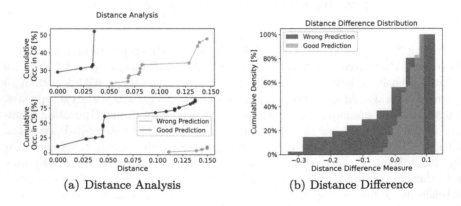

(a) Distance Analysis   (b) Distance Difference

Fig. 4. Distance Overlapping Analysis

Figure 4(b) has positive and negative values for distance difference. Positive values mean cases of intersection for good and wrong predictions, and negative values indicate a separation. We can see the overlapping of distance difference in the range of positive values.

Our findings show that 40% of wrong predictions occur when subsets have a distance difference below –0.05. Additionally, 60% of good predictions occur even with an overlapping before the 0.10 distance difference. Thus, databases should reduce the subsets imbalance and increase the distance per annotations cluster to improve the performance.

5   Related Work

Annotations Detection. Our research shows one empirical study catalogues developer issues and identifies annotations as the top category for components settings (30.3%) [8]. One systematic mapping study consolidates activities for detection and transition to microservices [3]. The research also shows previous studies that take advantage of the annotations to detect bad smells on microservice architecture [6] and evaluate the quality of the software through mutation testing [7]. Unlike those works, our approach identifies microservices and extracts annotations from a dataset from real open-source projects.

Table 1. Related work

Features	Related work									Our work
	[8]	[7]	[3]	[6]	[2]	[1]	[9]	[11]	[10]	
Annotations detection	✓	✓	✗	✓	✗	✗	✗	✗	✗	✓
Microservice detection	✗	✗	✓	✗	✗	✗	✗	✗	✗	✓
Granularity importance	✗	✗	✓	✗	✓	✓	✓	✗	✓	✓
Granularity metrics	✗	✗	✗	✗	✓	✓	✓	✓	✓	✓
Source code of samples	✗	✗	✗	✗	✗	✗	✓	✗	✓	✓
Semantics similarity	✗	✗	✗	✗	✗	✗	✗	✗	✗	✓
Operations collection	✗	✗	✗	✗	✗	✗	✗	✗	✗	✓
Granularity exploration	✗	✗	✗	✗	✗	✗	✗	✗	✗	✓

Granularity Importance. Several studies mentioned the *granularity importance* of determining the suitable size of microservices when splitting monolith applications [3]. Refactoring and Domain-Driven Design are used to find the optimal modularity of microservices [2,9,10]. Five works propose fourteen *granularity samples*, and only 22% have third-parties *source code* to calculate the *granularity metrics*. Unlike those works, our study explores different operation lengths among their semantics similarity to propose limits for good granularity.

Previous approaches do not consider the granularity by annotations. Then, we focus on the *operations collection, semantics similarity* and *granularity exploration* of size limits for fine-grained and coarse-grained operations with suitable amount of operations as suggested by Vural et al. [11] Table 1 shows how our work fits the state-of-the-art techniques.

6   Conclusion and Future Work

We elaborated a semantics-driven learning approach to suggest the granularity limits by learning the semantic relation between operations and their annotations and predicting the granularity limits. We are the first to propose a mechanism that detects the granularity limits of similar operations with their annotations.

We conclude that a database of operations is good enough to identify the granularity limits for unseen operations with annotations. Moreover, the analysis of overall results shows that increasing the unique annotations with overlapped operations would slightly reduce the overall accuracy. Increasing the distance between operations would minimize the impact on the overall accuracy.

In our ongoing research, we are including other granularity metrics and clustering mechanisms such as Hierarchical Clustering for advanced features.

References

1. Cojocaru, M., Uta, A., Oprescu, A.M.: MicroValid: a validation framework for automatically decomposed microservices. In: Proceedings of the International Conference on Cloud Computing Technology and Science, CloudCom **2019**, pp. 78–86 (2019)
2. Fritzsch, J., Bogner, J., Zimmermann, A., Wagner, S.: From monolith to microservices: a classification of refactoring approaches. In: Bruel, J.-M., Mazzara, M., Meyer, B. (eds.) DEVOPS 2018. LNCS, vol. 11350, pp. 128–141. Springer, Cham (2019). https://doi.org/10.1007/978-3-030-06019-0_10
3. Hassan, S., Bahsoon, R., Kazman, R.: Microservice transition and its granularity problem: A systematic mapping study. Softw. Pract. Exp. **50**(9), 1651–1681 (2020)
4. Jamshidi, P., Pahl, C., Mendonca, N.C., Lewis, J., Tilkov, S.: Microservices: The Journey So Far and Challenges Ahead. IEEE Softw. **35**(3), 24–35 (2018)
5. Perez, D., Chiba, S.: Cross-language clone detection by learning over abstract syntax trees. In: Proceedings of the 16th International Conference on Mining Software Repositories (MSR 2019), pp. 518–528. IEEE (2019)
6. Pigazzini, I., Fontana, F.A., Lenarduzzi, V., Taibi, D.: Towards Microservice smells detection. In: Proceedings of the 3rd International Conference on Technical Debt (TechDebt 2020), pp. 92–97. ACM (2020)
7. Pinheiro, P., Carlos Viana, J., et al.: Mutation operators for code annotations. In: Proceedings of the III Brazilian Symposium on Systematic and Automated Software Testing (SAST 2018), pp. 77–86. ACM (2018)
8. Ramirez, F., Mera-Gomez, C., Bahsoon, R., Zhang, Y.: An empirical study on microservice software development. In: Proceedings - 2021 IEEE/ACM Joint 9th International Workshop on Software Engineering for Systems-of-Systems and 15th Workshop on Distributed Software Development, Software Ecosystems and Systems-of-Systems, SESoS/WDES 2021, pp. 16–23 (2021)
9. Santos, A., Paula, H.: Microservice decomposition and evaluation using dependency graph and silhouette coefficient. In: ACM International Conference Proceeding Series, pp. 51–60 (2021)
10. Vera-Rivera, F.H., Puerto, E., Astudillo, H., Gaona, C.: Microservices backlog - a genetic programming technique for identification and evaluation of microservices from user stories. IEEE Access **9**, 117178–117203 (2021)

11. Vural, H., Koyuncu, M.: Does domain-driven design lead to finding the optimal modularity of a microservice? IEEE Access **9**, 32721–32733 (2021)
12. Wu, L., et al.: MicroDiag: fine-grained performance diagnosis for microservice systems. In: Proceedings of the International Workshop on Cloud Intelligence (CloudIntelligence 2021), pp. 31–36. IEEE (2021)
13. Zilberstein, M., Yahav, E.: Leveraging a corpus of natural language descriptions for program similarity. In: Onward! 2016: Proceedings of the 2016 ACM International Symposium on New Ideas, New Paradigms, and Reflections on Programming and Software, pp. 197–211. ACM (2016)

Service Personalization,
Recommendation, and Crowdsourcing

Balancing Supply and Demand for Mobile Crowdsourcing Services

Zhaoming Li[1] , Wei He[1,2](✉) , Ning Liu[1,2] , Yonghui Xu[1,2] ,
Lizhen Cui[1,2](✉) , and Kaiyuan Qi[3]

[1] School of Software, Shandong University, Jinan, China
`lizhaoming@mail.sdu.edu.cn`
[2] Jonit SDU-NTU Centre for Artificial Intelligence Research (C-FAIR), Jinan, China
`{hewei,liun21cs,clz}@sdu.edu.cn`
[3] State Key Laboratory of High-end Server & Storage Technology, Beijing, China
`qiky@inspur.com`

Abstract. Mobile crowdsourcing (MC) which has been developed
rapidly in recent years is playing an increasingly indispensable role in
people's daily lives such as taxi-hailing, food delivery and other services. The geographic equilibrium of service supply and demand is crucial so that the MC system could guarantee more promising matches in
a more regionally balanced way. However, due to the spatial dynamic
of MC environments, the emergence of supply and demand is unpredictable, asymmetric, and constantly changing among different regions
and throughout the day, presenting considerable challenges to the MC
platform. In this paper, we propose a hybrid reinforcement learning and
transformer-based balancing framework (HRB) to achieve geographically
balanced coverage of MC services, considering both the imbalanced state
of service supply-demand geographical distribution and the moving willingness of MC participants. The HRB framework is developed based
on the Deep Deterministic Policy Gradient strategy, which includes an
actor-critic network for generating migration strategies and a Willingness Transformer (WiT) model for predicting the migration willingness
of both mobile service providers and demanders among different regions.
Experimental results have validated the effectiveness by comparing the
proposed approach with other algorithms under multiple indicators.

Keywords: Mobile crowdsourcing service · Supply and demand
balance · Reinforcement learning · Transformer · Migration willingness

1 Introduction

With the popularity of mobile smart devices, Mobile Crowdsourcing (MC) [7]
assisted by smart mobile devices has developed rapidly. Multiple types of Mobile
Crowdsourcing Service (MCS) platforms are becoming more popular and integrating into people's daily life, such as taxi-hailing services, food delivery services, etc. In MC applications, a task publisher *requester* releases space-time

J. Troya et al. (Eds.): ICSOC 2022, LNCS 13740, pp. 285–299, 2022.
https://doi.org/10.1007/978-3-031-20984-0_20

related tasks on the platform, and one or more task performers *workers* similarly acquire tasks and perform them either actively (e.g. by grabbing orders) or passively (e.g. by being assigned by the platform) through the platform, and then get the corresponding reward. In this paper, the requester is referred to as *Service Demander* (e.g. the passenger in taxi-hailing services) and the worker as *Service Provider* (e.g. the driver in taxi-hailing services). Due to the personalized preference of both service demander and provider and the changeable contexts such as weather condition, urban traffic and geographic region, the service supplies and demands in MCS platform are asymmetrical, highly dynamic, and irregularly distributed. When there is an imbalance between supply and demand in a geographical region, it often happens that the provider cannot find a demander to be served or the demander cannot find a provider to offer the expected service. Therefore, the problem of mismatch and imbalance between service supply and demand has become a challenge for platforms, and the coverage balance of MCS is particularly important.

There have been some recent application-specific results on the balance of supply and demand services, which are mainly in the areas of WiFi hotspot sharing, bicycle-sharing and ride-hailing. Neiat *et al.* [14] proposed a system for WiFi service, which combines the participation probability model with an improved bipartite graph matching algorithm to achieve a geographically balanced coverage of services. Pan *et al.* [15] proposed a bicycle-sharing system with deep reinforcement learning methods to generate incentives encouraging users to participate in adjusting the number of bicycles among different subregions. Qin *et al.* [16] focused on taxi-hailing system, which uses deep reinforcement learning and transfer learning to improve efficiency. The above existing related works mostly balance the overall supply and demand situation through incentive mechanisms or maximizing benefits in platform-specific applications, ignoring the fact that the participant's autonomy and voluntariness play an essential role in general MC scenarios such as social-based, event-based or interest-based mobile services where incentives don't work very well. In fact, considering the willingness and preference of mobile participants will promote well-balanced distribution of service supply and demand, improve the matching efficiency and finally create more revenue for the MC platform.

In this paper, we propose a hybrid reinforcement learning and transformer-based balancing framework (HRB), to achieve the coverage balance of MC service supply and demand among multiple subregions. The basic idea is shown in Fig. 1, where the problem is formulated as a Markov Decision Process (MDP) based on interactions among the MC platform, the subregions and the participants. In the MDP, the "state" includes service supplies, demands, surplus, and shortage in different subregions, and each "action" corresponds to a decision on the migration direction of service providers or demanders in each subregion. Our HRB framework includes an actor-critic network for generating migration strategies and a Willingness Transformer (WiT) model for predicting the participants' migration willingness. Put simply, the actor-critic network and the WiT model are used to decide "how many participants should move from subregion sr_i to

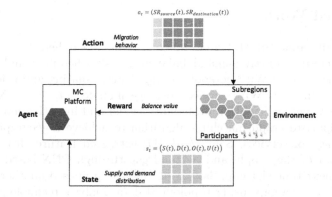

Fig. 1. An overview of the deep reinforcement learning framework for balancing supply and demand.

sr_j" and "who are most likely to move from subregion sr_i to sr_j", respectively. Specifically, the actor network is used to interact with the MC environment and generate migration decisions, meanwhile the critic network is used to evaluate the performance of the actor with a group of value functions and reward functions which can indicate the global supply-demand balance. Actions (i.e. user migration decisions) generated from the actor-critic network will be combined with the participants' willingness extracted by WiT model to effectively match the migration tasks with the participants. By this way, the distribution between MC service supply and demand can be adjusted continuously and thereby a relatively balanced state is maintained over the regions.

To summarize, the main contributions of the paper are as follows.

- We propose the hybrid reinforcement learning and transformer-based balancing (HRB) framework to achieve geographically balanced coverage of MC services by considering both the imbalanced state of service supply-demand distribution and the potential moving willingness of MC participants.
- We develop the Willingness Transformer (WiT) model to predict user intention and obtain the migration probabilities among different regions based on the historical trajectories of MC service participants.
- We conduct extensive experiments to validate the effectiveness of the proposed approach by comparing with other algorithms under multiple indicators, including the overall balance degree of supply and demand, geographical imbalance rate and supply-demand distribution etc.

The remainder of this paper is organized as follows: Sect. 2 summarizes the related work about adjusting service supply and demand for Mobile Crowdsourcing; Sect. 3 explains the definition of this problem; Sect. 4 introduces the proposed approach in detail; Sect. 5 presents the experimental results; Finally, Sect. 6 offers the conclusion of our work.

2 Related Work

Due to the dynamics of MC environments, some researchers have focused on problems including supply-demand balancing, task scheduling and allocation, mainly in the areas of WiFi hotspot sharing, bicycle-sharing and ride-hailing.

The literatures on WiFi service coverage include [14,17,18]. Neiat et al. [14] combined the participation probability model and incentive model with an improved bipartite graph matching algorithm to achieve a geographically balanced coverage of services. Said et al. [17] extracted features from historical sequence data of the supply and demand gap through CNN-based method to predict the next time slot gap. Said et al. [18] also proposed another prediction approach about the gap, using topological data analysis technology to generate a predictor from the original sequence data. The problem of supply and demand balance of bicycle-sharing has both theoretical research value and practical application value, and related literatures include [1,5,6,15,19,21]. Wang et al. [21] proposed a bike usage demand inference method, which estimates the demand of some regions and time intervals from the actual demand data of some bicycles, and then uses them as seeds to infer the regional bike usage demand of the entire city. By hiring workers to rebalance loads among bike stations, Duan et al. [6] first focused on the three-dimensional matching problem among workers, overflow and underflow stations from the perspective of workers' detour distance, and then considered the rebalancing frequency and target for each rebalancing operation. The authors also divided monetary incentives into source and destination incentives, and then combined reinforcement learning methods to solve the problem of bicycle rebalancing [5]. Pan et al. [15] also used a deep reinforcement learning algorithm to obtain the incentive value of each subregion hierarchically to adjust the distribution of bicycles. By modeling the relationships among bicycle stations, Chen et al. [1] used a dynamic cluster method to predict the over-demand. Singla et al. [19] designed a completely incentive system which adopts the optimal pricing policies using the approach of regret minimization and has been deployed in the real-world bicycle-sharing system. Compared to bicycle-sharing services, ride-hailing services appeared earlier. Related literatures mainly address two major problems in ride-hailing services, namely order dispatching and driver repositioning [9–11,16,22]. In [10], a practical framework based on deep learning and decision-making time planning was proposed to reduce the idle time of online drivers and improve the operating efficiency of the ride-hailing system. Qin et al. [16] set two optimization goals, i.e. driver-centric and passenger-centric, to maximize the total revenue of drivers on the platform, and propose a deep reinforcement learning approach to improve the order dispatch efficiency. Wang et al. [22] focused on matching passengers and drivers(i.e. order dispatching problem) by combining transfer learning and deep Q network reinforcement learning. Holler et al. [9] propose a decentralized solution for order dispatching problem by decomposing the single agent (system-centric) into multi-agents (driver-centric) which interact with the environment in reinforcement learning, and then use KL divergence optimization to accelerate the learning process. For the same purpose, Li et al. [11] use the approach of mean field approximation to simplify local interactions among multi-agents, and then take an average action among neighborhoods to capture dynamic changes in supply and demand.

3   Problem Definition

In this section, we present a formal model for the service coverage balance problem. The system of MC services consists of a central platform, which can be aware of the distribution of workers and users, that is service providers and service demanders. We use the following definitions to formulate the problem.

Definition 1. *(Region and Subregion)*

$$R = sr_1 \cup sr_2 \cup sr_3 \cup \cdots \cup sr_n \qquad (1)$$

In a location-based MC scenario, the entire region R is divided into a set of subregions $SR = \{sr_1, sr_2, sr_3, \cdots, sr_n\}$ (with different sizes), n is the number of subregions. Similarly, the entire interval τ when both the MC users and workers are available, is divided into a set of discrete time slots of equal fixed length. τ can be computed based on the maximum travel time between two subregions (e.g. using Google Map Distance Matrix API), denoted as $\{t_1, t_2, t_3, \cdots\}$.

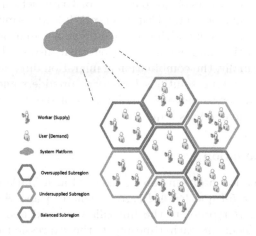

Fig. 2. Mobile crowdsourcing service scenario.

Definition 2. *(Region Coverage Equilibrium)*

$$RCE\left(P_{supply}, P_{demand}\right) = \sqrt{\sum_{i=1}^{n} (S_i - D_i)^2} \qquad (2)$$

We calculate the balance degree RCE based on the distribution of supply and demand in the region. And P_{supply}, P_{demand} represent supply distribution, demand distribution respectively. S_i and D_i are the number of service providers and demanders in subregion sr_i respectively. And n is the number of subregions. If RCE fluctuates within $[0, \alpha]$, it indicates the regional coverage balance. And the smaller RCE, the more balanced region. α depends on the distribution of supply and demand in experimental data.

Definition 3. (Mobile Crowdsourcing Coverage Balance Problem (MCCBP)) Given a time interval $\tau = \{t_1, t_2, t_3, \cdots\}$ and a set of subregions $SR = \{sr_1, sr_2, sr_3, \cdots, sr_n\}$, let $SP_{ij} = \{sp_1, sp_2, sp_3, \cdots\}$ be the set of service providers and $SD_{ij} = \{sd_1, sd_2, sd_3, \cdots\}$ be the set of service demanders in the time t_i in the subregion sr_j. As shown in Fig. 2, the MCCBP is to constantly redistribute service providers within subregions during the time interval τ to achieve optimal service coverage equilibrium in accordance with minimizing RCE, taking participants' willingness into account.

4   The HRB Framework

In this section, we propose a hybrid reinforcement learning and transformer-based balancing framework (HRB) to solve MCCBP. HRB not only takes the regional balance into account but also considers the autonomy of participants. As shown in Fig. 3, HRB consists of two parts: Actor-Critic network and Willingness Transformer (WiT) model. Actor-Critic network first determines the migration direction of service providers within each subregion based on the RCE. WiT then obtains the participants' willingness from their historical trajectory within the entire region. Finally, the combination of migration direction and willingness generates specific matching solutions for service providers and demanders, i.e., the plans for a provider to move to the location of the demander to provide a service to meet the demander's request.

4.1   MDP Formulation

The migration direction problem can be modeled as a Markov decision process (MDP) defined by a 5-tuple (S, A, Pr, R, γ), where S and A denote the set of states and actions, R represents the immediate reward and γ is the discount factor. In our problem, at each timestep t, the expression of **state** s_t is as follows:

$$s_t = (S(t), D(t), O(t), U(t)) \tag{3}$$

In subregion sr_i at the beginning of timeslot $t \in \tau$, let $S_i(t)$, $D_i(t)$, $O_i(t)$, $U_i(t)$ denote the supply, demand, oversupply, undersupply, i.e., the number of service provider, service demander, surplus provider, surplus demander. And we denote $S(t)$, $D(t)$, $O(t)$, $U(t)$ as the vector of supply, demand, oversupply, undersupply respectively. The **action** $a_t = (SR_{sou}(t), SR_{des}(t))$. At the beginning of timeslot $t \in \tau$, the MC service providers in subregion sr_j will migrate

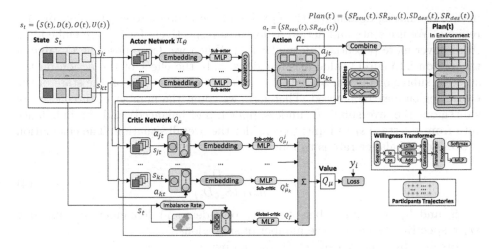

Fig. 3. The network of HRB framework.

to one of subregions $sr_{k1}, sr_{k2}, \cdots, sr_{km}$. And $sr_j \in SR_{sou}(t)$, $1 \leq j \leq n$, $sr_k \in SR_{des}(t)$, $1 \leq k \leq n$, $(sr_j, sr_{k1}, sr_{k2}, \cdots, sr_{km}) \in a_t$. An immediate reward $R(s_t, a_t)$ indicates the balance of region after a_t is executed on the basis of s_t, that is, the distribution of supply and demand. The **reward** $R(s_t, a_t) = -RCE(P_{supply}, P_{demand})$. As mentioned in Problem Definition, P_{supply}, P_{demand} represent supply distribution, demand distribution respectively. We use RCE to measure the similarity of the distribution of supply and demand, and negative RCE is used as the value of immediate reward. In conclusion, the platform takes an action a_t, and receives an immediate reward $R(s_t, a_t)$ in the whole area R at timestep t. $Pr(s_{t+1}|s_t, a_t)$ represents the transition probability from state s_t to state s_{t+1} under action a_t. The policy function $\pi_\theta(s_t)$ with the parameter θ, maps the current state to a deterministic action. The overall objective is to find an optimal policy to maximize the overall discounted rewards from state s_t following π_θ, denoted by $J_{\pi_\theta} = \mathbb{E}\left[\sum_{k=0}^{\infty} \gamma^k R(a_k, s_k)|\pi_\theta, s_0\right]$, where $\gamma \in [0,1]$ denotes the discount factor. The Q-value of state s_t and action a_t under policy π_θ is denoted by $Q^{\pi_\theta}(s_t, a_t) = \mathbb{E}\left[\sum_{k=t}^{\infty} \gamma^{k-t} R(a_k, s_k)|\pi_\theta, s_t, a_t\right]$. Note that J_{π_θ} is a discounted version of the targeting objective, and will serve as a close approximation when γ is close to 1.

4.2   Actor-Critic Network

Actor-Critic network based on DDPG [12] determine the migration direction of the service provider, i.e. the provider moves from the subregion where this provider is located to the subregion where the corresponding demander is located. The action space is high-dimensional and continuous. As the number of subregions increases, there will be a crisis of dimensionality. Inspired by [3], we decompose the original region critic network into multiple subregions critic networks, that is, decompose the Q-value of the region into sub-Q-value of sub-regions. We use state and action as features respectively for feature embedding to discover more potential information [2]. When we decompose the Q-value of the region into sub-Q-value of subregions, only the effect of the action on the state in subregions is considered, but the effect of the action on the state of the entire region may be ignored. Therefore, we count the number of three cases of subregions (i.e. oversupplied, undersupplied, and balanced) and the imbalance rate from the state s_t as input to consider the overall situation. The calculation process of imbalance rate is as follows:

$$ir_i = \frac{|S_i - D_i|}{max\,(S_i, D_i)} \tag{4}$$

S_i and D_i are the number of service providers and demanders in subregion sr_i respectively. And n is the number of subregions.

Inspired by [15], we can get $Q_\mu\,(s_t, a_t)$ by:

$$Q_\mu\,(s_t, a_t) = Q_f + \sum_{j=1}^{n} Q_{\mu_j}^j\,(s_{jt}, a_{jt}) \tag{5}$$

In time slot t, the input of global-critic are three numbers (i.e. the number of oversupplied, undersupplied, balanced subregions), the output is a global value Q_f. Each subregion has a sub-critic network. And the input is state s_{jt} and action a_{jt} of this subregion, the output is a sub-Q-value $Q_{\mu_j}^j$, so Q value of the entire region is $\sum_{j=1}^{n} Q_{\mu_j}^j$. As mentioned earlier, when the region is divided into subregions, Q-value will have a possible deviation, so Q_f makes up for this shortcoming.

Reinforcement learning uses the immediate rewards obtained during the interaction between the agent and the environment to guide the behavior of the agent. The Actor network will output actions based on the status of the environment feedback, and the Critic network will evaluate the actions output by the Actor network based on the status of the environment feedback and immediate rewards, and output the Q value. Due to the instability of a single network during training, drawing on the successful experience of DQN [13], the original Actor and Critic networks are expanded to four networks. These four networks are divided into the real network and the target network. The real network is the original one. In the Actor-Critic network, target network has the same structure as the real network. The real network will softly update the target network for a fixed period to improve the stability of the real network training. Intuitively speaking, during the training process, the Actor network updates its parameters according to the Q value output by the Critic network, that is, the goal of the Actor network is to maximize the Q value; the Critic network updates its own network parameters according to the immediate rewards feedback from the environment, that is, the real Critic network and the target Critic network do the mean square error.

The Actor network represents the policy π_θ parameterized by θ. It maximizes J_{π_θ} using stochastic gradient ascent. In particular, the gradient of J_{π_θ} over θ is given by:

$$\nabla_\theta J_{\pi_\theta} = \mathbb{E}_{s \sim \rho_{\pi_\theta}} \left[\nabla_\theta \pi_\theta (s) \nabla_a Q_\mu (s, a) |_{a=\pi_\theta(s)} \right], \tag{6}$$

where ρ_{π_θ} denotes the distribution of states.

The Critic network takes the state s_t and action a_t as input, and outputs the action value. Specifically, the critic network approximates the action-value function $Q^{\pi_\theta} (s, a)$ by minimizing the following loss [12]:

$$L (Q^{\pi_\theta}) = \mathbb{E}_{s_t \sim \rho_\pi, a_t \sim \pi} \left[(Q_\mu (s_t, a_t) - y_t)^2 \right], \tag{7}$$

where $y_t = R(s_t, a_t) + \gamma Q'_{\mu'} (s_{t+1}, \pi'_{\theta'} (s_{t+1}))$.

4.3   Willingness Transformer (WiT)

Inspired by Vision Transformer [4], we propose the Willingness Transformer (WiT) model based on Transformer [20]. Compared with Transformer, WiT inputs the subregions ID sequence during the training phase, and the label is the next subregion ID. After the training of WiT is completed, we can input the subregion ID sequence of the service provider to obtain the probabilities to subregions, that is, willingness. The principle is the consistency of behaviors, which means that human behaviors always follow a respective pattern and preference within a certain period. The subregion ID sequence first needs ID Embedding and Positional Encoding, then the two are added together. Convolutional Neural Network (CNN) and Long Short-Term Memory (LSTM) respectively extract the local features and long dependencies of the subregion ID sequence. And Transformer Encoder uses a self-attention mechanism to give these different features different attention levels. Finally, WiT outputs probabilities.

$$F_{input} = Concatenate(F_{CNN}, F_{LSTM}, F_{ie} + F_{pe}) \tag{8}$$

F_{ie} are the subregion ID embedding of the check-in sequence. Similarly, F_{pe} is the positional encoding. And F_{CNN}, F_{LSTM} respectively represent local features and long dependencies of ID sequence. F_{input} is fed into the Transformer Encoder. The encoder is a stack of N identical blocks. Each block contains a multi-head attention layer and a feedforward network layer. The attention function can be considered as mapping a set of key-value pairs (K-V) and a query (Q) to an output, where the key, value, and query all come from different transformations of feature integration. The output is the weighted sum of these values, where the weight of each value depends on the similarity of the query to the corresponding key. Residual connection [8] is used, which can alleviate the problem of vanishing or exploding gradients in deep neural networks as the depth increases, that is, to prevent information loss. The WiT's train loss $\mathcal{L} = CE(y_{id}, \hat{y}_{id})$, where CE is the Cross-Entropy function, y_{id} is the one-hot encoding of true next subregion ID, and $\hat{y}_{id}$ is the recommendation probabilities of all subregion ID. The training objective is to minimize the loss function $\mathcal{L}$.

5   Experiment

This section demonstrates the effectiveness of the proposed approach by conducting comparative experiments on benchmark datasets.

5.1   Datasets

We conduct our experiments on the following real-world datasets. Considering the diversity of experimental data, we select two types of datasets with different MC scenarios, including taxi-hailing and bike-sharing.

New York City Taxi Trip Duration[1]: We use the training set of this dataset to generate supply and demand data. The records include pick-up and drop-off time and pick-up and drop-off locations with their associated IDs. We consider each pick-up event as a demand record (i.e. passenger has a demand for a taxi) and each drop-off event as a supply (i.e. taxi has become available, and the driver can offer a service) to generate supply and demand data.

New York City Bike Sharing 2019[2]: We use this dataset to generate supply and demand data. The records include start and stop time and its corresponding locations in terms of latitude and longitude. We consider each start event as a demand record (i.e. passenger has a demand for a bike) and each stop event as a supply (i.e. bike has become available, and the bike can offer a service) to generate supply and demand data.

FourSquare - NYC and Tokyo Check-ins[3]: The dataset contains check-in records in two cities, NYC and Tokyo for about 10 months. It contains 227,428 check-ins in New York City and 573,703 check-ins in Tokyo. In the following experiments, we generate the trajectory data of MC service providers from this check-in dataset.

Two groups of datasets were used to evaluate the proposed HRB framework, namely the NYC Taxi and Check-ins datasets, the NYC Bike and Check-ins datasets. And the WiT model is evaluated with the NYC and Tokyo Check-ins datasets.

5.2   Evaluation Metric and Baselines

To comprehensively evaluate the performance of HRB over a period of time (one day), we summarize experimental data during this period of time and use the sum, mean, maximum and minimum values based on three metrics, including Region Coverage Equilibrium (RCE), accumulated service provider income (ASPI), and order response rate (ORR). RCE calculation formula is shown in

---

[1] https://tianchi.aliyun.com/dataset/dataDetail?dataId=94519.

[2] https://www.kaggle.com/datasets/ongks1986/new-york-city-bike-sharing-2019.

[3] https://www.kaggle.com/chetanism/foursquare-nyc-and-tokyo-checkin-dataset/version/2.

Eq. (2). ASPI and ORR inspired by [11] are proposed. To evaluate the performance of WiT, we use the probabilities output by the model and label to calculate the accuracy. If the correct label is among the top-k predicted values, the calculation result is increased by 1. We compare our HRB framework with the following baseline algorithms:

- No operations (NO). This method does not perform matching operations.
- Random (RAN). It only randomly assigns all active service providers with available demanders at each time step.
- Response-based (RES). During each time step, all available demanders starting from the same subregion will be sorted by the deadline. Multiple demanders with the same deadline will be further sorted by the service reward.
- Revenue-based (REV). The higher the reward is given by the service demander, the higher its priority when matched. Following the similar principle as described above, demanders with an earlier deadline will be assigned first if multiple demanders give the same reward.
- DDPG. [12].
- HRB-Hierarchical (HRB-H). Compared with HRB, HRB-H has no Global-critic and no Embedding in the network structure.
- HRB-Hierarchical-Global (HRB-HG). Compared with HRB, HRB-HG has no Embedding in the network structure.

To predict the migration willingness of MC participants among different regions, we compare the WiT module with the following algorithms:

- Convolutional Neural Network (CNNCom).
- Long Short-Term Memory (LSTMCom).
- TransformerCom (Imitating Vision Transformer [4]).

5.3   Performance Comparison

We first compare WiT with other related algorithms, then verify the effectiveness of the internal structure of Actor-Critic Network, and finally compare HRB with other related algorithms.

WiT Performance. We trained WiT and its' comparison algorithms on NYC and TKY datasets respectively. The Top-1 accuracy of these models on NYC and TKY test set are shown in Fig. 4. In detail, the training step and accuracy of these models to achieve the best results on the test set are shown in Table 1. We observe that WiT can achieve higher prediction accuracy in lesser training steps.

Effect of the Internal Structure with Actor-Critic Network. Respectively, we compare our HRB framework with the baseline algorithms, as well as conduct ablation experiments to verify the effectiveness of the different components (i.e. the Hierarchical structure, the Global-critic network and the Embedding layer) in the HRB framework. As shown in Tables 2 and 3 for the taxi-hailing

Table 1. Performance comparison for WiT in terms of training step and accuracy on Check-ins test set.

Datasets	Algorithm	Training step	Top-1	Top-2	Top-3	Top-4	Top-5
NYC Check-ins	**WiT**	**145500**	**51.42%**	**68.40%**	**75.88%**	**80.01%**	**82.89%**
	LSTMCom	207500	50.62%	67.65%	75.11%	79.28%	82.12%
	TransformerCom	214000	48.19%	66.25%	74.06%	78.64%	81.68%
	CNNCom	158500	47.03%	64.40%	72.01%	76.42%	79.26%
TKY Check-ins	**WiT**	**312000**	**57.22%**	**75.34%**	**82.79%**	**86.70%**	**89.22%**
	LSTMCom	786000	56.50%	74.75%	82.32%	86.37%	88.95%
	TransformerCom	597500	45.68%	66.04%	76.56%	82.48%	86.41%
	CNNCom	543000	44.25%	64.18%	74.19%	79.82%	83.52%

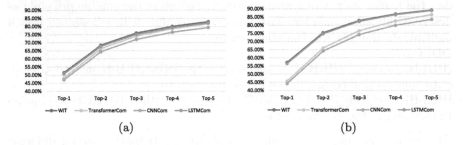

(a)   (b)

Fig. 4. Performance comparison for WiT in terms of accuracy on two test sets. (a) NYC test set. (b) TKY test set.

and bike-sharing datasets, we can observe the effectiveness of these three structures. The Hierarchical Structure can effectively improve the performance of HRB, so that the problem-solving perspective is changed from the entire region to subregions, paying more attention to each subregion. Global-critic makes up for the deficiencies of Hierarchical Structure and considers the connections between subregions from the perspective of imbalance rate. Embedding enables Actor-Critic Network to have the ability to mine more useful information from state s_t and action a_t.

Essentially, these DDPG-based algorithms are constantly exploring the best matching scheme to reduce RCE. In this exploration process, the ORR increases, which drives the increase of ASPI. Note that the smaller the RCE, the larger the ORR and ASPI, the better. And the relationship between ORR and ASPI is non-linear.

HRB Performance. As is shown in Tables 2 and 3 for Taxi and Bike datasets, traditional methods (i.e., RAN, RES and REV.) just mechanically perform matching operations in accordance with their own rules, ignoring participants' willingness, making ORR low. Although these methods can reduce RCE, the number of matches completed is too small. In contrast, HRB uses neural net-

Table 2. Performance comparison for HRB on NYC Taxi dataset.

Algorithm	ORR (mean)	ASPI (sum)	RCE (mean)	RCE (max)	RC E(min)
NO	0.00%	0.00	60.41	115.21	21.42
RAN	11.08%	604081.64	57.11	110.28	21.59
RES	11.01%	602223.01	56.88	105.25	21.38
REV	11.19%	626606.50	57.13	112.64	21.84
DDPG	73.71%	2773629.23	51.79	94.87	18.76
HRB-H	74.05%	2770291.25	51.51	93.39	18.57
HRB-HG	73.49%	2760943.73	51.52	92.99	19.18
HRB	**73.97%**	**2780334.14**	**50.92↓**	**89.24↓**	**18.76↓**

Table 3. Performance comparison for HRB on NYC Bike dataset.

Algorithm	ORR(mean)	ASPI(sum)	RCE(mean)	RCE(max)	RCE(min)
NO	0.00%	0.00	56.12	203.74	2.00
RAN	11.72%	622536.80	52.89	197.23	2.00
RES	12.41%	631632.78	53.26	196.15	2.00
REV	12.02%	656474.49	52.94	196.05	2.00
DDPG	66.40%	2882350.56	50.71	189.55	2.00
HRB-H	65.23%	2886530.42	50.56	187.57	2.00
HRB-HG	66.75%	2876824.91	50.22	189.51	2.00
HRB	**66.80%**	**2895037.73**	**49.91↓**	**175.31↓**	**2.00**

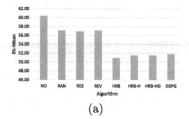 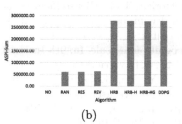

(a)   (b)

Fig. 5. Performance comparison for HRB in terms of two metrics on Taxi datasets. (a) RCE (mean). (b) ASPI (sum).

works to learn the relevant rules of migration direction of service providers and keeps trying to reduce RCE, that is, to maintain the relative balance of the region, to increase ORR, and thereby increase ASPI. As is shown in Figs. 5, compared with other algorithms, HRB matches providers and demanders taking the regional balance and the willingness of participants into account, which can effectively increase the number of transactions and thereby increase the total revenue of service providers.

6   Conclusion

In this paper, we propose a hybrid reinforcement learning and transformer-based balancing framework (HRB) to achieve geographically balanced coverage of MC services. Experimental results proved that HRB can continuously adjust supply and demand distribution among regions while taking participants' willingness into account, thereby increasing the overall number of successful MC supply and demand matches. In the future work, we will model participants in a more refined manner (e.g. interests in different contexts), and explore methods about reinforcement learning training for mobile user behavior prediction tasks.

Acknowledgements. This work was supported by National Key R&D Program of China (No.2021YFF0900802), Natural Science Foundation of China (No. 91846205) and Natural Science Foundation of Shandong Province (No. ZR2019LZH008).

References

1. Chen, L., et al.: Dynamic cluster-based over-demand prediction in bike sharing systems. In: Proceedings of the 2016 ACM International Joint Conference on Pervasive and Ubiquitous Computing, UbiComp 2016, Heidelberg, Germany, 12–16 September2016. pp. 841–852. ACM (2016)
2. Covington, P., Adams, J., Sargin, E.: Deep neural networks for YouTube recommendations. In: Proceedings of the 10th ACM Conference on Recommender Systems, Boston, MA, USA, 15–19 September 2016. pp. 191–198. ACM (2016)
3. Dietterich, T.G.: Hierarchical reinforcement learning with the MAXQ value function decomposition. J. Artif. Intell. Res. **13**, 227–303 (2000)
4. Dosovitskiy, A., et al.: An image is worth 16x16 words: transformers for image recognition at scale. In: 9th International Conference on Learning Representations, ICLR 2021, Virtual Event, Austria, 3–2 May 2021. OpenReview.net (2021)
5. Duan, Y., Wu, J.: Optimizing rebalance scheme for dock-less bike sharing systems with adaptive user incentive. In: 20th IEEE International Conference on Mobile Data Management, MDM 2019, Hong Kong, SAR, China, 10–13 June 2019. pp. 176–181. IEEE (2019)
6. Duan, Y., Wu, J.: Optimizing the crowdsourcing-based bike station rebalancing scheme. In: 39th IEEE International Conference on Distributed Computing Systems, ICDCS 2019, Dallas, TX, USA, 7–10 July 2019, pp. 1559–1568. IEEE (2019)
7. Hamrouni, A., Alelyani, T., Ghazzai, H., Massoud, Y.: Toward collaborative mobile crowdsourcing. IEEE Internet Things Mag. 4(2), 88–94 (2021)
8. He, K., Zhang, X., Ren, S., Sun, J.: Deep residual learning for image recognition. In: 2016 IEEE Conference on Computer Vision and Pattern Recognition, CVPR 2016, Las Vegas, NV, USA, 27–30 June 2016. pp. 770–778. IEEE Computer Society (2016)
9. Holler, J., et al.: Deep reinforcement learning for multi-driver vehicle dispatching and repositioning problem. In: 2019 IEEE International Conference on Data Mining, ICDM 2019, Beijing, China, 8–11 November 2019. pp. 1090–1095. IEEE (2019)
10. Jiao, Y., et al.: Real-world ride-hailing vehicle repositioning using deep reinforcement learning. CoRR abs/2103.04555 (2021)

11. Li, M., et al.: Efficient ridesharing order dispatching with mean field multi-agent reinforcement learning. In: The World Wide Web Conference, WWW 2019, San Francisco, CA, USA, 13–17 May 2019. pp. 983–994. ACM (2019)
12. Lillicrap, T.P., et al.: Continuous control with deep reinforcement learning. In: Bengio, Y., LeCun, Y. (eds.) 4th International Conference Track Proceedings on Learning Representations, ICLR 2016, San Juan, Puerto Rico, 2–4 May 2016 (2016)
13. Mnih, M., et al.: Human-level control through deep reinforcement learning. Nature **518**(7540), 529–533 (2015)
14. Neiat, A.G., Bouguettaya, A., Mistry, S.: Incentive-based crowdsourcing of hotspot services. ACM Trans. Internet Techn. **19**(1), 5:1–5:24 (2019)
15. Pan, L., Cai, Q., Fang, Z., Tang, P., Huang, L.: A deep reinforcement learning framework for rebalancing dockless bike sharing systems. In: The Thirty-Third AAAI Conference on Artificial Intelligence, AAAI 2019, pp. 1393–1400. AAAI Press (2019)
16. Qin, Z.T., et al.: Ride-hailing order dispatching at DIDI via reinforcement learning. INFORMS J. Appl. Anal. **50**(5), 272–286 (2020)
17. Said, A.B., Erradi, A.: Deep-gap: a deep learning framework for forecasting crowd-sourcing supply-demand gap based on imaging time series and residual learning. In: 2019 IEEE International Conference on Cloud Computing Technology and Science (CloudCom), Sydney, Australia, 11–13 December 2019. pp. 279–286. IEEE (2019)
18. Said, A.B., Erradi, A.: Multiview topological data analysis for crowdsourced service supply-demand gap prediction. In: 16th International Wireless Communications and Mobile Computing Conference, IWCMC 2020, Limassol, Cyprus, 15–19 June 2020. pp. 1818–1823. IEEE (2020)
19. Singla, A., Santoni, M., Bartók, G., Mukerji, P., Meenen, M., Krause, A.: Incentivizing users for balancing bike sharing systems. In: Proceedings of the Twenty-Ninth AAAI Conference on Artificial Intelligence, 25–30 January 2015, Austin, Texas, USA, pp. 723–729. AAAI Press (2015)
20. Vaswani, A., et al.: Attention is all you need. In: Advances in Neural Information Processing Systems 30: Annual Conference on Neural Information Processing Systems 2017, 4–9 December 2017, Long Beach, CA, USA, pp. 5998–6008 (2017)
21. Wang, S., Chen, H., Cao, J., Zhang, J., Yu, P.S.: Locally balanced inductive matrix completion for demand-supply inference in stationless bike-sharing systems. IEEE Trans. Knowl. Data Eng. **32**(12), 2374–2388 (2020)
22. Wang, Z., Qin, Z.T., Tang, X., Ye, J., Zhu, H.: Deep reinforcement learning with knowledge transfer for online rides order dispatching. In: IEEE International Conference on Data Mining, ICDM 2018, Singapore, 17–20 November 2018. pp. 617–626. IEEE Computer Society (2018)

Acceptance-Aware Multi-platform Cooperative Matching in Spatial Crowdsourcing

Xiaotong Xu[1], An Liu[1(✉)], Guanfeng Liu[2], Jiajie Xu[1], and Lei Zhao[1]

[1] School of Computer Science and Technology, Soochow University, Suzhou, China
`20204227022@stu.suda.edu.cn`, {`anliu,xujj,zhaol`}`@suda.edu.cn`
[2] Department of Computing, Macquarie University, Sydney, Australia
`guanfeng.liu@mq.edu.au`

Abstract. With the development of sharing economy, multi-platform cooperative matching (MPCM) is becoming popular as it provides an effective way to cope with the supply-demand imbalance in spatial crowdsourcing (SC). While cooperation between two SC platforms in MPCM has been intensively studied, competition among multiple SC platforms is largely overlooked by existing work. In particular, an idle worker may be requested by multiple platforms simultaneously, but he/she can only accept some of them due to capacity constraints. This partial acceptance will decrease the revenue of some platforms and thus should be addressed properly. Towards this goal, we investigate in this paper the problem of acceptance-aware multi-platform cooperative matching. We first design an algorithm called BaseMPCM to predict the acceptance rate of workers and calculate the utility scores of task-and-worker pairs. Considering that in BaseMPCM, the platforms make the decision from their own benefits, and this may lead to a sub-optimal total revenue, we further design an algorithm called DeepMPCM to predict the action of other platforms and calculate the utility scores globally. Extensive experiments on real and synthetic datasets demonstrate the effectiveness of our algorithms.

Keywords: Spatial crowdsourcing · Task allocation · Cooperative matching · Multiple platforms

1 Introduction

Spatial Crowdsourcing (SC) is an emerging paradigm of crowdsourcing in which SC platforms employ a crowd of workers to move to specific physical locations to perform spatiotemporal tasks. Many services in daily life are typical SC applications, for example, real-time taxi-calling services (e.g., DiDi and Uber), online meal-ordering services (*e.g.*, Ele.me and Meituan), citizen sensing services (e.g., Waze and OpenStreetMap), just to name a few.

© The Author(s), under exclusive license to Springer Nature Switzerland AG 2022
J. Troya et al. (Eds.): ICSOC 2022, LNCS 13740, pp. 300–315, 2022.
https://doi.org/10.1007/978-3-031-20984-0_21

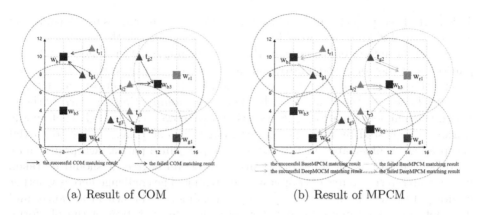

(a) Result of COM   (b) Result of MPCM

Fig. 1. An example of cooperative matching among three platforms

One critical problem in SC is matching, which assigns tasks to workers so that the total utility of an SC platform is optimized. Most existing studies focus on designing algorithms for a single platform to achieve optimal matching using different utility settings. For instance, the utility of a platform can be the total number of assigned tasks [9], the total moving distance of workers [15], the payoff difference among workers [21], and so on. All these methods can achieve good matching when the tasks and workers of a platform are evenly distributed. In the real world, however, this is not the case. Specifically, some tasks cannot be fulfilled because there are no idle workers nearby, while some idle workers at other locations may always be unoccupied since no executable tasks are around. The uneven distribution will bring a huge loss of performance to the existing methods. Fortunately, the distributions of tasks and workers in different platforms are typically various in real life [5]. It is likely that an unassigned task in one platform can be served by the idle workers of other platforms. If these platforms can cooperate in matching, the problem caused by uneven distribution will be alleviated, and the platforms will achieve a win-win situation.

Motivated by this, we investigate the Multi-Platform Cooperative Matching (MPCM) problem where n platforms cooperate in assigning their tasks with the aim of increasing their total revenue. A simple version of this problem has been studied in [5], where $n = 2$ and the aim is to maximize the revenue of only one platform. However, the proposed solution does not work well when $n > 2$ due to a phenomenon called worker competition. Let us illustrate this with a simple example shown in Fig. 1(a). Suppose there are three platforms G, B, and R. At some point, the platform B has some free workers (denoted by blue squares) but no task. On the contrary, platforms G and R have some tasks (denoted by green and red triangles) to complete, but no worker is available. Using the solution proposed in [5] which matches the nearest serviceable worker to a task, G and R will ask the worker w_{b_3} to perform their tasks t_{g_2} and t_{r_2}, respectively. The worker, however, can only accept one task say t_{r_2}, due to capacity constraint.

This partial acceptance will decrease the platform G's revenue since G could ask w_{r_1} for help if it knew w_{b_3} would reject it, albeit w_{r_1} is a little far away.

An important observation from the above example is that when $n > 2$, the platforms are not only cooperators but also competitors for workers. In [5], only two platforms are involved in the cooperation, so the idle workers of one platform can just be lent to the other. Clearly, there is no competition for workers there. When the number of platforms is more than two, however, it is likely that an idle worker is requested by multiple platforms at the same time, leading to partial acceptance, as illustrated in the above example. Since partial acceptance may decrease the revenue of some platforms to a certain degree, it should be taken into account in the course of cooperative matching. The challenge here is whether or not a task will be accepted by a worker cannot be known in advance, and it is determined by many factors, for example, the quotation of the platform, the distance between the task and the worker, and the number of requests that the worker receives at that time. Note that the last factor cannot be known in advance either, which makes the prediction of acceptance non-trivial.

To enable acceptance awareness in cooperative matching, we propose in this paper an algorithm called BaseMPCM which first employs the method of upper confidence bound to learn the relationship between the acceptance rate and the platform's quotation and then calculates utility scores for all task-and-worker pairs. In BaseMPCM, every platform makes the decision from its own benefit, which may lead to a sub-optimal total revenue. To overcome this shortcoming, we further design an algorithm called DeepMPCM which first predicts the action of other platforms and then calculates global utility scores for task-and-worker pairs. Specifically, we adopt a Convolutional Neural Network (CNN) to capture the spatial correlation between tasks and workers, which is useful to estimate the number of requests that workers may receive. We also construct a multi-layer perceptron (MLP) to predict global utility scores based on the contextual information of tasks and workers. In summary, we make the following contributions:

- To the best of our knowledge, this is the first study to consider the problem of worker competition in cooperative matching in spatial crowdsourcing. Worker competition will lead to partial acceptance, which in turn may decrease the revenue of some platforms and thus should be addressed.
- We propose two algorithms to predict the utility scores of task-and-worker pairs. Specifically, We first design the BaseMPCM algorithm to predict the acceptance rate of workers and calculate platform's expected revenue as the utility score. We further design the DeepMPCM algorithm to predict the action of other platforms and predict global utility scores by neural networks.
- We conduct extensive experiments on real and synthetic datasets to demonstrate the effectiveness of the proposed algorithms.

2   Related Work

Task-worker matching plays an important role in SC. Existing studies on matching can be divided into two categories: offline matching and online matching. In the former case, the spatiotemporal information, such as the arrival time and the location of tasks and workers, is known in advance. Based on the information, offline matching can be modeled as a typical bipartite matching and be solved by network flow algorithms [10,14].

Compared with offline matching, dynamic online matching is more practical, where tasks and workers arrive at a platform dynamically, and the platform needs to respond promptly to task requests. Existing works usually design dynamic matching algorithms [4] and greedy algorithms [7] to solve the online matching problem. In [16], the authors randomly choose task-and-worker pairs whose score is higher than an established threshold to obtain a competitive ratio of $1/2e\ln(1 + U_{\max})$ under the online adversarial model with U_{max} as the maximum edge weight in the bipartite graph and e as the natural constant. In addition, some algorithms based on road discovery, game theory and reinforcement learning [3,6,20,21] have been proposed to improve the matching quality and realize personalized matching based on workers' social graph [11–13].

Besides the traditional simple matching, some complex matching problems have been studied in recent years [3,8,18,19]. However, these solutions cannot be applied to our problem. On the one hand, although the acceptance rate of workers has been considered in [22], it is assumed to be known in advance and does not need to be predicted. On the other hand, in the MPCM scenario, partial acceptance is caused by worker competition on multiple platforms. Therefore, the acceptance rate of workers is also determined by the action of other platforms, which is different from the traditional acceptance rate in the single platform scenario.

3   Problem Statement

In this section, we introduce some basic concepts and present the formal definition of the MPCM problem.

Definition 1 (Task). *A task is a tuple $t = \langle t.s, t.e, t.l, t.p, t.c \rangle$ where $t.s$ and $t.e$ are the arrival time and due time of t respectively, $t.l$ is the location where t will be performed, and $t.p$ is the amount of money that the platform $t.c$ will receive after t is completed.*

Definition 2 (Worker). *A worker is a tuple $w = \langle w.s, w.l, w.r, w.c \rangle$ where $w.s$ is the arrival time of w, $w.l$ is the location of w, $w.r$ is the reachable range of w and $w.c$ is the platform to which w belongs.*

Definition 3 (SC Platform). *An SC platform is a tuple $sc = \langle sc.\boldsymbol{W}, sc.\boldsymbol{T} \rangle$, where $sc.\boldsymbol{W}$ and $sc.\boldsymbol{T}$ are the worker set and task set of sc, respectively.*

Definition 4 (Outer Payment). *When a worker from other platforms successfully serves a platform's spatial task t, the worker will be paid an outer payment $t.p'$ and $0 < t.p' \le t.p$.*

Definition 5 (Revenue). *For any pair $(t, w) \in M_{sc}$ where M_{sc} is the matching result set of sc, the revenue of platform sc on (t, w) is as follows:*

$$\text{rev}_{sc}(t, w) = \begin{cases} t.p & t.c = sc \text{ and } w.c = sc \\ t.p' & t.c \neq sc \text{ and } w.c = sc \\ t.p - t.p' & t.c = sc \text{ and } w.c \neq sc \end{cases} \tag{1}$$

If a task and a worker both come from the same platform *sc*, the revenue will be the original payment of the task. If *sc*'s internal task is performed by a worker from other platforms, the revenue will be the task's original payment minus its outer payment. If *sc*'s internal worker serves a task of other platforms, the revenue is the task's outer payment.

Definition 6 (The MPCM Problem). *Given a set of cooperative platforms $SC = \{sc_1, sc_2, ...sc_{|SC|}\}$, tasks and workers arrive at these platforms sequentially, and the platforms conduct matching over the shared tasks and workers. MPCM requires finding a matching result set M_i $(1 \leq i \leq |SC|)$ for each platform so that the platforms' total revenue is maximized under the following constraints:*

- *Spatial constraint: A worker can only serve tasks within his/her reachable range, that is, only the tasks in the circular area with w.l as the center and w.r as the radius can be served by worker w.*
- *Temporal constraint: A matched worker must arrive at the workplace of task t before the task's expiration time, i.e., before t.e.*
- *Capacity constraint: A crowd worker can serve only one task at a time, and a task can be performed by only one worker.*

4   Methodology

In this section, we present a general framework for solving the problem of MPCM and design two self-supervised algorithms for external matching.

4.1   Framework of Solving MPCM Problem

Our general framework mainly contains three components: internal matching, task pricing, and external matching, where the internal matching and external matching are respectively responsible for matching inner workers (*i.e.*, workers in the current platform) and outer workers (*i.e.*, workers in other platforms) for platform's tasks and the task pricing calculates the outer payments that platform would payoff the outer workers. It is clear that existing task matching algorithms proposed for a single platform can be applied to the internal matching problem as the problem only matches inner workers and tasks. In this paper, we adopt the online task assignment algorithm proposed in [16] for the internal matching, as the algorithm can give response to task requests promptly with a competitive ratio guarantee of $1/2e\ln(1 + U_{\max})$, where U_{max} is the maximum utility of task-and-worker pairs, and e is a natural constant.

Considering that the tasks' outer payments depend on the platforms' global supply-demand relationship, we utilize a variant of the existing matching-based task pricing approach (v-MAPS) [17] for task pricing in MPCM. The approach calculates rewards for tasks based on the platform's supply and demand curves to maximize the platform's total expected revenue. Specifically, our v-MAPS algorithm makes the following modifications.

- **The expected revenue:** For a cooperative spatial task t with payment $t.p$ and outer payment $t.p'$ and a set of outer workers W_{out}, the *expected revenue* of the task can be expressed as

$$E(t, W_{\text{out}}) = (t.p - t.p') \times A\_p(t.p', W_{\text{out}})   (2)$$

where $A\_p(t.p', W_{\text{out}})$ indicates the acceptance rate that the serviceable outer workers in W_{out} would like to serve task t with outer payment $t.p'$.
- **The acceptance rate:** In v-MAPS, a self-supervised approach is used to update the acceptance rate of workers for tasks with different outer payments. Specifically, we use the grid index to model location spaces in the real world. Every time receiving feedbacks of a current matching result, we use formula (3) to calculate the acceptance rate of workers under different outer payments in each grid and take the arithmetic mean of the calculated acceptance rates $\widehat{Acc_{g,p'}}$ of all grids as the overall acceptance rate $\widehat{Acc_{p'}}$ of specific outer payments, where g is a specific grid cell and p' is an outer payment.

$$\widehat{Acc_{g,p'}} = \frac{|t \text{ in } g \text{ and } t.p' = p' \text{ and } t \text{ is successfully accepted}|}{|t \text{ in } g \text{ and } t.p' = p'|}   (3)$$

After introducing the above basic steps, we focus on our primary work: external matching. As shown in Algorithm 1, the main workflow of our proposed external matching algorithm contains two steps, the utility prediction step (lines 3–5) and the task matching step (lines 6–8). In the utility prediction step, we call algorithms to predict the acceptance rate of workers and calculate comprehensive utility scores of task-and-worker pairs. The utility score combines the worker's acceptance rate and the platform's revenue. In the task matching step, we construct a bipartite graph of tasks and workers and use the Minimum Cost Maximum Flow (MCMF) algorithm to realize final matching. In the following two sections, we will detail the utility prediction algorithms.

4.2   The BaseMPCM Algorithm

For a set of inner tasks and a set of outer workers, BaseMPCM always renders higher scores to the valid pairs with higher revenue and greater acceptance rate. Inspired by the task pricing algorithm, we use *expected revenue*(formula (2)) to balance the worker's acceptance rate and the platform's obtained revenue in BaseMPCM. Specifically, for a valid pair (w_i, t_j), we use formula (4) to predict the acceptance rate of w_i for t_j, where $\alpha_1 \in [0, 1]$ is an adjustable parameter,

---

Algorithm 1. The main workflow of the external task matching algorithm.

Input: Inner task set T_{in}, outer task set T_{out} and outer worker set W_{out}
Output: The set of external matching results M_{out} and the obtained revenue rev_{out}
1: $M_{out} = \emptyset$; $rev_{out} = 0$
2: Traverse T_{in} and W_{out}, retrieve all the valid task-and-worker pairs to S
3: **for** each pair (t, w) in S **do**
4:     use *BaseMPCM* or *DeepMPCM* algorithm to calculate a utility score $s(t, w)$
5: Construct a bipartite graph in which a vertex represents a task or a worker, and there exists an edge between a worker w_i and a task t_j if they constitute a valid task-and-worker pair, the weight of the edge is $-s(w_i, t_j)$.
6: Add a source vertex and a sink vertex in the graph, the source vertex connects task vertexes and the sink vertex connects worker vertexes, the weight of the edge is 0.
7: Use the MCMF algorithm to get the final matching result M_{out} with 1 as each edge's capacity and the weight as the cost.
8: **for** each matching pair (w_i, t_j) in M_{out} **do**
9:     send the task request t_j to worker w_i
10:     **if** w_i receive the task t_j **then**
11:         $rev_{out} + = t_j.p - t_j.p'$
12:     **else**
13:         remove (w_i, t_j) from M_{out}
14: **return** M_{out}; rev_{out};

$Acc(t_j.p', t_j.g)$ is the upper confidence bound (UCB, *i.e.*, the upper bound of a confidence interval, which is defined as the sample mean plus a confidence radius) of the acceptance rate for the outer payment $t_j.p'$ in grid $t_j.g$, $1/c(w_i)$ measures the acceptance rate of w_i for t_j in the worst case (all of the $w_i's$ serviceable platforms send task request to him at the same time) in reality in which $c(w_i)$ calculates the number of platforms that w_i is serviceable for in the current time point. It's worth noting that we predict the acceptance rate via the method of calculating UCB (a classical solution to the multi-arm bandit (MAB) problem [2]), as the method well combines exploration (try to request workers in a new grid) and exploitation (automatically filter out workers in grids with low acceptance rate), and can find an appropriate grid cell to locate the optimal workers rapidly and effectively. The mathematical representation of UCB is shown in formula (5) where $\widehat{Acc_p}$ is the sample mean, N is the total number of tasks in g so far, $N(p)$ is the number of times that we use p in g and if $N(p) = 0$, we all have $\sqrt{\frac{2\ln N}{N(p)}} = 0$.

$$A\_p(w_i, t_j) = \alpha_1 \times Acc(t_j.p', t_j.g) + (1 - \alpha_1) \times \frac{1}{c(w_i)} \tag{4}$$

$$Acc(p, g) = \widehat{Acc_p} + \sqrt{\frac{2\ln N}{N(p)}} \tag{5}$$

To reduce the waiting time of tasks, we additionally take the distance between workers and tasks into consideration on the basis of *expected revenue*, and the final score of a task-and-worker pair is calculated as the following formula:

$$s\left(w_i, t_j\right) = \alpha_2 \times E\left(t_j, w_i\right) + (1 - \alpha_2) \times \left(max\_d - \text{dis}\left(w_i, t_j\right)\right) \qquad (6)$$

where $\alpha_2 \in [0, 1]$ is an adjustable parameter, $\text{dis}(w_i, t_j)$ calculates the euclidean distance between t_j and w_i, max_d is the maximum distance in all valid task-and-worker pairs.

In BaseMPCM, we predict the acceptance rate of workers to make the platforms with lower acceptance rates (*i.e.*, the inferior platforms) avoid selecting the same worker as other platforms with higher acceptance rates (*i.e.*, the superior platforms) so as to improve platform's revenue. However, the algorithm only focuses on the worker selection of inferior platforms but not on that of the superior platforms. With BaseMPCM, the superior platforms will assign the closest workers to their tasks without considering the impact of their matching results on other platforms. Considering the example in Fig. 1(b), for platform G (the superior platform), whichever worker (w_{b_1} or w_{b_5}) it sends request to, task t_{g_1} can be carried out because t_{g_1} is closest to both of the two workers (the acceptance rates of w_{b_1} and w_{b_5} for t_{g_1} are both 1). Thus, G will match the closer worker w_{b_1} to t_{g_1}. In this case, the task t_{r_1} will be rejected. However, if G matches w_{b_5} to t_{g_1}, both t_{g_1} and t_{r_1} can be served. Actually, the final matching of inferior platforms is usually decided by the matching result of superior platforms. In the following section, we additionally consider the impact of task-and-worker pairs on global matching results and propose the DeepMPCM algorithm to calculate the global utility score for valid pairs.

4.3   The DeepMPCM Algorithm

It is evident in the MPCM scenario that the selection strategy of a platform often depends on the action of others. If a platform gets the action of other platforms in advance, it can then infer the most favorable selection strategy for the global situation: the platform will avoid selecting the same worker with the platforms with high acceptance rates and try to select the workers with less impact on other platforms when there are more than one candidates. This can not only help the platform itself to improve the total revenue but also indirectly increase the revenue of other platforms. Inspired by this, we further propose the DeepMPCM algorithm to calculate the global utility score for platforms.

As shown in Fig. 2, the DeepMPCM model is mainly composed of two parts: the predictive layer and the evaluative layer. In the predictive layer, the model predicts the probability that each platform sends task requests to every worker based on the platforms' task and worker distribution. On this basis, in the evaluative layer, the model calculates the global utility score for valid pairs using a multi-layer perceptron (MLP). Specifically, we first encode the distribution information of the platforms' tasks and workers in the predictive layer. We use the grid index to model different location spaces in the real world and then take each grid as a unit to count each platform's task and worker distribution. Suppose that the number of the cooperative platforms is n and the entire space is divided into $k_1 \times k_2$ grids, each grid contains $k_3 \times k_4$ sub-grids. The feature vector of the overall distribution can be expressed as

$$D = \begin{bmatrix} D_1 & D_2 & \cdots & D_{k_2} \\ D_{k_2+1} & D_{k_2+2} & \cdots & D_{2k_2} \\ \vdots & \cdots & \ddots & \vdots \\ D_{(k_1-1)*k_2+1} & D_{(k_1-1)*k_2+2} & \cdots & D_{k_1*k_2} \end{bmatrix} \tag{7}$$

where $D_i(i \in [1, k_1 \times k_2])$ is the feature vector of the ith grid, it is expressed as

$$D_i = \begin{matrix} [num_{i,1}^t, x_{i,1,0}^t, y_{i,1,0}^t, \cdots num_{i,1}^w, x_{i,1,0}^w, \cdots, \\ num_{i,2}^t, x_{i,2,0}^t, y_{i,2,0}^t, \cdots num_{i,2}^w, x_{i,2,0}^w, \cdots, \\ \vdots \quad \vdots \quad \vdots \quad \ddots \quad \vdots \quad \vdots \quad \ddots \\ num_{i,n}^t, x_{i,n,0}^t, y_{i,n,0}^t, \cdots num_{i,n}^w, x_{i,n,0}^w, \cdots] \end{matrix} \tag{8}$$

in which $num_{i,j}^t$ is the total number of tasks platform sc_j contains in grid g_i, $x_{i,j,q}^t$ and $y_{i,j,q}^t$ $(q \in [0, k_3 \times k_4))$ are the average longitude coordinate and latitude coordinate of the tasks contained by sc_j in the sub grid g_{iq} of grid g_i.

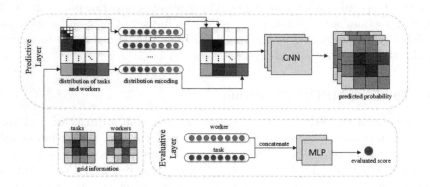

Fig. 2. The DeepMPCM model.

Considering the spatial correlation between tasks and workers, we then use a classical 3-layer Convolutional neural network (CNN) to conduct the prediction after encoding overall distribution. We can get the probability that each platform selects workers in different grids: $O = [O_1, O_2, ..., O_n]$, where O_i represents the selection probability matrix of platform sc_i.

Based on the platforms' worker selection probability obtained from the predictive layer, we encode both the task and the worker for each valid pair in the evaluative layer: we take the task's 2D location, platform id, original payment, the ratio of the outer payment to the original payment and the current time to constitute its feature vector **t**, and take the worker's 2D location, distance from the task, the number of each platform's tasks that the worker can serve and the probability that the worker is selected by each platform to constitute the worker's feature vector $\mathbf{w}$. Then we concatenate the task and worker's representation to obtain a joint representation $\mathbf{r} = \{\mathbf{t}; \mathbf{w}\}$ which will be fed into the MLP to predict the global utility score of the task-and-worker pair.

Every time receiving feedbacks of the current external task matching, both the predictive layer and the evaluative layer will learn their parameters in a self-supervised way. The predictive layer normalizes the counted number of workers in each grid selected by each platform as its real label, then calculates the cross entropy loss and uses the gradient descent method to optimize parameters. In the evaluative layer, we use the actual matching results of the platform to calculate the real label. For a task-and-worker pair $(t_i, w_j) \in M_i^{out}$, if the worker w_j accepts the task t_i, we use the following formula to represent their real utility score:

$$y_{t_i} = \max(1 - std, 0) \tag{9}$$

where 1 represents that the acceptance rate of w_j to t_i is 1, std is the standard deviation of the obtained revenue proportion of all platforms, which measures the difference between the platforms' revenues. In this way, on the premise of ensuring their own revenues, the platforms will try to improve the revenue of other platforms so as to narrow the difference between platforms' revenues. For a platform, the revenue proportion is the ratio of its obtained revenues from the inner tasks to the total payment of its inner tasks in the current turn. If the worker w_j rejects the task t_i, their real utility score will be 0, which means that the acceptance rate of w_j to t_i is 0 under the current distribution.

Similar to the predictive layer, cross-entropy is also used in the evaluative layer, and the gradient descent method is used to optimize the parameters.

5   Experiment

5.1   Dataset and Setup

The dataset used in the experiment is a real dataset from DiDi [1], which contains historical taxi records in Chengdu on November 14 and November 15, 2016. The data on November 14 is used for training, and the data on November 15 is used for evaluation. Since the original dataset comes from one platform, that is, DiDi, we divide workers and tasks into 5 groups. Each group simulates one platform, so we have 5 platforms in the experiment. For each platform, we consider two kinds of data distribution: even distribution and uneven distribution. Specifically, we divide the urban area of Chengdu into 2,790 grids. For even distribution, we randomly divide the workers into 5 groups and randomly select for each worker 10~15 tasks from the grid in which the worker locates. For uneven distribution, we randomly divide all the grids into 5 groups, and then for each grid, we retain either tasks or workers. We also generate synthetic datasets to verify the scalability of the proposed algorithms. We randomly generate 100~10k workers and 1000~100k tasks for each cooperative platform. The location of tasks and workers are randomly generated in the range of longitude 102°E~ 104°E and latitude $30°N \sim 31°N$. Besides, the speed of workers is set to $40km/h$, and the serviceable range of workers is random from $1km$ to $3km$. The details of the resulting datasets are shown in Table 1 and Table 2, where the default values are shown in bold.

Table 1. Real datasets

Dataset		Platform				
		A	B	C	D	E
Even	$|W|$	4728	4642	4510	4658	4661
	$|T|$	57792	58013	58418	57966	58005
Uneven	$|W|$	501	502	507	507	2391
	$|T|$	26724	28452	27404	29333	29952

Table 2. Synthetic datasets

Parameter	Value				
$|W|$	100	1 k	2 k	5 k	10 k
$|T|$	1000	10 k	20 k	50 k	100 k

We compare our algorithms with three baselines: 1) TOTA: an online task matching algorithm proposed for a single platform [16]; 2) COM: the latest cross online matching algorithm proposed for cooperation between two platforms [5]; and 3) V-MPCM: a variant of BaseMPCM which ignores the acceptance rate of workers. TOTA is used to demonstrate the effectiveness of cooperative matching, and the other two algorithms are used to verify the significance of dealing with worker competition. In particular, the idle worker list in COM is shared by all platforms to realize multi-platform cooperation, and the edge weights in the bipartite graph in V-MPCM are set to tasks' real payment.

We use three metrics for evaluation: 1) $AREV$: the average revenue of all platforms; 2) $ACOM$: the average completed task number of all platforms; 3) $AACP$: the average acceptance rate of all tasks, which is calculated by formula (10), in which M_{out} is the outer matching result set of all platforms and $\mathbf{c}(w)$ is the number of platforms that send requests to worker w at the same time.

$$AACP = \frac{|M_{out}|}{\sum_{w \in M_{out}} \mathbf{c}(w)} \tag{10}$$

5.2   Experiment Results

Effectiveness *w.r.t* AREV. As shown in Fig. 3(a) and Fig. 3(b), the revenues obtained by the four cooperation-based algorithms are all higher than that obtained by TOTA, which means the cooperation between platforms can indeed improve their revenues. In addition, it can be seen from Table 3 that our algorithms can achieve higher revenue than COM and V-MPCM over both datasets. This confirms that our algorithms are more effective in terms of revenue.

Table 3. Results on real datasets

Dataset	Algorithm	AREV ($\times 10^6$)	ACOM ($\times 10^4$)	AACP
Even	TOTA	1.622	5.186	/
	COM	1.686	5.109	0.657
	V-MPCM	1.690	5.040	0.629
	BaseMPCM	1.710	5.238	0.764
	DeepMPCM	1.736	5.386	0.845
Uneven	TOTA	0.421	1.405	/
	COM	0.579	1.683	0.431
	V-MPCM	0.590	1.715	0.454
	BaseMPCM	0.606	1.771	0.505
	DeepMPCM	0.619	1.856	0.566

Effectiveness *w.r.t* ACOM. As shown in Table 3, in the *even distribution dataset*, COM and V-MPCM complete the fewest tasks but obtain more revenue than TOTA. This is because the worker competition will lead to a huge amount of rejection of the tasks with lower outer payment. In addition, as shown in Fig. 3(c) and Fig. 3(d), the number of completed tasks is gradually increasing in TOTA (V-MPCM), BaseMPCM and DeepMPCM on both datasets, which indicates that our algorithms can effectively solve the problem of worker competition.

Effectiveness *w.r.t* AACP. As shown in Table 3, our algorithms achieve better acceptance rates than COM and V-MPCM, which directly confirms that our algorithms can solve the problem of worker competition effectively. Further, since DeepMPCM additionally considers the utility from a global point of view, the acceptance rate of DeepMPCM is higher than that of BaseMPCM.

AREV *w.r.t.* $|W|$ As shown in Fig. 4(a), the average revenue in all algorithms increases with the increase of $|W|$, and when $|W| > 2000$, the revenue increases slowly. This is because when $|W| < 2000$, the number of existing tasks is much larger than that of existing workers can serve. Therefore, with the increase of $|W|$, more tasks can be served. When $|W| > 2000$, the number of serviceable tasks reaches the peak, so the revenue increases slowly and then reaches the peak.

ACOM *w.r.t.* $|W|$ Fig. 4(b) shows the average number of completed tasks in the four algorithms w.r.t $|W|$. Similar to the average revenue, the number of average completed tasks calculated by the algorithms also increases with the increase of $|W|$, and when $|W| > 2000$, it increases slowly.

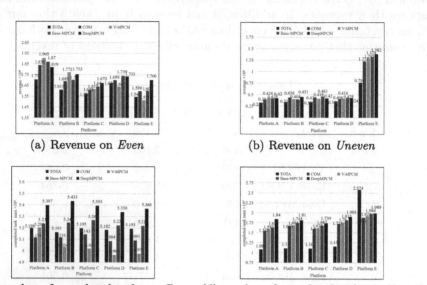

(a) Revenue on *Even*   (b) Revenue on *Uneven*

(c) number of completed tasks on *Even*   (d) number of completed tasks on *Uneven*

Fig. 3. Result of each platform on the real datasets

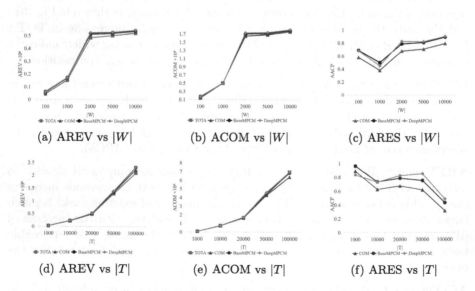

(a) AREV vs $|W|$ (b) ACOM vs $|W|$ (c) ARES vs $|W|$

(d) AREV vs $|T|$ (e) ACOM vs $|T|$ (f) ARES vs $|T|$

Fig. 4. Scalability of the proposed algorithms

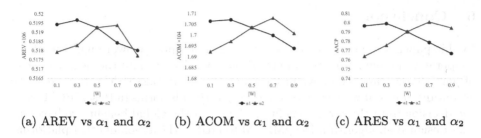

(a) AREV vs α_1 and α_2 (b) ACOM vs α_1 and α_2 (c) ARES vs α_1 and α_2

Fig. 5. Experiment results of parameter selection

AACP *w.r.t.* $|W|$ As shown in Fig. 4(c), the average acceptance rate in all the algorithms firstly decreases when $|W| < 1000$ and then increases. This is because when $|W| < 1000$, the number of existing tasks is much larger than that existing workers can serve, so all platforms will compete for workers. Thus, with the increase of $|W|$, the worker competition becomes more intense, and the acceptance rate decreases. When $|W| > 1000$, with the increase of workers, the platforms' demand for outer workers gradually decreases, while the number of serviceable outer workers is also increasing. Therefore, the worker competition between platforms will slow down, and the acceptance rate will increase.

AREV *w.r.t.* $|T|$ As shown in Fig. 4(d), when $|T| < 20000$, the number of existing tasks is much smaller than that of existing workers can serve. Hence, with the increase of tasks, idle workers are gradually engaged in the service, making the revenue correspondingly increase. When $|T| > 20000$, however, all the workers are involved in performing tasks, so the revenue will increase much faster with the increase of $|T|$.

ACOM *w.r.t.* $|T|$ Fig. 4(d) shows the average number of completed tasks in the algorithms w.r.t $|T|$. Similar to the revenue, the number of completed tasks in the four algorithms also increases with the increase of $|T|$, and when $|T| > 20000$, the amounts increase faster.

AACP *w.r.t.* $|T|$ As shown in Fig. 4(f), with the increase of tasks, the platforms' demand for outer workers gradually increases, and the worker competition becomes fierce, so the acceptance rate is on the decline. However, when $10000 \leq |T| \leq 50000$, the acceptance rate increases slightly. This is because there remain few unassigned tasks and workers on the platforms after internal matching. Therefore, the worker competition will be alleviated.

In addition to the above experiments on effectiveness and scalability, we also carry out verification experiments on involved parameters. Specifically, as shown in Fig. 5, we take an average of 5 values from 0 to 1 as candidates for the parameter α_1 and α_2 in BaseMPCM and then conduct experiments on the synthetic dataset. The experiment results show that when $\alpha_1 = 0.3$ and $\alpha_2 = 0.7$, our model can achieve the optimal experimental results on $AREV$, $ACOM$ and $AACP$. Therefore, we set α_1 as 0.3 and α_2 as 0.7 in our algorithms.

6   Conclusion

In this paper, we have studied the problem of acceptance-aware multi-platform cooperative matching in spatial crowdsourcing. To alleviate the negative effect of partial acceptance, we have proposed an algorithm BaseMPCM to predict the acceptance rates of workers. Considering that the platforms in BaseMPCM make the decision from their own benefits rather than the global benefit, we have further designed an algorithm DeepMPCM to predict the action of other platforms. Extensive experiments on both real and synthetic datasets have demonstrated the effectiveness of the proposed algorithms.

In real SC applications, we observe that users often have different preferences for platforms, and workers may have different preferences for tasks. Thus, we plan to consider the preference between tasks and workers to realize personalized cooperative matching. Besides, a fair cooperation scheme among platforms is worth exploring, as platforms may have different contributions to cooperation, and the revenue obtained by cooperation needs to be distributed properly.

Acknowledgements. This work is supported by Natural Science Foundation of Jiangsu Province (Grant Nos. BK20211307), by project Funded by the Priority Academic Program Development of Jiangsu Higher Education Institutions, and by NH33714722 Youth Team on Interdisciplinary Research Soochoow University - Research on Subjectivity and Reasoning Theory in Artificial Intelligence.

References

1. Gaia of didi. https://outreach.didichuxing.com/research/opendata/en/
2. Auer, P., Cesa-Bianchi, N., Fischer, P.: Finite-time analysis of the multiarmed bandit problem. Mach. Learn. **47**(2–3), 235–256 (2002)
3. Cheng, P., Lian, X., Chen, L., Han, J., Zhao, J.: Task assignment on multi-skill oriented spatial crowdsourcing. TKDE **28**(8), 2201–2215 (2016)
4. Cheng, P., et al.: Reliable diversity-based spatial crowdsourcing by moving workers. PVLDB **8**(10), 1022–1033 (2015)
5. Cheng, Y., Li, B., Zhou, X., Yuan, Y., Wang, G., Chen, L.: Real-time cross online matching in spatial crowdsourcing. In: ICDE, pp. 1–12 (2020)
6. Ding, P., Liu, G., Wang, Y., Zheng, K., Zhou, X.: A-MCTS: adaptive monte carlo tree search for temporal path discovery. In: TKDE, pp. 1–1 (2021)
7. Fan, J., Zhou, X., Gao, X., Chen, G.: Crowdsourcing task scheduling in mobile social networks. In: ICSOC, pp. 317–331 (2018)
8. Jiang, Y., He, W., Cui, L., Yang, Q.: User location prediction in mobile crowdsourcing services. In: ICSOC, pp. 515–523 (2018)
9. Li, B., Cheng, Y., Yuan, Y., Wang, G., Chen, L.: Simultaneous arrival matching for new spatial crowdsourcing platforms. In: IJCAI, pp. 1279–1287 (2020)
10. Liu, C., Gao, X., Wu, F., Chen, G.: QITA: quality inference based task assignment in mobile crowdsensing. In: ICSOC, pp. 363–370 (2018)
11. Liu, G., et al.: MCS-GPM: multi-constrained simulation based graph pattern matching in contextual social graphs. TKDE **30**(6), 1050–1064 (2018)

12. Liu, G., Wang, Y., Orgun, M.A.: Finding k optimal social trust paths for the selection of trustworthy service providers in complex social networks. TSC **6**(2), 152–167 (2013)
13. Liu, G., Wang, Y., Zheng, B., Li, Z., Zheng, K.: Strong social graph based trust-oriented graph pattern matching with multiple constraints. TETCI **4**(5), 675–685 (2020)
14. To, H., Shahabi, C., Kazemi, L.: A server-assigned spatial crowdsourcing framework. ACM Trans. Spat. Algorithms Syst. **1**(1), 2:1–2:28 (2015)
15. Tong, Y., She, J., Ding, B., Chen, L., Wo, T., Xu, K.: Online minimum matching in real-time spatial data: Experiments and analysis. PVLDB **9**(12), 1053–1064 (2016)
16. Tong, Y., She, J., Ding, B., Wang, L., Chen, L.: Online mobile micro-task allocation in spatial crowdsourcing. In: ICDE, pp. 49–60 (2016)
17. Tong, Y., Wang, L., Zhou, Z., Chen, L., Du, B., Ye, J.: Dynamic pricing in spatial crowdsourcing: a matching-based approach. In: SIGMOD, pp. 773–788 (2018)
18. Zhang, Z., Liu, A., Liu, S., Li, Z., Zhao, L.: Privacy-preserving worker recruitment under variety requirement in spatial crowdsourcing. In: ICSOC, pp. 302–316 (2021)
19. Zhao, B., Xu, P., Shi, Y., Tong, Y., Zhou, Z., Zeng, Y.: Preference-aware task assignment in on-demand taxi dispatching: An online stable matching approach. In: AAAI, pp. 2245–2252 (2019)
20. Zhao, Y., Guo, J., Chen, X., Hao, J., Zhou, X., Zheng, K.: Coalition-based task assignment in spatial crowdsourcing. In: ICDE, pp. 241–252 (2021)
21. Zhao, Y., Zheng, K., Guo, J., Yang, B., Pedersen, T.B., Jensen, C.S.: Fairness-aware task assignment in spatial crowdsourcing: game-theoretic approaches. In: ICDE, pp. 265–276 (2021)
22. Zheng, L., Chen, L.: Maximizing acceptance in rejection-aware spatial crowdsourcing. TKDE **29**(9), 1943–1956 (2017)

Combining User Inherent and Contextual Preferences for Online Recommendation in Location-Based Services

Haiting Zhong[1], Wei He[1,2(✉)], Lizhen Cui[1,2], and Lei Liu[1,2]

[1] School of Software, Shandong University, Jinan, China
zhonghaiting@mail.sdu.edu.cn
[2] Joint SDU-NTU Centre for Artificial Intelligence Research (C-FAIR), Shandong University and Nanyang Technological University, Jinan, China
{hewei,clz,l.liu}@sdu.edu.cn

Abstract. With the development of mobile internet and smart devices, location-based services (LBS) have developed rapidly and attracted more and more users. The availability of a large amount of user interaction data makes it possible to provide more personalized and accurate recommendation services. However, in mobile scenarios, multiple influencing factors such as the diversity of user preferences, the variability of user behavior, and the dynamics of spatiotemporal contexts bring great challenges to recommendation services. To accurately capture the preferences of mobile users in dynamic contexts, we propose an Inherent and Contextual Preference-aware Attention Network (ICPAN) for online recommendation in location-based services. Our ICPAN consists of an inherent-preference mining module with self-attention layers, a contextual-preference perception module with improved IR^2-tree-based index structures, and an online recommendation module. The inherent-preference and contextual-preference models are trained based on global historical behavior data and instantly selected context-sensitive data, respectively. And then the online recommendation module uses attention aggregation to couple the two preference representations to generate the final recommendation result. Extensive experiments are conducted on three real datasets, and the experimental results show that the proposed ICPAN outperforms existing state-of-the-art methods.

Keywords: Location-based service · Recommender system · Self-attention · IR^2-tree

1 Introduction

With the rapid development of location-based social networks and mobile devices, more and more people record and share their lives on different kinds of platforms, such as Yelp, Places, Foursquare etc. Recommendation of location-based services aims to recommend new locations to users according to their personalized preferences, which is beneficial for users to know new interested places and explore the cities, while for advertisers to launch advertisements to targeted users [1,2].

In mobile scenarios, each user's behaviors such as visiting a particular location are diversified due to many factors, including spatiotemporal context, geographical distance and user preferences etc. Also, even for the same user, they have different interests in different contexts. These influencing factors with their changeability and interaction bring considerable challenges to recommender system in location-based services. Current research on location-based services mainly focuses on capturing the users' sequential patterns from their historical check-in or trajectory data by training different types of models, with consideration of spatial-temporal features or time influence [3–5]. Essentially, there are still two vital issues that have not been solved particularly well, and consequently the performance of recommender systems in mobile scenarios cannot always be satisfactory.

- **RQ1.** How to accurately capture user preferences with diversity and variability in mobile environments? The sequence patterns of user-item interaction captured from historical data are not always reliable because the users expected behavior varies in different contexts, such as weekend at home, out on weekday evening etc. Additionally, the users preferences may not be continuously stable, that is, vary over time.
- **RQ2.** How does a model-based approach meet the demand of online recommendation for location-based services? An effective user preferences prediction model requires offline training and updating periodically because the behavioral data of mobile users emerge quickly at anytime and anywhere. There are conflicts between online recommendation efficiency requirements and current offline model-based approaches.

We investigate the above issues in recommender systems of location-based services, that is, accurate preferences perception and online recommendation efficiency for mobile users. The basic assumption here is that mobile user preferences are affected by both their inherent factors such as personality or likes, and variable external factors such as contexts. Unlike recent approaches, we model user behavioral preferences as a combination of constant interests and dynamic interests, which are referred to as *User Inherent Preferences* and *User Contextual Preferences*, respectively. To achieve recommendation efficiency, we use a context-sensitive online model to capture user contextual preferences.

In this paper, we propose an Inherent and Contextual Preference-aware Attention Network (ICPAN), which combines user constant interest mining (using an offline model) and dynamic interest perception (directly using a memory-based model). The offline module trains the model based on user historical data to achieve stable interest perception and performs periodic training and updating; while the online module learns user contextual preferences based on instantly selected context-sensitive data using the improved IR^2-tree-based index schema. And the improved IR^2-tree structure can provide logarithmic complexity for the retrieval of training data from extensive historical trajectories.

Then the online recommendation module uses attention aggregation to couple the two preference representations to generate the final recommendation result.

To summarize, our contributions are summarized as follows:

- We propose ICPAN, an attention model based on users inherent and contextual preferences, which fully considers the stability of users inherent preferences and the dynamics of contextual preferences.
- We design an improved IR^2-tree-based index structure for retrieval context-sensitive data from users historical trajectories.
- Extensive experiments were conducted on three real datasets. Experimental results show that our ICPAN performs better compared to state-of-the-art models.

The rest of this article is organized as follows. Section 2 introduces related work. Section 3 defines the problem and related terms. Section 4 introduces our recommendation model in location-based services based on self-attention mechanism in detail. Section 5 reports the experiment. Section 6 summarizes the paper.

2   Related Work

In recent years, there have been significant efforts to the recommendation algorithm for location-based services. One of the most common tactics in these efforts is the RNN-based method. In some early works, Wang et al. [6] proposed the SPENT method which used similarity tree to organize all POIs (Point-of-interests) and applied Word2Vec to perform POI embedding, and then used a recurrent neural network (RNN) to model users' successive transition behaviors. Similarly, Lu et al. [7] proposed a latent-factor and RNN-based successive POI recommendation method, named PEU-RNN, to integrate the sequential visits of items and user preferences to recommend items. Different from the previous works that model users' successive transition through various methods, we believe that the behavior of a user is mainly determined by her inherent preferences which are relatively stable and invariant, at the same time the current contexts (e.g., position, time, etc.) also have impact.

Nowadays, the attention mechanisms have been widely used in various fields, such as natural language processing [8], computer vision [9], recommender systems [4,5,10] and so on. The core of the attention mechanisms is to assign different weights to inputs, paying more attention to relevant information and ignoring irrelevant information. Recently, the transform based entirely on the attention mechanisms has been proposed, which completely eliminated recurrence and convolutions, and has achieved the best performance in machine translation [11].

The self-attention module of transform has been widely used in recommendation systems and has achieved very good performance. SASRec [12], a sequence model based on self-attention, can not only capture long-term semantics, but also make predictions based on relatively few actions. TiSASRec [13] uses self-attention to model the absolute positions of items in the sequence and their time intervals. SAE-NAD [14] uses a multi-dimensional attention mechanism to adaptively differentiate the user preferences degrees in multiple aspects.

3   Preliminaries

In this section, the symbolic representation and problem definition are given. The set of user, location, location category, and time are expressed as $U = \{u_1, u_2, \cdots, u_U\}$, $V = \{v_1, v_2, \cdots, v_V\}$, $C = \{c_1, c_2, \cdots, c_C\}$, and $T = \{t_1, t_2, \cdots, t_T\}$, respectively. Each location has its longitude and latitude and is associated with a location category.

Check-in Record. The set of check-ins is denoted as $CH = \{ch_1, ch_2, \cdots\}$. Each check-in record ch_i is represented as a quaternion (u, v_l, c_j, t_a), representing that user u checked in at location v_l at time t_a, and location v_l is associated with location category c_j.

Time Slot. In order to capture the influence of time on user preferences, both the time slot and day type of each check-in record are extracted and used to represent the temporal context. The time slot is defined similarly to [15], in which a day is divided into eight time slots by hours $\{h_1, h_2, \cdots, h_8\}$, i.e., each of which is 3 h 00:00:00–02:59:59, 03:00:00–05:59:59... Also, two day types $\{w_1, w_2\}$ are used to represent workday and non-working days respectively.

Recommendation of Location-Based Services. Given a user $u \in U$, the users' check-in records CH, the current location $v_l \in V$ of the user u, the location category $c_k \in C$ of the current location v_l, and the current time t, recommend to the user K locations that the user may visit in the next few hours.

4   Inherent and Contextual Preference-Aware Attention Network

In this section, we will detail the inherent and contextual preference-aware attention network (ICPAN) for online recommendation in location-based services. We first depict the architecture of the ICPAN model, as shown in Fig. 1. And then we demonstrate how to make the model inference.

4.1   Inherent Preferences Mining Module

Inherent Preferences Embedding Layer. As a carrier of information, vector is very important to the model. However, when one-hot encoding is used to represent each user, location, location category and time, it is difficult to capture user preferences due to its sparsity. Therefore, the user, location, location category and time are encoded into latent vectors. Latent vectors $U_u \in R^d$, $V_v \in R^d$, $C_c \in R^d$, and $T_t \in R^d$ represent the latent features of the user, location, location category, and time, respectively. Among them, the input dimensions of the embeddings $T_t \in R^d$ is 16 ($2 \times 8 = 16$), and the specific index scheme is in Sect. 3. The input dimensions of the embeddings $U_u \in R^d$, $V_v \in R^d$, $C_c \in R^d$ are U, V, C, respectively. In order to make the learned inherent preferences more stable, here we use the location category. The output of embedding layer

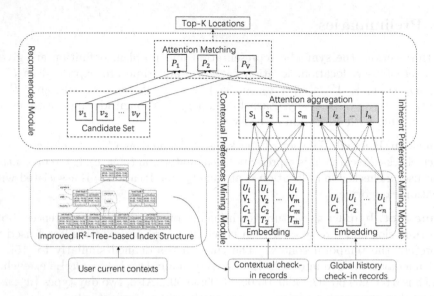

Fig. 1. The architecture of the proposed ICPAN model.

for each check-in j is the sum $H_j = U_j + C_j \in R^d$. For each user's check-in records $CH = \{ch_1, ch_2, \cdots\}$, we only consider $(n+m)$ check-ins. Among them, there are n user's historical check-in records, and m user's contextual check-in records. If the number of user's historical check-in records $ch_i > n$, the most recent n records are considered. If the user's historical check-in records $ch_i < n$, add zeros to the right end to n, and mask off the padding items during calculation. For the embedding of each user's historical check-ins, we express it as $E(u_i) = \{H_1, H_2, \cdots, H_n\} \in R^{n \times d}$.

Inherent Preferences Self-attention Aggregation Layer. In the online recommendation in location-based services, we argue that the user's next visit is mainly affected by two aspects: inherent preferences and contextual preferences. Since inherent preferences are generally relatively stable, they need to learn from more historical check-in records of users. In addition, the same location may have different effects on different users. For example, some people go to the cinema to watch a movie because they are interested, and some people go to the cinema to watch a movie to accompany their friends. In this case, the same location should have different weights for different users.

In order to meet the above requirements, we use self-attention mechanisms that have been successfully applied in many fields, such as natural language processing (NLP), computer vision (CV) and speech processing [16]. Let $E(u)$ with non-padding length n' represent the embedding matrix, that is $E(u) = \{H_1, H_2, \cdots, H_n\} \in R^{n \times d}$, where $H_i = U_i + C_i \in R^d$. First, we construct the mask matrix as $M \in R^{n \times n}$ with each element M_{ij} satisfying:

$$M_{ij} = \begin{cases} 1, & if \ i,j \leq n', \\ 0, & otherwise. \end{cases}$$

And then the new check-in records are calculated through different parameter matrices $W_1^Q, W_1^K, W_1^V \in R^{d \times d}$ as

$$I(u) = Attention(E(u)W_1^Q, E(u)W_1^K, E(u)W_1^V, M) \tag{1}$$

with

$$Attention(Q, K, V, M) = (M * softmax(\frac{QK^T}{\sqrt{d}}))V \tag{2}$$

We input $E(u)$ as query, key and value of self-attention, respectively. First, we project query, key and value to the same space through nonlinear transformation with shared parameters. Here, the mask and softmax attention are multiplied element by element and other elements use matrix multiplication. In order to avoid the small gradient of the softmax function when d is large, we scale the dot products by $\frac{1}{\sqrt{d}}$. We compute the potential correlation between different visits in the check-in record via the scaled dot product and assign a different weight to each visit. When predicting the $(n'+1)$-st visit, we only take the first $n' \in [1, ch]$ check-in records as input. During training, we control the check-in records used to learn user inherent preferences by adjusting the labels of the mask matrix M. Finally, we get $I(u) \in R^{n \times d}$ to represent the user's inherent preferences. In addition, to improve the real-time responsiveness of the model, the learning of user inherent preferences can be trained offline.

4.2 Contextual Preferences Perception Module

Improved IR²-Tree-Based Trajectory Index. To quickly retrieve the contextual trajectories from large-scale check-in data, we propose an improved IR²-tree [17] with a new signature generation strategy.

The IR²-tree is a combination of an R-tree [18] and signature files. In particular, each node of an IR²-tree contains both spatial and keyword information. The spatial information is in the form of a minimum bounding rectangle, and the keyword information is in the form of a signature. In general, an IR²-tree is a height-balanced tree data structure similar to R-tree. Each leaf node in an IR²-tree has entries of the form (ObjPtr, MBR, S). ObjPtr identifier refers to a tuple in the database(i.e. a check-in record in historical logs) and MBR is a minimum bounding rectangle which is the bounding box of the spatial object indexed. S is the signature of the object referred to by ObjPtr. A non-leaf node has entries of the form (NodePtr, MBR, S). NodePtr is the pointer of its child node, MBR covers all the rectangles in the lower node's entries, and S is the signature of the current node. A node's signature is the superposition of the signatures of all its entries. So the signature of a node is equivalent to the signatures of all trajectories in its subtree.

Table 1. Sample dataset of check-in records.

	UserId	LocationId	Category	Latitude	Longitude	Time
ch_1	470	49	Arts&Crafts Store	40.61	−73.81	Tue Apr 03 18:00:09 2012
ch_2	979	443	Bar	40.58	−73.92	Sat Apr 14 21:06:59 2012
ch_3	885	489	Coffee Shop	40.69	−74.11	Thu Apr 19 01:40:25 2012
ch_4	877	46	Medical Center	40.67	−74.28	Tue Apr 24 22:28:57 2012
ch_5	642	443	Building	40.63	−73.72	Fri Apr 27 19:39:55 2012
ch_6	73	93	Subway	40.65	−73.56	Sun May 06 17:47:50 2012
ch_7	461	340	Bridge	40.59	−74.31	Tue May 08 19:38:30 2012
ch_8	1021	921	Home (private)	40.62	−74.19	Sun May 13 23:56:45 2012

We improve the IR^2-tree with a new signature generation strategy. Both day type and time slot are hashed and then form a bitmap representation for the node signature. Figure 2(a) shows the structure of the newly generated signature. A node signature in the improved IR^2-tree is divided into two disjoint blocks holding the day of the week and the time slot which are defined in Sect. 3, respectively. Without loss of generality, the signature is assigned with 10 bits, in which the first 2 bits represent day of the week and the following 8 bits denote the corresponding time slot. For example, '10' and '01' represent the weekdays and weekends respectively. The bitmap representation of time for ch_1 is 00000010 according to the order of the 8 time slots. For the check-in records in Table 1, Fig. 2(b) shows an improved IR^2-tree for the sample dataset of Table 1.

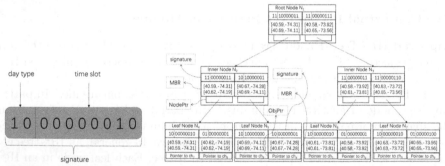

(a) The signature in improved IR^2-tree.

(b) An example of improved IR^2-tree for dataset of Table 1

Fig. 2. Improved IR^2-tree

The detailed contextual trajectory search algorithm is given in Algorithm 1. Concretely, given the user's contextual information, $d(loc, day, time, r)$ and a tree node *node*, *loc* is the current location and r is the range. For example, the user's current location is $(40.61, -73.81)$, then r is $(40.61\pm0.1, -73.81\pm0.1)$.

If $dist(d, node) \geq r$, the node *node* can be pruned as its location does not qualify the distance requirement. Given a non-leaf node *node* in an improved IR^2-tree and a contextual information $d(loc, day, time, r)$, *nsig* is the signature of *node*, and the signature of $d(loc, day, time, r)$ is *dsig*. For example, the current time is 19:00 on Tuesday. If $nsig.day \& dsig.day = 0$ or $nsig.time \& dsig.time = 0$, the node *node* can be pruned as it does not satisfy the time contexts.

Algorithm 1: Contextual Trajectory Search Algorithm.

Input : IR^2-tree tr, contextual information d
Output: A list of contextual trajectories

1 Initialize a FIFO Queue Q;
2 $Q.Enqueue(tr.RootNode)$;
3 **while** Q *is not empty* **do**
4   Node $n = Q.Dequeue()$;
5   **if** $minDist(d.loc, n.loc) < d.r$ *(r is the range)* **then**
6   **if** n *is a non-leaf node* **then**
7   **for** *each child node c in n* **do**
8   **if** $csig.day \& dsig.day! = 0$ *AND* $csig.time \& dsig.time! = 0$ **then**
9   Q.Enqueue(c);
10   **else**
11   **for** *each object o in n* **do**
12   **if** $osig.day = 10$ *AND* $osig.time = 00000010$ **then**
13   Q.Enqueue(o);

14 **return** Q

Contextual Preferences Embedding Layer. The user's next visit will be more affected by contextual factors, such as time, weather, position, etc. Here, the improved IR^2-tree-based trajectory index retrieves check-ins that match the contextual information according to the user's current location and time. We take the check-ins in the current time slot and the nearby area as the contextual check-ins. For each user, only m contextual check-ins are considered. If the number of user's contextual check-ins $m_i' > m$, the most recent m records are considered. If the user's contextual check-ins $m_i' < m$, add zeros to the right end to m, and mask off the padding items during calculation. Similar to the embedding layer in the inherent preferences mining module, the output of embedding layer for each check-in j is the sum $H_j' = U_j + V_j + C_j + T_j \in R^d$. For the embedding of contextual check-ins, we express it as $E'(u_i) = \left\{ H_1', H_2', \cdots, H_m' \right\} \in R^{m \times d}$.

Contextual Preferences Self-attention Aggregation Layer. Similar to the inherent preferences mining module, we still utilize the self-attention mechanism. Let $E'(u)$ represent the embedding matrix, that is $E'(u_i) = \left\{ H'_1, H'_2, \cdots, H'_m \right\} \in R^{m \times d}$, where $H'_i = U_i + V_i + C_i + T_i \in R^d$. First, we construct the mask matrix $M' \in R^{m \times m}$. If the number of user's contextual check-ins $m'_i > m$, the all elements of matrix M' are one. If the number of user's contextual check-ins $m'_i < m$, with each element M'_{ij} satisfying:

$$M'_{ij} = \begin{cases} 1, & if \ i, j \leq m' \\ 0, & otherwise \end{cases}$$

And then the new contextual check-in records are calculated through different parameter matrices $W_2^Q, W_2^K, W_2^V \in R^{d \times d}$ as

$$S(u) = Attention(E'(u)W_2^Q, E'(u)W_2^K, E'(u)W_2^V, M') \tag{3}$$

with

$$Attention(Q, K, V, M) = (M * softmax(\frac{QK^T}{\sqrt{d}}))V \tag{4}$$

Similarly, we assign a different weight to each contextual visit by scaling the dot product calculation. We can get $S(u) \in R^{m \times d}$ as a representation of the user's contextual preferences.

4.3   Recommendation Module

Attention Matching Layer. This module combines the user's inherent preferences with contextual preferences, and recalls the K locations that the user is most likely to visit next from the candidate set. The candidate set of V locations can be expressed as $V = \{v_1, v_2, \cdots, v_V\} \in R^{V \times d}$. We modify the scaled dot product attention [11] to calculate the similarity between the candidate set and the user's comprehensive preferences. This layer calculates the probability that each location in the candidate set will be visited in the future:

$$S_u = Concat(I(u), S(u)) \tag{5}$$

$$P(u) = Matching(V, S_u) = Sum(softmax(\frac{V S_u^T}{\sqrt{d}})) \tag{6}$$

Here, $S_u = Concat(I(u), S(u)) \in R^{(n+m) \times d}$, which represents a comprehensive representation of users' inherent preferences and contextual preferences. Calculate the attention score of V and S_u by scaling the dot product, and use softmax on it to get the attention weight. Finally, the Sum operation computes the weighted sum of the last dimension of the attention weights, transforming a two-dimensional matrix into an V-dimensional vector, $P(u) \in R^V$. The V values in $P(u)$ respectively represent the visited probability of V locations in the candidate set. As can be seen in Eqs. (5)–(6), we comprehensively consider the user's inherent preferences and contextual preferences, that is, take into account the updated representations of all the user's historical and contextual check-ins, and at the same time, do not treat them equally.

Model Inference and Learning. Given the user $i's$ check-in records, the matching probability of each candidate location $p_j \in P(u_i)$ for $j \in [1, V]$, and the label v_k with number of order k in the candidate set V. We adopt the binary cross entropy loss as the objective function:

$$L = -\sum_i \sum_{ch_i} [log\sigma(p_k) + \sum_{j=1, j\neq k}^{N} log\sigma(1 - \sigma(p_j))] \tag{7}$$

where σ is the sigmoid function. Moreover, for every positive sample p_k, we need to compute $(V - 1)$ negative samples in the meantime. We use the Adam optimizer to train the model, and the detailed learning algorithm is shown in Algorithm 2. Among them, $\Theta = \{\Theta_1, \Theta_2\}$ is the set of model parameters. $\Theta_1 = \{W_1^Q, W_1^K, W_1^V, W_2^Q, W_2^K, W_2^V\}$ is the parameters set of attention networks. $\Theta_2 = \{U_u, V_v, C_c, T_t\}$, which represents the embedding set of user, location, location category, and time respectively.

Algorithm 2: ICPAN Algorithm

    Input: check-in records, embedding dimension, learning rate, dropout rate
    Output: model parameters Θ
1 Draw Θ_2 from Normal Distribution N (0, 0.01);
2 Initialize parameters Θ_1;
3 **repeat**
4   shuffle the check-in records $\{(u, v_l, c_j, t_a)\}$;
5   **for** *each record* $\{(u, v_l, c_j, t_a)\}$ **do**
6   compute $I(u)$ according to Equation (1)-(2);
7   compute $S(u)$ according to Equation (3)-(4);
8   compute $P(u)$ according to Equation (5)-(6);
9   update model parameters with Adam optimizer;
10 **until** *converge*;
11 **return** Θ

---

5 Experiments

In this section, we conduct experiments to answer the following questions: 1) what's the performance of our model as compared to other state-of-the-art methods? 2) what's the influence of different components in our model? 3) how do the parameters affect model performance, such as the number of dimensions?

5.1 Experimental Setup

Datasets. We evaluated the model on three real data sets: Weeplaces[1], NYC and TKY[2]. Weeplaces dataset is collected from Weeplaces, a website that aims

---

[1] http://www.yongliu.org/datasets.
[2] http://www-public.it-sudparis.eu/~zhang_da/pub/dataset_tsmc2014.zip.

to visualize users' check-in activities in location-based social networks (LBSN). The NYC and TKY dataset include long-term (approximately 10 months) check-in data for New York City and Tokyo from April 12, 2012 to February 16, 2013 collected from Foursquare [19]. We preprocess these datasets by deleting users with fewer than 100 check-in records and locations with fewer than 10 check-in records because they are outliers in the data. The number of users, locations, location categories and check-ins of each data set after preprocessing are shown in Table 2.

Table 2. Basic dataset statistics after preprocessing.

	NYC	TKY	Weeplaces
#users	1083	2293	1467
#locations	5135	7873	8161
#location categories	209	292	481
#check-ins	147938	447570	134762

Baselines. We compare our ICPAN with the following baselines:

STRNN [20]: an invariant RNN model that incorporates spatio-temporal features between consecutive visits.

FPMC [21]: a model that subsumes both a common Markov chain and the normal matrix factorization.

SHAN [22]: a novel two-layer hierarchical attention network that combines user's long- and short-term preferences.

SAE-NAD [14]: a novel autoencoder-based model to learn the complex user-POI relations, which consists of a self-attentive encoder and a neighbor-aware decoder.

TiSASRec [13]: a method which models both the absolute positions of POIs as well as the time intervals between them in a sequence.

STAN [5]: a bi-layer attention architecture that firstly aggregates spatiotemporal correlation within user trajectory and then recalls the target with consideration of personalized item frequency

Matrices. In order to evaluate the performance of online recommendations in location-based services, we utilize two commonly used performance metrics, the top-k precision rates and recall rates. The higher the recall and precision, the better the recommendation performance of the model.

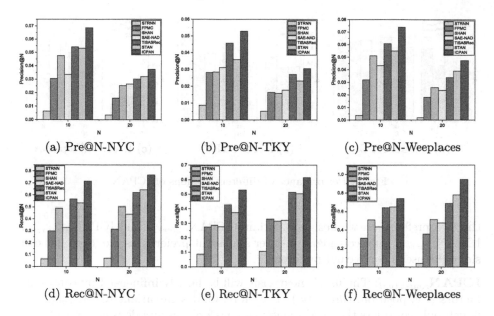

Fig. 3. Comparison of recommendation performance on three datasets.

5.2 Comparison of Performance

Figure 3 shows the recommendation performance of our ICPAN and baselines on the three datasets. We can see that our ICPAN outperforms all other baselines. Among all the baselines, STRNN performs the worst because RNN cannot solve the problem of long-term dependence. The poor performance of FPMC may be due to the fact that it only captures sequential effects and ignores spatiotemporal effects. The performance of SHAN is better than STRNN, FPMC and SAE-NAD. It employs a hierarchical attention network that combines the user's dynamic long-term and short-term preferences. STAN and TiSASRec outperform the other methods significantly, both of which take the time interval into account. Only ICPAN fully considers the user's inherent preferences and contextual preferences, and fully considers the location category, time and geographic influence. In addition, the six baselines did not consider the impact of category, and FPMC, SHAN did not consider the impact of temporal and spatial relationships, which may be the reason why the performance is slightly worse than ICPAN.

5.3 Influence of Components

In order to verify the effectiveness of several key modules designed in our model, we conducted more experiments to evaluate whether there are model variants of this type of design.

ICPAN$_{inherent}$: The user's stable inherent preferences and dynamic contextual preferences simultaneously affect the user's behavior. To verify the importance of

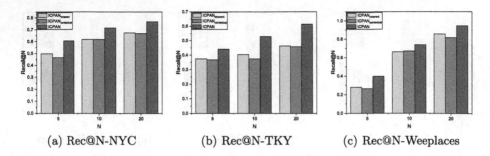

(a) Rec@N-NYC   (b) Rec@N-TKY   (c) Rec@N-Weeplaces

Fig. 4. Performance of different versions of ICPAN.

the two preferences, we designed variants $ICPAN_{inherent}$ and $ICPAN_{contextual}$. $ICPAN_{inherent}$ only considers the user's inherent preferences, i.e. does not consider the user's contextual preferences.

$ICPAN_{contextual}$: The user's next visit will be largely influenced by contextual factors (e.g. position, time, etc.). Therefore, we design variant $ICPAN_{contextual}$, which only considers the user's contextual preferences and does not consider the inherent preferences.

Figure 4 shows the experimental results of these ICPAN variants. In general, ICPAN performs better than its variants on the three data sets. This indicates that every part of the design plays an important role. The performance difference between $ICPAN_{inherent}$ and $ICPAN_{contextual}$ in the three datasets is very small.

5.4 Influence of Embedding Dimensions

In our model, we change the embedding dimension from 10 to 70 with a step size of 10. We use Rec@N as the evaluation criterion. Figure 5 shows that different embedding dimensions d lead to some differences in the experimental results. Figure 5(a) shows that $d = 20$ is the best dimension. Figure 5(b) shows that $d = 50$ is the best dimension of NYC and TKY, and $d = 30$ is the best dimension of Weeplaces. And Fig. 5(c) shows that $d = 50$ is the best dimension of NYC and

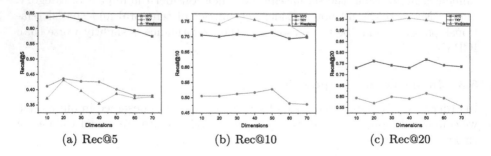

(a) Rec@5   (b) Rec@10   (c) Rec@20

Fig. 5. Effect of embedding dimensions.

TKY, and d = 40 is the best dimension of Weeplaces. In general, our model is relatively stable and is not greatly affected by the hyperparameter d.

6   Conclusion

In this paper, we proposed a model based on the self-attention mechanism, abbreviated as ICPAN, for online recommendation in location-based services. ICPAN combines the user's inherent preferences and contextual preferences. We conducted a lot of experiments on three real data sets. Experimental results showed that ICPAN outperformed other state-of-the-art models in terms of precision and recall.

Acknowledgement. This work was supported by Natural Science Foundation of China No. 61972230 and National Key R&D Program of China No. 2021YFF0900802.

References

1. Gao, H., Tang, J., Hu, X., Liu, H.: Exploring temporal effects for location recommendation on location-based social networks. In: Proceedings of the 7th ACM Conference on Recommender Systems, pp. 93–100 (2013)
2. Cheng, C., Yang, H., Lyu, M.R., King, I.: Successive point-of-interest recommendation. In: Twenty-Third International Joint Conference on Artificial Intelligence, Where you like to Go Next (2013)
3. Sun, K., Qian, T., Chen, T., Liang, Y., Nguyen, Q.V.H., Yin, H.: Where to go next: modeling long-and short-term user preferences for point-of-interest recommendation. In: Proceedings of the AAAI Conference on Artificial Intelligence **34**, 214–221 (2020)
4. Ying, H., et al.: Time-aware metric embedding with asymmetric projection for successive poi recommendation. World Wide Web **22**(5), 2209–2224 (2019)
5. Luo, Y., Liu, Q., Liu, Z.: Stan: spatio-temporal attention network for next location recommendation. In: Proceedings of the Web Conference 2021, pp. 2177–2185 (2021)
6. Wang, M.F., Lu, Y.S., Huang, J.L.: Spent: a successive poi recommendation method using similarity-based poi embedding and recurrent neural network with temporal influence. In: 2019 IEEE International Conference on Big Data and Smart Computing (BigComp) (2019)
7. Yi-Shu, L., Shih, W.-Y., Gau, H.-Y., Chung, K.-C., Huang, J.-L.: On successive point-of-interest recommendation. World Wide Web **22**(3), 1151–1173 (2019)
8. Galassi, A., Lippi, M., Torroni, P.: Attention in natural language processing. IEEE Trans. Neural Netw. Learn. Syst. **32**(10), 4291–4308 (2020)
9. Parmar, N., et al.: Image transformer. In: International Conference on Machine Learning, pp. 4055–4064. PMLR (2018)
10. Yin, J., Li, Y., Liu, Z., Xu, J., Xia, B., Li, Q.: ADPR: an attention-based deep learning point-of-interest recommendation framework. In: 2019 International Joint Conference on Neural Networks (IJCNN), pp. 1–8. IEEE (2019)
11. Vaswani, A., et al.: Attention is all you need. In: Advances in Neural Information Processing Systems, vol. 30 (2017)

12. Kang, W.-C., McAuley, J.: Self-attentive sequential recommendation. In: 2018 IEEE International Conference on Data Mining (ICDM), pp. 197–206. IEEE (2018)
13. Li, J., Wang, Y., McAuley, J.: Time interval aware self-attention for sequential recommendation. In: Proceedings of the 13th International Conference on Web Search and Data Mining, pp. 322–330 (2020)
14. Ma, C., Zhang, Y., Wang, Q., Liu, X.: Point-of-interest recommendation: exploiting self-attentive autoencoders with neighbor-aware influence. In: Proceedings of the 27th ACM International Conference on Information and Knowledge Management, pp. 697–706 (2018)
15. Zhao, S., Zhao, T., Yang, H., Lyu, M.R., King, I.: Stellar: spatial-temporal latent ranking for successive point-of-interest recommendation. In: Thirtieth AAAI Conference on Artificial Intelligence (2016)
16. Lin, T., Wang, Y., Liu, X., Qiu, X.: A survey of transformers. arXiv preprint arXiv:2106.04554 (2021)
17. De Felipe, I., Hristidis, V., Rishe, N.: Keyword search on spatial databases. In: 2008 IEEE 24th International Conference on Data Engineering, pp. 656–665 (2008)
18. Guttman, A.: R-trees: a dynamic index structure for spatial searching. In: Proceedings of the 1984 ACM SIGMOD International Conference on Management of Data, pp. 47–57 (1984)
19. Yang, D., Zhang, D., Zheng, V.W., Yu, Z.: Modeling user activity preferences by leveraging user spatial temporal characteristics in LBSNs. IEEE Trans. Syst. Man Cybern. Syst. **45**(1), 129–142 (2014)
20. Liu, Q., Wu, S., Wang, L., Tan, T.: Predicting the next location: a recurrent model with spatial and temporal contexts. In: Thirtieth AAAI Conference on Artificial Intelligence (2016)
21. Rendle, S., Freudenthaler, C., Schmidt-Thieme, L.: Factorizing personalized Markov chains for next-basket recommendation. In: Proceedings of the 19th International Conference on World Wide Web, pp. 811–820 (2010)
22. Ying, H., et al.: Sequential recommender system based on hierarchical attention network. In: IJCAI International Joint Conference on Artificial Intelligence (2018)

PD-SRS: Personalized Diversity for a Fair Session-Based Recommendation System

Naime Ranjbar Kermany[1,2](✉) ⓘ, Luiz Pizzato[2], Jian Yang[1], Shan Xue[3], and Jia Wu[1]

[1] Department of Computing, Macquarie University, Sydney, Australia
{naime.ranjbar-kermany,jian.yang,emma.xue,jia.wu}@mq.edu.au
[2] AI Labs, Commonwealth Bank of Australia, Sydney, Australia
luiz.pizzato1@cba.com.au
[3] University of Wollongong, Wollongong, Australia
emma.xue@mq.edu.au

Abstract. Session-based Recommender Systems (SRSs), which aim to recommend users' next action based on their current and historical sessions, play a significant role in many real-world online services. The existing session-based recommendation methods have mainly focused on the accuracy of recommendation, which biases to reinforce popular items/services and loses the recommendation diversity. Diversity is a positive aspect particularly in SRSs as the target user may like to be surprised and interact with a broader range of content in different sessions. In this work, we propose a Personalized Diversification strategy for a Session-based Recommender System (PD-SRS) using graph neural networks. Comprehensive experiments are carried out on two real-world datasets to demonstrate the effectiveness of PD-SRS in making a trade-off between accuracy and personalized diversity over the baselines.

Keywords: Session-based recommendation · Personalized diversity · Fairness · Long-tail recommendation · Graph neural network

1 Introduction

Recommender Systems (RSs) have been widely used to help users find the right services regarding their needs from masses of data on the Internet growing over time. Conventional RSs provide personalized recommendations based on users' explicit and/or implicit feedbacks, assuming that users' preferences are static [3]. However, this assumption is often invalid as users' interests may change over different time frames which are called sessions [13]. Session-based Recommender Systems (SRSs) have been emerged to predict user's next action (e.g., click, view, or purchase) based on their session sequence of interactions. In SRSs, users' actions in the current session imply their short-term interests, while historical session sequences reflect their long-term interests. Utilizing both short-term and long-term interests of users has achieved better performance in SRSs [12].

© The Author(s), under exclusive license to Springer Nature Switzerland AG 2022
J. Troya et al. (Eds.): ICSOC 2022, LNCS 13740, pp. 331–339, 2022.
https://doi.org/10.1007/978-3-031-20984-0_23

With the development of SRSs, lots of research efforts have focused on improving the accuracy of recommendation. However, it has been proved that accuracy is not the only quality criteria to create a good recommender system that will completely reflect a user's preferences [1,7,8]. Diversity is another significant criteria in recommendation since it enables users to discover unexpected and surprising services that are not similar to what they have previously experienced. Without diversity in recommendations, users are therefore likely to be exposed to repetitive and/or popular services.

To fill the research gap of diversity issues in SRSs, we aim to address the following challenges in this paper: Firstly, *how can diversity be supported in SRSs?* Diversity is a positive aspect in SRSs since users often spend considerable time in browsing the web to find different/new services [15]. Diversity can be studied at intra-user or inter-user level. Intra-user diversity is the average pairwise dissimilarity among recommended services in the list, whereas inter-user diversity focuses on providing different results for different users. It results in *popularity bias* problem which denotes high imbalanced distribution of recommendations based on interaction frequency of services [14]. Secondly, *how can popularity bias be tackled in SRSs?* In this study, we try to improve the inter-user level diversity, which is also known as long-tail recommendation [4,15]. Long-tail recommendation is the strategy of targeting unpopular services. It is a good mitigation for the common problem of popularity bias in recommender systems. It is also fair towards services since it does not favour only popular ones. However, simply recommending long-tail services with an identical diversification strategy towards all users may largely affect the accuracy and also be unfair towards some groups of users. Thirdly, *how can we consider user's level of interest in diversity in SRSs?* Diversity is a significant matter in SRSs as target user may be interested about specific content in one session while she may prefer to interact with a broader range of content in another session. It shows the importance of assessing users' level of interest in diversity to provide personalized diverse recommendation when user looks for it [9]. This can distribute users' utility loss fairly among all users so that accuracy gets the minimum impact.

In this work, we propose a Personalized Diversified Session-based Recommender System, called PD-SRS, using Graph Neural Networks (GNNs). GNNs are capable of capturing the complex service transitions. The proposed method generates fair recommendations by making trade-off between accuracy and personalized diversity. To the best of our knowledge, approaches considering a trade-off between accuracy and diversity in SRSs are very limited in the literature of service recommendation. In order to fill this gap and address the above four discussed main challenges in SRSs, we propose PD-SRS.

2 The Proposed Method: PD-SRS

2.1 Problem Definition

To predict users' next action based on their historical (long-term) and current (short-term) interests, the main goal of PD-SRS makes trade-off between

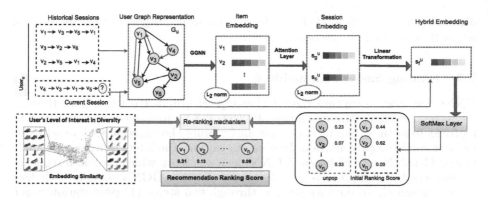

Fig. 1. The main framework of the proposed PD-SRS method. All user's session sequences are modelled as session graphs and then an embedding vector is obtained for each user session using GGNN, attention network, L_2 norms, and a linear transformation. Afterward, the initial recommendation ranking scores of all possible services are predicted. Finally, recommendations are re-ranked to include top-relevant long-tail services using a personalized diversification strategy.

accuracy and personalized diversity (Fig. 1). Let $V = \{v_1, v_2, \cdots, v_n\}$ and $U = \{u_1, u_2, \cdots, u_m\}$ denote the sets of n services and m users, respectively. For each service v, $e_v \in \mathbb{R}^d$ represents the d-dimension embedding vector. The clicked services by user u in session i are ordered by timestamps and shown as $s_i^u = \{v_{s_i,1}, v_{s_i,2}, \cdots, v_{s_i,n_v}\}$, where n_v is different for different users. Sessions are also normalized and ordered by timestamps so that the last session, s_l^u, is called current session and the others, $\{s_1^u, s_2^u, \cdots, s_{l-1}^u\}$ are called historical sessions. For convenience, we call the current session and historical session as S_c^u and S_h^u, respectively. These user's sessions form a user graph $\mathcal{G}_u$ so that GNN is used to capture the transitions among services with respect to each user. Given $\mathcal{G}_u$, we output probability $\hat{y} = \{y_1, y_2, \cdots, y_n\}$ for all candidate services, where y_i corresponds to the initial ranking score of service v_i. Then, we optimize the ranking scores of the services based on the proposed personalized diversification strategy to make trade-off between accuracy and diversity. To do so, we include the top-relevant long-tail services into the top-K recommendation list based on a user's level of interest in diversity (LID). We obtain how many long-tail services can be be picked for an individual explorer user based on a hyper parameter.

2.2 Constructing User Session Graph

All session sequences for user u can be modelled as a directed graph $\mathcal{G}_u = (\mathcal{V}_u; \mathcal{E}_u)$, where each node represents an service $v_i \in V$ and each edge $v_i \to v_j$ shows that user u clicked service v_j after service v_i in the same session. We represent $\mathcal{G}_u$ with adjacency matrix $A^u \in \mathbb{R}^{n \times 2n}$, which is a concatenation of two connection matrices $A_{in}^u, A_{out}^u \in \mathbb{R}^{n \times n}$; A_{in}^u, A_{out}^u denote weighted connections of incoming and outgoing edges in $\mathcal{G}_u$, respectively. Incoming edges of a node are directed edges that the node is the destination while outgoing edges are directed edges that the node is the origin.

2.3   Finding Session Embedding

GNNs are used to capture the relationships of graph-structured data through message passing among the nodes. In fact, GNNs iteratively aggregate latent features from the adjacent nodes and incorporate the aggregated data with the current service representation. In order to capture the latent features, we apply Gated Graph Neural Network (GGNN) as it can learn which data in a sequence is important to be preserved or discarded. We use GGNN to map each user session graph $\mathcal{G}_u$ to outputs passing through two steps: (1) propagation which calculates service and session embeddings; (2) output model which maps from embeddings and labels to an output using SoftMax function [6]. The recurrence of the propagation step is as follows:

$$a_i^{(t)} = A_i^u : [v_1^{(t-1)}, v_2^{(t-1)}, \cdots, v_n^{(t-1)}]^T H + b, \tag{1}$$

$$z_i^{(t)} = \sigma(W_z a_i^{(t)} + U_z v_i^{(t-1)}), \tag{2}$$

$$r_i^{(t)} = \sigma(W_r a_i^{(t)} + U_r v_i^{(t-1)}), \tag{3}$$

$$\tilde{v}_i^{(t)} = tanh(W_o a_i^{(t)} + U_o(r_i^{(t)} \odot v_i^{(t-1)})), \tag{4}$$

$$v_i^{(t)} = (1 - z_i^{(t)}) \odot v_i^{(t-1)} + z_i^{(t)} \odot \tilde{v}_i^{(t)} \tag{5}$$

To obtain the session embeddings, the combination of long-term interests and current preferences of the user's session is used for a better prediction on users' next action. We have all the services' vectors after feeding all users' session graphs into GGNN. Then, we show each user's session as a session embedding vector $s^u \in \mathbb{R}^d$ by defining local embedding (s_l^u) and global embedding (s_g^u) of user's session graph $\mathcal{G}_u$. The local embedding is the vector representation of last service of the user's session. The global embedding of the user's session graph is the aggregation of all service vectors with the use of soft attention mechanism to differentiate the importance of services. Then, a linear transformation on the concatenation of the local and global embeddings is used to calculate the final hybrid embedding: $s_f^u = [s_l^u, s_g^u]$.

2.4   Generating Initial Recommendation Scores

After obtaining user session embedding, score $\hat{z}_i$ is calculated by multiplying service' embedding e_{v_i} by user session embedding s_f^u as $\hat{z}_i = (s_f^u)^T v_i$. Next, we utilize a SoftMax function to get $\hat{y}$ and rank the services ($\hat{y} = \text{SoftMax}(\hat{z})$, where $\hat{y}$ represents the initial recommendation probability values of all possible services being the next click of the user in current session s_c^u). Then, we train our model by minimizing the loss function ($\mathcal{L} = -\sum_{i=1}^{n} y_i \log(\hat{y}_i) + (1 - y_i) \log(1 - \hat{y}_i)$), where y denotes one-hot encoding vector of the ground truth service.

2.5   Ranking Optimization and Personalized Diversification

The main goal of the proposed PD-SRS method is to recommend users' next action by considering both accuracy and diversity. Given a session s, user u may either look for a specific product (focused) or just browsing novel or diverse services (explorer). Thus, we propose a personalized diversification strategy to obtain user's level of interest in diversity (LID) in current session. To do so, we first obtain how many long-tail services can be picked by each user based on a hyperparameter, and then we re-rank the recommendation to include the top-relevant long-tail services into the top-K recommendation list. In the following, we explain the personalized diversification with more details.

First, we measure the unpopularity of services according to click frequency as:

$$\varphi(v) = 1 - \sum_{i=1}^{|S|} \frac{\text{number of clicks for service } v \text{ in session } i}{\text{number of clicks in session } i} \tag{6}$$

where $\varphi(v)$ is unpopularity of service v, and $|S|$ is total number of sessions. Note that, we differentiate between the service being clicked k times in a sequence with smaller length and the service being clicked the same k times in a sequence with longer length.

Then, we compute users' LID in their current sessions based on list-wise similarity of service embeddings in a user session as:

$$LID_s^u = 1 - \sum_{i=1}^{k} \sum_{j=1}^{k} \frac{Sim(v_i, v_j)}{\binom{k}{2}} \tag{7}$$

where k shows the number of clicked services by user u in current session s_c, and $Sim(v_i, v_j)$ is the embedding-based similarity between two services v_i and v_j. The similarity is calculated using the short random walks. Word2Vec is used to group the vectors of similar nodes together in vectorspace. We use it in this work to detect similarities among service embedding vectors. To do so, we form a directed graph with all clicked services by moving from one node (source) to another (target), where edges are weighted based on their counts of occurrences in the whole service networks. We then define the short random walks using Word2Vec parameters. We feed the walks into neural networks to train the Word2Vec models and generate service embeddings. These embeddings incorporate a notion of similarity among them i.e. two nodes who are similar to each other tend to be closer in the vector space.

Finally, we can say if services in user's current session are less similar (higher LID) to each other, user is exploring and more diverse recommendations can be offered. In contrast, if the LID_s^u value is small, the more similar are the services clicked by user u in session s, and accordingly the more focused the user u is in her current session. Finally, we re-rank the recommendations to be the next click of user u in current session. The re-ranking process depends on how explorer she is in her current session. Thus, we define a hyper parameter to find how many long-tail services can be included in the top-k recommendation list for user u as:

$$D = \lfloor \alpha \times LID_s^u \times K \rfloor \tag{8}$$

where α is a hyper parameter, $\lfloor . \rfloor$ returns the largest integer less than or equal to a given number, and D shows the number of unpopular services the top-K recommendations should contain for user u in session s. Therefore, the top-D relevant long-tail services are selected among a longer recommendation lists of size t to be included in the final top-K recommendation list ($K \leq t$).

Table 1. The performance of PD-SRS and five baselines in terms of Recall@K, MRR@K, and LT@K where $K = 5, 10, 20$ on Reddit and Xing data sets. *Change* shows the improvement and reduction over the best baseline. Note that, the best results among the baselines are indicated by star sign.

| Method | Reddit | | | | | | | | |
	Recall@5	Recall@10	Recall@20	MRR@5	MRR@10	MRR@20	LT@5	LT@10	LT@20
POP	4.14	8.97	10.75	4.02	5.04	5.36	0	0	0
Item-KNN	14.61	20.79	28.12	8.20	9.46	10.28	41.02*	49.22*	55.87*
NARM	28.85	34.76	40.47	19.95	20.14	20.57	28.86	36.98	41.28
SR-GNN	33.80	40.36	47.65	25.42	26.29	26.79	28.37	35.25	40.79
NISER	34.28*	41.18*	48.21*	25.61*	26.42*	27.03*	40.04	47.93	53.23
PD-SRS	**34.12**	**40.99**	**48.00**	**25.24**	**26.12**	**26.84**	**70.03**	**83.11**	**88.26**
Change	−0.47%	−0.46%	-0.44%	-1.47%	-1.15%	-0.70%	+70.72%	+68.85%	+57.97%

| Method | Xing | | | | | | | | |
	Recall@5	Recall@10	Recall@20	MRR@5	MRR@10	MRR@20	LT@5	LT@10	LT@20
POP	0.20	0.24	0.59	0.08	0.09	0.13	0	0	0
Item-KNN	3.79	6.15	7.31	1.86	2.31	2.52	46.67*	53.85*	64.04*
NARM	8.18	9.01	10.22	5.13	6.12	6.71	34.11	43.83	56.02
SR-GNN	15.47	18.85	22.50*	10.82*	11.27*	11.53*	34.76	44.60	56.05
NISER	15.89*	19.39*	22.47	10.71	11.18	11.40	45.32	52.16	63.35
PD-SRS	**15.56**	**19.11**	**22.23**	**10.54**	**11.02**	**11.30**	**72.61**	**80.11**	**89.48**
Change	−2.12%	−1.46%	−1.21%	−2.66%	−2.27%	−2.03%	+55.58%	+48.76%	+39.72%

3   Experiments and Discussions

3.1   Datasets

In order to evaluate the proposed method, we conducted a set of experiments on two real-world datasets. These datasets are Xing data from RecSys Challenge 2016[1] and Reddit[2]. These two datasets are manually split using a 30-minutes and a 60-minutes idle threshold, respectively. We hold the first 80% of each user's sessions as the training set and the remaining as test set for Xing and Reddit datasets. For both datasets, we segment each session S_u into a series of historical sessions and current session.

---

[1] http://2016.recsyschallenge.com/.
[2] https://www.kaggle.com/colemaclean/subreddit-interactions.

3.2   Baselines

We compared the performance of our PD-SRS with five existing methods.

- POP recommends the top-K services with the largest number of interactions.
- Item-KNN [10] calculates item-based similarity based on the co-incidence of items within sessions.
- NARM [5] uses an attention mechanism on RNN to capture the users' key purpose and sequential behavior
- SR-GNN [11] applies gated GNN to capture complex transition patterns of items for a session-based recommendation.
- NISER [2] normalizes the item and session-graph representations to alleviate the popularity bias problem in SRSs.

3.3   Evaluation Metrics

Recall@K: it computes recommendation accuracy by representing the percentage of correctly recommended items among the K items in recommendation list.

MRR@K (Mean Reciprocal Rank): it computes the average of reciprocal ranks of the correctly-recommended items.

LT@K (Long-Tail coverage): it measures how many long-tail items ever appear in the top-K recommendations. The larger the LT@K value is, the more long-tail items the recommendation lists have covered.

3.4   Experimental Results and Discussion

We compare the proposed PD-SRS method with baselines as shown in Table 1. Compared with the conventional method POP, our PD-SRS method performs far better. POP aims to recommend services only based on their frequency of appearance, which is not suitable for session-based recommendation scenarios. Item-KNN computes the similarity between services ignoring the sequences of interactions. As shown in Table 1, this method attains quite poor results on Recall@K and MRR@K in comparison with NARM. However, Item-KNN achieves the best LT@K result among the baseline methods, which confirms the importance of considering trade-off between accuracy and diversity in SRSs for evaluating the quality of recommendation model.

NARM applies RNN for sequence modeling and a self-attention to pay more attention to the last item of the session. This neural network-based method fails to preserve significant information during the propagation step (short-term memory problem) and they are also unable to consider complex item transitions.

SR-GNN applies GNNs to output embeddings and attention mechanism and generate session graph representations. Our PD-SRS method outperforms SR-GNN in most of the cases. NISER is the closest GNN-based literature to our work that aims to alleviate the popularity bias problem in SRSs. They demonstrate that GNN-based SRSs are biased towards recommending popular services and fail to recommend long tails, so they address this problem by normalizing the learned service and session embeddings. Comparing with all baselines, NISER achieves the best results in terms of accuracy and the closest results to Item-KNN in terms of LT@K .

Our PD-SRS method achieves the best results on LT@K among the baselines for all datasets. Table 1 shows improvement and reduction of PD-SRS over the best baselines. For instance, comparing with the closest baseline, NISER, our method has 74.90%, 73.40%, and 65.81% LT@K improvement in top-5, top-10, and top-20 recommendations for Reddit data respectively, with only 0.47%, 0.46%, and 0.44% reduction on Recall@K and 1.47%, 1.15%, and 0.70% reduction on MRR@K. Higher coverage of long-tail services while the accuracy is almost kept shows that the proposed PD-SRS method is fair towards services and users and also could better overcome the popularity bias issue in SRSs. PD-SRS attains a trade-off between accuracy and long-tail inclusion for SRSs. Comparing with the baselines, the range of accuracy fluctuation in our method is very small because of employing the proposed personalized diversification strategy.

4 Conclusion

In this paper, we propose PD-SRS to make a trade-off between accuracy and personalized diversity. We consider personalized diversity to include top-relevant long-tail services into the recommendations. Extensive experiments on two real-world datasets verify that the proposed PD-SRS method tackles popularity bias problem and achieves higher long-tail coverage with a small range of accuracy fluctuation.

References

1. Chen, L., Wu, W., He, L.: Personality and recommendation diversity. In: Tkalčič, M., De De Carolis, B., de de Gemmis, M., Odić, A., Košir, A. (eds.) Emotions and Personality in Personalized Services. HIS, pp. 201–225. Springer, Cham (2016). https://doi.org/10.1007/978-3-319-31413-6_11
2. Gupta, P., Garg, D., Malhotra, P., Vig, L., Shroff, G.M.: Niser: normalized item and session representations with graph neural networks. arXiv preprint arXiv:1909.04276 (2019)
3. Kermany, N.R., Alizadeh, S.H.: A hybrid multi-criteria recommender system using ontology and neuro-fuzzy techniques. Electron. Commer. Res. Appl. 21, 50–64 (2017)
4. Kermany, N.R., Zhao, W., Yang, J., Wu, J., Pizzato, L.: An ethical multi-stakeholder recommender system based on evolutionary multi-objective optimization. In: 2020 IEEE International Conference on Services Computing (SCC), pp. 478–480. IEEE (2020)
5. Li, J., Ren, P., Chen, Z., Ren, Z., Lian, T., Ma, J.: Neural attentive session-based recommendation. In: Proceedings of the 2017 ACM on Conference on Information and Knowledge Management, pp. 1419–1428 (2017)

6. Li, Y., Tarlow, D., Brockschmidt, M., Zemel, R.: Gated graph sequence neural networks. arXiv preprint arXiv:1511.05493 (2015)
7. Ranjbar Kermany, N., Pizzato, L., Min, T., Scott, C., Leontjeva, A.: A multi-stakeholder recommender system for rewards recommendations. In: Proceedings of the 16th ACM Conference on Recommender Systems, pp. 484–487 (2022)
8. Ranjbar Kermany, N., Yang, J., Wu, J., Pizzato, L.: Fair-srs: a fair session-based recommendation system. In: Proceedings of the Fifteenth ACM International Conference on Web Search and Data Mining, pp. 1601–1604 (2022)
9. Ranjbar Kermany, N., Zhao, W., Yang, J., Wu, J., Pizzato, L.: A fairness-aware multi-stakeholder recommender system. World Wide Web **24**(6), 1–24 (2021)
10. Sarwar, B., Karypis, G., Konstan, J., Riedl, J.: Item-based collaborative filtering recommendation algorithms. In: Proceedings of the 10th international conference on World Wide Web, pp. 285–295 (2001)
11. Wu, S., Tang, Y., Zhu, Y., Wang, L., Xie, X., Tan, T.: Session-based recommendation with graph neural networks. In: Proceedings of the AAAI Conference on Artificial Intelligence, vol. 33, pp. 346–353 (2019)
12. Zhang, M., Wu, S., Gao, M., Jiang, X., Xu, K., Wang, L.: Personalized graph neural networks with attention mechanism for session-aware recommendation. IEEE Trans. Knowl. Data Eng. **34**, 3946–3957 (2020)
13. Zhang, S., Yao, L., Sun, A., Tay, Y.: Deep learning based recommender system: a survey and new perspectives. ACM Comput. Surv. (CSUR) **52**(1), 1–38 (2019)
14. Zhao, Z., et al.: Popularity bias is not always evil: disentangling benign and harmful bias for recommendation. arXiv preprint arXiv:2109.07946 (2021)
15. Zheng, Y., Gao, C., Chen, L., Jin, D., Li, Y.: DGCN: diversified recommendation with graph convolutional networks. In: Proceedings of the Web Conference 2021, pp. 401–412 (2021)

TagTag: A Novel Framework for Service Tags Recommendation and Missing Tag Prediction

Wentao Chen[1], Mingyi Liu[1], Zhiying Tu[2], and Zhongjie Wang[1(✉)]

[1] Faculty of Computing, Harbin Institute of Technology, Harbin, China
22S003073@stu.hit.edu.cn, {liumy,rainy}@hit.edu.cn
[2] Faculty of Computing, Harbin Institute of Technology, Weihai, China
tzy_hit@hit.edu.cn

Abstract. Currently, service tag recommendation plays an important role in the study of services. As a result, there have been many service tag recommendation studies that have achieved significant achievements. However, existing studies mainly have two problems: they only recommend one tag and cannot determine whether new tags are needed. To help solve the above problems, we propose a novel graph neural framework named **TagTag** to make multi-tag recommendations and missing tag prediction, which relies on the idea of tag collaboration graph. We conduct experiments on the real-world dataset from ProgrammableWeb, and the results show that **TagTag** performs better than existing studies. The code used in this paper is fully accessible at https://github.com/HIT-ICES/TagTag.

Keywords: Web services · Tags collaboration graph · Service tags recommendation · Service tag prediction · Deep learning

1 Introduction

Nowadays, the rapid development of new technologies and increasingly sophisticated user requirements lead to the explosion of the number and diversity of services. A massive volume of services brings new challenges in service management and reuse. For users, it is becoming more and more difficult to find suitable services to satisfy their requirements; For service managers, the cost of keeping services in the right place for easy retrieval is also becoming higher and higher. Therefore, we need a simple and intuitive mechanism to help users and managers organize and retrieve services efficiently.

Service tags are chosen as a fundamental mechanism to solve the abovementioned problems due to their simplicity and high expressiveness. To reduce the annotation cost and make work more efficient, researchers started to study how to automatically tag services, a.k.a. service tag recommendation task. There have been many studies that have achieved remarkable performance, such as ServeNet [6]. However, these studies often simplify the reality of service tag annotation, which limits the scope of application of these methods:

© The Author(s), under exclusive license to Springer Nature Switzerland AG 2022
J. Troya et al. (Eds.): ICSOC 2022, LNCS 13740, pp. 340–348, 2022.
https://doi.org/10.1007/978-3-031-20984-0_24

1. The current methods only attach one tag to the service, such as ServeNet [6] and SRaSLR [7]. Such operations are obviously extremely inconsistent with reality. If only one tag is provided for a service, the cross-domain services, such as e-commerce and virtual fitness, will never be accurately described.
2. The existing tag recommendation methods cannot give a prompt for missing tags. However, services are in a period of rapid development, and the existing tags are not enough to describe all services. Therefore, if there is no timely reminder to add new tags, tags will become less and less descriptive, and the existence of tags will gradually lose their meaning.

In order to solve the above problems, we propose the following ideas. The essence of service tag recommendation is to match the service to the tag. Therefore, it will make more sense if we can extract features from the tag and match them with the service's features to determine whether the two are suitable. In fact, the tag has two main features. The first feature is the text information, which can concisely reflect the service's usage area. And the second feature is that there is an association between tags that appear in the same service. This association organizes tags into a graph called Tag Collaboration Graph. The tag collaboration graph can combine all tags and extract the features of tags as a whole and then match them with the target service. At the same time, the service features are derived from the textual features of the service description so that the tag can be matched with the service. Therefore, this approach, which takes service and tag perspectives, will be more convincing.

This paper proposes a novel graph neural framework for service tags recommendation and missing tag prediction named **TagTag**. **TagTag** combines the tag features extracted from the tag collaboration graph with the service description features and recommends all tags matching the service, then make predictions for missing tags. The experiment is performed on real-world data provided by *Programmable Web*[1], and the result shows that **TagTag** has achieved the best results in tags recommendation and missing tag prediction.

The remainder of this paper is organized as follows: In Sect. 2, we introduce the related works. In Sect. 3, we describe the formulation of the problem. In Sect. 4, we describe the architecture of the **TagTag** model. In Sect. 5, we introduce the details of the experiment. In Sect. 6, we present the experiment results. In Sect. 7, we conclude our work.

2   Related Works

At present, the research on service tags mainly focuses on extracting service features from the service description and finding the most relevant tag in the given tag set, so the service tag recommendation problem has been regarded as a text classification problem for a long time.

Text feature extraction has always been an important subject in natural language processing. In 2013, the Google team developed the word2vec tool. In 2018, Google launched a transformer-based training language model - BERT.

---

[1] https://www.programmableweb.com.

For tag classification, the deep learning method is widely used to classify the extracted features, for example, recurrent neural network [4] and convolutional neural network [3]. In addition, some methods use multiple networks. For example, ServeNet [6] combines the convolutional neural network and long-term and short-term memory network, achieving good service tag classification results.

Graph Representation Learning converts graph data into low-dimensional dense vectors. It is divided into the following two kinds: 1) Graph structure-based representation learning only learns the vector representation of nodes based on the graph's topological structure; 2) Graph feature-based representation learning, called graph neural network (GNN) [5], considers not only the graph's topology but also the nodes' initial eigenvectors.

3   Problem Formulation

Definition 1. *Services are defined as a set composed of individual service:* $S = \{s_1, s_2, \ldots\ldots, s_n\}$, *where* $s_i (1 \leq i \leq n)$ *is a service. For* $s \in S$, *we define:* $s = \{d_s, T_s\}$, *where* d_s *is the service description of this service and* T_s *is collection of tags for service s. Suppose the set of all tags currently owned is* T, T *is defined as:* $T = \{t_1, t_2, \ldots\ldots, t_m\}$, *where m is the number of all pre-defined tags. The set* T_s *of tags for service s is defined as:* $T_s = \{t | t \in T \land f_d(s, t) = 1\}$, *where* f_d *is the function to determine whether a tag can be used to describe a service.*

Definition 2. *Tags Collaboration Graph is a weighted and undirected graph. It is represented as:* $G = \{T, E\}$, *where* E *is the set of edges in graph.* E *is defined as:* $E = \{(u, v, \omega) | u \in T, v \in T, \omega \in N^+\}$. *For each* $(u, v, \omega) \in E$, *there is service* $s \in S$ *and tag* $u, v \in T_s$, *s is tagged with both u and v. Suppose the set of such services is* $S_{u,v}$. ω *is the weight of the edge* (u, v) *and its value is equal to the size of* $S_{u,v}$.

Definition 3. *Service Tags Recommendation Task is training a model named* F_r *to predict the tag set* $T_s \subseteq T$ *for a given service description* d_s *of* $s \in S$. *Its mathematical definition is as follows:* $T_s = F_r(s|T)$.

Definition 4. *Missing Tag Prediction Task is training a model named* F_p *to determine if the tag sets* T *could fully describe a given service* $s \in S$. *Its mathematical definition is as follows:* $F_p(s|T) \in \{0, 1\}$, *where 0 means no new tag is needed, 1 means new tag is needed.*

4   The Architecture of TagTag

Figure 1 shows the architecture of **TagTag**. **TagTag** inputs service text description and tag collaboration graph, then outputs tags recommended for the service and determines whether existing tags can fully describe the target service. Functionally, the model is divided into two parts: the joint embedding part and the task special part. The rest of this section will discuss each part in detail.

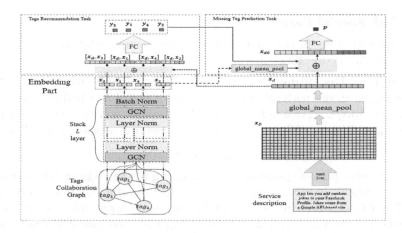

Fig. 1. The architecture of **TagTag**

4.1 Joint Embedding Part

There are two parts in joint embedding part: service description feature embedding and tag collaboration graph feature embedding.

Service Description Feature Embedding: Service text description feature extraction adopts the pre-training model word2vec for encoding. We choose word2vec as the text encoder instead of BERT for two reasons: 1) save compute resources to satisfy more scenarios; 2) create a fair comparison environment with the baselines to demonstrate the validity of **TagTag**. In the process of the experiment, it can use the description of all services to train the word2vec model. For service s with text description $d = \{w_1, w_2, \ldots\ldots, w_{|d|}\}$, the service description feature embedding $\mathbf{x_d}$ can be obtained the following equation:

$$\mathbf{x_d} = \frac{1}{|d|} \sum_{w \in d} f_{word2vec}(w) = \frac{1}{|d|} \sum_{w \in d} \mathbf{w} \tag{1}$$

where $f_{word2vec}(w)$ denotes convert word w into word embedding vector $\mathbf{w}$.

Tag Collaboration Graph Feature Embedding: For the tag collaboration graph, it has three characteristics: node characteristics, edges connecting nodes and edge weight. Graph convolution network (GCN) is used to get the final feature of nodes through the three features. At the same time, add a normalization layer behind each GCN layer. For node $t_i \in T$, it is initially characterized by the word embedding of the tag name and is constantly updated through the GCN and normalization layers, with the following expressions:

$$\mathbf{x_i^{(k)}} = Normalization \cdot GCN(\mathbf{x_i^{(k-1)}}) \tag{2}$$

where $\mathbf{x_i^{(k)}}$ is the feature vector of tag t_i after iteration k, moreover, GCN and $Normalization$ represent the GCN and normalization layers respectively. $\mathbf{x_i}^{(0)}$ is the word embedding of the tag.

4.2   Task Special Part

There are two parts in task part: service tags recommendation task part and missing tag prediction task part.

Service Tags Recommendation Task: After the joint embedding part, we put the target service with all tags one by one to determine whether each tag can describe the target service individually. Therefore, for service s with description feature $\mathbf{x_d}$ and tag t_i with tag feature x_i, the merging method is as follows:

$$\mathbf{x_{di}} = [\mathbf{x_d}, \mathbf{x_i}] \tag{3}$$

where [ ] means splicing operation. Then **TagTag** use three-layer fully connected layers for service tags recommendation task to get recommendation results. After that, **TagTag** converts the result of fully connected layers into the probability $\hat{y}_i$ of whether the tag t_i can describe the target service through sigmoid layer. For each input x_{di}, the processing is as follows:

$$\hat{y}_i = sigmoid \cdot FC(\mathbf{x_{di}}) \tag{4}$$

where FC is three-layer fully connected layers. **Missing tag prediction task:** **TagTag** adopts the layer_mean_pool converts feature of all tags into feature $\mathbf{x_G}$ of tag collaboration graph:

$$\mathbf{x_G} = \frac{1}{m} \sum_{i=1}^{m} \mathbf{x_i} \tag{5}$$

The graph-level vector $\mathbf{x_G}$ means the range of service features that all tags can describe. In addition to the features of all tags and the service description, the result of the recommendation task will also affect the prediction task. Therefore, the **TagTag** model will take the result $\{\hat{y}_1, \hat{y}_2, \ldots \ldots, \hat{y}_m\}$ of recommendation task as the input of prediction task. These can be expressed as:

$$\mathbf{x_{dG}} = [\mathbf{x_d}, \mathbf{x_G}, \hat{y}_1, \hat{y}_2, \ldots \ldots, \hat{y}_m] \tag{6}$$

TagTag also uses three-layer fully connected layers and the sigmoid layer converts $\mathbf{x_{dG}}$ into the probability $\hat{p}$ of whether the service needs add new tags:

$$\hat{p} = sigmoid \cdot FC(\mathbf{x_{dG}}) \tag{7}$$

4.3   Optimization Object

The **TagTag** uses binary cross entropy as the loss function. The mathematical expressions of the loss functions of the two tasks are as follows:

$$\mathcal{L}_1 = -\frac{1}{m} \sum_{i=1}^{m} \mathbf{y_i} \cdot log\hat{\mathbf{y}}_i + (1 - \hat{\mathbf{y}}_i) \cdot log\,(1 - \hat{\mathbf{y}}_i) \tag{8}$$

$$\mathcal{L}_2 = \mathbf{p} \cdot log\hat{\mathbf{p}} + (1 - \hat{\mathbf{p}}) \cdot log\,(1 - \hat{\mathbf{p}}) \tag{9}$$

For multi-task learning with multiple losses, the **TagTag** sets parameters, σ_1 and σ_2, for the two losses and handles them in the following method [2]:

$$\mathcal{L} = \frac{1}{2\sigma_1{}^2}\mathcal{L}_1 + \frac{1}{2\sigma_2{}^2}\mathcal{L}_2 + log\sigma_1 + log\sigma_2 \tag{10}$$

5   Experiment

A. Dataset

The experiment crawled an English dataset from *Programmable Web*. Then, the data set is pre-processed as follows:

1. Remove all services without description or tag.
2. Select the 50 tags with the most occurrences as a sample of multi-classification T. This operation is because **TagTag** not only recommends tags for services but also predicts whether new tags need to be added. The remaining tags are used as tags that need to be added.
3. Remove some tags appropriately so that T can fully cover more than 80% of the selected services. This operation is because, in practice, existing tags can fully describe most of the services. We set the total number of services to be 10,000. The tags contained in these 10,000 services, except for the selected 50 tags in T, are removed in descending order of occurrence until T can cover more than 8,000 services.

After the above processing, we divide the data set into the training set, validation set and test set in the ratio of 7:2:1.

B. Baselines and experimental setup

Three groups of 15 comparison methods are set up in the experiment. The first group is independent training for the recommendation task; The second group is independent training for the prediction task; The third group is joint training for two tasks. Each group uses five methods as baselines: FC, RNN [4], LSTM [1], TextCNN [3], ServeNet [6]. These methods were initially set up for single-tag recommendations. However, in experiments, we make modifications to enable them to make multi-tag recommendations and missing tag predictions.

Each method has done five independent experiments to eliminate contingency. In addition, early stop method is used in baselines to avoid overfitting during training. The results of baselines will be compared with those of **TagTag**.

The batch sizes of the three sets are 16, 8 and 4, respectively. A total of three GCN layers are set for graph feature extraction. The learning rate is set to 0.0001, and the weight decay is set to 0.00001.

C. Evaluation Metrics

In the experiments, we use F1, Precision, and Recall to evaluate the performance of the model on two tasks.

6   Results and Discussion

This section will show the experimental results of the proposed **TagTag** and comparison methods, then we do some ablation experiments, and finally, we analyze the experimental results. Table 1 shows the results of the experiment.

Table 1. Performance comparison of different methods. In each column, the best result is bolded, and the second is underlined. @I means the model is trained independently, and @J means the model is trained jointly for two tasks.

Model	Recommendation task			Prediction task		
	F1	Precision	Recall	F1	Precision	Recall
FC@I	0.2472 ± 0.0040	0.6137 ± 0.0082	0.1652 ± 0.0026	0.0000 ± 0.0000	0.0000 ± 0.0000	0.0000 ± 0.0000
RNN@I	0.2372 ± 0.0482	0.5740 ± 0.0380	0.1585 ± 0.0377	0.0216 ± 0.0304	0.0252 ± 0.0328	0.0200 ± 0.0293
LSTM@I	$\underline{0.3455 \pm 0.0260}$	$\underline{0.7015 \pm 0.0253}$	$\underline{0.2455 \pm 0.0232}$	0.0140 ± 0.0513	0.0176 ± 0.0624	0.0123 ± 0.0463
TextCNN@I	0.3064 ± 0.0099	0.6318 ± 0.0097	0.2205 ± 0.0134	$\underline{0.0585 \pm 0.0095}$	$\underline{0.0696 \pm 0.0124}$	$\underline{0.0543 \pm 0.0077}$
ServeNet@I	0.3400 ± 0.0254	0.6898 ± 0.0104	0.2418 ± 0.0217	0.0009 ± 0.0038	0.0016 ± 0.0064	0.0007 ± 0.0026
FC@J	0.2458 ± 0.0044	0.6104 ± 0.0180	0.1644 ± 0.0042	0.0000 ± 0.0000	0.0000 ± 0.0000	0.0000 ± 0.0000
RNN@J	0.2266 ± 0.0470	0.5816 ± 0.0561	0.1490 ± 0.0363	0.0005 ± 0.0022	0.0008 ± 0.0032	0.0004 ± 0.0016
LSTM@J	0.3395 ± 0.0571	$\mathbf{0.7019 \pm 0.0290}$	0.2394 ± 0.0567	0.0267 ± 0.0240	0.0320 ± 0.0280	0.0243 ± 0.0230
TextCNN@J	0.2953 ± 0.0127	0.6231 ± 0.0326	0.2128 ± 0.0102	0.0141 ± 0.0106	0.0168 ± 0.0112	0.0129 ± 0.0104
ServeNet@J	0.3233 ± 0.0163	0.6659 ± 0.0051	0.2284 ± 0.0146	0.0228 ± 0.0141	0.0288 ± 0.0168	0.0201 ± 0.0128
TagTag(improv.)	$\mathbf{0.3551 \pm 0.0099}$ (+1.03%)	0.3001 ± 0.0054	$\mathbf{0.4511 \pm 0.0074}$ (+183.75%)	$\mathbf{0.1568 \pm 0.0225}$ (+268.03%)	$\mathbf{0.1592 \pm 0.0239}$ (+228.74%)	$\mathbf{0.1780 \pm 0.0253}$ (+327.81%)

6.1 Results

For the recommendation task, the proposed **TagTag** model reaches the highest 0.3551 in the average value of F1 score, which is 1% higher than the sub-optimal methods; The error is also the smallest in the comparison method, which is less than 0.01. At the same time, it is worth noting that **TagTag** has leaped forward breakthrough in Recall, almost doubling the recall value. This means that more tags that should be tagged are recommended.

For the prediction task, the F1 score obtained from baselines is basically 0. This also verifies our previous conjecture: simple service features are not enough to judge whether a service needs new tags. This makes the **TagTag** significantly increase the F1 score to 0.1568. At the same time, the **TagTag** also has a precision of 15.92% and a recall of 17.8%.

6.2 Ablation Experiment

Figure 2(a) shows the variation of F1 with the number of GCN layers. The recommendation task reaches a maximum of 0.3556 at the number of GCN layers is 2, and the prediction task reaches a maximum of 0.1568 at the number of GCN layers is 3. Considering the result of **TagTag** with three-layer GCN is only 0.0005 less than the result of two-layer in the recommendation task but 0.01 higher in prediction task, **TagTag** with 3-layer GCN is the best performing one.

In addition, we set up the model αTagTag, which, in contrast to **TagTag**, does not use the results of the recommendation task as input to the prediction task. And independent training is training model with tag collaboration graph for one task independently. As can be seen from Fig. 2(b), **TagTag** achieves the best results on the recommendation task. At the same time, the significant improvement achieved by independent training proves the indispensable role of tag collaboration graph for prediction tasks.

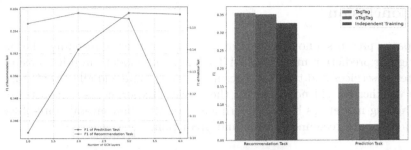

(a) Variations with number of GCN   (b) Variations with intimacy of tasks

Fig. 2. Ablation experiment

Table 2. Example of results

API name	Description	Existing tags	Missing tags	Recommended tags	Add tags
Open New York Liquor Authority Quarterly List of Active Licenses API	The Open **New York** ...... API ...... **New York's** data.ny.gov **open** _data_ initiative....... **an organization** that ......include: ...... address, city, state, ... geographic coordinates.	Government	Alcohol Open Data New York City	Government Transportation Data	✓
DNA Freight API	DNA **Freight** is an international technology integration **company** delivering **supply chain** technology solutions......with the DNA Freight Quote/Tracking and Billing systems	Enterprise	Supply Chain Shipping	Enterprise Business Financial eCommerce	×
Verizon ThingSpace Connectivity Management API	The Verizon ThingSpace Connectivity **Management** API integrates **telephony** connection features into **mobile** devices......_session_.	Telephony Mobile	Management Wireless	Messaging Telephony Mobile	×

Bold: judgment basis of the ground truth; Underline: judgment basis of **TagTag**

Add Tags: the results of the **TagTag**'s recommendation task: ✓ means need add tags; × means no need to add new tags

6.3   Discussion

From Table 1 and Fig. 2(b), we have two questions: 1) why the precision of **Tag-Tag** is lower than baselines on recommendation task; 2) why the F1 of independent training is higher than **TagTag** on prediction task.

This is because, to describe the service fully, the **TagTag** first looks for tags that can make up for the deficiency from the existing tag set for the service, rather than immediately judging that the service needs to add new tags. As a result, many service-related tags are recommended that are useful to describe the service but reduce the precision of recommendation, and **TagTag** thinks the service no longer needs new tags. As shown in Table 2, we can see **TagTag** replaces missing tags with existing ones. For example, **TagTag** uses "Data" to replace "Open Data", uses "Business" to summarize the meaning of "Supply Chain" and uses "Messaging" according to the word "session". **TagTag**'s prediction matches the description content, and some of the recommended tags have a similar or broader meaning for the missing tags. Although the tag used for substitution is somewhat broad, it can already help find and manage the service. Therefore, the lower-than-expected results can also be seen as a sign that **TagTag** can fully use existing tags.

7   Conclusion

This paper presents a novel tags relation aware service tag recommendation and missing tag prediction model, called **TagTag**. The model can fully consider the features of services and tags. As a result, it can recommend all suitable tags and judge whether to add new tags for the service. Experiments demonstrate that the **TagTag** model has better experimental results than several state-of-the-art methods in both recommendation and prediction.

Acknowledgement. The research in this paper is partially supported by the National Key Research and Development Program of China (No 2021YFB3300700) and the National Natural Science Foundation of China (61832014, 61832004).

References

1. Johnson, R., Zhang, T.: Supervised and semi-supervised text categorization using LSTM for region embeddings. In: Balcan, M., Weinberger, K.Q. (eds.) Proceedings of the 33nd International Conference on Machine Learning, ICML 2016, New York City, NY, USA, 19–24 June 2016. JMLR Workshop and Conference Proceedings, vol. 48, pp. 526–534. JMLR.org (2016). http://proceedings.mlr.press/v48/johnson16.html
2. Kendall, A., Gal, Y., Cipolla, R.: Multi-task learning using uncertainty to weigh losses for scene geometry and semantics. In: CVPR, pp. 7482–7491 (2018)
3. Kim, Y.: Convolutional neural networks for sentence classification. In: Moschitti, A., Pang, B., Daelemans, W. (eds.) The 2014 EMNLP, pp. 1746–1751. ACL (2014)
4. Liu, P., Qiu, X., Huang, X.: Recurrent neural network for text classification with multi-task learning. arXiv preprint arXiv:1605.05101 (2016)
5. Wu, Z., Pan, S., Chen, F., Long, G., Zhang, C., Philip, S.Y.: A comprehensive survey on graph neural networks. IEEE Trans. Neural Netw. Learn. Syst. **32**(1), 4–24 (2020)
6. Yang, Y., et al.: ServeNet: a deep neural network for web services classification. In: 2020 ICWS, pp. 168–175. IEEE (2020)
7. Zhu, Y., Liu, M., Tu, Z., Su, T., Wang, Z.: SRASLR: a novel social relation aware service label recommendation model. In: 2021 ICWS, pp. 87–96. IEEE (2021)

Blockchain

Non-disclosing Credential On-chaining for Blockchain-Based Decentralized Applications

Jonathan Heiss[1(✉)], Robert Muth[2], Frank Pallas[1], and Stefan Tai[1]

[1] Information Systems Engineering, Technische Universität, Berlin, Germany
{j.heiss,frank.pallas,tai}@tu-berlin.de
[2] Distributed Security Infrastructures, Technische Universität, Berlin, Germany
muth@tu-berlin.de

Abstract. Many service systems rely on verifiable identity-related information of their users. Manipulation and unwanted exposure of this privacy-relevant information, however, must at the same time be prevented and avoided. Peer-to-peer blockchain-based decentralization with a smart contract-based execution model and verifiable off-chain computations leveraging zero-knowledge proofs promise to provide the basis for next-generation, non-disclosing credential management solutions. In this paper, we propose a novel credential on-chaining system that ensures blockchain-based transparency while preserving pseudonymity. We present a general model compliant to the W3C verifiable credential recommendation and demonstrate how it can be applied to solve existing problems that require computational identity-related attribute verification. Our zkSNARKs-based reference implementation and evaluation show that, compared to related approaches based on, e.g., CL-signatures, our approach provides significant performance advantages and more flexible proof mechanisms, underpinning our vision of increasingly decentralized, transparent, and trustworthy service systems.

Keywords: Verifiable credential · Blockchain · Zero-knowledge proof

1 Introduction

Blockchain-based Decentralized Applications (DApps) are service systems where the backend code runs on a peer-to-peer blockchain network, using smart contracts for the application logic. DApps are increasingly applied in distrusted, multi-stakeholder environments to overcome reliance and dependence on trusted and often centralized third parties (TTPs) and associated risks of failure, manipulation, or opportunistic behavior. Traditional architectures are transitioned into decentralized ones in that core functionalities provided by previously centralized TTPs are now implemented in smart contracts, which are executed on the blockchain by each peer [32]. This way, involved stakeholders do not have to trust TTPs anymore to act as intended, resulting in a service system that is more transparent and manipulation-resistant.

Even when using permissionless blockchains, a DApp may still define roles, permissions, or assets and assign them to particular users and other parties. DApps therefore depend on reliably distinguishing the users by some kind of distinct *attributes* that only a single participant or a group of users possesses and for which a *proof* can be provided. In decentralized finance (DeFi) lending DApps [30], for instance, lenders and borrowers may be required to prove possession of a valid citizenship or tax number, in IoT DApps [25], devices may have to prove official calibration or certain configuration parameters, and participants of marketplaces [20] may be required to prove creditworthiness before they are allowed to engage into trading. The attestation of such attributes can come from different *issuers* such as tax offices, calibration authorities, or credit bureaus. Parties having to prove attributes can then do so by presenting *credentials* allowing another party to *verify* the fulfillment of attribute requirements.

In state-of-the-art service systems, DApps which need to verify user attributes typically employ some off-chain authority for this purpose acting as a TTP and providing respective services. For example, DApps running on permissioned blockchains rely on identity and access management (IAM) services that are provided at platform-level through a trusted committee of nodes, e.g., the Membership Service Providers authority in Hyperledger Fabric [18]. However, in many DApps, off-chain verification of user attributes is not appropriate as it violates design goals. DeFi and marketplace DApps, for example, implement cryptocurrency-based transaction logic that may depend on the on-chain verification of user attributes. In IoT DApps that typically characterize through uncertain, dynamic, and distrusted settings, it may simply not be possible to employ an off-chain TTP service for authentication that is tamper-resistant and always online. Furthermore, many DApps call for independent verifiability of all transactions, including attribute verification, e.g., for external auditing.

Alternatively, credential verification can be implemented as smart contract-based logic as well and be executed as part of the blockchain's consensus protocol [23]. This mitigates the problems described above, however, it also introduces other challenges originating from the blockchain's natural design, most importantly related to users' privacy: While users of DApps running on permissionless blockchains can veil their identity behind pseudonymous account addresses, on-chain credential verification threatens this pseudonymity since consensus-based validation reveals confidential user attributes to the blockchain network. Existing approaches that, for example, leverage *zero-knowledge proofs* (ZKP) to keep such attributes off the blockchain, either suffer from severe performance limitations making their usage impractical [23] or are limited to a specific use case and credential type which restricts general applicability [12,14,27].

In face of the on-going debate about measures for Know-Your-Customer (KYC) and Anti-Money Laundering (AML), and consequential blockchain regulations[1,2], we consider the need for on-chain credential verification as real and technical approaches essential to pave the way for general purpose adoption of DApps

---

[1] https://www.sec.gov/news/statement/crenshaw-defi-20211109.
[2] https://www.europarl.europa.eu/news/en/press-room/20220627IPR33919.

as well as presenting an alternative to using traditional off-chain IAM services. To this end, we herein provide an approach to make attribute-specific user credentials verifiable on the blockchain while preserving pseudonymity properties. We, thereby, make three individual contributions:

- First, we propose a novel credential on-chaining system. This system leverages *verifiable off-chain computations* (VOC) [9] for executing logic on confidential identity attributes through the holder and for only presenting a non-revealing ZKP to the peer network.
- Second, we show how the proposed model can be employed to solve typical computational identity-related problems by proposing different types of credential conditions to be verified.
- Third, we demonstrate technical feasibility by providing a reference implementation for each type of condition using ZoKrates [11], a tool for realizing VOC on Ethereum [31]. Our implementation exhibits significant performance advantages over on-chain verification of established *Camenisch-Lysyanskaya* (CL) signature-based ZKPs [23].

In the remainder of this paper, we first describe relevant concepts and related work in Sect. 2. Then, we present a general system design for credential on-chaining in Sect. 3. On this basis, in Sect. 4 we show how to apply the design to realize different proof types. Details on the implementation and an evaluation based on our proofs-of-concept (PoC) are described in Sect. 5. Finally, we conclude with some final remarks in Sect. 6.

2   Preliminaries

As relevant preliminaries, we first introduce the core idea of on-chaining credentials underlying our approach along with its benefits and challenges. Then, we describe existing concepts and approaches that are relevant to our contributions.

2.1   On-chaining Verifiable Credentials

Within this paper, on-chaining verifiable credentials describes the process of providing credentials originating from off-chain to smart contracts in a verifiable manner. Instead of having a blockchain-external entity checking the validity of an attribute-based credential (such as holding a particular citizenship or being creditworthy) and acting as a centralized TTP service provider, the issuer-generated credential is verified on-chain as a smart contract-based transaction that is validated through the blockchain's consensus protocol by each peer in the network.

Benefits: For DApps, on-chain credential verification has some considerable benefits over off-chain verification:

- *Transparency:* Credentials are independently verifiable throughout and, in public blockchains, even beyond the network.
- *Tamper-resistance:* While off-chain authorities could previously manipulate credential verification unnoticedly, on-chain verification prevents this.

- *Passive verification:* The credential verification is self-executed and automatically verified by all blockchain peers to maintain global consensus [1].
- *Availability:* It is not required to have an off-chain authority to be online all the time. Availability is guaranteed by the blockchain network.
- *Immediate usage:* The output of the credential verification can immediately be used on-chain as part of the smart contract-based application logic.

Challenges: On-chain credential verification also introduces challenges that originate from the nature of blockchains.

- *Privacy:* Given that the blockchain-based system is a fully replicated one with full transparency and an immutable, append-only data structure, confidential information contained in credentials must not be revealed on-chain.
- *Verification costs:* Given fully redundant transaction execution as part of expensive consensus protocols, e.g., Proof-of-Work, the computational costs for verifying credentials on-chain should be kept at a minimum.
- *On-/Off-chain interactions:* Given an isolated execution environment that restricts interactivity with off-chain systems, the DApp cannot directly call the issuer to check, e.g., credential authenticity. Therefore, credentials must become non-interactively verifiable and function without trusted oracles [16].

2.2   Related Work and Concepts

Our contributions build upon the concepts of *verifiable credentials* (VC), *anonymous credentials* (AC), and *verifiable off-chain computations* (VOC), and intersect with related work around these existing concepts.

Verifiable Credentials: The W3C recommendation for VCs [28] advocates a user-centric identity management model where claims on identity attributes are assumed to be attested by a trusted *issuer* and issued as VC to the *holder* where they are securely stored, e.g., in a wallet. The *holder* can then independently present a selection of verifiable attribute claims as a *verifiable presentation* (VP) to a *verifier*, as illustrated in Fig. 1. Different from the objective of this paper, the VC model assumes the verifier to be executed off the blockchain. Blockchains are applied only to realize *Verifiable Data Registries* (VDR) that are used to store public artifacts, such as identifiers, public keys, or *credential schemas* (CS) which describe what VC consist of and how they are verified.

Blockchain-based implementations of this model include credential management systems such as uPort [24], Jolocom [19], or Hyperledger Indy [17]. None of these does, however, implement on-chain credential verification.

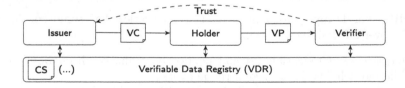

Fig. 1. W3C verifiable credential model

Anonymous Credentials: AC have been proposed to enable the verification of credentials without revealing confidential user attributes to the verifier. A ZKP is generated to convince a verifier about certain aspects of the credential. Common proof types for credentials include *range proofs* to verify that a value is within a given range or *set membership proofs* to verify that an element is part of a predefined set [3].

CL signature-based ZKPs [4] are a well-known approach to AC that have been implemented, for example, in IBM's attribute-based credential system, Identity Mixer [5], which, in turn, has been adopted in Hyperledger Indy [17]. As another zero-knowledge protocol class that distinguishes through non-interactivity and succinct proof size, zkSNARKs (zero-knowledge succinct non-interactive argument of knowledge) have also been applied to enable non-revealing credential verification [26].

Verifiable Off-chain Computation: Another essential concept for on-chain credential verification is VOC [9] which has been introduced to mitigate blockchain's limitations regarding privacy and scalability. Here, the result of any off-chain computation can be verified on-chain without revealing private inputs to the computation. VOC has conceptually be extended in [15] where it is considered as an intermediate pre-processing step in data on-chaining workflows between an off-chain data source and an on-chain verifier. To technically realize VOC, ZoKrates [11] has been proposed, a toolbox and language for the construction of on-chain verifiable ZKPs based on zkSNARKs.

ZoKrates has been adopted in various use-cases to enable non-revealing authentication of DApp users. Examples include smart vehicle authentication at charging stations [12], user authentication for car sharing [14], or patient authentication in health care [27]. These works so far do, however, focus on the verification of a specific identity attribute only, consider comparably trivial authentication schemes, or lack general applicability. A rather general approach to on-chain credential verification is described in [23]. Here, it has been shown how CL signature-based ZKPs can be verified on-chain, albeit with considerable performance limitations currently rendering the approach impractical.

3   System Design

Seizing on the previously described challenges and limitations of existing approaches, in this section, we present our credential on-chaining system that applies VOC [9] as pre-processing step [15] to the W3C recommendations for VCs [28]. Instead of verifying the issuer-generated VC directly on-chain, it is pre-processed by the user as a VOC that returns a ZKP which can be verified by the DApp in a non-disclosing manner.

As illustrated in Fig. 2, our system works along four stages, each of them executed by a different system role.

1. During **attestation** which is considered a pre-requisite of our system the issuer signs identity claims contained in a credential and sends them as VC to the user.

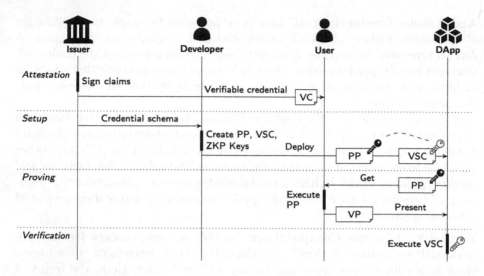

Fig. 2. Credential on-chaining system overview which demonstrates all steps from initial signing credentials to the verification of a corresponding verifiable presentation

2. The **setup** describes all activities executed by the developer to create the artifacts required for proving and verification, i.e., the *proof program* (PP) that implements the verification logic as a VOC, the *ZKP keys* used to sign and verify the verifiable presentation (VP), and the *verifier smart contract* (VSC) that is required by the DApp to verify the VP.
3. During **proving**, a DApp user creates a VP from her VC using the PP and the *proving key* (PP_{key}).
4. The **verification** of the VP consisting of a ZKP and a computational result is executed on-chain by the VSC using the verification key (VSC_{key}).

3.1   Attestation

During the attestation, the issuer creates a VC from a *credential* (CR) according to a public credential schema: $\texttt{Attest}(CR, SK) \rightarrow (VC)$. A CR consists of a set of *claims* (CL) such that $CR = \{CL_1, ..., CL_n\}$. A claim, in turn, consists of a 3-tuple comprising subject, attribute, and value, e.g., (Alice, age, 31). The issuer signs the credential with its individual *issuer secret key* SK which can be verified with the corresponding *issuer public key* PK. To enable users to select single claims from a VC (and, hence, enable *selective disclosure*) the issuer needs to sign each claim of a credential individually instead of all claims collectively. This results in a VC consisting of a set of *verifiable claims* (VCL) such that $VC = \{VCL_1, ..., VCL_n\}$. A VCL in turn consists of a claim-signature pair: $VCL = \{CL, SIG\}$. Once attested through the issuer, the VC is stored by the holder in her personal wallet. While VCs of different issuers may be used, for simplicity, we describe the following stages assuming a single issuer.

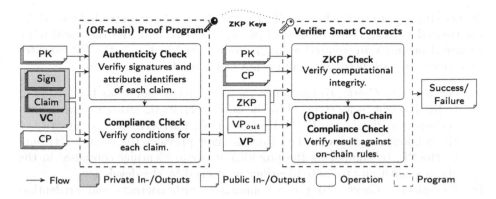

Fig. 3. In- and outputs of the proof program and the verifier smart contracts

3.2 Setup

During the setup, the developer creates required artifacts which enable the construction and verification of ZKPs. Therefore, she obtains the public credential schema from the issuer (or indirectly from a public VDR as described in Sect. 2.2). Without compromising generality of our approach, we consider a zkSNARKs-based setup that takes the technological capabilities of ZoKrates [11] into account and consists of the following three steps:

First, the verification logic and required input types are implemented for an execution environment that represents the PP and enables the assertion of computational correctness through a ZKP. Using ZoKrates, its high-level language can be leveraged for this purpose which compiles into an executable constraint system represented in the ZoKrates Intermediate Representation format [11].

Second, the developer generates the *ZKP keys* from the PP : $\text{KeyGen}(\text{PP}) \rightarrow (\text{PP}_{key}, \text{VSC}_{key})$. The ZKP keys are bound to the PP and enable a prover, here the user, to create a verifiable PP-specific ZKP with the proving key (PP_{key}) and a verifier, here the DApp, to verify the ZKP with the corresponding verification key (VSC_{key}).

As a third step, the developer implements the VPs-verification logic in the *verifier smart contracts* (VSC), integrates all artifacts, i.e., the PP, the PK, the VSC, the VSC_{key}, into the DApp and deploys it. While the deployed DApp only requires the VSC and the VSC_{key} for the verification, it makes the PP and PK, which are required for proving, accessible to the users.

3.3 Proving

In the proving stage, the user first obtains the PP and PP_{key} from the DApp and selects the required VCLs from her personal wallet. Based on that, she executes the proving: $\text{Prove}(\text{PP}_{key}, \text{In}_{pub}, \text{In}_{priv}) \rightarrow (\text{ZKP}, \text{VP}_{out})$. The PP takes two types of inputs: *public inputs* (In_{pub}) are required on-chain for ZKP verification and are, hence, revealed to the blockchain network whereas *private inputs* (In$_{priv}$) are kept off-chain. To keep confidential attributes hidden, VCLs are treated as In$_{priv}$, but *conditional parameters* (CP) and PKs that need to be reviewed on-chain are treated as In$_{pub}$. As depicted in Fig. 3, the PP executes two checks on each verifiable claim contained in a VC:

(i) *Authenticity Check*: To guarantee that a verifiable claim has been attested to by the right issuer (trusted by the developer), its signature is verified with the issuer's PK: F_{auth}: (VCL, PK) $\rightarrow$ (*bool*). Furthermore, the integrity of the attribute is reviewed, i.e., that the user provides the correct attribute to the PP, by comparing the provided attribute identifier contained in the claim against an attribute identifier predefined by the developer.

(ii) *Compliance Check*: To prove compliance with context- and credential-specific conditions that the developer defines based on the DApp logic, the CL's attribute value is checked against some CP, e.g., age higher than 21: F_{comp}: (CL, CP) $\rightarrow$ (*bool*)

The output is a VP that contains a ZKP for the correct ZKP execution and the corresponding *computional output* (VP$_{out}$), e.g., a boolean value indicating if the Authenticity and Compliance Checks succeed. The VP does not contain In$_{priv}$ anymore; hence, it can be presented without risking the VCs confidentiality.

3.4 Verification

The verification is executed on-chain through the verifier smart contracts (VSCs): Verify(VSC$_{key}$, ZKP, VP$_{out}$, CP, PK) $\rightarrow$ (*bool*). Inputs to the VSCs are the VP consisting of the ZKP and the VP$_{out}$ and the public inputs used for proving, i.e., the conditional parameters CP and the issuers' public key PK. As depicted in Fig. 3, the VSCs implement two checks:

(i) *ZKP Check*: To verify that the proving has correctly been executed on the expected public inputs, the ZKP Check is executed on the VP and the public inputs: F_{zkp}: (ZKP, VP$_{out}$, PK$_i$, CP) $\rightarrow$ (*bool*).

(ii) *Compliance Check*: Optionally, an additional on-chain Compliance Check is executed on VP$_{out}$ as, for example, required for the Uniqueness Proof mechanism presented in Sect. 4.4.

4 Application

Given the proposed credential on-chaining system, in this section, we demonstrate the system's proving abilities through a set of proof mechanisms. On the one hand, we show how established concepts, e.g., range and membership proofs [3], can be realized with our system, on the other hand, we introduce novel mechanisms to on-chain credential verification in DApps, namely, relative time-dependent proofs and uniqueness proofs.

To describe the proof mechanisms, we set a particular focus on the off- and on-chain Compliance Checks (CompCheck) and the conditional parameters

(CP) used to validate credential-specific conditions. In contrast to the off-chain Authenticity Check (AuthCheck) and the on-chain ZKP Check which are conceptionally application-agnostic, the CompChecks are application-specific.

4.1 Range and Equality Proofs

A DApp Requires a Numeric Attribute to be in a Specific Range Indicated Through an Upper and/or Lower Bound. This may, for example, be required in referendum DApps [22], to guarantee that only DApp users in a specific zip code range are eligible to participate.

Off-chain Proving: For range proofs, the CompCheck validates if the attribute value is within the range defined by the developer through one or two boundaries. Given a Turing-complete language as with ZoKrates, range proofs can be implemented as simple predicated statements. CPs are range boundaries that are provided as public inputs to the PP. Thereby, the same PP can be used for different ranges simply by setting different range boundaries as public inputs.

On-chain Verification: Since the range boundaries are required as public inputs for the ZKP Check, it can independently be verified that the range has been set correctly. No further on-chain CompCheck is required.

Discussion: A range proof will not reveal identity attributes to the verifier as they are defined as private inputs, but if the boundaries of a range proof are too small, the private attribute can be approximated or even completely exposed. It is also possible that past proofs with different boundaries can be combined, so that the intersections of all proofs reveal insights of the VC or even the exact attribute value. This is especially dangerous with a publicly available transaction history, e.g., in permissionless blockchains. To avoid this, proofs should not be linkable to each other or with a single blockchain account.

A special type of range is the *equality proof* which can be implemented with the described range proof mechanism. Here, the range is set to a single value that needs to match the user's attribute value. While we consider equality proofs with private attributes pointless since a successful verification discloses the attribute on-chain, DApps may have reasons to require clear text attributes from a user. However, once published, attributes are publicly revealed and cannot be removed due to the permanent nature of a blockchain, so we advise the greatest attention to privacy for such proofs. Also, it needs to be mentioned, that while equality proofs can easily be realized with our system, there are more efficient approaches, e.g., by verifying the issuer's signature directly on-chain.

4.2 Relative Time-Dependent Proofs

A DApp requires a date- or time-based attribute to be in a range that has boundaries relative to the current date or timestamp. This is, for example, required if the users' age needs to be checked or if an expiration date of a credential needs to be verified. Realizing such proofs with our system is challenging in that a timestamp is required off-chain for ZKP generation, however, the off-chain timestamp is not verified on-chain as part of the consensus protocol and, hence, can be manipulated unnoticedly. To describe our approach to that, we assume that a DApp needs to verify that the age of its users is above 21, i.e., a range proof with a single boundary, and the required time-dependent user attribute is the date of birth (cf. Fig. 4).

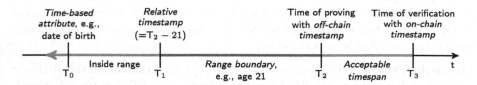

Fig. 4. Age verification scenario for time-dependent proof mechanisms

Off-chain Proving: CPs are the *range boundary*, e.g., age 21, that is predefined by the developer, and the *relative timestamp* that is pre-calculated by the user as the current date minus the range boundary, i.e., $2022 - 21 = 2001$. For simplicity, timestamps are here indicated in years, although more fine-grained timestamps are applicable. Both, the relative timestamp and the range boundary, are provided to the PP as public inputs. As part of the off-chain CompCheck, the PP compares the relative timestamp to the date of birth that is part of the VC and, hence, provided as private inputs to the PP. If the relative timestamp is larger than the date of birth, the off-chain CompCheck is successful.

On-chain Verification: On-chain, an additional CompCheck is required to make sure that the off-chain timestamp has not been faked by the user. Therefore, the DApp takes the on-chain timestamp from the current block header which can be considered trusted as it is validated through the blockchain's consensus protocol, and compares it against the off-chain timestamp. If on- and off-chain timestamp are within an *acceptable timespan* pre-determined by the developer the on-chain CompCheck succeeds.

Discussion: Relative time-dependent proofs are broadly applicable, especially considering their usage for validating expiration dates of credentials, e.g., for driver's licenses or credit cards. In this case, the expiration date needs to be signed by the issuer together with the corresponding attribute(s) to make sure that both belong together. However, it must also be noted that only rough periods can be verified with the proposed mechanism. For example, the acceptable time span between proving and verification is strongly dependent on peculiarities of the applied blockchain's consensus protocol, e.g., block interval and confirmation time, which may vary in orders of several minutes.

4.3   Set Membership Proofs

A DApp Requires that a Holder's Attribute Value val is in a predefined finite set $S = \{s_1, s_2, ..., s_n\}$ such that val $\in S$. Such proofs can be used to show that a holder belongs to a set of authorized users in permissioned settings as, for example, required in referendum DApps where eligible participants are, a priori, equipped with a referendum voucher. To prove set membership without revealing *val* on-chain, we leverage path proofs in Merkle Trees similar to the one described here[3].

Off-chain Proving: In addition to the user's set attribute contained in the set that is provided as private input, the PP requires three CPs that need to be pre-computed by the holder and are provided as public inputs to the PP: (1) the root hash of the Merkle Tree constructed over S, (2) an array of hash values situated on the path from the leaf hash (hashed attribute), to the root hash, and (3) a same-size array of left-right indicators that determine in which order two child hashes are concatenated as the pre-image of the parent hash. During the PP's CompCheck, first the attribute's hash is calculated. Then, the PP iterates over both, the hash and indicator arrays, and, in each iteration, calculates the next upper hash in the Merkle Tree. If the resulting hash is equal to the root hash provided as public input, set membership is proven.

On-chain Verification: On-chain, correctness of the PP computation and its public inputs is reviewed during the ZKP Check. No further on-chain CompCheck is required.

Discussion: Different types of set membership proofs are well-known and have extensively been discussed in the literature [2, 21]. We consider the set entries to be confidential such that they must not be revealed on the blockchain. An access list for DApp users generated off-chain, for example, must not reveal the user identifiers, e.g., to prevent attackers to simply use them for registration. In the proposed mechanism, only hashes of entries are revealed on-chain but the pre-images which are required for successful ZKP generation remain off-chain, kept secret by the user. It should be noted that privacy guarantees become stronger with an increasing size of set S, although the verification complexity grows only logarithmically due to the tree data structure.

In some cases, set membership proofs can be used interchangeably with range proofs. If DApp users need to prove that they live in a specific city without revealing it, a set membership proof can be leveraged that builds upon city identifiers in a given state or a range proof can be constructed based on the zip code applicable for the city.

4.4   Uniqueness Proof

A DApp Requires a Unique Pseudonymous Identifier (UPI), to Distinguish Different Users. This allows DApps to prevent Sybil-attacks [7] and to establish user accountability, e.g., function calls can be mapped to users even if different account addresses are used. Such UPIs are, for example, required if user-specific access control policies need to be verified as part of the DApp. However, with

---

[3] https://github.com/Zokrates/ZoKrates/tree/deploy/zokrates_cli/examples/merkleTree.

respect to the user privacy, the UPI must provide unlinkability (1) to off-chain activities of the user, i.e., a relation to the *real* off-chain identity must not be revealed, and (2) to on-chain activities of the user, i.e., UPIs of the same user used in different DApps must not be linkable with each other.

For this mechanism, we assume that a user can uniquely be identified through the issuer, either through a single unique identifier, e.g., a tax identification number, or through a set of attributes that jointly enable unique identification. Latter is assumed in the following. Furthermore, we assume that a unique DApp identifier is available, e.g., the address of the verifier smart contract.

Off-chain Proving: The set of predefined attributes is provided to the PP by the user as private inputs and individually validated as part of the AuthCheck. As a single conditional parameter, the unique DApp identifier is provided as public input. The UPI construction is executed as part of the CompCheck: The attribute values and the DApp identifier are concatenated in a predefined order and the resulting concatenation is hashed representing the UPI: $\mathrm{Hash}(att_1, ..., att_n, ID_{DApp})$. Together with the ZKP, the UPI is returned as VP.

On-chain Verification: On receiving the VP, first, the ZKP is checked together with all public inputs, i.e., the DApp identifier and the public keys. A successful validation attests correct construction of the UPI, but unique user registration has not yet been proven. Therefore, the DApp checks during the on-chain CompCheck if the UPI has already been registered in a *user registry* that is maintained by the DApp and contains the UPIs and account addresses of all registered users. If the UPI is already part of the list, the CompCheck fails. Otherwise, the UPI is recorded to the list and the user is officially registered.

Discussion: The proposed mechanism provides unlinkability to off- and on-chain activities of users: since the preimage of the hash is a concatenation of both, user attributes and the DApp identifier, the attributes applied for UPI construction cannot be traced back and the UPI changes for each DApp that a user registers at. This provides for user privacy and makes the mechanism applicable to various DApp contexts where uniqueness is required, e.g., votings, token airdrops, and access control.

However, the mechanism only provides uniqueness of users if the previous assumptions hold. If the attributes change, the user can create a different UPI and use it for registering twice with different blockchain accounts, which eliminates Sybil-resistance.

5   Evaluation

To evaluate our credential on-chaining system and its applicability to the proposed proof mechanisms, in this section, we first provide technical details for the ZoKrates-based implementations of the proof mechanisms, then analyze performance aspects, particularly in comparison with a similar CL-signature-based approach, and finally discuss open issues and refinements.

Table 1. Gas costs, artifact sizes, and execution times for proof generation and verification with ZoKrates.

Proof	TX cost (gas)	Witness (s)	Setup (s)	Proof (s)	Compiled (MB)	PP_{key} (MB)	VSC_{key} (KB)
Equality	511 k	4	63	13	352	38	8
Range	532 k	3	62	14	352	38	8
Uniqueness	675 k	8	89	27	864	47	12
Rel. time	627 k	4	61	14	352	38	8
Membership	532 k	6	147	26	656	90	8

5.1 Implementation

We implement each proof mechanisms prototypically to demonstrate the technical feasibility of our proposal and provide the source codes on GitHub[4].

For *attestation* we provide a Python script which constructs a EDDSA signature on a test credential – employing a Python library for ZoKrates-compatible cryptographic instructions[5] – and returns a VC. For the *setup*, we implement the PP using the ZoKrates language which can be compiled using the ZoKrates command line interface (CLI) which also enables the creation of the ZKP keys (i.e., PP_{key} and VSC_{key}) and the verifier smart contract VSC. Once the artifacts are created, the *proving* is executed in two CLI-aided steps: First, a *witness* is generated with the command `compute-witness` which represents an input-specific variable assignment of the executable constraint system. Second, the ZKP is created based on the witness and the proving key with the command `generate-proof`. For *verification*, a Solidity VSC that is automatically generated by means of the ZoKrates toolbox implements the routines required to verify the ZKP in the `verytx()` function using the integrated VSC_{key}. The optional on-chain Compliance Check is implemented in a separate smart contract.

To execute these processes we provide scripts that also measure the execution times, the artifact sizes, and the verification costs with the latter being enabled through a Truffle[6] test project on a simulated Ethereum [31] blockchain.

5.2 Performance Analysis

Based on our ZoKrates-based reference implementations, we execute an experimental test case for each proof mechanism using test credentials that consist of a single claim, such that, the Authenticity and Compliance check are only executed once. All experiments were executed on a MacBook Pro (13", 2018) with a 2.3 GHz Quad-Core Intel i5 and 8 GB memory.

ZoKrates-Based Credential On-chaining Proof Mechanisms. The measurements of our ZoKrates proof mechanism test cases are depicted in Table 1

---

[4] https://github.com/JonathanHeiss/ZoKrates-Credential-Verification.
[5] https://github.com/Zokrates/pycrypto.
[6] https://trufflesuite.com.

Table 2. Gas costs for on-chain proof verification with the same test credentials as in [23] for our implementation approach and with on-chain CL-signature verification.

Proof	ZoKrates	CL-signature
Test: equality	593 k	32,001 k
Test: range	521 k	84,826 k
Test: combined	870 k	84,033 k

which shows the corresponding blockchain transaction costs in Gas[7], execution runtimes in seconds, and artifact file sizes in MB.

The *transaction costs* range between 511 k and 675 k Gas. The costs are higher if more public inputs are passed to the PP, e.g., compared to the equality proof, the range proof additionally requires CPs. Furthermore, if an additional compliance check is executed as, for example, for uniqueness and relative time-dependent proofs, transaction costs increase as well.

Execution times are measured for the ZKP setup, which in ZoKrates is required for generating the ZKP keys, and the proving, which consists of the witness and proof generation. Most time-intensive is the setup which, however, is only executed once by the developer and, hence, does not impact the operation of the system where different users submit VPs to the DApp. For operations, the proof generation time takes the longest, however, the longest proving time does only slightly exceed half a minute considering witness and proof generation together. Regarding the different proving mechanisms, it can, as expected, be observed that with increasing computational complexity, the execution times increase as well. An in-depth analysis about the behavior of ZoKrates for varying inputs and computations can be found in [8].

The *artifacts size* varies between artifact types, e.g., the compiled PP size lies between 352 and 864 MB and the PP_{key} size between 38 and 90 MB, whereas the VSC_{key} size is considerably smaller, ranging between 8 and 12 KB. This makes the latter suitable to be used on-chain where resources are scarce. Consequences of large artifacts regarding the system deployment are discussed in Sect. 5.3.

Comparison to CL-Signatures. Furthermore, to establish comparability of performance behavior beyond our own proof mechanisms, we implement and conduct three test cases that mirror the experimental evaluation of smart contract-based verification with CL-signatures as described in [23]. These test cases are executed on multiple attributes and implement (1) an equality proof, (2) a range proof, and (3) a combination of both.

In comparison, as depicted in Table 2, with our approach, we are able to reduce the transactions costs in Gas by a factor of $\approx$ 50 to 100 in all three test cases. This distinct performance improvement shows that currently, in face of expensive on-chain computations, zkSNARKs are better suited for *on-chain* credential verification than CL-signatures-based approaches.

---

[7] Gas is an Ethereum-specific metric for measuring blockchain transaction complexity.

5.3   Discussion

Deployment: Referring to Table 1, we consider the size of the PP and the proving key as too large to be stored on the blockchain. Consequently, provisioning of both artifacts to the user needs to be solved differently. As one solution, we propose to apply a content addressable storage pattern [10] as for example realizable with IPFS and adopted for managing off-chain assets associated with Non-fungible Tokens (NFTs). Instead of storing both artifacts on-chain, only the artifacts' hash is stored on-chain and serves as a pointer to the artifacts that are stored off-chain in IPFS. By comparing the on-chain hash-based address with the hash of the off-chain stored artifacts, integrity can be reviewed. However, availability is not guaranteed per se [6]. Therefore, an additional protocol, e.g., Filecoin, could be applied that introduces redundant storage and provides incentives for keeping off-chain files available.

Revocation: A credential may be required to be revoked by the issuer, e.g., if a driver license is invalidated by a public authority. Since revocation is not in the scope of this work, we propose to leverage dedicated blockchain-based revocation systems as an extension to our credential on-chaining system similar to the ones proposed for educational credentials in [29]. Also, in some cases, revocation can be replaced with expiration dates on credentials which can be realized with the relative time-dependent proofs (see Sect. 4.2).

Attacks: For identification purposes, especially for secret credentials, *replay attacks* render a severe problem on blockchains. Since proofs become available to everyone on the blockchain after the on-chain verification, they can be used by anybody else on the blockchain to fake a different identity or to gain unauthorized access. To address this problem, developers can leverage the uniqueness proofs that enable the DApp to identify repeated submissions of the same proof from different users. Also, we recommend to use a proving scheme other than Groth16 [13] which is vulnerable to *malleability attacks*, or to implement countermeasures.

6   Conclusion

How can identity-related attribute information and computations on such information be shared in both a fully transparent but pseudonymity-preserving manner? This question is not easy to answer, especially in service systems that comprise multiple autonomous service providers and consumers for which no mutual trust assumptions can and should be made. State-of-the-art, typically centralized trusted third parties providing IAM services, stop short when it comes to the trust assumptions expected and the associated risks of manipulation or opportunistic behavior existing.

In this paper, we present a novel, non-disclosing credential management system that builds on peer-to-peer decentralization through blockchain, smart contract-based execution, and VOC using ZKPs. We introduce a W3C recommendation-compliant VC model, demonstrate and discuss typical identity-related computational problems that can now be addressed in such settings, and show technical feasibility through reference implementations with a cost and performance assessment. The significant transaction cost improvements towards a comparable approach based on established CL-signatures underline the relevance of our approach for its application in practical settings.

Our work is in line with prior work on data on-chaining and contributes to the larger question on what data and what computation to handle on-chain, that is, on the blockchain when a blockchain is part of a larger service system, and what data and what computation to handle off-chain – that is, anywhere but the blockchain – while ensuring and not violating key system properties related to performance, security, trustworthiness, and other system quality criteria.

References

1. Azouvi, S., Al-Bassam, M., Meiklejohn, S.: Who am I? Secure identity registration on distributed ledgers. In: Garcia-Alfaro, J., Navarro-Arribas, G., Hartenstein, H., Herrera-Joancomartí, J. (eds.) ESORICS/DPM/CBT -2017. LNCS, vol. 10436, pp. 373–389. Springer, Cham (2017). https://doi.org/10.1007/978-3-319-67816-0_21
2. Benarroch, D., Campanelli, M., Fiore, D., Gurkan, K., Kolonelos, D.: Zero-knowledge proofs for set membership: efficient, succinct, modular. In: Borisov, N., Diaz, C. (eds.) FC 2021. LNCS, vol. 12674, pp. 393–414. Springer, Heidelberg (2021). https://doi.org/10.1007/978-3-662-64322-8_19
3. Camenisch, J., Chaabouni, R., Shelat, A.: Efficient protocols for set membership and range proofs. In: Pieprzyk, J. (ed.) ASIACRYPT 2008. LNCS, vol. 5350, pp. 234–252. Springer, Heidelberg (2008). https://doi.org/10.1007/978-3-540-89255-7_15
4. Camenisch, J., Lysyanskaya, A.: A signature scheme with efficient protocols. In: Cimato, S., Persiano, G., Galdi, C. (eds.) SCN 2002. LNCS, vol. 2576, pp. 268–289. Springer, Heidelberg (2003). https://doi.org/10.1007/3-540-36413-7_20
5. Camenisch, J., Van Herreweghen, E.: Design and implementation of the idemix anonymous credential system. In: Proceedings of the 9th ACM Conference on Computer and Communications Security (2002)
6. Daniel, E., Tschorsch, F.: IPFS and friends: a qualitative comparison of next generation peer-to-peer data networks. IEEE Commun. Surv, Tutor. (2022)
7. Douceur, J.R.: The sybil attack. In: Druschel, P., Kaashoek, F., Rowstron, A. (eds.) IPTPS 2002. LNCS, vol. 2429, pp. 251–260. Springer, Heidelberg (2002). https://doi.org/10.1007/3-540-45748-8_24
8. Eberhardt, J.: Scalable and privacy-preserving off-chain computations. Doctoral thesis, Technische Universität Berlin (2021)
9. Eberhardt, J., Heiss, J.: Off-chaining models and approaches to off-chain computations. In: Proceedings of the 2Nd Workshop on Scalable and Resilient Infrastructures for Distributed Ledgers. SERIAL 2018. ACM (2018)
10. Eberhardt, J., Tai, S.: On or off the blockchain? Insights on off-chaining computation and data. In: De Paoli, F., Schulte, S., Broch Johnsen, E. (eds.) ESOCC 2017. LNCS, vol. 10465, pp. 3–15. Springer, Cham (2017). https://doi.org/10.1007/978-3-319-67262-5_1

11. Eberhardt, J., Tai, S.: ZoKrates - scalable privacy-preserving off-chain computations. In: IEEE International Conference on Internet of Things (iThings) and IEEE Green Computing and Communications (GreenCom) and IEEE Cyber, Physical and Social Computing (CPSCom) and IEEE Smart Data (SmartData) (2018)

12. Gabay, D., Akkaya, K., Cebe, M.: A privacy framework for charging connected electric vehicles using blockchain and zero knowledge proofs. In: IEEE 44th LCN Symposium on Emerging Topics in Networking, pp. 66–73 (2019)

13. Groth, J.: On the size of pairing-based non-interactive arguments. In: Fischlin, M., Coron, J.-S. (eds.) EUROCRYPT 2016. LNCS, vol. 9666, pp. 305–326. Springer, Heidelberg (2016). https://doi.org/10.1007/978-3-662-49896-5_11

14. Gudymenko, I., et al.: Privacy-preserving blockchain-based systems for car sharing leveraging zero-knowledge protocols. In: IEEE International Conference on Decentralized Applications and Infrastructures (DAPPS) (2020)

15. Heiss, J., Busse, A., Tai, S.: Trustworthy pre-processing of sensor data in data on-chaining workflows for blockchain-based IoT applications. In: Hacid, H., Kao, O., Mecella, M., Moha, N., Paik, H. (eds.) ICSOC 2021. LNCS, vol. 13121, pp. 133–149. Springer, Cham (2021). https://doi.org/10.1007/978-3-030-91431-8_9

16. Heiss, J., Eberhardt, J., Tai, S.: From oracles to trustworthy data on-chaining systems. In: IEEE International Conference on Blockchain (2019)

17. Hyperledger Indy-SDK Repository: Indy walkthrough - a developer guide for building indy clients using libindy (2018). https://github.com/hyperledger/indy-sdk/blob/master/docs/getting-started/indy-walkthrough.md

18. Hyperledger White Paper Working Group: An Introduction to Hyperledger (2018). https://www.hyperledger.org/wp-content/uploads/2018/07/HL_Whitepaper_IntroductiontoHyperledger.pdf

19. JOLOCOM: A decentralized, open source solution for digital identity and access management (whitepaper) (2019). https://jolocom.io/wp-content/uploads/2019/12/Jolocom-Whitepaper-v2.1-A-Decentralized-Open-Source-Solution-for-Digital-Identity-and-Access-Management.pdf

20. Klems, M., Eberhardt, J., Tai, S., Härtlein, S., Buchholz, S., Tidjani, A.: Trustless intermediation in blockchain-based decentralized service marketplaces. In: Maximilien, M., Vallecillo, A., Wang, J., Oriol, M. (eds.) ICSOC 2017. LNCS, vol. 10601, pp. 731–739. Springer, Cham (2017). https://doi.org/10.1007/978-3-319-69035-3_53

21. Merkle, R.C.: A digital signature based on a conventional encryption function. In: Pomerance, C. (ed.) CRYPTO 1987. LNCS, vol. 293, pp. 369–378. Springer, Heidelberg (1988). https://doi.org/10.1007/3-540-48184-2_32

22. Muth, R., Eisenhut, K., Rabe, J., Tschorsch, F.: BBBlockchain: blockchain-based participation in urban development. In: eScience. IEEE (2019)

23. Muth, R., Galal, T., Heiss, J., Tschorsch, F.: Towards smart contract-based verification of anonymous credentials. Cryptology ePrint Archive (2022). https://eprint.iacr.org/2022/492

24. Naik, N., Jenkins, P.: uPort open-source identity management system: an assessment of self-sovereign identity and user-centric data platform built on blockchain. In: International Symposium on Systems Engineering. IEEE (2020)

25. Peise, M., et al.: Blockchain-based local energy grids: advanced use cases and architectural considerations. In: IEEE 18th International Conference on Software Architecture Companion (2021)

26. Schanzenbach, M., Kilian, T., Schütte, J., Banse, C.: Zklaims: privacy-preserving attribute-based credentials using non-interactive zero-knowledge techniques. In: ICETE (2). SciTePress (2019)

27. Sharma, B., Halder, R., Singh, J.: Blockchain-based interoperable healthcare using zero-knowledge proofs and proxy re-encryption. In: International Conference on COMmunication Systems and NETworkS (COMSNETS) (2020)
28. Sporny, M., Longley, D., Chadwick, D.: Verifiable credentials data model v1.1 (2021). https://w3.org/TR/vc-data-model/
29. Vidal, F.R., Gouveia, F., Soares, C.: Revocation mechanisms for academic certificates stored on a blockchain. In: 15th Iberian Conference on Information Systems and Technologies (CISTI) (2020)
30. Werner, S.M., Perez, D., Gudgeon, L., Klages-Mundt, A., Harz, D., Knottenbelt, W.J.: SoK: Decentralized finance (DeFi). arXiv (2021). https://arxiv.org/abs/2101.08778
31. Wood, G.: Ethereum: a secure decentralised generalised transaction ledger, Berlin (2021). https://github.com/ethereum/yellowpaper/tree/fabef25
32. Wu, K., Ma, Y., Huang, G., Liu, X.: A first look at blockchain-based decentralized applications. Softw. Pract. Exp. (2021)

DeepThought: A Reputation and Voting-Based Blockchain Oracle

Marco Di Gennaro[1], Lorenzo Italiano[1], Giovanni Meroni[1,2],
and Giovanni Quattrocchi[1(✉)]

[1] Dipartimento di Elettronica, Informazione e Bioingegneria,
Politecnico di Milano, Milan, Italy
marco1.digennaro@mail.polimi.it,
{lorenzo.italiano,giovanni.quattrocchi}@polimi.it
[2] DTU Compute, Technical University of Denmark, Lyngby, Denmark
giom@dtu.dk

Abstract. Thanks to built-in immutability and persistence, the blockchain is often seen as a promising technology to certify information. However, when the information does not originate from the blockchain itself, its correctness cannot be taken for granted. To address this limitation, blockchain oracles—services that validate external information before storing it in a blockchain—were introduced. In particular, when the validation cannot be automated, oracles rely on humans that collaboratively cross-check external information. In this paper, we present *DeepThought*, a distributed human-based oracle that combines voting and reputation schemes. An empirical evaluation compares *DeepThought* with a state-of-the-art solution and shows that our approach achieves greater resistance to voters corruptions in different configurations.

Keywords: Blockchain oracles · Data certification services · Voting mechanisms · Human-based services

1 Introduction

The Web 2.0 revolution made extremely easy for anyone to publish, search and retrieve information [17]. As a consequence, organizations and individuals no longer rely on specific sources of information, such as a news agency. Instead, they typically rely on search engines and social media to collect information which, in turn, they may publish after processing, or simply republish as-is.

However, this change of paradigm has also made extremely easy for inaccurate, incorrect, and sometimes forged information to be spread. A clear example of this issue is represented by the so-called "fake news" and their detrimental effect they have on society. Thus, being able to easily track the provenance of the information available on the Web and to certify its authenticity becomes paramount. Also, to avoid potential conflicts of interests, and to minimize the risk of corruption, the certification process should be carried out independently by multiple subjects.

J. Troya et al. (Eds.): ICSOC 2022, LNCS 13740, pp. 369–383, 2022.
https://doi.org/10.1007/978-3-031-20984-0_26

To this aim, blockchain-based services are seen as a good candidate. Originally intended for exchanging cryptocurrency across untrusted entities, blockchain technology evolved to also support the trusted execution of arbitrary code and the exchange of any data. In particular, the blockchain provides immutability and persistence and, as reported by Gartner [9], it can be used to track the provenance of information without a centralized authority that validates it. For example, projects such as ANSAcheck [12] and SocialTruth[1] exploit this mechanism to certify if a news article comes from an accredited news agency. However, the blockchain alone cannot guarantee the authenticity of information that is not natively created on-chain. Instead, it must be coupled with an oracle.

Oracles are services that link a blockchain with the outside world. In particular, they are responsible for providing off-chain data that can be *trusted*, that is, they come from a reliable source [6]. A sub-class of such oracles is represented by distributed and human-based ones, where humans manually check the authenticity of off-chain information. These oracles are suited for checking information that cannot be automatically verified, such as a news article. One of the most famous oracles in this class is represented by ASTRAEA [1], which makes use of voting to determine the outcome. Other approaches, such as Witnet [8], rely on the reputation of the users. However, we are not aware of any approach that combines both a voting scheme and the reputation.

In this paper, we present *DeepThought*, a protocol derived from ASTRAEA that introduces the notion of reputation to increase the level of trust of the information being provided. Compared to *ASTRAEA*, *DeepThought* makes use of a different scheme to compute the voting outcome according to the reputation of the voters. Also, *DeepThought* implements a different mechanism to reward honest voters and to punish dishonest ones. *DeepThought* can be exploited by both traditional and blockchain-based services to validate information. For example, a news website can exploit *DeepThought* to publish only verified news. Based on an empirical evaluation, *DeepThought* is more robust than *ASTRAEA*, and makes the corruption of the voting game very difficult for dishonest users.

The rest of this paper is organized as follows: Sect. 2 provides some key background information, while Sect. 3 illustrates how DeepThought works. Section 4 presents the evaluation of *DeepThought*, Sect. 5 surveys the related work and Sect. 6 concludes the paper.

2   Blockchain and Oracles

A blockchain is a distributed, immutable ledger, where transactions are secured and verified using a completely decentralized peer-to-peer network [20]. Originally, blockchains were conceived to process monetary transactions without relying on a central trusted entity. Transactions are grouped inside blocks that are created using a decentralized consensus algorithm (e.g., proof of work [16]). Each block contains a digest (i.e., a hash) of the previous block, creating a cryptographic chain of blocks that is very hard to be changed by malicious users.

---

[1] See http://www.socialtruth.eu.

Nowadays, multiple general-purpose blockchains (such as Ethereum [4]) exist. Such blockchains allow users to write so-called smart contracts [18], computer programs whose code and state are stored in the blockchain [19]. In this way, developers can write "decentralized" applications that are transparent and secure, such as ones dedicated to finance [7], supply chain [10], and collectibles [2].

Smart contracts are executed in an isolated and deterministic environment and they cannot access information generated outside of the blockchain [6]. This limitation is needed because, while data generated within the blockchain are easily verifiable (i.e., they are the output of traced user transactions), off-chain data are not and cannot be validated in an automated, general-purpose way.

To address this limitation, *oracles* were introduced. An oracle is essentially a trusted service that connects smart contracts to the external world with validated information [14]. This allows the implementation of richer blockchain applications that can access, for example, stock market fluctuations or news headlines. Oracles can be implemented in different ways, ranging from ones that use only off-chain components, to others that are built with smart contracts themselves. In the first case, off-chain components obtain information in "traditional" ways, such as by calling a web service, and post the data to the interested smart contracts. In the second case, the information is validated by a smart contract (which is part of the oracle) before being submitted to the contracts that requested it.

Oracles can be categorized using four criteria [3]: software vs hardware, inbound vs outbound, human-based vs unmanned, and centralized vs decentralized. *Software oracles* can query online sources of information such as websites, web service APIs, and public databases to supply up-to-date information to smart contracts. *Hardware oracles*, instead, have the goal to send information measured from the physical world. For example, in supply chain management, information about a container (e.g., its temperature and location) can be collected by sensors and notified to a smart contract in charge of tracking goods. *Inbound oracles* supply smart contracts with external data, whereas *outbound oracles* allow smart contracts to interact with the outside world (e.g., opening a smart lock). *Human oracles* rely on people with deep knowledge of the domain of interest to manually verify the source of information (e.g., a news article) and feed the smart contract with data. Conversely, *Unmanned oracles* process and verify the information using rules and algorithms tailored for the given domain.

An oracle could be *centralized* or *decentralized*, depending on the number of nodes that validate the information. Given that one of the major advantages of the blockchain is to remove centralized parties, decentralized oracles are usually preferred to centralized ones [6]. However, since multiple parties have to agree on the outcome, decentralized oracles introduce a consensus problem. In the literature, two main approaches have been proposed to address this issue. *Reputation-based systems* rely on information provided by parties with a different reputation that measure their reliability. The reputation is usually increased if the information provided is in line with the majority of the other parties, and decreased otherwise. In *voting-based systems*, the parties vote on the correctness of a piece of information (e.g., if the events discussed in a news article are real) by betting an amount of money. To incentivize honest behavior, if the vote is in line with the majority, the user wins a reward. Otherwise, the initial bet is lost.

3   DeepThought

DeepThought is a decentralized blockchain oracle that allows users to validate plain text statements (e.g., to discriminate if a piece of news is legit or fake) that could be then used by other smart contracts in the blockchain. *DeepThought* is the first oracle that combines a voting system derived from ASTRAEA with users' reputations to reward the most honest users and to reduce the risk of corruption caused by adversarial users or lazy voters [13]. *DeepThought* is an inbound, software oracle, and it is implemented[2] as an Ethereum smart contract written in Solidity. Finally, it is human-based because it is assumed that only humans are able to vote rationally on the validity of a plain text statement.

3.1   Users and Phases

Figure 1 shows a high-level overview of *DeepThought* along with all the main entities and interactions. In *DeepThought* there are three types of users.

Submitters are users that publish in the system so-called *propositions*. A proposition is a plain text statement that must be verified through a voting-based process by the other types of users. For example, a proposition could be a piece of news that could be either legitimate or fake. To add a proposition to the system, submitters must pay a so-called *bounty*, a fixed fee that will be used to reward the most honest voters that participated in the verification process.

Voters are users that vote on randomly selected propositions. Voters must vote TRUE if they think that the proposition contains a valid statement, or FALSE otherwise. Before submitting a vote on proposition, each voter must *stake* (i.e., lock in the smart contract) an arbitrary amount of money as guarantee for their honesty. After the voting process, if the vote of a voter matches the final outcome and the voter results among the most honest users (more details in the following), the staked amount is sent back to the user along with a reward, otherwise, it is distributed to other users.

Certifiers are users in charge of certifying the outcome of the ballots. To do so, as voters, they vote (either TRUE or FALSE) on the proposition, but unlike voters, they can choose which proposition to work on. For each vote, they have to stake an amount of money which will be returned (plus a reward) to the certifiers only if the final outcome matches their vote.

For each proposition, the voting mechanism is organized in six main phases: *submission, staking, voting, certification, reveal,* and *closing.* Beforehand, users must subscribe to the system as either submitters, voters, or certifiers. When a new user subscribes, its identifier (i.e., its blockchain address) is stored in the *DeepThought* smart contract and its reputation is set to 1.

---

[2] Source code available at https://github.com/deib-polimi/deepthought.

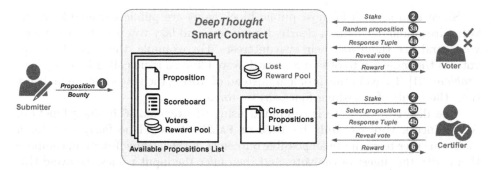

Fig. 1. *DeepThought* overview

Submission Phase. In this phase, a submitter submits a new proposition along with a bounty (action 1 in Fig. 1). The proposition is added to the list of *available propositions*, a data structure persisted by the *DeepThought* smart contract, and becomes available for the *voting phase*.

Staking Phase. Before being able to a vote a proposition, each voter and certifier must stake an arbitrary amount of money (action 2 in Fig. 1). That amount will be regained along with a reward in case of honest and correct votes. Voters must stake an amount s in the range (min_s_v, max_s_v) defined when the oracle is deployed. Instead, certifiers stake an amount s' in the range (min_c_v, max_c_v) where $min\_c_v > max\_s_v$. In this way, certifiers always stake more money than voters and they are incentivized to pick propositions that they are experts on. The reward sent (eventually) to certifiers is higher than the ones of voters (i.e., the higher the stake, the higher the risk, the higher the reward). In the next phases, each vote is weighted proportionally to the stake and the reputation of the user.

Voting Phase. Once the proposition is submitted, a set of N voters is randomly selected to participate in the voting phase (action 3a in Fig. 1). Note that a voter can be randomly selected multiple times for the same proposition and, in this case, will be able to vote more than once. Being smart contracts deterministic by design, pseudo-random functions are hard to be implemented with them. In our prototype, we implemented a pseudo-random function that relies on the digest of values that are very difficult, but not impossible, to be predicted. Such values are the timestamp reported in the current blockchain block, and the identifier of the node in the blockchain network that generated the current block.

When the proposition receives K votes, with $K \leq N$, the voting phase is concluded. To cast their vote, voters have to indicate the following two values.

– The actual *vote*, that is whether the proposition is TRUE or FALSE.
– A *prediction value*, which expresses the percentage of how much the voter believes that the outcome will be TRUE. For example, if the voter is certain that a news article is fake because he found some kind of evidence, he will vote False and he will set the prediction value to 0%.

Since transactions in most public blockchains are publicly available, if the votes are stored on-chain in cleartext, malicious and lazy voters could see others' votes and use them for their own interests. For example, they can decide to vote as the majority to obtain a reward, a well-known issue called *herd behavior problem* [21]. To avoid this problem, instead of storing the vote on-chain, a digest (i.e., the result of a hashing function) is stored.

The digest of the vote is computed using the keccak256 hashing function. Also, since a vote can only be TRUE or FALSE, it would be fairly easy for a malicious user to compute all possible outcomes of the hashing function, compare them with the digest of the vote, and then infer the input values. To avoid this issue, the hashing function takes as input also a *salt*, which is an arbitrary value selected by the voter and kept secret. The digest of the vote creates a so-called *response tuple* (RT), that submitted to the smart contract (action 4a in Fig. 1) and computed as follows:

$$RT = <kekkak256(\text{TRUE}|\text{FALSE}, prediction\ value, salt)> \tag{1}$$

Certification Phase. After the proposition has been submitted, and in parallel with the voting phase, certifiers can select the proposition (action 3b in Fig. 1) submit their votes (action 4b in Fig. 1) without a prediction value. Their response tuples are computed and stored in the *DeepThought* smart contract as follows:

$$RT = <kekkak256(\text{TRUE}|\text{FALSE}, salt)> \tag{2}$$

The protocol allocates a fixed amount of time (measured in the number of generated blockchain blocks within the smart contract) for the certification phase, since certifiers can decide whether to vote or not vote for a given proposition. Consequently, not all the propositions are guaranteed to have a certification.

Reveal Phase. When the certification phase ends, voters and certifiers must reveal their vote by submitting it to the smart contract (action 5 in Fig. 1) along with the *salt* used for computing the digest, and, only for the voters, the prediction value. To ensure that the revealed vote is consistent with the one cast during the voting phase, its digest is computed and compared to the one stored in the smart contract during the voting and certification phases.

Closing Phase. When all voters and certifiers reveal their vote, the proposition is moved from the *list of available propositions* to the *list of closed propositions* and its outcome is computed (either TRUE or FALSE or Unknown in case of a tie). Moreover, as detailed in the following, *DeepThought* calculates a score for each voter and creates a *scoreboard* that is used to reward (action 6 in Fig. 1) most honest users. Then, according to the outcome of the proposition, the reputation of each of all the users is updated. Being the votes revealed and stored in the smart contract, any user can check the outcome of the proposition and the voting process.

3.2 Proposition Outcome

In *DeepThought*, the reputation of voters and certifiers is key to compute the outcome of the voting and certification phases. Intuitively, reputation is used to privilege more reliable users that consistently vote correctly on past propositions. For each voter and certifier, the user reputation r ranges between 1 and max_r, which can be set during the first deployment of the *DeepThought* smart contract.

For each vote submitted by either a voter and a certifier, a *vote weight* f is computed as follows:

$$f(s, r) = [\alpha\sqrt{s} + (1 - \alpha)s]\sqrt{r} \tag{3}$$

where s is the stake submitted along with the vote and α is a value in the range $[0, 1]$ defined when the oracle is deployed. The vote weight is a sub-linear function of the submitted stake. In this way, a single voter is prevented from having dominant voting power [5] by using a larger stake. A value of α close to 1 is used to make the vote weight less dependent on the stake. Conversely, a value of α close to 0 causes the weight to be almost linear with respect to s. Instead, the reputation r scales sub-linearly. This does not affect the outcome between two users with similar reputations, but a user with a high reputation (e.g., 100), is much more significant (e.g., 10) with respect to a newly subscribed one.

Being $\bar{f}_{voters,\text{TRUE}}$ the sum of the vote weight f of all the voters that voted TRUE for a given proposition, and $\bar{f}_{voters,\text{FALSE}}$ the sum of the vote weight f of all the voters that voted FALSE, the voters outcome w_{voters} is computed as follows:

$$w_{voters} = \begin{cases} \text{TRUE} & , \ \bar{f}_{voters,\text{TRUE}} > \bar{f}_{voters,\text{FALSE}} \\ \text{FALSE} & , \ \bar{f}_{voters,\text{TRUE}} < \bar{f}_{voters,\text{FALSE}} \\ \text{Unknown} & , \ \bar{f}_{voters,\text{TRUE}} = \bar{f}_{voters,\text{FALSE}} \end{cases}$$

The certifiers outcome $w_{certifiers}$ is computed in the same way, by comparing the sum of weights of TRUE and FALSE votes.

Table 1. Proposition outcome.

Outcome			
w_{voters}	$w_{certifiers}$		
	TRUE	FALSE	Unknown
TRUE	TRUE	Unknown	TRUE
FALSE	Unknown	FALSE	FALSE
Unknown	Unknown	Unknown	Unknown

As shown in Table 1, the outcome of the proposition is computed from w_{voters} and $w_{certifiers}$. If w_{voters} coincides with $w_{certifiers}$, the proposition outcome is the same, otherwise, the outcome is Unknown. In case of the absence of certifiers, or their disagreement, the oracle outcome will be exclusively decided by voters.

Every time a proposition is closed, if the vote of a user matches the outcome the reputation is increased by one, or decreased by one otherwise. Note that a voter may vote multiple times on the same proposition. In this case, the voter is assumed to have voted TRUE (overall) if his/her/their sum of TRUE votes weight is greater than FALSE ones, or vice-versa. The reputation is then modified accordingly.

In the case of an Unknown outcome, the reputation of the voters is not modified, while the reputation of the certifiers is decremented by one.

3.3   Reward

After the computation of the proposition outcome, rewards are submitted to a subset of the voters and the certifiers. All the certifiers whose vote matches the outcome of the proposition are rewarded. Voters, instead, are first evaluated using a scoring mechanism, similar to the one reported in [5], and only the ones with a high score are rewarded.

The total score of a voter is based on two different parts:

- **Prediction Score:** A score based on the prediction of the result the voter submitted during the voting phase. RT_i is the response tuple provided by the voter i, while $RT_{i'}$ is the response tuple submitted by a randomly selected voter i'. PR is the prediction value (i.e., the percentage of how much the voter believes that the outcome will be TRUE) and IR is the vote (either TRUE or FALSE).

$$u_{i,PR} = R_q(RT_i.PR, RT_{i'}.IR)$$

R_q is a quadratic function, given q the prediction and w the outcome, the result will given by:

$$R_q(q, w) = \begin{cases} 2q - q^2 & , \ w = \text{TRUE} \\ 1 - q^2 & , \ w = \text{FALSE} \end{cases}$$

- **Information Score:** Score based on the information given by the voter.

$$u_{i,IR} = \begin{cases} 1 - (P_{-i,1} - RT_i.PR)^2 & , \ RT_i.IR = \text{TRUE} \\ -(P_{-i,0} - RT_i.PR)^2 & , \ RT_i.IR = \text{FALSE} \end{cases}$$

$P_{-i,q}$ is the arithmetic mean (G) of all the $RT.PR$ with $q = RT.IR$ excluding the voter i:

$$P_{-i,q} = A(RT_q - \{RT_i\})$$

DeepThought uses the arithmetic mean, being the only feasible aggregation mechanism that could be implemented in a smart contract in/with reasonable time/cost.

The total score of each voter is computed as

$$u_i = u_{i,PR} + u_{i,IR}$$

Each vote is inserted into a scoreboard that is stored in the smart contract. Each vote is added to the scoreboard as soon as it is computed, using algorithm *in-order insertion* in linear time. Given K voters, only the first $K * x$ voters in the scoreboard will earn a reward with x in the range $(0, 1)$. In our prototype, we set $x = 0.5$, so that half of the voters are rewarded.

The reward of the voters is computed using function g_v that, as f, depends on the stake s and the reputation r, and it is computed as follows:

$$g_v(s, r) = [\beta s^2 + (1 - \beta)s]\sqrt{r} \tag{4}$$

β is a value in the range $[0, 1]$ and is used to control the impact of the stake in the reward. The reward is a super-linear function with respect to s. On the one hand, this may incentivize high stakes to obtain very high rewards. On the other hand, the scoreboard acts as an opposite force, since only a subset of the voters is rewarded. This also mitigates *Sybil attacks*, where an attacker tries to control the outcome of the oracle by using multiple users [5]. The reward for voters is taken from a so-called *voters reward pool* that includes the submitter's bounty and all the stakes collected from the voters. The reward is sent to voters starting from the top of the scoreboard. If the funds in the voters reward pool are not enough to reward all the $x * K$ voters, part of them (the lower ranked on the scoreboard) are not rewarded. In the opposite case, when the voters reward pool exceeds the rewards to be distributed, the remaining part is stored in another pool called *lost reward pool*. This pool is shared among all the propositions, and it is used to reward certifiers.

Differently from the voters, the reward for certifiers is always guaranteed if the certification is done correctly (i.e., the vote matches the outcome). Otherwise, their stake is lost and stored in the *lost reward pool*. All the winning certifiers take back their stake and earn a portion (equal for all the certifiers) of the lost reward pool.

Being P the length of available propositions, R the total amount of money stored in the lost reward pool, and $\bar{s}_c$ the sum of all the certifier stakes that voted correctly on the given proposition, the reward g_c of a certifier depends on the submitted stake s and it is computed as follows:

$$g_c(s) = s + \frac{R}{P+1} * \frac{s}{\bar{s}_c} \tag{5}$$

In essence, if the certification is correct, the certifier gets back the stake s and a portion of the lost reward pool that is proportional to the staked amount over the certifiers' total staking. By design, the lost reward pool cannot be empty (apart from the very beginning when no proposition has ever been closed), since in the formula its total amount is divided by $P + 1$.

4   Evaluation

Our evaluation focused on the reliability of a decentralized voting oracle, that is, how difficult it is for malicious users to control the outcome of the voting.

Therefore, our experiments aimed to show if and how much a voting-based oracle extended with a reputation-based system could provide a lower level of corruptibility. In particular, we compared *DeepThought* to *ASTRAEA*, since the latter was used as the baseline when implementing *DeepThought*.

4.1 Experiment Setup

Although the authors of *ASTRAEA* opted for an analytical evaluation to validate their approach, we opted for an empirical evaluation and, consequently, we implemented a working prototype of *DeepThought*. This decision was taken to make easier for other researchers and practitioners to replicate the experiments, as well as to further extend the approach.

To this end, we implemented *ASTRAEA* as an Ethereum smart contract written in Solidity[3]. We run a set of experiments with different configurations using both *DeepThought* implementation and the one developed for *ASTRAEA*. All tests were performed using the Truffle Suite[4] to simulate an Ethereum Blockchain with 20 active users that interact with the protocol and to deploy the implemented smart contracts.

To validate both *ASTRAEA* and *DeepThought* we run a total of 400 experiments, with 10 different configurations and 20 repetitions for each approach. In each configuration, we considered 20 users and 100 different propositions. Each proposition, for the sake of simplicity, was set to have a correct answer equal to TRUE, but we would have obtained the same results with randomized outcomes. Moreover, we split the users into two parts: honest users and adversarial ones. Honest users do not always vote in the correct way. Thus, in each configuration, we varied both the percentage of adversarial users and the accuracy of honest ones. As an example, if the adversarial users are the 25% of the total and the honest users have an accuracy of 80%, this means that 75% of the users will vote TRUE (correct answer) with a probability of 80%, while the remaining 25% will always vote FALSE. These configurations are the ones used in the original *ASTRAEA* evaluation. Thus, our empirical evaluation not only compares *DeepThought* and *ASTRAEA* but also validates the analytical assessment of *ASTRAEA*. In particular, we focused on the configurations that involved 20 voters, being more challenging to preserve the robustness of the system in these cases. For the same reason, we also have added four new configurations, which were not presented in the evaluation of *ASTRAEA*, with a higher adversarial control.

All our tests were performed with a number of voters equals to 20, replicating all specific sub-cases (accuracy equal to 80% and 95%, adversary control equal to 0%, 5%, 25%, 35% and 45%. The four added configurations focus on an adversarial control equals to 35% and 45% while the others were the ones reported in the ASTRAEA evaluation.

---

[3] Source code available at https://github.com/deib-polimi/deepthought/blob/main/contracts/ASTRAEA.sol.

[4] https://trufflesuite.com.

Table 2. Results.

	Configuration				Approach	C-SPEC	C-ANY	STD	MIN	MAX
	V	PR	A	ADV						
#1	20	100	80	0	*ASTRAEA*	0.00	0.06	0.25	0	1
					DeepThought	0.00	0.14	0.35	0	1
#2	20	100	80	5	*ASTRAEA*	0.00	0.26	0.63	0	3
					DeepThought	0.00	0.30	0.55	0	2
#3	20	100	80	25	*ASTRAEA*	14.29	13.88	2.73	9	24
					DeepThought	0.00	2.13	1.25	0	4
#4	20	100	80	35	*ASTRAEA*	35.00	36.40	4.12	31	46
					DeepThought	8.00	5.28	3.00	1	13
#5	20	100	80	45	*ASTRAEA*	70.00	60.60	2.39	57	66
					DeepThought	75.00	68.55	37.42	8	99
#6	20	100	95	0	*ASTRAEA*	0.00	0.00	0.00	0	0
					DeepThought	0.00	0.00	0.00	0	0
#7	20	100	95	5	*ASTRAEA*	0.00	0.00	0.00	0	0
					DeepThought	0.00	0.00	0.00	0	0
#8	20	100	95	25	*ASTRAEA*	8.00	2.40	1.35	0	5
					DeepThought	0.00	0.00	0.00	0	0
#9	20	100	95	35	*ASTRAEA*	5.00	12.90	2.31	9	19
					DeepThought	0.00	0.15	0.36	0	1
#10	20	100	95	45	*ASTRAEA*	35.00	37.70	2.74	32	45
					DeepThought	5.00	1.15	1.08	0	3

4.2 Results

Table 2 shows the results obtained by *DeepThought* and *ASTRAEA* in the ten tested configurations. If we compare the behavior of *ASTRAEA* with the assessment reported in [1] (configurations #1, #2, #3, #6, #7 and #8), the results are comparable except for some smaller deviations that could have been introduced by statistical errors. In this way, we also made sure that our implementation of *ASTRAEA* is correct.

For each configuration, the table shows the number of voters (V), the number of proposition (PR), the accuracy of voters (A, in percentage), the adversarial control (ADV, in percentage), the percentage of times that a proposition selected by an adversarial user was corrupted (C-SPEC), the average number of corrupted propositions (C-ANY) along with the standard deviation (STD), minimum (MIN), and maximum (MAX) values. It must be noted that we considered corrupted also the propositions whose outcomes were incorrect for mistakes made by honest but inaccurate users.

In the configurations with ADV less than or equal to 25% *DeepThought* obtained zero cases where C-SPEC is greater than 0. On contrary, *ASTRAEA* obtained 14.29% and 8% in configurations #3 and #8 respectively where the

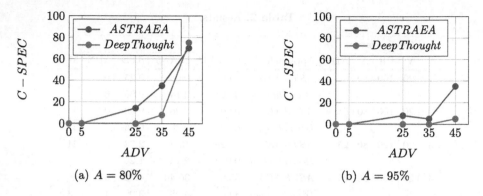

Fig. 2. Corruptibility of a specific proposition (C-SPEC).

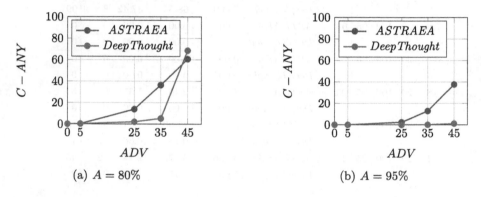

Fig. 3. Corruptibility of ANY proposition (C-ANY).

adversary control is equal to 25%. These data seem to indicate that *DeepThought* is more robust compared to *ASTRAEA* thanks to the usage of reputation.

Configuration #1 and #2 show that *ASTRAEA* obtain a smaller amount of corruptions on average compared to *DeepThought*. It must be noted that in these configurations, the adversarial control is quite small, 0% and 5% respectively. This shows that *DeepThought* is more sensible than *ASTRAEA* to the accuracy of honest voters. Intuitively, if voters with a higher reputation make mistakes, the chances of a wrong output are slightly higher compared to *ASTRAEA*. On this note, it must be noted that in the experiment the accuracy is equal to all the voters. However, in a real-world scenario voters with a higher reputation should tend to make fewer mistakes compared to others and make *DeepThought* perform better than *ASTRAEA* also in these cases. This behavior is also confirmed by configurations #6 and #7 where the adversarial control is equal to #1 and #2 respectively and *DeepThought* obtains zero corruptions in all the repetitions.

Configurations #3 and #8 show a significant difference between the behavior of *DeepThought* and *ASTRAEA*. These cases are quite challenging, since one-fourth of the voters are adversarial. In these cases, *DeepThought* obtained only

2.13 and 0.0 corrupted propositions on average, compared to the much higher data of *ASTRAEA* 13.88 and 2.4 respectively. These results clearly show the benefit of *DeepThought*.

Configurations #4, and #9 show a huge difference between *DeepThought* and *ASTRAEA*. In these newly introduced configurations, the adversarial control reaches 35%. In configuration #4 *DeepThought* is able to keep C-SPEC as low as 8% and obtained 5.28 corrupted propositions on average, while in configuration #5 (with a higher voters accuracy) the results are even lower with C-SPEC and C-ANY equal to 0% and 0.15 respectively. On contrary, *ASTRAEA* shows a very high level of corruptibility with C-SPEC and C-ANY equal to 35% and 36.40 in configuration #4 and 5% and 12.90 in configuration #5. A similar difference is obtained in configuration #10 where the adversarial control is 45% and the accuracy of voters is very high (95%). This shows how *DeepThought* is robust also in very edge cases when almost half of the total of voters is dishonest.

When the adversarial control is very high (45%) and the accuracy is lower (80%), the performance of our approach drops significantly (configuration #5). In this case, both *ASTRAEA* and *DeepThought* are not able to keep the system under control with a very high probability of corruption of a specific proposition ($> 70\%$) and more than 60 propositions corrupted on average. In this case, *DeepThought* shows slightly worse results compared to *ASTRAEA*. Our approach is more sensitive to the initial voting rounds, if honest voters outperform dishonest ones the system remains under control (MIN equals 8) since honest voters accumulate reputation. However, if dishonest voters are able to corrupt the initial propositions, their reputation increases and the low accuracy of honest voters is not enough to keep the system reliable (MAX equals 99). This behavior is also captured by the very high standard deviation of *DeepThought* (37.42) compared to *ASTRAEA*'s one (2.39).

Figures 2 and 3 help visualize the different behaviors of *DeepThought* and *ASTRAEA* when the adversarial control increases. By combining a voting-based approach with a reputation-based system, our solution is significantly more robust than *ASTRAEA* in avoiding corruptions of specific propositions (Fig. 2) and on average (Fig. 3) in almost all the cases.

5   Related Work

As already mentioned, one of the most successful voting-based oracles is represented by *ASTRAEA* [1]. Similarly to *DeepThought*, *ASTRAEA* also relies on submitters, voters and certifiers. However, it relies on a different scheme to determine the voting outcome and to compute the rewards. In particular, each vote has the same weight, regardless of who cast it. Also, two pools, containing the bounty of all the voters and certifiers who voted, respectively TRUE and FALSE, are used to compute the reward. However, these choices make *ASTRAEA* not so robust to adversary control. Similarly, *ASTRAEA* can be subject to the *Verifier's Dilemma*, that is, users always voting and certifying with a constant value in order to maximize their profit without expending any effort [13].

To address these limitations, several extensions of *ASTRAEA* have been proposed in the literature. Shintaku [11] removes the role of the certifier, leaving the certification of the voting result to the voters themselves. To counter the *Verifier's Dilemma*, a voter has to answer a pair of randomly selected propositions, instead of a single one. Voters are then eligible for rewards only if their votes for the two propositions differ. However, this approach has been criticized in [15] and [5] for being practically ineffective against lazy voting unless the penalties for disagreement are at least twice as large as rewards for agreement. Moreover, the honest voters are not incentivized because the payoffs are low.

Merlini et al. in [15] require a submitter to submit two antithetic propositions, posting a bond. Once votes are collected, the oracle checks whether the two questions converged to different answers. Cai et al. in [5] introduce a non-linear scoring scheme to weight the votes and compute the rewards. In particular, this approach collects for each vote a binary information answer and a popularity prediction. The oracle answer is determined by the majority of the information answer, weighted by the associated stakes and adjusted by a sub-linear function. Then, the oracle assigns a score to each report based on the accuracy and the degree of agreement with peers. Only the top-scored voters are awarded, while the share of award is determined by their stake adjusted by a super-linear function.

With respect to these approaches, *DeepThought* introduces the concept of reputation, which is absent in all of them. The reputation is used to determine the answer, the rewards and the penalties using a scoring scheme similar to [5].

Regarding reputation-based oracles, the most famous is Witnet [8]. This oracle runs on its own native customized blockchain, which provides support for smart contracts and relies on tokens named Wit. Miners, that are called *witnesses*, can earn Wits by retrieving and validating external information to be inserted into smart contracts. Witnesses contribute with their mining power, which is mainly determined by their reputation. Similar to *DeepThought*, Witnet rewards the successful majority consensus witnesses, while penalizing the contradicting witnesses. However, it does not have certifiers to counter-check the outcome of voters.

6   Conclusions

In this paper, we presented *DeepThought*, a decentralized human-based oracle that combines voting with reputation. CR*DeepThought* seeks to demonstrate how a reputation-weighted voting system could decrease the probability of outcome corruption compared to existing solutions available in the state-of-the-art that only rely on simpler voting mechanism or only on users' reputation. The results of the empirical evaluation, carried out through the implementation of two smart contracts, show that *DeepThought* presents a higher resistance to adversary control than *ASTRAEA*, which relies only on a voting scheme. In the future, we will implement other voting-based oracles available in the literature and compare them with *DeepThought*. Moreover, we will extend our evaluation with the assessment of a real-world use case and our reward mechanism.

References

1. Adler, J., et al.: ASTRAEA: a decentralized blockchain oracle. In: IEEE International Conference on Internet of Things, Green Computing and Communications, Cyber-Physical and Social Computing, and Smart Data, pp. 1145–1152 (2018)
2. Ali, M., Bagui, S.: Introduction to NFTs: the future of digital collectibles. Int. J. Adv. Comput. Sci. Appl. **12**(10) (2021)
3. Bisola, P.: Blockchain oracles explained (2018). https://www.mycryptopedia.com/blockchain-oracles-explained/
4. Buterin, V.: A next-generation smart contract and decentralized application platform (2014)
5. Cai, Y., Fragkos, G., Tsiropoulou, E.-E., Veneris, A.G.: A truth-inducing sybil resistant decentralized blockchain oracle. In: International Conference on Blockchain Research and Applications for Innovative Networks and Services, pp. 128–135. IEEE (2020)
6. Caldarelli, G.: Understanding the blockchain oracle problem: a call for action. Information **11**(11), 509 (2020)
7. Chen, Y., Bellavitis, C.: Blockchain disruption and decentralized finance: the rise of decentralized business models. J. Bus. Ventur. Insights **13**, e00151 (2020)
8. Crespo, A.S.d.P., Levi, D., García, L.I.C.: A decentralized oracle network protocol. In: Witnet (2017)
9. Gartner: Top strategic predictions for 2020 and beyond (2019)
10. Helo, P., Hao, Y.: Blockchains in operations and supply chains: a model and reference implementation. Comput. Ind. Eng. **136**, 242–251 (2019)
11. Kamiya, R.: Shintaku: an end-to-end-decentralized general-purpose blockchain oracle system (2018)
12. Lacity, M.C.: Blockchain: from bitcoin to the internet of value and beyond. J. Inf. Technol. 02683962221086300 (2022)
13. Luu, L., Teutsch, J., Kulkarni, R., Saxena, P.: Demystifying incentives in the consensus computer, pp. 706–719 (2015)
14. Mammadzada, K., Iqbal, M., Milani, F., García-Bañuelos, L., Matulevičius, R.: Blockchain oracles: a framework for blockchain-based applications. In: Asatiani, A., et al. (eds.) BPM 2020. LNBIP, vol. 393, pp. 19–34. Springer, Cham (2020). https://doi.org/10.1007/978-3-030-58779-6_2
15. Merlini, M., Veira, N., Berryhill, R., Veneris, A.G.: On public decentralized ledger oracles via a paired-question protocol. In: International Conference on Blockchain and Cryptocurrency, pp. 337–344. IEEE (2019)
16. Nakamoto, S.: Bitcoin: a peer-to-peer electronic cash system. Decentralized Bus. Rev. 21260 (2008)
17. O'reilly, T.: What is web 2.0: design patterns and business models for the next generation of software (2007)
18. Szabo, N.: Formalizing and securing relationships on public networks. First Monday **2**(9) (1997)
19. Wang, S., Ouyang, L., Yuan, Y., Ni, X., Han, X., Wang, F.-Y.: Blockchain-enabled smart contracts: architecture, applications, and future trends. IEEE Trans. Syst. Man Cybern. Syst. **49**(11), 2266–2277 (2019)
20. Wüst, K., Gervais, A.: Do you need a blockchain? In: Crypto Valley Conference on Blockchain Technology, pp. 45–54. IEEE (2018)
21. Çelen, B., Kariv, S.: Distinguishing informational cascades from herd behavior in the laboratory. Am. Econ. Rev. **94**, 484–498 (2004)

Blockchain-Oriented Services Computing in Action: Insights from a User Study

Giovanni Quattrocchi[1]([✉]), Damian Andrew Tamburri[2,3], and Willem-Jan Van Den Heuvel[3,4]

[1] Politecnico di Milano, Milan, Italy
giovanni.quattrocchi@polimi.it
[2] Eindhoven University of Technology, Eindhoven, Netherlands
d.a.tamburri@tue.nl
[3] Jheronimus Academy of Data Science, Den Bosch, Netherlands
W.J.A.M.v.d.Heuvel@jads.nl
[4] Tilburg University, Tilburg, Netherlands

Abstract. Blockchain architectures promise disruptive innovation but factually they pose many architectural restrictions to classical service-based applications and show considerable design, implementation, and operations overhead. Furthermore, the relation between such overheads and user benefits is not clear yet. To shed light on the aforementioned relations, a service-based blockchain architecture was designed and deployed as part of a field study in real-life experimentation. An observational approach was then performed to elaborate on the *technology-acceptance* of the service-based blockchain architecture in question. Evidence shows that the resulting architecture is, in principle, not different than other less complex equivalents; furthermore, the architectural limitations posed by the blockchain-oriented design demand a significant additional effort to be put onto even the simplest of functionalities. We conclude that further research shall be invested in clarifying further the design principles we learned as part of this study as well as any trade-offs posed by blockchain-oriented service design and operation.

Keywords: Blockchain software · Service-oriented architectures · Technology acceptance · Case-study research

1 Introduction

Blockchain technology is heralded as a silver bullet for a wide range of problems, yet the stylistic restrictions posed on top of more classical service-oriented architectures [14] that blockchain-oriented service design forces into the equation limit the throughput and latency of blockchain transactions [16]. For example, the Bitcoin network [12] can currently handle a maximum of 7 transactions per second, although the Ethereum network [18] offers a relatively higher number of 15 transactions per second (tps); to date, this rate is not compatible to

J. Troya et al. (Eds.): ICSOC 2022, LNCS 13740, pp. 384–391, 2022.
https://doi.org/10.1007/978-3-031-20984-0_27

the processing capacity of other networks such as VISA (2,000tps) and Twitter (5,000tps). Creating a new block that is required to assure the safety of the network requires 10 min which significantly slows down the time to complete one transaction, resulting in low latency.

As such, the usability of blockchain designs may need further attention than software designs following other architecture patterns [2]. More specifically, we are interested in studying the extent to which the intrinsic limitations of blockchain-oriented designs weigh on their perceived end-user effectiveness [19]. To look into blockchain usability from a design perspective, this article offers an empirical *invivo* field study designed using the guidelines defined in the Technology Acceptance Model (TAM) [1] and related frameworks [9]. First, we designed and prototyped a blockchain-based service-oriented transactional architecture. Second, we deployed and tested the architecture from the user perspective, by interviewing its end-users as part of a controlled experiment.

The results indicate that end-users do perceive several advantages (i.e., good information and transactions transparency, ease-of-use as well as user-friendliness) from using the blockchain but also that the blockchain imposes a *lock-in* which even comes at a cost of +30% development times and efforts. While the alternative transactive methods are perceived as no longer usable or obsolete by users, service architects may have to evaluate the resulting trade-offs a bit more carefully. Overall, these findings indicate a need to further understand the process of designing for blockchain-oriented service engineering [18].

The practical implications are at least twofold: on one hand, blockchain limitations need to be overcome with technical and design devices capable of addressing them, on the other hand, the risks of not involving end-users in the design might lead to the undesired circumstances we report in the results section, e.g., the lock-in condition we reported from our user study.

The rest of this paper is structured as follows. First, Sect. 2 outlines the related work. Beyond that, Sect. 3 outlines our research design, also providing a birds-eye view of the architecture we designed and implemented as a field-study device. Further on, Sect. 4 provides the *enfield* deployment and experimentation over our blockchain-oriented prototype. Finally, Sect. 5 concludes the paper.

2   Related Work

Technology acceptance by end-users is a well-established concept, and has been studied extensively in prior research [17]. One of the most used lenses to study technology acceptance is the well-known Technology Acceptance Model (TAM) [1]. Results from studies that employed the TAM suggest that when users are presented with new technology, at least two factors influence their decision about how and when they use it, namely: (1) perceived usefulness (PU)—defined by Davis [3] as "the degree to which a person believes that using a particular system would enhance his or her job performance"; (2) perceived ease-of-use (PEOU)—defined by Davis [3] as "the degree to which a person believes that using a particular system would be free from effort". In their variant DeLone and McLean

[4] introduce two additional variables: (3) perceived information quality (PIQ) and (4) user satisfaction. Although technology acceptance of the end-users of various IS has been thoroughly studied, except for a study conducted by Folkinshteyn and Lenon [6], no research has been conducted to gauge users' acceptance of blockchain technology. Moreover, the study carried out by Folkinshteyn and Lenon is limited to the use of the Bitcoin protocol and is based on literature rather than capturing the perceived user perception in practice.

3 Research Design

The problem addressed in this paper reflects the shortage of information concerning the user-acceptance of blockchain architectures. On one hand, such architecture poses a considerable strain on designers given their constraints and architectural limitations [18]. On the other hand, the end-user benefits and, more specifically, the *technology acceptance* [8] from such end-users is questionable at best. With technology acceptance, we indicate the information systems' architecture approach that focuses on establishing how users come to accept and use a specific technological architecture.

Given its early stage of adoption, we aim to articulate the effect of blockchain limitations to the above-mentioned dimensions of technology acceptance. More specifically, we pose the research questions below:

RQ1 *To what extent do blockchains enhance service application usefulness?*
RQ2 *To what extent is the blockchain transparent to direct service use?*

With the above RQs, we aim at understanding the *usefulness* and *transparency* of the blockchain design principles and restrictions; in so doing, we prototype a blockchain transaction system and execute a field-study featuring *enfield* questionnaires and web-surveys designed to evaluate usefulness as an essential dimension of the study.

3.1 Blockchain Technology Acceptance: Field Study Design

As previously mentioned, to attain our research results we conducted a field study using a *enfield*-deployed version of our research prototype. The prototype in question was deployed as production-ready—meaning that the prototype was in fully-working conditions and has been deployed in *practice* on several similar occasions (e.g. other festivals). The field experiment followed the guidelines of Singer et al. [11] and essentially involved: (1) end-use of the system in the context of a real-life event involving the active use of the prototype; (2) follow-up interviews featuring a web survey which followed a random sampling approach.

The data used for this research was collected during the pre-edition of a festival in the Netherlands[1]. The festival annually hosts 3000+ visitors and 200+

---

[1] For more information about the festival the reader should visit: https://www.welcometothevillage.nl.

volunteers who co-organize the festival. The volunteers were all asked to partic-ipate in this research in an *opt-in* fashion; the involvement in the context of this study was featuring the use of our blockchain platform. The platform in question allowed the participants of this research to (a) buy beverages using a token that was created on the blockchain platform and converted from real cash; (b) buy tokens with euros directly on the platform and upload them to their account using a QR-code wristband; (c) finally, check their account balance. Users can download a mobile app or surf an internet page to access the aforementioned features.

The study involved a total of 48 randomly-sampled end-users with a mean age of 23 (standard deviation of 4,37). The population involved a total of 23 male subjects and 18 female subjects. The population is skewed towards more tech-savvy people with a ratio of 1:3. The respondents for this study were administered a questionnaire consisting of 11 items to measure certain aspects detailed in the following. All questions were addressed by the studied subjects along a typical 5-factor Likert-scale [7] allowing for subsequent content analysis [10]. For the sake of reference and replicability, the questionnaire is available online[2]. All of the respondents filled in the survey albeit not completely.

The questions used for the survey (after the use of the platform was recorded) were derived from [13], which were in turn based on the DeLone and McLean model. Users Acceptance Testing questions are designed to evaluate the field use of the proposed technology along the typical criteria defined for technology acceptance, as defined previously in the prior sections.

1. *Perceived information quality* provided by the system (4 items), defined as the extent to which the system provides the respondents with accurate infor-mation, delivered in the format required by the users about their account balance,
2. *Perceived ease-of-use* as a concept to measure the systems' quality (1 item), which can be referred to as the degree to which the SIS is easy to use when making transactions to buy beverages and,
3. *Perceived usefulness of the system*, to gauge the perceived benefit of using the system (4 items), which we define for this research as the degree to which the user believes that the system caters to them in buying beverages, along with,
4. *Perceived user satisfaction* with regards to the architecture quality measured by one item evaluating the users' technical feedback on the architecture fea-tures [5] they tried out during their experimentation.

To rule out rivaling explanations for the results of the study, we have included two control variables in our model:

1. *Utilization*, defined as the degree to which a user is dependent on the IS to carry out his or her tasks, has been included to rule out that the users' perception of the system can be attributed to the fact that they cannot work around the system. One item was included to measure this variable

---

[2] https://tinyurl.com/ycha8282.

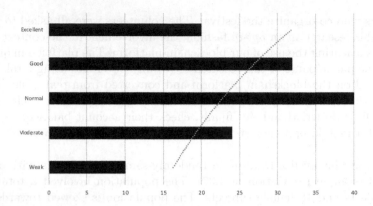

Fig. 1. Architecture information and transactions quality, that is, the extent to which the blockchain-oriented design is perceived as providing appropriate and useful transactions information; the y-axis indicates likert-scale levels while x-axis indicates #respondents.

2. *Technology Savviness* that is, questions designed to evaluate the users' perceived confidence with software technology along 5 evaluation criteria, namely, Search Engines (confidence with information retrieval and storage), Social Media (confidence with social networks, and online digital presence), Digital Content (confidence with knowledge-bases as well as general information management with different document formats), Software Security (knowledge and confidence against anti-viral, malware or other online security threats) and Software Care (confidence with software repair);

The data we obtained in our end-user survey featured 48 timestamped responses along a 5-dimensional Likert scale. To analyze available data, regular statistical modeling was adopted along with non-boosted logistic regression modeling. More specifically, in the scope of RQ1, namely, *to what extent do blockchains enhance information system usefulness?*, we produced combined Likert-scale responses to three specific questions. On one hand, we summed results from two questions: (1) *"the blockchain architecture offers me all the information I require to perform my transaction"*; (2) *"the possibilities that the blockchain platform offers to increase my balance are satisfactory"*. Subsequently, to avoid observer bias [15], we triangulated the two questions above with a control question, namely, *"the possibilities that the blockchain architecture offers to perform transactions are satisfactory"*; thus, the sum obtained above was decreased with the Likert-scale results from the above question. The results were plotted using a bar chart and a logistic regression trendline was fitted with the data (see Fig. 1).

Finally, in the scope of RQ2, namely, *to what extent is the blockchain transparent to direct use?*, we computed Pearson's product-moment correlation coefficient between the Likert-scale responses for question *"making transactions using the blockchain platform is easy and transparent."* and question *"I am depen-*

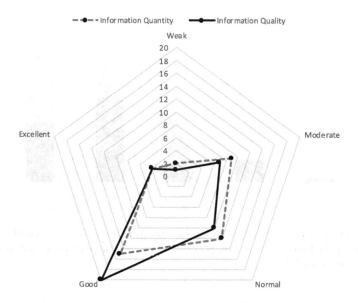

Fig. 2. Information Quantity vs. Quality, that is, the extent to which the blockchain-oriented design yields an appropriate quantity of information with respect to an appropriate quality of presented information—the data highlights a 78% overlap.

dent on the blockchain platform to perform my transactions."—our research assumption is that the significant correlation between the two responses indicates a strong dependency on the blockchain platform to perform transactions with respect to the regular transactional alternative.

4   Research Results

Figure 1 shows our results in the context of RQ1. More specifically, the figure shows a linear trend with respect to responses concerning architectural information and transaction quality within the blockchain-oriented design under study. Although the trend pends slightly by about 3% towards a positive transactional information quality, the data shows a rather inconclusive outcome with respect to the extent that the presence of a blockchain-oriented design reinforces transactions' quality. Our data indicate that the trend seems positive but there is little to no indication that the trend is connected to the blockchain and the effect size we report is non-significant.

With respect to transactions information quality and quantity in the scope of the blockchain-oriented design under study, Fig. 2 depicts a radial diagram to capture the overlap in question. The figure shows a definitive overlap between information quantity (dotted, smaller inner-line on the figure) and information quality (continuous black line). The overlap rests around 78% indicating a considerable perceived overlap between quality and quantity of information in the

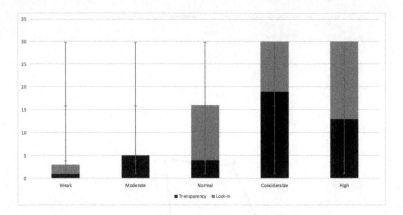

Fig. 3. perceived information transparency—the plot remarks the negative trend in transparency (black-area in the box-plot) with respect to perceived lock-in (greayed-out area in the box-plot).

context of performed transactions by the users in our study—this extent of over-lap between information quantity and quantity suggests that the presence of the blockchain underneath the implementation under study makes information and transactional quality/usefulness more explicit.

In terms of transparency, the data shows a mild correlation of 0.39 (P-value 0.012312<<0.05) between the extent to which the transactions performed by means of the proposed blockchain-oriented design are transparent and the extent to which the user feels constrained to use the blockchain-oriented design *only*, that is, instead of the classical transaction alternative. Concerning this apparent *lock-in* phenomenon, Fig. 3 provides an overview of the compulsive mutual effect size in the scope of the aforementioned lock-in.

The figure shows an increasing lock-in perception with a plateau around the *"considerable"* value but with a consequent negative trend immediately after-ward with a trade-off drop of 33%. This indicates that users perceive lock-in over transparency.

5   Conclusions

Blockchain-oriented applications are increasingly picking up interest in the more general audience both from the perspective of practice and academic research inquiry. Little is known, however, over the extent to which blockchain-oriented designs are perceived by their users.

Our study reported that i) blockchain-oriented designs support systems use-fulness, and ii) the formation of a significant *lock-in* phenomenon wherefore blockchain users seem to perceive transparency to the extent to which the blockchain becomes a lock-in with respect to conventional transactions system.

References

1. Bradley, J.: The technology acceptance model and other user acceptance theories. IGI Global, Hershey, PA, USA (2009)
2. Buschmann, F., Meunier, R., Rohnert, H., Sommerlad, P., Wiley, M., Stal, A.: System of patterns - pattern oriented software architecture (1996)
3. Davis, F.D.: Perceived usefulness, perceived ease of use, and user acceptance of information technology. MIS Q. **13**, 319–340 (1989)
4. Delone, W.H., McLean, E.R.: The DeLone and McLean model of information systems success: a ten-year update. J. Manage. Inf. Syst. **19**(4), 9–30 (2003)
5. Dhungana, D.: Integrated variability modeling of features and architecture in software product line engineering. In: ASE, pp. 327–330. IEEE (2006)
6. Folkinshteyn, D., Lennon, M.: Braving bitcoin: a technology acceptance model (tam) analysis. J. Inf. Technol. Case Appl. Res. **18**(4), 220–249 (2016)
7. Gil, M.A., Gonzalez-Rodriguez, G.: Fuzzy vs. likert scale in statistics. In: Trillas, E., Bonissone, P., Magdalena, L., Kacprzyk, J. (eds.) Combining Experimentation and Theory. Studies in Fuzziness and Soft Computing, vol. 271, pp. 407–420. Springer, Heidelberg (2012). https://doi.org/10.1007/978-3-642-24666-1_27
8. Kakar,A.K.,: How do perceived enjoyment and perceived usefulness of a software product interact over time to impact technology acceptance? Interact. Comput. **29**(4), 467–480 (2017)
9. King, W., He, J.: A meta-analysis of the technology acceptance model. Inf. Manage. **43**(6), 740–755 (2006)
10. Krippendorff, K.: Content Analysis: an Introduction to Its Methodology (second edition). Sage Publications (2004)
11. Lethbridge, T.C., Sim, S.E., Singer, J.: Studying software engineers: data collection techniques for software field studies. Empir. Softw. Eng. **10**, 311–341 (2005)
12. Lischke, M., Fabian, B.: Analyzing the bitcoin network: the first four years. Future Internet **8**(1), 7 (2016)
13. Rai, A., Lang, S.S., Welker R.B., Assessing the validity of is success models: an empirical test and theoretical analysis. Inf. Syst. Res. **13**(1), 50–69 (2002)
14. Richards, M.:Microservices vs. service-oriented architecture. Technical Report, July (2016)
15. Simons, T.R., Pollock, K.H., Wettroth, J.M., Alldredge, M.W., Pacifici, K., Brewster, J.: Sources of measurement error, misclassification error, and bias in auditory avian point count data. Environ. Ecol. Stat. **3**, 237–254 (2009)
16. Swan, M.: Blockchain: blueprint for a new economy. O'Reilly Media, Inc. (2015)
17. Venkatesh, V., Morris, M.G., Davis, G.B., Davis, F.D.: User acceptance of information technology: toward a unified view. MIS Quart. **27**(3), 425–478 (2003)
18. Wessling, F., Gruhn, V.: Engineering software architectures of blockchain-oriented applications. In: ICSA Companion, pp. 45–46. IEEE (2018)
19. Yli-Huumo, J., Ko, D., Choi, S., Park, S., Smolander, K.: Where is current research on Blockchain technology? a systematic review. PLOS ONE **11**(10), e0163477 (2016)

IoT and Green Computing

Maximizing Consumer Satisfaction of IoT Energy Services

Amani Abusafia[✉], Athman Bouguettaya, and Abdallah Lakhdari

The University of Sydney, Sydney, NSW 2000, Australia
{amani.abusafia,athman.bouguettaya,abdallah.lakhdari}@sydney.edu.au

Abstract. We propose a novel *Quality of Experience (QoE)*-aware framework to crowdsource IoT energy services efficiently. The proposed framework leverages the provisioning of energy services as an auxiliary to increase consumers' *satisfaction*. A novel QoE model is developed as a metric to assess the consumers' satisfaction with the provisioning of energy services. Two novel composition algorithms, namely, Partial-Based (PB) and Demand-Based (DB) approaches, are proposed to ensure the highest QoE for consumers. Both approaches leverage the providers' *flexibility* and *shareable* nature of energy services to efficiently allocate services and optimize the QoE. A set of extensive experiments is conducted to evaluate the proposed approaches' efficiency and effectiveness.

Keywords: Quality of experience · IoT services · Energy services · Energy sharing · Crowdsourcing · Incentive · IoT

1 Introduction

Internet of Things (IoT) is a paradigm that enables everyday objects (i.e., *things*) to connect to the internet and exchange data. IoT devices, such as smartphones and wearables, usually have augmented capabilities including sensing, networking, and processing [1]. Abstracting the capabilities of these IoT devices using the *service paradigm* may yield to multitude of novel *IoT services* [2]. These IoT services may be *exchanged* between IoT devices as *crowdsourced* IoT services. For example, an IoT device may offer WiFi hotspots or wireless energy services to charge other IoT devices [2]. These crowdsourced IoT services present a convenient and cost-effective solutions [2]. Our focus is on wireless energy sharing services among IoT devices.

Energy-as-a-Service (EaaS) is the abstraction of the wireless delivery of energy among nearby IoT devices [2,3]. *EaaS* is an IoT service where energy is delivered from an energy provider (e.g., a smart shoe or smartphone) to an energy consumer (e.g., a smartphone) through wireless means. *EaaS* may be deployed through the newly developed "Over-the-Air" wireless charging technologies [4,5]. Several companies, including Xiaomi[1], Energous[2], and ossia[3], are

---

[1] https://www.mi.com/.
[2] https://energous.com/.
[3] https://www.ossia.com/.

currently developing wireless charging technologies for IoT devices over a *distance*. For example, Energous developed a device that can charge up to 3 W power within a 5-m distance.

The crowdsourced EaaS ecosystem is a *dynamic* environment that consists of *providers* and *consumers* congregating in *microcells*. A microcell is any confined area where people may gather (e.g., coffee shops). In this ecosystem, IoT devices may share energy with nearby IoT devices. A key aspect to unlocking the full potential of the EaaS ecosystem is to design an *end-to-end* Service Oriented Architecture (SOA) to share crowdsourced energy. We identify three key components of the SOA: energy service *provider*, energy service *consumer*, and *super-provider*. In this architecture, providers advertise services, consumers submit requests, and super-provider (i.e., microcell's owner) manage the exchange of energy services between providers and consumers. This paper focuses on *managing energy sharing from the super-provider perspective*.

Super-provider typically focus on ensuring that customers keep coming back to their businesses. Their revenue is usually directly related to *foot traffic* [6]. Customer *satisfaction* is therefore paramount as a strategy to either maintain or increase the business target revenue [7]. A key objective is to ensure that customers have the *best experience*. We propose to use energy sharing as a key ingredient to provide customers with the best quality of experience when visiting the business. For example, a case study showed that "Sacred", a cafe in London, had a noticeable increase in foot traffic after installing wireless charging points[4].

We define a *Quality of Experience (QoE)* metric to represent the level of *satisfaction* across energy consumers over a period of time in a specific microcell. Note that QoE is different from Quality of Service (QoS). QoE uses QoS as a base to express satisfaction of a service over a period of time. QoE has traditionally been used in domains that assess how users perceive a service [8–10]. Our proposed environment requires the use of a different type of QoE. In particular, we identify the following three aspects that shape the new QoE definition: (1) crowdsourced environment resources are usually limited and cannot fulfill all consumers' requirements. Hence, assessing consumers' satisfaction should consider the limited available resources. Energy services may be provided partially due to the limited resources and the shareable nature of energy services, e.g., a single service may be split into smaller services and provided among multiple consumers. In a limited resource environment, consumers' experience with partial services differs from complete services. (3) Consumers' satisfaction with energy services will indirectly impact their experience with the super-provider's microcell. Therefore,our research focuses on the *super-provider's perspective* of QoE.

Assessing the QoE from a super-provider's perspective usually entails measuring the *aggregated* satisfaction of consumers over time. *Consumer's satisfaction* is defined as *meeting or exceeding* a set of expected service goals [11]. In this context, we define consumer satisfaction as *receiving the requested energy or part of it*. We focus on *optimizing* the *QoE* by efficiently provisioning and fulfilling the consumers' energy requirements.

---

[4] https://www.air-charge.com/.

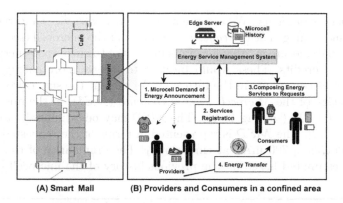

(A) Smart Mall   **(B) Providers and Consumers in a confined area**

Fig. 1. IoT energy services environment

The limited availability of energy is a key challenge that may hinder the super-provider from optimizing the consumers' QoE [2]. For instance, an energy consumer might not find their requested energy at a certain time in the microcell, resulting in an unsatisfying experience. In this context, using traditional resource allocation algorithms may incur uneven energy sharing for some consumers. Therefore, we propose a QoE-driven service provisioning framework to satisfy energy consumers in a crowdsourced IoT environment. The framework requires prior knowledge of providers' temporal preferences and the microcell energy demands. The proposed framework leverages the *shareable* nature of energy services to split the energy between consumers if the required energy is more than the available energy [3]. Intuitively, the super-provider may prefer to offer part of the required services to all consumers than offering it to some of them. Hence, we propose a heuristic Partial-Based (PB) approach which splits services among consumers in the case of low energy availability. Another possible solution is to leverage *flexible* providers that offer services on *multiple* time slots by allocating their services to the most demanding slots. Intuitively, this may ensure a better distribution of the available services. Therefore, we additionally propose a heuristic Demand-Based (DB) approach. The DB approach extends the PB approach by prioritizing the allocation of services based on the highest demanding time slots. The main contributions of this paper are:

- A novel Quality of Experience (QoE) model for crowdsourced energy services.
- A framework for QoE-driven composition of IoT energy services.
- An experimental analysis with two implementations of the proposed QoE-driven energy composition framework.

1.1 Motivating Scenario

We describe a scenario in a confined place (i.e., microcell) where people congregate, e.g., cafes,and restaurants (see Fig. 1(A)). Each microcell may have several IoT devices acting as energy providers or consumers (see Fig. 1(B)). The super-provider aims to leverage the crowdsourced energy services as a tool to enhance the consumers' *experience*. We assume all local energy services and requests are submitted and managed at the *edge*, e.g., a router in the microcell (see Fig. 1(B)). We assume that the super-provider offers incentives to encourage energy sharing in the form of credits. These would be used to receive more energy when the providers act as consumers in the future [2] We assume the super-provider has a prior knowledge of the *Microcell Energy Demand* ($\mathcal{MED}$) in the microcell over a period of time (T) (see Fig. 2(A)). The $\mathcal{MED}$ may be estimated based on previous history [12]. The $\mathcal{MED}$ is represented in terms of the requested energy in each time slot, e.g., 700 mAh at time slot t_1. The granularity of the time slots can also be estimated based on the previous history of the microcell [2].

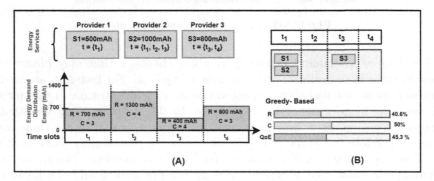

Fig. 2. (A) Microcell energy demand and providers services (B) Greedy energy provisioning approach

We also assume that the super-provider has prior knowledge of the providers preferences in terms of time and energy service attributes. An incentive model is employed to predict the amount of energy that would be available for consumption [13]. For instance, provider 1 in Fig. 2(A) wants to offer the energy service $S1$ with 500 mAh at time t_1. Another example, provider 2 wants to offer $S2$ at time slots t_1 , t_2, or t_3. We assume the provider would stay for the full-time slot. We also assume that the provider's service amount is fixed and can be split among multiple time slots. For instance, provider 2 may share part of their service $S2$ on t_1, e.g., 300 mAh, and the other part at t_2 or t_3. We also assume a single energy provider may share their spare energy with multiple energy consumers, within *a specific time interval*. The super-provider uses *rewards* to encourage providers to share energy. Rewards may come in the form of stored credits to providers. A provider receives a reward based on an incentive model [13].

The super-provider will allocate services to time slots to serve as many consumers as possible to *maximize* their quality of experience in the microcell. However, it is challenging to fulfill multiple energy requirements with limited energy services [2]. For example, in Fig. 2(A), the total energy demand ($\sum R$) is 3200 mAh, and the total available energy services ($\sum S$) is 2300 mAh. The available services may fulfill 71.9% of the energy requests which cannot be fully provisioned with the temporal constrains of services and requests.

Therefore, satisfying all consumers with their under-provisioned requests is *more challenging*.

Figure 2(B) presents the outcome of a greedy FCFS, i.e., first come first served, allocation strategy for the available energy [14]. In greedy, the time slots and services will be scheduled based on their start time. For instance, in Fig. 2(A) even though $S2$ can be offered in t_1, t_2 and t_3, $S1$ will be allocated to t_1 because it comes first in terms of time. The greedy strategy does not leverage the shareable nature of energy services or the providers' flexibility which may affect the energy allocation efficiency and impact the consumers' experience. Therefore, the greedy strategy may not be a good fit in this context. For example, in Fig. 2(B), the greedy-based approach could only fulfill 1300 mAh from the total demand which is equivalent to 40.6%. Moreover, the total number of consumers ($\sum C$) in Fig. 2(A) is 14 and the greedy approach could offer energy to 7 consumers which is equivalent to 50%. In this context, we consider the size of fulfilled requests and the number of fulfilled consumers in assessing the quality of experience. In this example, using the greedy approach resulted in 45.3% of consumers' QoE.

Allocating the limited available energy with the time constraints of both services and requests represents critical challenges for efficient and QoE-aware provisioning of IoT energy services. We propose a framework that will compose the energy services to maximize the consumers' experience. Our framework leverages leverage the providers' *flexibility* and *shareable* nature of energy services to efficiently allocate services and optimize the QoE.

2 Preliminaries

We consider the scenario of energy sharing in a microcell M during a time interval T. T is divided into a set of $\{t_1, ..., t_n\}$ where t_i is a predefined time period, e.g., one hour. We use the below definitions to formalize the problem.

Definition 1: Energy-as-a-Service (EaaS). We adopt the definition of $EaaS$ in [3]. An energy service ($EaaS$) is a tuple of $< E_{id}, E_{pid}, F, Q >$, where E_{id} is an energy service ID, E_{pid} is a provider ID, F is the function of sharing wireless energy, Q is a set of non-functional (QoS) attributes, including:

- p_{ae} is the amount of energy shared by the provider.
- p_{loc} is the location of the energy provider $< x, y >$.
- p_t is the set of time intervals $< t_s, t_e >$ a provider may offer their energy.

Definition 2: Energy Service Request (ER). We adopt the definition of ER in [13]. An ER is a tuple of $< E_{id}, E_{cid}, F, QR >$, where ER_id is an energy request ID, E_{cid} is a consumer ID, F is the function of receiving energy wirelessly by an IoT device, QR is a set of non-functional attributes, including:

- c_{re} is the amount of requested energy.
- c_{loc} is the location of the energy consumer $< x, y >$.
- c_t is the time interval $< t_s, t_e >$ of requiring energy.

Definition 3: Microcell Energy Demand $\mathcal{MED}$. $\mathcal{MED}$ is the total amount of requested energy during a time interval T (See Fig. 2). T is divided into time slots. We define $\mathcal{MED}$ by aggregating the amount of required energy per time slot. Therefore, the definition of $\mathcal{MED} = \{t_1, t_2, ..., t_n\}$ where t is a tuple of $< d, rwd, re, nc, ER >$. Here d is a predefined time in the time interval of the microcell T, e.g., [9:00 AM -10:00 AM]. rwd is the reward of providing the required energy re. We compute rwd using the incentive model proposed by [13]. We assume that the super-provider will use the microcell history to compute the energy demand in advance. nc is the number of consumers in the microcell at time slot t. ER is the set of available requests in the microcell at time slot t.

Definition 4: Quality of Experience (QoE). QoE is defined as an objective function to measure consumers' satisfaction with energy provisioning in a microcell M within a predefined time interval T. The function definition is:

$$QoE(M) = F(T, \mathcal{ES}, \mathcal{MED}) \tag{1}$$

where $\mathcal{ES}$ is the set of energy services and $\mathcal{MED}$ is the microcell energy demand.

2.1 Problem Definition

Given a set of n energy services $\mathcal{ES} = \{EaaS_1, EaaS_2, ..., EaaS_n\}$ and a set of m energy requests $\mathcal{ER} = \{ER_1, ER_2, ..., ER_m\}$ in a microcell M. The super-provider advertise the microcell energy demand $\mathcal{MED}$. Energy providers register their services in terms of: (1) the amount of energy p_{ae} (2) the time slots t_i to offer their services. The super-provider uses the providers preferences to allocate their services to time slots. The allocation approach aims at fulfilling the maximum number of requests and thereby maximize the QoE. We formulate the service composition problem to a time-constrained optimization problem as follows:

- Maximize $QoE(M) = F(T, \mathcal{ES}, \mathcal{MED})$,

Subject to:

- $t_i.re > 0$ for each $t_i \in T$,
- $EaaS_j.P_t \subset t_i.d$ for each $EaaS_j \in \mathcal{ES}$.

Where P_t is the time interval $< t_s, t_e >$ a provider of $EaaS_j$ may offer their energy, $t_i.d$ is the duration of a time slot i in the time interval of the microcell T, and $t_i.re$ is the required energy re at time slot i.

The goal of the composition is to efficiently allocate the available energy services to time slots. The objective function attempts to optimally assign energy services according to their spatio-temporal features, providers' preferences and required energy in time slots. The spatial aspect in energy service focuses on a geographical cell. The temporal aspect focuses on the times of energy service provisioning.

We use the following assumptions to formulate the problem.

- Providers energy size is fixed during composition.
- Providers are available in all their selected time slots.
- Providers may offer partial services to multiple consumers at the same time.
- Consumers' time windows do not overlap with time slots.
- Providers and consumers have fixed location during energy sharing.
- The microcell has *multiple* providers and *multiple* consumers.
- There is no energy loss in sharing. As the technology matures, we anticipate that the devices will be able to share more energy, and the energy loss of sharing will become minimal [2].
- The exact amount of required energy for a microcell is given [15].
- A reward system is used to incentivize providers to offer their service [13].
- A trust framework is used to preserve the privacy of the IoT devices [16].

3   Quality of Experience Model

The Quality of Experience (QoE) in a microcell is measured based on the *number of satisfied consumers* and the *amount of fulfilled requests*. Recall, the time interval of the microcell is divided into time slots. Therefore, QoE for each time slot t_i will be computed using the following attributes:

- **Satisfaction Ratio:** We define the Satisfaction Ratio ($\mathcal{SR}$) as the number of consumers who received their requested energy or part of it. We compute $\mathcal{SR}$ per time slot t as follows:

$$\mathcal{SR} = \frac{|\{ER \in \mathcal{ER} \mid ER \text{ is completed \& } c_t \in d\}|}{|\mathcal{ER}|} \qquad (2)$$

  Where $\mathcal{ER}$ is the set of all requests in time slot t, $|.|$ is the cardinality of the set, c_t is the request time, and d is the time duration of t.
- **Fulfillment Ratio:** The satisfaction ratio is not enough to measure QoE. For example, if we have a set of energy requests in mAh $\mathcal{ER} = \{10, 20, 20, 70\}$, serving the first 3 consumers is not equal to serving the last 3 due to the different amount of requested energy. Therefore, We define the Fulfillment Ratio ($\mathcal{FR}$) based on the percentage of fulfillment for each request. We compute FR per time slot t as follows:

$$\mathcal{FR} = \sum_{i=1}^{n} \left(w_i \times \frac{Received\_Energy_i}{Requested\_Energy_i} \right) \qquad (3)$$

  where n is the number of all energy requests in t, and w_i is the weight of the request over the total amount of requested energy in t.

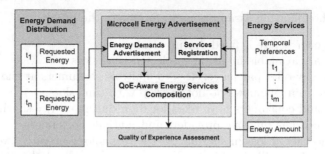

Fig. 3. Quality of experience driven service composition framework

Quality of Experience: As previously stated, We define the QoE in a microcell based on the satisfaction ratio $\mathcal{SR}$ and fulfillment ratio $\mathcal{FR}$ of each time slot t. Therefore, we compute the $QoE(M)$ as the following:

$$QoE(M) = \alpha \times \left(\sum_{i=1}^{m} SR_i \times \beta_i \right) + (1 - \alpha) \times \left(\sum_{i=1}^{m} FR_i \times \gamma_i \right) \qquad (4)$$

where m is the number of time slots in the microcell's time interval T. $\mathcal{SR}_i$ is the satisfaction ratio of a time slot computed by Eq. 2. β_i is the weight of a time slot t_i which is its number of consumers over the total number of consumers in T. $\mathcal{FR}_i$ is the ratio of fulfillment of the time slot computed by Eq. 3. γ_i is the weight of a time slot t_i which is its total required energy over the total amount of required energy in T. α is a user-defined weight between zero and one to define the weight of $\mathcal{SR}_i$ and $\mathcal{FR}_i$ in QoE.

4   Quality of Experience Framework

We introduce a quality of experience composition framework for managing energy services to enhance consumers' QoE (See Fig. 3). The framework is divided into three phases: (1) Microcell energy advertisement, (2) Composing energy services, and (3) Quality of experience assessment. In the first phase, the super-provider will advertise the energy demand of the microcell and receives providers' preferences. In the second phase, the super-provider will compose energy services to maximize the QoE. In the last phase, the super-provider will assess the QoE for the resulted composition.

4.1   Microcell Energy Demand Advertisement

In this phase, the super-provider computes the reward for each time slot based on the amount of required energy using the incentive model in [13]. Then, the system will announce the required energy and rewards for the whole microcell using Definition 3. Energy providers will register based on their preferences in terms of their energy amount and the time slots they will be available (See Fig. 2).

Algorithm 1. Partial-Based Composition of Services

Input: $\mathcal{MED}$, $\mathcal{ES}$, $threshold$
Output: $energy\_comp$

```
 1: for tᵢ in MED do
 2:    selectedES = {}
 3:    demand = tᵢ.re
 4:    for esⱼ in tᵢ.ES do
 5:       if demand > 0 then
 6:          demand = demand - esⱼ.pₐₑ
 7:          energy_comp.add(tᵢ, esⱼ)
 8:          selectedES.add(esⱼ)
 9:          if demand < 0 then
10:             esⱼ.pₐₑ =demand * -1
11:             demand = 0
12:          else
13:             Remove_Service(esⱼ, MED)
14:    if demand = 0 then
15:       Assign_Energy(tᵢ.ER, selectedES)
16:    else
17:       Assign_Partial_Energy(tᵢ.ER, selectedES, nc, threshold)
18: return energy_comp
```

1: for t_i in $\mathcal{MED}$ do
2:    $selectedES = \{\}$
3:    $demand = t_i.re$
4:    for es_j in $t_i.\mathcal{ES}$ do
5:       if $demand > 0$ then
6:          $demand = demand$ - $es_j.p_{ae}$
7:          $energy\_comp.add(t_i, es_j)$
8:          $selectedES.add(es_j)$
9:          if $demand < 0$ then
10:             $es_j.p_{ae} = demand$ * -1
11:             $demand = 0$
12:          else
13:             **Remove_Service**$(es_j, \mathcal{MED})$
14:    if $demand = 0$ then
15:       **Assign_Energy**$(t_i.\mathcal{ER}, selectedES)$
16:    else
17:       **Assign_Partial_Energy**$(t_i.\mathcal{ER}, selectedES, nc, threshold)$
18: **return** $energy\_comp$

4.2 Energy Services Composition

This phase aims to compose energy services to maximize the QoE. We propose two heuristic approaches to compose energy services: *Partial-Based* (PB) and *Demand-Based* (DB). The PB composition is inspired by the FCFS resource allocation algorithm [14]. The PB approach, splits services among consumers if the required energy is more than the available energy. Intuitively, offering part of the services will satisfy more consumers than offering it to some of them. The DB composition is inspired by the priority allocation algorithm [14]. The DB approach extends the PB approach by prioritizing slots with the highest demanding to ensure services availability. We discuss each approach below.

Partial-Based Energy Services Composition. The Partial-Based (PB) composition aims at maximizing the QoE by composing services for each time slot based on the first come first served approach. For example, if a provider offers their services on two-time slots, the algorithm will assign the service for the earlier time slot. If the time slot did not need the service, the service will be assigned to the next time slot. Moreover, PB chunks services between energy consumers if the available energy services are not enough to fulfill the total required energy in the time slot. Intuitively, offering part of the required services to all consumers is more satisfying than offering it only to some of them.

Algorithm 1 presents the PB service composition. For every time slot t_i, the algorithm retrieves the total required amount of energy (Line 3). Then, for

---

Algorithm 2. Demand-Based Composition of Services

Input: $\mathcal{MED}$, $\mathcal{ES}$, threshold
Output: energy_comp
1: $\mathcal{SMED} = \mathbf{sort}(\mathcal{MED}, nc : descending, re : descending)$
2: **for** t_i in $\mathcal{SMED}$ **do**
3:     selectedES = {}
4:     demand = $t_i.re$;
5:     sortedES = $\mathbf{sort}(t_i.\mathcal{ES}, nt : ascending)$
6:     **for** es_j in sortedES **do**
7:         **if** demand > 0 **then**
8:             demand = demand - $es_j.p_{ae}$
9:             energy_comp.add(t_i, es_j)
10:            selectedES.add(es_j)
11:            **if** demand < 0 **then**
12:                $es_j.p_{ae}$ =demand * -1
13:                demand = 0
14:            **else**
15:                **Remove_Service**($es_j, \mathcal{SMED}$)
16:        **if** demand = 0 **then**
17:            **Assign_Energy**($t_i.\mathcal{ER}$, selectedES)
18:        **else**
19:            **Assign_Partial_Energy**($t_i.\mathcal{ER}$, selectedES, nc, threshold)
20: **return** energy_comp

---

each registered service es in t, the algorithm keeps adding services to the set of selected services until the required energy is fulfilled or all the available services have been selected (Lines 4 - 13). Note that if a service was partially needed, then the service available amount will be updated to be used by other registered time slots (Lines 9 - 11). Moreover, if a service was fully used by a time slot, then it will be removed from other registered time slots (Lines 12 - 13). After processing all services, if the energy demand of the slot is zero, the algorithm assigns the selected services to requests (Lines 14 - 15). If the energy demand is not fulfilled, the algorithm distributes the available services among available requests (Line 17). If the service chunks are smaller than the threshold, consumers will be removed and the service will be shared among the rest. The threshold prevents dividing services into small neglectable chunks. The composition of the selected services will be returned in Line 18.

Demand-Based Energy Services Composition. The Demand-Based (DB) composition goal is to maximize QoE by giving priority to time slots with higher energy demand. The intuitive idea of the DB approach is that high-demanding time slots will require more services. Thus, services should be assigned to them prior to less demanding time slots which may ensure a better distribution of the available services. For instance, if a provider offers their service on two-time slots, the algorithm will assign the service to the more demanding time slot.

If that time slot does not need the service, the service will be assigned to the next time slot. This indicates that the order of time slots in composing services matters because if a service is used in a time slot, it will be removed from others. Removing a service from a time slot may affect the amount of available energy and thus the number of served and satisfied consumers. Moreover, DB approach maximizes the QoE by chunking services between energy consumers if the available services are not enough.

Algorithm 2 presents the DB service composition. The algorithm starts by sorting the time slots in a descending order based on the number of consumers nc, then the amount of requested energy re (Line 1). The goal of sorting is to start composing services for the most demanding time slots. As some services may be registered in multiple services, using these services for the most demanding time slots may offer a better experience. Line 4 retrieves the total required amount of energy for each time slot t_i. Then, for every time slot, the registered services will be sorted in ascending order based on the number of time slots a service was registered in. This sort will allow us to start with the least connected services. In other words, using such services may impact less number of time slots than using services that are registered in many time slots. Then, for each registered service es in t, the algorithm keeps adding services to the set of selected services until the required energy is fulfilled or all the available services have been selected (Lines 6 - 15). Similar to the PB approach, if a service was partially needed, then the service available amount will be updated to be used by other registered time slots (Lines 11 - 13). Moreover, if a service was fully used by a time slot, then it will be removed from other registered time slots (Lines 14 - 15). After processing all services, if the energy demand of the slot is zero, the algorithm assigns the selected services to requests (Lines 16 - 17). If the energy demand is not fulfilled, the algorithm distributes the available services among available requests (Line 19). If the service chunks are smaller than the threshold, consumers will be removed and the service will be shared among the rest. The threshold prevents dividing services into small neglectable chunks. Line 20 returns the composition of the selected services.

4.3 Assessing Quality of Experience

The super-provider assesses the QoE of each proposed composition in this phase. The QoE is computed using the model discussed in Sect. 3. The assessment of QoE gives an indicator of consumers' satisfaction in the microcell.

5 Evaluation

We compare the proposed composition approaches, Partial-Based composition (PB), and Demand-Based Composition (DB), with the resource allocation algorithms, namely, first come first served allocation (*Greedy*), and Max-Min Fair allocation (*Max-Min*) [2,14]. The *Greedy* approach is a modified FCFS algorithm where the time slots and services will be scheduled based on their start time.

The *Max-Min* is a modified Max-Min Fair allocation where services that can be offered in multiple time slots will be split among these time slots using the a Max-Min technique. We evaluate the *effectiveness* and the *efficiency* of each approach.

5.1 Dataset Description

We used a real dataset generated from the developed app in [17]. The dataset consists of energy transfer records between a provider (smartphone) and a consumer (smartphone). The records attributes are the provider ID, consumer ID, transaction date, time, energy services' and requests' amount, and transfer duration. We use the energy dataset to generate the QoS parameters for the energy services and requests. For instance, the amount of a wireless charging transfer in mAh is used to define the amount of requested/provided energy. In addition, the energy dataset records of a wireless charging transfer duration are used to define the end time of each request/service.

Table 1. Experiments Variables

Variables	Value
Energy dataset for coffee shop 8 in April	16830
Number of services & requests	[300–2000]/run
Number of time slots	6
Provided energy	5–100%
Requested energy	5–100%
Time interval	6 h
Service registration	[1–3] time slots/service

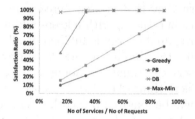

Fig. 4. The average of satisfaction ratio

We augmented the dataset of the energy sharing to mimic the behavior of the crowd within microcells by utilizing a dataset published by IBM for a coffee shop chain with three branches in New York city[5]. The dataset consists of transaction records of customers purchases in each coffee shop for one month. Each coffee shop consists of, on average, 560 transnational records per day and 16,500 transaction record in total. We use the IBM dataset to simulate the spatio-temporal features of energy services and requests. Our experiment uses the consumer ID, transaction date, time, location, and coffee shop ID from each record in the dataset to define the spatio-temporal features of energy services and requests, e.g., start and location of energy service or a request. We ran a total of 7000 experiments with 6-time slots each time slot was an hour long. In each run, the providers' temporal provision preferences were registered randomly to [1–3] time slots. In addition, the number of services and requests varied between 300 to 2000 per run depending on the experiments' setting. For each run, we used the proposed approaches to compose energy services. We then measured the QoE for each composition. Table 1 presents the experiments parameters.

---

[5] https://ibm.co/2O7IvxJ.

5.2   Evaluation of the Composition Framework

We ran six experiments to determine the effectiveness and efficiency of the proposed approaches. The experiments evaluated the approaches in terms of their satisfaction rate, fulfillment rate, quality of experience, impact of thresholds and computation cost. We run the approaches in different settings by changing the ratio of services to requests in the time interval T. We gradually increased the ratio from 15% to 90%. We repeated the experiment 1000 times at each point and considered the average value for each approach.

Quality of Experience Evaluation. As previously stated, we compute the QoE based on $\mathcal{SR}$ and $\mathcal{FR}$ (See Sect. 3). In this subsection, we study the impact of each ratio, then we evaluate the QoE.

The first experiment compares the $\mathcal{SR}$ of the proposed approaches PB and DB, against Greedy and Max-Min. As previously stated, $\mathcal{SR}$ represents the number of consumers who received energy fully or partially. Therefore, a high $\mathcal{SR}$ of a composition ensures a higher number of satisfied consumers and thereby a better QoE. The $\mathcal{SR}$ of a time slot is computed using Eq. 2 and then averaged for the microcell similar to the first part of Eq. 4. Figure 4 presents the average $\mathcal{SR}$ in the microcell for each approach. The x-axis in Figs. 4, 5, 6 and 7 represents the ratio of the number of energy services to requests. In Fig. 4, the $\mathcal{SR}$ increases when the number of available services increases for all the composition approaches. For instance, when the ratio of services to requests is 80%, all approaches provide a higher $\mathcal{SR}$ compared to the ratio is 20%. This observation can be explained by the availability of services to offer energy. The more services available, the more requests can be fulfilled. The proposed approach PB performs better than Greedy as it splits the available energy between the consumers as partial services, unlike the Greedy approach which fulfills a request fully before serving the next request. For the same reason PB also performs better than Max-Min. Even though, Max-Min has a better energy utilization by splitting energy services fairly between time slots (See Fig. 5), a fair distribution of energy does not necessarily result in equally satisfied consumers as in the time slots. This is due to the different energy requirements of consumers. In addition, the proposed

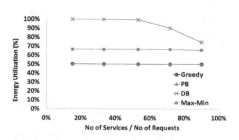

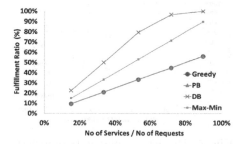

Fig. 5. The average of energy utilization   **Fig. 6.** The average of fulfillment ratio

approach DB gives the best results as it prioritizes the time slots that have the highest demand in terms of the number of consumers and amount of required energy. Recall the order of time slots in composing services is crucial because if a service is used in a time slot, it will be removed from others. Removing a service from a time slot may affect the amount of available energy and thus the number of served consumers. Prioritizing the most demanding time slots allows DB to have more services to use, and therefore increases $\mathcal{SR}$ by increasing the number of fulfilled consumers.

The second experiment compares the $\mathcal{FR}$ of each approach. As previously stated, $\mathcal{FR}$ presents the rate of fulfillment for each request. Therefore, a high $\mathcal{FR}$ of a composition ensures a higher level of satisfaction for consumers and thereby a better QoE. The $\mathcal{FR}$ of a time slot is computed using Eq. 3 and then averaged for the microcell similar to the second part of Eq. 4. Figure 6 represents the average $\mathcal{FR}$ in the microcell for each approach. In Fig. 6, the $\mathcal{FR}$ increases when the number of available services increases for all the approaches. This observation can be explained by the availability of services to offer energy. PB performs similar to Greedy in terms of $\mathcal{FR}$. This is an expected behaviour since both approaches start with the same time slots and, therefore, have the same set of available services. The difference between both approaches is in the way they share energy among consumers, i.e., complete services in Greedy and partial services in PB. Moreover, Max-Min has a better $\mathcal{FR}$ because it has better energy utilization (see Fig. 5). A higher energy utilization is achieved by splitting energy services fairly between time slots. DB gives the best results as it prioritizes the time slots that have the highest demand as discussed in the previous experiment.

The third experiment compares the QoE using all approaches. As previously stated, the QoE presents the overall satisfaction of consumers across time. Therefore, a high QoE of a composition indicates a higher level of satisfaction for consumers. The QoE is computed using Eq. 4. Note that we used $\alpha = 0.5$ to give equal weight for both $\mathcal{SR}$ and $\mathcal{FR}$. Figure 7 presents the average QoE using each approach. In Fig. 7, similar to the previous experiments, the QoE increases when the availability of services increase. PB approach performs better than Greedy in terms of QoE due to its higher $\mathcal{SR}$ as discussed in the first experiment.

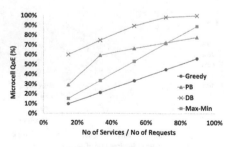

Fig. 7. The average of quality of experience

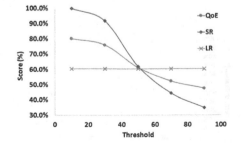

Fig. 8. The average of $\{QoE, \mathcal{SR}, \mathcal{FR}\}$ using PB composition

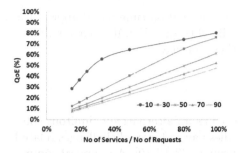

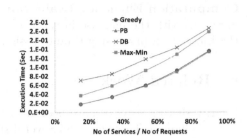

Fig. 9. The average of QoE using PB composition with various thresholds in a microcell

Fig. 10. The average execution time of all composition

Additionally, PB preforms better than Max-Min when the number of energy services is less than the request. This is because in a limited resources environment PB will satisfy more consumers (higher $\mathcal{SR}$) by partially fulfilling their requests. However, when there is enough services, Max-Min will better utilize the energy to completely fulfill requests (higher $\mathcal{FR}$). Moreover, the DB approach gives the best results due to its higher $\mathcal{SR}$ and $\mathcal{FR}$.

Threshold Impact Evaluation. The following two experiments study the impact of thresholds on the PB approach. Recall that PB and DB approaches split energy between consumers based on a defined threshold. The threshold prevents dividing services into small neglectable chunks. The experiments of both PB and DB gave the same behavior. Thus, we are only presenting the results of PB.

Figure 8 represents the impact of the threshold on the three previously tested attributes: $\mathcal{SR}$, $\mathcal{FR}$, and QoE. We tested the PB approach with a 99% ratio of services to requests. The x-axis in Fig. 8 represents the threshold of partial services. FR does not change as the threshold increases, because it relies on the order of time slots and not the size of distribution (threshold) as discussed in the previous experiment. Also, both $\mathcal{SR}$ and QoE decrease as the threshold increases due to the thresholds' size. When the threshold's size increases, fewer consumers will be served. A lower number of fulfilled consumers results in low $\mathcal{SR}$ and thereby a low QoE.

The fifth experiment compares the impact of the threshold on the QoE with different ratios of services to requests. We tested the PB approach with thresholds of {10, 30, 50, 70, 90}. In Fig. 9, the QoE increases when the number of available services increases for all threshold values. Additionally, the QoE for threshold 10 is the highest among all due to the threshold's size. When the size of the threshold is small, more consumers will be served. A higher number of fulfilled consumers results in high $\mathcal{SR}$ and thereby a high QoE.

Computation Efficiency Evaluation. The execution time for all approaches increases with the increase in services' availability (See Fig. 10). This is due to the increase in processing time to assign these services.

6   Related Work

Energy sharing services have been introduced as an alternative ubiquitous solution to charge IoT devices [18]. Several studies have addressed challenges related to fulfilling the requirements of energy consumers [3,16,19]. A temporal composition algorithm was proposed to compose energy services to fulfill a consumer's energy requirement [3]. The algorithm proposed the use of fractional knapsack to maximize the provided energy. An elastic composition was proposed to address the reliability of highly fluctuating energy providers [16]. The composition uses the concepts of soft and hard deadlines to extend the stay of a consumer and select more reliable services. The intermittent behavior of energy services was addressed by a fluid approach [19]. The approach uses the mobility patterns of the crowd to predict the intermittent disconnections in energy services then replace or tolerate theses disconnections. Other studies tackled challenges from a provider's perspective [13,20]. An context-aware incentive model was proposed to address the resistance in providing energy services [13]. Another article addresses the commitment of energy consumers to receive their initiated requests [20]. Existing literature in energy services addresses issues from a consumer or a provider perspective [18]. To the best of our knowledge, challenges related to the microcell perspective such as the QoE are yet to be addressed.

Quality of experience (QoE) has several definitions in the literature based on the field of research [8,21,22]. However, all existing definitions focus on assessing the quality of an application or a service based on the perception of the end-users. In addition, most of the literature focuses on assessing the QoE for multimedia applications. For instance, A method was proposed to gauge gaming QoE under system influencing factors such as delay, packet loss, and frame rates [23]. Another study proposed "Kaleidoscope" as an automated solution to evaluate Web features [10]. As previously stated, the existing research focuses on assessing the QoE of a service based on the perception of the end-users. To the best of our knowledge, assessing the QoE in energy services is not explored yet. In addition, using energy services as a tool to enhance QoE in other microcell-based services is yet to be addressed.

7   Conclusion

We proposed an energy service composition framework that evaluates QoE in a microcell. A new QoE based-assessment was proposed to capture the overall satisfaction across consumers over a period of time. A two QoE-driven composition of energy service were proposed. The Partial-Based (PB) approach uses partial services to maximize the number of satisfied consumers and thereby increase the QoE. The Demand-Based (DB) approach uses partial services and prioritizes the most demanding time slots to maximize the number of satisfied consumers and their level of fulfillment and thereby increase the QoE. Experimental results show that DB outperforms all the evaluated approaches. The efficiency of the proposed approaches was investigated against a Greedy approach. Future direction is to consider the probability of change in the microcell energy demand.

Acknowledgment. This research was partly made possible by LE220100078 and LE180100158 grants from the Australian Research Council. The statements made herein are solely the responsibility of the authors.

References

1. Whitmore, A., Agarwal, A., Da Li, X.: The internet of things-a survey of topics and trends. Inf. Syst. Front. **17**(2), 261–274 (2015)
2. Lakhdari, A., Bouguettaya, A.: Fairness-aware crowdsourcing of IoT energy services. In: Hacid, H., Kao, O., Mecella, M., Moha, N., Paik, H. (eds.) ICSOC 2021. LNCS, vol. 13121, pp. 351–367. Springer, Cham (2021). https://doi.org/10.1007/978-3-030-91431-8_22
3. Lakhdari, A., Bouguettaya, A., Neiat, A.G.: Crowdsourcing energy as a service. In: Pahl, C., Vukovic, M., Yin, J., Yu, Q. (eds.) ICSOC 2018. LNCS, vol. 11236, pp. 342–351. Springer, Cham (2018). https://doi.org/10.1007/978-3-030-03596-9_24
4. Lakhdari, A., et al.: Composing energy services in a crowdsourced IoT environment. IEEE TSC (2020)
5. Dolcourt, J.: Over-the-air wireless charging will come to smartphones (2019)
6. Muller, C.C., Woods, R.H.: An expanded restaurant typology. Cornell Hotel Restaurant Adm. Quart. **35**(3), 27–37 (1994)
7. Chao, T., et al.: C-flow: visualizing foot traffic and profit data to make informative decisions. Technical Report, University of Maryland (2013)
8. Fizza, K., et al.: QoE in IoT: a vision, survey and future directions. Discover Internet Things **1**(1), 1–14 (2021)
9. Möller, S., Raake, A. (eds.): Quality of Experience. TSTS, Springer, Cham (2014). https://doi.org/10.1007/978-3-319-02681-7
10. Wang, P., et al.: Kaleidoscope: a crowdsourcing testing tool for web quality of experience. In: ICDCS, pp. 1971–1982. IEEE (2019)
11. Farris, P.W., et al.: Marketing metrics: the definitive guide to measuring marketing performance. Pearson Education (2010)
12. Lakhdari, A., Bouguettaya, A.: Proactive composition of mobile IoT energy services. In: ICWS, pp. 192–197. IEEE (2021)
13. Abusafia, A., Bouguettaya, A., Mistry, S.: Incentive-based selection and composition of IoT energy services. In: IEEE SCC, pp. 304–311. IEEE (2020)
14. Kruse, R., et al.: Data structures and program design in C. Pearson (2007)
15. Huang, K., et al.: Predicting mobile application usage using contextual information. In: Ubiquitous Computing, pp. 1059–1065 (2012)
16. Lakhdari, A., et al.: Elastic composition of crowdsourced IoT energy services. In: MobiQuitous, pp. 308–317 (2020)
17. Yao, J., et al.: Wireless IoT energy sharing platform. In: PerCom, pp. 118–120. IEEE (2022)
18. Lakhdari, A., et al.: Crowdsharing wireless energy services. In: IEEE CIC, pp. 18–24. IEEE (2020)

19. Lakhdari, A., Bouguettaya, A.: Fluid composition of intermittent IoT energy services. In: SCC, pp. 329–336. IEEE (2020)
20. Abusafia, A., Bouguettaya, A.: Reliability model for incentive-driven IoT energy services. In: MobiQuitous, pp. 196–205 (2020)
21. Gong, Y., et al.: Model-based approach to measuring quality of experience. In: International Conference on Emerging Network Intelligence, pp. 29–32. IEEE (2009)
22. Abusafia, A., et al.: Quality of experience optimization in IoT energy services. In: ICWS. IEEE (2022)
23. Schmidt, S., et al.: Assessing interactive gaming quality of experience using a crowdsourcing approach. In: QoMEX, pp. 1–6. IEEE (2020)

A Multi-task Learning Approach for Predicting Intentions Using Smart Home IoT Services

Bing Huang[1], Boyu Zhang[2(✉)], Quan Z. Sheng[3], and Kwok-Yan Lam[1]

[1] Nanyang Technological University, Singapore, Singapore
{bing.huang,kwokyan.lam}@ntu.edu.sg
[2] Swinburne University of Technology, Melbourne, Australia
boyuzhang@swin.edu.au
[3] Macquarie University, Sydney, Australia
michael.sheng@mq.edu.au

Abstract. We propose a novel approach for predicting a resident's future *intentions* in terms of *what, how, when,* and *where* he will do next. The intention model is learned from his previous interactions with various types of IoT services. In particular, we propose a multi-task learning approach for predicting resident's future intention. The multi-task learning approach jointly learns the tasks of *what, how, when,* and *where* to boost the overall performance of the four tasks. We demonstrate the effectiveness and performance of our approach by conducting experiments on real-world datasets.

Keywords: IoT service · Multi-task learning · Intention · Activity prediction · Smart home

1 Introduction

Over the decades, the Internet is evolving from interconnecting computers to the current interconnection of people, and the rising interconnection of billions of things [8]. Things on the Internet are referred to as *IoT services* [1,3]. The proliferation of IoT services brings many opportunities to smart homes. A smart home is any regular home that is equipped with various types of IoT services [7]. A resident performs daily activities such as "making coffee" by interacting with different IoT services. The ultimate goal of the smart home is to make residents' home life to be more convenient, efficient, and enjoyable by automating repetitive and cumbersome interactions with IoT services [4]. In this regard, the smart home system should be capable of understanding a resident's potential needs and responding proactively at the right time and in the right place. To empower such high-level intelligence in smart homes, a key task is to predict residents' future *intentions*. A resident's future intention can be loosely defined as what activity he/she is going to perform, how he/she performs the activity, and when and where he/she will perform the activity. Specifically, the *what, how,*

J. Troya et al. (Eds.): ICSOC 2022, LNCS 13740, pp. 413–421, 2022.
https://doi.org/10.1007/978-3-031-20984-0_29

when, and *where* perspectives describe the category of the activity, a sequence of actions, the time information, and the location information of the activity, respectively. For example, a resident will make coffee at 8am in the kitchen by interacting with the fridge and the coffee maker. "Making coffee", "8am", "in the kitchen" and "< fridge, coffee maker >" are the corresponding *"what"*, *"when"*, *"where"* and *"how"* aspects of the resident's intention.

It is challenging to learn the intention model because it has four aspects including *what* (activity category), *how* (action), *when* (time), and *where* (location) regarding an activity. The four aspects are inter-dependent because a resident has the habit of performing an activity at a particular time and in a particular location by interacting with a collection of IoT services. We propose a novel multi-task learning approach to predict a resident's future intention by analyzing his/her previous interactions with IoT services. Our approach considers the latent inter-dependency between *what, how, when*, and *where* aspects of an activity and jointly train the four tasks. Our intention forecasting model can serve as a core component in an intelligent control system for anticipating future IoT services and automating these services for residents. To the best of our knowledge, there is not much research on predicting residents' intentions in smart homes. In a nutshell, the key contribution is a new approach of learning the intention model from the history of residents' interactions with IoT services.

2   Intention Model

We first introduce the notion of IoT service based on its functionalities and qualities [2]. Then we introduce the intention model that captures the spatio-temporal regularities of activities. Finally, we formalize the research problem.

Definition 1: IoT Service. An IoT service s_i is defined as a tuple $s_i =< id, F, Q >$ where:

- id is a unique IoT service identifier.
- $F = \{f_1, f_2, ..., f_n\}$ is a set of functionalities offered by the IoT service.
- $Q = \{q_1, q_2, ..., q_m\}$ is a set of qualities of the IoT service.

Definition 2: IoT Service Event. An IoT service event e_i describes an execution of an IoT service s_i at a time stamp t_i and in the location l_i. It is denoted as $e_i =< s_{id}, t_i, l_i >$. For example, the light *L100* is turned on at 2pm in the bedroom can be represented as "< *L100*, ON, 2pm, bedroom >".

Definition 3: IoT Service Event Sequence. An IoT service event sequence E is a set of IoT service events that are ordered by time stamps.

Definition 4: Intention. An intention is an occurrence of an activity. It describes *what, how, when*, and *where* the activity is performed. It is represented as a tuple $In_i =< id, lab_i, a_i, [t_s, t_e], loc_i >$ where:

- id is a unique identifier of the In_i.
- lab_i is an activity label associated with the intention. It corresponds to the *what* perspective.
- a_i is a sequence of IoT services involved in the activity. It corresponds to the *how* aspect of the intention.
- $[t_s, t_e]$ is the temporal aspect (i.e., corresponding to the *when* aspect) of the intention. It describes the start time t_s and end time t_e of the activity.
- loc_i is the spatial aspect (i.e., corresponding to the *where* aspect) of the intention. It describes the location of the activity.

Problem Formulation. Given an IoT service event sequence E, our goal is to learn an intention model In such that it can predict the next intention.

3   Multi-task Learning Approach

We propose a novel multi-task recurrent neural network approach for predicting the intentions in terms of *what, how, when,* and *where* aspects. Our choice of LSTM-based multi-task learning approach is based on two reasons. First, the tasks of predicting *what(activity)*, *how(action)*, *when(time)* and *where(location)* are highly inter-dependent. Multi-task learning is a promising paradigm to leverage useful information contained in multiple related tasks to improve the performance of the new relevant task [10]. Second, each aspect of the intention exhibits sequential patterns. Specifically, the resident performs a series of activities from time to time and she may travel from one place to another. Each activity constitutes a sequence of actions. *Long-short term memory* (LSTM) is a promising approach to capture such sequential patterns [6].

The detailed architecture of the LSTM-based multi-task learning model is shown in Fig. 1. The architecture has two main components including the LSTM layer and the task-specific layer. The LSTM layer is a share-bottom multitask structure for capturing the sequential patterns of the four tasks (i.e., the four tasks refer to predicting activity category, predicting action, predicting time, and predicting location.). The task-specific layers are fully-connected layers for predicting the four tasks.

Suppose we have an IoT service event sequence $E = \{< a_1, e_1, t_1, l_1 >, < a_2, e_2, t_2, l_2 > ... < a_n, e_n, t_n, l_n >\}$. For each event $e_i =< a_i, e_i, t_i, l_i >$, we convert a_i, e_i, t_i, and l_i to vectors using one-hot encoding technique and concatenate them as the input x_i to the model:

$$x_i = concat(a_i, e_i, t_i, l_i) \tag{1}$$

In time step i, the LSTM cell takes x_i and the last hidden state h_{i-1} as inputs and generates the next hidden state h_i. The hidden state h_i is used as input to the next time step of LSTM cell. It also serves as an input to the later task-specific layers. The h_i is computed by Eq. (2):

$$h_i = LSTM(x_i, h_{i-1}) \tag{2}$$

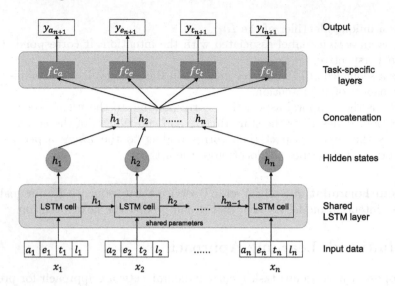

Fig. 1. The architecture of the multi-task model for learning intentions

We concatenate all the hidden states $\{h_i\}_{i=1}^n$ into a vector ch by Eq. (3). We use the vector ch as the input to the task-specific layers fc_a, fc_e, fc_t, fc_l for predicting the activity $y_{a_{n+1}}$, action $y_{e_{n+1}}$, time $y_{t_{n+1}}$ and location $y_{l_{n+1}}$ at time step $n+1$ by Eqs. (4)-(7).

$$ch = concat(\{h_i\}_{i=1}^n) \tag{3}$$

$$fc_a(ch) = w_a \cdot ch + b_a \tag{4}$$

$$fc_e(ch) = w_e \cdot ch + b_e \tag{5}$$

$$fc_t(ch) = w_t \cdot ch + b_t \tag{6}$$

$$fc_l(ch) = w_l \cdot ch + b_l \tag{7}$$

where w_a, w_e, w_t, and w_l are weights and b_a, b_e, b_t, and b_l are bias terms.

We define the four tasks as classification tasks and define the loss functions as below by using the cross-entropy loss.

$$\mathcal{L}_a = CrossEntropy(\hat{y}_{a_{n+1}}, y_{a_{n+1}}) \tag{8}$$

$$\mathcal{L}_e = CrossEntropy(\hat{y}_{e_{n+1}}, y_{e_{n+1}}) \tag{9}$$

$$\mathcal{L}_t = CrossEntropy(\hat{y}_{t_{n+1}}, y_{t_{n+1}}) \tag{10}$$

$$\mathcal{L}_l = CrossEntropy(\hat{y}_{l_{n+1}}, y_{l_{n+1}}) \tag{11}$$

where $\hat{y}_{a_{n+1}}$, $\hat{y}_{e_{n+1}}$, $\hat{y}_{t_{n+1}}$ and $\hat{y}_{l_{n+1}}$ are the one-hot encoded ground truth of activity, action, time, and location at time step $n+1$, respectively.

Finally, we linearly combine the loss functions as the overall loss function $\mathcal{L}$.

$$\mathcal{L} = \lambda_a \mathcal{L}_a + \lambda_e \mathcal{L}_e + \lambda_t \mathcal{L}_t + \lambda_l \mathcal{L}_l \tag{12}$$

where $\lambda_a, \lambda_e, \lambda_t, \lambda_l$ are the hyper-parameters to control the importance across activity, action, time, and location prediction. To avoid tedious optimal parameters searching for $\lambda_a, \lambda_e, \lambda_t$ and λ_l, we set them as 1 and use the MetaBalance technique [5] to automatically balance the gradients of four loss in the same magnitude to prevent some tasks from being too strong that dominate the learning process or too weak to contribute to the learning process. In the backward process, the gradients of the four losses, $\Delta \mathcal{L}_a$, $\Delta \mathcal{L}_e$, $\Delta \mathcal{L}_t$ and $\Delta \mathcal{L}_l$ w are used to update the parameters of their corresponding task-specific layers and jointly update the parameters of the shared LSTM layer. In this way, the task-specific information are shared across different tasks which contributes to improve the generalization.

4   Experimental Results

We evaluate our approach using three real-world datasets, namely, Data1, Data2, and Data3. The three datasets are summarized in Table 1. Both Data1 and Data2 are collected from smart home environments[1]. They are in the format of <date, time stamp, sensor ID, on/off> (e.g., <2008–02–27, 12:46:37, M13, OFF>). Data3 is collected from an old person's (i.e., subject 2) apartment for 17 days [9]. The Data3 is in the format of <id, start time, end time, location> (e.g., <light,7:00, 8:00, bedroom>)).

Table 1. Summary of real-world datasets

ID	No. of activity categories	No. of sensors	No. of locations	No. of events
Data1	5	25	2	6,424
Data2	8	47	4	8,147
Data3	23	70	9	3,501

For the time information in the three datasets, we divide each day into 24 time slots. In this regard, the granularity of the time aspect is the hour. For example, <L100-ON, 7:10am, bedroom> is converted into <L100-ON, 7, bedroom>. Each dataset is divided into training (70%) and testing(30%) portions. The detailed hyperparameter settings are shown in Table 2. We use a sliding window with 12 steps size in the model training and testing processes. We choose the Adam optimizer for the Gradient descent algorithm. We set the learning rate ε, batch size α, and epoch number β to be 0.001, 32, and 100, respectively. As mentioned earlier, we set all the hyper-parameters $\lambda_a, \lambda_e, \lambda_t, \lambda_l$ as 1 to guarantee the equal importance of the four tasks.

---

[1] http://casas.wsu.edu/datasets/.

Table 2. Hyperparameter settings for model training

Hyperparameters	Values
Window size (w)	12
Gradient descent algorithm (G)	Adam
Learning rate (ε)	0.001
Batch size (α)	32
Epoch number (β)	100
$< \lambda_a, \lambda_e, \lambda_t, \lambda_l >$	$< 1, 1, 1, 1 >$

We evaluate the performance of our proposed approach using four metrics including *accuracy, precision, recall* and *f1 score*. Since predicting activities, events, time, and locations are all multi-class classification tasks, we use macro average *precision, recall* and *f1 score* to calculate the overall metrics. In our case of simultaneously predicting multiple tasks, we treat it as multi-class classification and each unique combination of multiple task labels will be treated as one class. We conduct three sets of experiments on Data1, Data2, and Data3 to evaluate the performance of our model in predicting a single task, two-joint tasks, and four-joint tasks, respectively.

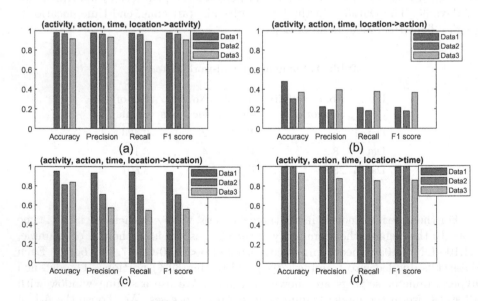

Fig. 2. Performance of predicting each individual task

Experiment I: Performance of Predicting Each Individual Task. We examine the performance of our model in predicting each aspect of the intention at a time. The model is trained using four aspects of the intention (i.e., *what,* *how, when, where*). The experimental results of predicting the single aspect of *what* (*activity*), *how* (*action*), *when* (*time*), and *where* (*location*) are shown in Figs. 2(a), (b), (c), (d), respectively. Specifically, Fig. 2(a) shows the average accuracy, precision, recall, f1 score in predicting the next activity category for Data1, Data2, and Data3. Our approach performs well in predicting the next activity category on all datasets. In particular, it performs the best on Data1, followed by Data2, and the least on Data3. For the three datasets, our approach achieves an average score of more than 90% in accuracy, precision, recall, and f1 score. For example, when Data1 is used, our approach's accuracy, precision, recall, and f1 score are 98.04%, 97.53%, 97.29%, and 97.40%, respectively. Our approach also performs well in predicting the *when* aspect of the intention as shown in Fig. 2(d). The score of accuracy, precision, recall, and f1 score for the three datasets is higher than 80%. The overall performance of our approach on Data2 is the best, with higher than 95% scores in accuracy, precision, recall, and f1 score. Figure 2(c) depicts the performance of predicting the *where* aspect of the intention. We can see that our approach performs the best on Data1 with 95.20% accuracy, 93.33% precision, 94.47% recall, and 93.88% f1 score. It achieves the lowest scores of accuracy (83.88%), precision (57.37%), recall (54.73%), and f1 score (55.89%) on Data3. Figure 2(b) shows the performance of predicting the *how* aspect of the intention on the three datasets. The score of accuracy, precision, recall, and f1 for the three datasets ranges from 20% to 40%. Our approach achieves higher precision, recall, and f1 score on Data3 than that of Data1 and Data2 and achieves lower accuracy than that of Data1.

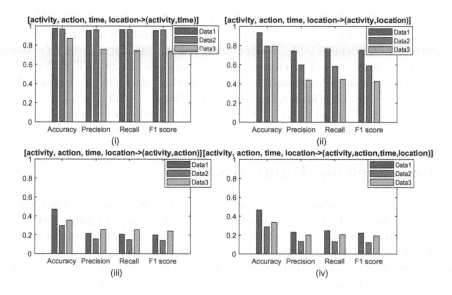

Fig. 3. Performance of predicting joint tasks

Experiment II: Performance of Predicting Two-Joint Tasks. We study the performance of our approach in predicting two-joint tasks at a time. In particular, we evaluate the following two-joint tasks: (i) [*activity, action, time, location -> activity, time*] (i.e., given a sequence of new events, *what* type of activity a resident will do next and *when* he will do it.), (ii) [*activity, action, time, location -> activity, location*] (i.e., given a sequence of new events, *what* type of activity a resident will do next and *where* he will do it.), and (iii) [*activity, action, time, location -> activity, action*] (i.e., given a sequence of new events, *what* type of activity a resident will do next, and *how* he will do it.). The experimental results for (i), (ii), and (iii) are shown in Fig. 3(i), (ii), and (iii), respectively. It can be seen that the overall performance of jointly predicting activity and time (Fig. 3(i)) is much better than that of jointly predicting activity and its location or action (Fig. 3(ii) and (iii)). For example, the scores of accuracy, precision, recall, and f1 for Data1 and Data2 are higher than 96%, which is an expected result. This result can be inferred from Fig. 2(a) and (d) which demonstrates the high performance of our approach in predicting respective activity and time. For the performance of jointly predicting activity and location, our approach performs better on Data1, achieving 93.29% accuracy, 74.23% precision, 77.11% recall, and 75.33% f1 score as shown in Fig. 3(ii). The task (iii) achieves the score of accuracy, precision, recall, and f1 ranging from 15% to 40% for the three datasets. It is obvious that the performance of the task (iii) is no better than that of the task (i) and (ii). The reason is that the feature space of action is larger than that of activity, time, and location.

Experiment III: Performance of Predicting Four-Joint Tasks. We conduct the third set of experiments to assess the performance of our approach in predicting the four-joint task (iv): [*activity, action, time, location -> (activity, action, time, location)*]. The experimental results are shown in Fig. 3(iv). The score of accuracy, precision, recall, and f1 for the three datasets falls between 15% and 40%. For example, the accuracy scores for Data1, Data2, Data3 are respective 46.62%, 28.78%, and 33.41%. It can be seen that the overall performance of our approach on Data1 outperforms that of Data2 and Data3.

5   Conclusion and Future Work

We addressed the problem of predicting a resident's future intention in terms of *what, how, when,* and *where* aspects of activities. We proposed a multi-task learning approach for predicting future intentions. The experimental results on real-world datasets demonstrate the performance of our proposed approach under different complexity of tasks. In the future, we plan to further improve the performance of predicting the intention. We will also use the intention model to explain IoT services' network behavior.

Acknowledgements. This research is supported by the Cyber Security Agency of Singapore (CSA), under its repertoire of initiatives leveraging on research institutes and think-tanks to contribute to the international community "towards a secure and trusted IoT ecosystem".

References

1. Huang, B., Bouguettaya, A., Dong, H., Chen, L.: Service mining for internet of things. In: Sheng, Q.Z., Stroulia, E., Tata, S., Bhiri, S. (eds.) ICSOC 2016. LNCS, vol. 9936, pp. 566–574. Springer, Cham (2016). https://doi.org/10.1007/978-3-319-46295-0_36
2. Huang, B., Bouguettaya, A., Neiat, A.G.: Discovering spatio-temporal relationships among IoT services. In: 2018 IEEE International Conference on Web Services (ICWS), pp. 347–350. IEEE (2018)
3. Bouguettaya, A., Sheng, Q.Z., Benatallah, B., Neiat, A.G., Mistry.: An internet of things service roadmap. Commun. ACM **64**(9), 86–95 (2021)
4. Hamdan, Y.B., et al.: Smart home environment future challenges and issues-a survey. J. Electron. **3**(01), 239–246 (2021)
5. He, Y., Feng, X., Cheng, C., Ji, G., Guo, Y., Caverlee, J.: Metabalance: improving multi-task recommendations via adapting gradient magnitudes of auxiliary tasks. In: The ACM Web Conference 2022, pp. 2205–2215 (2022)
6. Hochreiter, S., Schmidhuber, J.: Long short-term memory. Neural Comput. **9**(8), 1735–1780 (1997)
7. Huang, B.: Enabling Convenience in IoT-based Smart Homes, Ph. D. Thesis (2021)
8. Sheng, M., Qin, Y., Yao, L., Benatallah, B.: Managing the web of things: linking the real world to the web. Morgan Kaufmann (2017)
9. Tapia, E.M., Intille, S.S.: Activity recognition in the home using simple and ubiquitous sensors. In: International Conference on Pervasive Computing, pp. 158–175 (2004)
10. Vandenhende, S., Georgoulis, S., Van Gansbeke, W., Proesmans, M., Dai, D., Van Gool, L.: Multitask learning for dense prediction tasks: a survey. IEEE Transactions on Pattern Analysis and Machine Intelligence (2021)

Joint Optimization of Trajectory and Frequency in Energy Constrained Multi-UAV Assisted MEC System

Zhuohan Xu[1], YanPing Yang[2], and Bing Shi[1,3](✉)

[1] School of Computer Science and Artificial Intelligence,
Wuhan University of Technology, Wuhan 430070, China
[2] Beijing Institute of Computer Technology and Applications, Beijing 100039, China
[3] Shenzhen Research Institute of Wuhan University of Technology,
Shenzhen 518000, China
bingshi@whut.edu.cn

Abstract. Mobile edge computing (MEC) is a promising technology to enhance the computation capability of smart devices (SDs) in the Internet-of-Things (IoT). However, the performance of MEC server is limited due to the fixed location and constrained coverage. In order to address this issue, a multiple unmanned aerial vehicles (UAVs) assisted MEC system is studied in this paper. We consider an energy constrained multi-UAV assisted MEC system where multiple UAVs collaborate with each other to provide computing services, and UAVs can dynamically change the frequency according to the computing task size. We aim to maximize the computation bits, SDs' fairness and UAVs' load balancing in multi-UAV MEC system by jointly optimizing the trajectory and frequency. To address this problem, we model it as a Partially Observable Markov Decision Process, and propose a joint optimization strategy based on multi-agent deep reinforcement learning. Finally, we evaluate our strategy against some typical benchmark strategies on the realistic dataset. The experiment results show that our strategy can outperform other strategies.

Keywords: Mobile edge computing · Unmanned aerial vehicle · Multi-agent deep reinforcement learning

1 Introduction

With the rapid development of Internet-of-Things (IoT) technology, smart devices (SDs) play an essential role in various applications [6]. These applications are usually computing-intensive, which results in dramatically increased demands for computing resources, posing a great challenge to SDs due to their limited computing resources and battery capacity. Mobile edge computing (MEC) has been identified as a promising technique to tackle this challenge, which allows SDs to offload their computation-intensive applications to the edge

J. Troya et al. (Eds.): ICSOC 2022, LNCS 13740, pp. 422–429, 2022.
https://doi.org/10.1007/978-3-031-20984-0_30

servers [1]. However, the location of the terrestrial MEC server is usually fixed and cannot be changed or moved according to users' demands. In addition, some MEC server may be damaged by natural disasters or military attacks, causing computing resource scarcity and offloading performance degradation [9]. Due to the highly flexible mobility, easy deployment, low cost and line-of-sight (LoS) connections of unmanned aerial vehicle (UAV), UAV-assisted MEC systems have been widely analyzed in recent years. In the UAV-assisted MEC system, UAV can be used as a MEC server to provide computing services for SDs.

There also exist many challenges in UAV-assisted MEC systems. Due to the mobility and limited onboard energy of UAV, UAVs should maximize their energy efficiency by planning their trajectory in the limited service time. Some works [2] have showed that UAV can adopt dynamic voltage and frequency scaling technique, which can adjust the CPU frequency based on the scale of the computation tasks. Such dynamic approach can achieve better performance than the constant computing technique in terms of the energy consumption, throughput and latency. In addition, the MEC assisted by a single UAV may result in some deficiencies in network scalability. Therefore, multiple UAVs can be used to extend the network coverage and serve more SDs. However, the existing research on UAV-assisted MEC system rarely considers the joint optimization of trajectory and frequency of multiple UAVs under the constraint of energy.

To address the above challenges, an energy constrained multi-UAV assisted MEC system is studied in this paper, where multiple UAVs work together to provide SDs with computing services. We consider the scenario that multiple UAVs fly according to the designed trajectory, collect computing tasks from the SDs within their coverage and each UAV can dynamically adjust its CPU frequency according to the task size. Similar to work in [10], we intend to jointly optimizing the computation bits, SDs' fairness and UAVs' load balancing. Since UAVs need to make decisions in each time slot, and the decisions of UAVs will affect the location and energy of the next time slot, it is a sequential decision-making problem. Thus, we propose a joint optimization strategy based on multi-agent deep reinforcement learning to maximize the computation bits, SDs' fairness and UAVs' load balancing in multi-UAV assisted MEC system. We further evaluate our strategy against some typical benchmark strategies on the realistic dataset. The experiment results show that our strategy can achieve better performance than other strategies.

The rest of this paper is organized as follows. In Sect. 2, we describe the system model and problem formulation. In Sect. 3, we introduce our strategy in multi-UAV assisted MEC system based on MADDPG. The experimental analysis is shown in Sect. 4. Finally, we conclude the paper in Sect. 5.

2   System Model

As shown in Fig. 1, a multi-UAV assisted MEC system is considered, which consists of M UAVs and K SDs, denoted as $\mathcal{M} \triangleq \{1, 2, \ldots, M\}$ and $\mathcal{K} \triangleq \{1, 2, \ldots, K\}$, respectively.

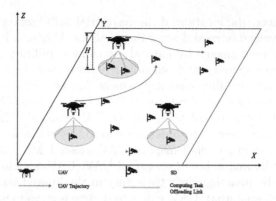

Fig. 1. The multi-UAV assisted MEC system.

We assume that the system operation duration is divided into T time slots, which is indexed by $t \in \mathcal{T} \triangleq \{1, 2, \ldots, T\}$. UAVs can fly through a small distance and provide computing services for SDs within their coverage in each time slot. We list the main notations used in this paper in Table 1.

Table 1. List of main notations.

Notation	Description
M	The number of UAVs
K	The number of SDs
T	The number of time slots
l_{max}	The side length of rectangular area where SDs are located
L_{max}	The maximal size of tasks allowed to be stored in the queue of single SD
C_k^{sd}	The horizon coordinate of SD k
$C_{m,t}^{uav}$	The horizon coordinate of UAV m in time slot t
$d_{\max}$	The maximal flying distance of UAV in each time slot
$R_{\max}$	The maximal horizontal coverage of UAV
$R_{\min}$	The minimal distance leading to collision of UAVs
r_{tran}	The wireless transmission rate of the offloading link
p_{tran}	The wireless transmission power of the offloading link
$E_{m,t}^{total}$	The total energy consumption of UAV m in time slot t
w_{uav}	The weight of UAV
v_{uav}	The speed of UAV
E_{uav}	The energy capacity of UAV

2.1 UAV Computing Model

If SD k generates a computing task at the beginning of time slot t, we define the size of this task as $l_{k,t}$. Let $L_{k,t}$ be the total size of tasks in the queue of SD k waiting to be offloaded in time slot t, which is updated by:

$$L_{k,t+1} = \min\{L_{k,t} + l_{k,t}, L_{max}\} \tag{1}$$

We use the boolean variable $z_{m,k,t}$ to indicate whether SD k is served by UAV m in time slot t:

$$z_{m,k,t} = \begin{cases} 1, R_{m,k,t} \leq R_{max} \text{ and } \forall m' \in \mathcal{M}, m' \neq m, z_{m',k,t} = 0 \\ 0, otherwise \end{cases} \quad (2)$$

Thus, the total size of tasks collected by UAV m in time slot t is:

$$N_{m,t} = \sum_{k=1}^{K} z_{m,k,t} \cdot \min\{L_{k,t} + l_{k,t}, L_{max}\} \quad (3)$$

Then, we update Eq. (1) to:

$$L_{k,t+1} = \begin{cases} 0, \exists m \in \mathcal{M}, z_{m,k,t} = 1 \\ \min\{L_{k,t} + l_{k,t}, L_{max}\}, \forall m \in \mathcal{M}, z_{m,k,t} = 0 \end{cases} \quad (4)$$

we define $Z_{m,k,t}$ as the cumulative service times of UAV m to SD k in time slot t, as:

$$Z_{m,k,t} = \sum_{i=1}^{t} z_{m,k,i} \quad (5)$$

We apply a fairness indicator $F_{m,t}^{sd}$ reflects the level of fairness of UAV m to all SDs in time slot t:

$$F_{m,t}^{sd} = \frac{\left(\sum_{k=1}^{K} Z_{m,k,t}\right)^2}{K \sum_{k=1}^{K} \left(Z_{m,k,t}\right)^2} \quad (6)$$

Similar to [7], we also consider the load balancing between UAVs, for which we define the fairness indicator F_t^{uav} as:

$$F_t^{uav} = \frac{\left(\sum_{m=1}^{M} \sum_{k=1}^{K} Z_{m,k,t}\right)^2}{M \sum_{m=1}^{M} \left(\sum_{k=1}^{K} Z_{m,k,t}\right)^2} \quad (7)$$

2.2 UAV Energy Consumption Model

We assume that the transmission power is p_{tran}, and then the energy consumption of offloading tasks is:

$$E_{m,t}^{tran} = p_{tran} \cdot T_{m,t}^{tran} \quad (8)$$

The computing energy consumption is given by:

$$E_{m,t}^{com} = k_1 \left(f_{m,t}\right)^{k_2} T_{m,t}^{com} \quad (9)$$

The flying energy consumption is given by:

$$E_{m,t}^{fly} = \frac{1}{2} w_{uav} v_{uav}^2 T_{m,t}^{fly} \quad (10)$$

where w_{uav} is the weight of UAV. Finally, we denote the total energy consumption of UAV m in time slot t as:

$$E_{m,t}^{total} = E_{m,t}^{tran} + E_{m,t}^{com} + E_{m,t}^{fly} \quad (11)$$

2.3   Problem Formulation

In this paper, we intend to maximize the total computation bits, SDs' fairness and UAVs' load balancing in multi-UAV assisted MEC system by optimizing UAVs trajectory and frequency while satisfying the UAVs' energy constraints. We formulate our optimization problem as follows:

$$\mathcal{P} : \max \sum_{t=1}^{T} \sum_{m=1}^{M} N_{m,t} F_{m,t}^{sd} F_{t}^{uav} \tag{21}$$

$$s.t.\ z_{m,k,t} = \{0,1\}, \forall m \in \mathcal{M}, k \in \mathcal{K}, t \in \mathcal{T} \tag{C1}$$

$$z_{m,k,t} \cdot R_{m,k,t} \le R_{max}, \forall m \in \mathcal{M}, k \in \mathcal{K}, t \in \mathcal{T} \tag{C2}$$

$$\sum_{m=1}^{M} z_{m,k,t} \le 1, \forall k \in \mathcal{K}, t \in \mathcal{T} \tag{C3}$$

$$\left(x_{m,t}^{uav}, y_{m,t}^{uav}\right) \in [0, l_{max}], \forall m \in \mathcal{M}, t \in \mathcal{T} \tag{C4}$$

$$\left(x_{k}^{sd}, y_{k}^{sd}\right) \in [0, l_{max}], \forall k \in \mathcal{K} \tag{C5}$$

$$R_{m,m',t} \ge R_{min}, \forall m, m' \in \mathcal{M}, m \ne m' \tag{C6}$$

$$\sum_{t=1}^{T} E_{m,t}^{total} \le E_{uav}, \forall m \in \mathcal{M} \tag{C7}$$

In this optimization problem, constraints C1 and C2 mean that UAV can only provide service to SDs within its coverage. Constraint C3 mean that each SD can only be served by at most one UAV at each time slot. Constraints C4 and C5 limit the locations of the UAVs and SDs. Constraint C6 means the minimal distance between UAVs. Constraint C7 means the energy capacity.

3   Joint Optimization Strategy Based on MADDPG

As discussed in Sect. 2, UAVs need to make decisions in each time slot in sequence, and the decisions of UAVs will affect the location and energy of the next time slot, and then affect future decisions. Therefore, the optimization problem in multi-UAV assisted MEC system is a sequential-decision problem, and we model it as a Markov Decision Process (MDP). In addition, since this problem involves multiple agents, and each agent can only observe partial information in the environment, we model it as a Partially Observable Markov Decision Process (POMDP) [4]. We define the observation, action and reward function for each agent in time slot t as follows:

- Observation: we define the observation that UAV m perceives in time slot t as: $o_{m,t} = (C_{m,t}^{uav}, \mathcal{F}_{m,t}^{sd}, \mathcal{F}_t^{uav}, \mathcal{R}_{m,t})$, where $C_{m,t}^{uav}$ is the coordinate of UAV, $\mathcal{F}_{m,t}^{sd} = (\sum_{i=1}^t Z_{m,k,i}, k \in \mathcal{K})$ is the cumulative service times of UAV m to each SD in time slot t, $\mathcal{F}_t^{uav} = (\sum_{i=1}^t \sum_{k=1}^K Z_{m,k,i}, m \in \mathcal{M})$ is the cumulative service times of each UAVs in time slot t, $\mathcal{R}_{m,t} = (R_{m,m',t}, m' \in \mathcal{M}, m \neq m')$ is the distances between UAV m and other UAVs.
- Action: we define the action as: $a_{m,t} = (d_{m,t}, \theta_{m,t}, f_{m,t})$, which consists of flying distance, flying direction and computing frequency of UAV m in time slot t.
- Reward function: we define the reward function as $r_{m,t} = N_{m,t} F_{m,t}^{sd} F_t^{uav} - p_{m,t}$. where $r_{m,t}$ is the immediate reward obtained by the UAV m in time slot t, $p_{m,t}$ is the penalty coefficient if UAV m flies out of the border or UAV m is collided with another UAV in time slot t.

Based on the previous description, we propose the joint optimization strategy based on Multi-Agent Deep Deterministic Policy Gradient (MADDPG) [5], which is called Computing Efficient Joint Optimization in Multi-UAV assisted MEC system (CEJOMU), as shown in Algorithm 1.

Algorithm 1. Computing Efficient Joint Optimization in Multi-UAV assisted MEC system (CEJOMU)

Input: The state s in each time slot
Output: The action a in each time slot
1: **for** $m = 1$ to M **do**
2:     Initialize actor network $\pi_m(\cdot)$, critic network $Q_m(\cdot)$ with parameters θ_m^π and θ_m^Q
3:     Initialize target network $\pi'_m(\cdot)$ and $Q'_m(\cdot)$ with parameters $\theta_m^{\pi'} = \theta_m^\pi$ and $\theta_m^{Q'} = \theta_m^Q$
4: **end for**
5: Initialize random noise function $\mathcal{N}$ and experience replay pool $\mathcal{P}$
6: **for** $episode = 1$ to $episode_{max}$ **do**
7:     Receive the initial state $s_1 = \{o_{m,1}, m \in \mathcal{M}\}$
8:     **for** $t = 1$ to T **do**
9:         **for** $m = 1$ to M **do**
10:            Select the action of UAV m: $a_{m,t} = \pi_m(o_{m,t}) + \mathcal{N}$
11:        **end for**
12:        Execute action $a_t = \{a_{m,t}, m \in \mathcal{M}\}$ and observe reward $r_t = \{r_{m,t}, m \in \mathcal{M}\}$ and next state s_{t+1}
13:        Store (s_t, a_t, r_t, s_{t+1}) in replay buffer $\mathcal{P}$
14:        $s_t \leftarrow s_{t+1}$
15:        **if** $t > episode_{before}$ **then**
16:            **for** $m = 1$ to M **do**
17:                Random sampling from P
18:                Update critic network
19:                Update actor network
20:                Update target networks with updating rate τ:
                        $\theta_m^{\pi'} \leftarrow \tau\theta_m^\pi + (1 - \tau)\theta_m^{\pi'}$
                        $\theta_m^{Q'} \leftarrow \tau\theta_m^Q + (1 - \tau)\theta_m^{Q'}$
21:            **end for**
22:        **end if**
23:    **end for**
24: **end for**

---

4   Experiment Analysis

In order to evaluate the effectiveness and expansibility of the algorithm, we run the experiments on the well-known real-world edge environment dataset Telecom [3,8] as testbeds to conduct our experiments.

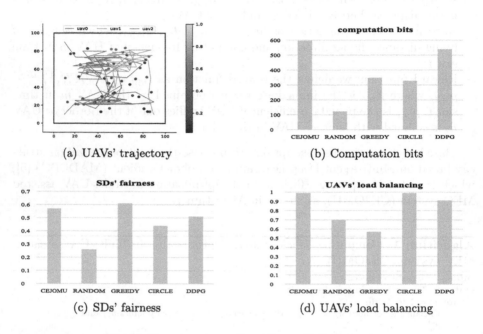

(a) UAVs' trajectory

(b) Computation bits

(c) SDs' fairness

(d) UAVs' load balancing

Fig. 2. Experiment results of the realistic dataset

The experiment results are shown in Fig. 2. The subfigure (a) of each figure is the UAV trajectory drawn by our proposed strategy, and we apply a heat map to reflect the task occurrence rate of each SD. The subfigure (b)-(d) is the performance of different strategies in computation bits, SDs' fairness, and UAVs' load balancing. It can be seen from Fig. 2(a) that UAVs will prefer to serve particular areas. The GREEDY's performance in the realistic dataset is poor, because the number of SDs with high task occurrence rate in the realistic dataset is rare and the location is concentrated, which will cause GREEDY without long-term vision to go to the same location for a long time, resulting in most SDs not being served and energy waste. Note that GREEDY needs to know all SDs' information in advance, and it may be infeasible in real scenarios. CEJOMU based on RL does not need to know SDs' information in advance. It can learn SDs' information through interaction with the environment.

5   Conclusion

In this paper, we analyze the joint optimization problem of trajectory and frequency in multi-UAV assisted MEC system with energy constraints. We model the problem as a Partially Observable Markov Decision Process, and then propose a joint optimization strategy CEJOMU based on multi-agent reinforcement learning MADDPG. Finally, we run experiments to evaluate our strategy against four typical algorithms on the realistic dataset. The experiment results show that CEJOMU achieves the best performance in terms of the computation bits, SDs' fairness and UAVs' load balancing. This research can provide some useful insights for UAV-assisted MEC system in real-world scenarios.

References

1. Chen, Y., Deng, S., Zhao, H., He, Q., Li, Y., Gao, H.: Data-intensive application deployment at edge: a deep reinforcement learning approach. In: 2019 IEEE International Conference on Web Services (ICWS), pp. 355–359. IEEE (2019)
2. Jeong, S., Simeone, O., Kang, J.: Mobile edge computing via a UAV-mounted cloudlet: optimization of bit allocation and path planning. IEEE Trans. Veh. Technol. **67**(3), 2049–2063 (2017)
3. Li, Y., Zhou, A., Ma, X., Wang, S.: Profit-aware edge server placement. IEEE Internet Things J. **9**(1), 55–67 (2021)
4. Littman, M.L.: Markov games as a framework for multi-agent reinforcement learning. In: Machine Learning Proceedings 1994, pp. 157–163. Elsevier (1994)
5. Lowe, R., Wu, Y.I., Tamar, A., Harb, J., Pieter Abbeel, O., Mordatch, I.: Multi-agent actor-critic for mixed cooperative-competitive environments. In: Advances in Neural Information Processing Systems 30 (2017)
6. Wang, F., Xu, J., Cui, S.: Optimal energy allocation and task offloading policy for wireless powered mobile edge computing systems. IEEE Trans. Wireless Commun. **19**(4), 2443–2459 (2020)
7. Wang, L., Wang, K., Pan, C., Xu, W., Aslam, N., Hanzo, L.: Multi-agent deep reinforcement learning-based trajectory planning for multi UAV assisted mobile edge computing. IEEE Trans. Cogn. Commun. Netw. **7**(1), 73–84 (2020)
8. Wang, S., Guo, Y., Zhang, N., Yang, P., Zhou, A., Shen, X.: Delay-aware microservice coordination in mobile edge computing: a reinforcement learning approach. IEEE Trans. Mob. Comput. **20**(3), 939–951 (2019)
9. Zhang, K., Gui, X., Ren, D., Li, D.: Energy-latency tradeoff for computation offloading in UAV -assisted multiaccess edge computing system. IEEE Internet Things J. **8**(8), 6709–6719 (2020)
10. Zhou, F., Wu, Y., Hu, R.Q., Qian, Y.: Computation rate maximization in UAV -enabled wireless-powered mobile-edge computing systems. IEEE J. Sel. Areas Commun. **36**(9), 1927–1941 (2018)

Services for Cloud, Edge, and Fog Computing

Dual-Tree Genetic Programming for Deadline-Constrained Dynamic Workflow Scheduling in Cloud

Yifan Yang$^{(\boxtimes)}$, Gang Chen, Hui Ma, and Mengjie Zhang

School of Engineering and Computer Science, Victoria University of Wellington,
Wellington 6140, New Zealand
{yifan.yang,aaron.chen,hui.ma,mengjie.zhang}@ecs.vuw.ac.nz

Abstract. Dynamic workflow scheduling (DWS) aims to allocate abundant cloud resources to process a large number of heterogeneous workflows in order to minimize total operation cost and the penalty for violating deadline constraints. Instead of using manually designed heuristics that cannot work effectively across different problem instances, we develop a new Genetic Programming Hyper-Heuristic (GPHH) algorithm to automatically design scheduling heuristics for a newly formulated deadline-constrained dynamic workflow scheduling in cloud (DCD-WSC) problem. Different from previous works, our GPHH algorithm can design a pair of rules for Virtual Machine selection and task selection. A new dual-tree representation is proposed to jointly evolve the rule pair, enabling the algorithm to effectively control the inter-dependencies of the two rules. Experimental results show that our new algorithm can significantly outperform three baseline algorithms on a wide range of testing scenarios.

Keywords: Dynamic workflow scheduling · Genetic programming hyper-heuristic · Cloud computing · Deadline constraint

1 Introduction

Many organizations are increasingly relying on cloud computing to process their workflows due to abundant heterogeneous computing resources and secure data storage in cloud [2]. For example, MetService in New Zealand uses multiple cloud resources to process its workflows for daily weather forecasting. Each *workflow* consists of a set of *tasks* with sophisticated *inter-dependencies* [13] and can be provided to numerous customers [2] based on pre-determined *Service Level Agreements* (SLAs). Effective methods are needed to help organisations to decide proper cloud resources for processing workflows to minimize the total cloud resource rental costs and SLA penalties [1,17,22]. In this paper, we use *brokers* to refer the agents who provide workflows as services in cloud.

© The Author(s), under exclusive license to Springer Nature Switzerland AG 2022
J. Troya et al. (Eds.): ICSOC 2022, LNCS 13740, pp. 433–448, 2022.
https://doi.org/10.1007/978-3-031-20984-0_31

For many brokers in cloud, *workflow scheduling* is a vital issue for them to lease and allocate suitable cloud computing resources (i.e., *Virtual Machines* or VMs) to execute a series of dynamically requested workflows in order to achieve important objectives, such as to minimize the total makespan and cost [16]. Many previous studies proposed various scheduling heuristics to tackle such workflow scheduling problems on the fly. However, manual design of scheduling heuristics demands for extensive human labor and domain expertise [7,15,21]. Further, manually designed heuristics can quickly lose effectiveness due to the increasing variety of cloud computing resources and workflow workloads. Furthermore, existing heuristics did not consider penalties resulted from violations of deadline constraints defined by SLA.

Hyper-heuristic techniques can automatically design a wide variety of heuristics and have been extensively utilized to solve diverse combinatorial optimization problems in recent years [11,14,25]. Particularly, a few research works recently developed *Genetic Programming Hyper-Heuristic* (GPHH) algorithms to tackle *dynamic workflow scheduling* (DWS) problems successfully. In [5,6,22], GPHH is explored to evolve a single rule/heuristic to select appropriate VM instances to process each workflow task. However, due to the highly dynamic nature of workflow execution in cloud, using VM selection rule alone is often insufficient (see Subsect. 3.1 and Fig. 1 for detail). Hence, [20] developed a cooperative coevolution GP (CCGP) approach to evolve a pair of task prioritizing rule and VM selection rule. Nevertheless, this method was designed to execute a single workflow without explicitly controlling the inter-dependencies between the two evolved rules. Effective methods are needed to cooperatively generate two rules to schedule a sequence of workflows dynamically arriving the cloud.

The goal of this paper is to develop a new dual-tree GP (DTGP) algorithm to jointly evolve *VM selection rules* (VMSRs) and *task selection rules* (TSRs) to effectively solve the deadline-constrained dynamic workflow scheduling in cloud (DCDWSC) problem. Three major contributions have been achieved:

1. We formally model the DCDWSC problem and demonstrate its practical importance. Different from existing problems, the new problem model considered for the first time the possibility of reordering pending tasks in VM queues to reduce the total cost involved in executing multiple heterogeneous workflows.
2. We develop a DTGP algorithm that uses a new dual-tree representation to effectively support the joint evolution of VMSRs and TSRs and explicitly control their inter-dependencies. Multiple new terminal types (i.e., features used for making scheduling decisions) have also been proposed to facilitate the design of effective VMSRs and TSRs.
3. We conduct extensive experimental evaluation on diverse DCDWSC problem scenarios with a variety of heterogeneous workflows to verify the effectiveness of DTGP. DTGP is experimentally shown to significantly outperform several existing approaches.

2   Related Work

Workflow scheduling aims to allocate cloud resources to process all tasks of one or multiple workflows [16]. All the previously studied workflow scheduling problems are either *static* or *dynamic*.

Most of the static problems concern mainly about scheduling a single workflow [4,15]. Dynamic resource provisioning is often neglected in the problem formulation. In view of the highly dynamic cloud computing environment, the research community is starting to pay more attention to the DWS problems [1,8,19] that consider either dynamic workflow arriving time [1,19] or dynamic resource provisioning [8] based on pre-determined workflow patterns. In fact, existing DWS problems rarely handle multiple heterogeneous workflows simultaneously. Although some studies [6,9] considered several different workflows patterns, a common assumption is to handle each workflow pattern one at a time. As far as we know, no existing studies considered the general and realistic problem for brokers to process a series of dynamically requested workflows with previously unknown patterns.

Most of existing research works focused on VM selection [5,8]. In this paper, we study the DWS problem with deadline constraints that aims to maximize the total profit. On the one hand, it is challenging to decide the number and type of VM instances to rent. To address this issue, we use GPHH to evolve a *VM selection* rule to select VMs to process each task in order to balance the VM rental fees and deadline penalties. On the other hand, it is critical to determine suitable orders to process all tasks pending for execution on a VM instance. Therefore, we further use GPHH to evolve a *task selection* rule to control the processing order of pending tasks so as to reduce deadline violations and shorten the workflow makespan. To the best of our knowledge, this is the first work to jointly consider VM selection and task selection for DWS.

3   Problem Description

3.1   Problem Overview

We assume that workflow requests arrive at a cloud data center dynamically over time. There are a fixed number of VM types available at the data center. An unlimited number of instances can be rented with respect to each VM type. Every workflow consists of a number of tasks and has a workflow pattern and size (see Fig. 1), which are unknown before arrival. Any task can be allocated to either an existing VM instance or any newly leased instance.

Figure 1 illustrates how a *scheduling heuristic* is used to schedule the execution of workflow tasks in the cloud. Different from several existing works [6,20,22], the scheduling heuristic in this paper is composed of a VMSR and a TSR. They are used to jointly support two interdependent scheduling decisions, which are highlighted as *VM selection* and *task selection* in Fig. 1, respectively.

Whenever one or multiple workflows arrive at the cloud, all the *ready tasks* within these workflows will be identified. For each ready task, the VMSR selects

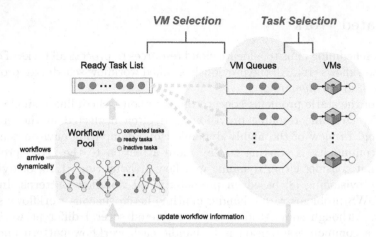

Fig. 1. The procedure of using a heuristic to schedule dynamic workflow execution.

from all candidate VM instances the instance with the highest-priority to process it. We do not only consider existing leased VM instances but also VM instances of any type that can be further leased for workflow execution. In other words, when a task is assigned to a VM instance that was not leased previously, we will lease the VM instance immediately. Upon allocating a task to a VM instance, if the VM instance is idle and has no pending task in its VM Queue, it immediately executes the allocated task; otherwise, the task is added into the instance's VM queue.

Whenever a VM instance completes its execution of one task, the TSR will be activated to select a pending task with the highest priority in its VM queue to be executed next. After a task is processed, some of its successor tasks in the same workflow will become ready. They will be subsequently allocated to either existing VM instances or newly leased VM instances. The above process will be repeated until all tasks of all workflows are processed. Afterwards, the VM rental fees in Eq. (9) and the deadline violation penalties in Eq. (11) will be computed to quantify the performance of the workflow scheduling process.

3.2   Formulation

The broker has no access to the size and pattern of any workflow before its arrival. The broker will also compensate its users if the execution of any workflow violates its deadline constraint specified in the respective SLA.

We consider a collection of dynamically arriving workflows for the DWS problem, denoted as $\mathcal{W} = \{W_1, W_2, ..., W_m\}$. A workflow W_i is defined as:

$$W_i = (DAG_i, AT_i, NOR_i, DL_i, RDL_i) \tag{1}$$

where DAG_i capture the workflow pattern, AT_i denotes the arriving time of the workflow, NOR_i is the total number of unassigned tasks remaining in the workflow, and DL_i denotes the deadline of the workflow. Additionally, RDL_i is the remaining time before the deadline is due, which is calculated by

$$RDL_i = DL_i - current\_time \tag{2}$$

These workflows will be processed by a time varying set of VM instances, denoted as $\mathcal{V} = \{V_1, V_2, ..., V_n\}$. A VM instance V_k is defined as a tuple below:

$$V_k = (TYPE_k, NIQ_k, TIQ_k, VMR_k) \tag{3}$$

where $TYPE_k = (CU_k, MEM_k PRICE_k)$ denotes its VM type. CU_k is the compute unit (i.e., computation capacity), MEM_K is the memory size, and $PRICE_k$ is the hourly rental fee charged by cloud providers. NIQ_k refers to the number of pending tasks in the VM Queue of V_k, TIQ_k is the total execution time of all pending tasks in the queue, and VMR_k is the remaining lease period of V_k of its current lease.

Given the set of all tasks $\{t_{i1}, t_{i2}, ..., t_{iq}\}$ that belong to a workflow W_i, each task $t_{ij} = (NOC_{ij}, TS_{ij})$. NOC_{ij} is the number of its successor tasks. TS_{ij} refers to its size, i.e., the execution time of t_{ij} on a VM instance with the compute unit $CU = 1$. Accordingly, the actual execution time of t_{ij} on V_k is

$$ET_{ij}^k = \frac{TS_{ij}}{CU_k} \tag{4}$$

Furthermore, we can obtain the time RT_{ij} when the task t_{ij} is assigned to an VM instance:

$$RT_{ij} = \max_{z \in pred(t_{ij})} \{FT_z\} \tag{5}$$

where FT_z refer to the finish time of its predecessors. Equation (5) implies that t_{ij} is assigned immediately to a VM instance when all its predecessor tasks are completed. Meanwhile, the ready time of the entry task is equal to the arrival time of its workflow, i.e., $RT_{i1} = AT_i$.

Let ST_{ij}^k be the time that the VM instance V_k starts to execute t_{ij}. The waiting time period WT_{ij}^k of t_{ij} and the finish time FT_{ij}^k of t_{ij} on V_k are defined as:

$$WT_{ij}^k = ST_{ij}^k - RT_{ij} \tag{6}$$

$$FT_{ij}^k = ST_{ij} + ET_{ij}^k \tag{7}$$

Through processing all workflows, we aim to minimize the *total cost* incurred for workflow execution, which consists of both *VM rental fees* and *workflow deadline penalties*, as formulated below

$$TotalCost = \sum_{k \in LVMS} RentFee_k + \sum_{i \in \mathcal{W}} Penalty_i \tag{8}$$

where $LVMS$ is the set of leased VM instances. $\mathcal{W}$ is the set of all workflows to be executed within a given period of time. $RentFee_k$ denotes the rental fee of the VM instance V_k, and $Penalty_i$ denotes the deadline violation penalty of the workflow W_i, as defined below.

1. *RentFee$_k$*: We use the prevailing hourly-based cost model supported by the global cloud market [1,7,18]. The cost of renting any VM instance V_k is calculated by

$$RentFee_k = PRICE_k \times \left\lceil \frac{FT_{t_{last}^k} - ST_{t_{first}^k}}{3600} \right\rceil \tag{9}$$

where t_{first}^k and t_{last}^k are the first task and the last task executed on V_k. Thus, the numerator in Eq. (9) gives the total time period measured in seconds between the start time of t_{first}^k and the finish time of t_{last}^k. The denominator and the ceiling function in Eq. (9) together convert this time period into the total number of leased hours.

2. *Penalty$_i$*: We first define the deadline of a workflow, denoted as $Deadline_i$, below:

$$Deadline_i = AT_i + \xi \times MinMakespan_i \tag{10}$$

where AT_i represents the arrival time of the workflow W_i, and ξ is a *relaxation coefficient* [1]. $MinMakespan_i$ refers to the theoretical shortest completion time of workflow W_i by executing all of its tasks on the fastest VM instances without any delay. Whenever $Deadline_i$ is violated due to delay in executing workflow W_i, penalties will be incurred as determined below:

$$Penalty_i = \delta \max\{0, AT_i + Makespan_i - Deadline_i\} \tag{11}$$

where δ is a *penalty coefficient* [23]. The smaller the value of δ, the greater the tolerance for violating the deadline.

4   Algorithm

To enable GPHH to generate effective rules for the DCDWSC problems, in this paper we propose two distinct sets of terminals to be utilized to design *VMSRs* and *TSRs*, respectively (see Subsect. 4.1 for an introduction of all terminals used in these rules). Note that these sets are different from terminals that are used by existing works [6,20,24], which only focus on building VMSRs, since we include the features related to deadline constraint of workflows. Specifically, we propose multiple new terminals for VMSR and a new set of terminals for building TSRs. These terminals enable us to develop a new DTGP algorithm to simultaneously evolve VMSRs and TSRs for DCDWSC.

In line with Algorithm 1, details regarding the solution representation, initialization, fitness evaluation of DTGP are presented below.

4.1   Representation

In DTGP, both VMSR and TSR are represented as GP trees. Different from [20], a pair of GP trees, one for VMSR and one for TSR, jointly form a single individual in this paper. As illustrated in the left of Fig. 2, each GP tree is a

---

Algorithm 1: DTGP Algorithm for DCDWSC

Input: Training instances, parameter settings
Output: The best scheduling rule consisting of a VMSR and a TSR
`// Representation`
1 Determine the terminal set and the function set
`// Initialization`
2 **while** $N < PopSize$ **do**
3 | Randomly initialize an individual
4 **end**
5 $gen \leftarrow 0$
6 **while** $gen < MaxGen$ **do**
    | `// Fitness Evaluation`
7 | **for** ind in Pop **do**
8 | | $fitness(ind) \leftarrow 0$
9 | | **for** $i = 1$ to $EvalNumber$ **do**
10 | | | $fitness(ind) \leftarrow fitness(ind) + objective(ind)$
11 | | **end**
12 | | $fitness(ind) \leftarrow fitness(ind)/EvalNumber$
13 | **end**
    | `// Evolution`
14 | Generate new population by genetic operators
15 | $gen \leftarrow gen + 1$
16 **end**
17 **Return** the best individual/heuristic/rule

---

syntax tree with one root node and multiple leaf nodes. The intermediate nodes, such as $+, -, \times, \div$, are called the *function* nodes. Every leaf node must be a *terminal* that extracts problem-dependent features from the DCDWSC problem, such as TS, NIQ and ET in Table 1.

Following many existing works [6,12,20], we consider $\{+, -, \times, \div, max, min\}$ as *function* nodes in the GP trees. We introduce new VMSR terminals as well as a new terminal set particularly designed for TSR. Table 1 summarizes the two terminal sets for building VMSRs and TSRs. Depending on the feature types captured by each terminal, all terminals are divided into task-related, VM-related, workflow-related, and problem-specific terminals (see Table 1).

This paper considers five commonly used terminals for VMSR, i.e., TS, ET, CU, $PRICE$ and LFT [5,20,24]. Apart from that, we introduce three new VM-related terminals, TIQ, VMR, and NIQ. They enable VMSRs to evaluate the priority of processing any task on a VM instance based on the instance's current workload and remaining capacity. Two additional terminals, NOC and NOR, are also introduced to provide workflow-related information to VSMRs. RDL allows VSMRs to assign near-expire tasks to fast VM instances.

Among all terminals for designing TSRs, RWT is a time-varying terminal whose value can only be determined in the task selection phase instead of the VM selection phase. It enables a task with a long waiting time to have relatively high priority in the VM Queue. We also use two VM-related terminals TIQ and NIQ to capture

Table 1. The terminal set of VMSR and TSR.

	VMSR		TSR	
	Terminal	Definition	Terminal	Definition
Task-related	TS	The size of a task	ET	The execution time of a task
	ET	The execution time of a task	RWT	The relative waiting time of a task in a VM queue
VM-related	CU	The compute unit of a VM	TIQ	Total execution time of all tasks in a VM queue
	PRICE	Price of renting a VM for one hour	NIQ	Number of tasks in a VM queue
	TIQ	Total execution time of all tasks in a VM queue		
	VMR	The remaining available time for a VM		
	LFT	The latest finish time of a task on a VM		
	NIQ	Number of tasks in a VM queue		
Workflow-related	NOC	Number of successor tasks (children) of a task	NOC	Number of successor tasks (children) of a task
	NOR	Number of remaining tasks in a workflow	NOR	Number of remaining tasks in a workflow
Problem-specific	RDL	Remaining deadline time of a workflow	RDL	Remaining deadline time of a workflow

the competition level among all tasks in the VM queue. NOC is expected to give high priority to those tasks with many successor tasks. NOR helps to shorten the completion time of those workflows with less pending tasks. RDL is important for satisfying deadline constraints. The usefulness of all the newly introduced terminals will be further analyzed experimentally in Subsect. 5.6.

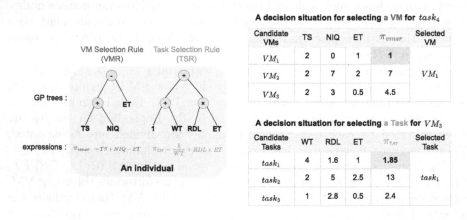

Fig. 2. Examples of how to use an individual to make scheduling decisions.

4.2 Initialization

The initial population is randomly generated by the widely used *Ramped half-and-half* approach [12] where half of the population is constructed by the *grow* method (e.g., VMSR in Fig. 2) and half by the *full* method (e.g., TSR in Fig. 2). In the *grow* method, a GP tree grows by adding randomly selected function and terminal nodes to the tree until it reaches the initial depth limit (6 in our experiments). The *full* method randomly adds function nodes to the tree until it reaches the maximum tree depth.

4.3   Fitness Evaluation

Each evolved GP individual is evaluated on multiple problem instances (3 in our experiments) to determine its average performance in terms of Eq. (8) as its fitness. Each problem instance involves a set of m heterogeneous workflows randomly sampled from multiple different workflow patterns (see Subsect. 5.2 for more details).

Figure 2 illustrates how to use a GP individual with a pair of VMSR and TSR to schedule workflow execution in the cloud. Specifically, it shows a decision situation that needs to select the optimal VM instance for $task_4$ from three candidate VM instances $\{VM_1, VM_2, VM_3\}$. We use VMSR to calculate the corresponding priority values of the three VM instances, i.e., $\{(2 + 0 - 1), (2 + 7 - 2), (2 + 3 - 0.5)\}$. Then, $task_4$ is allocated to the VM Queue of VM_1 which has the lowest priority value. Similarly, the priority values of all pending tasks on VM_3 are first calculated by TSR. $task_1$ with the lowest priority value is then selected for execution.

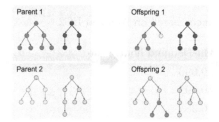

Fig. 3. Crossover operator.

Fig. 4. Mutation operator.

4.4   Evolution

The evolution process relies on *crossover* and *mutation*, as demonstrated in Fig. 3 and Fig. 4. We use *single-point crossover* to process any two parent GP individuals, each represented as a rule pair. Specifically, crossover is applied to either the VMSRs or TSRs of the two individuals (or rule pairs) with a probability of 0.5. Similar to crossover, *mutation* is also applied to one randomly selected tree/rule of a GP individual. For the chosen tree/rule (either VSMR or TR), its sub-tree rooted at a randomly selected mutation point is replaced by a randomly generated new sub-tree.

5   Experiments

We conduct experimental evaluations to demonstrate the effectiveness of our proposed GPHH approach in generating high quality of heuristics for DCDWSC. This section begins by describing the parameter setting of GP and the simulation configuration. The effectiveness of the proposed approach is then verified experimentally, followed by terminal analysis and rule analysis.

5.1   Parameter Setting

Following [12], we set the population size of DTGP to 1024, the number of generations to 51, and the tournament size to 7. Crossover, mutation, and reproduction rates are 85%, 10%, and 5%, respectively. We also limit the initial depth of a GP tree to between 2 and 6, and its maximum depth to 10.

5.2   Simulation Configuration

A simulated cloud environment with five key components below is used to experimentally compare the performance of DTGP against several baseline approaches.

VM Types: The simulated cloud data center is equipped with 6 different VM types according to Amazon EC2[1], as summarized in Table 2. The number of instances of each VM type is unlimited.

Table 2. Configurations of 6 VM instances based on Amazon EC2

Instance name	vCPU	Memory	On-Demand hourly rate
m5.large	2	8 GiB	$0.096
m5.xlarge	4	16 GiB	$0.192
m5.2xlarge	8	32 GiB	$0.384
m5.4xlarge	16	64 GiB	$0.768
m5.8xlarge	32	128 GiB	$1.536
m5.12xlarge	48	192 GiB	$2.304

Workflow Set: Four popular workflow patterns[2] (i.e., CyberShake, Inspiral, Montage, and SIPHT) are employed for our experiments. Each is available with three different sizes (i.e., number of tasks in a workflow), including 30, 50, and 100. Using these workflows patterns, three scenarios (*Mix_Small*, *Mix_Medium* and *Mix_Large*) are created in Table 3.

---

[1] https://aws.amazon.com/ec2/pricing/on-demand/.

[2] https://confluence.pegasus.isi.edu/display/pegasus/Deprecated+Workflow+Gener
ator.

Training Scenario: The *Mix_Large* in Table 3 is utilized for training in GP-based approaches. Each GP individual will be evaluated on 3 problem instances randomly created from this scenario to calculate its fitness. Consequently, it takes 51×3 problem instances to run a GP-based algorithm till completion.

Testing Scenario: All generated heuristics are tested on three *testing scenarios*, i.e., *Mix_Small*, *Mix_Medium* and *Mix_Large*, each containing 30 problem instances.

Table 3. Workflow patterns contained in three workflow sets.

Scenario	Workflow set	# of Workflows
Mix_Small	CyberShake_30, Inspiral_30, Montage_25, Sipht_30	30
Mix_Medium	CyberShake_30, Inspiral_30, Montage_25, Sipht_30 , CyberShake_50, Inspiral_50, Montage_50, Sipht_60	30
Mix_Large	CyberShake_30, Inspiral_30, Montage_25, Sipht_30 , CyberShake_50, Inspiral_50, Montage_50, Sipht_60, CyberShake_100, Inspiral_100, Montage_100, Sipht_100	30

Request Generation: Workflow requests arrive at the cloud data center over time following a Poisson distribution with $\lambda = 0.01$ [10]. The penalty coefficient in Eq. (11) is $\delta = \$0.24/h$ according to [23]. Moreover, the deadline relaxation coefficient in Eq. (10) is set to $\xi \in \{1, 12, 24, 36\}$, where a larger ξ implies more relaxed deadline which can be fulfilled by using relatively cheaper VMs.

5.3   Baseline Algorithms

This paper compares three baseline algorithms listed below, including two GP-based algorithms [20,22] and one well-known heuristic approach [3,15]. All GP-based algorithms will run independently for 30 times using the same set of problem instances. The final performance of any GP-based algorithm is then calculated as the average total cost achieved by the 30 best scheduling heuristics obtained from each of the 30 runs on all testing scenarios.

- *HEFT-FCFS* [3,15] uses HEFT for VM selection and FCFS for task selection.
- *SGP* [5] is a GPHH approach that can evolve VMSRs for DWS.
- *CCGP* [20] is a cooperative coevolution GPHH approach that evolves a combination of one VMSR and one TSR via two evolutionary sub-populations.

5.4   Performance Comparison

The test performance of all algorithms on three scenarios (see Table 3) with four deadline relaxation coefficients ($\xi = 1, 12, 24, 36$) is summarized in Table 4, which records the best and mean total costs in (8) across 30 independent runs. To identify whether there is a statistically significant difference among all competing

444   Y. Yang et al.

algorithms, a Wilcoxon test with a significance level of 0.05 is performed between each pair of algorithms. All statistically significant results are indicated as "+", "−" or "=" in Table 4. The optimal value in each row is also bolded.

Compared to other baselines, DTGP achieved the lowest overall costs on most of the testing scenarios and performed effectively under both tight ($\xi = 1$) and loose ($\xi = 24, 36$) deadlines because it can prioritize tasks with high overdue risks through reordering all pending tasks in the VM queues. Furthermore, for GP-based algorithms, the total cost decreases upon increasing ξ since they allow workflows with loose deadlines to be processed on cheaper VM instances.

Table 4. The best and mean (standard deviation) objective values of 4 algorithms on 12 testing scenarios across 30 independent runs.

Scenarios		HEFT-FCFS		SGP		CCGP		DTGP	
		Best	Mean (std.)	Best	Mean (std.)	Best	Mean (std.)	Best	Mean (std.)
$\xi = 1$	S	87.55	103.58(9.12)	58.12	60.84(2.25)(+)	57.51	60.94(3.07)(+)(=)	57.26	**59.65(1.68)**(+)(+)(+)
	M	145.15	164.20(10.07)	70.02	73.72(3.31)(+)	69.64	73.48(3.17)(+)(=)	69.01	**71.74(2.03)**(+)(+)(+)
	L	246.53	283.93(17.98)	86.36	91.10(4.45)(+)	85.04	91.20(4.8)(+)(=)	84.65	**88.76(3.45)**(+)(+)(+)
$\xi = 12$	S	91.39	101.50(6.57)	26.34	**31.91(3.59)**(+)	27.41	34.27(3.62)(+)(−)	27.24	33.71(4.70)(+)(−)(+)
	M	152.06	167.94(11.34)	39.01	**45.26(4.23)**(+)	39.08	49.51(5.4)(+)(−)	39.06	48.50(7.05)(+)(−)(+)
	L	248.06	283.47(22.43)	54.91	**65.30(5.84)**(+)	56.74	70.4(7.85)(+)(−)	57.29	69.30(10.63)(+)(−)(+)
$\xi = 24$	S	89.86	104.68(8.78)	25.74	28.49(1.53)(+)	24.34	29.27(1.96)(+)(−)	23.62	**26.16(1.79)**(+)(+)(+)
	M	139.78	167.14(13.28)	37.23	42.13(2.98)(+)	35.34	44.01(3.08)(+)(−)	34.91	**38.46(2.72)**(+)(+)(+)
	L	243.46	272.54(20.32)	52.84	62.51(4.93)(+)	51.8	65.60(4.84)(+)(−)	50.76	**57.05(5.34)**(+)(+)(+)
$\xi = 36$	S	90.62	103.45(6.93)	24.65	62.51(4.93)(+)	23.36	25.97(2.26)(+)(+)	23.09	**23.76(0.53)**(+)(+)(+)
	M	148.22	167.45(10.44)	36.63	38.95(1.70)(+)	33.95	38.35(3.55)(+)(+)	32.98	**34.53(0.96)**(+)(+)(+)
	L	246.53	270.85(17.29)	52.33	56.85(2.44)(+)	50.12	58.03(7.51)(+)(−)	48.88	**51.27(1.84)**(+)(+)(+)

* (+), (−) or (=) indicates that the matching result is significantly better, worse, or equivalent to its counterpart.

Interestingly, SGP outperforms CCGP and DTGP when $\xi = 12$. We notice that when the deadline is at a moderate level, tasks are normally processed in a FCFS order on any VM instances [3,22]. Hence, without evolving TSRs, SGP can concentrate fully on evolving more effective VMSRs with a much smaller search space than that of CCGP and DTGP. Comparing CCGP and DTGP, the results in Table 4 clearly indicate that simultaneously evolving VMSR and TSR as a dual-tree is more effective than evolving them separately in two sub-populations. By using the best GP tree in one sub-population (e.g., the best VMSR) to evaluate the fitness of all GP trees in another sub-population (e.g., TSRs), CCGP does not explore all potentially useful combinations of VMSRs and TSRs from both sub-populations.

5.5 Ablation Study

To demonstrate the necessity and effectiveness of jointly using both VSMR and TSR, we compare the performance of a rule pair designed by DTGP with the performance achieved by using only VMSR in the same rule pair on 12 testing scenarios. The observed performance difference is captured by a percentage metric defined in Eq. (12).

$$\frac{fitness(VMSR) - fitness(VMSR, TSR)}{fitness(VMSR, TSR)} \times 100\% \tag{12}$$

Table 5. Percentage increase in total cost when using VMSRs alone.

	Mix_Small	Mix_Medium	Mix_Large
$\xi = 1$	6.31%	6.96%	6.96%
$\xi = 12$	53.00%	43.45%	32.47%
$\xi = 24$	87.10%	75.12%	59.18%
$\xi = 36$	123.40%	103.16%	80.35%

Table 5 shows the percentage increase in total costs when using the VMSR of a rule pair evolved by DTGP alone. The results demonstrate that using two rules to schedule workflows is substantially better than using VMSR only on all testing scenarios. TSR therefore plays an essential role in solving the DCDWSC problem.

5.6   Terminal Analysis

We further analyze the distribution of terminal nodes among the best 30 rule pairs generated by DTGP in 30 runs to verify whether the newly proposed terminals in Subsect. 4.1 are effective. Specifically, VMR, NIQ, NOC, NOR and RDL are newly developed terminals for designing VMSRs. We calculate the percentage of the number of each terminal with respect to the total number of terminals in a rule, and report the average percentage among the 30 rules in Fig. 5 and Fig. 6.

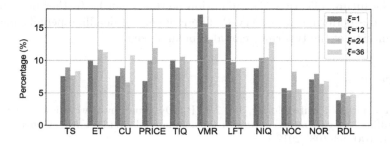

Fig. 5. Terminal statistic of VMSRs.

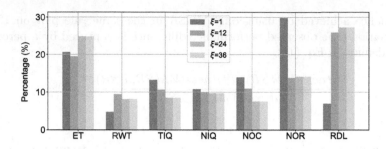

Fig. 6. Terminal statistic of TSRs.

In Fig. 5, the top three terminal types used in VMSRs are VMR, LFT and NIQ. They capture the real-time information of the VM. This is because VM-related information has a significant impact on the performance of VMSRs. Figure 6 shows that ET, NOR and RDL are the top three terminal types in TSRs. Clearly, with tight deadlines (i.e., $\xi = 1$), the number of unassigned tasks remaining in a workflow (NOR) has a strong influence on the TSR. The remaining time before the deadline of a workflow (RDL) also affects strongly the processing order of those tasks waiting at a VM queue.

6   Conclusions

In this paper, we investigated the DCDWSC problem where a series of hetero-geneous workflows can arrive dynamically over time with varied deadline con-straints. To address this problem, we proposed the DTGP algorithm to jointly design a pair of VMSR and TSR. Both VMSR and TSR are supported by newly developed terminals. As far as we know, TSR has never been used in previ-ous studies. Experimental results confirm that DTGP can outperform several competing algorithms under both tight and loose deadlines. Moreover, we found experimentally that better performance can be achieved by using both VSMR and TSR, instead of using VMSR alone. Evolving VSMRs and TSRs in the form of dual-trees was proved to be more effective than evolving them in separate sub-populations.

In the future, effective recombination methods can be further developed to improve the performance of DTGP. The influence of deadline penalty factor on the formation of the two rules can also be analyzed.

References

1. Arabnejad, V., Bubendorfer, K., Ng, B.: Dynamic multi-workflow scheduling: a deadline and cost-aware approach for commercial clouds. Futur. Gener. Comput. Syst. **100**, 98–108 (2019)
2. Armbrust, M., et al.: Above the clouds: a Berkeley view of cloud computing. Tech-nical report (2009)

3. Chen, W., Deelman, E.: Workflowsim: a toolkit for simulating scientific workflows in distributed environments. In: 2012 IEEE 8th International Conference on E-Science, pp. 1–8. IEEE (2012)
4. Djigal, H., Feng, J., Lu, J., Ge, J.: IPPTS: an efficient algorithm for scientific workflow scheduling in heterogeneous computing systems. IEEE Trans. Parallel Distrib. Syst. **32**(5), 1057–1071 (2020)
5. Escott, K.-R., Ma, H., Chen, G.: Genetic programming based hyper heuristic approach for dynamic workflow scheduling in the cloud. In: Hartmann, S., Küng, J., Kotsis, G., Tjoa, A.M., Khalil, I. (eds.) DEXA 2020. LNCS, vol. 12392, pp. 76–90. Springer, Cham (2020). https://doi.org/10.1007/978-3-030-59051-2_6
6. Escott, K.R., Ma, H., Chen, G.: A genetic programming hyper-heuristic approach to design high-level heuristics for dynamic workflow scheduling in cloud. In: 2020 IEEE Symposium Series on Computational Intelligence, pp. 3141–3148. IEEE (2020)
7. Faragardi, H.R., Saleh Sedghpour, M.R., Fazliahmadi, S., Fahringer, T., Rasouli, N.: GRP-HEFT: a budget-constrained resource provisioning scheme for workflow scheduling in IaaS clouds. IEEE Trans. Parallel Distrib. Syst. **31**(6), 1239–1254 (2020)
8. Ismayilov, G., Topcuoglu, H.R.: Neural network based multi-objective evolutionary algorithm for dynamic workflow scheduling in cloud computing. Futur. Gener. Comput. Syst. **102**, 307–322 (2020)
9. Rasouli Kenari, A., Shamsi, M.: A hyper-heuristic selector algorithm for cloud computing scheduling based on workflow features. Opsearch **58**(4), 852–868 (2021). https://doi.org/10.1007/s12597-021-00508-6
10. Liu, J., et al.: Online multi-workflow scheduling under uncertain task execution time in IaaS clouds. IEEE Trans. Cloud Comput. **9**(3), 1180–1194 (2019)
11. Liu, Y., Mei, Y., Zhang, M., Zhang, Z.: A predictive-reactive approach with genetic programming and cooperative coevolution for the uncertain capacitated arc routing problem. Evol. Comput. **28**(2), 289–316 (2020)
12. O'Neill, M.: Riccardo Poli, William B. Langdon, Nicholas F. Mcphee: a field guide to genetic programming (2009)
13. Rizvi, N., Dharavath, R., Wang, L., Basava, A.: A workflow scheduling approach with modified fuzzy adaptive genetic algorithm in IaaS clouds. IEEE Trans. Serv. Comput. (2022). https://doi.org/10.1109/TSC.2022.3174112
14. Tan, B., Ma, H., Mei, Y., Zhang, M.: A cooperative coevolution genetic programming hyper-heuristics approach for on-line resource allocation in container-based clouds. IEEE Trans. Cloud Comput. **10**(3), 1500–1514 (2022). https://doi.org/10.1109/TCC.2020.3026338
15. Topcuoglu, H., Hariri, S., Wu, M.Y.: Performance-effective and low-complexity task scheduling for heterogeneous computing. IEEE Trans. Parallel Distrib. Syst. **13**(3), 260–274 (2002)
16. Versluis, L., Iosup, A.: A survey of domains in workflow scheduling in computing infrastructures: community and keyword analysis, emerging trends, and taxonomies. Futur. Gener. Comput. Syst. **123**, 156–177 (2021)
17. Wang, Z.J., et al.: Dynamic group learning distributed particle swarm optimization for large-scale optimization and its application in cloud workflow scheduling. IEEE Trans. Cybern. **50**(6), 2715–2729 (2020)
18. Wu, Q., Ishikawa, F., Zhu, Q., Xia, Y., Wen, J.: Deadline-constrained cost optimization approaches for workflow scheduling in clouds. IEEE Trans. Parallel Distrib. Syst. **28**(12), 3401–3412 (2017)

19. Xiao, J.-P., Hu, X.-M., Chen, W.-N.: Dynamic cloud workflow scheduling with a heuristic-based encoding genetic algorithm. In: Yang, H., Pasupa, K., Leung, A.C.-S., Kwok, J.T., Chan, J.H., King, I. (eds.) ICONIP 2020. LNCS, vol. 12533, pp. 38–49. Springer, Cham (2020). https://doi.org/10.1007/978-3-030-63833-7_4

20. Xiao, Q.Z., Zhong, J., Feng, L., Luo, L., Lv, J.: A cooperative coevolution hyperheuristic framework for workflow scheduling problem. IEEE Trans. Serv. Comput. **15**(1), 150–163 (2022)

21. Xie, Y., Gui, F.X., Wang, W.J., Chien, C.F.: A two-stage multi-population genetic algorithm with heuristics for workflow scheduling in heterogeneous distributed computing environments. IEEE Trans. Cloud Comput. (2021). https://doi.org/10.1109/TCC.2021.3137881

22. Yang, Y., Chen, G., Ma, H., Zhang, M., Huang, V.: Budget and SLA aware dynamic workflow scheduling in cloud computing with heterogeneous resources. In: 2021 IEEE Congress on Evolutionary Computation, pp. 2141–2148 (2021)

23. Youn, C.H., Chen, M., Dazzi, P.: Cloud Broker and Cloudlet for Workflow Scheduling. Springer, Singapore (2017). https://doi.org/10.1007/978-981-10-5071-8

24. Yu, Y., Feng, Y., Ma, H., Chen, A., Wang, C.: Achieving flexible scheduling of heterogeneous workflows in cloud through a genetic programming based approach. In: 2019 IEEE Congress on Evolutionary Computation, pp. 3102–3109. IEEE (2019)

25. Zhang, F., Mei, Y., Nguyen, S., Zhang, M.: Correlation coefficient-based recombinative guidance for genetic programming hyperheuristics in dynamic flexible job shop scheduling. IEEE Trans. Evol. Comput. **25**(3), 552–566 (2021)

Cost-Aware Dynamic Multi-Workflow Scheduling in Cloud Data Center Using Evolutionary Reinforcement Learning

Victoria Huang[1]([✉]), Chen Wang[1], Hui Ma[2], Gang Chen[2],
and Kameron Christopher[1]

[1] National Institute of Water and Atmospheric Research, Wellington, New Zealand
{victoria.huang,chen.wang,kameron.christopher}@niwa.co.nz
[2] Victoria University of Wellington, Wellington, New Zealand
{hui.ma,aaron.chen}@ecs.vuw.ac.nz

Abstract. The Dynamic Multi-Workflow Scheduling (DMWS) problem aims to allocate highly complex tasks modeled as workflows to cloud resources while optimizing workflow brokers' interests. A workflow broker offers workflow execution services to end-users with agreed Service Level Agreements (SLA) while reducing its total VM rental fees in the meantime. Most existing DMWS-related research works focus on minimizing the workflow makespan by using either heuristics or hyper-heuristics techniques. However, these techniques were either designed for static workflow scheduling based on prior workflow information and/or the simplified cloud environment. In this paper, the DMWS problem is formulated to collectively minimize VM rental fees and SLA violation penalties. Moreover, we introduce a novel priority-based deep neural network scheduling policy that can flexibly adapt to a changing number of VMs and workflows. To train the new policy, a new Evolutionary Strategy based Reinforcement Learning (ES-RL) is developed and implemented. Different from gradient-based deep reinforcement learning algorithms, ES-RL has its advances in effectively training population based and generally applicable policies in parallel as well as robustness to hyper-parameter settings. Our experiments with real-world datasets show that ES-RL can effectively train scheduling policies that can significantly reduce the costs by more than 90% compared to the state-of-the-art scheduling policies.

Keywords: Dynamic workflow scheduling · Cloud computing · Reinforcement learning · SLA violation · Evolutionary strategy

This work is in part supported by the NZ Government's Strategic Science Investment Fund (SSIF) and the New Zealand Marsden Fund with the contract number (VUW1510), administered by the Royal Society of New Zealand.

J. Troya et al. (Eds.): ICSOC 2022, LNCS 13740, pp. 449–464, 2022.
https://doi.org/10.1007/978-3-031-20984-0_32

1   Introduction

Large-scale and highly complex computational applications (e.g., weather fore-casting and Tsunami prediction) are usually modeled as workflows in cloud [17, 18]. A workflow consists of a set of inter-dependent tasks connected by directed edges. These workflows are often outsourced to workflow brokers that offer work-flow execution services to users [29,31]. A workflow broker usually uses computa-tion resources, e.g., Virtual Machines (VMs), leased from cloud providers [10,28] to reduce the maintenance cost [28,29]. Service Level Agreements (SLAs) are often established between the users and the workflow brokers [28]. Brokers are highly motivated to comply with the commitments in SLAs, e.g., deadline con-straints, in order to avoid paying SLA violation penalties [28,30].

The process of *Workflow Scheduling* (WS) starts from users dynamically submitting workflows to brokers along with specified deadlines. Upon receiving a workflow, the broker makes scheduling decisions in real time which include the selection of VM resources (e.g., the VM number and types) and allocation from workflow tasks to VMs. Often, a broker needs to schedule multiple workflows for a customer. The goal of the broker is to maximize its profit by minimizing the VM rental fees and SLA violation penalties.

The WS problem is known to be NP-hard [9,15] and has been widely inves-tigated [9,10]. For example, GRP-HEFT [9] schedules a given workflow to mini-mize the makespan under a VM rental budget. ProLiS [29] proportionally assigns a sub-deadline to each task and allocates tasks to VMs that can meet the dead-line constraint as well as minimize the VM rental fees. However, existing meth-ods [5,9] were mostly designed for *static* WS where the workflow information (e.g., the arrival time, the number, and types of workflows) is known in advance. Moreover, many methods have been proposed with different goals and con-straints, such as minimizing the workflow makespan with a budget constraint in GRP-HEFT [9] or minimizing the budget while satisfying the deadline constraint in ProLiS [29]. Different from these works, in this paper a workflow broker aims to strike a desirable trade-off between reducing the SLA penalty and the total VM rental fee such that the overall cost involving both of the two can be mini-mized. Moreover, existing algorithms focus on developing heuristics [3,5,9,15,29] or hyper-heuristics [1,8,16,31] based on simplified cloud environment as well as prior information of all workflows to be scheduled. Some works only considered scheduling one workflow at a time [7].

In this paper, we consider a *Cost-aware Dynamic Multi-Workflow Scheduling (DMWS)* problem for workflow brokers, where different workflows are dynam-ically sent to brokers for execution. The broker needs to rent proper VMs and schedule workflows on the rented VMs in real-time to minimize VM rental fees and SLA violation penalties. Note that the number of VMs also needs to accom-modate the workflow dynamics. Therefore, DMWS involves decisions of dynami-cally adjusting the number of rented VMs and allocating workflow tasks to VMs. Since WS decisions at a given time are affected by previous decisions and the cur-rently available VM resources, this is a sequential decision problem. Therefore, Deep Reinforcement Learning (DRL) is a promising direction towards tackling this challenging problem. However, existing Q-learning or gradient-based DRL approaches for WS [7,13,20,25] have certain limitations: (1) They do not guarantee high scalability due to the assumption that the number of VMs is predetermined and remains fixed [13,20,25]. (2) Their performance is sensitive to hyper-parameter settings while hyper-parameter search is difficult.

The aim of this paper is to propose an effective approach for training newly designed scheduling policies to handle a changing number of VMs and workflows to address the cost-aware DMWS. Specifically, we design a new Deep Neural Network (DNN) based scheduling policy to dynamically rent new VMs and allocate simultaneously any tasks ready for execution to the rented VMs. We show that the designed scheduling policies can be used to efficiently assign a priority value to each candidate VM for a given task. The VM with the highest priority will be selected for renting and/or task execution. In line with the new policy network design, a new training approach called Evolutionary Strategy based Reinforcement Learning (ES-RL) for DMWS is proposed. Our new training approach features the use of Evolutionary Strategy (ES), a deep neuroevolution algorithm, to achieve stable and effective training of our policy network. Meanwhile, ES-RL is not sensitive to hyper-parameter settings and offers significant performance gain and time reduction through its parallel training capabilities.

Specifically, the key contributions of this paper are listed as follows:

- A Priority-based Deep Neural Network (DNN) scheduling policy design is proposed to flexibly adapt to a changing number of VMs and workflows.
- An evolutionary DRL approach called Evolutionary Strategy based Reinforcement Learning (ES-RL) is proposed to achieve robust and time-efficient training of new policy networks that can solve the DMWS problem effectively.
- Extensive experiments with real-world datasets have been conducted to show that the scheduling policies trained by ES-RL can significantly reduce the costs by more than 90% compared to the state-of-the-art WS approaches.

2   Related Work

Problem Formulation: Existing Workflow Scheduling (WS) studies can be divided into *static* and *dynamic* WS.

Static WS assumes the workflow information (e.g., arrival time, workflow type, and the number of workflows) is known in advance. Given the workflow information, the scheduling decisions are made offline and remained fixed during the workflow execution. Most of the existing works belong to this category [3,5,9, 29]. However, the assumption on prior knowledge of the workflow information in a cloud environment may not be practical because users can submit their workflows at any time and the workflows from one user can also vary in terms of structure and size from time to time [6,15]. Although an alternative way is to schedule the workflows periodically (e.g., batch scheduling) [2], deciding a suitable scheduling period is critical and challenging. For example, a short scheduling period can significantly increase VM rental fees due to low VM utilization (see GRP-HEFT performance in Sect. 6.2) while a long scheduling period introduces long workflow waiting time, potentially leading to high SLA violation penalties.

Dynamic WS makes scheduling decisions at run-time according to the current cloud environment. Unlike static WS, dynamic WS only received limited research interests [6,15]. For example, the existing studies [6,15] considered the workflow scheduling problem with the goal of minimizing the VM rental costs while treating the workflow deadline as a hard constraint. However, sometimes it can be more cost-efficient by paying the SLA penalties rather than renting additional/expensive VMs (see the comparison between ES-RL and ProLiS in Sect. 6.2). The trade-off between VM rental fees and SLA violation was not captured by the models proposed in existing works [9,29]. Motivated by [11,31], in this paper, we study the dynamic WS problem with the aim to optimize both VM rental fees and SLA violation penalties. That is, we consider the trade-off between rental fees and SLA violation fees to minimize the overall cost of brokers and therefore maximize their profits.

Algorithm Design: Most existing works focus on developing heuristics or hyper-heuristics to generate approximate or near-optimal solutions for the NP-hard WS problem with constraints. For example, GRP-HEFT [9] was proposed which selected VMs using a greedy heuristic under a budget constraint and allocated tasks using a modified HEFT [26]. To solve the deadline constrained WS problem of a single workflow, ProLiS [29] distributed the user-assigned deadline to each task in the workflow and subsequently allocated the tasks to VMs in order to meet their sub-deadlines. Other heuristics can also be found in [3,5,15]. However, most of them rely on a simplified cloud environment and full knowledge of all workflows to be scheduled, which potentially limits their practical applicability. Apart from that, many of them [3,5,9] are designed for static workflow scheduling. Alternatively, meta-heuristic (e.g., Particle Swarm Optimization) [19,21] and hyper-heuristic methods (e.g., Genetic Programming) [8,31] have been applied to WS. However, these approaches either assume the workflow information is known in advance (i.e., static WS) or generate heuristics based on historical data.

Deep Reinforcement Learning (DRL) has been applied for WS due to its ability to optimize a solution via interacting with an unknown environment [7,13,20,25,27]. For example, a deep-Q-network based DRL algorithm was proposed [27] to optimize the workflow makespan and user's cost. However, existing works have certain limitations. First, they are usually designed with a given and fixed number of VMs. However, the given number of VMs may not be optimal to handle the changing workloads [13,20,25,27]. Second, the performance of most DRL algorithms [23,24] is sensitive to the hyper-parameter setting while hyper-parameter search is difficult [14].

To cope with these limitations, Evolutionary Strategy (ES) is leveraged in this paper to train the scheduling policy. ES is a population-based approach that evolves DNNs by simulating the process of natural selection. Existing studies [22] have shown that ES can achieve competitive performance with DRL algorithms.

Moreover, ES is highly parallelizable and has fewer hyper-parameters needed to be tuned compared to DRL algorithms.

3 Problem Formulation

In this paper we study the cost-aware Dynamic Multi-Workflow Scheduling (DMWS) problem. This section presents a formal definition of the problem.

Cloud Environment: We consider a cloud data center equipped with a set of VM types. Thanks to the elasticity feature in the cloud, we assume that the number of VMs with each VM type for renting is "unlimited". A *VM* v with type $Type(v)$ can be described as:

$$v = \langle Type(v), Capa(v), Price(v) \rangle$$

where $Capa(v)$ is the VM processing capacity measured in Compute Units [9] and $Price(v)$ is the rental fee of each time unit depends on $Type(v)$. Following existing studies [9,31], we consider the rental time unit as one hour in this paper.

VM Rental Fee: For the DMWS problem, we consider a time interval $T = (t_s, t_e)$ where t_s and t_e are the starting and ending time. Within T, the same type of VM can be rented for multiple times. We denote the set of *rental periods* for a VM v with type $Type(v)$ within T as $RT(v, T)$:

$$RT(v, T) = \{(VMST(v, k, T), VMFT(v, k, T)) | k = 1, ...\}$$

where $(VMST(v, k, T), VMFT(v, k, T))$ is the kth time pair for v within time period T. $VMST(v, k, T)$ is the rental start time which begins when a workflow task is allocated at v and $VMFT(v, k, T)$ is the corresponding rental finish time. The VM rental fees under a scheduling policy π can be calculated as follows:

$$RentFee(\pi, T) = \sum_{v \in I(\pi, T)} \left(Price(v) \times \sum_{(t_1, t_2) \in RT(v, T)} \left\lceil \frac{t_2 - t_1}{3600} \right\rceil \right)$$

where $I(\pi, T)$ is the set of VMs being rented within the time period T.

Workflow Model: A *workflow* w is represented as a Directed Acyclic Graph associated with its arrival time $ArrT(w)$ and a user-specified deadline $DL(w)$.

$$w = \langle DAG(w), ArrT(w), DL(w) \rangle$$

where $DAG(w)$ includes a set of tasks $\{Task(w, i) | i \in \{1, 2, ...\}\}$ and directed edges connecting the tasks to enforce their execution order. Note that $Task(w, i)$ is associated with execution time $RefT(Task(w, i))$ and can only be executed if all its predecessor tasks $Pre(Task(w, i))$ are completed. $Task(w, i)$ is an entry task if $Pre(Task(w, i)) = \emptyset$. Similarly, the successors of $Task(w, i)$ are denoted as $Suc(Task(w, i))$. A task with no successors is an exit task.

In this paper, we assume that the arrival time of any new workflows is not known in advance. To avoid SLA violation and flexibly utilize the VM resources, scheduling decisions are made in real time, e.g., whenever a task is ready. In particular, a task $Task(w, i)$ is defined as *ready* if it is either an entry task of a workflow (i.e., $Pre(Task(w, i)) = \emptyset$) or a task with all its predecessors $Pre(Task(w, i))$ completed. We define a set of candidate VMs as $CVM(t)$ which includes all leased VMs at time t and a set of VM options with all VM types that can be created. Whenever $Task(w, i)$ is ready at time t, π selects a VM v from $CVM(t)$ for $Task(w, i)$ allocation.

Following π, the start time for $Task(w, i)$ is $ST(Task(w, i), \pi)$ and the completion time is

$$CT(Task(w, i), \pi) = ST(Task(w, i), \pi) + \frac{RefT(Task(w, i))}{Capa(v(\pi))}$$

Thus, the completion time WCT of a workflow w is the maximum completion time among all tasks:

$$WCT(w, \pi) = \max_{Task(w,i) \in DAG(w)} \{CT(Task(w, i), \pi)\}$$

SLA Penalty: Following existing works [28,31], the SLA violation penalty of workflow w can be defined as follows:

$$Penalty(w, \pi) = \begin{cases} 0, & \text{if } WCT(w, \pi) \leq DL(w) \\ \epsilon + \beta(w) \times (WCT(w, \pi) - DL(w)), & \text{otherwise} \end{cases}$$

where ϵ is a constant and $\beta(w)$ is the penalty rate for w.

The goal of the cost-aware DMWS problem is to find π to schedule a set of workflows $W(T) = \{w | ArrT(w) < t_e\}$ that arrive during T, so as to minimize SLA violation penalties and VM rental fees:

$$\underset{\pi}{\text{argmin}} \sum_{w \in W(T)} Penalty(w, \pi) + RentFee(\pi, T) \tag{1}$$

4   Priority-Based DNN Policy Design

In the DMWS problem, the scheduling decision needs to be made in real time with minimum delay. Therefore, π must select a suitable VM quickly whenever a task is ready. Meanwhile, in order to tackle environment dynamics and capture the most recent information (e.g., how close is the workflow deadline), the scheduling decision is made as soon as the task is ready and before it is assigned to a VM.

In this paper, a design of priority-based Deep Neural Network (DNN) policy is proposed. As shown in Fig. 1, the policy π consists of three major components:

the state extraction function O, the priority function f_θ parameterized by θ, and the mapping function Φ. Whenever a task is ready at time t, the policy π examines the VM status $z(v,t)$ extracted by O for $\forall v \in CVM(t)$. Then π assigns a priority value $p(v,t)$ to each VM v using f_θ. Based on the priorities, a VM is selected using Φ.

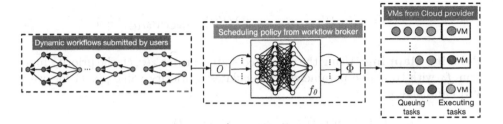

Fig. 1. The dynamic workflow scheduling system.

State Extraction: At time t, we use $S(t)$ to capture the state information of the current cloud environment including static information (e.g., the VM rental price) and dynamic information (e.g., VM rental period, availability, workflow processing information, etc.). To allow the policy to be applied to a varying number of VMs, a state extraction function O is proposed to extract essential information regarding any given VM v from $CVM(t)$ and the ready task to be scheduled:

$$z(v,t) = O(S(t), v)$$

Whenever a task is ready, only information of one VM instead of all VM is fed into f_θ. Therefore, f_θ can be flexibly applied with a changing number of VMs.

Intuitively, the priority value of a VM depends on the ready task and the VM. Therefore, $z(v,t)$ includes both workflow-related and VM-related information. Given a ready task $Task(w,i)$ from a workflow w, we identify the following workflow-related information to estimate the workflow remaining processing time and predict future workload:

- the number of its successors $|Suc(Task(w,i))|$
- the workflow completion ratio[1]
- the estimated workflow arrival rate

For VM-related information, we estimate whether a VM is a good fit depending on if it will satisfy the deadline, introduce additional rental fees, and remain any rental time:

---

[1] The workflow completion ratio is the ratio of the number of completed tasks to the total number of tasks from the workflow.

- a Boolean value indicating whether the VM can satisfy the task deadline[2]
- the potential cost of using the VM[3]
- the VM remaining rental time after allocating the ready task
- a Boolean value indicating whether the current VM is the one with the lowest cost and can satisfy the deadline.

The state extraction process can be formulated as follows:

$$Z(t) = [z(v,t)]_{v \in CVM(t)} = [O\left(S(t), v\right)]_{v \in CVM(t)}, t \in T \qquad (2)$$

Priority Mapping: Using the extracted state features $z(v,t)$, the priority function f_θ with trainable parameters θ calculates a priority value $p(v,t)$ for every VM candidate v:

$$P(t) = [p(v,t)]_{v \in CVM(t)} = [f_\theta\left(z(v,t)\right)]_{v \in CVM(t)}$$

In this paper, DNN is adopted to implement the priority function. Meanwhile, neural engines and similar hardware technologies can quickly process our neural networks for priority mapping during practical use.

VM Selection: Given the priorities, a VM $a(t)$ with the highest priority value is selected by Φ:

$$a(t) = \Phi(P(t)), \text{ i.e., } a(t) = \underset{v \in CVM(t)}{\arg\max}\left(P(t)\right)$$

The scheduling policy can be represented as follows:

$$a(t) = \pi(S(t)) = \Phi\left([f_\theta\left(O\left(S(t), v\right)\right)]_{v \in CVM(t)}\right) \qquad (3)$$

5   Evolutionary Reinforcement Learning

Training a policy can be considered as a DRL task. However, as we discussed in Sect. 2, existing DRL-based approaches for WS assume the number of VMs is pre-determined and fixed. Therefore, they cannot scale to a network with a different number of VMs. Meanwhile, their performance highly relies on hyperparameter tuning.

To tackle these problems, we introduced a new Evolutionary Strategy based Reinforcement Learning (ES-RL) approach for DMWS. The pseudo-code of ES-RL is presented in Algorithm 1. In particular, ES-RL adopts the ES framework introduced by OpenAI in [22] for training scheduling policies. ES-RL is a population-based optimization method that runs iteratively, as shown in Fig. 2.

---

[2] Motivated by ProLiS [29], we assign a deadline to a task based on the proportion of its computational time to the overall workflow computational time.
[3] The potential cost is the sum of new VM rental fee and deadline violation penalty.

At each iteration, given the current policy parameters $\hat{\theta}$, ES-RL samples a population of N individuals $[\theta_i]_{i=1,..,N}$ from an isotropic multi-variance Gaussian with mean $\hat{\theta}$ and fixed covariance $\sigma^2 I$, i.e., $\theta_i \sim \mathcal{N}(\hat{\theta}, \sigma^2 I)$, which is equivalent to

$$\theta_i = \hat{\theta} + \sigma\epsilon_i, \epsilon_i \sim \mathcal{N}(0, I)$$

The fitness value $F(\hat{\theta} + \sigma\epsilon_i)$ of each individual $\hat{\theta} + \sigma\epsilon_i$ is evaluated by applying the perturbed policy $\pi_{\hat{\theta}+\sigma\epsilon_i}$ in the cloud environment as discussed in Sect. 4. In line with our objective function in Eq. (1), we define the fitness function $F(\hat{\theta} + \sigma\epsilon_i)$ as the total cost incurred over T:

$$F(\hat{\theta} + \sigma\epsilon_i) = \sum_{w \in W(T)} Penalty(w, \pi) + RentFee(\pi, T) \tag{4}$$

The goal of ES-RL is to find θ that can minimize the total cost defined in Eq. (4) through minimizing the expected objective value over the population distribution, i.e., $\mathbb{E}_{\epsilon\sim\mathcal{N}(0,I)} F(\theta + \sigma\epsilon_i)$. To achieve this goal, ES updates θ using the following estimator:

$$\nabla_\theta \mathbb{E}_{\theta\sim p_\psi} F(\theta) = \nabla_\theta \mathbb{E}_{\epsilon\sim\mathcal{N}(0,I)} F(\theta + \sigma\epsilon) = \frac{1}{\sigma} \mathbb{E}_{\epsilon\sim\mathcal{N}(0,I)} \left[F'(\theta + \sigma\epsilon)\epsilon \right]$$
$$\approx \frac{1}{N\sigma} \sum_{i=1}^{N} \left[F(\theta + \sigma\epsilon_i)\epsilon_i \right] \tag{5}$$

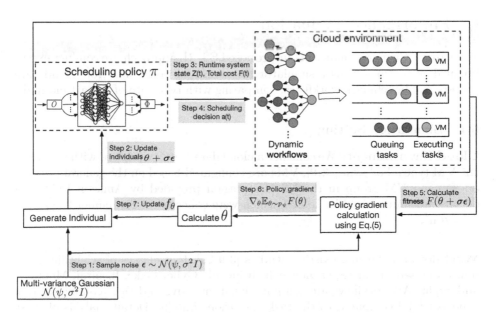

Fig. 2. Scheduling policy training using ES-RL.

Algorithm 1. ES-RL for DMWS

1: **Input**: Population size N, initial policy parameter $\hat{\theta}$, learning rate α; Gaussian noise standard deviation σ
2: **Output**: Scheduling policy
3: **while** the number of generations < the max number of generations: **do**
4:     **for** each individual $i = 1, ..., N$ **do**
5:         Sample $\epsilon_i \sim \mathcal{N}(0, I)$
6:         Update the WF scheduling policy π_i using $\theta_i = \hat{\theta} + \sigma\epsilon_i$
7:         Evaluate fitness $F(\theta_i)$ in cloud environment using Eq. (4)
8:     **end for**
9:     Estimate policy gradient $\nabla_\theta \mathbb{E}_{\theta \sim p_\psi} F(\theta)$ using Eq. (5)
10:    Update $\hat{\theta} \leftarrow \hat{\theta} + \alpha \nabla_\theta \mathbb{E}_{\theta \sim p_\psi} F(\theta)$
11: **end while**

Table 1. VM Setting based on Amazon EC2

Type	vCPU	Compute unit	Memory (GB)	Cost ($ per hour)
m5.large	2	10	8	0.096
m5.xlarge	4	16	16	0.192
m5.2xlarge	8	37	32	0.384
m5.4xlarge	16	70	64	0.768
m5.8xlarge	32	128	128	1.536
m5.12xlarge	48	168	192	2.304

6   Performance Evaluation

To evaluate the performance of our proposed ES-RL approach, we conduct experimental evaluations using a simulator based on real-world data from cloud data centers and benchmark workflows, comparing with two state-of-the-art methods.

6.1   Simulation Setting

Cloud Environment: We consider a cloud data center equipped with six different VM types. Following [3,9], VMs are configured based on the general-purpose on-demand VM group in the US East region provided by Amazon EC2. VM details are summarized in Table 1 which were collected in September 2020 from Amazon[4].

Workflows: Following existing studies [3,9,29], four classes of scientific workflows are used in our experiment which include CyberShake, Inspiral, Montage, and Sipht. All workflows are computational intensive and their communication time is trivial compared to the task execution time [9]. Detail analysis of these

---

[4] https://aws.amazon.com/ec2/pricing/on-demand/.

workflows can be found in [4, 12]. Note that workflows in each class share similar structures but can differ from the numbers of their tasks (e.g., ranging from 25 to 50). During our training, we simulate small workflows from four classes where each of them contains 25 to 30 tasks. Nevertheless, our trained scheduling policy is generalized well and can be directly applied to large workflows with 50 tasks without retraining. Following [6, 15], we simulate the dynamic arrival of workflow applications by randomly sampling 30 workflows from four classes of workflows in each simulation. The arrival time of workflows follows a Poisson distribution with $\lambda = 0.01$ [15]. The penalty rate β is set to be \$0.24 per hour for each workflow [32].

To compare the algorithm performance under different deadlines, a deadline relaxation factor η is used. Similar to [3], we consider η changes from 1 to 2.25. Given η, the deadline of a workflow w is set as below:

$$DL(w) = ArrT(w) + \eta \times MinMakespan(w)$$

where $MinMakespan(w)$ is the shortest makespan of each workflow w as its execution time when its tasks are executed by the fastest VM v from Table 1 (i.e., m5.12xlarge).

Algorithm Implementation: We implement ES-RL based on the code released by OpenAI[5]. In terms of parameter settings, we set the Gaussian noise standard deviation $\sigma = 0.05$ and the learning rate $\alpha = 10^{-2}$. The population size N is 40 and each individual is evaluated for 1 episodes (i.e., N_E=1). The maximum generation number is 3000. For the priority function design, we follow the DNN architecture used by OpenAI baselines. Specifically, it is a fully connected multilayer feed-forward neural network with two hidden layers. Each hidden layer consists of 64 nodes with the tanh activation function.

Baseline Algorithms: We compared ES-RL with two state-of-the-art scheduling algorithms (GRP-HEFT [9] and ProLiS [29]) which have similar objectives as (1). As we discussed in Sect. 2, both GRP-HEFT and ProLiS were designed for static WS of one single workflow. We need to adapt them to the DMWS problem. To enable GRP-HEFT to be comparable with ES-RL, we minimize the budget constraint for every newly arriving workflow by incrementally increasing the budget that is passed to GRP-HEFT as a constraint until the workflow satisfies its deadline. To enable ProLiS to be applicable for dynamic workflow arrival, ProLiS is triggered to assign deadlines to all tasks once a workflow arrives. Whenever a task is ready, the cheapest VM from $CVM(t)$ that can meet the task deadline will be selected.

6.2   Simulation Results

To demonstrate the effectiveness of ES-RL, we compare its performance (i.e., overall cost) with GRP-HEFT and ProLiS under different η (i.e., deadline relax-

---

[5] https://github.com/openai.

ation factor) as shown in Table 2. Note that a smaller η implies a tighter deadline. We also analyze the testing performance among all algorithms with respect to VM cost (\$), SLA penalty (\$), and VM utilization (%), as shown in Fig. 3. Note that GRP-HEFT causes a high VM cost which ranges from \$830 to \$1988. Thus, to show the difference in VM rental cost in Fig. 3(a), we set the y-axis limit to an upper value (i.e., 420).

As shown in Table 2, we can observe that the overall cost of ProLiS and GRP-HEFT increases as η decreases (i.e., a tighter deadline). This is mainly because both ProLiS and GRP-HEFT consider the workflow deadline as a hard constraint. In other words, they always select VMs that can satisfy the workflow deadlines. This explanation also matches well with our observation in Fig. 3(b) where the SLA penalty remains 0 regardless of the η changes. With a tight deadline, more powerful VMs in terms of computational capacity are required. As a result, an increase in VM cost can be observed in Fig. 3(a) as η decreases.

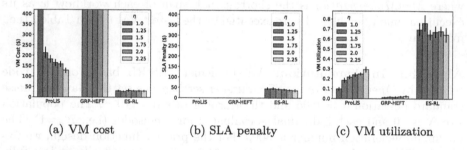

(a) VM cost   (b) SLA penalty   (c) VM utilization

Fig. 3. Comparison of GRP-HEFT [9], ProLiS [29], and ES-RL on different factors with respect to different η with small workflows.

Table 2. The average fitness values (i.e., total cost) tested over multiple runs for GRP-HEFT [9] and ProLiS [29], and ES-RL with different η with small workflows. (Note: a lower value is better)

η	ProLiS	GRP-HEFT	ES-RL
1.00	395.5520 ± 11.633617	-	**74.490828 ± 7.060981**
1.25	108.5184 ± 15.815567	1775.9232 ± 161.077450	**71.817811 ± 7.664415**
1.50	91.7376 ± 12.662934	1171.8144 ± 75.565892	**73.737249 ± 6.339560**
1.75	83.4304 ± 10.828026	1258.9056 ± 90.980289	**71.436684 ± 5.725663**
2.00	76.9088 ± 10.752586	1164.7488 ± 76.973755	**68.036960 ± 5.993622**
2.25	68.3456 ± 10.332963	969.9840 ± 102.602041	**65.590513 ± 7.967546**

In comparison, ES-RL consistently outperforms both ProLiS and GRP-HEFT with the lowest overall cost as highlighted in Table 2. This is achieved by balancing the trade-off between VM rental fees and SLA penalties. As demonstrated in Fig. 3, ES-RL maintains the low overall costs by renting cost-effective VMs (see Fig. 3(a)) as well as utilizing existing VMs (see Fig. 3(c) for the high VM utilization). As a result, ES-RL can violate the workflow deadlines and therefore introduces SLA penalties (see Fig. 3(b)). Meanwhile, when η increases, the SLA penalty decreases because when the deadline becomes looser, VM selection has less impact on the SLA penalty.

Another interesting observation is that GRP-HEFT has the highest overall cost among the three approaches. This is mainly because GRP-HEFT is designed for static WS. In a scenario when two tasks from the same workflow are assigned to the same VM, the idle time slot between the two tasks cannot be utilized by a different workflow, leading to low VM utilization. This also matches our observation in Fig. 3(c) where GRP-HEFT presents the lowest VM utilization.

We also investigate the generalization capability of our trained scheduling policy. In particular, we define the generalization capability as the policy that was trained using small workflows can still be able to effectively schedule large workflows. The results are shown in Fig. 4. From the figures, we can see that ES-RL still managed to reduce the overall cost by balancing the trade-off between VM rental fees and SLA penalties. Meanwhile, compared to ProLiS, ES-RL can achieve significantly higher VM utilization. In general, our observations of ES-RL

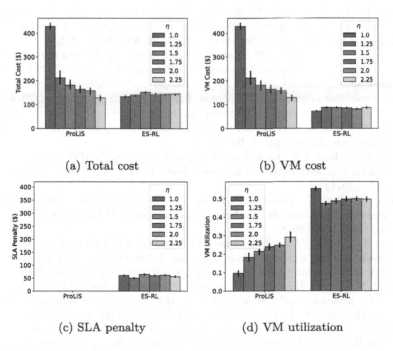

(a) Total cost   (b) VM cost

(c) SLA penalty   (d) VM utilization

Fig. 4. Comparison of ProLiS [29] and ES-RL on different factors with respect to different η with large workflows.

with large workflows are consistent with the results with small workflows shown in Fig. 3. Our results demonstrate that ES-RL can effectively train a generalized scheduling policy that can flexibly adapt to not only the changing number of VMs but also workflows with different sizes.

7   Conclusions

In this paper, we proposed an effective ES based approach for the cost-aware dynamic multi-workflow scheduling (DMWS) problem. In particular, we formulate a dynamic multi-workflow scheduling problem with the goal of minimizing both the VM rental cost and SLA violation penalties. To effectively solve this problem, we proposed a new scheduling policy design of a priority-based deep neural network that can be used in a dynamic environment with a changing number of VMs and workflows. Meanwhile, a new Evolutionary Strategy based RL (ES-RL) algorithm for DMWS is proposed to efficiently train a generally applicable scheduling policy in parallel. Our experiments with real-world datasets showed that the scheduling policies trained by ES-RL can effectively reduce the overall costs compared to two state-of-the-art algorithms.

References

1. Ahmad, S.G., Liew, C.S., Munir, E.U., Ang, T.F., Khan, S.U.: A hybrid genetic algorithm for optimization of scheduling workflow applications in heterogeneous computing systems. J. Parallel Distrib. Comput. **87**, 80–90 (2016)
2. Alsurdeh, R., Calheiros, R.N., Matawie, K.M., Javadi, B.: Hybrid workflow scheduling on edge cloud computing systems. IEEE Access **9**, 134783–134799 (2021)
3. Arabnejad, V., Bubendorfer, K., Ng, B.: Budget and deadline aware e-science workflow scheduling in clouds. IEEE Trans. Parallel Distrib. Syst. **30**(1), 29–44 (2019)
4. Bharathi, S., Chervenak, A., Deelman, E., Mehta, G., Su, M., Vahi, K.: Characterization of scientific workflows. In: 2008 Third Workshop on Workflows in Support of Large-Scale Science, pp. 1–10 (2008)
5. Byun, E.K., Kee, Y.S., Kim, J.S., Deelman, E., Maeng, S.: BTS: resource capacity estimate for time-targeted science workflows. J. Parallel Distrib. Comput. **71**(6), 848–862 (2011)
6. Chen, H., Zhu, X., Liu, G., Pedrycz, W.: Uncertainty-aware online scheduling for real-time workflows in cloud service environment. IEEE Trans. Serv. Comput. **14**(4), 1167–1178 (2018)
7. Dong, T., Xue, F., Xiao, C., Zhang, J.: Workflow scheduling based on deep reinforcement learning in the cloud environment. J. Ambient. Intell. Humaniz. Comput. **12**(12), 10823–10835 (2021). https://doi.org/10.1007/s12652-020-02884-1
8. Escott, K.-R., Ma, H., Chen, G.: Genetic programming based hyper heuristic approach for dynamic workflow scheduling in the cloud. In: Hartmann, S., Küng, J., Kotsis, G., Tjoa, A.M., Khalil, I. (eds.) DEXA 2020. LNCS, vol. 12392, pp. 76–90. Springer, Cham (2020). https://doi.org/10.1007/978-3-030-59051-2_6
9. Faragardi, H.R., Saleh Sedghpour, M.R., Fazliahmadi, S., Fahringer, T., Rasouli, N.: GRP-HEFT: a budget-constrained resource provisioning scheme for workflow scheduling in IaaS clouds. IEEE Trans. Parallel Distrib. Syst. **31**(6), 1239–1254 (2020)

10. Genez, T.A.L., Bittencourt, L.F., Madeira, E.R.M.: Workflow scheduling for SaaS/PaaS cloud providers considering two SLA levels. In: 2012 IEEE Network Operations and Management Symposium, pp. 906–912 (2012)
11. Hoseiny, F., Azizi, S., Shojafar, M., Tafazolli, R.: Joint QoS-aware and cost-efficient task scheduling for fog-cloud resources in a volunteer computing system. ACM Trans. Internet Technol. (TOIT) **21**(4), 1–21 (2021)
12. Juve, G., Chervenak, A., Deelman, E., Bharathi, S., Mehta, G., Vahi, K.: Characterizing and profiling scientific workflows. Futur. Gener. Comput. Syst. **29**(3), 682–692 (2013)
13. Li, H., Huang, J., Wang, B., Fan, Y.: Weighted double deep q-network based reinforcement learning for bi-objective multi-workflow scheduling in the cloud. Clust. Comput. **25**(2), 751–768 (2022)
14. Liessner, R., Schmitt, J., Dietermann, A., Bäker, B.: Hyperparameter optimization for deep reinforcement learning in vehicle energy management. In: ICAART (2), pp. 134–144 (2019)
15. Liu, J., et al.: Online multi-workflow scheduling under uncertain task execution time in IaaS clouds. IEEE Trans. Cloud Comput. **9**(3), 1180–1194 (2019)
16. Lopez-Garcia, P., Onieva, E., Osaba, E., Masegosa, A.D., Perallos, A.: GACE: a meta-heuristic based in the hybridization of genetic algorithms and cross entropy methods for continuous optimization. Expert Syst. Appl. **55**, 508–519 (2016)
17. Masdari, M., ValiKardan, S., Shahi, Z., Azar, S.I.: Towards workflow scheduling in cloud computing: a comprehensive analysis. J. Netw. Comput. Appl. **66**, 64–82 (2016)
18. Oliver, H., et al.: Workflow automation for cycling systems. Comput. Sci. Eng. **21**(4), 7–21 (2019)
19. Pandey, S., Wu, L., Guru, S.M., Buyya, R.: A particle swarm optimization-based heuristic for scheduling workflow applications in cloud computing environments. In: 2010 24th IEEE International Conference on Advanced Information Networking and Applications, pp. 400–407 (2010)
20. Qin, Y., Wang, H., Yi, S., Li, X., Zhai, L.: An energy-aware scheduling algorithm for budget-constrained scientific workflows based on multi-objective reinforcement learning. J. Supercomput. **76**(1), 455–480 (2020)
21. Rodriguez, M.A., Buyya, R.: Deadline based resource provisioning and scheduling algorithm for scientific workflows on clouds. IEEE Trans. Cloud Comput. **2**(2), 222–235 (2014)
22. Salimans, T., Ho, J., Chen, X., Sidor, S., Sutskever, I.: Evolution strategies as a scalable alternative to reinforcement learning. arXiv preprint arXiv:1703.03864 (2017)
23. Schulman, J., Levine, S., Abbeel, P., Jordan, M., Moritz, P.: Trust region policy optimization. In: International Conference on Machine Learning (ICML), pp. 1889–1897 (2015)
24. Schulman, J., Wolski, F., Dhariwal, P., Radford, A., Klimov, O.: Proximal policy optimization algorithms. arXiv preprint arXiv:1707.06347 (2017)
25. Suresh Kumar, D., Jagadeesh Kannan, R.: Reinforcement learning-based controller for adaptive workflow scheduling in multi-tenant cloud computing. Int. J. Electr. Eng. Educ. 0020720919894199 (2020)
26. Topcuoglu, H., Hariri, S., Wu, M.-Y.: Performance-effective and low-complexity task scheduling for heterogeneous computing. IEEE Trans. Parallel Distrib. Syst. **13**(3), 260–274 (2002)
27. Wang, Y., et al.: Multi-objective workflow scheduling with deep-q-network-based multi-agent reinforcement learning. IEEE Access **7**, 39974–39982 (2019)

28. Wu, L., Garg, S.K., Versteeg, S., Buyya, R.: SLA-based resource provisioning for hosted software-as-a-service applications in cloud computing environments. IEEE Trans. Serv. Comput. **7**(3), 465–485 (2014)
29. Wu, Q., Ishikawa, F., Zhu, Q., Xia, Y., Wen, J.: Deadline-constrained cost optimization approaches for workflow scheduling in clouds. IEEE Trans. Parallel Distrib. Syst. **28**(12), 3401–3412 (2017)
30. Xiaoyong, Y., Ying, L., Tong, J., Tiancheng, L., Zhonghai, W.: An analysis on availability commitment and penalty in cloud SLA. In: 2015 IEEE 39th Annual Computer Software and Applications Conference, vol. 2, pp. 914–919 (2015)
31. Yang, Y., Chen, G., Ma, H., Zhang, M., Huang, V.: Budget and SLA aware dynamic workflow scheduling in cloud computing with heterogeneous resources. In: 2021 IEEE Congress on Evolutionary Computation (CEC), pp. 2141–2148. IEEE (2021)
32. Youn, C.H., Chen, M., Dazzi, P.: Cloud Broker and Cloudlet for Workflow Scheduling. Springer, Singapore (2017). https://doi.org/10.1007/978-981-10-5071-8

Extending the Kubernetes Platform with Network-Aware Scheduling Capabilities

Angelo Marchese[✉] and Orazio Tomarchio

Department of Electrical Electronic and Computer Engineering, University of
Catania, Catania, Italy
angelo.marchese@phd.unict.it, orazio.tomarchio@unict.it

Abstract. Kubernetes is today the de-facto standard container orchestration platform for the lifecycle management of microservices-based applications on Cloud environments. However it is not yet ready to be adopted on node clusters distributed in the Cloud-to-Edge continuum. In particular its scheduling strategy is not suitable for the placement of modern latency-sensitive applications on Edge environments, characterized by frequent node failures and network partitions. In this work we propose a network-aware scheduling extension of the default Kubernetes scheduler that takes into account the ever changing infrastructure network conditions and the dynamic communication interactions between microservices, with the aim to optimize the placement of application containers.

Keywords: Edge computing · Containers technology · Kubernetes scheduler · Network-aware scheduling

1 Introduction

In recent years, new and challenging application scenarios are emerging from different domains such as smart cities, autonomous vehicles, smart agriculture, streaming services and so on. One common features of many applications in these areas include the production of a huge quantity of data together with the need of near real-time analytics for effective decision making [6]. To effectively support such requirements, traditional approaches that send data to centralized cloud infrastructure can no longer be used: they need to leverage the computational resources that are close to the nodes where data are generated in order to reduce response time and satisfy stringent latency requirements of applications, while at the same time optimizing resource usage. Such new paradigms, commonly referred to as Cloud-to-Edge continuum or simply Computing Continuum [2], are nowadays increasingly supported by container technology [11] which, on its turn, is gaining tremendous popularity among developers. To execute complex container based applications on clouds, container orchestration platforms that manage containers automatic deployment, their scaling, and operation on the underlying cluster have appeared [16], being Kubernetes the most widespread today [7].

J. Troya et al. (Eds.): ICSOC 2022, LNCS 13740, pp. 465–480, 2022.
https://doi.org/10.1007/978-3-031-20984-0_33

However, the default scheduling system of Kubernetes has not been designed to work in distributed and heterogeneous clusters such as the aforementioned Cloud-to-Edge infrastructures [8,9]. In particular, the Kubernetes scheduler does not deal with the ever changing network conditions of Edge environments, neither the run time communication relationships between the containers that compose a microservices-based application [1]. The mechanism of inter-Pod affinity represents a first attempt to define network-aware scheduling policies. However this is mainly a static scheduling mechanism that requires application architects to know container relationships before the run time phase.

To deal with those limitations, leveraging on our previous preliminary work presented in [10], in this paper we propose a network-aware extension of the default Kubernetes scheduler, able to take into account run time communication interactions between microservices and node-to-node network latencies to establish an optimal placement for containers. The rest of the paper is organized as follows. In Sect. 2 we provide background information about the base Kubernetes scheduler architecture. Section 3 deeply discusses the motivations of our work. In Sect. 4 the design of our proposed scheduler is presented, while in Sect. 5 we provide results of our prototype evaluation on a simple testbed. In Sect. 6 we examine some related works comparing them with our approach and, finally, Sect. 7 concludes the work.

2   Kubernetes Scheduler

Kubernetes[1] is a container orchestration platform which automates the management of distributed applications on large-scale computing infrastructures [3]. A Kubernetes cluster consists of a control plane and a set of worker nodes. The control plane is made up of different management components that run inside a master node. The worker nodes are responsible for the execution of containerized application workloads. In Kubernetes, minimal deployment units consist of *Pods*, which in turn contain one or more containers.

Kube-scheduler[2] is a control plane component that is in charge of selecting a cluster node for each Pod to run them on, taking into account Pod requirements and resource availability on cluster nodes. Each Pod scheduling attempt goes through a multi-phase process, where the filtering and scoring phases represent the main execution logic. Each phase is implemented by one or more plugins, which in turn can implement one or more phases. In the filtering phase each plugin executes a filtering function for each cluster node to check if that node satisfies a specific constraint. The output of the filtering phase is a list of candidate nodes that contains any suitable node to run the Pod on. In the scoring phase each plugin executes a scoring function for each candidate node to assign a score to that node according to a specific criterion. The final score of each node is determined by the weighted sum of the individual scores assigned to that node by each scoring plugin. The Pod is assigned to the node with the

---

[1] https://kubernetes.io.

[2] https://kubernetes.io/docs/concepts/scheduling-eviction/kube-scheduler.

highest final score and if there is more than one node with equal scores, one of these is randomly selected. The Kubernetes scheduler is meant to be extensible. In particular, each scheduling phase represents an extension point which one or more custom plugins can be registered at.

Among the default Kubernetes scheduler plugins, the *InterPodAffinity* plugin evaluates inter-Pod affinity constraints specified in the Pod configuration file. Inter-Pod affinity rules constrain which nodes Pods can be scheduled on based on the labels of Pods already running on that node. Two types of inter-Pod affinity rules could be specified: *requiredDuringSchedulingIgnoredDuringExecution*, in which case the scheduler can't schedule the Pod unless the rule is met and *preferredDuringSchedulingIgnoredDuringExecution*, in which case the scheduler still schedules the Pod, though a matching node is not available.

```
podAffinity:
  preferredDuringSchedulingIgnoredDuringExecution:
  - weight: 50
    podAffinityTerm:
      labelSelector:
        matchExpressions:
        - key: svc
          operator: In
          values:
          - s2
        topologyKey: topology.kubernetes.io/region
```

Listing 1: Example of an inter-Pod affinity rule

Listing 1 shows an example of a preferredDuringSchedulingIgnoredDuringExecution inter-Pod affinity rule in a Pod configuration file. The rule says that the scheduler should try to schedule the Pod onto a node in the same region as one or more existing Pods with the label *svc* set to the value *s2*. Inter-Pod affinity rules are meant to specify topological constraints during Pod scheduling, and can be used mainly to express communication relationships between Pods. The *topologyKey* parameter determines how far Pods should be placed near to each other, while the *weight* parameter represents the priority of the affinity rule. The greater this value, the greater the score assigned to the nodes that satisfy the rule and thus the probability that Pods are placed near to each other.

3   Motivation

As described in Sect. 2 the Kubernetes inter-Pod affinity rules can be used to express locality constraints during Pod scheduling, forcing the relative position of two Pods with some communication relationships between them. However this mechanism is not sufficient alone to implement an effective network-aware scheduling solution for modern deployment scenarios, characterized by complex applications and highly distributed and dynamic infrastructure. In particular we devise two main limitations on the default Kubernetes inter-Pod affinity mechanism.

The first limitation is related to the fact that the InterPodAffinity plugin doesn't evaluate run time network latencies between cluster nodes to determine their network proximity. Instead it partitions the cluster into different topology domains (eg. regions or availability zones) based on node labels assigned by cluster administrators.

Kubernetes has been initially thought as a container orchestration platform for Cloud environments, typically characterized by low communication latencies and high network bandwidth. On these environments cluster nodes are typically located in the same Cloud provider region that corresponds to a latency-constrained topology domain. In this case, scheduling Pods in the same Cloud provider region guarantees a limited network latency between them. With the recent diffusion of Fog and Edge computing paradigms and the need to move computation near to the end-users, new Kubernetes distributions have emerged suitable to be deployed on Cloud-Edge environments. Edge environments consist of geographically distributed nodes with high heterogeneity in terms of computational resources and network connectivity. In particular, network latency between nodes represents a not negligible and variable factor for Cloud-Edge clusters, especially for Edge nodes for which a reliable network connectivity is not guaranteed. In this scenario, it becomes difficult for cluster administrators to identify latency-constrained topology domains and an initial assignment of node labels may not reveal accurate at run time because of the frequently changing network conditions.

The second limitation is related to the fact that inter-Pod affinity rules allow to define only static communication relationships between Pods, by manually specifying a pre-defined value for the weight parameter that represents the priority of the affinity rule. The priority of an affinity rule is typically related to the degree of communication between services. The greater the communication intensity between two services the greater the priority value that should be assigned to the corresponding affinity rule in order to improve the probability that they are placed near to each other. This requires that in order to define weights of affinity rules an estimate of the degree of communication between services should be done by application architects before the deployment phase, a difficult task for modern application scenarios.

The shift from monolithic applications towards microservices-architectures that consist of complex application graphs, made by microservices and communication channels between them, makes network communication a critical factor to optimize in order to improve application performances, in terms of end-to-end response latency. In a microservices-based application a generic user request consists of a chain of sub-requests and its end-to-end latency is affected by the latencies of each service call in the chain. The communication channels involved in a specific user request may change depending on the application endpoints requested by end users. In order to improve the average application response time it becomes necessary to improve the response time of the most frequently requested application endpoints and then to reduce the network latency of the most involved communication channels where the highest traffic amount is exchanged. By using inter-Pod affinity rules this can be done by assigning to these communication channels the highest affinity weight values. The problem with this approach is that an accurate assignment of affinity weight values cannot be done ahead of time because the rate at which application endpoints are requested by end users may change over time, with some endpoints more requested than others, and therefore also the traffic amount exchanged over each communication channel is a variable factor. In general, considering the two limitations described above, the main problem with the Kubernetes inter-Pod affinity mechanism is that it is a static network-aware scheduling mechanism and then it is not sufficient to cope with the ever changing infrastructure network conditions and traffic distribution among services of a microservices-based application.

4   Proposed Approach

4.1   Overall Design

Considering the limitations described in Sect. 3 related to the default Kubernetes scheduler and its InterPodAffinity plugin not being able to implement an effective network-aware placement strategy, we propose an extension of the Kubernetes platform to cope with those limitations. The main goal of the proposed approach is to devise a dynamic scheduling solution for the Pods that compose a microservices-based application aimed to reduce the application response time of end user requests. The basic reasoning behind our approach is that the greater the communication intensity between two Pods, the greater the need to schedule them in the same node or in nodes with limited network distance between them in order to reduce the average application response time. As discussed in Sect. 3, in a microservices-based application an end user request may traverse multiple channels in the application graph. If the mean traffic amount exchanged between two Pods is high, this means that many user requests hit the communication channel between the two Pods: in order to ensure that this path does not represent a bottleneck in the request chain, the two Pods should be placed near to each other.

Figure 1 shows a general model of the proposed approach. The network-aware scheduler extends the default Kubernetes scheduler by implementing a custom scoring plugin. As in the case of the default InterPodAffinity plugin, the proposed scheduler evaluates the affinity rules specified in the resource configuration of the Pod to be scheduled in order to determine the communication relationships and their weights between the Pod and all the other Pods that compose a microservices-based application. However, differently from the default InterPodAffinity plugin that takes into account node labels statically assigned by cluster administrators in order to determine what nodes belong to the same topology

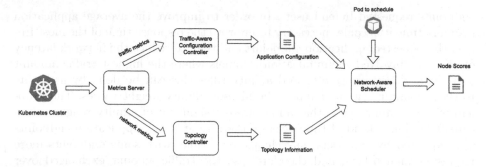

Fig. 1. General model

domain, the proposed scheduler makes use of dynamically assigned node labels that represent current network latencies between cluster nodes. These labels are continously updated by a topology controller that fetches network latency metrics from a metrics server. Therefore, the concept of static topology domain (eg. cloud provider availability zone or region) expressed by the topologyKey parameter and the corresponding node labels is extended by a more fine-grained node labelling process that allows the scheduler to know the current network distance between cluster nodes.

However a scheduling strategy that takes into account only the run time network latencies between cluster nodes is not sufficient to implement an effective network-aware placement solution. A critical aspect in our approach is the requirement to continously tune the placement of application Pods based on the dynamic infrastructure network conditions and the run time interactions between the microservices that compose an application graph. Kubernetes clusters, especially those distributed on the Cloud-to-Edge continuum, are highly dynamic environments with frequent network partitions and changes on node-to-node network latencies. Furthermore, application usage patterns can change over time, determining that different Pod-to-Pod channels can represent bottlenecks in request chains over different time periods. This causes that a placement decision for application Pods taken in a specific point in time may not be an optimal one later. In this context it becomes necessary to adapt to the ever changing cluster network conditions and Pods communication interactions and reschedule Pods if better scheduling decisions can be taken over time. However the Kubernetes platform currently lacks of an automatic Pod rescheduling strategy aware of the runtime cluster and application state changes.

Considering this limitation we propose a traffic-aware configuration controller, that continuously monitors traffic exchanged between Pods and updates their configuration by tuning the weights of their affinity rules based on traffic metrics fetched from the metrics server. By using the Kubernetes rolling update mechanism, changes to Pod configurations cause them to be recreated allowing for better placement decisions to be taken based on current Pods communication requirements and network conditions. Further details on the proposed controllers and the custom scheduler are provided in the following subsections.

4.2   Kubernetes Controllers

The traffic-aware configuration controller and the topology controller showed in Fig. 1 are implemented as Kubernetes operators written in the Java language by using the Quarkus Operator SDK. A Kubernetes operator is an application-specific controller configured through Kubernetes *custom API resources*.

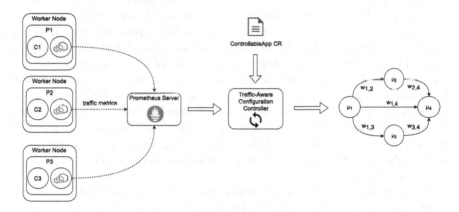

Fig. 2. Traffic-aware configuration controller

Figure 2 shows how the proposed traffic-aware configuration controller works. The controller executes a set of run time control-loops each activated by one *ControllableApp* Kubernetes custom resource that refers to a microservices-based application that has to be managed by the controller. In particular an application consists of a set of Deployment resources that in turn create and manage Pods each running an independent microservice instance. In Kubernetes a microservice is represented by a Deployment resource whose Pods represent the microservice replicas. Pods managed by a Deployment are instances of the Pod template section of the Deployment. A Pod template may contain a set of affinity rules as illustrated in Listing 1.

When a ControllableApp resource is created in the Kubernetes cluster, the controller starts a control-loop whose period is specified by the *runPeriod* property in the *spec* section of the resource. In each iteration the controller queries the Kubernetes API server to get the set of Deployments located in the namespace as specified by the *namespace* property and with an *app* label whose value is equal to the value of the *name* property. Deployments that compose an application must have the same value of the app label and a *svc* label has to be set on each one whose value is equal to the corresponding microservice name. After receiving the set of Deployments of an application, the controller determines an application graph configuration that represents the control-loop output for the current iteration. An application graph consists of the set of microservices μ_i each associated with the corresponding application Deployment and the communication relationships between them represented as a set of affinity rules. In particular, for each pair of Deployments D_i and D_j with $j \neq i$, the controller updates their corresponding Pod template section with a preferredDuringSchedulingIgnoredDuringExecution affinity rule with a weight $w_{i,j}$ and a label selector that matches the values of the app and svc labels of D_j. The value of the weight $w_{i,j}$ is directly proportional to the traffic amount, averaged over a configurable time period, exchanged between the microservices μ_i and μ_j. In particular for each microservice μ_i, the set of relative traffic metrics are queried from a Prometheus metrics server. The returned values represent the traffic exchanged between the microservice μ_i and all the other microservices in the application and, after being normalized as integer values in the range between 0 and 100, these values are assigned to the corresponding affinity rule weights of the Deployment D_i.

As showed in Fig. 2 traffic exchanged between microservices is collected by the Istio platform, a service mesh implementation, whose control plane is installed in the Kubernetes cluster. The Istio control plane injects a sidecar container running an Envoy proxy on each Pod when they are created. All the traffic between Pods is intercepted by their corresponding Envoy proxies that in turn expose traffic statistics through metrics exporters that can be queried by the Prometheus server.

The application graph configuration with the set of updated affinity rules is then submitted by the controller to the Kubernetes API server. If at least one affinity rule in the Pod template section of a Deployment has changed with respect to the last iteration, a rolling update process is activated and new Pods with the updated resource configuration are created. This way Pod affinity rules are updated with values that reflect the run time traffic exchanged between Pods that in turn are dynamically rescheduled allowing to find better placement decisions for them. Furthermore a rolling update consists of a progressive deployment process, where old Pods are deleted only after new ones are in a ready state. This allows to reduce application downtime to a minimum also in case of frequent updates.

A rolling update process for a Deployment is not activated if no affinity rule in its Pod template section is updated. This means that if traffic amounts exchanged between microservices do not change over a time period, application Pods would not be rescheduled. Considering the ever changing network latencies between nodes in Cloud-Edge Kubernetes clusters, this may cause a degradation in the application response time. In order to give Pods the opportunity to be rescheduled also in case of stationarity in the traffic amount exchanged between them, the controller adds a *rValue* label with a random value in the Pod template section of each application Deployment, with the aim to force a rolling update process. The random value is selected from the integer range between 0 and the value of the *updateFactor* property of the ControllableApp resource. The greater this value, the greater the probability that a rolling update process is activated.

Figure 3 shows how the proposed topology controller works. As in the case of the traffic-aware configuration controller, a control-loop in the topology controller is activated by a Kubernetes custom resource, in this case the *Topology* custom resource.

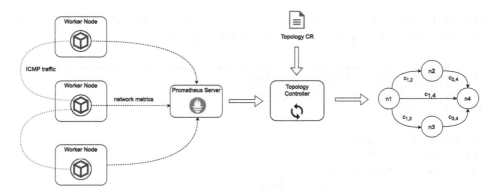

Fig. 3. Topology controller

The *runPeriod* property in the *spec* section of a Topology custom resource determines the period of the control-loop, while the *nodes* property represents the list of nodes in the cluster. For each iteration, the controller fetches the list of *Node* resources whose names are specified in the nodes property from the Kubernetes API server. For each node n_i the controller assigns to it a set of labels *network.cost.n_j* each with a value proportional to the network latency, averaged through a configurable time period, between nodes n_i and n_j and normalized in the range between 1 and 100. The network.cost.n_i label for node n_i is assigned a value of 1. Network latency metrics are fetched by the operator from the Prometheus metrics server. As showed in Fig. 3 network latencies between nodes are collected by a network probe agent deployed on each cluster node and configured to send ICMP traffic to all the other cluster nodes to measure the round trip time value. The output of each iteration of the control-loop is a topology graph with the updated network cost values that is then submitted to the Kubernetes API server.

4.3   Network-Aware Scheduler

The proposed network-aware custom scheduler extends the default Kubernetes scheduler by implementing an extension of the default *InterPodAffinity* plugin in the form of a custom scoring plugin. The custom scheduler is a program written in the Go language and runs as a Deployment in the Kubernetes control plane. For each Pod to be scheduled, the custom plugin assigns a score to each candidate node of the cluster that has passed the filtering phase. The scores calculated by the plugin are then added to the scores of the other scoring plugins. As in the case of the *InterPodAffinity* plugin, the custom plugin processes inter-Pod affinity rules, where in our approach affinity rules are specified by the traffic-aware application configuration operator. However, unlike the *InterPodAffinity* plugin, the custom plugin doesn't evaluate the *topologyKey* parameter in the affinity rules, but it takes into account network costs specified by the topology operator on each cluster node as *network.cost.x* labels. Algorithm 1 shows the details of the scoring algorithm of the proposed plugin.

Algorithm 1. Node scoring algorithm

Input: p, n, $cNodes$, $netCosts$, $affWeights$
Output: *score*

1: $cmCost \leftarrow 0$
2: **for** cn in $cNodes$ **do**
3:     $pcmCost \leftarrow 0$
4:     **for** cnp in $cn.pods$ **do**
5:         **if** $areNeighbors(p, cnp)$ **then**
6:             $pcmCost \leftarrow pcmCost + netCosts[n, cn] \times affWeights[p, cnp]$
7:         **end if**
8:     **end for**
9:     $cmCost \leftarrow cmCost + pcmCost$
10: **end for**
11: $score \leftarrow -cmCost$

The algorithm takes as inputs the following arguments:

- p: the Pod to be scheduled.
- n: the node to be scored.
- *cNodes*: the set of nodes in the cluster, including node n.
- *netCosts*: the network costs between node n and all the other nodes *cNodes*.
- *affWeights*: the set of weights associated with the Pod p affinity rules.

The algorithm starts by initializing the variable $cmCost$ to zero. The variable $cmCost$ represents the cost of communication between the Pod p and all its neighbors when the Pod p is placed on node n. A Pod $P1$ is considered a neighbor of another Pod $P2$ if there exists an affinity rule in Pod $P2$ resource configuration whose label selector matches Pod $P1$. The algorithm iterates through the list of cluster nodes *cNodes*. For each cluster node cn the $pcmCost$ variable value is calculated. The $pcmCost$ variable represents the cost of communication between the Pod p and all its neighbors running on node cn when the Pod p is placed on node n. For each neighbor Pod the weight of the corresponding affinity rule is multiplied by the network cost between node n and node cn and added to the $pcmCost$ variable. The $pcmCost$ variable value is then added to the $cmCost$ variable. The final node score is represented by the opposite of the $cmCost$ variable value.

By excluding the scoring results of the other Kubernetes scoring plugins and taking into account the result of the proposed custom plugin only, the node n selected for the placement of the Pod p is the node that minimizes the communication cost for the Pod p as shown in Equation (1):

$$n : cmCost(p, n) = \min_{n_i \in cn} \left(\sum_{n_j \in cn} (netCost(n_i, n_j) * \sum_{p_k \in n_j} affWeight(p, p_k)) \right) \quad (1)$$

The scoring algorithm assigns a score to each cluster node so that the Pod to be scheduled is placed on the node, or in a nearby node in terms of network latency, where the Pods with which the Pod has the greatest affinity are executed. For each affinity rule the default *InterPodAffinity* plugin assigns a score different from zero only to the nodes that belong to a topology domain matched by the *topologyKey* parameter of the rule. Our custom plugin instead scores all the cluster nodes based on the current relative network distance between them. This allows to implement a more fine-grained node scoring approach able to take into account the ever changing network conditions in the cluster instead of using node labels statically assigned before the application deployment phase.

5   Evaluation

The proposed solution has been validated using a sample microservices-based application executed on a test bed environment. The application, whose structure is depicted in Fig. 4, is composed of different microservices and database servers. The application can be thought of as composed of different independent service chains, each activated by a specific application endpoint. We conduct black box experiments by evaluating the end-to-end response time of the test application when HTTP POST requests are sent to the *apigateway* service, each with an equally sized message body. Requests to the application are sent through the k6 load testing utility[3]. We compare both cases when our network-aware scheduler and custom controllers are deployed on the Kubernetes cluster and when only the default scheduler is present. Each experiment consists of 20 trials, during which the k6 tool sends requests to the *apigateway* service with a specific number of virtual users for 32 min. For each trial, statistics about the end-to-end application response time are measured and are averaged with those of the other trials of the same experiment. The trial interval is partitioned into 4 min sub-intervals, during witch the k6 tool sends requests to different application endpoints. This way variability in application usage patterns is simulated by activating different microservice channels at different time intervals. In order to simulate network latencies between cluster nodes the traffic control (*tc*) Linux utility[4] is used. In particular, the tc tool is executed every 30 s and configured to add random delays in the virtual network cards of cluster nodes.

When evaluating the performance of the default scheduler we consider the case in which no inter-Pod affinity rules are specified and the case in which the affinity rules are statically defined for each service. In particular, for a service s_i that interacts with n services, n preferredDuringSchedulingIgnoredDuringExecution affinity rules are defined in its Pod template, each with a topologyKey parameter equal to *kubernetes.io/hostname* and a weight equal to 100 (the maximum allowed weight value) divided by n. This way the scheduler will try to co-locate Pods with affinity relationships on the same nodes. For our approach a ControllableApp custom resource with a runPeriod of 60 s and an updateFactor

---

[3] https://k6.io/.
[4] https://man7.org/linux/man-pages/man8/tc.8.html.

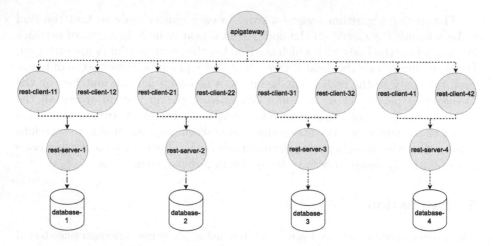

Fig. 4. Sample microservice application

of 10 s, and a Topology custom resource with a runPeriod of 60 s are created to configure the custom controllers.

We evaluate how the application response time varies depending on the network latencies between cluster nodes and the memory resource requirements for each Pod. The first factor impacts on the communication latency between Pods located on different nodes, while the latter determines how many Pods can be placed on the same node. The greater this value, the smaller the number of Pods that can be co-located on the same node and therefore the fewer the intra-node communications.

Figure 5 illustrates the results of the experiments performed, showing the 95th percentile of the application response time as a function of the maximum network latencies between nodes and the memory resource requirements of the application Pods. Three scenarios are considered in which 256MB, 512MB and 800MB of memory requests are configured for each Pod respectively. In all the cases, the proposed approach performs better than the default scheduler without statically defined inter-Pod affinity rules, with average improvements of 43%, 39% and 35% in the three scenarios respectively.

In the case of 256 MB Pod memory requests the default scheduler with statically assigned inter-Pod affinities performs better than our network-aware scheduler, with an average difference of 13% in the response times. Two main reasons may explain this kind of behaviour. First, considering the low Pod memory requests, more Pods can be scheduled on the same nodes. While the default scheduler gives a non zero score only to nodes that satisfy affinity rules, our scheduler scores all nodes based on run time network costs. This results in a greater distribution of Pods between nodes and therefore a lower amount of intra-node communications. The second reason is related to the fact that our approach determines inter-Pod affinity relationships by using run time information only, requiring that traffic and network metrics have to be collected before

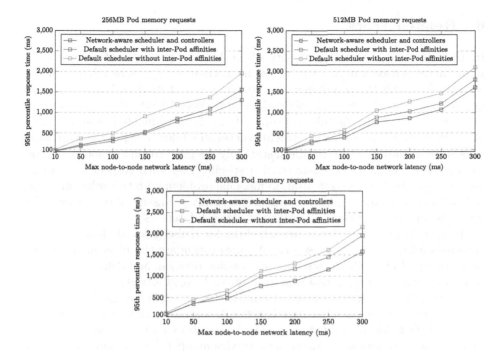

Fig. 5. Experiments results

our network-aware scheduler can take optimal decisions. While our scheduler is able to consider also statically assigned inter-Pod affinity rules, the task of defining proper affinity rules is not always a simple one as discussed in Sect. 3, especially considering the graph complexity of modern applications.

By increasing Pods memory requests to 512 MB and 800 MB, our approach starts to perform better. For network latencies less than or equal to 50 ms the default scheduler with affinity rules continues to obtain lower response times with an average difference of 14% and 3% for the second and third scenarios respectively. However, in the case of network latencies greater than 50 ms, our approach obtains lower response times with average improvements of 15% and 29% for the two scenarios respectively. This behaviour can be explained by the fact that the greater the memory requested by Pods, the lesser the amount of Pods that can be co-located on the same node. The same reasoning can be done for the number of Pods: the greater the number of Pods that compose an application, the lesser the portion of them that can be placed on the same node. This means that the default scheduler fails to find optimal decisions for a greater number of Pods because the number of candidate nodes that satisfy affinity rules decreases. Our network-aware scheduler instead tries to place the Pods with affinity relationships on nearby nodes in terms of network distance, though they can't be co-located on the same node.

6   Related Work

In the literature, there is a variety of works that propose extensions of the Kubernetes platform in order to devise network-aware Pod scheduling solutions able to deal with the communication requirements of modern latency-sensitive applications and the dynamic network conditions of Cloud-Edge environments.

A network-aware scheduler is proposed in [14], implemented as an extension of the filtering phase of the default Kubernetes scheduler. The proposed approach makes use of round-trip time labels, statically assigned to cluster nodes, in order to minimize the network distance of a specific Pod with respect to a target location specified on its configuration file. One problem with this solution relates to the fact that round-trip time labels are statically pre-assigned to cluster nodes, not reflecting the run-time variability of network latencies.

In [12] Pogonip, an edge-aware scheduler for Kubernetes, designed for asynchronous microservices is presented. Authors formulate the placement problem as an Integer Linear Programming optimization problem and define an heuristic to quickly find an approximate solution for real-world execution scenarios. The heuristic is implemented as a set of Kubernetes scheduler plugins. Also in this work, there is no Pod rescheduling if network conditions change over time.

In [5] Nautilus is presented, a run-time system that includes, among its modules, a communication-aware microservice mapper. This module divides the microservice graph into multiple partitions based on the communication overhead between microservices and maps the partitions to the cluster nodes in order to make frequent data interaction complete in memory. While the proposed solution migrates application Pod if computational resources utilization is unbalanced among nodes, there is no Pod rescheduling in the case of degradation on the communication between microservices.

NetMARKS [17] is a Kubernetes scheduler extender that uses dynamic network metrics collected with Istio Service Mesh to ensure an efficient placement of Service Function Chains, based on the historical traffic amount exchanged between services. The proposed scheduler however does not consider run-time cluster network conditions in its placement decisions.

In [4] an extension to the Kubernetes default scheduler is proposed that uses information about the status of the network, like bandwidth and round trip time, to optimize batch job scheduling decisions. The scheduler predicts whether an application can be executed within its deadline and rejects applications if their deadlines cannot be met. Although information about current network conditions and historical job execution times is used during scheduling decisions, communication interactions between microservices are not considered in this work.

In [13] an extension of the Kubernetes orchestration strategy with an adaptive autoscaler and a network-aware scheduler is proposed. The autoscaler uses a reinforcement learning approach that dynamically scales container replicas on the basis of application response time. Container replicas are then scheduled using a greedy heuristic that takes into account node-to-node latencies to optimize the application placement. The proposed solution however optimizes the placement of each microservice independently from the communication relationships with other microservices.

Finally, [15] presents a Kubernetes edge-scheduler that considers inter-node network latencies and services communication requirements in order to optimize, using an heuristic algorithm, the placement of containerized applications in geographically distributed clusters. A re-scheduler is also proposed that is responsible for container migration in order to improve resource utilization in the cluster. In this work, however, exchanged traffic amount between microservices is not taken into account during scheduling decisions.

7   Conclusions

In this work we proposed an extension of the Kubernetes platform in order to implement an effective network-aware Pod scheduling strategy aimed to deal with the ever changing network conditions in Cloud-Edge Kubernetes clusters and the dynamic communication relationships between the microservices of modern distributed applications. A traffic-aware configuration operator is in charge of dynamically updating inter-Pod affinity rules based on the traffic amount exchanged between Pods, while a topology operator encodes node-to-node network latencies on node labels. A network-aware custom scheduler makes Pod placement decisions based on current weights of Pods affinity rules and network costs between nodes.

As a future work we plan to improve the assignment mechanism for affinity rules weights. In this work only direct relationships between Pods are evaluated by measuring the traffic exchanged between them. However in a microservices-based application a user request consists of a chain of sub-requests where multiple services may be involved. Placing Pods that belongs to the same request chain near to each other may improve the application response time. For this reason we plan to make use of distributed tracing techniques to find more insightful information about communication relationships between Pods.

References

1. Ahmad, I., AlFailakawi, M.G., AlMutawa, A., Alsalman, L.: Container scheduling techniques: a survey and assessment. J. King Saud Univ. - Comput. Inf. Sci. (2021). https://doi.org/10.1016/j.jksuci.2021.03.002
2. Bittencourt, L., et al.: The internet of things, fog and cloud continuum: integration and challenges. Internet Things 3–4, 134–155 (2018). https://doi.org/10.1016/j.iot.2018.09.005
3. Burns, B., Grant, B., Oppenheimer, D., Brewer, E., Wilkes, J.: Borg, omega, and kubernetes. ACM Queue 14, 70–93 (2016). http://queue.acm.org/detail.cfm?id=2898444
4. Caminero, A.C., Muñoz-Mansilla, R.: Quality of service provision in fog computing: network-aware scheduling of containers. Sensors 21(12) (2021). https://doi.org/10.3390/s21123978

5. Fu, K., et al.: Qos-aware and resource efficient microservice deployment in cloud-edge continuum. In: IEEE International Parallel and Distributed Processing Symposium (IPDPS), pp. 932–941 (2021). https://doi.org/10.1109/IPDPS49936.2021.00102

6. Goswami, S.A., Padhya, B.P., Patel, K.D.: Internet of things: applications, challenges and research issues. In: 2019 Third International conference on I-SMAC (IoT in Social, Mobile, Analytics and Cloud) (I-SMAC), pp. 47–50 (2019). https://doi.org/10.1109/I-SMAC47947.2019.9032474

7. Jawarneh, I.M.A., et al.: Container orchestration engines: a thorough functional and performance comparison. In: ICC 2019–2019 IEEE International Conference on Communications (ICC), pp. 1–6 (2019). https://doi.org/10.1109/ICC.2019.8762053

8. Kayal, P.: Kubernetes in fog computing: feasibility demonstration, limitations and improvement scope: invited paper. In: 2020 IEEE 6th World Forum on Internet of Things (WF-IoT), pp. 1–6 (2020). https://doi.org/10.1109/WF-IoT48130.2020.9221340

9. Manaouil, K., Lebre, A.: Kubernetes and the Edge? Research Report RR-9370, Inria Rennes - Bretagne Atlantique (2020). https://hal.inria.fr/hal-02972686

10. Marchese, A., Tomarchio, O.: Network-aware container placement in cloud-edge kubernetes clusters. In: 2022 22nd IEEE International Symposium on Cluster, Cloud and Internet Computing (CCGrid), Taormina, Italy, pp. 859–865 (2022). https://doi.org/10.1109/CCGrid54584.2022.00102

11. Pahl, C., Brogi, A., Soldani, J., Jamshidi, P.: Cloud container technologies: a state-of-the-art review. IEEE Trans. Cloud Comput. (2017). https://doi.org/10.1109/TCC.2017.2702586

12. Pusztai, T., Rossi, F., Dustdar, S.: Pogonip: scheduling asynchronous applications on the edge. In: IEEE 14th International Conference on Cloud Computing (CLOUD), pp. 660–670 (2021). https://doi.org/10.1109/CLOUD53861.2021.00085

13. Rossi, F., Cardellini, V., Lo Presti, F., Nardelli, M.: Geo-distributed efficient deployment of containers with kubernetes. Comput. Commun. **159**, 161–174 (2020). https://doi.org/10.1016/j.comcom.2020.04.061, https://www.sciencedirect.com/science/article/pii/S0140366419317931

14. Santos, J., Wauters, T., Volckaert, B., De Turck, F.: Towards network-aware resource provisioning in kubernetes for fog computing applications. In: IEEE Conference on Network Softwarization (NetSoft), pp. 351–359 (2019). https://doi.org/10.1109/NETSOFT.2019.8806671

15. Toka, L.: Ultra-reliable and low-latency computing in the edge with kubernetes. J. Grid Comput. **19**(3), 1–23 (2021). https://doi.org/10.1007/s10723-021-09573-z

16. Tomarchio, O., Calcaterra, D., Modica, G.D.: Cloud resource orchestration in the multi-cloud landscape: a systematic review of existing frameworks. J. Cloud Comput. **9**(1), 1–24 (2020). https://doi.org/10.1186/s13677-020-00194-7

17. Wojciechowski, L., et al.: Netmarks: network metrics-aware kubernetes scheduler powered by service mesh. In: IEEE INFOCOM 2021 - IEEE Conference on Computer Communications, pp. 1–9 (2021). https://doi.org/10.1109/INFOCOM42981.2021.9488670

DeepSCJD: An Online Deep Learning-Based Model for Secure Collaborative Job Dispatching in Edge Computing

Zhaoyang Yu[1,2], Sinong Zhao[1], Tongtong Su[1], Wenwen Liu[1],
Xiaoguang Liu[1(✉)], Gang Wang[1], Zehua Wang[2], and Victor C. M. Leung[2]

[1] College of Computer Science, TJ Key Lab of NDST, Nankai University,
Tianjin, China
{yuzz,zhaosn,sutt,liuww,liuxg,wgzwp}@nbjl.nankai.edu.cn
[2] Department of Electrical and Computer Engineering, WiNMos Lab,
University of British Columbia, Vancouver, Canada
{zwang,vleung}@ece.ubc.ca

Abstract. Edge computing enhances the processing capabilities of edge networks for processing mobile users' jobs. Approaches that dispatch jobs to a single edge cloud are prone to cause task accumulation and excessive latency due to the uncertain workload and limited resources of edge servers. Offloading tasks to lightly-loaded neighbors, which are multiple hops away, alleviates the dilemma but increases transmission cost and security risks. Hence, how to realize the trade-off between computing latency, offloading cost and security during job dispatching is a great challenge. In this paper, we propose an online Deep learning-based model for Secure Collaborative Job Dispatching (DeepSCJD) in multiple edge clouds. Specifically, we first utilize bi-directional long short-term memory to predict the workload of edge servers and apply the graph neural networks to aggregate the features of directed acyclic graph jobs as well as undirected weighted topology of edge servers. Based on the state composed of these two features, a deep reinforcement learning agent including a simple deep Q network and linear branch, generates a final dispatching decision of tasks, aiming to achieve the smallest average weighted cost. Experiments on real-world data sets demonstrate the efficiency of proposed model and its superiority over traditional and state-of-the-art baselines, reaching the maximum average performance improvement of 54.16% relative to K-Hop. Extensive evaluations manifest the generalization of our model under various conditions.

Keywords: Collaborative job dispatching · Security · Deep reinforcement learning · Graph neural network · Multi-hop

This research is supported in part by the NSF of China (No. 62141412, 61872201), the Science and Technology Development Plan of Tianjin (20JCZDJC00610, 19YFZCSF00900, the Fundamental Research Funds for the Central Universities, China Scholarship Council (CSC). The first author is supported by CSC (Grant No.202106200061) as a visiting Ph.D. student at the University of British Columbia, Canada under the supervision of Prof. Victor C.M. Leung.

J. Troya et al. (Eds.): ICSOC 2022, LNCS 13740, pp. 481–497, 2022.
https://doi.org/10.1007/978-3-031-20984-0_34

1   Introduction

Edge computing alleviates the dilemma of insufficient abilities in mobile devices as well as great latency and bandwidth pressure in remote cloud. It is estimated that 70 million small cells will be deployed in 2025[1] and 90% of data will be processed at edge [9]. End users offload jobs to edge servers for various services. An End-Edge-Cloud architecture is illustrated as Fig. 1. Each edge cloud is likely to be collocated an Access Point (AP). The edge clouds are connected with each other as well as remote cloud and includes three modules. The Control Module is to receive user requests and decide their execution positions. The Dispatching Module determines specific destination edge servers and forwards jobs to Execution Module for calculation. The submitted jobs are of high explosiveness leading to the uncertain workload of machines. The load affects servers' calculation speed and results in variable computing latency of jobs in turn. Also, there is a delay in computing latency, which can only be aware after the job is completed. Besides, the jobs submitted by devices are heterogeneous with various objective functions. So efficient job dispatching in edge is a critical issue.

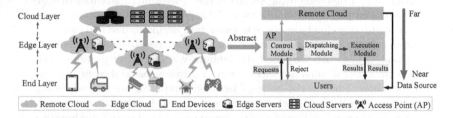

Fig. 1. The scenario of job dispatching in Internet of Things.

Prior research assumes that jobs are offloaded to a single edge cloud [20], resulting in resource contention between accumulated jobs. So we explore the cooperation resource sharing among multiple edge clouds and dispatch jobs to lightly-loaded distant neighbors. Nevertheless, increased number of hops makes offloading cost and security risks grow. Consequently, performing job dispatching to realize the trade-off between computing latency, energy consumption and security while ensuring users' Quality of Service (QoS) is a complicated challenge.

Static model-based algorithms are inapplicable in dynamical edge environment due to the long decision-making time and significant computational overhead [5]. While Deep Reinforcement Learning (DRL) makes job dispatching decisions in a global view adapting to the variations in edge and doesn't require manually labeled training samples. Furthermore, jobs are in the form of Directed Acyclic Graph (DAG). And the Graph Neural Network (GNN) effectively transmits node information and extracts features over graphs to achieve relational reasoning and combinatorial generalization. It makes up the shortcomings of prerequisite data independence in universe deep learning methods.

---

[1] Small Cell Market Status Statistics Dec 2017. scf.io. Retrieved 2018-02-19.

We propose an online **D**eep learning-based **S**ecure **C**ollaborative **J**ob **D**ispatching model (DeepSCJD) in edge computing. We employ Graph Attention Network (GAT) to aggregate the features of DAG jobs and network topology of edge servers. Workload is predicted through Bi-directional Long Short-Term Memory (BiLSTM) as one of the attributes of servers. A two-branch DRL agent integrating linear and Deep Q-Network (DQN) is built for multi-hop dispatching decisions for tasks. The contributions are as follows:

- We exert a two-branch deep reinforcement learning method to address the secure collaborative job dispatching problem in multiple edge clouds under co-provisioning the computing latency, offloading cost and security risks.
- We introduce a Prediction Module to evaluate the impact of servers' workload on the computing latency, and the predicted workload, as one of edge server features, is of benefit for making task offloading decisions.
- We verify the effectiveness of the proposed model based on a real-world data trace. The results prove that DeepSCJD outperforms traditional and state-of-the-art approaches. Moreover, extensive experiments under various configurations confirm that the model is of great generalization and well adapted to diverse objective requirements in the dynamic edge circumstances.
- Ablation experiments are conducted to prove the significance of load prediction, GNN feature aggregation and linear branch for offloading decisions.

2   Related Work

Traditional Offloading Strategies: Job dispatching in edge was usually formulated as an Mixed Integer Programming problem, and solved by heuristic local search [1]. Authors presented computation offloading using approximate dynamic programming [10] and game theoretic [3]. Nonetheless, these conventional methods were costly to perform lots of iterations and could not adapt to edge environments with high dynamics. Instead, we apply DRL to make job dispatching decisions, which constructs a reward mechanism to interact with the environment and accommodates the variety with great generalization.

Deep Learning-Based Offloading Methods: Generative Adversarial Networks (GAN) was utilized to forecast user requests [19], and authors put forward a RL-based framework to decrease offloading latency [17]. Scholars applied an Actor-Critic mechanism for offloading DAG tasks to reduce the average energy-time [2]. However, their works either failed to take into account the impact of server load on task execution, or ignored the data safety during offloading. Hence, we perdict the workload through BiLSTM to assist describing server characteristics and add the security in the formulation of offloading cost.

Dispatching of Single Edge Cloud: Researchers realized the workload balance of servers [20] and Nash equilibrium of computation offloading [3], respectively. Another investigation jointly considered communication and calculation resources for offloading [15]. Nevertheless, the constrained computing resources

Table 1. Table of notations

Type	Nota.	Representations	Type	Nota.	Representations
Edge cloud	$\mathcal{Z}$	Set of edge clouds	Job	$\mathcal{M}$	Job set in a certain priod
	Q_z	Number of edge servers in z		N_m	Number of vertexes in job m
	p_z	Fees to perform tasks of z		$\mathcal{W}_m$	Adjacency matrix of job m
	s_z	The security risk of z	Task	n_m	The nth task within m
Edge server	q_z	The qth edge server in z		b_{n_m}	Begin time of task n_m
	e_{q_z}	Disaster domain level of q_z		d_{n_m}	Deadline time of task n_m
	$u_{q_z}^{\text{cpu}}$	CPU cores available of q_z		ϵ_{n_m}	CPU cycles requested by n_m
	$u_{q_z}^{\text{mem}}$	Residual Memory size in q_z		$r_{n_m}^{\text{cpu}}$	CPU cores required by n_m
	$u_{q_z}^{\text{disk}}$	Disk volume unoccupied in q_z		$r_{n_m}^{\text{mem}}$	Memory size demanded of n_m
	$c_{q_z}^{\text{cpu}}$	Total CPU cores of q_z		$r_{n_m}^{\text{disk}}$	Amount of data carried by n_m
	$c_{q_z}^{\text{mem}}$	Maximum Memory size of q_z		$\mathcal{V}_{n_m}$	Parents index list of n_m
	$c_{q_z}^{\text{disk}}$	The entire Disk capacity of q_z		ϑ_{n_m}	Located edge server of n_m
	y_{q_z}	Predicted workload of q_z		ι_{n_m}	Destination edge server of n_m
	ψ_{q_z}	The cycle frequency of q_z		ω_{n_m}	Actual completion time of n_m

in a single edge cloud led to task accumulation, which resulted in high procras-
tination and affected the QoS of latency-sensitive jobs especially. In our design,
we are oriented to make further collaborative offloading among multiple edge
clouds to alleviate this situation.

Cooperative Dispatching of Multiple Edge Clouds: Authors delegated
tasks to edge servers located fixed-hops away [13]. Other studies proposed heuristic methods like evolutionary scheme [16] and Lyapunov optimization [11], which
were easy to fall into local optimum and failed to adapt to edge scences. We
exert the DAG network to extract the features of DAG jobs and edge servers
for better offloading decisions. The DRL-based cooperative task offloading in [6]
didn't consider the possible frauds between edge clouds, which posed threats
to users' data security. The proposed DeepSCJD comprehensively pay attention
to dynamic environment variations, computing workload, offloading cost, data
security for accomplishing efficient collaborative job dispatching.

3   Problem Definition

As displayed in Fig 1, numerous mobile devices like autonomous vehicles, phones,
cameras, etc. continuously submit diverse jobs to edge clouds for services. At a
busy traffic intersection, there may be substantial target detection requirements
at the same time. These explosive jobs are of strict delay demands. If we fail
to get timely feedback, our life safety will be threatened. Furthermore, we must
guarantee the accuracy of calculation results and security of user data. A single
edge cloud bears great stress due to the limited computing resource. Although
distant lightly-loaded neighbors with abundant available resources obtain smaller
calculation delay, the offloading cost (transmission delay, energy consumption
and security risk) grows with the increase of the number of hops.

Consequently, the secure collaborative job dispatching in edge can be defined
as: for each subtask in the job, we make a dispatching decision about its execution

location (the destination edge server to perform this task and the corresponding transmit path), while achieving a trade-off between computing latency and offload cost to ensure users' QoS and service providers' profits. Tasks are executed on a certain edge server either in the local edge cloud or a non-local one beyond several hops. Related representations are shown in Table 1.

Edge Cloud: Let $\mathcal{Z} \triangleq \{1, \ldots, Z\}$ denote the set of edge clouds and denote Q_z as the number of edge servers in edge cloud $z \in \mathcal{Z}$. Different edge clouds apply different fees and security risks to tasks. The network topology information is maintained and updated regularly by edge service providers.

Edge Server: Let $q_z \in \mathcal{Q}_z \triangleq \{1, \ldots, Q_z\}$ denote the qth server of edge cloud $z \in \mathcal{Z}$. Due to the interoperability among edge clouds, all edge servers form an undirected but weighted topology, in which each server represents a node.

Job: Each job is independent but contains multiple dependent tasks. Denote $\mathcal{M} \triangleq \{1, \ldots, M\}$ as the jobs in a certain period. So the job m can be defined by a DAG graph $\mathcal{G}_m = \{N_m, \mathcal{W}_m\}$, in which each vertex stands for a subtask, and the directed edges signify the relationships of reliance between tasks.

Task: The nth task in job m is $n_m \in \mathcal{N}_m \triangleq \{1, \ldots, N_m\}$. Only when the parent tasks are accomplished, can the child tasks be executed. Due to the long-tail effect of start and end time, each task in a job has its own separate deadline.

Security: In network with diameter D, there are K_{n_m} paths for task n_m from the located server to destination server. $p_{n_m}^k$ stands for the kth path and $l_{n_m}^k$ represents its length. The security cost increases with the hop grows $\text{Sec}_{n_m}^k = \sum_{j=0}^{l_{n_m}^k}(1-\zeta)^j \times s_z^j, l_{n_m}^k \in \{0, 1, 2, \cdots, D\}$, where ζ indicates the data transmission security decay factor, s_z^j is the security risk of edge cloud z at the jth hop.

Latency: We assume a static network and ignore the time spent between terminal devices and local servers. Users' mobility has no impact on task dispatching decisions. For task n_m, let $f_{n_m}^{k,j}$ and $t_{n_m}^{k,j}$ represent the from-node and to-node at the jth hop, and $\text{W}(f_{n_m}^{k,j}, t_{n_m}^{k,j})$ denotes the weight between them. The transferring latency of path $p_{n_m}^k$ is the sum of transmit all data $\text{Lat}_{n_m}^k = \sum_{j=0}^{l_{n_m}^k} \text{W}(f_{n_m}^{k,j}, t_{n_m}^{k,j}) \times r_{n_m}^{\text{disk}} \times \tau, \forall f_{n_m}^{k,j}, t_{n_m}^{k,j} \in p_{n_m}^k$, where $r_{n_m}^{\text{disk}}$ means the data carried by task n_m, and τ is the time of transmitting a unit of data per distance.

Energy: The energy consumption during task offloading is the sum of energy expenditure of all senders, receivers and transmission paths, which is displayed as $\text{Eng}_{n_m}^k = \sum_{j=0}^{l_{n_m}^k} \text{W}(f_{n_m}^{k,j}, t_{n_m}^{k,j}) \times \xi \times r_{n_m}^{\text{disk}} + r_{n_m}^{\text{disk}} \times \left[\rho_0 l_{n_m}^k + \rho_1 \sum_{j=0}^{l_{n_m}^k} \text{W}^\gamma(f_{n_m}^{k,j}, t_{n_m}^{k,j}) \right] + \rho_0 \times r_{n_m}^{\text{disk}} \times l_{n_m}^k$. The first item indicates the energy required for path transmission carrying data $r_{n_m}^{\text{disk}}$ and ξ depicts the power of transferring unit data per distance [8]. The second and third items demonstrate the energy of senders and receivers, where γ represents the path attenuation index. ρ_0 and ρ_1 denote power expenditure of sending and modulation coding unit of data, separately [7].

So the total cost of offloading task n_m with path $p_{n_m}^k$ is represented as (1)

$$\text{Cost}_{n_m}^k = \text{Sec}_{n_m}^k + \text{Lat}_{n_m}^k + \text{Eng}_{n_m}^k. \tag{1}$$

Any task cannot be migrated between edge servers once it starts to be performed due to relocation expense. We decide the destination server ι_{n_m} (i.e. server q_z) for each task n_m. The server's actual processing speed is affected by the future workload y_{q_z}. The computing latency of task n_m when being executed on q_z is

$$\text{Comp}_{n_m}^{q_z} = x^{y_{q_z}} \times \epsilon_{n_m} \times \frac{1}{\psi_{q_z}}, \tag{2}$$

where x is the skewness between workload and processing speed [11], ϵ_{n_m} means required CPU cycles and ψ_{q_z} indicates the cycle frequency of server q_z.

Therefore, the weighted cost (WC) of task n_m for the kth path is represented as (3), where α and β are weight coefficients

$$\text{WC}(n_m, q_z, k) = \alpha \times \text{Cost}_{n_m}^k + \beta \times \text{Comp}_{n_m}^{q_z}. \tag{3}$$

Optimization Objective: In a period of time, the total number of processed tasks T is calculated as $T = \sum_{m=1}^{M} N_m$. We make decisions Π for all incoming tasks, realizing the smallest average weighted cost (AWC):

$$
\begin{aligned}
&\Pi(T) = \arg\min \frac{1}{T} \sum_{m=1}^{M} \sum_{n=1}^{N_m} \text{WC}(n_m, q_z, k), \\
&\quad \text{C}_1 : 0 < \omega_{n_m} < d_{n_m}, && \forall m \in \mathcal{M}, \forall n_m \in \mathcal{N}_m, \\
&\text{s.t.} \, \text{C}_2 : \sum_{z=1}^{Z} \sum_{q=1}^{Q_z} \pi_{q_z} = 1, \pi_{q_z} \in \{0,1\}, && \forall z \in \mathcal{Z}, \forall q_z \in \mathcal{Q}_z, \\
&\quad \text{C}_3 : \sum r_{n_m} < c_{q_z}, && \forall z \in \mathcal{Z}, \forall q_z \in \mathcal{Q}_z, \forall m \in \mathcal{M}, \forall n_m \in \mathcal{N}_m.
\end{aligned}
\tag{4}
$$

As C_1 claims, the completion time of any task cannot surpass its deadline to ensure QoS. C_2 means that any task can only be performed locally or be offloaded to one neighbor edge server exclusively. The dispatching decision of task n_m is $\pi_{n_m} = \{\pi_{1,1}, \cdots, \pi_{1,Q_1}, \cdots, \pi_{Z,1}, \cdots, \pi_{Z,Q_Z}\}$, which is a D-dimension vector. π_{z,q_z} is a binary indicator corresponding to server q_z. Value 1 means the task will be executed on this server, while 0 indicates not. C_3 indicates that the sum of the resource requests of all tasks on an edge server cannot exceed its resource capacity limitation. Finally, the offloading behavior should be effective. In a long term view, the decisions of migrating tasks to neighbors beyond multiple hops should produce a smaller AWC than executing them in local. That is to say, a shorter computing latency is obtained through paying tolerable offloading cost.

4   System Overview

4.1   Framework

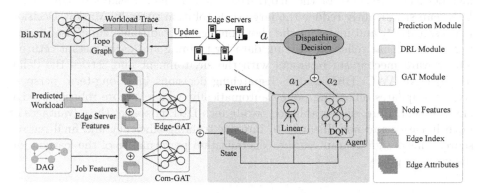

Fig. 2. The framework of DeepSCJD

The workflow of the system is shown as Fig. 2. In Prediction Module, the historical data of resource utilization of edge servers is input into BiLSTM model to predict the workload situation at the next moment, which is regarded as one of dimensions of servers' characteristics. In the meantime, we process the network topology to obtain initial features of the edge servers, including edge index properties, weight attributes and so on. The GAT Module consists of two graph neural networks Com-GAT and Edge-GAT, which extracts and aggregates the features of jobs and edge servers separately, deriving high-dimensional abstract ones. These two outputs are concated to compose the current state. In DRL Module, a two-branch agent involving a linear and DQN branch makes job dispatching decisions. Based on the trained policy, the state is input into each branch, acquiring action a_1 and a_2. Finally, we add the two actions and attain the ultimate dispatching decision action a.

Next, tasks are offloaded and performed on destination edge servers to generate a reward. The agent detects this reward to adjust the dispatching behavior at the next step. Moreover, we update the current load of edge servers and the time window of BiLSTM slides one bit backward. The new workload is applied to the next round prediction. The occupancy conditions of CPU, Memory and Disk of edge servers also vary, resulting in server attributes modifying accordingly.

Due to resource contention, the servers' computing speed and tasks' completion delay are affected by the workload in future continuous slots [11]. And Bi-LSTM can precisely capture the certain correlation between adjoining slots in the workload time series from forward and backward directions to explore temporal dynamic behaviors, which provides feature basis for job dispatching. Besides, the DAG job data with dependent edges is of Non-Euclidean structure. It is inconsistent with the assumption in conventional learning techniques.

While GNN effectively transmits node knowledge to conduct feature aggregation over graphs. Here, we adopt GAT that introduces an attention mechanism
based on Graph Convolution Network (GCN). What's more, the job dispatching problem is NP-hard [20], which is arduous for heuristic algorithms to make
fast decisions. Because of the arbitrariness and memorylessness of DAG jobs,
DRL can significantly reduce the large-scale solution space by Markov Decision
Process (MDP) and make up the shortcomings of traditional supervised learning methods that relies on existing data for training and cares instant returns.
The reward mechanism interacts with the environment and settles the delay
of objective AWC. DRL makes dispatching decisions in a long-term perspective and updates offloading policy automatically, which is more robust for edge
environment. Here, our established two-branch DRL possesses the advantages of
both linearity and non-linearity to improve training efficiency and final reward
score. This design guarantees the generalization performance of the learned job
dispatching policy.

4.2   Prediction Module

We consider CPU, Memory and Disk as main factors influencing the workload.
Then we perform Min-max normalization and assign different weights to formu-
late workload $y = \eta \times y^{\mathrm{cpu}} + \mu \times y^{\mathrm{mem}} + (1 - \eta - \mu) \times y^{\mathrm{disk}}$. Most of submitted jobs
are computation-intensive or latency-sensitive rather than storage-intensive. We
designate higher values of η and μ (both are 0.4) for CPU and Memory to reflect
their greater influences on machine workload relative to Disk.

The history data of previous E moments (sliding window), with step length S,
is used to predict the load of next L moments. We randomly select trace data of
1000 machines containing 61252584 time series in Cluster-trace-v2018[2]. Through
pre-experiments, we have $S = L = 1, E = 4$. The training set, validation set and
test set are divided according to the ratio of 7:2:1. Moreover, we exert early
stopping in order to prevent over-fitting and improve generalization.

As seen in Fig. 3(a), the loss of BiLSTM decreases on training set while it
gradually stabilizes after a short fluctuation on validation data. Through 27 iterations, the losses both on the training and validation sets converge progressively.

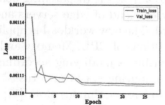 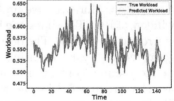

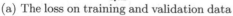

(a) The loss on training and validation data   (b) The prediction results of workload

Fig. 3. Losses and prediction results of BiLSTM

---

[2] https://github.com/alibaba/clusterdata/.

The first 200 moments of prediction results on test set are displayed in Fig. 3(b). We observe that the real workload fluctuates randomly with no certain periodicity. Our BiLSTM can forecast load variations including peaks and troughs, with an average variance of 1.08×10^{-3} between the predicted and true values.

4.3   GAT Module

1) **Feature extraction of DAG graphs:** Supposing that the feature vector of node i is $\vec{v}_i$ with G_i neighbors, the weight assigned by node i to its neighbor j can be formulated as $\varphi_{i,j}$. Here, we apply the *softmax* function for normalization and the activation function *LeakyReLU* to provide non-linearity. The new representation $\vec{v}_i{'}$ of node i aggregates the attributes of itself and all its neighbors. A multi-head attention mechanism is exploited to learn the attention weights of different subspaces for stable learning. As equation (5) shows, we perform H times of operations, in which $\varphi_{i,j}^h$ and $\mathbf{W}^h$ are the normalization attention coefficient and weight matrix by using the hth head

$$\vec{v}_i{'} = \sigma(\frac{1}{H}\sum_{h=1}^{H}(\varphi_{i,i}^h \mathbf{W}^h \vec{v}_i + \sum_{j \in G_i} \varphi_{i,j}^h \mathbf{W}^h \vec{v}_j)). \tag{5}$$

Edges in DAG jobs are directed but unweighted, the adjacency matrix of which is asymmetric. The GAT performing job feature extraction is called Com-GAT.

2) **Feature extraction of topology graph:** The edges among edge servers are undirected but weighted, indicating the distance between node pairs. So we regard the weight of edge $e_{i,j}$ between node i and its neighbor j as a certain dimension attribute of node j, $\vec{v}_j{'} = \vec{v}_j \parallel e_{i,j}, \forall j \in G_i$. Then we implement the same multi-head attention operation as the mechanism when processing DAG jobs. The GAT conducting feature aggregation on servers is named Edge-GAT.

4.4   DRL Module

There are three indispensable elements in a DRL model, state, action and reward. The agent selects an action a based on current state s, obtaining next sate s'. After action a is executed, we receive a reward r from the environment and move to the next round of action selection.

1) **State:** The state includes the attributes of DAG jobs output by Com-GAT and the features of edge servers output by Edge-GAT. Features of edge server q_z are $(p_z, e_{q_z}, u_{q_z}^{\mathrm{cpu}}, u_{q_z}^{\mathrm{mem}}, u_{q_z}^{\mathrm{disk}}, c_{q_z}^{\mathrm{cpu}}, c_{q_z}^{\mathrm{mem}}, c_{q_z}^{\mathrm{disk}}, y_{q_z}, \psi_{q_z})$. And task n_m is featured by $(b_{n_m}, d_{n_m}, \epsilon_{n_m}, r_{n_m}^{\mathrm{cpu}}, r_{n_m}^{\mathrm{mem}}, r_{n_m}^{\mathrm{disk}})$. We assume that there is only one service provider offers identical edge clouds and servers in our system.

2) **Action:** The outputs of DQN and Linear branch are the probabilities of selecting each server and action a refers to the one with the highest probability. In a period of time, there are T tasks totally with a diameter of network D. We reduce the action space from exponential D^T to $D \times T$.

3) **Reward:** Task n_m will be dispatched from the located edge server to the destination server q_z according to action a_{n_m}. We find all paths between two nodes, calculate corresponding weighted costs and select the path $p_{n_m}^{k^*}$ with the smallest cost. This cost is regarded as the reward $R(n_m, a_{n_m}) = -WC(n_m, q_z, k^*)$. A negative sign is added, because we tend to gain a smaller weighted cost while the network is trained for a larger reward.

In DQN branch, the Target Q-network Q' computes target Q-value $\mathcal{Q} = r + \delta \max_{a'} Q'(s', a'; \theta')$, where δ indicates the impact of further moments on present. The Q network updates each iteration while Q' is modified with the parameters of Q network every ς steps, which eliminates the divergence and oscillations during update. The loss is calculated as $\mathcal{L}(\theta) = \mathbb{E}[(\mathcal{Q} - Q(s, a; \theta))^2]$.

As Algorithm 1 shows, each graph is regarded as an episode and each task as a step. We use ε-greedy strategy (Lines 16–17) to explore new state-action sampling pairs outside known information and gets the maximum reward from known information, preventing the model falling into local optimum. Experience replay is exerted (Lines 31–32) to build a replay buffer to store training samples (s', a, r, s). We select a λ-size mini-batch data for iterative update each time. This manner reuses the historical data with reduced complexity, eliminates the correlation between training samples and accelerates the speed of model convergence.

5   Evaluation and Analysis

5.1   Experiment Setup

We use GT-ITM[3] to produce network topo graphs in a recursive manner. First, a flat random graph is generated. Then each node is represented as a transit domain (edge cloud) and replaced with a flat random graph. The number of nodes in this graph is the quantities of edge servers in relevant edge cloud. Preprocessed cloud task data can be applied in edge for simulation [12]. We apply the data in Cluster-trace-v2018 (see footnote 2), which contains jobs and machine usage data on 4000 machines in 8 days. The data volume attribute r^{disk} is generated obeying normal distribution $\mathcal{N}(10, 4)$. We conduct normalization on each element in the AWC objective function. Regarding the parameters, we set x to 1.04 [11], ρ_0 and ρ_1 both to 0.5 [7]. And γ and ξ are set to 3 [8]. The initial values in the sliding window of BiLSTM are randomly selected from one machine's workload over four consecutive moments, which are 0.5636, 0.5367, 0.5597 and 0.5557. The values of δ, ε, λ and ς are 0.999, 0.9, 128 and 10, respectively.

5) **Baselines:** We choose three representative algorithms as our baselines to verify the performance of proposed DeepSCJD. Rand converges by probability, K-Hop is a heuristic technique and GRL stands for deep learning method.

---

[3] http://www.cc.gatech.edu/projects/gtitm/.

Algorithm 1. Algorithm of DeepSCJD

1: Initialize replay buffer A; attenuation factor δ; initial probability ε; batch size λ; step ς; the sum of AWC Rwd_{sum}; the average AWC V; task number T;

2: Initialize Network Q with θ and Target Q-network Q' with $\theta' = \theta'$

3: Set initial workload of sliding windows

4: Put jobs into priority queue $\mathbb{L}$ according to arriving times

5: **while** $\mathbb{L}$ is not empty **do**

6:     Obtain current job $\mathcal{G}_m$ from $\mathbb{L}$

7:     $T{+}=N_m$

8:     Aggregate job features $\vec{g_1}$ through *Com-GAT*

9:     **for** each server q_z in topology **do**

10:         Predict workload y_{q_z} using *Prediction Module*

11:     **end for**

12:     Add y_{q_z} to servers' attributes

13:     Aggregate server features $\vec{g_2}$ through *Edge-GAT*

14:     Contact features to form current state $s = (\vec{g_1} \parallel \vec{g_2})$

15:     **for** each subtask n_m in job m **do**

16:         With probability ε, choose a_{n_m}

17:         Otherwise $a_1 = \arg\max Q(s, a_1; \theta)$

18:         Determine a_2 through *Linear*

19:         Get $a_{n_m} = a_1 + a_2$

20:         Get destination server $\iota_{n_m}\ (q_z)$

21:         **for** each path from ϑ_{n_m} to ι_{n_m} **do**

22:             Compute $\text{WC}(n_m, q_z, k)$

23:         **end for**

24:         Select the optimal path $p_{n_m}^{k^*}$

25:         Perform action $a = a_{n_m}$

26:         Dispatch n_m to q_z

27:         Update edge server topo status $\vec{g_2}'$

28:         Get reward $r = \text{R}(n_m, a_{n_m})$

29:         $\text{Rwd}_{\text{sum}} \mathrel{+}= r$

30:         Form new state $s' = (\vec{g_1} \parallel \vec{g_2}')$

31:         Store transition(s', a, r, s) in A

32:         Randomly sample minibatch of transitions (s_{j+1}, a_j, r_j, s_j) from A

33:
$$Q = \begin{cases} r_j, & \text{for terminal } s_{j+1} \\ r_j + \delta \max_{a'} Q'(s_{j+1}, a'; \theta'), & \text{otw.} \end{cases}$$

34:         Perform a gradient descent step on Loss value

35:     **end for**

36:     Every ς steps, update Q' using $\theta' = \theta'$

37: **end while**

38: **return** average AWC, $V = \text{Rwd}_{\text{sum}}/T$

- K-Hop: Select the edge server randomly which is K hops away from the located server of the task and the value of K is set to 3 in later experiments [14].
- Rand: Randomly select a server in global topo map [4].
- GRL: Utilize GCN to extract DAG job features and make dispatching decisions through DRL [18].

5.2 Experiment Results

1) **Effect of job number:** We extract 10000 jobs (38051 tasks) arbitrarily to train the model. Then treat 4 various data sets including 10 jobs (50 tasks), 50 jobs (178 tasks), 100 jobs (347 tasks) and 200 jobs (763 tasks) as test sets. We give the offloading cost and computing latency equal weights ($\alpha = \beta = 0.5$) and fix the number of edge clouds to 3 (15 server nodes). As shown in Fig. 4(a), DeepSCJD obtains the best AWC performance on all test sets, achieving maximum average performance improvement of 54.16% relative to K-Hop. As the jobs increases, the gaps between DeepSCJD and other baselines decrease gradually. Because a small job set is poorly representative. But the AWC

results are still better than K-Hop, Rand and GRL on 200 jobs by 53.21%, 3.63% and 3.97%, respectively.

The effect of K-Hop is worst, which offloads tasks with fixed hops and limited range of selected edge servers. When the job set is extensive, it results in task accumulation. Heavy workload affects the servers' processing speed, leading to the growth of calculation delay and higher AWC. Besides, the distance between edge servers is not taken into account. Some tasks may obtain the optimal solutions within K hops. A fixed number of dispatching hops increases the offloading cost to a certain extent, resulting in a higher AWC.

Rand takes a global view of topology and obtain a relatively balanced AWC. Generally, the performance of GRL is close to that of Rand on a larger data set. Because it applies GNN to extract jobs features. However, compared with DeepSCJD, GRL neglects the impact of servers' workload on computing latency and ignores the influence of weights between servers on offloading cost. Our model not only analyses the features of jobs, exploits an additional load attribute to edge server but also aggregates the topology of servers. Moreover, the GCN used in GRL gives all neighbors same weights when extracting node features. While DeepSCJD introduces an attention mechanism to explore more valuable information, thereby further improving the performance.

2) **Effect of edge cloud number:** We expand the number of edge clouds to 4 and 5, involving 20 and 25 edge servers respectively. As displayed in Table 2, there is not much difference among the AWC of K-Hop. Because we apply same seeds to generate edge clouds, and the weights between servers are similar gaining comparable results on same job sets. DeepSCJD still surpasses the other three baselines, the performance improvement of which are 49.56%–54.46% relative to K-Hop, 5.73%-13.45% compared with Rand, and 4.83%-7.32% contrast with GRL. When facing a larger job set, the AWC obtained by all baselines under 4 edge clouds is lower than that under 5 edge clouds. Because for K-Hop and Rand, moderate-scale servers fully satisfy users' requests. Tasks may be offloaded to neighbors farther away in a greater network, increasing the offloading expense and AWC. Additionally, GRL doesn't work well in a large-scale topo for ignoring the distance between pair nodes. However, DeepSCJD still performs excellently under greater network size, which demonstrates its universality.

3) **Effect of edge server capacity:** We change configurations of edge servers to perform further evaluation under fixed 4 edge clouds with 20 nodes.
   - High-CPU: In above experiments, we assign edge server configurations randomly according to machine meta data. Through experimental statistics, different machines have equivalent capacities of CPU and Memory but diverse volumes of Disk. The largest resource request of jobs accounts for 90% and 40% of capacities of CPU and Memory, and only 2%-5% for Disk.
   - High-Mem: Increase all servers' CPU capacities and reduce Memory capacities, so that the highest resource demands occupy 40% and 90%. The volumes of Disk are the same as settings in the case of High-CPU.

– High-Disk: Raise CPU capacities and remain Memory capacities unchanged, so that the largest resource requests both account for 40% of CPU and Memory capacities. Reduce the sizes of Disk in order that the maximum Disk demands occupies 50% of Disk capacities.

Table 2. AWC ($\times 100$) of explorations in various cases

Item	Edge server numbers						Edge server configs					
Cases	Nodes = 25 High-CPU			Nodes = 20 High-CPU			Nodes = 20 High-Mem			Nodes = 20 High-Disk		
Jobs	10	50	100	10	50	100	10	50	100	10	50	100
K-Hop	4.601	4.457	4.556	4.603	4.546	4.550	4.601	4.546	4.557	4.603	4.540	4.550
Rand	3.408	3.173	3.197	3.381	3.237	3.172	3.384	3.177	3.160	3.287	3.236	3.185
GRL	3.227	3.154	3.155	3.198	3.162	3.145	3.196	3.226	3.158	3.373	3.276	3.178
DeepSCJD	3.043	2.980	3.010	2.980	3.010	3.040	3.043	2.983	3.019	3.015	2.890	3.018

As shown in Table 2. For K-Hop and Rand, their effects under High-CPU and High-Mem are worse than High-Disk. Because the servers' CPU or Memory resources are limited in the former two cases, which is the primary bottleneck affecting the computing latency of tasks and gaining higher AWC. The GRL and DeepSCJD alleviate the pressure of insufficient resources through adjusting dispatching strategies based on extracted features of jobs and edge servers. Furthermore, DeepSCJD achieves the best average performance enhancement when CPU and Memory are fully abundant (High-Disk). It further shows the little effect of Disk on task execution. Under diverse configurations of edge servers, DeepSCJD exceeds baselines when ensuring users' QoS, reaching maximum improvement of 53.46% compared with K-Hop. This manifests our model is of great generalization and well adapted to edge scenarios of various configurations.

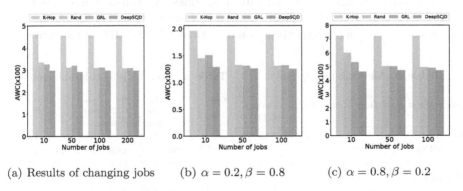

(a) Results of changing jobs   (b) $\alpha = 0.2, \beta = 0.8$ (c) $\alpha = 0.8, \beta = 0.2$

Fig. 4. Experimental results under various conditions

4) **Effect of weights in objective:** Similarly, we alter the proportions of computing latency and offloading cost in the objective function. The results in

Figs. 4(b) and 4(c) reveal the optimal effect of DeepSCJD on different numbers of job sets and verify its generalization in diverse applications. As a result, service providers can adjust the target functions as needed. Delay-sensitive jobs can be given a higher weight to calculation latency and computation-intensive jobs can be paid more attention to offloading cost, while meeting users' QoS requirements.

We analyze the algorithm complexity in Table 3. Although K-Hop has the least path selection complexity, it acquires the worst result and is 48.77%–57.09% inferior to DeepSCJD. The computation complexity of our DeepSCJD due to feature extraction or workload prediction increases $\mathcal{O}(T)$ compared with GRL, $\mathcal{O}(M) + \mathcal{O}(T)$ relative to Rand, which is acceptable. The gain is 3.45%–17.20% and 3.63%–29.44%, respectively without a substantial increase in algorithm complexity. The effect is significant in a long-term view, not to mention K-Hop. Because computing latency is crucial, particularly for application like autonomous driving, which even threatens life safety. Furthermore, the drop in offloading cost means substantial savings for service providers. Hence, the performance improvement of DeepSCJD will benefit both mobile users and service providers. Moreover, Rand is not easy to produce near-optimum solutions with high randomness. DeepSCJD is superior after utilizing the predicted workload through BiLSTM and aggregated features through GAT. The slight increase in complexity will not affect the actual deployment of DeepSCJD in edge computing.

5.3   Ablation Studies

We conduct ablation studies to verify the effectiveness of sub-modules in Deep-SCJD. No-Pre removes BiLSTM, No-GNN detaches GAT, No-Lin takes off Linear, and Bi-RL excludes GAT and Linear modules. As Tables 4 and 5 show, we change the number of job requests and edge servers, server configurations and weight parameters in objective function to evaluate DeepSCJD comprehensively.

Table 3. Algorithm complexity

Operations	K-Hop	Rand	GRL	Deep SCJD
Feature extraction	–	–	$\mathcal{O}(M)$	$\mathcal{O}(M)$
Job dispatching	$\mathcal{O}(T)$	$\mathcal{O}(T)$	$\mathcal{O}(T)$	$\mathcal{O}(T)$
Path selection	$\mathcal{O}(K)$	$\mathcal{O}(D!)$	$\mathcal{O}(D!)$	$\mathcal{O}(D!)$
Workload prediction	–	–	–	$\mathcal{O}(T)$

Table 4. AWC ($\times 100$) ablation results

Cases	Jobs	No-Pre	No-GNN	No-Lin	Bi-RL	Deep SCJD
High-CPU, Nodes = 20						
$\alpha = 0.8$ $\beta = 0.2$	10	4.901	4.770	5.041	5.072	**4.649**
	50	4.853	4.961	4.893	4.823	**4.738**
	100	4.897	4.895	4.901	4.868	**4.725**
$\alpha = 0.5$ $\beta = 0.5$	10	3.224	3.399	3.413	3.412	**2.980**
	50	3.205	3.294	3.252	3.234	**3.010**
	100	3.290	3.161	3.130	3.176	**3.040**
$\alpha = 0.2$ $\beta = 0.8$	10	1.804	1.367	1.329	1.450	**1.290**
	50	1.385	1.320	1.348	1.318	**1.261**
	100	1.396	1.318	1.300	1.309	**1.256**

We see that each sub-module has a performance improvement for the final decisions in all cases. In general, the Prediction Module has a greater improvement, achieving the maximum effect of 13.80% under High-CPU and 25 nodes. When the computing latency accounts for proportion at 0.8, the enhancement compared with No-Pre reaches 39.84% for 10 jobs. Because server load influences calculation speed. Effective workload prediction avoids tasks being allocated to heavily-loaded servers. This manner trades off tolerable offloading cost for computing latency, reducing AWC. GAT extracts the features of jobs and edge servers, increasing the model performance by 0.81%–14.90%. Similarly, the Linear branch achieves promotion of 2.96%–14.53%, which explores the possibilities beyond the view of DQN. It ensures that DeepSCJD has the advantages of linearity and non-linearity. On the whole, the effect of Bi-RL is worse than that of No-GNN and No-Lin. Although the workload prediction is considered, it sets the aggregation of jobs features and server characteristics aside. The lack of Linear branch also leads to performance degradation of performance. Last but not least, there are mutual influences between these sub-modules. The final performance is not obtained by the simple addition of all sub-module effects.

Table 5. AWC (x100) of ablation studies under various cases

Cases	Jobs	No-Pre	No-GNN	No-Lin	Bi-RL	Deep SCJD	Cases	No-Pre	No-GNN	No-Lin	Bi-RL	Deep SCJD
		High-CPU, $\alpha = 0.5$, $\beta = 0.5$						Nodes $= 20$, $\alpha = 0.5$, $\beta = 0.5$				
Nodes = 15	10	3.311	3.432	3.278	3.261	**2.987**	High-CPU	3.224	3.399	3.413	3.412	**2.980**
	50	3.297	3.171	3.185	3.198	**2.910**		3.205	3.294	3.252	3.234	**3.010**
	100	3.107	3.083	3.083	3.154	**2.976**		3.290	3.161	3.130	3.176	**3.040**
Nodes = 20	10	3.224	3.399	3.413	3.412	**2.980**	High-Mem	3.343	3.226	3.225	3.135	**3.043**
	50	3.205	3.294	3.252	3.234	**3.010**		3.175	3.132	3.110	3.148	**2.983**
	100	3.290	3.161	3.176	3.176	**3.040**		3.143	3.135	3.116	3.195	**3.010**
Nodes = 25	10	3.463	3.288	3.380	3.287	**3.043**	High-Disk	3.192	3.348	3.144	3.146	**3.015**
	50	3.176	3.178	3.198	3.130	**2.980**		3.172	3.157	3.130	3.226	**2.890**
	100	3.248	3.153	3.206	3.172	**3.010**		3.159	3.179	3.128	3.171	**3.018**

6 Conclusion

In this paper, we have presented a DeepSCJD model for secure collaborative job dispatching problem among multiple edge clouds, realizing the trade-off between latency and offloading cost. We use BiLSTM model to forecast the workload, GNN to aggregates features of jobs and servers, and DRL to make dispatching decisions. The experiments under various conditions demonstrate DeepSCJD surpasses traditional and state-of-the-art approaches with the maximum average improvement of 54.16% and great generalization. Ablation studies manifest the effectiveness of each sub-module to improve the performance of DeepSCJD.

References

1. Bi, S., Zhang, Y.J.: Computation rate maximization for wireless powered mobile-edge computing with binary computation offloading. IEEE Trans. Wirel. Commun. **17**(6), 4177–4190 (2018)
2. Chen, J., Yang, Y., Wang, C., Zhang, H., Qiu, C., Wang, X.: Multi-task offloading strategy optimization based on directed acyclic graphs for edge computing. IEEE Internet of Things J. **7**, 1678–1689 (2021)
3. Chen, X., Jiao, L., Li, W., Fu, X.: Efficient multi-user computation offloading for mobile-edge cloud computing. IEEE/ACM Trans. Netw. **24**(5), 2795–2808 (2015)
4. Eshraghi, N., Liang, B.: Joint offloading decision and resource allocation with uncertain task computing requirement. In: IEEE INFOCOM 2019-IEEE Conference on Computer Communications, pp. 1414–1422. IEEE (2019)
5. Guan, W., Zhang, H., Leung, V.C.: Customized slicing for 6g: enforcing artificial intelligence on resource management. IEEE Netw. **35**(5), 264–271 (2021)
6. He, X., Lu, H., Huang, H., Mao, Y., Wang, K., Guo, S.: QOE-based cooperative task offloading with deep reinforcement learning in mobile edge networks. IEEE Wirel. Commun. **27**(3), 111–117 (2020)
7. Heinzelman, W.B., Chandrakasan, A.P., Balakrishnan, H.: An application-specific protocol architecture for wireless microsensor networks. IEEE Trans. Wirel. Commun. **1**(4), 660–670 (2002)
8. Huang, L., Bi, S., Zhang, Y.J.A.: Deep reinforcement learning for online computation offloading in wireless powered mobile-edge computing networks. IEEE Trans. Mob. Comput. **19**(11), 2581–2593 (2019)
9. Kelly, R.: Internet of things data (2015). https://campustechnology.com/articles/2015/04/15/internet-of-things-data-to-top-1-6-zettabytes-by-2020.aspxd
10. Lei, L., Xu, H., Xiong, X., Zheng, K., Xiang, W.: Joint computation offloading and multiuser scheduling using approximate dynamic programming in NB-IOT edge computing system. IEEE Internet Things J. **6**(3), 5345–5362 (2019)
11. Li, Y., Wang, X., Gan, X., Jin, H., Fu, L., Wang, X.: Learning-aided computation offloading for trusted collaborative mobile edge computing. IEEE Trans. Mob. Comput. **19**(12), 2833–2849 (2019)
12. Liu, L., Tan, H., Jiang, S.H.C., Han, Z., Li, X.Y., Huang, H.: Dependent task placement and scheduling with function configuration in edge computing. In: 2019 IEEE/ACM 27th International Symposium on Quality of Service (IWQoS), pp. 1–10. IEEE (2019)
13. Liu, Y., Yu, H., Xie, S., Zhang, Y.: Deep reinforcement learning for offloading and resource allocation in vehicle edge computing and networks. IEEE Trans. Veh. Technol. **68**(11), 11158–11168 (2019)
14. Pu, L., Chen, X., Xu, J., Fu, X.: D2D fogging: an energy-efficient and incentive-aware task offloading framework via network-assisted D2D collaboration. IEEE J. Sel. Areas Commun. **34**(12), 3887–3901 (2016)
15. Saleem, U., Liu, Y., Jangsher, S., Li, Y.: Performance guaranteed partial offloading for mobile edge computing. In: 2018 IEEE Global Communications Conference (GLOBECOM), pp. 1–6. IEEE (2018)
16. Saleem, U., Liu, Y., Jangsher, S., Li, Y., Jiang, T.: Mobility-aware joint task scheduling and resource allocation for cooperative mobile edge computing. IEEE Trans. Wirel. Commun. **20**(1), 360–374 (2020)
17. Sun, M., Bao, T., Xie, D.: Towards application-driven task offloading in edge computing based on deep reinforcement learning. Micromachines **12**(9), 1011 (2021)

18. Tang, Z., Lou, J., Zhang, F., Jia, W.: Dependent task offloading for multiple jobs in edge computing. In: 2020 29th International Conference on Computer Communications and Networks (ICCCN), pp. 1–9. IEEE (2020)

19. Xu, Z., et al.: Learning for exception: Dynamic service caching in 5g-enabled MECS with bursty user demands. In: 2020 IEEE 40th International Conference on Distributed Computing Systems (ICDCS), pp. 1079–1089. IEEE (2020)

20. Yu, Z., Liu, W., Liu, X., Wang, G.: Drag-JDEC: a deep reinforcement learning and graph neural network-based job dispatching model in edge computing. In: 2021 IEEE/ACM 29th International Symposium on Quality of Service (IWQOS), pp. 1–10. IEEE (2021)

The Extreme Counts: Modeling the Performance Uncertainty of Cloud Resources with Extreme Value Theory

Mengjuan Li[1], Jinshu Su[2], Hongyun Liu[3], Zhiming Zhao[3], Xue Ouyang[1(✉)], and Huan Zhou[1(✉)]

[1] National University of Defense Technology, Changsha, China
{limj,ouyangxue08,huanzhou}@nudt.edu.cn
[2] Academy of Military Sciences, Beijing, China
sjs@nudt.edu.cn
[3] University of Amsterdam, Amsterdam, The Netherlands
{h.liu,z.zhao}@uva.nl

Abstract. Although Cloud techniques developed rapidly in the last decade, most of the applications running on Cloud are still web-based. It is the performance uncertainty of Cloud resources that hinders the further migration of other applications, such as quality critical applications. Hence, an accurate Cloud performance model is crucial for optimized resource allocation to satisfy the quality requirements of the quality critical applications. However, the existing efforts of Cloud performance modeling focus more on the mean and variance, which cannot be leveraged to guarantee meeting the deadline miss rate of quality critical applications. To tackle the issue, a new modeling method is proposed to build performance uncertainty model of Cloud resources based on Extreme Value Theory, which can generate a proper threshold to guarantee the application's Quality of Service (QoS). Based on our experimental data and studies, the threshold calculated by our proposed model can make the average miss rate become lower than the required 5% deadline miss rate and reduced by 77% compared with the traditional modeling method. The number of times that the deadline miss rate cannot be satisfied is also reduced by 84%.

Keywords: Cloud performance · Modeling · Uncertainty · Extreme value theory · Quality critical

1 Introduction

Although the Cloud techniques develop rapidly in recent years, the applications running on Clouds are still mainly web services. Other types of applications, such as quality critical applications [1], are difficult to migrate to the Cloud. Because quality critical applications require critical constraints on resource performance for QoS guarantee. But compared with real-time applications, quality critical

J. Troya et al. (Eds.): ICSOC 2022, LNCS 13740, pp. 498–512, 2022.
https://doi.org/10.1007/978-3-031-20984-0_35

applications do not need to meet the hard deadline, i.e., 0% deadline miss rate. It is allowed that a certain deadline miss rate is met for quality critical applications. For example, most of the scientific workflow applications, such as the disaster early warning systems [2], need to complete most of their tasks in a specific time window, otherwise the results would be meaningless. As a result, it requires CPU, memory access and other processing performance to be guaranteed to a certain extent for running quality critical applications.

However, Cloud service providers usually promise the quantity of the Cloud resources they offered, instead of the quality of the Cloud resources, i.e., the performance standard of Cloud resources, such as the CPU execution speed or the disk memory access speed. Furthermore, there are severe performance fluctuations for the same quantity of Cloud resources from different Clouds, even different data centers and at different moments. Hence, the uncertainty of Cloud resources performance is the main issue that hinders the migration of quality critical applications running on the Cloud. To tackle the challenge of performance uncertainty, we need a reliable performance uncertainty model for Cloud resources first.

Current efforts on Cloud resources performance uncertainty modeling can be divided into two ways. One is to model the Cloud system from the perspective of the data center as the Cloud service provider, based on the queuing theory. However, the model of this method is bounded to a specific Cloud platform and cannot be extended to the multi-cloud environment. From the perspective of Cloud users, a non-parametric statistical method is leveraged to predict the Cloud performance based on the observed probability distribution. However, most of the current uncertainty modeling methods are based on the classical central statistical method, which pays more attention to the mean and variance of the performance. Quality critical applications, on the other hand, need to ensure that each execution is done within a specific time window, and more attention should be paid to the worst cases of performance rather than the mean cases.

To solve this problem, we use the powerful statistical tool of Extreme Value Theory (EVT) [3]. In statistics, EVT focuses on the tail shape of random variable distribution and studies the statistical characteristics of extreme values. In particular, for sample extremum, the EVT gives an asymptotic theory that is similar to the central limit theorem. In other words, the distribution of extreme values is almost independent of the distribution of data. Moreover, due to the complex Cloud environment and the numerous influencing factors, it is hard to find a specific data distribution to analyze extreme values. EVT is therefore more accurate in dealing with extreme cases than other specific distributions. Using EVT, the performance of Cloud resources in extreme cases can be characterized, and a performance threshold can be calculated based on the deadline miss rate. Quality critical applications can refer to the threshold when selecting Clouds and resources to avoid the impact of performance uncertainty.

In this paper, we first develop an automatic multi-datacenter performance monitoring application based on the Cloud infrastructure operation code of

CloudsStorm [4], which is a framework for seamless Cloud virtual infrastructure programming and control. With an interval of 10 min between each test, 1500 tests were simultaneously performed on four real data centers to retrieve the performance information. Then we pre-process the observed performance data using k-means to distinguish different physical hosts in the same data center. Finally, the performance uncertainty model of Cloud resources is built with EVT to obtain the performance threshold of the data center. We use the k-fold cross-validation method to verify that the threshold obtained based on the EVT theory dramatically reduces the miss rate compared with the threshold calculated by the Normal distribution. In summary, the contributions of this paper can be summarized as follows.

- We develop the Cloud performance monitoring application using the infrastructure operation code, and retrieve the Cloud performance information from four real data centers continuously lasting for one month.
- We propose a Cloud performance modeling method based on k-means and the Extreme Value Theory to analyze and model the extreme situation of Cloud performance.
- We conduct experiments using the K-fold cross-validation method and the experimental studies demonstrate the superiority of our proposed model.

The rest of this paper is organized as follows. Section 2 discusses the related work. Section 3 introduces the background of the EVT, followed by a detailed description of our contribution in Sect. 4. And in Sect. 5, we perform experiments to validate the effectiveness of our EVT-based method. Conclusions and future research directions are presented in Sect. 6.

2   Related Work

The QoS improvement for Cloud applications is well studied through the methods of modeling and scaling, but most of them do not take into account the performance uncertainty of Cloud resources. For example, El Kafhali et al. [5] model the CDC (Cloud Data Centers) platforms with an open queuing system that can be used to estimate the expected QoS parameters. Hwang et al. [6] present generic Cloud performance models for evaluating IaaS, PaaS, SaaS, and hybrid Clouds, and they focus more on the mechanism of scaling to guarantee the application QoS.

To describe the Cloud performance, one way is trying to find the causes of performance uncertainty, and setup a model inferring the performance behaviour from the possible factors. Khazaei et al. present a performance model which uses interacting stochastic models to quantify the uncertainty of Cloud [7]. Antonelli et al. [8] model the Cloud computing system by adding parameter uncertainty to the queuing model. But in practice, the performance of Cloud resources is not only affected by the Cloud system itself, but also affected by shared users and other factors. Consequently, these models are not suitable for public Cloud and cannot be extended to multi-cloud environments.

The other way of modeling the Cloud performance is to treat Cloud as a black box. The Cloud performance is modeled through monitoring data with statistical approaches. He et al. [9] used the non-parametric statistical method to obtain the probability distribution of the execution performance of the application in a Cloud data center. Wang et al. [10] mainly obtain the general execution time by repeatedly executing benchmark programs for different resource types, and use this data to estimate the execution time of the target application. The Smart CloudBench platform presented by Chhetri et al. [11] can measure its performance levels under different workload conditions through the automated execution of representative benchmarks on multiple IaaS Clouds. These works all use non-parametric statistical methods to test Cloud resources as a black box without considering the underlying factors, so as to measure performance uncertainty more directly.

However, the current non-parametric statistical methods mostly focus on the mean and variance of performance, so the estimated time given cannot guarantee that the application can be completed in a certain time window. Meanwhile, most current works retrieve the Cloud performance through an on-premise VM, which is fixed and cannot sufficiently explore the Cloud performance, since there are a mass of physical hosts inside one data center.

3   Background

This section gives a brief introduction to some basic knowledge of Extreme Value Theory. Because the proof of relevant theorems is too tedious and not the focus of this paper, we do not elaborate here (readers who want to know the details can read [3]). Due to the page limit, we neglect the proof and only explain the general principles to show how the EVT can be applied.

There are many ways to calculate the performance threshold (quantile) we need. One of the most common methods is to assume that the performance data is coincident with an empirical distribution, such as Normal, Poisson, exponential etc., and then calculate the threshold. However, real data hardly follows a specific distribution due to the complex Cloud environment, which leads to complex modeling steps and even an inappropriate model. In addition, when predicting a rare event (such as a hurricane), the empirical distribution would assume that the probability is adjacent to zero, which means that the estimates of extreme cases given by empirical distributions are often inaccurate. The extreme value theory infers the distribution of the extreme events that we have already known, and does not make assumptions about the original distribution of the events, so as to avoid the above-mentioned problems.

3.1   Generalized Extreme Value Distribution

Extreme value theory is a branch of statistical research to study the tail distribution characteristics of random variables, and one of its important research tools is the generalized extreme value distribution. The landmark development of

EVT was in 1928. Fisher and Tippett gave a famous theorem after analysis and research, which we call the extreme value type theorem. The theorem points out that all the extreme events follow the same type of distribution under weak conditions, regardless of the initial distribution, which means that the distribution of extreme values is almost independent of the distribution of data. These distributions are called the Extreme Value Distribution (EVD). Moreover, Jenkinson gives a unified form of these distributions after transformation, as follows:

$$H_{(x;\mu,\sigma,\xi)} = exp\left\{ -\left[1 + \xi\left(\frac{x-\mu}{\sigma}\right)\right]^{-1/\xi}\right\}, 1 + \xi(x-\mu)/\sigma > 0 \qquad (1)$$

where μ is the location parameter, σ the scale parameter, and ξ the shape parameter, $\mu, \xi \in \mathbb{R}$, $\sigma > 0$. H is called the generalized extreme value distribution, usually abbreviated as the GEV distribution.

To sum up, all the extreme events follow the GEV distribution under weak conditions. For example, the distribution of the maximum rainfall and maximum wind level is basically the same, even though we know that the distribution of rainfall and the wind level itself are almost never be same. This conclusion may sound very counterintuitive, but we can try to understand the idea. In fact, most distributions have a low probability of events in extreme cases. What H mainly simulates is the shape of the tail of these distributions, and there are not many possible shapes of this tail. Figure 1 shows the density function graph of the GEV distribution under different shape parameters (ξ). Figure 1 also illustrates that the Type I distribution has a light tail, the Type II distribution has a heavy tail, and the tail of the Type III distribution is somehow bounded.

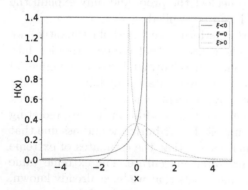
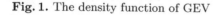
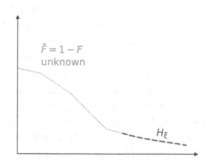

Fig. 1. The density function of GEV   **Fig. 2.** EVD fit of an unknown cdf

3.2   Find the Quantile

Using the above results, we can calculate the probability of extreme events more accurately regardless of the actual complex initial distribution. In fact, EVT just shows that the extreme values of n i.i.d. random variables converge to EVD, which is similar to the conclusion of the central limit theorem about the mean.

The tail of the input data distribution can be fitted by using EVD (see Fig. 2), so that the probability of extreme events can be calculated. Mathematically speaking, it is to find the quantile of the probability p. Specifically, when the probability p is given, x_p can be obtained such that $P(X > x_p) < p$. Assuming we get estimates of the parameters of the GEV distribution (our method is described in Sect. 3.3), the quantile can be calculated by the following formula:

$$\hat{x}_p = \begin{cases} \hat{\mu} - \dfrac{\hat{\sigma}}{\xi}(1 - y_p^{-\xi}), & \xi \neq 0; \\ \hat{\mu} - \hat{\sigma} \log y_p, & \xi = 0. \end{cases} \tag{2}$$

where $y_p = -\log p$.

There are many methods to estimate the three parameters of GEV distribution. The most classical methods are the Probability Weighted Moment(PWM), the Method of Moments Estimate(MME) and the Maximum Likelihood Estimation(MLE). MLE is adopted for parameter estimation in this paper.

3.3   Maximum Likelihood Estimation

The Maximum Likelihood Estimation is a widely used parameter estimation method in statistics. Compared with other estimation methods, it achieves higher efficiency and better robustness. Especially with the emergence of high-level languages such as R language and MATLAB, program optimization and operation speed have been greatly improved, and the Maximum Likelihood Estimation is more dominant in practical applications. The following is the likelihood function expression of the GEV distribution.

Assuming that $X_1, X_2, ..., X_n$ are i.i.d. random variables obeying the GEV distribution, the log-likelihood function of the GEV distribution is (when $\xi \neq 0$):

$$l(\mu, \sigma, \xi) = -n \log \sigma - \left(1 + \frac{1}{\xi}\right) \sum_{i=1}^{n} \log h_{(\mu,\sigma,\xi)} - \sum_{i=1}^{n} h_{(\mu,\sigma,\xi)}^{-1/\xi} \tag{3}$$

where

$$h_{(\mu,\sigma,\xi)} = \left[1 + \xi\left(\frac{x_i - \mu}{\sigma}\right)\right] > 0, i = 1, ..., n.$$

When $\xi = 0$, the log-likelihood function is:

$$l(\mu, \sigma) = -n \log \sigma - \sum_{i=1}^{n}\left(\frac{x_i - \mu}{\sigma}\right) - \sum_{i=1}^{n} exp\left\{-\left(\frac{x_i - \mu}{\sigma}\right)\right\} \tag{4}$$

By maximizing the above log-likelihood function with respect to the parameter vector (μ, σ, ξ), the maximum likelihood estimation of GEV distribution can be obtained. Although there is no analytical solution, the maximum likelihood estimation can be obtained by numerical algorithms for the given data.

4   Our Contribution

In this section, we describe the overall steps for performance uncertainty modeling of Cloud resources, as shown in Fig. 3. First of all, we introduce the application we developed to retrieve the real Cloud performance and show the performance uncertainty. Secondly, we use the K-means clustering method to preprocess the data, mainly to cluster the performance data generated by physical hosts with different performance in the data center, so that the performance of Cloud resources can be characterized in a fine-grained manner. Finally, we introduce the EVT-based Cloud performance model, through which the performance characterization of Cloud resources in extreme cases and the threshold based on the deadline miss rate can be calculated. The obtained results can be utilized by quality critical applications as a reference for choosing a proper Cloud data center.

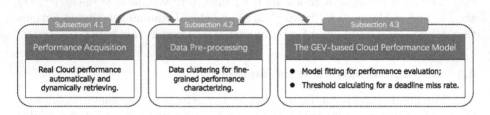

Fig. 3. The overview of our contribution in Cloud performance uncertainty modeling

4.1   Cloud Performance Acquisition and Description

CloudsStorm[1] [4] is a multi-cloud resources management and control framework. The framework provides infrastructure programmability for applications at the topology design level, infrastructure level and application logic level. Among them, at the infrastructure level, based on the YAML format, CloudsStorm provides the "Cloud infrastructure operation language" for Cloud application operation and maintenance, which is used to describe the operations required by the Cloud infrastructure. The language can be used to develop performance monitoring applications for multi-cloud resources [12].

In order to obtain the real performance data of Cloud resources, we select several data centers from ExoGENI, which is a federated Cloud contributed and used by a number of Universities around the world. The selected four data centers are located in the University of Sydney (in Australia, referred to as SYD), the University of Amsterdam (in Europe, referred to as UVA), Boston University (in eastern United States, referred to as BBN), and Oakland Scientific Facility (in western United States, referred to as OSF). The task of the application is to provide a VM in each of the above data centers and use "sysbench [13]" to test the CPU/memory performance of each data center. For comparison, we use the

---

[1] https://cloudsstorm.github.io/.

same type of virtual machines for all the tests, which is the "XOMedium" type of ExoGENI with the capacity of one virtual CPU and 3GB memory. Meanwhile, there were other applications running from other clients at the same time. It means that we acquire the Cloud performance purely as a normal Cloud client.

We utilize the "infrastructure execution code" to define the whole process of executing tests on the selected data centers of ExoGENI Cloud. The pseudo code is shown in Algorithm 1. We leverage "loop" code to repeat the test task. In this case, all test results are recorded in the log of infrastructure code. Afterwards, we can directly extract the test results from the log for analysis.

Algorithm 1. Performing tests with the Infrastructure Execution Code

---
1: **for** a certain time period or a certain count **do**
2:     Provision VM_x
3:     Execute **CPU test** simultaneously on the VM_x of OSF‖SYD‖BBN‖UvA
4:     Execute **memory test** simultaneously on the VM_x of OSF‖SYD‖BBN‖UvA
5:     Get the results
6:     Terminate VM_x
7:     Wait for executing another round of tests
8: **end for**

We use CloudsStorm framework to continuously track and perform tests on the four data centers lasting for nearly one month. The interval between each test is about 10 min, and a total of 1500 tests were performed. All the raw data of performance information is retrieved in the form of log files[2]. Then we extract all the performance information for analysis. The data extracted from CPU performance tests is the execution time with the unit of seconds, and the data extracted from memory performance test is the throughput in unit time with the unit of "MB/sec". To show the performance uncertainty, we generate box plot from the test results, as shown in Fig. 4.

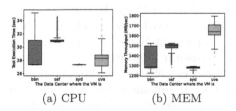

(a) CPU   (b) MEM

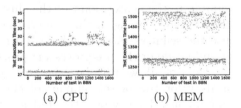

(a) CPU   (b) MEM

Fig. 4. Box plot of test results

Fig. 5. Scatter plot of test results in BBN

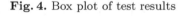

---

[2] https://anonymous.4open.science/r/CloudPerformanceData-6203/.

As shown in Fig. 4, the box of SYD data center is very narrow no matter in the sub-figure of CPU or in the one of memory, which indicates that the performance of the data center is relatively stable. Similarly, the box of the OSF data center is also narrow, but there are more abnormal values, indicating a sudden and large fluctuation in performance. Thirdly, the performance of UVA data center is revealed as a wide box with a large fluctuation of outliers. The biggest fluctuation of Cloud performance appears in the BBN data center, where the box is the widest among the four data centers.

Additionally, the performance data of BBN data center is clearly differentiated into two clusters as shown in Fig. 5. It is known that data centers typically have multiple physical hosts. As shown in Algorithm 1, we terminate the VM after each test and dynamically provision the VM again before the next test. This is different from the traditional test method which does not terminate the VM. If the VM is not terminated, the VM would remain on the same physical host and the performance of the Cloud data center cannot be fully explored. Hence, for our testing in the BBN data center, it is the provisioned VMs randomly appear on two physical hosts with different performance that cause the phenomenon of stratification. This also requires us to pre-process the data for carrying out a fine-grained performance modeling.

4.2 Data Pre-processing

Since there may be a phenomenon of performance stratification in the data center, we use the K-means clustering method to cluster the performance data. And the performance of the clustered data would be modeled respectively, which can provide applications with fine-grained performance characterization of Cloud resources.

K-means algorithm is by far the most widely used clustering tool used in scientific and industrial applications. Its basic idea is to find a solution that divides a group of data into k clusters through iteration, so as to minimize the corresponding loss function of the clustering results. Among them, the loss function can be defined as the sum square error (SSE) of the distance from each sample to the center point of the cluster to which it belongs. In the process of data pre-processing in this paper, the K-means algorithm is mainly used. We use the scikit-sklearn module in Python to implement K-means clustering, the pseudo code of the pre-processing process is shown in Algorithm 2.

First of all, we calculate the average silhouette coefficient of the sample separately for the preset number of clusters (the minimum value is 2, and the maximum value can be estimated according to the situation of the data center). The silhouette coefficient is a method to evaluate the quality of clustering. The best value is 1, and the worst value is -1. As a result, the cluster number k with the largest silhouette coefficient would be the best division scheme. And then, we use the k-means cluster again to calculate the cluster label with k as the number of clusters. Also, since the built VM appear randomly on each physical host, the amount of data after classification should be average. Hence, if the data contained in each category after clustering is not average, it is determined

Algorithm 2. Data Pre-processing with K-means Algorithm

```
1: function KMEANS(data,maxnum)
2:     index_list ← CalSilhouette(data, 2, ..., maxnum)
3:     k ← max(index_list[:])
4:     k_clusters ← Cluster(data, k)
5:     if The size of k clusters is average then
6:         No clustering is required
7:     else
8:         Output K clusters respectively
9:     end if
10: end function
```

that there is no need for clustering, which also indicates that the performance of physical host in the data center is relatively average. If the amount of data tends to be average, the clustering results are deemed available, and the clustered data would be output. This is also the data input for subsequent modeling. Figure 6 shows the clustering results of the test results in the BBN data center.

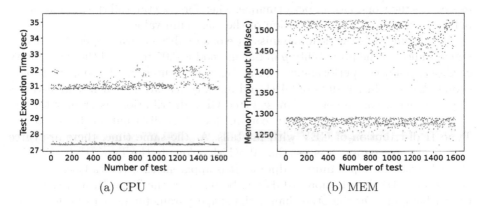

(a) CPU   (b) MEM

Fig. 6. Clustering results in the BBN

4.3   The EVT-Based Cloud Performance Model

Let us summarize the basic idea of our uncertainty model with EVT. We have n test results $X_1, X_2, ..., X_n$, and the probability p is determined according to the requirements (i.e., the deadline miss rate) of the quality critical application. The goal is to calculate the threshold x_p such that $P(X > x_p) < p$ by fitting a GEV distribution. In this way, we can make resource recommendations for quality critical applications based on x_p, or we can describe the uncertainty of Cloud resources performance more accurately of the Cloud data center.

Algorithm 3. GEV (Generalized Extreme Value)

1: **function** GEV$(data, p)$
2:     $M_i \leftarrow$ Maximum per hour of data
3:     $l(\mu, \sigma, \xi) \leftarrow CalLogLikelihoodFunction(M_i)$
4:     $\hat{\mu}, \hat{\sigma}, \hat{\xi} \leftarrow \text{MAX}_{\mu, \sigma, \xi} l(\mu, \sigma, \xi)$
5:     $x_p \leftarrow CalThreshold(\hat{\mu}, \hat{\sigma}, \hat{\xi}, y_p)$
6:     **return** x_p
7: **end function**

This modeling method is summarized in Algorithm 3. First, we need to group the test results. Considering the size of the data, we group them in hours. The extreme value of performance per hour is obtained, and the set of these extreme values is recorded as M_i. Then, the log-likelihood function of the GEV distribution is calculated according to Eq. (3) and (4), and an estimate of the parameter μ, σ, ξ is obtained. Finally, we use Eq. (2) to calculate x_p, which is the threshold we desired.

In particular, the result of memory resource performance we extracted from the test is the throughput in unit time, so the minimum value of this data represents the worst case of performance. Therefore, we take all the data negative before fitting the GEV distribution of the maximum value.

We assume that the deadline miss rate of a quality critical application is 5%, which indicates the probability p in our method is 0.05 to model the uncertainty of Cloud resources performance of the four data centers in this paper. Table 1 shows the modeling results of CPU and memory resources, which demonstrates that the shape parameter ξ of most fitted GEV distributions is greater than 0. According to the Fisher-Tippett theorem, all of these distributions belong to the Type II distribution of GEV with fat tails. At the same time, there are three groups of shape parameters less than 0, which belong to the Type III distribution of GEV with an upper finite endpoint. It is apparent that the tail performance of the Type III distribution of GEV is better than the Type II, and the Type I is in between. On the other hand, the shape parameter (ξ) can be leveraged to somehow characterize and evaluate certain Cloud performance. Then we can calculate the corresponding threshold in the next step.

For the threshold x_p of resource performance modeling, the CPU resource performance in extreme cases of SYD data center is the best. It has the minimum test execution time of about 27.38 s under the deadline miss rate of 5%. And in the extreme case of memory resource performance, the UVA data center performs best with a throughput rate of 1484.33MB/s.

The distribution type fitted in extreme cases and the threshold calculated based on deadline miss rate can be used as a reference for quality critical applications when selecting Cloud and making corresponding resource recommendation. Suppose a developer of a quality critical application wants to migrate his application to the Cloud, and make a choice among the four data centers in this paper. Since our work pays more attention to the performance uncertainty modeling of multi-cloud resources and does not address the related issues of specific

Table 1. Worst-case Performance Distributions of four data centers with GEV fitting

Data center	CPU				MEM			
	$\hat{\mu}$	$\hat{\sigma}$	$\hat{\xi}$	x_p	$\hat{\mu}$	$\hat{\sigma}$	$\hat{\xi}$	x_p
BBN0	27.35	0.02	0.15	27.44	−1278.91	8.07	−0.03	−1256.05
BBN1	30.99	0.21	0.55	32.59	−1497.46	21.20	0.07	−1427.50
OSF	31.01	0.26	0.99	35.63	−1483.53	30.34	0.36	−1322.67
SYD	27.34	0.01	0.18	27.38	−1277.70	8.06	0.03	−1252.48
UVA	28.13	1.17	−0.17	30.87	−1643.37	70.36	−0.19	−1484.33

Note: distributions of BBN0 and BBN1 belong to the same data center, but are classified as two clusters.

application optimization, we assume that the resource requirements of applications are already known. For example, this performance critical application is known to be purely computational and requires more stable and higher CPU performance. According to our modeling results, the SYD data center will be the best choice. In addition, Cloud resources recommendation can be made based on modeling results, assuming that the required resources are linearly related to the execution time (which is generally approximate). For example, if the application needs to complete the task within 10 s and the minimum miss rate is 5%. Then when migrating to the SYD data center, it needs to be expanded to 2.738 virtual CPU to guarantee QoS. Here we only give a simple example, the more specific details of Cloud selection and resource recommendation are not the main research content of this article.

5   Experiments and Results

In this section, we introduce our experimental verification method, and illustrate the superiority of Extreme Value Theory for performance uncertainty modeling of Cloud resources according to the experimental comparison results.

5.1   K-fold Cross-validation

In order to make full use of the limited real data, we choose the K-fold cross-validation for experimental verification. K-fold cross-validation first divides all data into k subsets, and selects one of the subsets as the test set without repetition, and the other $K - 1$ subsets are used for training. A total of k times are repeated to ensure that each subset participates in training and is tested. K-fold cross-validation takes advantage of the non-repetitive sampling technique, so we can extend a limited set of real performance data into k sets for experiments. In this way, we can verify the advantages of the GEV modeling method for performance modeling of Cloud resources in extreme cases more comprehensively.

Our experiment mainly compares our EVT-based model with the widely-used Normal distribution model. The process of this experiment is shown in Algorithm 4. First, group the data according to the volume of experimental data to determine the k value. In this experiment, we take 200 data as a group. As a consequence, except for the special BBN data center, the k value is taken as 8, and the 8-fold cross-validation experiment is carried out. Then, 8 subsets are selected as the test set in turn, and the other subsets together form the training set for 8 cycle experiments. In each cycle, our EVT-based modeling method and the traditional Normal distribution method are used to calculate the threshold. The probability p used in the threshold calculation is still assumed to be 0.05. It is worth mentioning that p can be other values according to the demand. Finally, the calculated threshold is substituted into the test set for testing, and the miss rate of the two modeling methods can be obtained.

Algorithm 4. Experiment with K-fold Cross-Validation

1: **function** K-FOLD CROSS-VALIDATION$(data, k, p)$
2:     **for** $i = 1 \rightarrow k$ **do**
3:         Select the i fold as the test set (the future unknown performance)
4:         The other k-1 fold is used as train set (the already known performance)
5:         $X_p\_gev \leftarrow$ threshold calculated with GEV using train set
6:         $X_p\_norm \leftarrow$ threshold calculated with Normal Distribution using train set
7:         $mr\_gev \leftarrow$ test X_p_gev in test set
8:         $mr\_norm \leftarrow$ test X_p_norm in test set
9:         **return** mr_gev, mr_norm
10:     **end for**
11: **end function**

5.2   Result Analysis

The bar graph in Fig. 7 shows the comparison of the experimental results of the K-fold cross-validation experiments of the four data centers. The green column represents the test results of the Normal distribution modeling method, the orange represents our EVT-based method, and the purple baseline is the deadline miss rate of 5%. Figure 7 demonstrates that our EVT-based method can give an appropriate threshold to ensure a low miss rate in most cases, no matter how variable the Cloud environment is.

In addition, we extract the experimental results from three angles. From the number of times exceeding the maximum miss rate, the verification experiment has been tested 66 times in all, the Normal distribution modeling method has 25 times that do not satisfy the maximum miss rate, and the GEV method has only 4 times, an optimization by 84%. From the worst-case of the miss rate, the highest miss rate of Normal distribution modeling method is 28.5%, and that of our GEV-based method is only 8.5%, which is reduced by 70%. From the overall average of the miss rate, the average value of the Normal distribution modeling method is 6.85%, which does not meet the requirement of the maximum miss

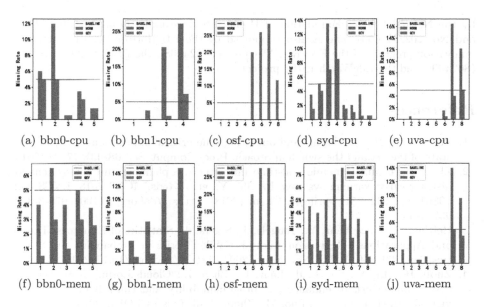

(a) bbn0-cpu   (b) bbn1-cpu   (c) osf-cpu   (d) syd-cpu   (e) uva-cpu

(f) bbn0-mem   (g) bbn1-mem   (h) osf-mem   (i) syd-mem   (j) uva-mem

Fig. 7. Comparison of test results between Normal Distribution method and our EVT-based method

rate of 5%. The total average value of our EVT-based method is 1.56%, which is lower than deadline miss rate and reduced by 77% compared with Normal distribution modeling method.

In summary, when the performance distribution of the Cloud data center is unknown, our EVT-based modeling method can describe the extreme situation more accurately, thereby ensuring the QoS of quality critical applications. Whereas, methods such as Normal distribution need to make assumptions about the actual distribution in advance, are not sensitive to extreme values, and cannot give a suitable threshold in complex and changeable Cloud environments.

6   Conclusion

This paper proposes a new method for modeling Cloud resources performance uncertainty. Our Extreme Value Theory (EVT) based method can generate a proper threshold to ensure the QoS for quality critical applications. Comparing to the traditional modeling methods, our method does not focus on the mean performance, and we do not need to assume the actual distribution of the performance. Therefore, our method can describe the extreme cases of Cloud resources performance more accurately, and it is also suitable for complex Cloud and multi-cloud environments. To the best of our knowledge, this is the first time that EVT is applied to performance uncertainty modeling of Cloud resources.

Acknowledgment. The work is supported by the National Natural Science Foundation of China under grant No. 62102434 and No. 62002364, and is partially supported by the Natural Science Foundation of Hunan Province under grant No. 2020JJ3042 and No. 2022JJ30667, and is also supported by the EU Horizon 2020 research and innovation program of the ENVRI-FAIR project (824068), the BLUECLOUD project (862409), and the LifeWatch ERIC project.

References

1. Zhao, Z., et al.: Developing and operating time critical applications in clouds: the state of the art and the switch approach. Proc. Comput. Sci. **68**(43), 17–28 (2015)
2. Zhou, H., et al.: Dynamic real-time infrastructure planning and deployment for disaster early warning systems. In: Shi, Y., et al. (eds.) ICCS 2018. LNCS, vol. 10861, pp. 644–654. Springer, Cham (2018). https://doi.org/10.1007/978-3-319-93701-4_51
3. Beirlant, J., Goegebeur, Y., Teugels, J., Segers, J.: Statistics of Extremes: Theory and Applications—Regression Analysis. [Wiley Series in Probability and Statistics], pp. 209–250. Wiley, New York (2004). https://doi.org/10.1002/0470012382
4. Zhou, H., Hu, Y., Su, J., de Laat, C., Zhao, Z.: CloudsStorm: an application-driven framework to enhance the programmability and controllability of cloud virtual infrastructures. In: Luo, M., Zhang, L.-J. (eds.) CLOUD 2018. LNCS, vol. 10967, pp. 265–280. Springer, Cham (2018). https://doi.org/10.1007/978-3-319-94295-7_18
5. El Kafhali, S., Salah, K.: Modeling and analysis of performance and energy consumption in cloud data centers. Arab. J. Sci. Eng. **43**(12), 7789–7802 (2018)
6. Hwang, K., Bai, X., Shi, Y., Li, M., Chen, W.G., Wu, Y.: Cloud performance modeling with benchmark evaluation of elastic scaling strategies. IEEE Trans. Parallel Distrib. Syst. **27**(1), 130–143 (2015)
7. Khazaei, H., Miic, J., Miic, V.B., Mohammadi, N.B.: Modeling the performance of heterogeneous IAAS cloud centers. In: 2013 IEEE 33rd International Conference on Distributed Computing Systems Workshops, pp. 232–237. IEEE (2013)
8. Antonelli, F., Cortellessa, V., Gribaudo, M., Pinciroli, R., Trivedi, K.S., Trubiani, C.: Analytical modeling of performance indices under epistemic uncertainty applied to cloud computing systems. FGCS **102**, 746–761 (2020)
9. He, S., Manns, G., Saunders, J., Wang, W., Pollock, L., Soffa, M.L.: A statistics-based performance testing methodology for cloud applications. In: Proceedings of the Joint Meeting on European Software Engineering Conference and Symposium on the Foundations of Software Engineering, pp. 188–199 (2019)
10. Wang, W., et al.: Testing cloud applications under cloud-uncertainty performance effects. In: ICST, pp. 81–92. IEEE (2018)
11. Chhetri, M.B., Chichin, S., Vo, Q.B., Kowalczyk, R.: Smart cloudbench-automated performance benchmarking of the cloud. In: 2013 IEEE Sixth International Conference on Cloud Computing, pp. 414–421. IEEE (2013)
12. Zhou, H., et al.: Fast resource co-provisioning for time critical applications based on networked infrastructures. In: International Conference on Cloud Computing, pp. 802–805. IEEE (2016)
13. Kopytov, A.: Sysbench manual. In: MySQL AB, pp. 2–3 (2012)

Scalable Discovery and Continuous Inventory of Personal Data at Rest in Cloud Native Systems

Elias Grünewald$^{(\boxtimes)}$ ⓘ and Leonard Schurbert

Information Systems Engineering, Technische Universität Berlin, Berlin, Germany
{gruenewald,schurbert}@tu-berlin.de

Abstract. Cloud native systems are processing large amounts of personal data through numerous and possibly multi-paradigmatic data stores (e.g., relational and non-relational databases). From a privacy engineering perspective, a core challenge is to keep track of all exact locations, where personal data is being stored, as required by regulatory frameworks such as the European General Data Protection Regulation. In this paper, we present TEIRESIAS, comprising i) a workflow pattern for scalable discovery of personal data at rest, and ii) a cloud native system architecture and open source prototype implementation of said workflow pattern. To this end, we enable a continuous inventory of personal data featuring transparency and accountability following DevOps/DevPrivOps practices. In particular, we scope version-controlled Infrastructure as Code definitions, cloud-based storages, and how to integrate the process into CI/CD pipelines. Thereafter, we provide iii) a comparative performance evaluation demonstrating both appropriate execution times for real-world settings, and a promising personal data detection accuracy outperforming existing proprietary tools in public clouds.

Keywords: Privacy · Data protection · Transparency ·
Accountability · Data loss prevention · Privacy engineering · DevOps

1 Introduction

The European General Data Protection Regulation (GDPR) or, similarly, the California Consumer Privacy Act (CCPA) define strong regulatory frameworks following the principle Privacy[1] by Design and by Default (PbD). At the same time, various services collect personal data from countless data subjects and enterprises face the challenges of aligning to all regulatory obligations to avoid severe fines. In particular, data controllers are required to establish technical and organizational measures as safeguards against potential misuse or data breaches. Supervisory authorities are also expanding their activities to audit data

---

[1] For the sake of simplicity, we use the terms *privacy* and *data protection* interchangeably, being aware of their different notions in other contexts.

© The Author(s), under exclusive license to Springer Nature Switzerland AG 2022
J. Troya et al. (Eds.): ICSOC 2022, LNCS 13740, pp. 513–529, 2022.
https://doi.org/10.1007/978-3-031-20984-0_36

controllers and processors [1]. Meanwhile, cloud native systems follow polyglot microservice architectures and multi-cloud strategies and are therefore especially hard to account for personal data. Due to their inherent complexity, they lack transparency and because of their evolutionary development, they might contradict present accountability requirements.

In practice, personal data are found in multi-paradigmatic storage and processing settings (e.g., SQL, NoSQL). Effective means need to be found that identify common patterns or context-specific indicators of personal data as such in the vast amount of present data at rest. For instance, the GDPR requires comprehensive records of processing activities (RoPA, inventory) according to Art. 30.Such a procedure consists of technical and organizational measures, which, in turn, have to take into account the state of the art (Art. 25). So far, we observe laborious and primarily manual tasks of information collection and documentation, often inflexibly supported by simplistic spreadsheets or burdensome written documents [2]. Consequently, we identify a collective need for what data protection officers and supervisory authorities need to enhance transparency and accountability of large-scale cloud native systems: A scalable discovery and continuously updated inventory of personal data. Furthermore, we observe the need for tools to guarantee data protection at runtime to meet the prevailing software development and operations (DevOps) lifecycle of constantly evolving systems and not only ex-ante assumptions. From that follows, the technical scope should align with both the regulatory obligations and the development practice. A key research question here is: *How to (i) discover personal data in large-scale cloud native systems and (ii) how to inventory respective findings?*

We herein present the (to the best of our knowledge) first model, architecture, and implementation that jointly leverages Infrastructure as Code definitions, multi-paradigmatic data stores, and CI/CD pipelines in cloud native systems to inventory personal data at rest. To this end, we provide in this paper:

- A workflow pattern for the scalable discovery of personal data in cloud native systems.
- TEIRESISAS, an architecture and open source prototype implementation of said workflow pattern.
- An experimental evaluation of our approach in comparison to two widely used baseline systems.

Therefore, the remainder of this paper is structured as follows: In Sect. 2 we provide relevant background and related work. Thereafter, in Sect. 3 we present the general approach for a scalable and continuous inventory procedure. We elaborate on the implementation in Sect. 4. On this basis, our approach is evaluated in Sect. 5. In Sect. 6 we discuss the current limitations. Finally, Sect. 7 concludes.

2   Background and Related Work

2.1   Personal Data in Cloud Native Systems

Hereinafter, we refer to personal data as defined in Art. 4(1) which states "'personal data' means any information relating to an identified or identifiable natural person ('data subject')". Looking at real-world data sets, this classification is, however, often far from trivial [3]. The presence of personal data can be constituted by existing field such as a data subject's name, (email) address, social security number, (under certain circumstances) IP address [4] or more complex data structures such as social media profiles, location data, personal preferences, health records, and many others. Usually, these data are stored in relational or non-relational (NoSQL) databases, e.g., as basic *string* values or more complex objects.

From a legal perspective, several obligations need to be implemented by the data controller as imposed by the GDPR. For this paper, four guiding privacy principles are central: First, for the processing of personal data the *transparency* principle according to Art. 5(1a) applies. This implies the controller needs to provide detailed transparency information to signal categories of personal data being collected, their retention time, legal basis, purposes, third country transfers, and many more (see, e.g., [5]). Second, Art. 5(1f) requires appropriate *security* measures (incl. integrity and confidentiality) against unauthorized or unlawful processing or accidental loss (cf. Sect. 2.2). Third, the controller needs to be able to demonstrate compliance with (not only) the aforementioned principles, i.e. the responsibility and liability (see also Recital 74) for *accountability* (Art. 5(2)). To this end, data controllers shall maintain a record of processing activities (Art. 30) with a special focus on the above-mentioned security of processing (Art. 32). While carrying out Data Protection Impact Assessments (DPIAs), the risks associated with the processing of personal data shall be determined and regularly reviewed (Art. 35 GDPR). Fourth, the overarching principle of privacy by design and by default (Art. 25) needs to be taken into account. It applies to all obligations laid out in the GDPR and requires "both at the time of the determination of the means for processing and at the time of the processing itself [('at runtime')] [to] implement appropriate technical and organizational measures". For the following considerations, we use the term *inventory* to describe the aforementioned documentary measures concerning where personal data are being stored.

Through the technical lens, cloud native systems are built to scale applications for millions of concurrent users. For this, horizontal scaling techniques are used and infrastructure (compute, storage, and network) is provisioned automatically on demand [6]. Public cloud providers such as Amazon Web Services, Google Cloud Platform, Microsoft Azure, or IBM Cloud are appreciated for their elasticity and (seemingly) infinite resources. Consequently, privacy engineering has to examine this generation of technology intensively.

Moreover, the architectural paradigm of microservices is pervasive. Through cohesive, independently encapsulated services that interact through API-enabled messaging, scalable microservice architectures can be implemented [7]. Within such microservices, the choice of data storage strongly depends on the functionality needed and the skills of the development team. Considered in its entirety, a multitude of polyglot microservices and multi-paradigmatic data stores are then in use. In larger distributed systems, we can observe thousands of such individual processing entities. From a transparency perspective, observing all of these concurrently for their (personal data) processing activities is a still-unsolved task.

Besides these aspects, the degree of automation is rising. A best practice is to provide infrastructure as code (IaC) definitions. In particular, DevOps teams declaratively describe the desired state of compute, network, and storage components. Advanced configuration management and orchestration tools then transform the current state. For instance, an auto-scaling mechanism runs additional virtual machines or replicates a database under high load. From a privacy perspective, this continuous process – being triggered by load, external events, and new code developments – needs to be examined carefully. If a database instance was replicated to a new data center, possibly personal data were suddenly being stored in a third country. The GDPR would then require the controller to inventory this storage separately, implement adequate safeguards, and transparently inform data subjects.

2.2   Data Loss Prevention

As mentioned above, Art. 5(1f) GDPR explicitly demands technical and organizational measures against accidental loss of personal data. This is why dedicated Data Loss Prevention systems (DLP) have been designed in several iterations. Most of these have in common that they examine *data at rest*. Remarkably, *data in transit* or *data in use* will not be the core subject of this work. Existing DLP systems are mostly security-centric. Related work covers also user behavior analysis, such as profiling of document, database and network access [8], file and network traffic analysis [9] and protection from misuse of email communication [10], as well as content tagging for export prevention [11] or access policies that hinder an adversary from accessing data stores. With DLP, the discovery of sensitive data has been demonstrated by the utilization of different NLP techniques, through which documents become classifiable [12]. Additionally, document classification has been discussed in the context of machine learning [13]. Meanwhile, cloud providers developed proprietary DLP systems, namely there are AWS Macie [14] and Google Cloud Data Loss Prevention [15]. However, they are substantially limited to the extent they only support the provider's storage system (such as S3 for AWS) or they lack algorithmic transparency. Hence, multi-cloud and on-premise infrastructure are not covered at all. Neither meaningful evaluation establishing more trust has been published. Therefore, a data controller cannot meet the accountability requirements as imposed by, e.g., the GDPR [16].

In summary, the major drawback of these systems is the necessity to provide contextual information on where suspected data are located at. In microservice infrastructures, this step is far from easy. This is why we present a new general approach to identifying sensitive information, in particular personal data, with less necessary prior knowledge about the underlying system in the following sections.

3   General Approach

3.1   Requirements

Hence, the system must be designed with a strong focus on the regulatory givens, which are in our example the information obligations from the GDPR. To clarify up front what is often misunderstood: the discovery and inventory system is not required to store *copies* of the personal data records persistently. Since the system is to be built to safeguard data protection rather than introducing novel threats, neither have the entities to be stored permanently in the inventory nor for analysis activities. Rather, the data minimization principle from Art. 5(1c) GDPR has to be ensured. This implies the system will only need to store meta data, e.g., database and records references. Thus, the system is to be built with a Privacy by Architecture [17] approach, not least to avert possible linkability attacks which arose from the presence of a personal record within the system [18].

Moreover, the system should cover a wide range of technological concepts, such as multi-paradigmatic infrastructures, storage alternatives, data types, etc., which all likely depend on the present infrastructure provider in a real cloud-native system. To support these concepts, the system shall be flexible and extensible with little effort. The system must therefore interact through well-documented application programming interfaces (APIs) that power-efficient communication and promote the extensibility and connection with existing parts of the system or their development and operations (DevOps) tech stack.

Furthermore, multi-faceted automation potentials can unfold. These will help to replace existent laborious manual tasks and human errors (read: sending emails around, waiting for replies, and then manually creating spreadsheets that are outdated at the moment of their completion). The inventory process must therefore happen continuously and should scale out to larger infrastructures to meet the givens of current system architecture practice.

On a non-functional level, the system itself should be created and behave transparently to enable independent assessments, identify architectural and functional limitations, and determine scalability, accuracy, security, and usability – also for a non-technical audience, since naturally multidisciplinary stakeholders are involved.

3.2   Introducing a Workflow Pattern for Scalable Discovery of Personal Data

When studying data loss prevention systems, there is a lot of attention on the detection methods but less on the practical integration of such systems. All too often, monolithic tools are proposed that are suitable to operate as standalone entity. However, these cannot meet the givens of modern heavily distributed systems consisting of numerous services, all potentially dealing with sensitive information. In these scenarios, we need to delegate the complexity of scheduling classification and inventorying tasks to dedicated algorithms. Therefore, we propose the application of the workflow pattern. Having also the requirements listed above in mind, we propose the following general four-step workflow as depicted in Fig. 1:

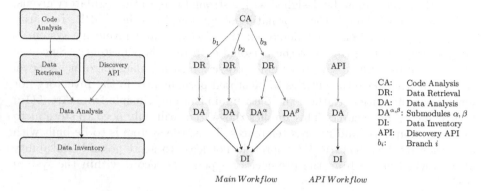

Main Workflow   *API Workflow*

Fig. 1. Workflow pattern and exemplary workflows.

1. Code Analysis (CA): Discover storages in cloud native systems by analyzing version-controlled code repositories. With this module, an approach to finding storages in unknown distributed systems environments shall be implemented (black-box approach). By analyzing code repositories, it is possible to find traces, definitions, or encoded connection strings of storages such as databases or disk storages. Repositories may contain the program's code, but also relevant Infrastructure as Code (IaC) definitions. Both of them potentially comprise information about personal data storages. The aspired outcome of the code analysis is a list of connection details for each storage found, which then enables the following retrieval component to read from. The list of connections must consist of a Uniform Resource Identifier (URI), login credentials if required, and the storage type. To successfully achieve the task of connection information extraction, the module would need to be able to clone code repositories and parse relevant code, including parameters of software packages used for storage connection (e.g., frequently used object-relational mappers). Incomplete connection information – for instance in case of missing passwords or dynamically assigned IP addresses or host names – should be adequately marked in the inventory. Given these pieces of information, a data controller can take action to include them manually in future audits/analyses.

2. Data Retrieval (DR): Manage to access the deployed storages and retrieve relevant (meta) data. The Data Retrieval directly depends on the Code Analysis. With the given storage information, this component should be able to connect to the storages and fetch data and meta data from them. Structured and potentially unstructured data have to be extracted in the form of database entities or files. The whole process must stay reliable, and therefore a data subset selection (sampling) could optionally guarantee the timely termination of the following processing steps for very large data sets. In addition, to provide a system that is applicable for as many scenarios and architectures as possible, a Discovery API needs to be added. This API listens for data requests, which will then be analyzed, to overcome the issue that storages were not found, or their connection information was incomplete. That includes external storages that are not under development of the data controller. The implementation of middlewares which actively send data to the Discovery API allows the analysis of these prior hidden data collections. Alternatively, it may be used to analyze data that is not stored at rest, such as samples from stream processing frameworks.

3. Data analysis (DA): Detect personal data using heuristics and data analysis methods. The Data Analysis component accepts data and meta data as incoming parameters. The actual analysis is carried out in a multistep approach, which results in indicators for a personal or non-personal data classification which includes entity and storage references to be inventoried. It is preferable to yield false-positive rather than false-negative classifications. For example, if verbose meta data – which can be categorically similar to a personal field's data type, but also natural language such as field names – exist, an analysis of the meta data can result in false-positive indicators. Primarily, sensitive information shall not be overlooked. It is safe to assume that these results are, before any optimizations, still preferred over overlooking sensitive information. Moreover, all analysis techniques which are convenient for meta data, especially pattern matching and lookup tables, should be also applied to data in the initial phase.

4. Data Inventory (DI): Inventory findings while meeting the regulatory givens. The results of all prior steps are then written into the Data Inventory which can serve as input for Data Protection Impact Assessments, Records of Processing Activities, or any other external or internal supervisory activity. Since the discovery job results can be highly diverse, a flexible and non-relational document store is considered the best fit here. The results can be transformed to meet the form specifications of necessary legal documents, potential visualizations, or summaries of transparency information (Art. 12–14 GDPR).

Continuous software engineering relies on the concept of CI/CD pipelines, which are usually triggered by the version control system [19]. Therefore, most likely, the process shall be started each time relevant code changes are detected or due to changes in the underlying architecture of a system.

3.3   Workflow Engineering

For large architectures and consequently many appearing triggering events, this four-step workflow needs to be properly orchestrated. In the probable event of detecting multiple storages under examination, the execution of the aforementioned steps needs then to be parallelized. Therefore, an efficient execution yielding timely results needs horizontal scalability. The components presented above are, in turn, dependent on each other. On a conceptual level, these dependencies can be modeled as a Directed Acyclic Graph (DAG). We therefore propose an orchestration implementing the *workflow pattern* [20]. That means, each component performs a dedicated task for separation of concerns in an independent or dependent (and consequently sequential) flow.

Figure 1 depicts an example of an instantiated *Main Workflow* with parallelization of the sub-graphs. Supposing the Code Analysis returns a list of three storages, the workflow is forked afterward into three execution branches. Then, the Data Retrieval component is instantiated in each of the branches and takes responsibility for the sub-tasks. For more complex scenarios, forking can even be nested to introduce even more parallelism. Assuming the Data Retrieval of branch b_3 has returned complex data that should be analyzed by multiple techniques, DA^α and DA^β would fork the sub-graph to handle the data sets separately. Finally, all branches are joined and the workflow terminates after storing the findings successfully. Besides, the *API Workflow* happens on requesting the Discovery API and could also be forked (not shown).

In a cloud native environment, such workflows can be implemented through workflow management platforms [20]. Their implementations depend on DAGs as they manage workflow orchestration (i.e., the concurrent and distributed task execution while meeting the ordering dependencies). Letting such a tool take the responsibility for task execution and scheduling of the discovery and inventory process promises reliability, scalability, and high automation potential, meeting the above-mentioned requirements. Keeping these aspects in mind, we now continue with the concrete software architecture and implementation in the upcoming sections.

4   Software Architecture and Implementation

We will now synthesize the conceptual workflow pattern and engineering considerations to elaborate on the design and implementation of a prototype system called TEIRESIAS. The complete implementation is available under the MIT License as open source software in a public code repository.[2]

4.1   Overview

In Fig. 2 we provide an overview of the proposed system architecture. As indicated above, we heavily rely on the concepts of workflow management platforms. For our implementation we chose the open-source workflow platform Apache Airflow (for more details, see Sect. 4.2). It is mainly responsible for the correct execution of all workflow steps. Within the TEIRESIAS system boundary ❶, Apache Airflow is integrated as an Airflow Celery Cluster ❷, consisting of a message broker, database, (Airflow) API, scheduler, and worker nodes. An Airflow Worker ❸ is executing the code of each discovery component. Hence, it gets allocated their needed processing resources automatically. A data controller or supervisory authority can initialize the discovery and inventory process by

---

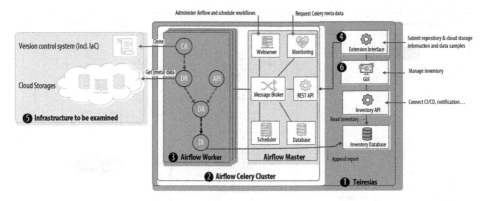

Fig. 2. System Architecture

passing (meta) data to the Extension Interface ❹. Such data will then be passed on into the workflow, where modules are listening for incoming data (*Discovery API*). Alternatively, they access them during a workflow execution, which may include fetching data from the data controller's infrastructure ❺ under examination through both the *Code Analysis* and *Data Retrieval* modules. Finally, discovered meta data are stored in the Inventory Database. These findings can afterward be accessed through the Inventory GUI ❻, which requests the reports from the Inventory Database through the Inventory API. Meanwhile, all the Airflow subcomponents can be administered through the Web Server (incl. GUI). For instance, workflows and rules for their scheduling, such as the determination of an examination on a regular basis, can be fine-tuned. Through these settings, TEIRESISAS can be precisely parameterized to fit the users' needs.

4.2 Workflow Management

We run the workflow management platform in a Celery cluster deployment. Celery handles tasks asynchronously based on a job queue, which communicates through message passing. We employ Redis as a broker to exchange messages between the scheduler and worker services. For all tasks, we implemented *PythonOperators* for executing the logic of all components.The DAG for orchestrating the workflow is defined in Python. The definition of the DAG focused on scalability for the examination of larger infrastructures and extensibility for handling paradigmatically different services (e.g., different storages or IaC definitions). Conditional branching (as indicated in the example above) is introduced by placing a *BranchPythonOperator* instance in front of the branches, which is chosen during DAG execution by conditional context evaluation. Moreover, parallelization of sub-workflows can be achieved by iterating over Airflow variables, and – once per iteration – the instantiation and linking (defining the execution order) of tasks are dynamically set. During runtime, the system would instantiate a *clone_and_analyze_code* function to examine a code repository for storage definitions and afterward create a task for each *process_code_analysis* task, all

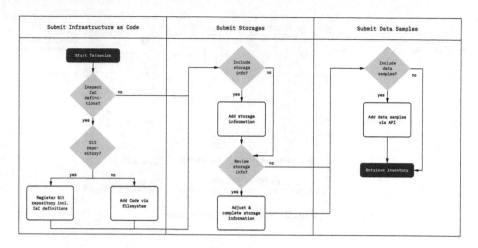

Fig. 3. Interaction flow

of which can then run in parallel. Throughout the iterative prototypical implementation, stability could be improved by the re-implementation of the tasks by adding atomicity and idempotency as per best practice. For that, several more little DAG definitions (chunking them in smaller units) worked best. Failing tasks would then not prevent the main enclosing DAG to continue. Each error is logged for debugging and highlighted in the Airflow administration interface. We provide documentation along with the code.

4.3   Components

We now briefly explain the implementation of the core components. We provide Fig. 3 to show the basic interactions with the system.

Code Analysis: This component allows discovering and semantically parsing IaC definitions. In particular, we chose to support Ansible and Docker Compose encoded in YAML files. The analysis extracts, among others, details such as Docker images or Ansible module names. Through a look-up table and several storage & IaC dependent regular expressions we identify, for demonstration purposes, PostgreSQL and MongoDB storages. There we fulfill the requirement of multi-paradigmatic storage identification. The analysis factors in structural information, retrieving the storages' contexts and resolves any variables that might be distributed over several IaC files. Moreover, the component can utilize repository information passed through the extension interface and clone Git repositories. Non-Git code bases can also be passed to the module by semi-automatically pulling the contents into a specific directory, in which a listener detects any changes and hence triggers the analysis. In doing so, (parts of) repositories can be analyzed without having access privileges to the version control system, which could be preferred from a security.

Data Retrieval and Analysis: The component collects meta data about different data stores. At the core, an object-relational mapper (SQLAlchemy) allows for easy integration of a variety of storages, such as MySQL, Google BigQuery, or IBM DB2. While running, any analysis is performed *in place* through the engines of the data storages. For example, the *Meta data Analysis* of a PostgreSQL database fetches the list of columns per table, data types, number of entities, and primary key definitions. An *INET*-typed table would then indicate the storage of IP addresses, which will often be considered relatable to a person. Throughout the analysis, a look-up table is compared to the attributes using simple named-entity recognition (NER) methods. For instance, the similarity is measured by the Levenshtein distance on a per attribute level. Finally, proximity lists are sorted and filtered using a 0.6 threshold, which is, according to our experiments, a viable trade-off between a low false-positive rate (i.e., excluding sub-string matches with few characters) and the best possible true positive rate (i.e., including matches of declined or compound words which hint at personal data semantically). Afterward, the *Data Analysis* is implemented through regular expression-based search patterns (e.g., for social security, ID, or credit card numbers). The result is a list of references (e.g., *ObjectIds* in a MongoDB) , which is appended to the report. Finally, the discovery comprises a binary classification of whether personal data have been detected. Since several meaningful insights originate from the analysis, such as the number of matched entities, the proximities from the meta data's analysis, and the total number of entities in the collection, should be weighted differently. For this purpose, we propose and implement the T metric:

$$T := \underbrace{min(1, n)}_{= 0 \vee 1} \cdot max(\underbrace{\alpha_{\text{hasMatch}}}_{= 0 \vee 1}, \underbrace{\beta_{\text{meanProx}}/100}_{= 0 \vee x \in [0.6, 1]})$$

$$n := \text{total number of entities in collection}$$
$$\alpha_{\text{hasMatch}} := min(1, \text{total number of data matches})$$
$$\beta_{\text{meanProx}} := mean(\text{proximities of attribute names to keywords})$$

In short, we propose a binary classification based on T which enables a quick assessment of data stores. However, we store the underlying measures because they are helpful for later possibly manual verification.

Discovery API: The API accepts any valid JSON document, which will then be analyzed. The pattern matching works the same way as described above. A report will be written with a user-provided identifier. Using the REST API of the Airflow web server, interoperability with other systems can be easily achieved.

Data Inventory: The reports are persistently stored in a MongoDB database, since the schemaless approach fits best to the potentially heterogeneous report structures. A specialized reporting Airflow operator is responsible for appending report portions from the different discovery steps into one bundled report per discovery execution. This is done by using a common DAG execution identifier, which is passed to the reporting operator. Each part is written, regardless of whether the following discovery steps are failing or succeeding, to provide full transparency and indicate necessary manual interaction.

Extension Interface and GUI: Furthermore, the inventory consists of a RESTful API and a graphical interface (GUI), through which the reports can be requested by the data controller or supervisory authority. Initially, the users register the repository URI and branch name, to start the workflow. Next, additional storage information which was not accessible during execution can be completed. This includes the addition of externally managed data stores. Such information is then provided to the discovery via Airflow variables. Furthermore, storages can be temporarily excluded from the workflows or eventually be deleted. Such deletion is helpful when infrastructure has been redefined, and bypassing storages with huge amounts of known non-personal content can help to limit unnecessary processing costs. Such changes remain consistent between multiple code analysis executions.

4.4   Deployment and Integration

The deployment works as follows. First, all services are deployed through Docker containers. Referencing production-ready Docker images enable a quick, maintainable, repeatable, and deterministic deployment.Second, all critical system partsare only accessible after successful authentication. The communication with all accessible servers is encrypted using TLS, which was achieved by adding a reverse proxy server, which handles encryption with the utilization of a user-generated private key and certificate. The inventory database separates users for read and write access. It is additionally advised to provision a virtual private network to add another security layer. More extensive details are provided as software documentation in the repository.

Recommended integration scenarios include automated and recurrent triggering (e.g., hourly schedule) of the workflow through the management platform. Alternatively, the Discovery API can be triggered through CI/CD pipelines. Moreover, to align with DevPrivOps / DevSecOps [21,22] practices, the reports can be updated based on the workload. For example, each time the monitoring system registers changes, the inventory process should be triggered to check for unforeseen new sources of personal data.

5   Evaluation

To evaluate our approach, we first compare our prototype to two widely used baseline systems, namely AWS Macie and Google CDLP, with regard to the performance of personal data discovery. Therefore, we compile three data sets to evaluate both (personal) data and meta data discovery in a single analysis task. Hence, we assume a single column of 5k values (i.e., potential personal data) with a meaningful column type and name (i.e., meta data). The first two data sets are composed of a synthetic personal data generatorwhich outputs IP addresses using a regular expression and, through lookup tables, forenames, and surnames, which we combine (full names) to get a higher number of unique values. Besides these, we prepare a random subset of scraped personal handles from Twitter.[3] Moreover, we create a set of labeled noise to not give the veneer of heuristics, since it would be feasible to drop empty data sets from the analysis queue in the systems. In particular, the labeled noise has four columns named *user_name, email, address* and *ip*. It is expected that *IPv4* addresses can be discovered by pattern matching, whereas *Full Names* are a use case for classification tasks or comprehensive lookup tables. Furthermore, *Twitter Names* can only be found during classification and *Labeled Noise* entities should not be detected as personal data at all.

Since AWS Macie exclusively scans files within its S3 storage, and Google CDLP does not cover non-proprietary databases,*csv* files have been used for the cloud service evaluationAvoiding interference between the experiment iterations, each *csv* file has been deployed individually to a freshly provisioned storage. For the prototype's evaluation, the same data sets have been deployed to different tables of a managed PostgreSQL database within the Google Cloud Platform (PostgreSQL 13, 2 vCPUs, 3.75 GB Memory).The Google CDLP parameter *Percentage of included objects scanned within the bucket* was set to 100% and the *Sampling method* was set to *No Sampling*. No other preferences have been set in AWS Macie's console since comparable defaults were set. In both the Google CDLP and the AWS Macie console, for each iteration, a one-time scan with a pointer to the specific bucket was submitted. The prototype ran on a MacBook Pro 2019 (2.4 GHz Intel i5 CPU, 16 GB RAM).

Table 1 summarizes the first experimental results. For both proprietary services, there is not an indication that meta data have been analyzed at all. Google CDLP has correctly found the 5 000 *IPv4* entities per regular expression. Our prototype is, in addition, able to find proximity between *IPv4* and *IP* through the meta data lookup attribute. There is some vagueness in the interpretation of which techniques have been used to classify the *Full Name* entities correctly as personal data, which only AWS Macie was able to do. It is most likely that only pre-trained machine-learning models can achieve that task TEIRESIAS again correctly classified the data set via the meta data analysis. *Twitter Names* entities have not been recognized as personal data by any of the compared systems, but, the data set was classified by TEIRESIAS' meta data analysis workflow. In turn, the cloud services have correctly classified the *Labeled Noise* as non-personal data, and the TEIRESIAS analysis classified it incorrectly as personal data, which is a result of the found meta data proximities and a non-empty data set. To overcome this false positive, the weighting of the terms of T could be refined in future work. However, yielding false positives rather than false negatives rather strengthens the comprehensiveness of the discovery, since it prevents

---

[3] https://github.com/danibram/mocker-data-generator,
   https://kaggle.com/hwassner/TwitterFriends.

overlooking sensitive data. Balancing the results in a F1 measure, the proprietary services both reached a 0.57 score, each with one true positive, one true negative, and two false negatives. The prototype's score of 0.86 can be ascribed to the true positive classifications of the meta data analyses. In these first experiments, TEIRESIAS outperforms AWS Macie and Google CDLP. Still, regarding the data analysis, only a section of personal data can be discovered with pattern matching and other rule-based detection mechanisms. Promising classification technologies should therefore be considered to be added to the system as future work.

In our second experiment, we measure the runtime performance, for which we re-used the experimental setup described above. However, this time we cannot compare AWS Macie and Google CDLP, since their underlying compute resources are not publicly known and this would contradict fairness in performance benchmarks.For the experiment, four different data sets with four columns each, and different total numbers of entities (0.5–500k) have been deployed. Afterward, we measured the execution time for the different samples. To limit the workload to one specific data set at a time, the PostgreSQL instance was registered to the system, containing one table per iteration, and the DAG for data analysis was scheduled exclusively.

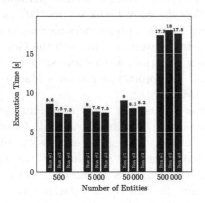

Fig. 4. Execution times of three runs for different sample sizes.

Table 1. Comparative evaluation results of DLP systems.

	AWS Macie				Google CDLP				TEIRESIAS			
	TP	TN	FP	FN	TP	TN	FP	FN	TP	TN	FP	FN
IPv4				❶	❷				❸❹			
Full Name	❶							❷	❹			
Twitter Name				❶				❷	❹			
Labeled Noise		❶				❷						❹
F1-Score	0.57				0.57				0.86			

TP True Positive   ❶ See [14]
TN True Negative   ❷ See [15]
FP False Positive   ❸ Data analysis
FN False Negative   ❹ Meta data analysis

The results are presented in Fig. 4. We show that there is a non-linear growth, with 8.4 s for 50k and 17.6 s for 500k entities, which is nearly a doubling of the required time for a tenfold higher number of entities. It can be assumed that, with a very high number of entities, the mean execution time depends largely on the in-place data analysis query processing costs. In contrast, with a low number of entities, the costs for the system core functionalities and the meta data handling make up a major part of the execution time and stay almost constant. In summarizing, we demonstrate the applicability of our approach in a real-world setting, since these execution times allow for discovery operations without major time or resource consumption.

Note, we publish all test data sets used for the evaluation to enhance both repeatability and verifiability of our work.[4]

6 Limitations and Discussion

Without a doubt, the system provides a scalable framework, which illustrates an automation concept using the proposed workflow pattern. However, for now, it only supports a limited set of data at rest storages and types of IaC definitions. To be used in more environments, support to connect to more popular *at rest* systems should be implemented. More and more relevant processing happens also in stream processing systems and ephemeral storages, which could be included as well. Moreover, static code analysis techniques would complement the code analysis features to discover also some of these additional components. Furthermore, the detection and analysis methods should be extended. Lookup tables and regular expressions are well-functioning tools to detect many critical categories of personal data. Nevertheless, with the help of mature natural language processing and advanced machine learning models, better classification results can be yielded for all kinds of unpredictable data sets. This is especially important for audit scenarios and data that are provided by the data subject. This limitation, however, was not within the scope of the paper, but recent related work could complement our approach [23]. Future work should also focus on data linkage attacks and anonymization or minimization methods [24]. Since the GDPR requires data controllers to consider if it is reasonably likely (cf. Recital 26) that personal data get de-anonymized, a DLP system could also try to (re-)combine records from different storage systems.

TEIRESIAS is expected to discover and inventory personal data continuously at runtime. Related work shows how to formalize machine-readable transparency information (encoding the purpose, legal bases, third country transfers, categories of personal data, etc.) [5,25]. At the same time, observability measures (such as logging, distributed tracing, monitoring) can create precise data flow models. Future research should concentrate on combining such practical privacy engineering practices to harvest accurate and transparent information at runtime [26,27]. Especially growing and constantly evolving microservice architectures are not to be inventoried manually anymore. Therefore, there is an urgent need for more automated tools that help data controllers to keep track of their processing activities.

7 Conclusion

In this paper, we presented a DLP approach that monitors a system under examination for personal data at runtime continuously. With these contributions,

---

[4] https://github.com/teiresias-personal-data-discovery/evaluation.

data controllers are provided with working measures for aligning with regulatory frameworks such as the GDPR. Moreover, supervisory authorities can utilize TEIRESIAS to audit infrastructures. Practical applicability has been demonstrated through a comparative evaluation. We emphasize that the approach primarily targets cloud native systems, but is also applicable to cloud-enabled ones. The latter, e.g., in legacy-cloud hybrids, would only need a lightweight custom middleware component to be connected to the proposed APIs. Within the wider prospects, our workflow could be extended to not only detect personal data (and other kinds of sensitive information) but also support efficient distributed data deletion.

Acknowledgements. The work behind this paper was partially conducted within the project DaSKITA, supported under grant no. 28V2307A19 by funds of the Federal Ministry for the Environment, Nature Conservation, Nuclear Safety and Consumer Protection (BMUV) based on a decision of the Parliament of the Federal Republic of Germany via the Federal Office for Agriculture and Food (BLE) under the innovation support programme.

References

1. Ruohonen, J., Hjerppe, K.: The GDPR enforcement fines at glance. Inf. Syst. **106**, 101876 (2021)
2. Huth, D., Tanakol, A., Matthes, F.: Using enterprise architecture models for creating the record of processing activities (Art. 30 GDPR). In: 2019 IEEE 23rd Intl. Enterprise Distributed Object Computing Conference, pp. 98–104 (2019)
3. Finck, M., Pallas, F.: They who must not be identified-distinguishing personal from non-personal data under the GDPR. Int. Data Priv. Law. **10**(1), 11–36 (2020)
4. Zuiderveen Borgesius, F.: Breyer case of the court of justice of the European union: IP addresses and the personal data definition (Case Note). Eur. Data Protect. Law Rev. **3**(1), 130 (2017)
5. Grünewald, E., Pallas, F.: TILT: a GDPR-aligned transparency information language and toolkit for practical privacy engineering. In: Proceedings of the 2021 ACM Conference on Fairness, Accountability, and Transparency, pp. 636–646 (2021)
6. Gannon, D., Barga, R., Sundaresan, N.: Cloud-native applications. IEEE Cloud Comput. **4**(5), 16–21 (2017)
7. Dragoni, N., et al.: Microservices: yesterday, today, and tomorrow. In: Present and Ulterior Software Engineering, pp. 195–216 (2017)
8. Shabtai, A., Elovici, Y., Rokach, L.: Data leakage detection/prevention solutions. In: A Survey of Data Leakage Detection and Prevention Solutions. SpringerBriefs in Computer Science, pp. 17–37. Springer, Boston, MA (2012). https://doi.org/10.1007/978-1-4614-2053-8_4
9. Li, H., Peng, Z., Feng, X., Ma, H.: Leakage prevention method for unstructured data based on classification. In: Niu, W., et al. (eds.) ATIS 2015. CCIS, vol. 557, pp. 337–343. Springer, Heidelberg (2015). https://doi.org/10.1007/978-3-662-48683-2_30
10. Alneyadi, S., Sithirasenan, E., Muthukkumarasamy, V.: A survey on data leakage prevention systems. J. Netw. Comput. Appl. **62**, 137–152 (2016)

11. Marecki, J., Srivatsa, M., Varakantham, P.: A decision theoretic approach to data leakage prevention. In: 2010 IEEE Second International Conference on Social Computing, pp. 776–784. IEEE (2010)
12. Trieu, L.Q., Tran, T.-N., Tran, M.-K., Tran, M.-T.: Document sensitivity classification for data leakage prevention with twitter-based document embedding and query expansion. In: International Conference on Computational Intelligence and Security (CIS), pp. 537–542. IEEE (2017)
13. Ghouse, M., Nene, M.J., Vembuselvi, C.: Data leakage prevention for data in transit using artificial intelligence and encryption techniques. In: 2019 International Conference on Advances in Computing, Communication and Control (ICAC3), pp. 1–6. IEEE (2019)
14. Amazon Macie - Amazon Web Services. https://aws.amazon.com/de/macie/
15. Google Cloud Data Loss Prevention. https://cloud.google.com/dlp
16. Kaul, A., Kesarwani, M., Min, H., Zhang, Q.: Knowledge & learning-based adaptable system for sensitive information identification and handling. In: 2021 IEEE 14th International Conference on Cloud Computing, pp. 261–271. IEEE (2021)
17. Spiekermann, S., Cranor, L.F.: Engineering privacy. IEEE Trans. Softw. Eng. **35**(1), 67–82 (2008)
18. Pfitzmann, A., Hansen, M.: A terminology for talking about privacy by data minimization: anonymity, unlinkability, undetectability, unobservability, pseudonymity, and identity management (2010)
19. Shahin, M., Babar, M.A., Zhu, L.: Continuous integration, delivery and deployment: a systematic review on approaches, tools, challenges and practices. IEEE Access **5**, 3909–3943 (2017)
20. Mitchell, R., et al.: Exploration of workflow management systems emerging features from users perspectives. In: 2019 IEEE International Conference on Big Data, pp. 4537–4544 (2019)
21. Grünewald, E.: Cloud native privacy engineering through DevPrivOps. In: Friedewald, M., Krenn, S., Schiering, I., Schiffner, S. (eds.) Privacy and Identity 2021. IAICT, vol. 644, pp. 122–141. Springer, Cham (2022). https://doi.org/10.1007/978-3-030-99100-5_10
22. Myrbakken, H., Colomo-Palacios, R.: DevSecOps: a multivocal literature review. In: Mas, A., Mesquida, A., O'Connor, R.V., Rout, T., Dorling, A. (eds.) SPICE 2017. CCIS, vol. 770, pp. 17–29. Springer, Cham (2017). https://doi.org/10.1007/978-3-319-67383-7_2
23. Wei, Y.-C., Liao, T.-Y., Wu, W.-C.: Using machine learning to detect PII from attributes and supporting activities of information assets. J. Supercomput. **78**, 1–22 (2022)
24. Pallas, F., Hartmann, D., Heinrich, P., Kipke, J., Grünewald, E.: Configurable per-query data minimization for privacy-compliant web APIs. In: Proceedings of the 2022 ICWE International Conference on Web Engineering, Bari (2022)
25. Grünewald, E., Wille, P., Pallas, F., Borges, M.C., Ulbricht, M.-R.: TIRA: an OpenAPI extension and toolbox for GDPR transparency in RESTful architectures. In: European Symposium on Security and Privacy Workshops (EuroS&PW) (2021)
26. Sion, L., Van Landuyt, D., Joosen, W.: An overview of runtime data protection enforcement approaches. In: 2021 IEEE European Symposium on Security and Privacy Workshops (EuroS&PW). IEEE, pp. 351–358 (2021)
27. Flittner, M., Balaban, S., Bless, R.: CloudInspector: a transparency-as-a-service solution for legal issues in cloud computing. In: 2016 IEEE Intl. Conference on Cloud Engineering Workshop (IC2EW), pp. 94–99 (2016)

Cheops, a Service to Blow Away Cloud Applications to the Edge

Marie Delavergne$^{(\boxtimes)}$ ⓘ, Geo Johns Antony ⓘ, and Adrien Lebre ⓘ

Inria, Nantes, France
{marie.delavergne,geo-johns.antony,adrien.lebre}@inria.fr

Abstract. One question to answer the shift from the Cloud to the Edge computing paradigm is: how distributed applications developed for Cloud platforms can benefit from the opportunities of the Edge while dealing with inherent constraints of wide-area network links? Leveraging the modularity of microservice-based applications, we propose to deploy multiple instances of the same service (one per edge site) and deliver collaborations between them according to each request. Collaborations are expressed thanks to a DSL and orchestrated in a transparent manner by the Cheops runtime. We demonstrate the relevance of our proposal by geo-distributing Kubernetes resources.

Keywords: Edge computing · Service composition · Service mesh

1 Introduction

Nowadays, there is an indubitable shift from Cloud Computing to the Edge [8].

The assumptions that are generally taken to develop Cloud applications are not valid anymore in the Edge context. For instance, the intermittent network connections should be considered as the norm rather than the exception. If you consider the Google Doc service, users in the same vicinity cannot work on the same document if they cannot reach the datacenter, even though they are close to each other. To reckon with the Edge constraints, and thus be able to satisfy requests locally, the most straightforward approach is to deploy an entire, independent instance of the application on every Edge sites. This way, if one site is separated from the rest of the network, it can still serve local requests[1]. The next step is to offer collaboration means between these instances when needed.

Git is an application that fulfills such requirements (even though it has not been designed specifically for this paradigm): Git operations can be performed locally and pushed to other instances when required.

We proposed the premises of a generalization of these Git concepts by presenting how an application can be geo-distributed without intrusive changes in

---

[1] We underline we do not consider disconnections between users and their Edge location. Edge elements are supposed to be as close as possible to prevent this situation.

© The Author(s), under exclusive license to Springer Nature Switzerland AG 2022
J. Troya et al. (Eds.): ICSOC 2022, LNCS 13740, pp. 530–539, 2022.
https://doi.org/10.1007/978-3-031-20984-0_37

its business logic thanks to a service mesh approach [3]. A service mesh is a layer over microservices that intercepts requests in order to decouple functionalities such as monitoring or auto-scaling [4]. Concretely, we proposed to leverage the modularity and REST APIs of cloud applications to allow collaborations in an agnostic manner between multiple instances of the same system.

In this paper, we extend our proposal to deliver a complete framework that allows multiple instances of a Cloud microservice based application to behave like a single one. Thanks to our framework, called *Cheops*, DevOps can *share*, *replicate*, and *extend* resources between the different instances in agnostic manner. A service managed by Cheops can be seen as a *Single Service Image*. We found this analogy with past activities on Single System Images [5] relevant as *the interest of SSI clusters was based on the idea that they may be simpler to use and administer*. With Cheops, the challenge related to the collaboration between multiple instances of a system (the geo-distribution aspects) is reified at the level of the DevOps and externally from the business logic of the system itself.

The contributions of this article are as follows:

- A nonintrusive approach relying on service mesh concepts to achieve three kind of collaborations between services: *sharing*, *replication*, and *cross*.
- A model of the different kind of relationships between resources that may exist in a microservice based applications.
- A detailed description of the current Cheops prototype.
- A demonstration of the feasibility of the proposed framework and collaboration strategies in the Kubernetes ecosystem.

The rest of this paper is organized as follows: Section 2 presents the generalization idea of our proposal, while Sect. 3 deals with the current architecture we followed to implement our proof-of-concept. Section 4 presents related works. Finally, Sect. 5 concludes and discusses future work.

2   Towards Generic and Noninvasive Collaborations

2.1   Scope-lang

Scope-lang is a language introduced in [3], that extends the usual requests made from users to their application in order to reify the locality aspects. A scope-lang expression, which we call *scope*, contains information on the location where a specific request, or part of the request, will be executed. As an example, a scope defined as "$s : App_1, t : App_2$" specifies to use service s from App_1 (the application *App* on Site 1), and the service t from

$$
\begin{aligned}
App_i, App_j &::= \text{application instance} \\
s, t &::= \text{service} \\
s_i, t_j &::= \text{service instance} \\
Loc &::= App_i \qquad \text{single location} \\
&\mid Loc\&Loc \quad \text{multiple locations} \\
&\mid Loc\%Loc \quad \text{cross locations} \\
\sigma &::= s : Loc, \sigma \quad \text{scope} \\
&\mid s : Loc
\end{aligned}
$$

$$\mathcal{R}[\![s : App_i]\!] = s_i$$

$$\mathcal{R}[\![s : Loc\&Loc']\!] = \mathcal{R}[\![s : Loc]\!] \text{ and } \mathcal{R}[\![s : Loc']\!]$$

$$\mathcal{R}[\![s : Loc\%Loc']\!] = \mathcal{R}[\![s : Loc]\!] \text{ spread to } \mathcal{R}[\![s : Loc']\!]$$

Fig. 1. Scope-lang expressions σ and the function that resolves service instance from elements of the scope $\mathcal{R}$.

App₂ (on Site 2). Users defines the scope of the request to specify the exact collaboration between instances required for the execution of their request. The scope is interpreted during the execution of the request workflow to decide the execution location accordingly. A more formal definition of the language is available in Fig. 1, which has been extended to allow cross collaborations.

2.2   Collaboration Implementations for Elementary Resources

Figure 2 depicts the three collaborations implemented in *Cheops*.

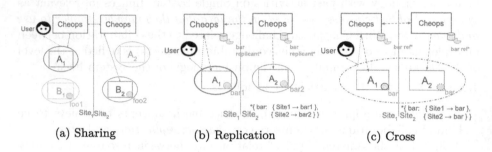

(a) Sharing   (b) Replication   (c) Cross

Fig. 2. The different Cheops collaborations

Sharing. *Sharing* is the collaboration which allows a service instance to use a resource from a service which is not the one assigned to its application instance.

The typical example is getting a resource from a service B on another site for a service A as presented by the red arrows in Fig. 2a. :

`application create a --sub-resource foo2 --scope {A: `*Site₁*`, B: `*Site₂*`}`

1. A user requests to create a resource on service A from *Site₁* (Service A_1), using a sub-resource foo_2 from service B on *Site₂* (Service B_2).
2. The request is intercepted and transferred to Cheops.
3. Cheops extracts the scope from the request and interprets it.
4. Cheops transfers the request to service A, until A needs the sub-resource.
5. The outgoing request is intercepted, and at this point, is transferred to *Site₂*.
6. Cheops on *Site₂* uses its catalog to find Service B endpoint and transfer the request to this service to get foo_2.
7. The service response (containing the resource itself) is finally transferred back to Service A through Cheops.

Replication. *Replication* is the ability for users to create and have available resources on different Edge sites to deal with latency and split networks. Replication main action is duplication: transfer the request to every involved sites and let the application execute the request locally. The operation does not simply consists in forwarding the request to the different instances, though. Cheops keeps track of the different replicas in order to ensure that future CRUD operations achieved on any replica will be applied on all copies, maintaining eventually the consistency over time. To do that, Cheops relies on a data scheme, called the replicant, that links a meta-ID to the different replica IDs and their locations.

Figure 2b sums up the workflow to create a replicated resource on two sites:
`application create a --name bar --scope` {A: $Site_1$ & $Site_2$}.

1. A user sends a request on $Site_1$ to create two replicas of the *bar* resource.
2. The request is intercepted and transferred to Cheops.
3. Cheops extracts the scope and interprets it.
4. Cheops creates the replicant, and passes the request to create it to Cheops on the other involved site ($Site_2$), as well as the request of creation of *bar* on both sites, which is simply the request without the scope.
5. Both Cheops execute the request of creation; the response is intercepted to fill the local IDs on the replicants and the response is transferred to the user, replacing the local ID by the meta-ID of the replicant.

To provide eventual consistency, Cheops follows the Raft protocol, with one replicant acting as the leader.

Cross. *Cross* is the last collaboration we identified. The idea is to create a resource over multiple sites. The main difference with respect to the aforementioned replication concept is related to the aggregation/divisibility property. In the replication, each copy is independent, even if they all converge eventually based on the CRUD operation. A cross resource can be seen as an aggregation of all resources that constitutes the cross-resource overall. Some resources which cannot be divided by an application API will require an additional layer in the business logic to satisfy the divisibility property.

Similarly to the replicant data scheme, Cheops keeps tracks of the different resources in order to perform CRUD operations in the expected manner. A `CREATE` operation for instance can distribute the resource over different sites (if this resource is divisible), while a `READ` will be performed on each "sub-resource" composing the cross-resource in order to return the aggregated result.

How Cheops deals with split-brain issue for cross resource is left as future work. However, it is worth noting that the unreachability of one site that hosts a part of the cross resource faces multiple challenges.

An illustration of Cross is depicted in Fig. 2c:
`application create a --name bar --scope` {A: $Site_1$% $Site_2$}.

1. A user sends a request to create a resource specifying the involved sites.
2. The request is intercepted and transferred to Cheops.
3. Cheops extracts the scope and interprets it.
4. Cheops creates the resource on the first site ($Site_1$) and passes the request to other involved sites.
5. Cheops on $Site_2$ identifies the extended resource and creates an identifier within Cheops to forward to the deployed resource site

2.3   Relationship Model

Many resources have dependencies with each other (a virtual machine in the OpenStack ecosystem depends on an image, a network, an IP, etc.; a deployment file in Kubernetes is linked to several pods; etc.).

Hence, it is mandatory to rely on a relationship model for replication and cross operations. This model will be used to keep track on each critical resource and ensure that CRUD operations are performed thoroughly. We have identified and formulated three dependencies, depicted in Fig. 3.

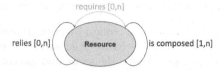

Fig. 3. The different dependencies

Requirement defines a relationship between two resources that is not critical for the survival of either of the resource but rather is a necessary link during a particular operation. The operation can be any operation performed upon either of the resource and while it is performed, the link is vital. If it is severed, the operation will terminate and not succeed. If the link is maintained and no external factors affect the operation, the operation will be a success and after this the link between these resources is insignificant. Hence, a broken link after the operation does not affect either of the resource. An example for OpenStack is a VM requires an image, for the creation operation.

Reliance defines a relationship between two resources that is critical for the survival of either one of the resource or both. If the link between these resources is cut at some point during the lifetime of these resources it will impact the existence of the resources and can lead to a failure condition. Involved resources are independent and one resource cannot alter the other resource. For example, in Kubernetes, a pod, when created with a secret, relies on this secret.

Composition consists of intrinsic dependencies between resources: the life cycle of the two resources are linked. The creation of resource A implies the creation (and respectively the destruction) of resource B. Composition is obviously wider, as one resource can be linked to a collection of other resources, which in their turn can also depend on sub-resources. For example, in OpenStack a stack can be composed of VMs, and in Kubernetes, a deployment is composed of pods.

2.4   Creation Patterns for Replication/cross Operations

As mentioned, the goal of the relationship model is to ensure that Cheops operations are done thoroughly when the manipulated resource is not elementary, but depends on other resources. We discuss in this paragraph the various cases.

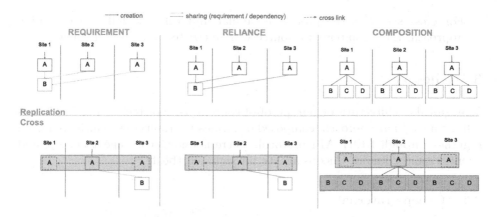

Fig. 4. Behaviors to observe following the dependencies

Requirement. For a replication or a cross scenario, the user have the choice to first replicate B everywhere A will be; in this case, the creation of A can be executed without specifying the location of B, it will be executed locally on each site. The other choice is to specify the dependency in the creation request, which is represented in Fig. 4.

1. Using sharing, the user specifies that a resource B required is on *Site*1.
2. Cheops intercepts the request to get a resource from another site when it will be sent by the service needing it.
3. Cheops transfers the request to get resource B from *Site*1.
4. Resource B is received and the usual flow is executed.
5. Since Resource B is only required for some operations, this dependency is stored in Cheops database for further usage (in these operations).

Reliance. This relationship follows a similar approach from requirement for replication and cross. The primary objective being to preserve the strong relationship between the resources A and B, Cheops needs to ensure the reachability of Resource B.

As before, a user can still replicate Resource B to ensure that Resource A will not suffer from a network partition. Otherwise, the process is the same as the requirement, except for: first, the dependency information needs to be stored in Cheops database for resource B to warn users against resources failures in replicas in case of a deletion of B. Second, Cheops needs to warn the users of affected resources (replicas of resource A) in case of network partition that affects B, because they will be in a failure state.

Composition. For replication scenario, a copy of resource A is created on the involved sites which in turn creates resources B, C and D on each of these sites with a *cascading effect* from the normal, local execution of the creation of A. An update on resource A for a secondary layer resource B, C or D is propagated across the involved sites and also follows normal execution on each site. Network split brain is managed through the Raft protocol that ensures eventual consistency between all replicas.

For cross scenario, the process is similar and will also follow a cascading approach. Each compound resource will be created in a cross manner.

3 Cheops

The global architecture of our proof-of-concept is depicted in Fig. 5. Cheops follows a modular approach, composed of various microservices, which are linked together through REST API protocol. There is one Cheops agent per site and agents monitor known Cheops agents through heartbeats.

3.1 Cheops Internals

Cheops agents are divided into two main components which are Cheops Core API and Cheops Glue.

Cheops Core consists of the communication, interface and database modules. The communication module creates a service mesh around the involved sites. This module also talks with the core API module in the core. Core API is a management module created for the framework that acts as a service which interconnects all the services inside Cheops.

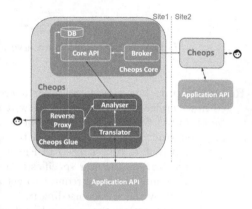

Fig. 5. Cheops architecture

Cheops Glue is designed to help Cheops Core translate Cheops API requests into the respective application API and vice-versa. Since each application has its own pattern for intercepting API, Glue helps in understanding these patterns and convert them to an agnostic API for Core. It is developed independently to an application. The analyser service in Glue evaluates the request from scope-lang and converts it into a generic request understandable by the Core API service, while the translator do the reverse operation. Cheops Glue also manages the creation of extra business logic for divisibility property of cross collaboration for specific types of resource. It also handles the network requirements and implements the relationship model.

3.2 Validation

We demonstrated the correctness of our proposal on Kubernetes. The feasibility for the collaborations were studied for replication and cross operations:

- For replication, we manipulated replicated pods across two sites.
- For cross, we created a namespace and performed a few operations to validate the existence of the namespace across the two sites.

Experiments have been performed over two sites of the Grid'5000 experimental testbed [1] (Rennes and Nantes). These instances were completely independent of each other and local to the infrastructure. On each site, we deployed a Kubernetes cluster, composed of one master and one worker node, as well as a Cheops agent.

The goal of the experiments was to validate the expected behaviour. Table 1 and Table 2 presents the results.

Table 1. Replication Kubernetes CLI requests

Operation	Location	Result
Kubectl create pod purple –scope{Site1&Site2}	Site1	Pod *purple* created on Site1 and Site2
Kubectl create pod violet –scope{Site1&Site2}	Site2	Pod *violet* created on Site1 and Site2
Kubectl get pod violet	Site1	Pod *violet* from Site1 is displayed
Kubectl get pod violet	Site2	Pod *violet* from Site2 is displayed

Table 2. Cross Kubernetes CLI requests

Operation	Location	Result
Kubectl create ns foo –scope{Site1%Site2}	Site1	Namespace created on Site1 and Site2
Kubectl create pod blue -n namespace foo –scope{Site1}	Site2	Pod created under namespace *foo* in Site1 extended to Site2
Kubectl create pod yellow -n namespace foo –scope{Site2}	Site1	Pod created under namespace *foo* in Site2 extended to Site1
Kubectl get pods -n namespace foo	Site1	Shows all resources from *foo* namespace from Site1 and Site2
Kubectl create pod yellow -n namespace foo	Site1	Error: Pod already exist in Site2 under namespace *foo*

4   Related Work

Popular solutions such as Rancher[2], Volterra[3] or Google Anthos[4] geo-distribute a service to the Edge with a centralised approach. In these approaches, sites are not autonomous, centralised single source of truth and additional details are added to the business logic. Our solution focuses on forming a decentralized P2P set of autonomous application instances without changing the application code.

---

[2] https://rancher.com Accessed 2022-07-06.
[3] https://medium.com/volterra-io/tagged/kubernetes Accessed 2022-03-20.
[4] https://cloud.google.com/anthos Accessed 2022-07-06.

Istio[5] uses a sidecar mechanism to intercept all the requests at the resource level. It creates an individual sidecar or a broker for each service as opposed to Cheops which manages all microservices at each site with a single broker.

MiCADO-Edge [9] extends cloud operator to edge. It uses the KubeEdge [10] to orchestrate. Mck8s [7] is another similar solution with geo-distribution application deployments. The solution is created as a wrap around KubeFed[6]. These Framework provides primarily a centralised approach to manage the resources without the Edge sites autonomy like our solution.

Hybrid control planes such as OneEdge [6] brings autonomony to the Edge. This solution is quite similar to our proposal but the centralised aspect still makes this solution an unsuitable candidate for us.

TOSCA [2] is a framework which standardises a deployment pattern across platforms. Our solution aims not at avoid creating any additional code, but to allow collaborations between sites without changes in code.

5   Future Work and Conclusion

In this paper we presented our service-mesh like framework, Cheops, that allows Devops to geo-distribute a micro-services based application following a REST API without requiring intrusive changes in the business logic. This service mesh relies on these applications modularity and the deployment of instances of the application on each site composing the Edge infrastructure.

Cheops relies on scope-lang, a DSL we previously introduced to allow users to explicit the execution location of their requests as well as the type of collaborations between the different service instances. To ensure the correctness of each collaboration, Cheops relies also on a relationship model we introduced. Finally, we demonstrated the relevance our approach on simple collaborations across different sites.

We are currently working on a model to introduce patterns for application code for cross collaboration which requires a step further. As discussed above, we also need to focus on tolerance for intermittent networks across collaborations. Finally, one future area of focus will be to add control loops in Cheops in order to optimize the placement of resources. In our current version of the approach, DevOps need to manually specify the location, and finding the optimal site may be an additional overhead. We claim our approach to bring existing Cloud applications to the Edge without entangling any geo-distribution code in the business logic is crucial to stimulate the shift to include Edge sites in the global capabilities of the Cloud.

---

[5] https://istio.io Accessed 2022-07-06.
[6] https://github.com/kubernetes-sigs/kubefed Accessed 2022-07-06.

References

1. Balouek, D., et al.: Adding virtualization capabilities to the grid'5000 testbed. In: Ivanov, I.I., van Sinderen, M., Leymann, F., Shan, T. (eds.) CLOSER 2012. CCIS, vol. 367, pp. 3–20. Springer, Cham (2013). https://doi.org/10.1007/978-3-319-04519-1_1

2. Binz, T., Breitenbücher, U., Kopp, O., Leymann, F.: Tosca: portable automated deployment and management of cloud applications. In: Bouguettaya, A., Sheng, Q., Daniel, F. (eds.) Advanced Web Services, pp. 527–549. Springer, New York (2014). https://doi.org/10.1007/978-1-4614-7535-4_22

3. Cherrueau, R.-A., Delavergne, M., Lèbre, A.: Geo-distribute cloud applications at the edge. In: Sousa, L., Roma, N., Tomás, P. (eds.) Euro-Par 2021. LNCS, vol. 12820, pp. 301–316. Springer, Cham (2021). https://doi.org/10.1007/978-3-030-85665-6_19

4. Li, W., et al.: Service mesh: challenges, state of the art, and future research opportunities. In: 2019 IEEE International Conference on Service-Oriented System Engineering (SOSE), pp. 122–1225 (2019)

5. Lottiaux, R., et al.: OpenMosix, OpenSSI and Kerrighed: a comparative study. In: IEEE International Symposium on Cluster Computing and the Grid, CCGrid 2005, vol. 2, pp. 1016–1023. IEEE (2005)

6. Saurez, E., Gupta, H., Daglis, A., Ramachandran, U.: OneEdge: an efficient control plane for geo-distributed infrastructures. In: Proceedings of the ACM Symposium on Cloud Computing, pp. 182–196 (2021)

7. Tamiru, M., Pierre, G., Tordsson, J., Elmroth, E.: mck8s: an orchestration platform for geo-distributed multi-cluster environments. In: 30th International Conference on Computer Communications and Networks, ICCCN 2021 (2021)

8. Tran, T.X., Hajisami, A., Pandey, P., Pompili, D.: Collaborative mobile edge computing in 5G networks: new paradigms, scenarios, and challenges. IEEE Commun. Mag. **55**(4), 54–61 (2017)

9. Ullah, A., Dagdeviren, H., Ariyattu, R.C., DesLauriers, J., Kiss, T., Bowden, J.: MiCADO-Edge: towards an application-level orchestrator for the cloud-to-edge computing continuum. J. Grid Comput. **19**(4), 1–28 (2021)

10. Xiong, Y., Sun, Y., Xing, L., Huang, Y.: Extend cloud to edge with KubeEdge. In: 2018 IEEE/ACM Symposium on Edge Computing (SEC), pp. 373–377 (2018). https://doi.org/10.1109/SEC.2018.00048

GreenFog: A Framework for Sustainable Fog Computing

Adel N. Toosi[1]($\boxtimes$)(iD), Chayan Agarwal[1], Lena Mashayekhy[2](iD),
Sara K. Moghaddam[1](iD), Redowan Mahmud[3](iD), and Zahir Tari[4](iD)

[1] Department of Software Systems and Cybersecurity, Faculty of Information
Technology, Monash University, Clayton, VIC, Australia
`adel.n.toosi@monash.edu`
[2] Department of Computer and Information Sciences, University of Delaware,
Newark, USA
`mlena@udel.ed`
[3] School of Electrical Engineering, Computing and Mathematical Sciences, Curtin
University, Perth, Australia
`mdredowan.mahmud@curtin.edu.au`
[4] School of Computing Technologies, STEM College, RMIT University, Melbourne,
Australia
`zahir.tari@rmit.edu.a`

Abstract. The alarming rate of increase in energy demand and carbon
footprint of Fog environments has become a critical issue. It is, therefore, necessary to reduce the percentage of brown energy consumption
in these systems and integrate renewable energy use into Fog. Renewables, however, are prone to availability fluctuations due to their variable
and intermittent nature. In this paper, we propose a new Fog framework
and design various optimization techniques, including linear programming optimization, linear regression estimation, and Multi-Armed Bandit (MAB) learning to optimize renewable energy use in the Fog based
on a novel idea of load shaping with adaptive Quality of Service (QoS).
The proposed framework, along with the optimization techniques, are
tested on a real-world micro data center (Fog environment) powered by
solar energy sources connected to multiple IoT devices. The results show
that our proposed framework significantly reduces the difference between
renewable energy generation and total energy consumption while efficiently adjusting the QoS of applications.

1 Introduction

The rise of IoT and Fog computing elicits an increase in global energy consumption and has a massive impact on the carbon footprint of the ICT (Information
Communication Technology) industry. Therefore, Fog computing requires inno-
vations in energy supply, management, and use [13]. To further lower the carbon
footprint of the IoT ecosystem, it is widely accepted that renewable or green
energy sources must be used as the primary power supply of Fog environments.

© The Author(s), under exclusive license to Springer Nature Switzerland AG 2022
J. Troya et al. (Eds.): ICSOC 2022, LNCS 13740, pp. 540–549, 2022.
https://doi.org/10.1007/978-3-031-20984-0_38

Many researchers have proposed using green energy to power Fog micro data centers [3–5,7,10,12]. They focused on various techniques to optimize renewable energy use. Li *et al.* [7] suggested task placement and scheduling. Karimiafshar *et al.* [3,5] proposed load balancing, and Toor *et al.* [10] and Karimiafshar *et al.* [4] proposed dynamic voltage and frequency scaling.

Nevertheless, the primary challenge of powering Fog environments with renewable energy sources such as solar is the *intermittency* and *variability* of power input. While different methods have been proposed to address this, a promising solution of matching demand to supply of green and renewable energy via load shaping has received little attention. In this paper, we propose a framework called *GreenFog* that conducts load shaping of a Fog environment powered by on-site renewable energy. This framework operates without the usage of a battery as we believe the installation of battery storage for Fog environments is often prohibitive [2]. Our proposed load shaping method happens through dynamic adjustment of Quality of Service (QoS) for IoT applications. According to the adjusted QoS, GreenFog horizontally scales the application software containers, the latest norm for building IoT applications. At the same time, GreenFog controls the QoS of tasks submitted to the gateway, e.g., the frame rate or image quality at which the video streaming data must be processed. Thus, the **key contributions** of the paper are as follows:

- A framework called *GreenFog* for dynamic QoS management of the IoT application based on load shaping in a renewable-powered Fog environment.
- The optimal offline model for load shaping with prior knowledge of renewables availability that sets the required QoS for the hosted IoT application.
- A fast and lightweight reactive heuristic approach based on a linear regression model and profiling to overcome the complexity of the optimal model and lack of prior knowledge of energy availability.
- A machine learning technique using Multi Armed Bandit (MAB), which automatically learns how QoS adjustment affects energy consumption and dynamically adapts QoS to maximize renewable energy utilization.
- The performance evaluation of the proposed load shaping algorithms in a practical implementation using real-world traces of renewable energy and an object detection application demonstrator in live video streams.

2   System Overview and GreenFog Framework

Our Fog environment is powered by an on-site renewable energy generation system with a grid-tied inverter that can work without batteries. The Fog environment is a multi-server cluster that monitors its own power consumption and can trace the amount of generated renewable power available for usage. It is connected to both the grid (brown energy) for reliability and an on-site renewable energy system (green energy) to reduce its carbon footprint. Note that grid energy is used whenever renewable energy is insufficient.

Figure 1 illustrates the architecture of our proposed software framework and its various software components. IoT devices are connected to a gateway device through which they send their processing tasks (requests) to Fog. In our proposed framework, the IoT devices have APIs that allow gateway software to dynamically adapt QoS requirements remotely by setting configurations at the IoT devices. The QoS adjustment is performed within an acceptable Service Level Agreement (SLA) via a comparison between the available renewable power and the current power consumption.

We assume that the Fog environment hosts the IoT applications in the form of containerized micro-services (e.g., Docker). Fog is equipped with a cluster manager and container orchestrator software (e.g., K3s[1]) for automating deployment, scaling, and management of containers. A *master node* runs a *scheduler* program interacting with the gateway software, thereby informing the expected QoS. The scheduler also

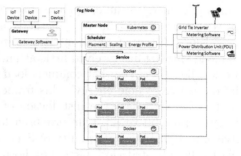

Fig. 1. GreenFog software system overview

interacts with the energy metering software (*energy profile*), which monitors the available green energy and the current power consumption. Through its placement algorithm, the scheduler makes a decision regarding the *placement* of container instances (Pods in Kubernetes terminology) on different worker nodes. Another major component of GreenFog is the *scaling* component, which is responsible for the autoscaling of resources.

Due to the high volume of data generated by cameras and the low latency requirements of real-time video analytics, in this paper, we mainly focus on detecting objects in live video streams [1,8]. For many video analytics applications, the data quality directly drives the QoS and resource demand. For instance, the accuracy of an object detection algorithm in a pest bird repellent system can be lowered to reduce resource usage of energy constraint devices [9]. Therefore, we set the image rate as QoS for our video analytics. In the following, we propose different optimization techniques to scale resources and adjust QoS in GreenFog.

3   Optimization Model

Assuming time is divided into time slots, we have $t = \{0, \ldots, T\}$, where T is the decision horizon. The green energy system $\mathcal{G}$ at any time t generates e^t units of electricity. We assume that the value of e^t for any time slot t is known *a priori* considering the optimal model is offline and only used as the baseline. The Fog environment $\mathcal{F}$ is a Kubernetes cluster that consists of N nodes (or worker machines). Each node $n_i \in N$ hosts at most P pods, where each pod holds a single container. Therefore, the Fog environment has the maximum of $C = P \times N$ containers in full capacity, and at each time t only some containers ($\leq C$) become

---

[1] K3s is a lightweight Kubernetes distribution suitable for resource-constrained environments such as Fog or Edge.

active to match the demand based on available energy e^t for that time slot. When the demand exceeds the renewable power availability, the gateway adjusts QoS to match demand with the available power. Each pod requires e_p units of electricity. Each node runs on a different virtual machine. If a node is not needed, the system simply puts the machine in a shutdown state. Each physical machine requires e_b units of energy in a shutdown state, while a running machine requires additional e_n units of energy. Each task requires e_j units of energy added to other energy terms. Moreover, there is an upper limit on the total energy consumption when running all the containers (r_{max}) and a lower limit when running one container (r_{min}). Note that in our formulations, for the sake of simplicity, we consider request rate as the only QoS factor, e.g., frame rate in our video analytics example. Other QoS factors, such as resolution, can be included in our model similarly. We also assume that each request is mapped to an IoT task in the system, e.g., an image (frame) to an image processing task.

We consider a set of homogeneous tasks generated by the IoT application. The required processing time of a task is denoted by c. The goal of GreenFog is to choose the best rate for the IoT tasks and adjust them accordingly based on the available renewable power input. We define sets of decision variables: x_i^t to determine the number of active pods at node n_i; y^t to determine the arrival rate of requests from IoT devices; and z_i^t to determine if node n_i should be on or off. Our objective is to minimize excess energy usage (brown energy usage) and determine the arrival rates of IoT tasks. We formulate this problem as an Integer Program (IP) as follows:

$$\text{Minimize} \sum_{t=1}^{T} E^t, \text{where } E^t = \sum_{n_i \in N} (e_p \cdot x_i^t + e_n \cdot z_i^t + e_b) + (e_j \cdot y^t) \qquad (1)$$

Subject to:

$$E^t \geq e^t \qquad \forall t \in T \qquad (2)$$

$$x_i^t \leq P \qquad \forall n_i \in N, t \in T \qquad (3)$$

$$x_i^t \leq \mathbf{M} \cdot z_i^t \qquad \forall n_i \in N, t \in T \qquad (4)$$

$$\sum_{n_i \in N} z_i^t \leq N \qquad \forall t \in T \qquad (5)$$

$$r_{min} \leq y^t \leq r_{max} \qquad t \in T \qquad (6)$$

$$c \cdot y^t = \sum_{n_i \in N} x_i^t \qquad \forall t \in T \qquad (7)$$

$$x_i^t \in \mathbb{Z}_{\geq 0} \qquad \forall n_i \in N, t \in T \qquad (8)$$

$$y^t \in \mathbb{Z}_{\geq 0} \qquad \forall t \in T \qquad (9)$$

$$z_i^t \in \{0, 1\} \qquad \forall n_i \in N, t \in T \qquad (10)$$

The objective function minimizes the total brown energy consumption subject to the following constraints. Constraint (2) guarantees that all generated renewable energy must be used. Constraint (3) guarantees that each node has at most P pods. Constraint (4) ensures that the energy cost of turning on a node should be calculated only once. This means that if any pod has already been deployed on a node, there is no additional cost for the node but for new pods. We model this using the *Big M* method.[2] Constraint (5) ensures that the Fog environment does not exceed its capacity of N nodes. Constraint (6) ensures that the selected rate for the IoT tasks is between its minimum and maximum rates in SLA. Constraint (7) ensures that enough pods are running to service all the incoming tasks. To ensure this, we multiply the processing time for each job c with the rate of incoming tasks at time t, which is denoted by y^t, and we match this product with the total number of pods running at time t denoted by $\sum_{n_i \in N} x_i^t$. Constraints (8) and (9) guarantee that the decision variables x_i^t and y^t are non-negative integers, respectively. Constraints (10) guarantee that decision variable z_i^t is binary.

4   Linear Regression Algorithm

It is challenging to use the proposed IP model in practice. Therefore, we propose a heuristic approach based on a regression model using profiling to set QoS and scale resources. Since such a regression model only gives the rate of tasks as output, we propose a threshold-based autoscaling algorithm in Sect. 5 to scale the Kubernetes cluster. Profiling is necessary to gather the data needed to develop regression. For profiling, we identify the power consumption at different task rates. Our profiling results show that there is a simple linear correlation between the power consumption and the rate of tasks (See Sect. 7.1). Accordingly, we set α (y-intercept) and β (the slope) of the linear regression equation. We first read the current availability of green power generation. Then, we set the acceptable rate of the tasks at the gateway software in a way that Fog can fully utilize the available green energy.

5   Threshold-Based Linear Autoscaler

We propose a threshold-based autoscaler with two thresholds to keep the average pending number of tasks between the minimum and the maximum pod load thresholds. The creation/removal of a pod is performed linearly in a way that nodes should be fully packed/emptied before adding/removing a new node. If all of the currently switched-on nodes are fully utilized, and we require to add pods, we switch on a new machine (a node) and start allocating new pods to it. Using this method, we increase the number of pods allocated to a node until it cannot host any more pods; then, we add a node to the list. At any given time, there may be a node with no pods allocated to it. These nodes are removed, and we switch off machines with no active nodes to save energy. As we need to iterate through all P pods running on maximum N nodes, the time complexity of the Autoscaler algorithm is $O(NP)$.

6   Multi-Armed Bandit Approach

Specific knowledge, preliminary to the implementation, is required by the IP and linear regression algorithms. To address this problem, we propose an online

---

[2] Big M method is a method of solving linear programming problems using simplex.

machine learning model based on the Multi-Armed Bandit (MAB) approach [6] using the Upper Confidence Bound (UCB) method. In our MAB problem, the agent needs to choose among five different actions (arms) referring to varying the rate of tasks (QoS): 1) increase rate high, 2) increase rate low, 3) do nothing, 4) decrease rate low, and 5) decrease rate high. All these actions have rewards set between 0 to 1, initially valued at 0.5. The obtained rewards depend on the difference between the available renewable energy and the energy consumed. When the system is stable, our MAB-based algorithm computes the reward for the last choice made using a reward function. The stable condition is achieved when there is no change in the number of pods by the Autoscaler for the last four consecutive time slots. MAB algorithms generally have polynomial time complexity.

7 Performance Evaluation

Hardware: The setup contains 3 Dell servers managed by OpenStack and connected to Eaton ePDUs, allowing us to monitor the power consumption of the servers. A total of 5 Virtual Machines (VMs) can be hosted, out of which one acts as a Kubernetes master and others as Kubernetes nodes (workers). The master VM runs on the main server alone, and the rest are running on the other two physical servers (2 VMs on each physical server). Each VM has 16 GB of Memory, 8 VCPUs and 160 GB of Disk space. We limit the maximum resources (CPU, Memory, etc.) that can be used by each pod. Every VM can accommodate up to 5 pods, including the master VM, with a total of 25 pods for all VMs. Apart from the servers, we use a group of three Raspberry Pi Model 3B+ to act as IoT devices. The Raspberry Pis use the Pi Camera Module v2.

Software: The Raspberry Pis run a client code taking images and sending them to the Kubernetes service running on the master node. They also run a flask server with RESTful APIs through which we can set the image rate. The flask server accepts the interval in seconds that images are sent (minimum of 0.3 s). The maximum power consumption of our system is around 1 KW, whereas the maximum renewable energy available in the traces is also roughly 1 kWh as anything above will not be utilized by the servers. We have not taken into account the energy needed for cooling or other power consumption sources and renewable power is solely utilized for server power consumption. We deploy YOLO V3 (You Only Look Once), an object detection technology, as a service in the pods to process the image data sent by the Raspberry Pis to the endpoint of the Kubernetes service. We implemented the Gateway software which interacts with the master node and the Raspberry Pis, that evenly sets the rate provided by the master node across all three Raspberry Pis.

Renewable Energy Trace: The renewable energy traces used for all the experiments are based on the availability of solar energy for a location of a data center in Lyon, France. We used the data traces for the Global Horizontal Irradiance (GHI) at the location to calculate the output for the solar photovoltaics (PV) power with one-hour granularity between the 20th and 21st of September, 2007. For more details see our previous paper [11].

7.1   Results

Linear Regression with Linear Autoscaling: The linear regression model requires profiling for different rates of images while the Autoscaler changes the number of pods according to the average number of pending tasks. The lower and upper thresholds for the Autoscaler are set at 10 and 15, respectively. Then, we identify the power consumption for different rates. For each rate, we wait until the Fog environment becomes stable. We fit a linear regression model where the power consummation is the explanatory variable and the rate (Images per Second) is the dependent variable. Figure 2 shows how well the regression model predicts the power consumption compared to the actual data (α (y-intercept) = -0.2535 and β (slope) = 0.00324).

We ran the linear regression model with the Autoscaler. To reduce the duration of experiments, we scale every hour in renewable energy traces into a 15-min interval. However, we report the results based on the 24-h scale. The total absolute energy difference between the available renewable energy and the energy consumed in the 24-h test is 4.886 kWh as shown by the shaded area in Fig. 3(a). The sudden spikes and dips deviating from the renewable energy are due to Autoscaler's performance. As it increases the

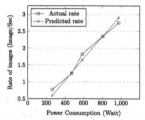

Fig. 2. Regression model predictions vs actual values

number of pods linearly (1 after another), getting the correct number of pods to handle the incoming tasks might take some time. Therefore, the average pending tasks in each pod could fluctuate to extreme limits. In addition, a node shutdown might take 10–12 min, adding a considerable latency to reach stability.

IP Model with Linear Autoscaling: We use the IP model from Sect. 3 with the default Linear Autoscaler from Sect. 5. The IP model requires certain information about the system, such as energy consumed per pod, energy consumed by the servers when running or shut down, the energy needed to service a task, and the processing time it takes for a task. To obtain the energy consumed per pod, we ran the system with one VM (master) with two pods running, and then we scaled the deployment by adding another pod to the same VM

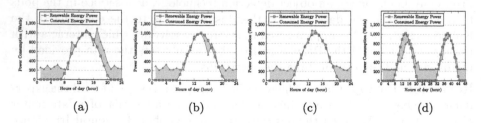

| (a) | (b) | (c) | (d) |

Fig. 3. GreenFog with different optimization methods: (a) Linear regression with linear autoscaler, (b) IP with linear autoscaler, (c) IP with direct scaler, and (d) MAB with linear autoscaler

to record the rise in energy consumption. For energy consumed by the servers, we first switched off the server and recorded the power consumption; then, we switched on the system and noted the difference in power consumption. To figure out the energy needed to service a task, we ran GreenFog with Linear Autoscaler and then we sent one image every second and waited until the cluster becomes stable and noted down the power consumption; from this value we subtracted the values obtained previously like the energy per pod and the energy per node in On/Off state appropriately to get the energy per task.

If such information is known, this model can provide the number of servers that should be running, how many pods in each server are required, and also the acceptable rate of jobs which helps in setting QoS. In this experiment, we ignore scaling information provided by the IP model and we use the Linear Autoscaler instead. The results are shown in Fig. 3(b), illustrating that the IP model with Linear Autoscaler has 16% less absolute energy consumption difference compared to the Linear Regression model for the same data by being 4.095 kWh compared to the 4.886 kWh, respectively. In the next section, we investigate the performance of the IP model if scaling information is provided by the model itself.

IP with Direct Scaler: Figure 3(c) shows the results of the experiments for the IP model with its scaling information called *Direct Scaler*, which utilizes all the decision variables from the IP model. The Direct Scaler receives the information owing to which nodes are to be switched On/Off, and the number of pods that should be running in each node from the IP model. The IP model also sets the rate of images (QoS) that should be sent to the gateway software. Figure 3(c) shows a considerably smooth power consumption pattern with a lower number of spikes compared to the previous methods. The IP model with Direct Scaler has 25% less absolute energy consumption difference compared to the Linear Regression model for the same data by being 3.677 kWh compared to the 4.886 kWh, respectively. Similarly, it is 10% less compared to 4.095 kWh for the IP model with Linear Autoscaler.

MAB Model with Linear Autoscaling: Figure 3(d) depicts power consumption for the GreenFog Framework, where the MAB model with the Linear Autoscaler is used. We conducted two days of experiments, where the first day would provide the MAP model with the opportunity to learn the system's patterns. The renewable energy data is the same across two days to show the best achievable results by MAB. The total absolute energy difference in the second day is 4.164 kWh. This is 14% better than the linear regression model and about the same as the IP model with Linear Autoscaler. However, as we expected, the baseline IP model with Direct Scaler outperforms the MAB model by 11%. Given proper training data, the MAB model outperforms other approaches.

8   Conclusions and Future Work

We proposed GreenFog, a framework to optimize green energy use for Fog environments with on-site renewable electricity generation. We designed and implemented an Integer Programming optimization model with exact energy requirements knowledge for different components to use as a baseline. We proposed a heuristic approach based on linear regression to overcome the limitations of the IP. Since the performance of the Linear Regression model relies on accurate profiling, we proposed a machine learning model based on the Multi-Armed Bandit problem. We evaluated and validated the GreenFog framework equipped with these optimization techniques on a real testbed. We measured the actual power usage and response times with a practical IoT application and realistic traces of renewable energy. In the future, we are interested in developing a model to work based on forecasting future renewable energy availability. We further look into solving this problem with other machine learning methods, such as deep reinforcement learning.

References

1. Ananthanarayanan, G., et al.: Real-time video analytics: the killer app for edge computing. Computer **50**(10), 58–67 (2017)
2. Goiri, I.N., et al.: GreenSlot: scheduling energy consumption in green datacenters. In: Proceedings of 2011 International Conference for High Performance Computing, Networking, Storage and Analysis, SC 2011. Association for Computing Machinery, New York (2011). https://doi.org/10.1145/2063384.2063411
3. Karimiafshar, A., Hashemi, M.R., Heidarpour, M.R., Toosi, A.N.: An energy-conservative dispatcher for fog-enabled IIoT systems: when stability and timeliness matter. IEEE Trans. Serv. Comput., 1 (2021). https://doi.org/10.1109/TSC.2021.3114964
4. Karimiafshar, A., Hashemi, M.R., Heidarpour, M.R., Toosi, A.N.: Effective utilization of renewable energy sources in fog computing environment via frequency and modulation level scaling. IEEE Internet Things J. **7**(11), 10912–10921 (2020)
5. Karimiafshar, A., Hashemi, M.R., Heidarpour, M.R., Toosi, A.N.: A request dispatching method for efficient use of renewable energy in fog computing environments. Futur. Gener. Comput. Syst. **114**, 631–646 (2021)
6. Lattimore, T., Csaba, S.: Bandit Algorithms. Cambridge University Press, Cambridge (2020)
7. Li, W., et al.: On enabling sustainable edge computing with renewable energy resources. IEEE Commun. Mag. **56**(5), 94–101 (2018)
8. Ma, W., Mashayekhy, L.: Quality-aware video offloading in mobile edge computing: a data-driven two-stage stochastic optimization. In: Proceedings of the 14th IEEE International Conference on Cloud Computing, pp. 594–599 (2021)
9. Mahmud, R., Toosi, A.N.: Con-Pi: a distributed container-based edge and fog computing framework. IEEE Internet Things J. **9**(6), 4125–4138 (2022)
10. Toor, A., et al.: Energy and performance aware fog computing: a case of DVFS and green renewable energy. Future Gener. Comput. Syst. **101**, 1112–1121 (2019)
11. Toosi, A.N., Qu, C., de Assunção, M.D., Buyya, R.: Renewable-aware geographical load balancing of web applications for sustainable data centers. J. Netw. Comput. Appl. **83**, 155–168 (2017)

12. Zeng, D., Gu, L., Yao, H.: Towards energy efficient service composition in green energy powered cyber-physical fog systems. Futur. Gener. Comput. Syst. **105**, 757–765 (2020)
13. Zhang, G., Chen, Y., Shen, Z., Wang, L.: Distributed energy management for multiuser mobile-edge computing systems with energy harvesting devices and QoS constraints. IEEE Internet Things J. **6**(3), 4035–4048 (2019)

Artificial Intelligence and Machine Learning for Service Computing

FedHF: A High Fairness Federated Learning Algorithm Based on Deconfliction in Heterogeneous Networks

Zhipeng Gao[✉], Yingwen Duan, Yang Yang, Lanlan Rui, and Chen Zhao

State Key Laboratory of Networking and Switching Technology,
Beijing University of Posts and Telecommunications, Beijing 100876, China
{gaozhipeng,ywduan,yyang,llrui,zc_zhaochen}@bupt.edu.cn

Abstract. In large-scale machine learning, federated learning (FL) is considered as a promising paradigm to address the problem of data privacy breach. Previous works have focused on improving fairness in terms of fair resource allocation. However, this is not sufficient considering that federated learning is essentially distributed training with average aggregation. Because low-contributing nodes, even if they are assigned more computational resources, are diluted by large-weighted nodes in aggregation. In particular, fair resource allocation for sophisticated systems is not realistic for real scenarios. In this paper, we propose FedHF, a new hierarchical fair federated learning framework with robust convergence and high fairness. FedHF improves upon naive combinations of federated learning and fair resource allocation with a hierarchy-based optimization of client selection algorithm and a conflict elimination method for fairness and discriminatory incentives. Through extensive experimental validation of our approach, we show that FedHF outperforms previous state-of-the-art methods.

Keywords: Distributed machine learning · Federated learning · Fairness

1 Introduction

Federated learning (FL) [1] produces efficient and private statistical models by aggregating knowledge from different data sources [2], which is mainly the gradients of the models rather than users' private data. However, many constraints (fairness, robustness, and privacy security, etc.) in real-world scenarios hinder federated learning algorithm from being deployed in practice [3]. In this paper, we focus on how to satisfy simultaneously the fairness and accuracy of federated learning.

Fairness refers to ensuring that the performance variance of all nodes in the system is constrained to a certain bound [4–7], whereas statistical heterogeneity is the root cause of unfairness [8]. There is significant variability in system

© The Author(s), under exclusive license to Springer Nature Switzerland AG 2022
J. Troya et al. (Eds.): ICSOC 2022, LNCS 13740, pp. 553–566, 2022.
https://doi.org/10.1007/978-3-031-20984-0_39

characteristics (network outages, temporary withdrawals, etc.) and differences in hardware and data sources (i.e., heterogeneity) lead to the existence of strong and weak nodes in the network [9,10]. Strong nodes typically possess abundant resources and network conditions, while weak nodes possess the opposite. During the iterative process of the central aggregation model, strong nodes are granted a superior chance of selection and considerable weights. As a result, they are afforded the ability to retain their contributions in each round of aggregation, which helps to subsequent personalized model generate. Weak nodes, on the other hand, often find it difficult to enjoy this positive feedback. This unfairness can reduce the willingness of weak nodes to participate in federated aggregation significantly.

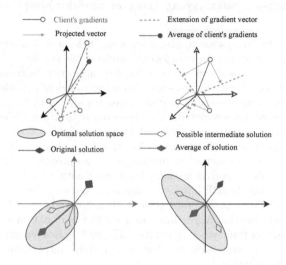

Fig. 1. Aggregation results from different optimization strategies (in 3D and 2D respectively). The 3D diagram illustrates that when multiple conflicting gradients ($g_a \cdot g_b < 0, g_a \cdot g_c < 0, g_b \cdot g_c < 0$) are aggregated, the magnitude and direction of the final gradient will be determined by the gradient of the strong node [8], which will violate the principle of fairness. Consider projecting the gradient onto the normals of other gradients, which can resolve the conflict between this gradient and other gradients, thus improving the fairness principle of the aggregation algorithm. The 2D diagram illustrates that resolving the conflict of potential solutions can restrict the mean range of potential solutions, thus shrinking the magnitude of the solution space, which facilitates the convergence process.

Yu et al. [11] reveal a potential approach to solve the unfair problem, i.e., to ameliorate the discrimination suffered by weak nodes in the aggregation process by eliminating the conflict between model gradients. Yu considers that the two gradients are in conflict with each other when $g_a \cdot g_b < 0$. As shown in Fig. 1, the magnitude and direction of the final gradient after aggregation will be predetermined by the gradient of the strong node, which contravenes the fairness principle. Gradients project is a method to eliminate gradient conflict by projecting the gradient onto the normal of the target gradient to mitigate the ramifications of the gradient update on the adversary gradient [8,12–17]. Wang et al. [8] adopt an iterative method to eliminate conflicts between gradients in order to achieve a fair federal system. However, the method sacrifices too much accuracy in exchange for fairness, which will compromise the usability of the federated system. So it is eminently necessary to achieve a high fair federated learning framework under the premise of ensuring sufficient accuracy.

In this paper, we demonstrate a **Fed**erated Learning framework with **h**igh **f**airness, FedHF, which achieves a tradeoff between fairness and accuracy through a hierarchy-based optimization of a client selection algorithm and a conflict elimination approach with fair and discriminatory incentives. Then we propose a stage-based order to resolve conflicts between gradients, which limits the performance variance of strong and weak nodes by eliminating intra-layer and extra-layer conflicts. Finally we combine this into a federated aggregation workflow and conduct extensive experiments on multiple federation datasets to validate the advantages of our FedHF in terms of fairness and accuracy.

We summarize our contributions below:

– We propose a fair hierarchical client selection algorithm that improves the likelihood that weak nodes retain their original gradients.
– We eliminate the conflict between gradients to improve the discrimination of weak nodes during aggregation.
– We conduct extensive experiments on federated datasets and propose a pioneering experimental method to test the true fairness, verifying the effectiveness of our FedHF algorithm.

2   Preliminaries

In this section, we will present some background knowledge on federated learning and gradient conflict.

2.1   Federated Learning

In essence, federated learning is a special kind of distributed learning. Thousands of remote devices send their own local training parameter vectors or gradients to the curators. Under the coordination of centralized servers as aggregators, the participating learners collectively train a global shared model and conduct t rounds of iterations until the central model converges. The ultimate goal of the traditional FedAvg algorithm [1] is to find the optimal set of model parameters w^* that minimizes the global objective function:

$$w^* = \arg\min_w f(w) \quad where \quad f(w) = \sum_{i=1}^{N} \frac{p_i}{\mathcal{P}} F_i(w) \tag{1}$$

where $F_i(w)$ denotes the local objective of the remote client i. N is the total number of participating learners, and p_i is the contribution value of device i, where $\mathcal{P} = \sum_{i=1}^{N} p_i$. The FedAvg algorithm effectively minimizes the target at low communication cost, but the difference in p_i leads to an unfair result [4], which significantly impairs the fairness of the federated system.

2.2 Gradient Conflict

We use the definition in [14]. Consider two model gradients g_a and g_b:

Definition 1. *Suppose ϕ_{ab} is the angle between two model gradients g_a and g_b. We believe that the two gradients conflict with each other when $\cos\phi_{ab} < 0$, i.e., $g_a \cdot g_b < 0$.*

Definition 2. *We define Φ_{ab} is the gradient magnitude similarity between two gradients g_a and g_b where $\Phi_{ab} = \frac{2\|g_a\|_2 \cdot \|g_b\|_2}{\|g_a\|_2{}^2 + \|g_b\|_2{}^2}$.*

When two gradients have the same magnitude, this value is equal to 1. As the magnitudes of the gradients become dissimilar, this value becomes 0.

3 The FedHF System Workflow

In this section, we introduce the main workflow of FedHF and how it improves the fairness of the federation system in stages.

We assume that the federation system has a fraction of weak nodes endowed with meager computational resources and valid data. The overall scheme of FedHF is to minimize gradient conflicts, so as to keep the model updates of weak nodes from being compromised in weighted aggregation.

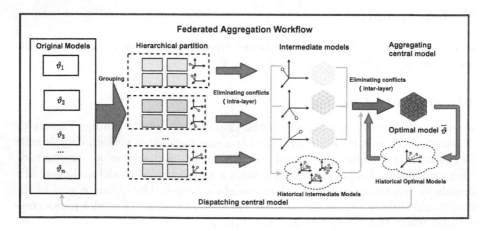

Fig. 2. A graphical representation of the federated aggregation workflow with four modules: local update, hierarchical partition, deconfliction, and central aggregation.

First, all clients perform local model update, which is consistent with other FL algorithms. Second, the central curator stratifies all user model parameters according to the magnitude of training accuracy. And after selecting a certain number of clients, the curator performs the work on eliminating intra-layer conflicts and historical intermediate model conflicts. Third, before participating in the central model aggregation, the representative updates of each layer should eliminate the extra-layer conflicts and conflicts of historical optimal models. Of course, the current results need to be piggybacked after each conflict elimination to be saved as historical model records.

Then we will present how FedHF works and Algorithm 1 reveals the detail.

Algorithm 1: Federated Aggregation Workflow

Server Execution:

Initialize: w_0, historical optimal gradients H_o^t.

while $t < T$ **do**

    for *each client $i \in Z_t$ **in parallel*** **do**

        $\Delta w_i^{t+1}, loss_i, acc_i \leftarrow$ **ClientUpdate**(i, w_i^t);

    $\overline{G_l} \leftarrow$ Hierarchical Stochastic Client Selection Workflow ;

    $G_L \leftarrow \{ \overline{G_1}, \dots \overline{G_L} \}$;

    $\overline{G_o^t} \leftarrow$ ExtraLayerDeconflict(G_L, H_o^t);

    Compute the optimal model $\theta_{t+1} \leftarrow \theta_t - \overline{G_o^t}$;

ClientUpdate (i, w_i^t):

    while $t < T_{threshold}$ **do**

        for $b \in \mathcal{B}$ **do**

            $w_i^{t+1} = w_i^t - \eta \nabla F_k(w_t; b) - \eta \cdot \mu(w_k^t - w_c^t)$

    return w_i^{t+1} ;

ExtraLayerDeconflict (G_L, H_o^t):

    $\overline{G_0} = \frac{1}{L} \sum_{k=1}^{L} G_k$;

    for *each $g_i \in \overline{G_L}, i = 1, 2, .. L_{num}$* **do**

        if $g_i \cdot \overline{G_0} < 0$ **then**

            $g_i = g_i - \frac{g_i \cdot \overline{G_0}}{||\overline{G_0}||^2} \cdot \overline{G_0}$

    $\overline{G_0^t} = \frac{1}{L} \sum_{k=1}^{L} \overline{G_k}$;

    for *round $t = T - i, i = 1, 2, .. T - 1$* **do**

        if $H_o^t \cdot \overline{G_o^t} >= 0$ **then**

            break;

        $\overline{G_o^t} = \overline{G_o^t} - \frac{\overline{G_o^t} \cdot H_o^t}{||H_o^t||^2} \cdot H_o^t$

    return $\overline{G_o^t}$;

3.1 Local Client Update

Because federated learning is essentially a kind of distributed learning, the training results of distributed nodes may be close to the locally optimal objective function but far from the global, failing that objective function being convergent. And the use of non-iid data for training, which makes the local objective function different for each node, exacerbates this situation. In this paper, we try to add constraints to the local subproblem to make the local devices closer to the global objective function:

$$h_i(w_i) = F_i(w_i) + \frac{\lambda}{2}||w_i - w||^2 \tag{2}$$

where w_i, w are the local model of client i and server model, respectively.

3.2 Hierarchical Partition

As described in Fig. 2, all participants send model information to the server rather than pre-selecting certain clients. This approach decouples the server from the clients to avoid accidental crashes of pre-selected clients. We propose a fair and incentivized strategy for efficient client selection. The central curator sequentially sorts the users according to their training accuracy and stratifies the sorting results. Obviously, the accuracy of all nodes in layer i is less than that in layer j, where $i < j$. We assign an intrinsic probability value to each node, on which the reward probability is assigned according to the loss value of each node, and then a client is randomly selected with this probability value.

The essence of this algorithm is to convert the competition between weak vs. strong nodes to strong vs. strong and weak vs. weak nodes. The hierarchical selection of participants ensures that weak nodes can also participate in federated aggregation. Figure 3 shows that this is a way to encourage devices to actively participate in the system, as it encourages each client to devote more computing power to aggregation. The scheme contributes to a fair distribution of resources.

The user gradients selected in round t are a mixed set of strong and weak gradients, and as discussed in Fig. 1, these gradients may conflict with each other. Since strong nodes always dominate in the conflict, we need to solve the conflict problem of strong and weak nodes beforehand. Consider a strong node a and a weak node b with conflicting gradients, where $||g_a|| >> ||g_b||$. Because federal learning uses average aggregation, the direction of the gradient after aggregation is always biased toward node a with a size close to $||g_a|| - ||g_b||$, i.e., $||g_a||$. We use gradient projection to resolve the conflict between strong and weak gradients by projecting the gradient of one client onto the normal plane of another client with conflicting gradients, and Theorem 1 demonstrates the feasibility of this.

Theorem 1. *Consider two conflicting model gradients g_a and g_b, we obtain an intermediate gradient $g_a^{(c)}$ by projecting g_a onto the normal of g_b. Thus, we get :*

$$g_a^{(c)} = \frac{g_a \cdot g_b}{||g_b||^2} g_b, \ a \neq b, g_a \cdot g_b < 0 \tag{3}$$

Algorithm 2: Hierarchical Stochastic Client Selection Workflow

---

Input: Clients fraction C and number N, number of layers L, historical
    gradients H_l^t, acc_i, $loss_i$.
Output: Intermediate clients' gradients $\overline{G_L}$.
Initialize: $M = C \cdot N$, $\alpha = M/L$, $L_{num} = N/L$;
Sort the clients' gradients by their accuracy and divide them into L layers,
    where $acc_{L_i}^t < acc_{L_{i+1}}^t$;
for *each layer $l \in L$ **in parallel*** **do**
    for $i < L_{num}$ **do**
        $V_i = tanh(loss_{l_i}^t)$;
        $V' = \sum_{i \in l} V_i$;
        $P_{l_i} = P_{base} + \frac{1-P_{base}}{L_{num}} \cdot \frac{V_i}{V'}$;
    $G_l^t \leftarrow$ Select α clients with the probability of P_{l_i} ;
    $\overline{G_l} \leftarrow$ **IntraLayerDeconflict**(G_l^t, G^t, H_l^t) ;
return $\overline{G_L}$;
IntraLayerDeconflict (G_l^t, G^t, H_l^t):
    for *each gradient $g_{l_k}^t \in G_l^t$ **in parallel*** **do**
        for *each $g_i^t \in G^t, i = 1, 2..L_{num}$* **do**
            if $i \neq k$ *and* $g_i^t \cdot g_{l_k}^t < 0$ **then**
                $g_{l_k}^t = g_{l_k}^t - \frac{g_{l_k}^t \cdot g_i^t}{||g_i^t||^2} \cdot g_i^t$

        for *roundt* $= T - i, i = 1, 2..T - 1$ **do**
            if $H_l^t \cdot g_{l_k}^t >= 0$ **then**
                break;
            $g_{l_k}^t = g_{l_k}^t - \frac{g_{l_k}^t \cdot H_l^t}{||H_l^t||^2} \cdot H_l^t$
    $\overline{G_l} \leftarrow \frac{1}{\alpha} \cdot \sum_{k=1}^{\alpha} g_{l_k}^t$;
    return $\overline{G_l}$;

Then we subtract $g_a^{(c)}$ from g_a to get g_a'.

$$g_a' = g_a - \frac{g_a \cdot g_b}{||g_b||^2} \tag{4}$$

Now g_a has been rectified to g'_a, which doesn't conflict with g_b:

$$g'_a \cdot g_b = g_a \cdot g_b - \frac{g_a \cdot g_b}{||g_b||^2} \cdot (g_b)^2 = 0 \tag{5}$$

We first propose a stage-based order to resolve conflicts between gradients. Each node $a \in$ *selected set* needs to resolve conflicts with the nodes $\in$ *selected set* first, which is called intra-layer conflict, to prevent the gradients from conflicting with each other in future central aggregation. Also, we notice that the gradients of each round of the selected set will also conflict with the gradients of the previous round, and if this conflict is not resolved, it will make the state update of each round lack of memorability. We add the historical intermediate model as a time factor to resolve the historical gradient conflicts. Finally we need to scale the length of the update because resolving the conflict between the gradients deflates the length of the gradients. See Algorithm 2 for the specific algorithm.

3.3   Global Discriminative Model Generation

With the hierarchical partition, we obtain a batch of intermediate gradients representing each layer. These gradient values are also subject to conflicts, which we call extra-layer conflicts. Obviously the conflicts are more intense than intra-layer conflicts, because the gradient gap is larger. Direct deconfliction will cause the aggregated model to deviate from the correct direction. Therefore, we adopt a compromised strategy to let the representative nodes and model averages undergo deconfliction. According to Theorem 1 (the later the customer gradient is used as the projection target, the less conflict between it and the final average gradient), consider node a in layer i and node b in layer j, where $i < j$ and $acc_a < acc_b$, if the node in layer j is used as the projection target later than the node in layer i, then the final average gradient value obtained will be less vulnerable to conflict. Therefore, we eliminate the conflict of gradient update between each layer and other layers in hierarchical order. Similarly, to ensure the memorability of the elimination work, we likewise need to eliminate its conflicts with the historical model.

3.4   The Analysis of the Principle of FedHF

The main ideology of FedHF is a combination of the previous deconfliction algorithms and the classical clustering algorithms K-Means [18] and NetVLAD [19]. From the data perspective, K-Means clusters similar sample points together and aggregates a large number of samples into multiple clusters. The same cluster has similar characteristics to each other. The K-Means algorithm uses the distance between two sample points to characterize the similarity between nodes.

Likewise, we use the gradient magnitude similarity mentioned in Sect. 2.2 to measure the degree of difference between two gradients. If gradient projection and deconfliction are performed on two gradients with excessive differences, the deconfliction will fail briefly (the deconflicted gradient will be towards the strong gradient node, violating the fairness principle). It can be effectively avoided by stratifying the nodes with similar characteristics for deconfliction. The hierarchical sampling algorithm helps to mitigate the instability brought by environmental heterogeneity to the deconfliction algorithm.

4 Experimental Evaluation

4.1 Experiment Setup

In this paper, we conduct an extensive experimental evaluation of different fair federated learning frameworks on heterogeneous systems. We use three standard datasets, MNIST, CIFAR-10, and FMNIST with a federation consisting of 100 and 1000 participants. And We mainly compare our FedHF with the previous state-of-the-art framework:

- a fair and accurate framework using a double momentum gradient *FedFA* [11].
- a novel and fair framework by resolving gradient conflicts *FedFV* [8].

We use the same model parameters and local data distribution in the same environment settings to draw a fair comparison. We use python of version 3.8.3 and Pytorch of version 1.6.0 to build our federated framework. And we use a single GPU, GeForce RTX 2080 Ti, for hardware acceleration.

Non-IID Setting. We use 2 classes of non-IID. i.e., each participant has only two classes of data [20]. We divide the entire training set into 20 parts, and each client is randomly given two partitions from two different classes. In the case of 100 clients, for MNIST and FMNIST settings, every single device is assigned 600 images while the number is 500 for CIFAR-10. For 1000 clients, data points are repeated.

Systems Heterogeneity Simulations. We assume that there are strong and weak nodes in the federation system and that the strong nodes have stronger training accuracy by virtue of their abundant resources and data. To simulate this part of heterogeneity, we used an improved version of the method used in FedProx [21]. 0%, 30% and 50% heterogeneity implies that the system has a corresponding proportion of weak nodes, respectively We set the epoch of strong nodes to E_s and weak nodes to E_w, where $E_w <= E_s <= 2E_w$. We set $E = 10$ and $E = 8$ for CIFAR-10, FMNIST respectively.

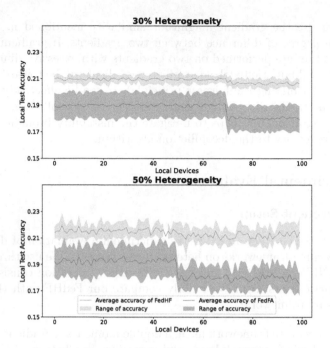

Fig. 3. The range distribution of local test accuracy on FedFA and FedHF algorithms, test at 30% heterogeneity and 50% heterogeneity.

4.2   Performance

Fairness. As shown in Table 1, FedHF outperforms the two baseline algorithms on different heterogeneities, suggesting that the FedHF workflow is effective in promoting fairness of the federated system. We note that FedHF improves the average accuracy of the central model by 5.06% (30% heterogeneity) and 5.01% (50% heterogeneity) on the CIFAR-10 dataset compared to FedFA, which implies that FedHF brings a significant improvement.

To more concretely compare the fairness of the federated system, we performed additional test experiments. We conducted local test experiments on 100 devices to compare the true fairness of FedFA and FedHF, respectively. Figure 3 shows the respective test accuracy on different devices when the global curator sends back the central model in the penultimate round. We recorded the maximum and minimum values of model accuracy for each local device to characterize the range of accuracy. Because we used 2 classes of non-IID with only two data labels on each device, the client-side local test accuracy should be around 20%. The level of heterogeneity determines the distribution of the accuracy range of the devices, i.e., the local test accuracy of strong nodes should be higher than that of weak nodes. As can be seen in Fig. 3, FedHF can effectively balance the gradient difference between strong and weak nodes, and the local test accuracy of weak nodes can be comparable to that of strong nodes even under high heterogeneity. In contrast, the true fairness of the FedFA algorithm is weaker

Table 1. The central model test accuracy performance of FedHA and FedHV and FedHF on CIFAR-10 with different system heterogeneities.

Method	Heterogeneity	Acc	Var	Best 10%
FedFA	30%	47.23 ± 0.78	16.01 ± 1.88	69.99 ± 2.43
	50%	47.25 ± 1.01	16.55 ± 1.78	70.62 ± 2.57
FedFV	30%	50.21 ± 0.65	$\mathbf{10.35 \pm 1.50}$	71.39 ± 2.11
	50%	50.19 ± 0.99	13.01 ± 1.93	72.11 ± 2.79
FedHF	30%	$\mathbf{52.29 \pm 0.75}$	10.39 ± 1.01	$\mathbf{73.57 \pm 2.19}$
	50%	$\mathbf{52.26 \pm 0.98}$	$\mathbf{11.74 \pm 1.43}$	$\mathbf{73.43 \pm 2.55}$

because the local accuracy of weak nodes is significantly weaker than that of strong nodes.

Robustness. Figure 4 shows the convergence of the three algorithms under different system heterogeneities. It is clear that the presence of strong and weak nodes in our simulated system leads to a harder convergence of the central model compared to the ideal case, and the jitter magnitude improves with increasing heterogeneity. From the figure, we can see that the convergence speed, jitter magnitude and trial accuracy variance (especially under high heterogeneity) of the FedHF algorithm are better than the other two algorithms. The main reason is that we adopt a clustering-like algorithm to deconflict similar samples in layers. The nodes with large differences are isolated first, and then the representative nodes and the model averages are deconflicted to avoid gradient skewing, so this algorithm is naturally resistant to heterogeneity. FedHF can effectively improve the overall fairness of the system when there is severe heterogeneity leading to discrimination in the aggregation model. Thus, our algorithm is robust and fair.

Effects of Hierarchical Partition. To demonstrate the effectiveness of the conflict elimination algorithm, we compare FedHF with the other two cases separately: 1) without any conflict elimination. 2) Only intra-layer conflicts are eliminated. Table 2 shows the results of the three algorithms. It can be seen that the elimination of both extra-layer and intra-layer conflicts reduces the variance of the test accuracy. There are some differences between intra-layer and extra-layer deconfliction. It's well known that one of the features of clustering algorithms is: high intra-class similarity and low inter-class similarity. Analogously, when we use a clustering-like approach (i.e., hierarchical partition), FedHF benefits more from extra-layer deconfliction than from intra-layer deconfliction, because the former resolves more dramatic gradient conflicts. In summary, both the two conflict elimination algorithms strengthen the performance of the federated system.

Table 2. The three algorithms respectively represent the result of no conflict resolution, intra-layer conflict resolution only, and all conflict resolution, testing on CIFAR-10.

Method	Acc	Var
FedHF_{Bare}	50.26 ± 1.87	12.56 ± 0.88
FedHF_{Intra}	50.91 ± 1.77	12.29 ± 0.75
FedHF_{All}	$\mathbf{52.29 \pm 0.75}$	$\mathbf{10.39 \pm 1.01}$

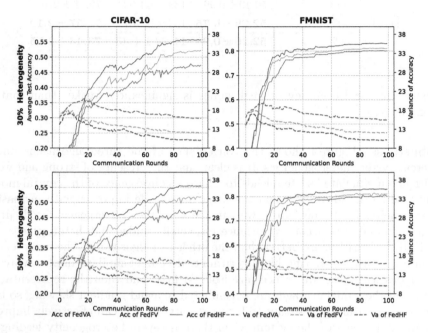

Fig. 4. The accuracy curves of FedFA, FedFV and FedHF on CIFAR-10 and FMNIST with 100 clients.

5   Conclusion

With the goal of increasing the fairness of the federation system under the premise of guaranteeing the accuracy of the central model, we propose a high fairness federated learning workflow, which operates well in heterogeneous data networks.

FedHF performs hierarchical partition-based deconfliction optimization using fair aggregation architecture. Hierarchical client selection and elimination of intra-layer conflicts and extra-layer conflicts improve the retention of weak nodes' model updates after federated iteration and aggregation. This clustering-like approach, which is stratified by gradient magnitude similarity and uses an eclectic deconfliction strategy to minimize model update conflicts, naturally improves the fairness of the federated system.

Our empirical evaluation shows that our FedHF workflow outperforms previous state-of-the-art frameworks in terms of fairness and accuracy trade-offs.

References

1. McMahan, B., Moore, E., Ramage, D., Hampson, S., Arcas, B.A.: Communication-efficient learning of deep networks from decentralized data. In: Artificial Intelligence and Statistics, pp. 1273–1282. PMLR (2017)
2. Sattler, F., Wiedemann, S., Müller, K.R., Samek, W.: Robust and communication-efficient federated learning from non-IID data. IEEE Trans. Neural Netw. Learn. Syst. **31**(9), 3400–3413 (2019)
3. Yang, Q., Liu, Y., Chen, T., Tong, Y.: Federated machine learning: concept and applications. ACM Trans. Intell. Syst. Technol. **10**(2) (2019)
4. Li, T., Sanjabi, M., Beirami, A., Smith, V.: Fair resource allocation in federated learning. In: 8th International Conference on Learning Representations, ICLR 2020, Addis Ababa, Ethiopia, 26–30 April 2020 (2020). OpenReview.net
5. Li, T., Hu, S., Beirami, A., Smith, V.: Ditto: fair and robust federated learning through personalization. In: International Conference on Machine Learning, pp. 6357–6368. PMLR (2021)
6. Rehman, M.H.U., Dirir, A.M., Salah, K., Damiani, E., Svetinovic, D.: TrustFed: a framework for fair and trustworthy cross-device federated learning in IIoT. IEEE Trans. Ind. Inf. **17**(12), 8485–8494 (2021)
7. Hashimoto, T., Srivastava, M., Namkoong, H., Liang, P.: Fairness without demographics in repeated loss minimization. In: International Conference on Machine Learning, pp. 1929–1938. PMLR (2018)
8. Wang, Z., Fan, X., Qi, J., Wen, C., Wang, C., Yu, R.: Federated learning with fair averaging. In: Zhou, Z. (ed.) Proceedings of the Thirtieth International Joint Conference on Artificial Intelligence, IJCAI 2021, Virtual Event/Montreal, Canada, 19–27 August 2021, pp. 1615–1623 (2021). ijcai.org
9. Wu, W., He, L., Lin, W., Mao, R., Maple, C., Jarvis, S.A.: SAFA: a semi-asynchronous protocol for fast federated learning with low overhead. IEEE Trans. Comput. **70**, 655–668 (2020)
10. Chen, Y., Ning, Y., Slawski, M., Rangwala, H.: Asynchronous online federated learning for edge devices with non-IID data. In: 2020 IEEE International Conference on Big Data (Big Data), pp. 15–24. IEEE (2020)
11. Huang, W., Li, T., Wang, D., Du, S., Zhang, J., Huang, T.: Fairness and accuracy in horizontal federated learning. Inf. Sci. **589**, 170–185 (2022)
12. Yu, T., Kumar, S., Gupta, A., Levine, S., Hausman, K., Finn, C.: Gradient surgery for multi-task learning. Adv. Neural. Inf. Process. Syst. **33**, 5824–5836 (2020)
13. Li, J., He, L., Ren, S., Mao, R.: Developing a loss prediction-based asynchronous stochastic gradient descent algorithm for distributed training of deep neural networks. In: 49th International Conference on Parallel Processing-ICPP, pp. 1–10 (2020)
14. Farajtabar, M., Azizan, N., Mott, A., Li, A.: Orthogonal gradient descent for continual learning. In: International Conference on Artificial Intelligence and Statistics, pp. 3762–3773. PMLR (2020)
15. Guo, Y., Liu, M., Yang, T., Rosing, T.: Learning with long-term remembering: following the lead of mixed stochastic gradient (2019)

16. Désidéri, J.A.: Multiple-gradient descent algorithm (MGDA) for multiobjective optimization. C.R. Math. **350**(5-6), 313–318 (2012)
17. Wang, Q., Du, X., Gao, Z., Guizani, M.: An optimal channel occupation time adjustment method for LBE in unlicensed spectrum. IEEE Trans. Veh. Technol. **68**(11), 10943–10955 (2019)
18. Krishna, K., Murty, M.N.: Genetic k-means algorithm. IEEE Trans. Syst. Man Cybern. Part B (Cybernetics) **29**(3), 433–439 (1999)
19. Arandjelovic, R., Gronat, P., Torii, A., Pajdla, T., Sivic, J.: NetVLAD: CNN architecture for weakly supervised place recognition. In: Proceedings of the IEEE Conference on Computer Vision and Pattern Recognition, pp. 5297–5307 (2016)
20. Kairouz, P., et al.: Advances and open problems in federated learning. Found. Trends® Mach. Learn. **14**(1-2), 1–210 (2021)
21. Li, T., Sahu, A.K., Zaheer, M., Sanjabi, M., Talwalkar, A., Smith, V.: Federated optimization in heterogeneous networks. Proc. Mach. Learn. Syst. **2**, 429–450 (2020)

A Collaborative Framework for Ad Click-Through Rate Prediction in Mobile App Services

Xianjin Rong, Jinghua Zhu$^{(\boxtimes)}$, and Heran Xi

School of Computer Science, HeilongJiang University, Harbin, China
2201852@s.hlju.edu.cn,{zhujinghua,xiheran}@hlju.edu.cn

Abstract. Recent embedding techniques have shown remarkable effectiveness in CTR prediction. However, such methods heavily rely on centralized storage and work poorly on cold-start users and items. In reality, historical data of users or ads are heterogeneously distributed across multiple platforms and not directly accessible due to business competition and privacy issues, leading to cold start problems with CTR predictions for each application server. In this paper, we learn federated meta embedding (FME) based on the cooperation of the user-server-advertiser (H-USA), which completes the CTR prediction task in two stages. In the federated phase, we learn richer semantic information about hot IDs under the collaboration of the USA. We treat each cold id in the meta phase as a learning task. And then, the application server learns embedding for cold IDs using federated embeddings through gradient-based meta-learning. Extensive experiments on real-world datasets show that FME learned in H-USA can significantly improve the prediction performance of cold IDs.

Keywords: CTR prediction · Cold-start · Federated-learning · Heterogeneous distribution

1 Introduction

Click-through rate (CTR) prediction plays a crucial role in industrial production, such as online advertising system [8]. Recently proposed deep learning-based models such as [2,6,7,12,14] demonstrated that well-learned embeddings could improve CTR prediction for they can capture richer semantics. However, behavioral data exists heterogeneously in many different application servers and are not directly accessible due to business competition and privacy issues, which leads to the data isolated islands [15]. For example, if the user installs multiple apps on his phone, he may be a YouTube fan, but when he opens the Amazon app, he has no idea what to buy. How does Amazon use the user's historical data on YouTube to make personalized recommendations for the user? Meanwhile, the advertisers might put their ads on multiple servers to maximize the exposure of their products and increase sales, such as the book may be a cold

© The Author(s), under exclusive license to Springer Nature Switzerland AG 2022
J. Troya et al. (Eds.): ICSOC 2022, LNCS 13740, pp. 567–574, 2022.
https://doi.org/10.1007/978-3-031-20984-0_40

item on Taobao but popular on Amazon. Similarly, how should the advertiser cooperate with Taobao to promote products?

We need to tackle the cold-start problem from a novel perspective; that is, predicting click behavior requires the involvement of three parties: users, servers, and advertisers. Firstly, we store user privacy data (such as gender and age) on the user's device (e.g., mobile phone); servers and advertisers do not have direct access to this private data. Secondly, we design a cooperation framework constructed by the user-server-advertiser in the heterogeneous scenarios (H-USA) on which we learn federated meta embedding (FME) to solve the problem, which mainly consists of two phases. In the federated phase, USA collaborative learns federated embeddings for hot IDs in a privacy-preserving manner. Concretely, the application server pre-trains a base CTR model, like WideDeep [2], DCN [14], PNN [12], using local incomplete hot IDs, and sends the model to devices and advertisers. Then device locally optimizes user-side embedding of the pre-trained model using private user data. At the same time, advertisers execute weight aggregation on the ad side. Finally, during the meta phase, we learn embedding for cold IDs on application servers through gradient-based meta-learning [3] by using federated embeddings. Finally, we construct a unified optimization objective that balances both hot and cold ID performance [11]. In this way, the generated embeddings (i.e., FME) not only incorporate the hot IDs' information but also link the adequate semantics of the federation stage.

To summarize, the contributions of this paper are as follows:

(1) We generalize the real-world click-through prediction problem and argue that a perfect click-through behavior prediction requires perfect collaboration among three parties. To our knowledge, it is the first work in CTR prediction to propose a collaborative framework in a heterogeneous scenario constructed by User-Server-Advertiser (H-USA).
(2) We revisit the problem of cold-start CTR prediction from a new perspective and learn FME with the cooperation of the H-USA. First, we address the problem for hot IDs based on a federated setting. Then, in the meta phase, we focus on solving the cold ID problem without compromising the performance of hot IDs.
(3) Experimental results on three real-world datasets with heterogeneous distributions showed that FME could significantly improve the performances of the hot and cold IDs for four existing CTR prediction models.

2   Problem Formulation

Assume that each user has a device (e.g., a cell phone) to store private data and provide computing services and that it communicates only with the installed app. The apps do not store the user's private characteristic data, but only the user's click history on the ad and the relevant characteristics of the ad, and cannot communicate directly with other apps. Besides, any user and advertisers cannot communicate with each other either. In this way, H-USA ensures the privacy of users and anonymity of advertisers, as unrelated app servers do not perceive their presence.

Then H-USA is made up of set servers $\mathcal{S} = \{s_1, s_2 \ldots\}$, devices $\mathcal{U} = \{u_1, u_2, \ldots\}$ and advertisers $\mathcal{A} = \{a_1, a_2, \ldots\}$. For user u and advertiser a, the servers they can connect to, can be a set of $u^{(s)}$, and $a^{(s)}$ respectively, and also, for the server s, devices and advertisers it can connect to, can be a set of $s^{(u)}$, and $s^{(a)}$, where $s \in \mathcal{S}, u \in \mathcal{U}, a \in \mathcal{A}$. Each user and ad has an id and associated features, and we refer to $e^s_{u_{id}}$, $e^s_{u_{fea}}$ and $e^s_{v_{id}}, e^s_{v_{fea}}$ as id embedding and feature embedding of user u and ad v on server s. The Log-loss is often used as the optimization target: $l = -y\log\hat{y} - (1-y)\log(1-\hat{y})$.

3   Framework Design

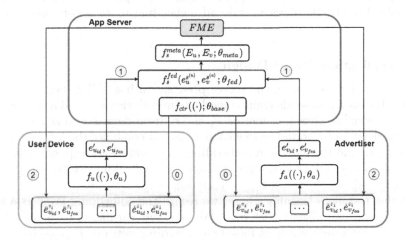

Fig. 1. The architecture of the collaborative framework H-USA and training workflow of FME.

3.1   User Device Design

The user receives the base CTR models from app servers $u^{(s)}$, which can be a set $f_u^{(s)} = \{f_{ctr}^{s_1}, f_{ctr}^{s_2}, \cdots\}$. In particularly, the embeddings of user u in $f_u^{(s)}$ can be a set $e_{u_{id}}^{(s)} = \{e_{u_{id}}^{s_1}, e_{u_{id}}^{s_2}, \cdots\}$, and $e_{u_{fea}}^{(s)} = \{e_{u_{fea}}^{s_1}, e_{u_{fea}}^{s_2}, \cdots\}$. Next, we build a multi-output network $f_u(\cdot)$ based on $f_u^{(s)}$. First, we initialize E_u of $f_u(\cdot)$ with: $E_u = \frac{1}{I} \sum_{i=1}^{I} E^{s_i}$, where E_u is embedding layer of $f_u(\cdot)$ and is shared by each $f_{ctr}^{(s_i)}$. Then we take the user's features data stored on the device as input, and evaluate loss l_{s_i}, we define final loss as: $l_u = \frac{1}{I} \sum_{i=1}^{I} l_{s_i}$. Note that the device only updates user-related embeddings, so we freeze the ad-related embedding

E_v during device training. By computing the gradient of l_u and taking a step of gradient descent, we get a new adapted user embedding $e'_u(\cdot)$: $e'_{u_{id}} = e_{u_{id}} - \alpha \frac{\partial l_u}{\partial e_u}$ and $e'_{u_{fea}} = e_{u_{fea}} - \alpha \frac{\partial l_u}{\partial e_{u_{fea}}}$, where $\alpha > 0$ is the step size of gradient descent, then device sends updated user embeddings e'_u to correspond app servers $u^{(s)}$.

3.2   Advertiser Platform Design

Advertisers receive ad-related embedding from servers $a^{(s)}$, and the accuracy of the ad on the validation data of each server s_i, which can be a set $e_v^{(s)} = \{e_v^{s_1}, e_v^{s_2}, \cdots\}$ and $acc_v^{(s)} = \{acc_v^{s_1}, acc_v^{s_2}, \cdots\}$. Then, advertiser take a accuracy aggregation strategy $f_a(\cdot)$ [13] to update ad embedding, which can be denoted as:
$$e'_{v_{id}} = \frac{\sum \delta(acc_v^{s_i}, p) \times e_{v_{id}}^{s_i}}{\sum \delta(acc_v^{s_i}, p)}, e'_{v_{fea}} = \frac{\sum \delta(acc_v^{s_i}, p) \times e_{v_{fea}}^{s_i}}{\sum \delta(acc_v^{s_i}, p)},$$ where $\delta(acc, p)$ is an indicator function, $\delta(acc, p) = 1$, if $acc > p$; otherwise, $\delta(acc, p) = 1$, and p is a dynamic threshold. Finally, the device sends ad embedding e'_v to a corresponding app server.

3.3   Application Server Design

Before the federated phase, the server pre-trains a base CTR model $f_{ctr}^{s_i}$ based on local hot data and sends trained model to user device $s^{(u)}$ and advertiser $s^{(a)}$.

After server receives parameters e'_u and e'_v from devices and advertisers, the server performs a federated aggregation $f_{fed}(\cdot)$, it combines the local embedding vector e_u, e_v and the federated embedding e'_u, e'_v via its corresponding accuracy acc, to accuracy weighted update [13] the new embedding vector e_{fed}: $e_{fed}^u = e_u \times acc_u + e'_u \times (1 - acc_u)$, $e_{fed}^v = e_v \times acc_v + e'_v \times (1 - acc_v)$.

During the meta-learning phase, we regard the embedding layer as a meta-learner [4] and initialize it with e_{fed}. We view the learning of each cold ID as a task and build a use a gradient-based meta-learning network $f_{meta}(\cdot)$ to optimize it. Specifically, for server s, we take a portion of the hot IDs as the support set D_{sprt}, and treat the cold IDs as a query set D_{cold}. We first make predictions on D_{sprt}, calculate the loss l_{sprt}, and take a step of gradient descent to get a new adapted embedding e'_{fed}. We then test the new adapted federated embedding on the query data D_{cold} and obtain the loss l_{cold}.

To unify these two losses, we deploy the final loss function for the meta phase as a weighted sum of l_{sprt} and l_{cold}: $L_{meta} = \beta \times l_{sprt} + (1 - \beta) \times l_{cold}$, where $\beta \in [0, 1]$ is a coefficient to balance the two phases. By computing the gradient of L_{meta} and taking a step of gradient descent, we get the federated meta embedding $e^{meta}(\cdot)$: $e_{meta} = e'_{fed} - \alpha \frac{\partial L_{meta}}{\partial e'_{fed}}$, where $\alpha > 0$ is the step size of gradient descent.

3.4   H-USA Framework and Train Workflow of FME

The overall framework is shown in Fig. 1. Step 0, prior to federation, each server pre-trains a basic model, such as [2,6,12,14], with its incomplete hot data and sends it to $s^{(u)}, s^{(a)}$. Step 1, during the federated, the user device receives the models from the apps $u^{(s)}$ and only updates user-related embeddings and sends them back. At the same time, the advertiser receives ad embeddings from $a^{(s)}$, does a local aggregation, and sends them back. Step 3, when the app receives the federated parameters from $s^{(u)}, s^{(a)}$, it performs a weighted update-based strategy to update the embedding of hot ids and learns embeddings of cold ids based on federated embeddings through gradient-based meta-learning. Then, the server sends federated meta embedding(FME) to the users and advertisers. Repeat the process above until the model converges. In this way, we learn FME in the H-USA, allowing the model to achieve good performance in both hot and cold id.

4   Experiments

4.1   Experimental Setup

Datasets and Metrics. To evaluate the effectiveness of FME in H-USA, we conduct extensive experiments on three real-world datasets, namely ML-1M[1], Tencent[2] and Taobao[3]. Besides, we leverage the most commonly-used evaluation metrics in CTR prediction, namely AUC and LogLoss.

Models and Embedding. Since the H-USA framework is model-independent, it can be applied to various existing CTR prediction models in the Embedding & MLP paradigm, and we conduct experiments upon the four representative models, namely PNN [12], DCN [14], DeepFM [6], and WideDeep [2]. To thoroughly test the effectiveness of FME, we evaluate the following embedding types. InitEmb, initial embedding, generated using Xavier initialization [5] and used as a baseline. FedEmb, federated embedding, it only performs federated phase. MetaEmb, meta embedding, it only considers meta phase. FME, federated meta embedding, is generated based on the collaboration of H-USA, taking into account both the federated phase and the meta-learning phase.

Heterogeneous Data Splites. Methods for heterogeneous distributions widely used in federal learning include Dirichlet Distribution [1] and Mixed Distribution [10]. First, we partition the dataset into multiple application servers using the method mentioned above to meet the heterogeneous distribution. Next, we partition devices and advertisers based on user and ad attributes. Besides, for an ID, if the number of labeled instances is larger than a threshold, we regard it as an old ad. This threshold is set to 25, 50, and 130 for the three datasets. Then we divide the data distribution of 80%/20% again from the hot data and use 80% as federated training data and 20% for meta training support data.

Hyper-parameters Settings. We set the step size of gradient descent α of as 0.001, coefficient β 0.1, and weight decay as 0.0001. Each device trains two

---

[1] http://www.grouplens.org/datasets/movielens/.

[2] https://algo.qq.com/archive.html.

[3] https://tianchi.aliyun.com/dataset.

epochs locally during the federated phase, and the application service learns twice per batch during the meta-phase. Moreover, we set the dimension of the embedding as 16. We report the average results for all servers as a metric. All the models are optimized by the Adam algorithm [9].

4.2   Experimental Analysis

Table 1. Test AUC and Loss on Cold IDs. Model: Base prediction model. Emb: ID embedding type. AUC (↑) is thelarger the better. Loss (↓) **is the smaller the better.**

Model	Emb	ML-1M		Tencent		TaoBao	
		LOSS	AUC	LOSS	AUC	LOSS	AUC
PNN	InitEmb	0.6564	0.6675	0.6625	0.6296	0.3448	0.5446
	FedEmb	0.6310	0.7193	0.6337	0.6521	0.3301	0.5603
	MetaEmb	0.6227	0.7264	0.6222	0.6691	0.3385	0.5781
	FME	**0.5887**	**0.7423**	**0.6113**	**0.7019**	**0.3114**	**0.5901**
DCN	InitEmb	0.6535	0.6642	0.6635	0.6212	0.3487	0.5412
	FedEmb	0.6382	0.7114	0.6311	0.6505	0.3315	0.5605
	MetaEmb	0.6278	0.7282	0.6254	0.6691	0.3376	0.5766
	FME	**0.5876**	**0.7428**	**0.6147**	**0.7015**	**0.3124**	**0.5912**
DeepFM	InitEmb	0.6508	0.6623	0.6628	0.6241	0.3415	0.5435
	FedEmb	0.6301	0.7135	0.6311	0.6552	0.3389	0.5613
	MetaEmb	0.6249	0.7219	0.6225	0.6651	0.3311	0.5712
	FME	**0.5856**	**0.7439**	**0.6122**	**0.7043**	**0.3178**	**0.5926**
WideDeep	RndEmb	0.6576	0.6683	0.6687	0.6277	0.3441	0.5419
	FedEmb	0.6366	0.7175	0.6392	0.6545	0.3362	0.5611
	MetaEmb	0.6236	0.7244	0.6224	0.6674	0.3321	0.5779
	FME	**0.5841**	**0.7477**	**0.6154**	**0.7042**	**0.3136**	**0.5958**

Overall Performance. Table 1 and Table 2 list experimental results of the four base CTR models using FME on the mixture distribution. We observed that when using FedEmb, FedEmb, and MetaEmb, models yielded better AUC and LOSS results than the random InitEmb. For example, when using DCN, Wide&Deep, PNN, and DeepFM as the base models, FME provides nearly 8% and 4% AUC improvement on ML-1M, respectively.

Contribution to Cold IDs. Table 1 lists the performance of FME on cold IDs based on four popular CTR prediction models. We observed that using FME models yielded better AUC and LOSS results than the other three embeddings. Then comparing FedEmb and MetaEmb, we will find that MetaEmb has a more obvious improvement on cold id. We believe that while FedEmb learned more about the valid semantics of hot IDs by working with other participants in H-USA during the federal phase, these were only for hot IDs and not for cold IDs. In contrast, MetaEmb learned cold IDs specifically in the basic model of each server.

Table 2. Test AUC and Loss on Hot IDs. Model: Base prediction model. Emb: ID embedding type. AUC (↑) **is thelarger the better. Loss** (↓) **is the smaller the better.**

Model	Emb	ML-1M		Tencent		TaoBao	
		LOSS	AUC	LOSS	AUC	LOSS	AUC
PNN	InitEmb	0.6283	0.7108	0.6215	0.6696	0.3348	0.5611
	FedEmb	0.6089	0.7493	0.6137	0.6821	0.3101	0.5894
	MetaEmb	0.6201	0.7279	0.6202	0.6779	0.3285	0.5734
	FME	**0.5737**	**0.7523**	**0.6013**	**0.7119**	**0.3014**	**0.6121**
DCN	InitEmb	0.6233	0.7179	0.6291	0.6623	0.3342	0.5631
	FedEmb	0.6024	0.7418	0.6154	0.6865	0.3155	0.5859
	MetaEmb	0.6211	0.7270	0.6241	0.6703	0.3252	0.5797
	FME	**0.5765**	**0.7547**	**0.6062**	**0.7113**	**0.3081**	**0.6136**
DeepFM	InitEmb	0.6266	0.7133	0.6215	0.6648	0.3303	0.5659
	FedEmb	0.6007	0.7397	0.6163	0.6819	0.3167	0.5897
	MetaEmb	0.6215	0.7279	0.6275	0.6774	0.3295	0.5706
	FME	**0.5753**	**0.7523**	**0.6029**	**0.7151**	**0.3005**	**0.6169**
WideDeep	InitEmb	0.6276	0.7187	0.6227	0.6641	0.3387	0.5672
	FedEmb	0.6075	0.7432	0.6145	0.6807	0.3112	0.5853
	MetaEmb	0.6239	0.7279	0.6236	0.6743	0.3226	0.5774
	FME	**0.5706**	**0.7523**	**0.6031**	**0.7106**	**0.3013**	**0.6132**

Contribution to Hot IDs. Table 2 shows the results for the hot id, and we can conclude that when we use the hot id to improve the cold id, it does not degrade the model's performance on the hot id but slightly improves it. Therefore, in the framework of H-USA, we can significantly improve the performance of cold start iD in heterogeneous environments without losing the performance of hot id.

5   Conclusion

This paper discusses cold-start problems in CTR prediction of heterogeneous environments from a novel perspective; we argue that a perfect click-through prediction cannot be separated from the cooperation of the three parties, namely the user, server, and advertiser. Moreover, we propose a collaborative framework (H-USA) and learn FME for CTR prediction in mobile app services. Experimental results show that FME can significantly improve prediction performance. In the future, we will further consider enhancing the gradient safety of FME during the federated process in the H-USA framework. We also plan to deploy FME to the online ad system and test its online performance.

References

1. Bouguila, N., Ziou, D., Vaillancourt, J.: Novel mixtures based on the Dirichlet distribution: application to data and image classification. In: Perner, P., Rosenfeld, A. (eds.) MLDM 2003. LNCS, vol. 2734, pp. 172–181. Springer, Heidelberg (2003). https://doi.org/10.1007/3-540-45065-3_15
2. Cheng, H.T.: Wide & Deep Learning for Recommender Systems. ACM (2016)
3. Finn, C., Abbeel, P., Levine, S.: Model-agnostic meta-learning for fast adaptation of deep networks. In: Precup, D., Teh, Y.W. (eds.) Proceedings of the 34th International Conference on Machine Learning, ICML 2017, Sydney, NSW, Australia, 6–11 August 2017, Proceedings of Machine Learning Research, vol. 70, pp. 1126–1135. PMLR (2017)
4. Finn, C., Abbeel, P., Levine, S.: Model-agnostic meta-learning for fast adaptation of deep networks. In International Conference on Machine Learning (2017)
5. Glorot, X., Bengio, Y.: Understanding the difficulty of training deep feedforward neural networks. In: Teh, Y.W., Titterington, D.M. (eds.) Proceedings of the Thirteenth International Conference on Artificial Intelligence and Statistics, AISTATS 2010, Chia Laguna Resort, Sardinia, Italy, 13–15 May 2010, JMLR Proceedings, vol. 9, pp. 249–256. JMLR.org (2010)
6. Guo, H., Tang, R., Ye, Y., Li, Z., He, X., Dong, Z.: DeepFM: an end-to-end wide & deep learning framework for CTR prediction. CoRR, abs/1804.04950 (2018)
7. He, X., Liao, L., Zhang, H., Nie, L., Chua, T.S.: Neural collaborative filtering. In: The 26th International Conference (2017)
8. He, X., et al.: Practical Lessons from Predicting Clicks on Ads at Facebook. ACM (2014)
9. Kingma, D.P., Ba, J.: Adam: a method for stochastic optimization. In: Bengio, Y., LeCun, Y. (eds.) 3rd International Conference on Learning Representations, ICLR 2015, San Diego, CA, USA, 7–9 May 2015, Conference Track Proceedings (2015)
10. Marfoq, O., Neglia, G., Bellet, A., Kameni, L., Vidal, R.: Federated multi-task learning under a mixture of distributions. In: Ranzato, M., Beygelzimer, A., Dauphin, Y.N., Liang, P., Vaughan, J.W. (eds.) Advances in Neural Information Processing Systems 34: Annual Conference on Neural Information Processing Systems 2021, NeurIPS 2021, 6–14 December 2021, Virtual, pp. 15434–15447 (2021)
11. Pan, F., Li, S., Ao, X., Tang, P., He, Q.: Warm up cold-start advertisements: improving CTR predictions via learning to learn ID embeddings. ACM (2019)
12. Qu, Y., Han, C., Kan, R., Zhang, W., Wang, J.: Product-based neural networks for user response prediction. In: 2016 IEEE 16th International Conference on Data Mining (ICDM) (2016)
13. Wang, Q., Fangai Liu, P., Huang, S.X., Zhao, X.: A hierarchical attention model for CTR prediction based on user interest. IEEE Syst. J. 14(3), 4015–4024 (2020)
14. Wang, R., Fu, B., Fu, G., Wang, M.: Deep & cross network for ad click predictions. In: ADKDD 2017 (2017)
15. Yang, Q., Liu, Y., Chen, T., Tong, Y.: Federated machine learning: concept and applications. ACM Trans. Intell. Syst. Technol. 10(2), 1–19 (2019)

Process-Oriented Intents: A Cornerstone for Superimposition of Natural Language Conversations over Composite Services

Sara Bouguelia[1]([✉])(ID), Auday Berro[1](ID), Boualem Benatallah[2](ID),
Marcos Báez[3](ID), Hayet Brabra[4](ID), Shayan Zamanirad[5](ID),
and Hamamache Kheddouci[1](ID)

[1] LIRIS - University of Claude Bernard Lyon 1, Villeurbanne, France
{sara.bouguelia,auday.berro,hamamache.kheddouci}@univ-lyon1.fr
[2] Dublin City University, Dublin, Ireland
boualem.benatallah@dcu.ie
[3] Bielefeld University of Applied Sciences, Bielefeld, Germany
marcos.baez@fh-bielefeld.de
[4] SAMOVAR - Telecom SudParis, Institut Polytechnique de Paris, Palaiseau, France
hayet.brabra@telecom-sudparis.eu
[5] University of New South Wales (UNSW), Sydney, Australia
shayanz@cse.unsw.edu.au

Abstract. Task-oriented conversational assistants are in very high demand these days. They employ third-party APIs to serve end-users via natural language interactions and improve their productivity. Recently, the augmentation of process-enabled automation with conversational assistants emerged as a promising technology to make process automation closer to users. This paper focuses on the superimposition of task-oriented assistants over composite services. We propose a Human-bot-Process interaction acts that are relevant to represent natural language conversations between the user and multi-step processes. In doing so, we enable human users to perform tasks by naturally interacting with processes.

Keywords: Task-oriented conversational bots · Rest APIs · Software-enabled services · Composite services · Process-oriented intents

1 Introduction

Task-oriented conversational services (or simply chatbots) emerged as engines for transforming online service-enabled digital assistance and powering natural interactions between humans, services, and things [15]. Recently, organizations leveraged chatbots in a variety of assistance tasks. For instance, the augmentation of process-enabled automation with task-oriented chatbots emerged as a promising technology to make process automation even closer to users [1,5]. This evolution

J. Troya et al. (Eds.): ICSOC 2022, LNCS 13740, pp. 575–583, 2022.
https://doi.org/10.1007/978-3-031-20984-0_41

promises to increase the benefits of automation by simplifying access and reuse of concomitant capabilities across potentially large number of evolving and heterogeneous data sources, applications and things [5,9]. While today's chatbots may automate some tasks, bot developers have recently started investigating the incorporation of robotic process automation (RPA) to increase automation [14]. For instance, Devy chatbot was proposed to provide automated support in DevOps processes [6]. Authors in [13] developed a chatbot for agile software development teams which analyzes teams' project data to provide insights into their performance. In [12], the authors proposed an approach that automatically builds a chatbot from a process model to query process structure. Another work proposed a chatbot to query event data allowing users to get insights into specific process executions [11]. All these works are either about domain-specific chatbots or about querying the process execution or structure but do not focus on performing process tasks. Other works propose approaches to interact with business processes and perform process tasks through chatbots. For instance, Google proposes the use of a chatbot in so-called communication-enabled business process applications [8]. However, no specific details about the internals of the chatbot infrastructure are provided. The closest work to ours is [10], which proposed a methodology that takes a business process model as input and generates a chatbot to help the users interact with the process. However, the work does not focus on the recognition of process-oriented intents. In our previous work, we proposed various techniques for the superimposition of task-oriented chatbots on top of APIs [3,4,16,17].

In this paper, we focus on the superimposition of task-oriented chatbots over *composite services*. In doing so, we enable users to perform tasks by naturally interacting with service orchestrations involving multiple actions. Orchestrating human-machine conversations over composite services requires rich abstractions and knowledge to: (i) interact with a multi-step processes using natural language utterances, (ii) automatically recognise nuanced, context sensitive and possibly ambiguous process-aware user intents including starting a new task, inquiring about task progress, switching from one task to another and exceptional behavior such as canceling. Specifically, we identify fine-grained Human-bot-Process (HP) interaction acts that are relevant to represent natural language conversations between user and multi-step processes. In a nutshell, interaction acts are dialogue acts that characterise process-oriented intents in user utterances.

2   Preliminaries and Architecture

In this section, we first introduce some process-related concepts and assumptions. Second, we present a scenario illustrating interactions between a user and multi-step processes. Finally, we present the architecture.

Preliminaries. A *business process* is a collection of coordinated tasks to achieve a concrete goal [7]. The *schema* of a process can be represented in a variety of forms, such as Petri nets and Event-Driven Process Chains [7]. For simplicity, we represent the process schema as a directed acyclic graph. Figure 1 shows an example of a Travel Booking Process graph. The process graph nodes represent

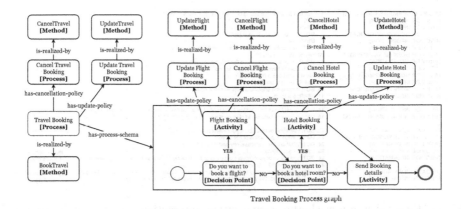

Fig. 1. Example of a Travel Booking Process Model

activities and *decision points*. A process is associated with a set of *exception handling policies*. Exception handling policies are directives that model exceptional situations together with a set of actions that are used to handle exceptions (e.g., cancel a travel booking) [2]. In this paper, we consider that a process is realized by a composite service. Furthermore, a composite service is accessible through an API that includes: a main method to invoke the normal process behavior (e.g., *BookTravel* method), and exception handling methods to handle exceptional behaviors of a process (e.g., *CancelTravel* method) or an activity (e.g., *CancelHotel* method). We also consider that a process has a set of *correlation attributes* that uniquely identify an *instance* [7].

Scenario. Figure 2 shows an example of a user-chatbot conversation in which the user is interacting with the Travel Booking process illustrated in Fig. 1. There are interactions that are triggered by the user and others by the chatbot. During normal process execution (e.g., booking travel): (i) the chatbot can *ask for more information to fulfill a task* (message 10) or *provide information* about a performed task (message 6), (ii) the user can *provide information* (message 11) or *inquire about task progress* (message 23). As mentioned before, a process is associated with possible run-time exceptions. In message 27, the user wants to change the check-out date. This interaction (changing date) is triggered by the user and involves the update of a previously performed task. However, exception interactions can also be triggered by the chatbot. For example, assume that the airline company canceled the user's flight. The chatbot can trigger an interaction that involves notifying the user about the cancellation and proposing alternatives such as changing the travel date. In this paper, we focus on interactions from the user side; chatbot-initiated interactions are outside the paper scope.

Architecture. To support natural language conversations with processes, the chatbot needs a set of services to initiate, monitor, and control task-related conversations. The *Natural Language Understanding (NLU)* service aims to extract HP interaction acts and slot-value pairs from the utterance. The *Process*

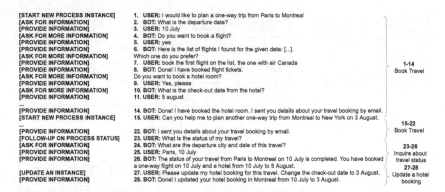

Fig. 2. Example of a user-chatbot conversation. Interaction acts in blue are triggered by the user and those in green are triggered by the chatbot. (Color figure online)

Embedding Service (PES) aims to identify the *process* that corresponds to the utterance. The *Dialogue Manager (DM)* service aims to infer the dialogue state in terms of user intent and its slot-value pairs. This DM relies on the *Context Knowledge Service (CKS)* to recognize user intent and infer missing information. Once the DM recognizes the intent and collects all required information, it performs the corresponding action and sends the results to the *Natural Language Generator (NLG)*. The NLG generates then human-like responses to the user. In what follows, we describe PES and CKS.

The PES aims to identify processes from natural language utterances. It has (i) a process knowledge model and (ii) a set of services to leverage this knowledge. The process knowledge model is denoted as a process knowledge graph (P-KG) with specific types of nodes and relationships. In particular, nodes can describe *Processes*, *Paths*, and *Activities*. Part of the information in the P-KG is the graph representation of what we find in the process model definition. Such information typically includes the process *name*, the process *description*, activity *name*, and activity *description*. Furthermore, a *Process* node has relationships such as *is-realized-by* that denotes that a process is performed by an API method (refer to Fig. 1). The PES features the following three services:

- *Vector generation Service* is used to construct vector embeddings for process elements. It takes as input a process element e and generates its vector embedding. It generates: (i) an *activity vector* by aggregating the information from activity *name* and its *description*; (ii) a *path vector* by aggregating vectors of activities in this path; and (iii) a *process vector* by averaging the information from process *name*, process *description* and all path vectors.
- *Process Identification Service* aims to identify the corresponding process of a given utterance u. First, it generates the embedding vector of the utterance. Second, it calculates the cosine similarity between this utterance vector and the vector of each process in the P-KG. Then, according to a predefined threshold, processes with similarities greater than this threshold are kept and ordered. Finally, the service returns the process scoring the highest similarity.

– *Method Identification Service* aims to identify a process API method that corresponds to a given process intent. It takes as input a process p (e.g., *Travel Booking*), a process intent i (e.g., *canceling task*) and an activity a (e.g., *Hotel Booking*) and returns the corresponding API method.

In [3], we proposed the CKS that enables to capture contextual knowledge from different sources. We extend the CKS with two additional services:

– *Process Instance Identification Service* returns the list of instances for a given process. It takes as input a process p and returns the list of instances of p.
– *Correlation attribute Value Retrieval Service* provides values of correlation attributes for a given process instance id. It takes as input an instance id and returns an array of attribute-value pairs.

3   Process-Aware User Intents

Conversations regarding a given process-aware task may involve several turns (e.g., starting a travel booking, later inquiring about booking status, modifying travel dates, or canceling the booking). We propose HP interaction acts to characterize a set of elementary user intents in conversations between users and multi-step processes. Specifically, we derive four types of process-oriented intents: *start new process instance* intent, *follow-up on process status* intent, *canceling task* intent, and *task update* intent.

We propose five general steps to recognize these process-oriented intents from an utterance u: (i) detect the *HP interaction act class* expressed in u; (ii) invoke the *Process Identification PES* service to get the corresponding process p; (iii) invoke the *Process Instance Identification CKS* service to retrieve the set of instances set_i of p; (iv) extract the values of correlation attributes of the instance that the user is referring to; (v) compare the extracted values of correlation attributes with those of set_i to check if the identified instance already exists or not. In what follows, we describe the process-oriented intents and define rules that combine detection of HP interaction acts with additional context and process knowledge to recognize and realize each of these intents.

Start New Process Instance. This intent allows to identify whether the user utterance expresses a task that requires the creation of a new process instance. In general, when users ask for a new task, they provide general information describing this task, and sometimes they provide more detailed information about this task. The chatbot needs this information to identify the process and to check if the utterance concerns the creation of a new process instance. Figure 3 shows the specification of the rule related to *start-new-process-instance* intent. This rule consists of *trigger* and *action* clauses. The trigger clause defines three boolean conditions. (1) The condition IS_START() checks if the utterance u expresses a *start new instance* HP interaction act. (2) The condition IS_SIM() checks if the process p corresponds to the utterance u. (3) The last condition

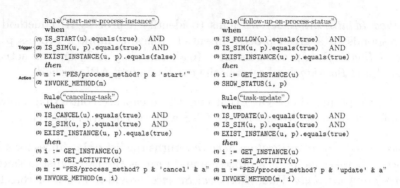

Fig. 3. Rules to recognize and realize the identified process-oriented intents.

EXIST_INSTANCE() compares values of the correlation attributes with those of the existing instances to check if the identified instance does not exist. If the conditions are satisfied, the chatbot (1) invokes the *Method Identification PES* service to get the method m and (2) triggers m to start the process execution.

Follow-up on Process Status. This intent allows inquiring about process instance status (e.g., pending, in-progress or completed). For example, in Fig. 2 utterance 23, the user is inquiring about travel status. Figure 3 shows the specification of the rule related to this intent. The conditions are the same as those defined in the previous rule, except that this rule needs to detect a *follow-up* HP interaction act and the process instance should exists. If all conditions are satisfied, the chatbot (1) retrieves the corresponding instance and (2) lists the status of this instance.

Task Update. This intent allows to identify whether the user wants to update an existing process instance (e.g., update the hotel check-out date). A user can request to update an information in the whole process, or a specific activity in the process. We model an activity as an input parameter of the intent *task update*, thus the chatbot can extract from the user utterance the activity that the user wants to update. The conditions are the same as those defined in the first rule, except that this rule needs to detect a *task update* HP interaction act and the process instance should exists. If all conditions are satisfied, the chatbot (1) retrieves the corresponding instance, (2) extract the value of the *activity* parameter, (3) invokes the *Method Identification PES* service to get the corresponding method m and (4) triggers m to update the corresponding task.

Canceling a Task. This intent allows to identify whether the user utterance expresses a task cancellation of an existing process instance. The user can request to cancel the whole process (e.g., canceling travel bookings), or a specific task in the process (e.g., canceling hotel booking). The steps to recognize and realize *canceling task* intent are the same as those in the *task update* intent (Fig. 3).

4   Implementation and Experiments

The first objective of the study was to explore the *effectiveness* of the proposed approach, i.e., its capability of recognizing correctly the process-oriented intents presented in Sect. 3 and reducing unnecessary interactions. The second objective was to assess the impact of enabling interaction with a process as opposed to leaving users to orchestrate services themselves to fulfill their goals.

Experimental design.[1] Participants were recruited via email from the extended network of contacts of the authors. The call for volunteers resulted in a total of 17 participants. The evaluation scenario required participants to perform tasks associated with three underlying processes (Travel Booking, Shopping and Scheduling an appointment). Participants were asked to complete 4 tasks in this scenario (T1: starting new process instances, T2: updating information of process instances, T3: following up on process statuses, T4: canceling process instances). We followed a within-subjects design tasking participants to complete the above tasks by interacting with two chatbots representing the following conditions: (i) *Baseline-bot* that implements a standard conversational management; (ii) *Process-bot* that support PES and CKS services as well as the defined rules.

Procedure. The study was conducted online. After reading the informed consent and agreeing to participate, participants were introduced to the evaluation scenario and tasks (T1-T4). They were asked to perform those tasks with the two chatbots, in a counter-balanced design. After interacting with each chatbot, participants were asked: to select their preferred chatbot, to specify why, and provide quantitative feedback on their experience along three dimensions: *naturalness* (ability to fulfill user tasks in natural language), *repetitiveness* (ability to avoid redundant questions) and *understanding* (ability to interpret requests).

Data analysis. We performed an analysis of conversation logs so as to assess the effectiveness of our approach in recognizing the process-oriented intents. These are computed in relation to optimal conversation scenarios (i.e., scenarios assuming ideal accuracy of process-oriented intent recognition) that we designed based on participants conversations. The effectiveness is calculated by considering the following metrics: number of (M1) conversation turns, (M2) prompts asking for missing information, (M3) process correctly identified and (M4) process-oriented intents correctly recognized.

Results. Table 1 shows the relative performance by task of both baseline-bot and process-bot in relation to the optimal reference scenario. For the four tasks, we can see that process-bot experienced a boost in performance M1 and M2, approaching the efficiency of the reference scenario in terms of number of turns

---

[1] Experimental materials: https://tinyurl.com/ICSOC22StudyMaterials.

Table 1. Performance of experimental conditions for each task according to the relevant metrics. Values in bold denote best performance.

Task	Baseline-bot			Process-bot			
	M1 TURNS	M2 PROMPTS	M4 INTENT	M1 TURNS	M2 PROMPTS	M3 PROCESS	M4 INTENT
T1 (new)	54,14%	45,59%	51,75%	**95,73%**	**91,67%**	**92,86%**	**88,68%**
T2 (update)	31,58%	26,67%	25,00%	**85,71%**	**80,00%**	**91,67%**	**83,33%**
T3 (follow up)	47,15%	51,28%	27,86%	**82,61%**	**88,89%**	**85,71%**	**85,71%**
T4 (cancel)	27,27%	18,75%	33,33%	**80,00%**	**75,00%**	**91,67%**	**83,33%**
Mean	40,04%	35,57%	34,49%	**86,01%**	**83,89%**	**90,48%**	**85,27%**

(M1) and prompts (M2). This level of performance is possible thanks to the PES and CKS services and the defined rules that allow to perform a mean relative performance across tasks for process identification (M3) and intent recognition (M4) of 90,48% and 85,27% respectively. In contrast, not supporting these rules leads the baseline-bot to perform poorly in comparison, with the best performance being at around 36,70% for the considered metrics. Regarding the user experience, all but two participants (15/17 participants) expressed a preference towards the process-bot as opposed to the baseline-bot. The feedback to the specific user experience questions, highlighted the reasons behind the preference. The majority of participants reported that process-bot interactions described *naturalness* (11/17), less *repetitiveness* (11/17) and *understanding* (12/17), whereas the baseline-bot was poorly rated on these fronts (2/17).

5   Conclusions and Future Work

We proposed process-oriented intents that are relevant to represent natural language conversations between the user and multi-step processes. We devised an approach that combines recognition of these intents from user utterances with additional context and process knowledge to enable users to perform tasks by naturally interacting with service orchestrations. Future work includes identifying a new pattern that allows selecting a service based on subjective attributes.

References

1. Barukh, M.C., et al.: Cognitive augmentation in processes. In: Aiello, M., Bouguettaya, A., Tamburri, D.A., van den Heuvel, W.-J. (eds.) Next-Gen Digital Services. A Retrospective and Roadmap for Service Computing of the Future. LNCS, vol. 12521, pp. 123–137. Springer, Cham (2021). https://doi.org/10.1007/978-3-030-73203-5_10
2. Benatallah, B., et al.: The Self-Serv environment for Web services composition. IEEE Internet Comput. **7**(1), 40–48 (2003)
3. Bouguelia, S., et al.: Context knowledge-aware recognition of composite intents in task-oriented human-bot conversations. In: Proceedings of the CAiSE (2022). https://doi.org/10.1007/978-3-031-07472-1_14

4. Bouguelia, S., Brabra, H., Zamanirad, S., Benatallah, B., Baez, M., Kheddouci, H.: Reusable abstractions and patterns for recognising compositional conversational flows. In: La Rosa, M., Sadiq, S., Teniente, E. (eds.) CAiSE 2021. LNCS, vol. 12751, pp. 161–176. Springer, Cham (2021). https://doi.org/10.1007/978-3-030-79382-1_10

5. Brabra, H., et al.: Dialogue management in conversational systems: a review of approaches, challenges, and opportunities. IEEE Trans. Cognitive Dev. Syst. **14**, 783–798 (2021)

6. Bradley, N., et al.: Context-aware conversational developer assistants. In: 2018 IEEE/ACM 40th ICSE, pp. 993–1003. IEEE (2018)

7. Dumas, M., et al.: Fundamentals of Business Process Management, vol. 1. Springer (2013). https://doi.org/10.1007/978-3-642-33143-5

8. Gaulke, D., et al.: Interactive user interface to communication-enabled business process platforms method and apparatus (2015), US Patent 9,043,407

9. Hofmann, P., et al.: Robot. Process Autom. **30**(1), 99–106 (2020)

10. Kalia, A.K., Telang, P.R., Xiao, J., Vukovic, M.: Quark: a methodology to transform people-driven processes to chatbot services. In: Maximilien, M., Vallecillo, A., Wang, J., Oriol, M. (eds.) ICSOC 2017. LNCS, vol. 10601, pp. 53–61. Springer, Cham (2017). https://doi.org/10.1007/978-3-319-69035-3_4

11. Kobeissi, M., et al.: An intent-based natural language interface for querying process execution data. In: Proceedings of the ICPM, pp. 152–159. IEEE (2021)

12. López, A., Sànchez-Ferreres, J., Carmona, J., Padró, L.: From process models to chatbots. In: Giorgini, P., Weber, B. (eds.) CAiSE 2019. LNCS, vol. 11483, pp. 383–398. Springer, Cham (2019). https://doi.org/10.1007/978-3-030-21290-2_24

13. Matthies, C., et al.: An additional set of (automated) eyes: chatbots for agile retrospectives. In: Proceedings of the BotSE, pp. 34–37. IEEE (2019)

14. Rizk, Y., et al.: A unified conversational assistant framework for business process automation. arXiv preprint arXiv:2001.03543 (2020)

15. Sheth, A., et al.: Cognitive services and intelligent chatbots: current perspectives and special issue introduction. IEEE Internet Comput. **23**(2), 6–12 (2019)

16. Zamanirad, S., et al.: Hierarchical state machine based conversation model and services. In: Proceedings of the CAiSE (2020)

17. Zamanirad, S., et al.: Programming bots by synthesizing natural language expressions into API invocations. In: Proceedings of the ASE (2017)

A Bi-directional Category-Aware Multi-task Learning Framework for Missing Check-in POI Identification

Junhang Wu[1,2], Ruimin Hu[1,2(✉)], Dengshi Li[1,3], Lingfei Ren[1,2], Wenyi Hu[1,2], and Yilong Zang[1,2]

[1] National Engineering Research Center for Multimedia Software, School of Computer Science, Wuhan University, Wuhan 430072, China
hurm1964@gmail.com
[2] Hubei Key Laboratory of Multimedia and Network Communication Engineering, Wuhan University, Wuhan 430072, China
[3] School of Artificial Intelligence, Jianghan University, Wuhan 430056, China

Abstract. The prevalence of Location-based Social Networks (LBSNs) services makes next personalized Point-of-Interest (POI) prediction become a research topic. However, due to device failure or intention camouflage, geolocation information missing prevents existing POI-oriented studies for advanced user preference analysis. Herein, we proposed a Bi-directional category-aware multi-task learning (Bi-CatMTL) framework, which fuses bi-direction spatiotemporal transition patterns and personalized dynamic preference to identify where the user has been at a past specific time, namely missing POI identification. Specifically, Bi-CatMTL introduces: (1) a two-channel encoder, i.e., spatial-aware POI encoder and temporal-aware category encoder, to capture user bidirectional dual-grained mobility transition patterns; (2) a task-oriented decoder to fuse learned transition patterns and personalized preference for multi-task prediction; (3) a POI2Cat matrix to make full use of both types of sequential dependencies. Extensive experiments demonstrate the superiority of our model, and it can also be adaptively extended to next POI prediction task with the convincing performance.

Keywords: Missing check-in POI identification · Spatial-aware POI encoder · Temporal-aware category encoder

1 Introduction

The prevalence of LBSN attracts numerous users to share their real-life experiences in the form of check-ins, and data accumulated from LBSN is effectively utilized for POI-oriented applications (e.g., next POI recommendation or prediction) to facilitate the sharing between users and POIs.

However, due to device failure or user cheating, data quality issues (e.g., geolocation information missing) always limit above POI-oriented studies for

© The Author(s), under exclusive license to Springer Nature Switzerland AG 2022
J. Troya et al. (Eds.): ICSOC 2022, LNCS 13740, pp. 584–599, 2022.
https://doi.org/10.1007/978-3-031-20984-0_42

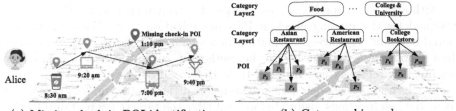

(a) Missing check-in POI identification   (b) Category hierarchy

Fig. 1. An example of missing check-in POI identification and category hierarchy.

advanced user mobility patterns understanding. Existing POI-oriented studies mainly focus on where to go (e.g., recommending or predicting the POI where a user may go in the future), which models user mobility patterns and preferences, and assumes that all users' check-ins have been specified to the exact POIs without considering check-in POI missing. Unfortunately, it has been found that over half of user check-ins are POIless (i.e., associated POIs are missing) in Twitter and Foursquare [5].

To the end, we focus on identifying where the user has been at a specific time in the past, that is, missing check-in POI identification. As shown in Fig. 1 (a), given an observed check-in subsequence for Alice, assuming that one check-in POI is missing between two successive check-ins, the task is to identify possible candidate POIs the target user might visit at a past specific time. The task is non-trivial due to the following reasons. First, given the distribution of candidates for the missing POI, it helps alleviate data sparsity issues. It can also be used for some social good, such as suspects tracing or missing population searching analysis. Moreover, by identifying which venues the patient has visited during his/her past disconnection, we can track persons who are within a certain spatiotemporal range with him/her to avoid a risk of cross-infection and help precision prevention.

So far, much progress has been made in next POI recommendation or prediction problem, which is related to our task. Earlier works primarily focused on feature engineering, and explored conventional collaborative filter and sequential approaches, such as Matrix Factorization (MF) models and Markov Chains (MC) model [7,9]. However, the sparsity of the user-POI matrix and cold-start issue are great challenges, causing significant degradation in POI recommendation performance. With the development of embedding techniques, it is heuristically developed to learn POI embeddings in a low-dimension vector space for the next POI prediction by treating each venue in the sampled sequence as a word, and it appears many embedding-based methods, such as GE [14], EDHG [3], HME [2], and so on. However, these existing embedding models can not well model user evolving preference and local temporal contexts when dealing with user chronological activities, and suffer from the large number of parameters and the inextricability of the learning framework. Since RNN and long-Short Term Memory (LSTM) are advantageous in mining sequential information, RNN- [8,16,19] and LSTM- [6,12] based methods are widely employed in POI recommendation [4].

Although these methods have achieved satisfactory results, they are not designed for the missing check-in POI identification task. The task needs to model check-in sequences information before and after the specific time rather than from a single perspective, so the methods of current POI-oriented methods can not be directly extended to our task. Bi-STDDP [13] is most relevant to our work, which jointly models user preference and the spatiotemporal dependence given the two locations visited before and after the targeted timestamp to identify the missing POI. Bi-G^{2}AN [13] is the advanced method for missing POI identification, which designed a GAN-based framework to generate the candidate POIs according to the same distribution as historical check-ins. However, Bi-STDDP and Bi-G^{2}AN fails to make full use of rich bi-directional spatiotemporal context, and can not reflect the dynamic importance of history.

Actually, missing check-in POI identification is essentially a sequence prediction promblem, and it is naturally studied using RNN. However, the RNN was originally designed for language modeling, and it can not be used directly to deal with user mobility traces due to sparsity. Therefore, most existing studies resort to incorporating spatiotemporal information with the temporal- and spatial-specific transition matrices into the RNN layer to model local spatiotemporal influence [8]. Though they have achieved satisfactory performance, they may oversimplify the spatial regularity of mobility and neglect the temporal periodicity of personalized preference. Additionally, people tend to decide which category of POIs they are going to at a specific time and then determine the specific POI, which naturally reflects personalized hierarchical mobility preferences [18]. However, most current methods directly model POI-level user preference and sequential transition on sparse data without considering the hierarchical structure in user mobility data (e.g., category taxonomy). We thus model the hierarchical transition pattern and personalized preference for the identification task. Figure 1 (b) depicts a POI-category structure example tree. For simplicity, we only consider the semantic POI categories on leaf nodes, as illustrated in category layer 1.

Against this background, we propose a novel bi-directional category-aware multi-task learning (Bi-CatMTL) framework, which explicitly exploits bi-directional rich spatiotemporal context to search items with high predictive power using attention mechanism. The main contributions are as follows:

(1) A two-channel encoder, i.e., spatial-aware POI transition encoder and temporal-aware category transition encoder, is developed to capture user bi-directional dual-grained mobility transition patterns.

(2) A POI2Cat matrix is introduced to facilitate the interactive multi-task learning framework, which makes full use of both types of sequential dependencies (i.e., POI and category)

(3) Extensive experiments demonstrate the superiority of our model, and it can also be adaptively extended to next POI prediction task with convincing performance.

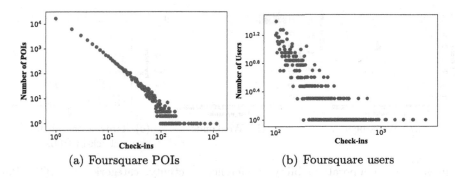

(a) Foursquare POIs   (b) Foursquare users

Fig. 2. Frequency of check-ins for users and POIs.

2   Perlimimaries

In this section, we focus on the preliminary work, and explore the characteristics of the LBSN datasets here. Two available public datasets used in the paper are Foursquare NYC and TKY. More details about them will be provided in Sect. 4. To facilitate the understanding, we also present the definition of key concepts and problems formulation next.

2.1   Data Analysis

In this subsection, based on the dataset, we investigate user mobility patterns from check-in frequency, temporal mobility preference, and transition mobility preference.

Analysis on the Distributions of the Check-in Frequency We first study the distribution of check-in frequency for POIs and users, as depicted in Fig. 2(a) and (b). We can observe that a handful of users and POIs with many check-in records (short head) and many users and POIs with a handful of check-in records (long tail), which follows the power-law distribution. Theoretically, it suggests a hierarchical structure, such as category taxonomy [2]. Actually, people tend to decide which category of POIs they are going to at a specific time and then determine the specific POI, which naturally reflects personalized hierarchical mobility preferences. Based on this, we model both POI- and category-level user mobility pattern to facilitate the identification task.

Analysis on User Temporal Mobility Preference In Fig. 3 (a) and (b), it shows the users' temporal preference for user activities and depict the different preferences for weekdays and weekends. Intuitively, it exhibits a strong temporal cyclic for users' mobility patterns. On weekdays, people usually work in the office from 9 am to 7 pm and have a cup of coffee at 11 am. Interestingly, some people choose to Gym/Fitness Center at noon or midnight. At weekends, most

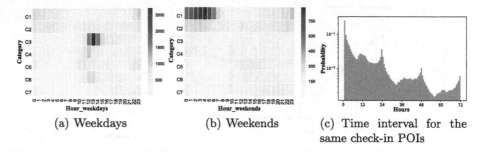

(a) Weekdays   (b) Weekends   (c) Time interval for the same check-in POIs

Fig. 3. User temporal mobility preference. Activity categories = {C1: Bar, C2:Home(private), C3: Office, C4:Subway, C5: Gym/Fitness Center, C6:Coffee Shop, C7: Food&Drink Shop}

people don't have to work, and they may choose some nightlife spots (bar) to relax at night or early morning, while some people decide to stay at home or go out for some food and drink at a later time. It shows the periodicity and preference variance of temporal characteristics. To capture the above personalized temporal mobility patterns, we incorporate temporal influence into the model by dividing the timestamp into day slots(seven days for a week) and time slots(several sessions for a day).

In Fig. 3 (c), it shows the return probability of user check-ins over time, defined as the probability of a user re-checking in at a POI within a certain period of time after her last check-in at that POI. A clear periodic re-checking pattern can be observed. For our task, such a periodicity indicates that contextual check-ins with a temporal distance (taken from the time with POI missing) closer to the periodic peaks provide a higher predictive ability.

Analysis on User Transition Preference Figure 4(a) plots the sequence transition statistics between user successive activities. It can be observed that sequence transition patterns exist between activity items; for instance, "Office" is more likely checked in after "Coffee Shop", and "Food & Drink Shop" is usually visited before going "Home(private)". Intuitively, an activity item can be deployed into two roles: the departure itself and the destination of others. To preserve the "double role" for each activity item in the sequence, we use Bidirectional Recurrent Neural Networks(Bi-RNN) [10] for sequence modeling, which takes both forward and backward information into account when they encode the same sequence input.

In Fig. 4(b), we can observe that "Train Stations" looks like the spider web across the whole city, "Offices" are concentrated in the centre of the city and "Home(private)" are located around the city and close to the "Train Stations". Actually, the city is divided into several regions with certain implicit "functions", such as working and resting. Therefore, the closer the user is to such a region the more predictable her behavior is. It implies that the closer a POI check-in is

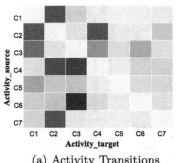

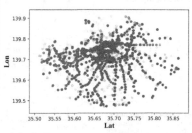

(a) Activity Transitions   (b) Activity spatial distribution

Fig. 4. User temporal mobility preference. In the left figure, Activity categories = {C1: Bar, C2:Home(private), C3: Office, C4:Subway, C5: Gym/Fitness Center, C6:Coffee Shop, C7: Food&Drink Shop}. In the right figure, Activity categories = {Red: Train Station, Blue: Office, Yellow: Home(private)}

located to the current location, the more helpful it is for next loction prediction [16], which can be heuristically extended to our task.

2.2 Problem Definition

In this subsection, we will formulate some key definition and notations which we use in the paper.

Let U, P and C be a set of LBSN users, POIs and categories, denoted as $\{u_1, u_2, ..., u_N\}$, $\{p_1, p_2, ..., p_M\}$ and $C = \{c_1, c_2, ..., c_Q\}$, respectively. Note that each POI is geoencoded by coordinate (lat, lon), and associated with one of the categories without overlap items.

Definition 1 (Check-in Activity). The check-in activity $A_{t_\tau}^u$, denoted as a quadruple (u, p_i, c_j, t_τ) where $u \in U$, $p_i \in P$, $c_j \in C$, means the user u made the check-in at POI p_i with category c_j at time t_τ.

Definition 2 (Check-in Activity Sequence). It is a chronological ordered sequence, denoted as $\langle A_{t_1}^u, A_{t_2}^u, ..., A_{t_T}^u \rangle$, and it can also be split into the POI check-in sequence $\langle p_{t_1}^u, p_{t_2}^u, ..., p_{t_T}^u \rangle$ and the according category check-in sequence $\langle c_{t_1}^u, c_{t_2}^u, ..., c_{t_T}^u \rangle$.

Definition 3 (POI2Cat Matrix). Given M POIs and Q categories, a matrix $\mathbf{M}^{p2c}$ of size $M \times Q$ is constructed. When a POI p_i falls into a category c_j, $\mathbf{M}_{ij}^{p2c}$ is set to 1.

Problem (Missing Check-in POI Identification). Given user u's check-in activity sequence, it is assumed that the ith check-in $p_{t_i}^u$ with $c_{t_i}^u$ is lost. The target is to identify which check-in POI that the user u visited at time t_i with the help of the forward sequence before t_i: $\langle A_{t_1}^u, A_{t_2}^u, ..., A_{t_{i-1}}^u \rangle$ and backward sequence after $\langle A_{t_1}^u, A_{t_2}^u, ..., A_{t_{i-1}}^u \rangle$.

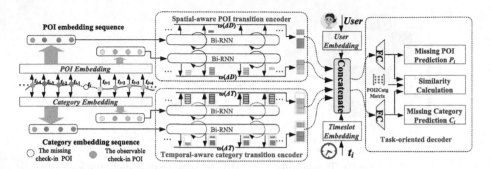

Fig. 5. The diagram of proposed Bi-CatMTL architecture for missing POI identification, composed of the temporal-aware category and spatial-aware POI transition ecoder, and the task-oriented decoder.

Problem (Next POI prediction). Given only the forward sequence information $\left\langle A_{t_1}^u, A_{t_2}^u, ..., A_{t_{i-1}}^u \right\rangle$, it is to predict user's next check-in POI $p_{t_i}^u$ at time t_i.

3   Proposed Methodology

3.1   Model Framework

To solve the above-defined problem, we devise a novel method named Bi-CatMTL, as shown in Fig. 5. We can observe that Bi-CatMTL consists of three main components, namely temporal-aware category transition encoder, spatial-aware POI transition encoder, and task-oriented encoder. It models bi-direction dual-granularity mobility transition patterns for missing check-in POI identification. Next, we will introduce them in detail.

3.2   Bi-directional Recurrent Neural Networks

As the sequential prediction problem, it is naturally studied using RNN, which learns the sequence transition pattern by taking information from current input e_{p_i} and prior hidden state h_{i-1} to influence the output h_i, denoted as:

$$h_i = f\left(\mathbf{M} \cdot e_{p_i} + \mathbf{N} \cdot h_{i-1}\right), \tag{1}$$

where $f(x)$ refers to the sigmoid activation function. To better model the forward and reverse sequence transition, we exploit Bi-RNN for sequence modeling, which takes both future and current information into account when they encode the sequence input. It concatenate both forward and backward RNN hidden states h_i^f and h_i^b at the ith time point, that is, $h_i = \left[h_i^f, h_i^b\right]$.

3.3 Temporal-Aware Category Transition Encoder

From a temporal perspective, users' mobility behavior shows the strong cyclical and concomitant nature. To model above factors, we first use Havercosin function as the periodic function to parameterize ΔT_{ij} (in days):

$$\lambda^c_{period}(\Delta T_{ij}) = havercos(2\pi\Delta T_{ij}), \tag{2}$$

where $havercos(x) = \frac{cos(x)+1}{2}$, and it is used to model user daily periodicity. Besides that, our mobility behavior is of concomitance (e.g. going home after shopping), and the longer the interval between check-ins, the smaller the concomitant effect it makes for prediction. Therefore, we add a temporal exponential decay weight to model this factor:

$$\lambda^c(\Delta T_{ij}) = \lambda^c_{period}(\Delta T_{ij}) \cdot e^{-\beta\Delta T_{ij}}, \tag{3}$$

where β is the temporal decay rate, which controls the speed of weight decreasing over time interval ΔT_{ij}. Given the corresponding semantic category forward sequence, we conduct the temporal-aware hidden search as follows:

$$c^F_i = \frac{1}{S(\cdot)}\left(\sum_{n=1}^{w}\lambda^c(\Delta T_{i,i-n}) \cdot h^c_{i-n}\right), \tag{4}$$

where $S(\cdot) = \sum_{n=1}^{w}\lambda^c(\Delta T_{i,i-n})$, w is the length of subsequence, h^c_{i-n} is the hidden state at t_{i-n} for POI sequence, and c^F_i denotes the integrated features which have selected hidden states with high predictive power from the forward semantic category sequence using temporal-aware attention cell. Similarly, c^B_i can be derived from the backward category sequence.

3.4 Spatial-Aware POI Transition Encoder

From a spatial perspective, users' check-ins in their frequently visited regions are highly biased toward certain POIs, and the closer a related check-in POI is located to the current location, the more helpful it becomes for the next POI prediction [16]. Specifically, the weights for the related Bi-RNN hidden states are parameterized by spatial distance as follows:

$$\omega^p(\Delta D_{ij}) = e^{-\alpha\Delta D_{ij}}, \tag{5}$$

where ΔD_{ij} is the $L2$ distance between the GPS coordinates of POIs p_i and p_j, and α is the spatial decay rate which controls the decrease speed of weight over spatial distance ΔD_{ij}. Given the forward POI sequence before t_i, we conduct spatial-aware hidden state search as follows:

$$p^F_i = \frac{1}{Z(\cdot)}\left(\sum_{n=1}^{w}\omega^p(\Delta D_{i-1,i-n}) \cdot h^p_{i-n}\right), \tag{6}$$

where $Z\left(\cdot\right) = \sum_{n=1}^{w} \omega^p \left(\Delta D_{i-1,i-n}\right)$, and p_i^F denotes the integrated features which have selected hidden states with high predictive power from the forward POI sequence using spatial-aware attention cell. Following that, we derive p_i^B from the backward POI sequence.

3.5   Task-Oriented Encoder

To model user personalized preference and temporal preference variance, we introduce user learnable embeddings e_u and timeslot embeddings e_τ. Note that a timestamp is split into the day and hour slot, and we split a week into seven days and a day into six sessions, and it totals 42 distinct timeslots τ for a week. Finally, we concatenate the features as follows:

$$x_{input} = \left[e_u,\ e_\tau,\ p_i^F,\ p_i^B,\ c_i^F,\ c_i^B\right]. \tag{7}$$

Considering the interplay between users' mobility category and POI visit, we thus perform the major task (missing POI identification) with the help of an auxiliary task(missing semantic category identification). That is mainly because of two reasons: (1) it is of complementarity for both prediction tasks; (2) jointly learning both tasks facilitates to enhance the model generalization. We thus perform the multi-task as:

$$\hat{y}_p = softmax\left(\mathbf{W_p} \cdot x_{input} + \mathbf{b_p}\right)$$
$$\hat{y}_c = softmax\left(\mathbf{W_c} \cdot x_{input} + \mathbf{b_c}\right), \tag{8}$$

where $\hat{y}_p \in R^{M \times 1}$ and $\hat{y}_c \in R^{Q \times 1}$ denote the prediction of missing POI and semantic category with $softamx$ function.

Actually, each POI is associated with a certain category, so the distribution of predicted POI can be transformed into the distribution of category as follows:

$$\hat{y}_c' = softmax(\hat{y}_p^T \cdot \mathbf{M}_j^{p2c}), \tag{9}$$

where $\mathbf{M}^{p2c} \in R^{M \times Q}$ is the relation matrix which indicates the affiliation between each POI and category, and $\hat{y}_c' \in R^{1 \times Q}$ is the category distribution generated by generated predicted POI distribution. As for two category distributions $\hat{y}_c$ and $\hat{y}_c'$, we should learn the model to make them close with maximizing their distribution similarity as follows:

$$D_{JS}\left(\hat{y}_c' \| \hat{y}_c\right) = \frac{1}{2}(D_{KL}(\hat{y}_c' \left\| \frac{\hat{y}_c' + \hat{y}_c}{2}\right) + D_{KL}(\hat{y}_c \left\| \frac{\hat{y}_c' + \hat{y}_c}{2}\right)), \tag{10}$$

where $D_{JS}\left(\cdot\right)$ is the Jensen-Shannon Divergence (JS) to measure the distributions of different facets diverging from each other entropically with symmetry, and it circumvents the asymmetry issue and bounds to $[0,1]$. The larger the value, the better the coordination between tasks. $D_{KL}\left(\cdot\right)$ is the Kullback-Leibler Divergence which measures the observed distribution of facet P_1 diverging from distribution of facet P_2, and it is denoted as follows:

$$D_{KL}\left(P_1 \| P_2\right) = \sum P_1 log\frac{P_1}{P_2}. \tag{11}$$

For these two tasks, they are both independent but also inherently interdependent, so we define the coordination between them as $Coor\left(\hat{y}_p,\ \hat{y}_c\right)$:

$$Coor\left(\hat{y}_p,\ \hat{y}_c\right) = D_{JS}\left(softmax(\hat{y}_p \cdot \mathbf{M}_j^{p2c})\|\hat{y}_c\right). \tag{12}$$

The larger $Coor\left(\cdot\right)$), the better coordination of two tasks.

3.6 Model Optimization

Given the training samples, the model is trained to make the prediction distribution fit the ground distribution more closely by minimizing the loss value as follows:

$$J_p = -\frac{1}{R}\sum_{i=1}^{R}\sum_{j=1}^{|P|} y_{ij}^p \cdot \log\left(\hat{y}_{ij}^p \,|x_{input},\ \theta\right), \tag{13}$$

where J_p refers to the cross-entropy loss between the prediction and the ground truth. R and $|P|$ are the number of training samples and candidate POIs, repectively, and θ is the involved parameters set. y_{ij}^p is either equal to 1 or 0 for the ground truth, and $\hat{y}_{ij}^p$ refers to the identification probability for the p_j outputted by the model. Following that, the loss function of missing check-in category identification can be denoted as:

$$J_c = -\frac{1}{R}\sum_{i=1}^{R}\sum_{k=1}^{|C|} y_{ik}^c \cdot \log\left(\hat{y}_{ik}^c \,|x_{input},\ \theta\right). \tag{14}$$

In addition, we incorporate the coordination influence into consideration and seek to minimize the sum loss as:

$$J = (2 - Coor\left(\hat{y}_p,\ \hat{y}_c\right)) \cdot (\lambda_p J_p + \lambda_c J_c) + \frac{\lambda}{2}\|\theta\|^2, \tag{15}$$

where λ_p and λ_c ($\lambda_p + \lambda_c = 1$) are the weights to balance the importance of different task losses. $\|\theta\|^2$ is the regularization term to avoid over-fitting, and λ controls the power of regularization. Note that, $Coor\left(\cdot\right)$ acts an scaling factor for loss penalty. When $Coor\left(\cdot\right)$ is small, the loss penalty becomes large and it brings large magnitude grandient update.

4 Evaluation

4.1 Dataset

Two public LBSN datasets, i.e., NYC and TKY [17] are used for performance evaluation. These two datasets[1] are collected in New York and Tokyo from 12 Apr 2012 to 16 Feb 2013, respectively. The statistic of the two datasets is shown in Table 1. Note that, the involved data has been strictly decrypted to avoid any risk of information leakage. Following [13], POIs checked in by fewer than 10

---

[1] https://sites.google.com/site/yangdingqi/home/foursquare-dataset.

users and users with fewer than 10 check-ins are eliminated. Each user' check-ins are sorted chronologically, and then we take the first 80% for training, the next 10% for validation, and the rest for testing. The source code of our model is available.[2]

Table 1. Dataset statistics

Dataset	#User	#POI	#Category	#Check-in
NYC	1083	38333	251	227428
TKY	2293	61858	247	573703

4.2 Baseline Method

- **PRME-G** [1] is a widely used personalized ranking-based method, which jointly models sequential transition, personalized preference and geographical for POI Recommendation;
- **ST-RNN** [8] is an RNN-improved method that models local spatiotemporal influence by incorporating both distance- and time interval-specific transition matrix into each RNN layer;
- **PACE** [15] is a deep network-based method, which first models sophisticated interactions between them by embedding users and POIs into a shared space, then it is used to predict the preference of users for POIs;
- **Flashback** [16] is the state-of-the-art RNN-based model for next location prediction by doing flashbacks on past hidden states in RNNs;
- **Bi-STDDP** [11] is the pioneer work which is specially developed for missing POI identification by modeling personalized preference and the spatiotemporal dependence given the two adjacent POIs visited before and after the targeted timestamp.
- **Bi-G^{2}AN** [13] is the state-of-the-art method for missing POI identification, which designed a GAN-based framework to generate the candidate POIs obeying the same distribution as historica check-ins.

4.3 Implementation Details

For such two datasets, we deploy batch size of 256, embedding dimension of 32, window size of 8, regularization weight of 0.5, initial learning rate of 0.005. As for spatial decay rate α temporal decay rate β, we set $\alpha = 100$ and $\beta = 0.1$, respectively. These values are chosen via a grid search on the validation set, and the key parameter sensitively analysis will be introduced in Sect. 4.7.

---

[2] https://github.com/Shzuwu/Missing-POI-Identification3.

Table 2. Evaluation for missing POI identification.The best result in each column is in bold, while the second is underlined

Method	NYC				TKY			
	Acc@1	Acc@5	Acc@10	MAP	Acc@1	Acc@5	Acc@10	MAP
PRME-G [1]	0.1077	0.2836	0.3717	0.1912	0.0870	0.2003	0.2557	0.1436
STRNN [8]	0.1302	0.3225	0.4055	0.2250	0.1612	0.3665	0.4492	0.2543
PACE [15]	0.1287	0.3226	0.4033	0.2199	0.1608	0.3605	0.4469	0.2518
Flashback [16]	0.1345	0.3351	0.4090	0.2246	0.1637	0.3832	0.4721	0.2671
Bi-STDDP [13]	0.1743	0.3476	0.4176	0.2533	0.2049	0.4107	0.4838	0.2991
Bi-G^{2}AN [11]	0.1830	0.3686	0.4358	0.2674	0.2145	0.4367	0.4908	0.3120
Bi-CatMTL	**0.1864**	**0.3872**	**0.4816**	**0.2890**	**0.2181**	**0.4458**	**0.5172**	**0.3189**

Table 3. Performance of missing check-in POI identification on different sequences in NYC dataset.

	Acc@1	Acc@5	Acc@10	MAP
F-CatMTL	0.1684	0.3652	0.4672	0.2536
B-CatMTL	0.1645	0.3663	0.4614	0.2547
Bi-CatMTL	**0.1864**	**0.3872**	**0.4816**	**0.2890**

4.4 Evaluation Metrics

Accuracy@N(Acc@N, where N=1,5,10) and Mean Average Precision (MAP) are employed for performance evaluation. Specifically, for a test case, we define $hit@N$ as either 1, if the ground truth POI appears in the top-N predicted POIs or categories list, or the value 0, if otherwise. The Acc@N is computed as follows:

$$Acc@N = \frac{\sum hit@N}{|D_{test}|}, N = \{1, 5, 10\}, \tag{16}$$

where $\sum hit@N$ denotes the sum of all hits, and $|D_{test}|$ is the number of test samples. As for the predicted item, we not only want it in the top-N list but also want it to be at the top of this list. MAP is used to measure the position of ground truth POI in the ranked predicted list. Overall, the larger Acc@N and MAP value, the better model performance.

4.5 Performance Comparison

Extensive experiments are conducted to evaluate our Bi-CatMTL with other state-of-the-art baseline models as shown in Table 2, and we have following observations.

First, PRME-G, as the rule-based model, fails to achieve high Acc@N and MAP on two datasets because the historically check-in POIs and moving constraints with geographical distance can help missing POI identification, but simply leveraging them cannot achieve satisfactory performance as they are deficient in modeling complex mobility regularity. Second, RNN-based methods(STRNN,

Flashback) and deep network-based approaches (PACE) achieve similar performance, and they generally perform better than rule-based methods, demonstrating their strong capability of sequence and complex relation modeling. Third, Bi-CatMTL, Bi-G^{2}AN, and Bi-STDDP, as the missing POI identification methods, deliver decent performance on both datasets. Because it is different from traditional POI recommendation or prediction tasks, missing POI identification models richer context with both forward and backward sequential information instead of from a single directional sequence. Last, compared to the advanced missing POI identification method Bi-STDDP and Bi-G^{2}AN, Bi-CatMTL performs better because: (1)Bi-CatMTL exploits the interplay between POI and semantic category via an interactive multi-task learning framework which models the hierarchical dependencies between these two items; (2)Bi-CatMTL adopts the spatiotemporal-aware attention encoder to search the hidden states with high predictive power bilaterally across both POI and semantic category granularity, which helps make full use of bi-directional rich context.

4.6   Imapct of Forward and Backward Sequences

Intuitively, a bi-directional sequence contains more useful context information and brings performance improvement. Hence, we conduct a comparison experiment evaluated by Acc@k and MAP on the NYC dataset, as shown in Table 3. Similar results can also be observed on TKY. Not surprisingly, compared with F-CatMTL and B-CatMTL which only use the backward or forward sequence information, Bi-CatMTL performs best. It is worth pointing out that the performances of our method F-CatMTL which only models the forward sequence is still superior to the baseline models containing the next POI recommendation and prediction. Significantly, Bi-CatMTL can be naturally applied to next POI prediction tasks with competitive performance.

4.7   Effect of Hyper-parameter Settings

In this section, we will study the impact of key hyper-parameters on NYC, including batch size, embedding size d, window length w, and regularization weight λ_p, and the similar results can also be observed on TKY.

To study the impact of batch size on final identification, we vary the value of batch size in the range of [8, 512]. For clarity, we adopt the log_2^N coordinate axis. The result is depicted in Fig. 6 (a), and It can be observed that the performance gets improved with the batch size increasing and becomes stable when it is greater than 128. Actually, too small a batch size causes the instability of network convergence. Too large a batch size takes less time but makes large running memory requirements and easily falls in a local optimum. To make a trade-off between the above effects, we finally set the batch size as 256.

To investigate the effect of embedding size d, we vary it in the range of [2, 64]. As shown in Fig. 6 (b), we can observe that performance improves with the increasing dimension of embedding, as it gradually fits the data distribution sufficiently. However, when $d \geq 16$, the improvement gradually becomes marginal.

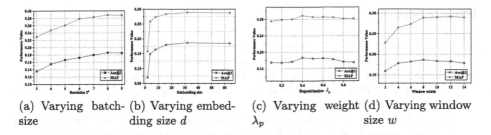

(a) Varying batch-size (b) Varying embedding size d (c) Varying weight λ_p (d) Varying window size w

Fig. 6. Performance of missing POI identification on NYC dataset with varying embedding size d and window size w evaluated on Acc@1 and MAP.

Considering the larger embedding dimension means higher computational complexity and converges to local optimum, we set d to 32.

To study the impact of regularization weight λ_p, which is used to weigh the importance of POI-level and category-level loss, we report the experimental results by varying λ_p in the range of $[0.1, 0.9]$ stepped by zero point one in Fig. 6 (c). In the figure, it shows a small unimodal distribution where the performance first gradually climbs up and reaches the peak, then it declines and tends to become stable. Taken overall, the performance comprehensively gets the best when λ_p is set to 0.5.

To investigate the effect of window size w, we vary it in the range of $[2, 14]$ stepped by two. As shown in Fig. 6 (d), it first makes gradual improvement with w increasing, as it gets the richer context. When $w \geq 8$, the performance of MAP is with less fluctuation while the performance of Acc@1 has some degradation as too long a searching window length may make some noise incorporated. For overall performance, we finally set w to 8.

5   Conclusion

Herein, we proposed a bi-directional category-aware multi-task learning (Bi-CatMTL) framework to address the problem of missing check-in POI identification. Specifically, we modeled bi-directional dual-grained sequences to capture user mobility transition patterns. To make full use of rich context from sparse traces, we developed the spatiotemporal-aware encoder to explicitly weigh bi-directional hidden states with high prediction capability. The task-oriented decoder performs both missing POI and category tasks, and a POI2Cat matrix is introduced to model the interdependence between them. Experimental results show the superiority of Bi-CatMTL over state-of-the-arts and it can be naturally applied to next POI prediction tasks with convincing performance.

Acknowledgments. We first gratefully acknowledge anonymous reviewers who read this draft and make any helpful suggestions. The work is supported by the National Nature Science Foundation of China (No. U22A201181, U1803262, U1736206), National Social Science Fund of China (No. 19ZDA113), and the Application Foundation Frontier Project of Wuhan Science and Technology Bureau (No. 2020010601012288).

References

1. Feng, S., Li, X., Zeng, Y., et al.: Personalized ranking metric embedding for next new poi recommendation. In: Proceedings of IJCAI, pp. 2069–2075 (2015)
2. Feng, S., Tran, L.V., Cong, G., et al.: HME: a hyperbolic metric embedding approach for next-POI recommendation. In: Proceedings of SIGIR, pp. 1429–1438 (2020)
3. Hang, M., Pytlarz, I., Neville, J.: Exploring student check-in behavior for improved point-of-interest prediction. In: Proceedings of SIGKDD, pp. 321–330 (2018)
4. Islam, M., Mohammad, M.M., Das, S.S.S., et al.: A survey on deep learning based point-of-interest (POI) recommendations. arXiv preprint arXiv:2011.10187 (2020)
5. Li, H., Deng, K., Cui, J., et al.: Hidden community identification in location-based social network via probabilistic venue sequences. Inf. Sci. **422**, 188–203 (2018)
6. Li, R., Shen, Y., Zhu, Y.: Next point-of-interest recommendation with temporal and multi-level context attention. In: Proceedings of ICDM, pp. 1110–1115. IEEE (2018)
7. Li, X., Cong, G., Li, X.L., et al.: Rank-GeoFM: a ranking based geographical factorization method for point of interest recommendation. In: Proceedings of SIGIR, pp. 433–442 (2015)
8. Liu, Q., Wu, S., Wang, L., et al.: Predicting the next location: a recurrent model with spatial and temporal contexts. In: Proceedings of AAAI, pp. 194–200 (2016)
9. Rendle, S., Freudenthaler, C., Schmidt-Thieme, L.: Factorizing personalized Markov chains for next-basket recommendation. In: Proceedings of the 19th International Conference on WWW, pp. 811–820 (2010)
10. Schuster, M., Paliwal, K.K.: Bidirectional recurrent neural networks. IEEE Trans. Signal Process. **45**(11), 2673–2681 (1997)
11. Shi, M., Shen, D., Kou, Y., Nie, T., Yu, G.: Missing POI check-in identification using generative adversarial networks. In: Jensen, C.S., et al. (eds.) DASFAA 2021. LNCS, vol. 12681, pp. 575–590. Springer, Cham (2021). https://doi.org/10.1007/978-3-030-73194-6_38
12. Sun, K., Qian, T., Chen, T., et al.: Where to Go Next: modeling Long- and Short-Term user preferences for point-of-interest recommendation. Proc. AAAI **34**, 214–221 (2020)
13. Xi, D., Zhuang, F., Liu, Y., et al.: Modelling of bi-directional spatio-temporal dependence and users' dynamic preferences for missing POI check-in identification. Proc. AAAI **33**, 5458–5465 (2019)
14. Xie, M., Yin, H., Wang, H., et al.: Learning graph-based POI embedding for location-based recommendation. In: Proceedings of CIKM, pp. 15–24 (2016)
15. Yang, C., Bai, L., Zhang, C., et al.: Bridging collaborative filtering and semi-supervised learning: a neural approach for POI recommendation. In: Proceedings of KDD, pp. 1245–1254 (2017)
16. Yang, D., Fankhauser, B., Rosso, P., et al.: Location prediction over sparse user mobility traces using RNNs: flashback in hidden states! In: Proceedings of IJCAI, pp. 2184–2190 (2020)
17. Yang, D., Zhang, D., Zheng, V.W., et al.: Modeling user activity preference by leveraging user spatial temporal characteristics in LBSNs. IEEE Trans. Syst. Man Cybern.: Syst. **45**(1), 129–142 (2014)

18. Zhang, L., Sun, Z., Zhang, J., Kloeden, H., Klanner, F.: Modeling hierarchical category transition for next POI recommendation with uncertain check-ins. Inf. Sci. **515**, 169–190 (2020)
19. Zhao, K., Zhang, Y., Yin, H., et al.: Discovering subsequence patterns for next POI recommendation. In: Proceedings of IJCAI, pp. 3216–3222 (2020)

Performance and Cost-Aware Task Scheduling via Deep Reinforcement Learning in Cloud Environment

Zihui Zhao[1,2], Xiaoyu Shi[1,3(✉)], and Mingsheng Shang[1,3]

[1] Chongqing Key Laboratory of Big Data and Intelligent Computing, Chongqing Institute of Green and Intelligent Technology, Chinese Academy of Sciences, Chongqing 400714, China
xiaoyushi@cigit.ac.cn
[2] Beihang University, Beijing 100191, China
[3] School of Automotive Software, Chongqing School, University of Chinese Academy of Sciences, Chongqing 400714, China

Abstract. In the cloud computing environment, task scheduling with multiple objectives optimization becomes a highly challenging problem in such a dynamic and bursty environment. Previous studies have mostly emphasized assigning the incoming tasks in a specific scenario, with a weak generalization ability to various objectives automatically. Thus, they suffer the inefficient issue under large-scale and heterogeneous cloud workloads. To address this issue, we propose a deep reinforcement learning (DRL)-based intelligent cloud task scheduler, which makes the optimal scheduling decision only dependent on learning directly from its experience without any prior knowledge. We formulate task scheduling as a dynamical optimization problem with constraints and then adopt the deep deterministic policy gradients (DDPG) network to find the optimal task assignment solution while meeting the performance and cost constraints. We propose a correlation-aware state representation method to capture the inherent characteristics of demands, and a dual reward model is designed to learn the optimal task allocation strategy. Extensive experimental results on Alibaba cloud workloads show that compared with other existing solutions, our proposed DDPG-based task scheduler enjoy superiority and effectiveness in performance and cost optimization.

Keywords: Cloud computing · Task scheduling · Deep reinforcement learning · Cost optimization · Performance improvement

1 Introduction

Cloud computing is the most popular computing paradigm in IT society [1]. With virtualization technologies, the data center can easily abstract the different hardware infrastructures as a larger resource pool and provides elastic hardware resources as services to users through the Internet. For instance, Amazon EC2[1],

---

[1] https://aws.amazon.com/ec2/.

© The Author(s), under exclusive license to Springer Nature Switzerland AG 2022
J. Troya et al. (Eds.): ICSOC 2022, LNCS 13740, pp. 600–615, 2022.
https://doi.org/10.1007/978-3-031-20984-0_43

Microsoft Azure[2], and Alibaba Cloud[3] offers customized hardware resource to customers in the form of virtual machine (VM), and charge based on actual usage. As a result, increasingly services have migrated to the cloud environment for fast development and cost-saving.

Regarding of cloud environment, the effective task scheduling of cloud services is one of the key enablers of large-scale cloud systems [2]. However, the unique features of the cloud environment make task scheduling among VMs more challenging. Firstly, the cloud workload featured highly dynamic variation and unexpected bursts. Thus, it requires a designed task scheduler with the characteristic of robustness against the unexpected burst in incoming cloud tasks. Secondly, the problem of task scheduling in cloud environment is NP-hard problem. Furthermore, the datacenter usually offers users various types of VM instances to meet users' customized requirements. Each type of VM has its own pricing model. Thus, the large-scale task scheduling problem becomes more complicated in such a heterogeneous environment. Last but not least, task scheduling in the cloud environment is a multi-objective optimization problem and is related to the profits of multiple stakeholders. For the date center, it is expected to maximize the utilization ratio of hardware resources. The cloud services providers emphasize minimizing the usage cost of rented VM instances, while the end users concern more about the service experience offered by cloud services providers. Thus, how to design an efficient task scheduler to guarantee the profits of different stakeholders is also an important problem.

Following this, several solutions have been proposed with using heuristic-based algorithms [3–7]. Some of these methods focus on scheduling problems for offline or static batch tasks, which are not incapable of the dynamic workloads in real-time scenarios. For the online task scheduling method, existing solutions using meta-heuristic algorithms can only assign tasks sequentially, which is inefficient to deal with the massive and dynamic workload case. Meanwhile, heuristic-based task scheduling methods emphasize on a specific scenario, lacking the generalization ability to adapt to a wide range of objectives. Meanwhile, they cannot utilize the inherent characteristics of workloads to improve the optimization effect.

To this end, we propose an effective task scheduling based on the deep reinforcement learning (DRL) framework in this paper. We consider online task scheduling as a constrained dynamical optimization problem. We formulate it as a Markov decision process (MDP) model, then adopt the deep deterministic policy gradient (DDPG) network to find the optimal task assignment solution. It can learn directly from its experience without any prior knowledge, making the appropriate scheduling decision for VMs for continuous online task requests. The main contributions of this paper include:

– We propose an RL model of the task scheduling problem in cloud environments. We also formulate the state representation and rewards to train DRL

[2] https://azure.microsoft.com/en-ca/.
[3] https://www.alibabacloud.com/.

agents to satisfy load balancing, reduce average response time and optimize the usage cost of a cloud cluster.

– We design a correlation-aware state representation method that leverages the Pearson's correlation coefficient (PCC) and standard deviation of the resources demands (STD) to help perceive the feature of the workloads. A dual-reward model is designed to improve the effectiveness of learning the optimal policy.
– We conduct extensive experiments on real-world workload trace. It clearly demonstrates the superiority of our method over other state-of-the-art approaches.

2   Related Works

Scheduling tasks in the cloud environment is an essential and challenging problem, which has been studied for decades. To improve the performance of cloud datacenter under the constraints of the Service Level Agreements (SLAs), various task assignment algorithms and approaches are proposed [8–10]. Several solutions view the task scheduling problem as an NP-hard problem, whose goal is to optimize the task assignment in a stable environment. Hence, some heuristic or meta-heuristic methods have been proposed to solve the task scheduling problem, such as SARO [6] and hybridized BA [7]. For instance, Luo et al. [5] proposed a Correlation-Aware Heuristic Search(CAHS) method to detect the inherent correlations of the demands of different types of computing resources. Note that, most heuristic-based solutions only focus on specific scenarios, which limits their generalization ability in a highly dynamic environment.

Recently, several reinforcement learning (RL) methods have been applied to cloud task scheduling [11,12]. Compared to the heuristic-based methods that focus on maximizing the immediate (short-term) reward, RL-based method can help cloud services learn the long-term optimal task scheduling policy on-the-fly. For example, Wei et al. [13] proposed a QoS-aware job scheduling method for applications in a cloud deployment. DeepRM [14] used REINFORCE, a policy gradient DeepRL algorithm for multi-resource packing in cluster scheduling. Rjoub et al. [15] combined DRL with LSTM to address large-scale workloads. However, the cluster of this model is assumed to be homogeneous. Therefore, they can not adapt to various scenarios easily and be widely used in the real-world environment.

In summary, most of the existing methods can only schedule single task at a time. Furthermore, these works only focus on performance improvement. In addition, most of the previous solutions only adapt to some specific scenarios, and cannot be generalized to adapt to various scenarios. In contrast, our method can schedule multiple tasks simultaneously. By perceiving the status of the batch tasks as a whole, it can use Pearson's correlation coefficient (PCC) and standard deviation of the resource demand to evaluate the feature of the workload and therefore come up with better strategies. What's more, it can adapt to multiple optimization objectives such as task response time and cost-efficiency.

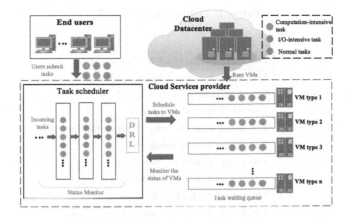

Fig. 1. Task scheduling framework in the cloud environment

3   System Architecture and Problem Statement

3.1   Overview of System Architecture

A typical cloud computing scenario is considered in this paper. It involves three
stakeholders: datacenter, cloud services providers and end users. Figure 1 is the
system architecture. On the cloud side, each VM maintains a task wait queue
for received tasks. Here, we assume that each VM executes all assigned tasks
in a non-preemptive way (i.e.,the first come first served way). On the other
hand, users are allowed to submit multiple types of tasks at the same time.
These tasks can be of different types, such as Computation-intensive tasks, I/O-
intensive tasks ,and normal tasks. These tasks can be assigned to different VMs
through the designed task scheduler. Please note that the arrival time, quantity,
and type of tasks submitted by users are all unpredictable.

The task scheduler consists of three core components: a task queue (TQ)
module, a status monitor (SM) module ,and a DRL-based scheduler module.
The function of TQ is mainly to store heterogeneous tasks submitted by different end-users over time. The SM is used to collect status information of all
assigned tasks and VMs, including task length, CPU utilization of each task,
VM's MIPS (Million Instructions Per Second), RAM utilization, and waiting
time of a task. For scheduler module, it is responsible for calculating the optimal
task assignment solution, based on the collected status information from SM.
After that, according to the result of the scheduler module, the tasks in TQ are
assigned to suitable VM instances automatically for execution.

3.2   Problem Formulation

For the convenience of expression, we first define the related symbol in our
model, as shown in Table 1. Then we formalize the cloud task scheduling as a
constrained dynamic optimization problem.

Table 1. Definition of symbols

Symbol	Definition
J	The total number of VMs in the cluster
I	The total number of tasks in a batch
$speed$	The data transportation speed
vm_j	The jth VM in the cluster $1 \leq j \leq J$
$mips_j$	The speed that the vm_j executes the instructions
ram_j	The size of $vm_j's$ memory
$price_j$	The price of the vm_j per second
$task_i$	The ith task in the task batch $1 \leq i \leq I$
mi_i	The task length of $task_i$
cpu_i	The required cpu utilization rate of $task_i$
$data_i$	The data size of $task_i$
$coreNum_j$	The number of cores in the jth VM

To provide personal services and maximize resource utilization, the data center usually offers various types of VM instances with varied resource configurations. Hence, the VM instance can be described as $vm_j = (mips_j, ram_j, price_j)$ $(0 \leq j \leq J)$, where j indicates the id of the VM instance.

Generally, the tasks are submitted by numerous end-users simultaneously. On the other hand, the cloud services providers have no prior knowledge of the incoming workloads in advance, e.g., the amount and type of submitted tasks. Hence, in our model, a task is identified as $task_i = (mi_i, cpu_i, data_i)$ $(0 \leq i \leq I)$, where i is the task id.

The task scheduler is responsible for assigning user tasks to suitable VM instances. When a task is allocated to a specific VM instance, it firstly enters the corresponding waiting queue in a first-come-first-sever (FCFS) manner. The response time of task i deployed on VM j (i.e., RT_{ij}) is defined as the total amount of time that task i stays in VM j. In detail, it can be divided into the duration of task i will spend in the waiting queue (i.e., Q_j^{queue}) and the execution time in the CPU (P_{ij}^{exe}). Considering the transportation of $data_i$ consumes some time, the RT_{ij} can be defined as:

$$RT_{ij} = P_{ij}^{exe} + max\left(Q_j^{queue}, \frac{data_i}{speed}\right) \qquad (1)$$

Based on the above assumption, the execution time P_{ij}^{exe} is defined as $P_{ij}^{exe} = \frac{mi_i}{mips_j \times cpu_i}$, and the waiting time Q_j^{queue} is $Q_j^{queue} = \sum_{k=1}^{C} P_{kj}^{exe}$, where C means the number of tasks (arrival earlier than task i) that are waiting in the queue of vm_j. Furthermore, the average response time of total $I(t)$ tasks at time t is:

$$AT(t) = \sum_{i=1}^{I(t)} \frac{RT_{ij}}{mi_i} \qquad (2)$$

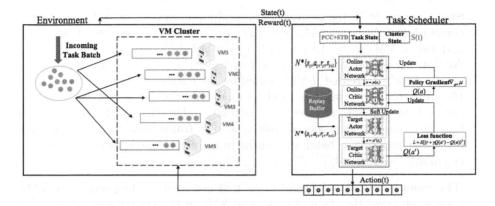

Fig. 2. The structure of DRL-based Task scheduler

Given the price of rented VM_j, the cost of executing $task_i$ is evaluated as $EC_i = P_{ij}^{exe} \times price_j$. Thus, the total cost of executing $I(t)$ tasks at time t is:

$$EC(t) = \sum_{i=1}^{I(t)} EC_i \tag{3}$$

Based on (2) and (3), the optimal target of the task scheduler can be defined as minimizing the average response time and total cost of all tasks during the whole running time K, it can be expressed as:

$$minimize \quad \beta \times \sum_{t-1}^{K} AT(t) + (1 - \beta) \times \sum_{t=1}^{K} EC(t) \tag{4}$$

4   Performance and Cost-Aware Task Scheduler

In this section, we propose a DDPG-based method for performance and cost-aware task scheduling in the high dynamic cloud environment. The objectives of our method are to optimize the average response time and total cost when executing large-scale tasks in VM cluster. Considering the time-varying characteristics of workload, the dynamic tasking scheduling problem is constructed as a Markov decision process (MDP), then the DDPG algorithm is employed to obtain the optimal task scheduling strategy. Specifically, the correlation-aware state representation and dual rewards design are introduced.

4.1   MDP Model

In the cloud environment, the workloads are unpredictable and highly dynamic. Thus, it is impossible for us to adapt traditional scheduling methods to such flexible scenarios. In this scenario, we model the task scheduling in the cloud environment as a Markov Decision Process (MDP). Formally, we define the tuple of three elements (S, A, R) of MDP in the cloud task scheduler as follows:

- **State space** S: In the scheduling algorithm, a state $s \in S$ is defined by the correlation of the batch tasks s^{cor}, the current status of submitted tasks s^{Task} and rented VMs s^{VM}, i.e., $s = s^{cor} \bigcup s^{Task} \bigcup s^{VM}$.
- **Action Space** A: An action $a = \{vm^1, vm^2, \ldots, vm^J\} \in A$ is to assign a batch of tasks to rented J VMs based on the current state s.
- **Reward** R: The reward is used to guide the task scheduler to make the optimal assignment solution (i.e., action) under current states, based on the objective of the proposed task scheduler framework. In our model, the reward of assigning a batch of I tasks to a cluster of J VMs is: $reword_{IJ} = reward_{IJ}^{prior} + reward_{IJ}^{posterior}$.

The agent is to assign different tasks that users submit to appropriate VMs. The agent observes the state of tasks and VMs in the cluster and takes action according to trained police π. After that, it receives a reward immediately from the environment. In detail, the proposed DDPG-based task scheduling framework consists of two parts, i.e., online net and target net, to train and test the task assignment policy based on the online environment and offline historical data. For each part, it includes an Actor net and Critic net. The structure of our proposed task scheduler is illustrated in Fig. 2.

4.2 Correlation-Aware State Representation

State representation plays an important role in the DRL algorithms because it describes the current information of the cloud environment. In [5], it revealed the effectiveness of considering correlations while scheduling the tasks. Therefore, we propose a correlation-aware state representation method to help the agent better perceive the workload. In detail, PCC is an effective matrix to evaluate the correlation of any two task, and has been widely applied in various fields. Hence, in this paper, we adopt PCC to measure demand correlation. Considering the demand for three types of resources $(mi, cpu, data)$ in batch tasks, the PCC of the batch tasks can be calculated by:

$$\rho(mi, data) = \frac{cov(mi, data)}{\sigma(mi) \times \sigma(data)}, \tag{5}$$

$$\rho(mi, cpu) = \frac{cov(mi, cpu^{util})}{\sigma(mi) \times \sigma(cpu)}, \tag{6}$$

$$\rho(cpu, data) = \frac{cov(cpu, data)}{\sigma(cpu) \times \sigma(data)}, \tag{7}$$

Here, $cov(\cdot)$ and $\sigma(\cdot)$ represent the covariance and standard deviation, respectively. In addition, to evaluate the distributions of the resource demands between different tasks, we also employ the standard deviation(STD) of $std(mips)$, $std(data)$, and $std(cpu)$, which can be calculated by:

$$std(mips) = \sqrt{\frac{\sum_{i=1}^{I}(mips_i - \overline{mips})^2}{I}} \tag{8}$$

$$std(cpu) = \sqrt{\frac{\sum_{i=1}^{I}(cpu_i - \overline{cpu})^2}{I}} \tag{9}$$

$$std(data) = \sqrt{\frac{\sum_{i=1}^{I}(data_i - \overline{data})^2}{I}} \tag{10}$$

We applied the PCC and STD to the state space to let the agent make better decisions according to the feature of the batch tasks. Therefore the correlation part of the state s is:

$$s^{cor} = [\rho(mi, data), \rho(mi, cpu), \rho(cpu, data), std(mi), std(data), std(cpu)] \tag{11}$$

The second part of the vector is the batch's specification. Suppose there are in total I tasks in a batch, the batch can be described as:

$$s^{task} = [task_{mi}^1, task_{cpu}^1, task_{data}^1, ..., task_{mi}^I, task_{cpu}^I, task_{data}^I] \tag{12}$$

The third part of the vector represents the state of the VMs. Suppose there are in total J VMs in the cluster. Note that each vm_j may have a Task Queue waiting to be executed, therefore it has a feature that represents the time that a new task will wait in line Q_j^{queue}, so the cluster can be described as:

$$s^{VM} = [vm_{mips}^1, vm_{price}^1, vm_Q^1, ..., vm_{mips}^J, vm_{price}^J, vm_Q^J] \tag{13}$$

These three parts make up the state space vector. After each action, the cluster state will be updated and the next batch will come and make up the new space state.

4.3   Dual Rewards

To better guide the agent in learning an optimal task allocation scheme, we define a dual reward model for the proposed DDPG method, which includes a prior and a posterior rewards. Specifically, the prior reward means the agent can know the reward of a specific action before the VMs execute the tasks. We use $reward_{IJ}^{prior}$ to represent the total prior reward of a batch task:

$$reword_{ij}^{prior} = \begin{cases} reward_{pri}/I, & \text{if } Q_j^{queue} \text{ is not empty} \\ 0, & \text{if } Q_j^{queue} \text{ is empty} \end{cases} \tag{14}$$

$$reward_{IJ}^{prior} = \sum_{i=1}^{I} reword_{ij}^{prior} \tag{15}$$

Here, $reward_{pri}$ is a constant that is used to control the maximum of prior reward. The posterior reward means the agent can only know the reward after the VMs execute the tasks. Our posterior reward has two elements, one is the total cost of the tasks EC_{IJ}, the other is the average response time AT. For a specific task in the batch, the execution of it will have a certain cost and a certain response time ratio, which are EC_{ij} and AT_{ij} respectively.

To make the training process stable, we normalized the EC and AT in a batch. We define the maximum and minimum AT in a batch as AT_{max} and AT_{min}, and the maximum EC in a batch as EC_{max}. Therefore, the normalized AT and $cost$ are:

$$AT^*_{ij} = \frac{AT_{ij} - AT_{min}}{AT_{max} - AT_{min}} \tag{16}$$

$$EC^*_{ij} = \frac{EC_{ij}}{EC_{max}} \tag{17}$$

Hence, the posterior reward of this batch is:

$$reward^{posterior}_{IJ} = \beta \times \sum_{i=1}^{I} AT^*_{ij} + (1 - \beta) \sum_{i=1}^{I} EC^*_{ij} \tag{18}$$

Note that $\beta \in [0, 1]$. β can be used to adjust the agent's optimization objectives. For example, if $\beta = 1$, then an agent is trained to reduce the average response time.

The two rewards are applied simultaneously to train the agent. We can adjust the value of $reward_{pri}$ to control the size relationship between two rewards. The goal of the DDPG agent is to minimize the rewards.

4.4   Algorithm Training

In the following, we introduce our proposed DDPG-based task scheduling algorithm (see Algorithm 1). Offline training can not only make the critic network evaluate the actions more accurately, but also let the action network generate higher scored actions. To achieve this, we applied experience replayed strategy and target network [16].

Experience replay's main purpose is to solve the problem of correlation and non-stationary distribution of empirical data. We introduced a fixed-size memory replay buffer $\mathfrak{R}$. At each time step, we will store the latest (a_t, s_t, r_t, s_{t+1}) sets to the replay buffer $\mathfrak{R}$, and randomly sample a mini-batch from the buffer to train the agent. Because the DDPG algorithm is an off-policy algorithm, the replay buffer can be relatively large which allows the algorithm to learn across a set of uncorrelated transitions. Therefore, the parameters of the actor network are updated by:

$$\begin{aligned}
\nabla_{\theta^\mu} \mu &\approx E_{\mu'}[\nabla_{\theta^\mu} Q(s, a|\theta^Q)|_{s=s_t, a=\mu(s_t|\theta^\mu)}] \\
&= E_{\mu'}[\nabla_a Q(s, a|\theta^Q)|_{s=s_t, a=\mu(s_t)} \nabla_{\theta^\mu} \mu(s|\theta^\mu)|_{s=s_t}]
\end{aligned} \tag{19}$$

Directly implementing Q-learning with a neural network is proved unstable in many situations. Introducing a target network can significantly reduce the oscillations of the neural network's parameters caused training process. The target network is a copy of the online network (actor and critic network), but it is

Algorithm 1. DDPG-based task scheduling Algorithm

1: Randomly initialize online critic network $Q(s, a|\theta^Q)$ and online actor network $\mu(s|\theta^\mu)$ with parameters θ^Q and θ^μ
2: Initialize target network Q' and μ' with parameters $\theta^{Q'} \leftarrow \theta^Q$, $\theta^{\mu'} \leftarrow \theta^\mu$
3: Initialize memory replay buffer $\mathfrak{R}$
4: Initialize exploration probability ϵ and exploration warm up steps n
5: **for** each batch of I tasks arrive at time $t = 1, ..., T$ **do**
6:    **if** $t > n$ **then**
7:       Sample a mini-batch of $\mathcal{N}$ transitions (s_i, a_i, s_{i+1}) from $\mathfrak{R}$, which all the selected tasks have been completed
8:       Calculate $reward^i_{IJ}$ according to responseTime and exT
9:       Calculate r_i according to $reward^i_{IJ}$
10:      Set $y_i = r_i + \lambda Q'(s_{i+1}, \mu'(s_{i+1}|\theta^{\mu'})|\theta^{Q'})$
11:      Update the critic by minimizing the loss:
      $L = \frac{1}{N}\sum_i(y_i - Q(s_i, a_i|\theta^Q))^2$
12:      Update the actor policy using the sampled gradient:
      $\nabla_{\theta^\mu}\mu|s_i \approx \frac{1}{N}\sum_i \nabla_a Q(s, a|\theta^Q)|_{s=s_i,a=\mu(s_i)}\nabla_{\theta^\mu}\mu(s|\theta^\mu)|_{s=s_i}$
13:      Update the target networks:
      $\theta^{Q'} \leftarrow \tau\theta^Q + (1-\tau)\theta^{Q'}$
      $\theta^{\mu'} \leftarrow \tau\theta^\mu + (1-\tau)\theta^{\mu'}$
14:      With probability $1 - \epsilon$ generate an action $a_t = \mu(s_t|\theta^\mu)$ and ϵ generate a random action a_t
15:    **else**
16:       Generate a random action a_t
17:    **end if**
18:    Complete task scheduling according to action a_t and observe reward
19:    Store transition (s_t, a_t) in $\mathfrak{R}$
20:    Store completed task's RT and P^{exe} in $\mathfrak{R}$
21: **end for**

---

updated slower instead of copying the weights directly, which ensures the neural network higher stability. At each time step, the parameters of the target network are updated by:

$$\theta' = \tau\theta + (1 - \tau)\theta' \tag{20}$$

5 Performance Evaluation

5.1 Experimental Settings

Cluster Resources. We consider that there are 20 VMs deployed in the public cloud and provide services to the end-users. Meanwhile, we set four types of VM instances with various pricing models in the cluster. The details of cluster resources and price are shown in Table 2. Note that, the pricing model of the VM instances is identified with the Enterprise level Computation type(c7) (in China) provided by Alibaba Cloud. Following [17,18]. We also adopt Cloudsim Plus to build the cloud environment.

Table 2. Cluster resource details

Instance Type	CPU cores	Memory(GB)	Quantity	Price
m1	16	32	5	$0.3624/h
m2	12	24	5	$0.2739/h
m3	4	8	5	$0.0972/h
m4	2	4	5	$0.0530/h

Workloads. *Alibaba-Cluster-trace-v2018* is used to test the performance of the task scheduler, which contains 4000 VMs under workload of 8 d. To simplify the problem, we use the data of the second day. To make the model stable, there are up to 50 tasks can be submitted by the end-users in one second, which will not miss the feature of the workload according to our observation.

Parameter Settings. In our DDPG-based task scheduling algorithm, we employ four deep neural networks, which are Actor_online, Critic_online, Actor_target, Critic_target. Each one has four fully connected layers. Both two online networks are updated with each round of training, whereas the two target networks are updated by (20) with $\tau = 0.01$. We set the capacity of memory replay buffer $\Re = 10000$, the size of mini-batch $\mathcal{N} = 16$. We apply Adam optimizer to optimize the network and the learning rate for Actor_online and Critic_online networks are 0.0006 and 0.001 respectively. To store some memory before the training, the network begins to train after 400 steps. All experiments are conducted on a tower server, which includes 2.1GHz Intel Xeon E5 CPU, 250GB RAM, Ubuntu 18.04LTS operation system, JDK1.8, Python3.6, PyTorch 1.0 and CloudSim Plus 4.0.

Baseline Schedulers. We compare our DDPG-based task scheduler with four baseline approaches. There are 1)Random, randomly selects a VM for each job; 2) Round-Robin(rr), assigns tasks to each VM in turn; 3) Earliest, assigns a task to the first idle VM according to the arrival time; 4) DQN, the newest DRL-based task scheduling method, and the design of the DQN method is similar to [11].

Note that, our proposed DDPG-based scheduler and all the baselines make dynamic decisions from the current state of the cluster and workload, and do not have prior knowledge of the whole workload. We performed 10 repeated experiments on each algorithm and recorded the average results.

Evaluation Metrics. In this paper, we apply three indicators to evaluate the performance of different methods in terms of satisfying different stakeholders profiles, which are response time ratio, total cost and the standard deviation of CPU utilization. Among them, response time ratio $ResTR = \frac{\sum_{m=1}^{M} \frac{mi_m}{RT_{mj}}}{M}$ describes the average response time of executing M tasks in total. Total costs represents the monetary cost of the cloud services provider during the whole execution time K. According to (3), the total costs can be defined as $Cost = \sum_{t=1}^{K} EC(t)$.

CPU utilization standard deviation among the cluster, which means the standard deviation of average CPU utilization of each VM instance in the cluster. The CPU utilization standard deviation can represent the level of load balance among the cluster. For the data center, a lower one means better resource utilization:

$$\Delta cpu = \sqrt{\frac{\sum_{j=1}^{J}(AvgCpu_j - \overline{AvgCpu_j})}{J}} \qquad (21)$$

Here, $AvgCpu_j$ represents the average cpu utilization of VM_j in the time period of K time steps.

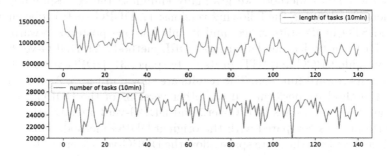

Fig. 3. The changes of Alibaba-Cluster-trace-v2018 workload on the second day.

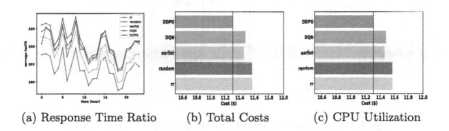

(a) Response Time Ratio   (b) Total Costs   (c) CPU Utilization

Fig. 4. Performance comparison on real-world workload.

5.2   Performance on Real-World Workload

First, we evaluate the performance of DDPG in the face of real-workload with the characteristic of high dynamical. Figure 3 shows the average total task number and average total task length of Alibaba-Cluster-trace-v2018 every 10 min.

Figure 4 shows the experiment result of the comparison of these methods. We can summarize the following three conclusions: 1). Our proposed DDPG-based method has the best performance on all of those three metrics, this is because the reinforcement learning methods and our design of PCC and STD in the state space allows it to detect the feature of the workload efficiently. The dual rewards allow it to learn to adapt to proper strategy to realize global optimization. 2).

The RL methods (DDPG, DQN) have better performance than traditional methods, because they can learn from their interaction with the environment, whereas traditional methods are incapable of changing their strategies according to the environment. 3). Our proposed DDPG-based method has a better performance than the DQN method, especially on the metric of cost the average CPU utilization standard deviation. This is because the DDPG method can schedule the whole batch of tasks simultaneously, and DQN can only do a one-by-one schedule. This ability of DDPG is strengthened by the design of PCC and STD in the state space.

Ablation Study. To prove the effectiveness of each component in our refinement of the DDPG method, we gradually eliminate the corresponding model components by defining the following versions: 1). DDPG-ver1: it does not have PCC and STD in its state space, and it only has one posterior reward for the agent, which is a typical model for most DRL methods. 2). DDPG-ver2: In this model, we added PCC and STD in its state space. 3). DDPG-ver3: It has dual rewards as its reward function. The results are shown in Fig. 5. As expected, our proposed method outperforms all the other versions of the DDPG method. In detail, our refined versions DDPG-ver2 and DDPG-ver3 already achieved quite good performances compared with the original DDPG method. This is because the PCC and STD in the state space allow the DDPG-ver2 agent to better detect

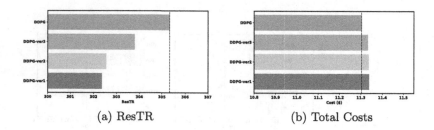

(a) ResTR   (b) Total Costs

Fig. 5. Comparison of DDPG methods in different versions

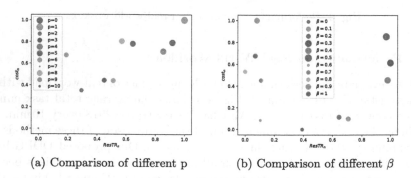

(a) Comparison of different p   (b) Comparison of different β

Fig. 6. Influence of changing $reward_{pri}$ and β. The size of the points represents the sum of the two value.

the intrinsic correlation of the workload efficiently, and the dual rewards allow the DDPG-ver3 agent to adapt to a more balanced global optimization strategy. Lastly, our proposed method combines the advantages of DDPG-ver2 and DDPG-ver3 can reach the best performance among these versions.

As the optimization priority β and the $reward_{pri}$ of prior reward are pivotal for the agent to learn a proper strategy, we investigated the impact of changing the value of them. To better evaluate these two objectives, we normalized both of them. Among all of these algorithms, we can define the $ResTR_{max}$, $ResTR_{min}$ and $cost_{max}$, $cost_{min}$. Therefore, each one's $ResTR^* = \frac{ResTR-ResTR_{min}}{ResTR_{max}-ResTR_{min}}$, and $cost^* = 1 - \frac{cost-cost_{min}}{cost_{max}-cost_{min}}$. It is clear that a greater $ResTR^*$ and $cost^*$ means a better performance.

Effect of changing $reward_{pri}$. We use p in the figure to denote $reward_{pri}$. We changed $reward_{pri}$ in a range of $[0, 10]$. Figure 6a shows the experiment results. We have the following observations: 1). $p = 0$ does not have the best overall performance because it completely ignores the prior reward. 2). As the growing of p, the performance of the model declines. This is because the excessive large value of p will let the agent adapt to the strategy more like the earliest method which can not reach a global optimization strategy. 3). $p = 1(reward_{pri} = 1)$ has the best performance on both $ResTR$ and $cost$, which indicates that this is the most proper value of the prior reward.

Effect of changing β. To evaluate which value of β can help the algorithm reach the best overall performance, we changed β in a range of $[0, 1]$. Figure 6(b) shows the experiment results. We have the following observations: 1). $\beta = 0$ and $\beta = 1$ do not have good performances on either metric, because these two are strongly correlated, and ignoring any of them will prevent the algorithm from finding the most proper strategy. 2). When $\beta = 0.5$, the overall performance is the best because it is in the upper right corner. This is because it can better balance the two optimization objectives and learn to adapt to the most appropriate strategies. 3). $\beta = 0.3$ has the best performance on $ResTR$ and $\beta = 0.9$ has the best performance on $cost$. According to different scenarios, these are also applicable choices of β.

6   Conclusion

Efficient task scheduling in the cloud environment is always an important and challenging problem because of its high dynamic and unpredictable workload and complex inherent VM characteristics. Traditional methods and heuristic-based approaches only focus on some specific scenarios with particular objectives. In this paper, we introduce an RL model for the problem of multiple-objective optimization-based task scheduling in the cloud datacenter. In addition, we apply this model to our DDPG-based algorithm. We have designed correlation-aware state representation and advanced reward signals, which help the DDPG agent to learn the task schedule performance and the total cost of VM cluster. The agents can learn to optimize multiple objectives under high dynamic workloads without previous knowledge of the VM cluster and the workload, but only from its interaction with the environment and the rewards. Extensive experimental results have shown that our proposed method overperforms the baseline methods on response time and total cost when facing high dynamical workloads.

Acknowledgements. This work is partly supported by the key cooperation project of chongqing municipal education commission (HZ2021017,HZ2021018), in part by the "Fertilizer Robot" project of Chongqing Committee on Agriculture and Rural Affairs, in part by the Chongqing Research Program of Technology Innovation and Application under grants cstc2019jscx-zdztzxX0019, in part by West Light Foundation of The Chinese Academy of Sciences.

References

1. Arunarani, A., Manjula, D., Sugumaran, V.: Task scheduling techniques in cloud computing: a literature survey. Future Gener. Comput. Syst. **91**, 407–415 (2019)
2. Zhu, Q.-H., Tang, H., Huang, J.-J., Hou, Y.: Task scheduling for multi-cloud computing subject to security and reliability constraints. IEEE/CAA J. Automat. Sinica **8**(4), 848–865 (2021)
3. Houssein, E.H., Gad, A.G., Wazery, Y.M., Suganthan, P.N.: Task scheduling in cloud computing based on meta-heuristics: review, taxonomy, open challenges, and future trends. Swarm Evol. Comput. **62**, 100841 (2021)
4. Tawfeek, M.A., El-Sisi, A.B., Keshk, A.E., Torkey, F.A.: Cloud task scheduling based on ant colony optimization. In: 2013 8th International Conference on Computer Engineering & Systems (ICCES), pp. 64–69 (2013)
5. Luo, C., et al.: Correlation-aware heuristic search for intelligent virtual machine provisioning in cloud systems. In: Proceedings of the AAAI Conference on Artificial Intelligence **35**, 12363–12372 (2021)
6. Shu, W., Cai, K., Xiong, N.N.: Research on strong agile response task scheduling optimization enhancement with optimal resource usage in green cloud computing. Future Gener. Comput. Syst. **124**, 12–20 (2021)
7. Bezdan, T., Zivkovic, M., Bacanin, N., Strumberger, I., Tuba, E., Tuba, M.: Multi-objective task scheduling in cloud computing environment by hybridized bat algorithm. J. Intell. Fuzzy Syst. **42**(1), 411–423 (2022)
8. Gill, S.S., Chana, I.: A survey on resource scheduling in cloud computing: issues and challenges. J. Grid Comput. **14**, 06 (2016)
9. Mathew, T., Sekaran, K.C., Jose, J.: Study and analysis of various task scheduling algorithms in the cloud computing environment. In: 2014 International Conference on Advances in Computing, Communications and Informatics (ICACCI), pp. 658–664 (2014)
10. Liu, X., Tong, W., Zhi, X., ZhiRen, F., WenZhao, L.: Performance analysis of cloud computing services considering resources sharing among virtual machines. J. Supercomput. **69**(1), 357–374 (2014)
11. Islam, M.T., Karunasekera, S., Buyya, R.: Performance and cost-efficient spark job scheduling based on deep reinforcement learning in cloud computing environments. IEEE Trans. Parallel Distrib. Syst. **33**(7), 1695–1710 (2021)
12. Ran, L., Shi, X., Shang, M.: SLAs-Aware online task scheduling based on deep reinforcement learning method in cloud environment. In: 2019 IEEE 21st International Conference on High Performance Computing and Communications; IEEE 17th International Conference on Smart City; IEEE 5th International Conference on Data Science and Systems (HPCC/SmartCity/DSS), pp. 1518–1525, IEEE (2019)

13. Wei, Y., Pan, L., Liu, S., Wu, L., Meng, X.: DRL-scheduling: an intelligent QoS-aware job scheduling framework for applications in clouds. IEEE Access **6**, 55112–55125 (2018)
14. Mao, H., Alizadeh, M., Menache, I., Kandula, S.: Resource management with deep reinforcement learning. In: Proceedings of the 15th ACM workshop on hot topics in networks, pp. 50–56 (2016)
15. Rjoub, G., Bentahar, J., Abdel Wahab, O., Saleh Bataineh, A.: Deep and reinforcement learning for automated task scheduling in large-scale cloud computing systems. Concurrency and Computation: Practice and Experience, vol. 33, no. 23, p. e5919 (2021)
16. Lillicrap, T.P., et al.: Continuous control with deep reinforcement learning. In: 4th International Conference on Learning Representations, ICLR 2016, San Juan, Puerto Rico, May 2–4, 2016, Conference Track Proceedings (Y. Bengio and Y. LeCun, eds.) (2016)
17. Abreu, D.P., et al.: A rank scheduling mechanism for fog environments. In: 2018 IEEE 6th International Conference on Future Internet of Things and Cloud (FiCloud), pp. 363–369, IEEE (2018)
18. Silva Filho, M.C., Oliveira, R.L., Monteiro, C.C., Inácio, P.R., Freire, M.M.: CloudSim Plus: a cloud computing simulation framework pursuing software engineering principles for improved modularity, extensibility and correctness. In: 2017 IFIP/IEEE symposium on integrated network and service management (IM), pp. 400–406, IEEE (2017)

IDGL: An Imbalanced Disassortative Graph Learning Framework for Fraud Detection

Junhang Wu[1,2], Ruimin Hu[1,2(✉)], Dengshi Li[1,3], Lingfei Ren[1,2], Wenyi Hu[1,2], and Yilong Zang[1,2]

[1] National Engineering Research Center for Multimedia Software, School of Computer Science, Wuhan University, Wuhan 430072, China
`hurm1964@gmail.com`
[2] Hubei Key Laboratory of Multimedia and Network Communication Engineering, Wuhan University, Wuhan 430072, China
[3] School of Artificial Intelligence, Jianghan University, Wuhan 430056, China

Abstract. The thriving growth of Internet service not only facilitates our daily lives but also incubates various fraudulent activities with concealment. The traceable interactive behaviors forming the graph-like data provide a great opportunity for graph-based fraud detection. Owing to the stellar performance of assortative graph learning, GNN-based fraud detection methods escalate much attention. However, the fraud graph is not always assortative but more likely disassortative as the fraudsters usually camouflage themselves via building numerous connections with normal users. Additionally, the GNN-based fraud detection methods also suffer from graph imbalance issues as the number of fraudsters is far less than that of the normal users. To address these problems, an imbalanced disassortative graph learning framework (IDGL) is proposed with two key components. First, an adaptive dual-channel convolution filter is developed to adaptively combine the advantage of low- and high-frequency signals from its neighbors so as to assimilate the nodes with assortative edges and discriminate the nodes with disassortative edges. Second, a label-aware nodes and edges sampler is designed with the consideration of nodes' popularity and corresponding label class frequency, which helps the model simultaneously eliminate the bias towards the major classes and pay more attention to the valuable connections (fraud-fraud, fraud-benign). Extensive experiments on two public fraud datasets demonstrate the effectiveness of our method.

Keywords: Fraud detection · Graph disassortativity · Graph imbalance · Adaptive frequency filter · Label-aware sampler

J. Troya et al. (Eds.): ICSOC 2022, LNCS 13740, pp. 616–631, 2022.
https://doi.org/10.1007/978-3-031-20984-0_44

1   Introduction

With the thriving growth of Internet services facilitating our daily life, there also brings various kinds of fraudulent behaviors. The fraudsters or attackers disguise as the benign users to do some malicious activities and conceal themselves within the mass of data, which has caused great damage to finance security [10,16,20], cyber security [4] and comment management [3,14]. Fortunately, our online behavior is always traceable no matter whether we are benign or fraudulent, and we can transform these interactive behaviors as graph-like data where the users and their interactions are treated as the nodes and the edges, respectively. Recently, the emerging graph neural network (GNN) has shown its great representation power of graph data, which makes GNN-based fraud detection methods escalate extensive attention.

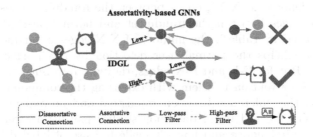

Fig. 1. Illustration of graph disassortativity and imbalance

Although these GNN-based fraud detection methods have made much progress, there still exist the following two main challenges.

Graph Disassortativity. Generally, GNNs update the representation of nodes by aggregating the signals from their neighbors, which can be treated as a low-pass filter to retain the commonality between the connected nodes [9,18]. Benefiting from the smoothness of the low-frequency filter, it works well for assortative graphs, i.e., similar nodes tend to make the connections [1], which makes GNN-based fraud or anomaly detection effective as it assumes that the fraudulent or abnormal nodes with the same malicious goals tend to make the connections with each other. However, some studies [5,7,14,19] have shown that the fraud graphs are not always assortative but more likely disassortative as the fraudsters often camouflage themselves by making many connections with the benign users to make them look normal with less suspiciousness, which makes the fraud graph flood with numerous disassortative connections, i.e., the entities from different classes tend to make the connections. Consequently, the low-pass smoothing aggregation mechanisms of GNNs are insufficient to support the inference for these disassortative graphs as it enables the fraudsters to achieve their intentions, i.e., the fraudulent features are concealed within the myriads of benign ones. As shown in Fig. 1, given a query user who has far more connections with the normal user than the fraudster, the assortativity-based GNNs tend to classify him/her into the normal user as its behavior features have been concealed by his numerous benign neighbors within the low-pass smoothing aggregation. Under this circumstance, the high-frequency signals (i.e., the difference between entity nodes) are more suitable for these disassortative graphs.

Graph Imbalance. First, the number of fraudsters is generally far less than that of the benign users, which causes the graph node imbalance issues. According to Amazon and YelpChi datasets, only 9.50% and 14.53% of labeled entities are the fraudulent ones respectively, as introduced in Table 1. The graph node imbalance may make the training bias towards the majority class (i.e., the benign users) with the reduction of model generalization ability. Expect for node imbalance, the edge imbalance is more urgent as it directly guides the node aggregation process. There are three types of edges in the fraud graph: edges between normal entity nodes (denoted as N-N), edges between the fraudulent ones (denoted as F-F), and the edges between the fraudulent and normal ones (denoted as F-N). As introduced in Table 2, the number of N-N edges is far more than that of others, which helps the normal user detection by retaining commonalities between them. But for F-F and F-N edges, they are rare but valuable, and we should pay more attention to them with exploring the commonalities between fraudsters and the difference between fraudsters and normal users. However, most current GNN-based fraud detection studies pay little attention to both nodes and edges imbalance and haven't made full use of labeled F-F and F-N edges to detect the new fraudsters. Unfortunately, the graph imbalance issues further exacerbate the disassortativity of the graph with more difficulties for discrimination.

To address the above challenges, we propose an Imbalanced Disassortative Graph Learning framework (IDGL) to simultaneously adaptively aggregate low- and high-frequency signals from assortative and disassortative connections on the imbalanced fraud graph. Specifically, IDGL is composed of four module layers: 1) a re-embedding layer. Some recent studies [2] have emphasized that the performance and robustness of the model may be hurt by the entanglement of graph filters and parameter matrices, and the fraudsters usually camouflage themselves with the similar raw features to the normal users. Therefore, a non-linear re-embedding layer is applied to relearn the representations of nodes; 2) an adaptive dual-channel convolution layer, which is used to adaptively combine the advantage of dual-channel (i,e., the low- and high-frequency) signals from its neighbors to assimilate the nodes with assortative edges and discriminate the nodes with disassortative edges; 3) a representation fusion layer, which combines the intermediate embeddings to be the final representation of nodes; 4) an imbalanced-oriented classification layer. To alleviate the effects of graph imbalance, a label-aware nodes and edges sampler is designed with the consideration of nodes' popularity (i.e., degree) and corresponding label class frequency. Sampled nodes are used for classification training to eliminate the bias towards the major classes, and the sampled edges are treated as the supervision information to facilitate the training of adaptive filters and make the model pay more attention to the valuable edges (i.e., F-F and F-N layers). The contributions of the paper can be listed as follows:

- We formulate the graph-based fraud detection problem as an imbalanced disassortative node classification task and propose an imbalanced disassortative graph learning framework to deal with the disassortativity and graph imbalance issues on the graph.
- An adaptive dual-channel convolution filter is further developed for fraud detection to assimilate the nodes with assortative edges and discriminate the nodes with disassortative edges. A label-aware node and edge sampler is proposed to relieve graph imbalance issues with more attention to the valuable edge information.
- Experiments on two public real-world datasets demonstrate the effectiveness of our proposed IDGL for fraud detection.

2 Preliminaries

2.1 Definition

Definition 1 (Assortativity and disassortativity). Given a graph, if two nodes (e.g., v_i and v_j), which make the connection as an edge, belong to different classes, then we treat the connection as a disassortative edge, denoted as ε_{ij}^-, and if they belong to the same class, the connection is an assortative edge, denoted as ε_{ij}^+. The larger disassortativity of the graph, the more nodes from different classes tend to connect with each other, and vice versa. For our task, the fraud graph is of both assortativity and disassortativity at the same time.

Definition 2 (Graph). Consider a graph $G = \{V, X, \{\varepsilon^+, \varepsilon^-\}, A, Y\}$, $V = \{v_1, v_2, ..., v_N\}$ is the set of nodes, N is the number of nodes; $X \in \mathbb{R}^{N \times d}$ is the original d-dimension feature vector of all of N nodes; For $\{\varepsilon^+, \varepsilon^-\}$, ε^+ and ε^- represent the assortative and disassortative edge sets respectively where $\varepsilon^+ \cup \varepsilon^- = \varepsilon$ and $\varepsilon^+ \cap \varepsilon^- = \emptyset$; A is the corresponding adjacency matrice of the graph where $A_{ij} = 1$, if $e_{ij} \in \varepsilon$; Y is the set of labels for the nodes, and each one has a label $y_i \in \{0, 1\}$ where 1 represents the *fraudster* and 0 represents the *benign*.

Definition 3 (Multi-relation Graph). There are different relations among the nodes, and $G = \left\{V, X, \{\varepsilon_r^+, \varepsilon_r^-\}\big|_{r=1}^R, \{A_1, A_2, ..., A_R\}, Y\right\}$ is defined as a multi-relation graph, where $e_{ij}^r \in \{\varepsilon_r^+, \varepsilon_r^-\}$ represents the edge between the node v_i and v_j under the relation $r \in \{1, 2, ..., R\}$ and A_r is the corresponding adjacency matrix.

2.2 Problem Formulation

Definition 4 (Graph-based Fraud Detection). Considering a multi-relation graph G, which has been defined in definition 2, the task is to detect the fraud nodes from the benign ones in the given graph. Specifically, given the structural information of the graph $\{A_1, A_2, ..., A_R\}$ and the original feature information X, we need to learn the function f to map the nodes into a d-dimension feature vector $z_i \in \mathbb{R}^d$ across the multi-relation graph where $d \ll N$. With the learned embedding and the labeled nodes, a classifier is trained to detect whether a given unlabeled node is a fraudster.

3   Overview Framework of Method

In this section, we present the proposed IDGL framework, as shown in Fig. 2. IDGL includes four module layers: the re-embedding embedding layer, adaptive dual-channel convolution layer, representation fusion layer, and the imbalance-oriented classification layer. For the first module layer, it is used to add some uncertainty by the dense and dropout layer to relieve the effect of feature camouflage. Furthermore, the second module layer is introduced to make full use of low- and high-pass signals to deal with the graph disassortativity issue. The third module layer makes the fusion of the intermediate representation to be the final features of nodes. The final module layer is used to deal with the graph imbalance and detect the fraudsters.

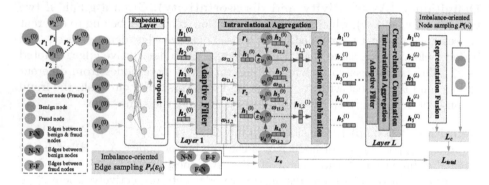

Fig. 2. An illustration of proposed framework of IDGL

3.1   Re-embedding Layer

Fraudsters usually learn the normal users to camouflage themselves, so the original attribute features between the fraudsters and the normal users are of great similarity. Therefore, it is highly desirable to add some uncertainty into the original features to re-learn the feature similarity between nodes to cater downstream fraudster detection tasks. In the paper, a dense-based dropout layer is introduced to encode the embeddings of the nodes without depending on the network topology, and it is denoted as follows:

$$h_i^{(0)} = \sigma \left(dropout \left(x_i, \eta \right) \cdot \mathbf{W}_0 \right), \tag{1}$$

where x_i is the original feature vector of node v_i, $dropout\,(\cdot,\eta)$ is the function which drops the neurons from the network with a certain probability η during network training, $\mathbf{W}_0$ is a learnable weight matrix, $h_i^{(0)}$ represents the embedding of node v_i, and $\sigma\,(\cdot)$ is the non-linear **ReLU** activation function. Based on the above components, the difference between the fraudsters and the normal users will be further amplified via network topology based on the improved convolution and aggregation strategies.

3.2 Adaptive Dual-channel Convolution Layer

Dual-channel Graph Convolution. Following GCN [8], from the perspective of graph signal processing, the graph convolution $*_G$ between the given signal x and filter f are denoted as:

$$f*_G x \approx \theta\left(I_N + D^{-\frac{1}{2}}AD^{-\frac{1}{2}}\right)x, \tag{2}$$

where $I_N \in \mathbb{R}^{N\times N}$ denotes the identity matrix and $D = diag\{d_1, d_2, ..., d_N\}$ is the diagonal degree matrix $(d_i = \sum_j A_{ij})$. From Eq. 2, we can observe that $I_N + D^{-\frac{1}{2}}AD^{-\frac{1}{2}}$ can be considered to smooth the central node by its adjacent nodes' information via summation between signals, and it can be treated as a low-pass filter to capture the commonalities between the central node and its adjacent nodes [1]. Naturally, for a high-pass graph filter, it should be used to capture the difference between them. Heuristically, a low-pass filter f_L and a high-pass filter f_H are designed as follows:

$$
\begin{aligned}
f_L*_G x &\approx \theta\left(\varepsilon I_N + \hat{D}^{-\frac{1}{2}}A\hat{D}^{-\frac{1}{2}}\right)x \\
f_H*_G x &\approx \theta\left(\varepsilon I_N - \hat{D}^{-\frac{1}{2}}A\hat{D}^{-\frac{1}{2}}\right)x,
\end{aligned}
\tag{3}
$$

where $\hat{D} = I + D$, and $\varepsilon \in [0, 1]$ is a scaling factor. We can generalize Eq. 3 to the signal $X \in \mathbb{R}^{N\times d}$ (i.e., a d-dimension representation for each node) as follows:

$$
\begin{aligned}
Z_L &= (\varepsilon I_N + \hat{D}^{-\frac{1}{2}}A\hat{D}^{-\frac{1}{2}})X\Theta \\
Z_H &= (\varepsilon I_N - \hat{D}^{-\frac{1}{2}}A\hat{D}^{-\frac{1}{2}})X\Theta,
\end{aligned}
\tag{4}
$$

where $\Theta \in \mathbb{R}^{d\times M}$ is the matrix of learnable filter parameter, and $Z_L \in \mathbb{R}^{N\times M}$ and $Z_H \in \mathbb{R}^{N\times M}$ are the signal matrix convolved by low-pass and high-pass filters, respectively. Then the low-pass and high-pass convolution of the node i can be denoted as:

$$
\begin{aligned}
(F_L X)_i &= \left(\varepsilon X_i + \sum_{j\in N(i)} \frac{1}{\sqrt{\hat{D}_{ii}\hat{D}_{jj}}} X_j\right)\Theta \\
(F_H X)_i &= \left(\varepsilon X_i - \sum_{j\in N(i)} \frac{1}{\sqrt{\hat{D}_{ii}\hat{D}_{jj}}} X_j\right)\Theta,
\end{aligned}
\tag{5}
$$

where $N(i)$ is the set of one-hop neighborhoods of node i.

Learnable Channel Fusion Aggregation. Given the above low- and high-pass graph filters, the next step is how to aggregate both low- and high-frequency information from the node's neighbors, respectively. Naturally, a basic idea is to add the weight parameter $\alpha_{ij,r}$ to balance the importance between such two filters under the relation r:

$$\tilde{h}_{i,r} = \alpha_{ij,r}(F_L H)_{i,r} + (1 - \alpha_{ij,r})(F_H H)_{i,r}, \tag{6}$$

where $\alpha_{ij,r} \in [0,1]$, and Eq. 6 can be further expanded as follows:

$$\tilde{h}_{i,r} = \left(\varepsilon h_{i,r} + \sum_{j \in N_r(i)} \frac{2\alpha_{ij,r} - 1}{\sqrt{\hat{D}_{ii,r}\hat{D}_{jj,r}}} h_{j,r} \right) \Theta_r, \tag{7}$$

where $\tilde{h}_{i,r}$ is the aggregated embedding of node v_i under the relation r. Here, we set a learnable coefficient $\omega_{ij,r} = 2\alpha_{ij,r} - 1$, where $\omega_{ij,r} \in [-1,1]$. For $\omega_{ij,r}$, it decides whether a low or high-frequency signal should be extracted between the node v_i and v_j, and thus the features of both the node itself v_i and its neighbor v_j should be considered together. Naturally, a shared self-gating mechanism is used to learn $\omega_{ij,r}$ as follows:

$$\omega_{ij,r}^{(l)} = \tanh \left(\left(\mathbf{W}_r^{(l)} \right)^T \left[h_i^{(l-1)} || h_j^{(l-1)} \right] \right), \tag{8}$$

where $h_i^{(l-1)} \in \mathbb{R}^{d_{v_i} \times 1}$ and $h_j^{(l-1)} \in \mathbb{R}^{d_{v_j} \times 1}$ are the representations of the nodes v_i and v_j at l-th layer, $\mathbf{W}_r^{(l)} \in \mathbb{R}^{(d_{v_i}+d_{v_j}) \times 1}$ is a trainable matrix, $||$ is the concatenation operation, and $\tanh(\cdot)$ is the *hyperbolic tangent* function, which makes the value ω_{ij} in the range of $(0,1)$. Finally, the aggregation of node i can be denoted as follows:

$$h_{i,r}^{(l)} = \sigma \left(\left(\varepsilon h_i^{(l-1)} + \sum_{j \in N_r(i)} \frac{\omega_{ij,r}^{(l)}}{\sqrt{\hat{D}_{ii,r}\hat{D}_{jj,r}}} h_j^{(l-1)} \right) \Theta_r^{(l-1)} \right). \tag{9}$$

Layer Architecture and Cross-relation Combination. In the previous sections, we have introduced the message passing paradigm of our method. Here, we formally define the convolution layer of our method under the r-th relation, and the mathematical formulation is denoted as follows:

$$
\begin{aligned}
&h_i^{(0)} = \sigma \left(dropout \left(x_i, \eta \right) \cdot \mathbf{W}_0 \right) \\
&\dots \\
&\omega_{ij,r}^{(l)} = \tanh \left(\left(\mathbf{W}_r^{(l)} \right)^T \left[h_i^{(l-1)} || h_j^{(l-1)} \right] \right) \\
&h_{i,r}^{(l)} = \sigma \left(\left(\varepsilon h_i^{(l-1)} + \sum_{j \in N_r(i)} \frac{\omega_{ij,r}^{(l)}}{\sqrt{\hat{D}_{ii,r}\hat{D}_{jj,r}}} h_j^{(l-1)} \right) \Theta_r^{(l-1)} \right) \\
&h_i^{(l)} \leftarrow [h_{i,1}^{(l)}, h_{i,2}^{(l)}, \dots, h_{i,R}^{(l)}] \\
&\dots
\end{aligned}
\tag{10}
$$

In Eq. 10, we can observe that $h_{i,r}^{(l)}, r \in [1, 2, ..., R]$ (i.e., the signal of node i learned under the different relation at the l-th layer) is concatenated as a new signal $h_i^{(l)}$, and it will be the input of node feature for the next layer.

3.3   Representation Fusion Layer

In our model, the node embedding outputted by different neural network layers has different smoothness and sharpness. In the model, the designed low- and high-pass filters make the node embedding outputted by different convolution layers have different smoothness and sharpness, and they can help facilitate the downstream classification task. Thus, we combine the intermediate embeddings outputted by the different layers as the final representation of the node:

$$z_i = [x_i, h_i^{(0)}, h_i^{(1)}, ..., h_i^{(L)}], \qquad (11)$$

where L is the number of convolution layer.

3.4   Imbalance-Oriented Classification Layer

As introduced in Eq. 9, for each graph neural layer l under the relation r, $\alpha_{ij,r}^{(l)}$ can be directly calculated by the learnable weight $\omega_{ij,r}^{(l)}$ as: $\alpha_{ij,r}^{(l)} = 0.5 \left(\omega_{ij,r}^{(l)} + 1 \right) \in [0, 1]$, and it can be used to measure the assortativity and disassortativity of the edge e_{ij}, so as to be the supervised information to balance the weight between low- and high-pass filters. Actually, the supervision signal from the known label nodes can be treated as the ground truth to make an auxiliary loss:

$$\mathcal{L}_r^{(l)} = - \sum_{e_{ij,r} \in \varepsilon_{t,r}} \left[y_{ij,r} \log \left(\alpha_{ij,r}^{(l)} \right) + (1 - y_{ij,r}) \log \left(1 - \alpha_{ij,r}^{(l)} \right) \right], \qquad (12)$$

where $y_{ij,r} \in \{0, 1\}$ is the label of the assortative edge (i.e., $y_{ij,r} = 1$) or the disassortative edge (i.e., $y_{ij,r} = 0$) under the relation r, and $\varepsilon_{t,r}$ is the edge set whose source nodes and target nodes have been labeled under the relation r. For each layer and each relation, the final loss for assortative and disassortative edges can be formulated as follows:

$$\mathcal{L}_\varepsilon = \frac{1}{L \times R} \sum \mathcal{L}_{\varepsilon_{t,r}}^{(l)}, \qquad (13)$$

where L and R are the number of layers and relations, respectively.

Additionally, given the final embedding of nodes z_i, the fraud detection problem can be treated as a binary node classification problem, and we use cross-entropy loss function to model it:

$$\mathcal{L}_c = - \sum_{i \in V} [y_i \log (p_i) + (1 - y_i) \log (1 - p_i)]$$
$$p_i = softmax (MLP(z_i)). \qquad (14)$$

To sum up, we define the overall loss of our method as follows:

$$\mathcal{L}_{total} = \gamma_c \mathcal{L}_c + \gamma_\varepsilon \mathcal{L}_\varepsilon + \gamma \|\Theta\|^2, \tag{15}$$

where γ_c, and γ_ε ($\gamma_c + \gamma_\varepsilon = 1$) are the weights to balance the importance of different losses, $\|\Theta\|^2$ is the regularization term to avoid over-fitting and γ is the control coefficient. Note that, to alleviate the influence of sample imbalance problem (i.e., the number of normal users is significantly larger than that of the fraudsters), a label-aware sampler is proposed to take the nodes' label frequency and degree information into consideration, which make the minority class of relatively high sampling probability. First, as to the node sampling for classification, the sampling probability is denoted as follows:

$$P(v_i) \propto \frac{\sqrt{d_i}}{Z(\mathcal{C}(v_i))}, \tag{16}$$

where $d_i = \sum_{r=1}^{R} \sum_j A_{ij,r}$ is the degree of node v_i under all relations, and $Z(\mathcal{C}(v_i))$ represents the label frequency of class $\mathcal{C}(v_i)$. Note that, $\sqrt{d_i}$ means that more "popular" nodes are more likely to selected, and $Z(C(v_i))$ means the more "rare" nodes are more likely to be selected.

Table 1. Datasets statistic information

YelpChi					Amazon				
#nodes (Fraudster%)	Relation type	Relations	Class	#Class	#nodes (Fraudster%)	Relation type	Relations	Class	#Class
45954 (14.53%)	R-U-R	49315	1	6677	11944 (10.5%)	U-P-U	175608	1	821
	R-T-R	573616	0	39277		U-S-U	3566479	0	7818
	R-S-R	3402743	–	0		U-V-U	1036737	–	3305
	ALL	3846979				ALL	4398392		

[1] For Class: 1: spam or fraudulent; 0: legitimate or benign; -: unlabeled.

The set of the sampled nodes is denoted as V_s. Next, for the edge sampling under the relation r, the sampling probability is defined as follows:

$$P(\varepsilon_{ij,r}) \propto \frac{\sqrt{d_{i,r} d_{j,r}}}{Z(\mathcal{C}(\varepsilon_{ij,r}))}, \tag{17}$$

where $d_{i,r} = \sum_k A_{ik,r}$ is the degree of node v_i under the relation r, and $Z(\mathcal{C}(\varepsilon_{ij,r}))$ is the edge label (i.e., the assortative or disassortative edge) frequency of class $\mathcal{C}(\varepsilon_{ij,r})$. The sets of the sampled edge under all relations are marked as: $\{\varepsilon_{s,r}\}|_{r=1}^{R}$. Similarly, $\sqrt{d_{i,r} d_{j,r}}$ and $Z(C(\varepsilon_{ij,r}))$ represents the popularity and rareness of the edge e_{ij} under the relation r. For the edges between fraudsters (F-F) and the edges between the fraudsters and the normal users (F-N), they are rare but valuable. Thus, $P(\varepsilon_{ij,r})$ can make F-N and F-F edges be selected at a higher probability.

4   Experiments

4.1   Experiment Setup

Datasets. Two public real-world fraud detection datasets (i.e., Yelp review dataset and Amazon dataset[13]) are used to validate the performance of IDGL. **YelpChi** dataset collects the reviews of hotels and restaurants on the Yelp platform, and the reviews are treated as the node with three relations: 1) R-U-R represents the reviews, which are provided by the same user, are linked; 2) R-T-R represents the reviews, which are given to the same product within the same month; 3)R-S-R represents the reviews, which are given to the same product with the same star-rating, are linked. The nodes are labeled by Yelp's filter (spam) and recommendation (legitimate). For **Amazon**, it is composed of users with their comments on the musical instruments. Here, users are treated as the node with three different types of relations: 1) U-P-U represents the users, who make the comments on at least one same product, are linked; 2) U-S-U represents the users, who give at least one same star-rating within a same week, are linked; 3) U-V-U represents the users, who have top-5% mutual review TF-IDF similarities, are linked. Note that the user is labeled the normal user or the fraudster according to more than 80% or less than 20% helpful votes. The statistics of such two datasets are shown in Tab. 1.

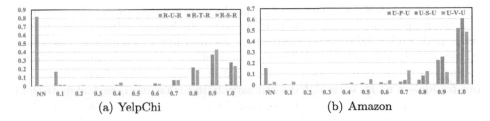

Fig. 3. Disassortativity Evidence. X-axis is the proportion of disassortative edges in the neighborhood of fraud nodes. Y-axis is the proportion of the corresponding fraudulent nodes among all fraudsters. NN is the fraudulent node without any neighbor.

Baselines. In this section, several state-of-the-art GNN-based methods and their variants are compared to verify the effectiveness of our proposed method. The source code of our model is available.[1]

GCN [8] is a general GNN model which aggregates the embedding information of node's first-order neighours. GAT [15] is an attention-based graph neural network which takes the attention mechanism into the process of aggregation. GraphSAGE [6] is an inductive graph neural network which takes the multi-order node sampling strategy into node aggregation. GEM [12] is an improved graph neural network for malicious accounts detection which constructs the heterogeneous account-device graphs by summarizing the weakness of the attackers.

---

[1] https://github.com/Shzuwu/IDGL.

FdGars [17] is a GCN-based method for fraud detection which reconstruct a relational graph between the fraudsters and the normal users based on multi-context information. GraphConsis [11] is a heterogeneous GNN-based method that aims to address the inconsistency problems of context, feature, and relation. CARE-GNN [3] is a GNN-based method that investigates the camouflage behavior of fraudsters and their negative influence on GNN-based fraudster detectors, and proposes a label-aware similarity measure and a similarity-aware selector. FRAUDRE [19] is an improved GNN method that focuses on the graph inconsistency and imbalance issues of the camouflaged fraudsters.

Note that we perform GCN, GAT, GraphSAGE, and FdGars on the graphs characterized by Definition 2 (i.e., ALL in Table 1), and perform the other methods on multi-relation graphs characterized by Definition 3.

Evaluation Metrics. Since YelpChi and Amazon datasets have imbalanced classes, following previous work, we use AUC, Macro-Recall and Macro-F1 for performance evaluation. As a widely used binary classification metric, AUC is computed based on the relative ranking of prediction probabilities of all samples, and it could eliminate the influence of class imbalance.

4.2 Evidence of Graph Disassortativity and Imbalance

First, we investigate the existence of graph disassortativity. Specifically, we calculate the proportion of disassortative edges to all one-hop neighbors of each fraudulent node under different relation subgraphs, and further count the proportion changes of these fraudulent nodes among all of them with the growth of disassortativity proportion, as shown in Fig. 3. We can observe that there are numerous fraudulent nodes with high disassortativity in such subgraphs, and more than half-past of fraudsters are with larger than 80% disassortativity proportion. Consequently, the fraud graph is of disassortativity naturally, and we need to take the separation of assortativity and disassortativity into consideration.

Table 2. Edge type statistic information

Edge	YelpChi			Amazon		
	R-U-R	R-T-R	R-S-R	U-P-U	U-S-U	U-V-U
N-N	48,261	420,783	2,539,220	112,330	2,670,843	665,149
F-F	878	14,781	88,406	3,397	4,474	925
F-N	176	138,052	775,117	31,655	124,232	26,970

[1] N-N: edges between normal users; F-F: edges between fraudsters; F-N: edges between fraudsters and normal users.

Next, we further study the imbalance of the fraud graph, and we find that the imbalance of nodes and edges is widespread. Specifically, for node imbalance, we have counted it in Table 1, and we can observe that only 14.53% and 9.50% of labeled nodes are fraudsters, which makes the model dominated by the majority class (i.e., the benign users) with the reduction of model generalization ability. Furthermore, we also investigate the edge imbalance of fraud graphs. Specifically, we first classify the edge type into three classes, namely N-N(edges between normal users), F-F(edges between fraudsters), and F-N(edges between the normal users and fraudsters), and then count their numbers under the different relational subgraphs, as shown in Table 2. We can observe that the number of N-N edges is of maximum quantity, which may make the node aggregation dominated by N-N edges and weaken the ability to model differences (between fraudsters and normal users) and commonalities (between the fraudsters) while they are the keys to fraud detection. Consequently, the imbalance of nodes and edges is widespread in fraud detection, and we need to design an imbalanced-oriented nodes and edges sampling strategy to eliminate bias toward the majority classes.

4.3 Performance Comparison

In this section, we compare our proposed method IDGL with the state-of-the-art methods on both Amazon and YelpChi datasets. Note that we also perform the metrics (i.e., AUC, Macro-Recall, and Macro-F1) under different ratios (from 10% to 40%) of both datasets, as shown in Table 3, and we have the following observations.

First, compare the methods which are performed on the single graph (i.e., GCN, GAT, GraphSage, and FdGars) with the ones which are performed on the multi-graph (i.e., GME, GraphConsis, CARE-GNN, FRAUDRE, and IDGL), the latter is mostly better than formers, expect for GME, which brings two aspects of inspiration. On the one hand, the multi-relation graph contains richer

Table 3. Performance under various ratios of Amazon and YelpChi training sets. Recall and F1 are the abbreviation of Macro-Recall and Macro-F1.

Data	Method	10%			20%			30%			40%		
		AUC	Recall	F1	AUC	Recall	F1	AUC	Recall	F1	AUC	Recall	F1
Amazon	GCN	77.26	50.00	47.51	77.42	50.00	47.51	76.99	50.00	47.51	77.94	50.00	47.51
	GAT	76.96	50.00	47.50	76.99	50.00	47.51	76.61	50.00	47.50	77.35	50.00	47.50
	GraphSage	69.87	50.00	47.50	71.75	50.00	47.50	72.51	50.00	47.51	71.49	50.00	47.50
	GME	70.24	69.56	75.52	72.05	71.55	75.53	73.99	72.12	68.48	74.44	70.66	74.42
	FdGars	81.10	73.41	55.32	81.19	73.47	55.31	80.91	72.90	55.01	80.82	72.82	55.14
	GraphConsis	82.67	82.63	75.97	84.22	84.21	81.93	84.46	84.37	79.06	85.15	85.10	77.98
	CARE-GNN	88.16	88.19	88.21	88.25	87.95	85.80	87.41	84.89	75.70	87.36	83.90	88.36
	FRAUDRE	90.37	89.12	91.02	88.99	88.71	90.67	90.67	91.51	88.01	91.11	88.18	91.10
	IDGL	**95.09**	**89.37**	**91.22**	**96.42**	**89.76**	**91.17**	**96.98**	**90.61**	**91.65**	**97.58**	**90.73**	**91.23**
YelpChi	GCN	52.12	50.00	46.08	53.88	50.00	46.08	52.62	50.00	46.08	53.12	50.00	46.08
	GAT	50.14	50.00	46.08	49.94	50.00	46.08	49.97	50.00	46.08	49.67	50.00	46.08
	GraphSage	52.94	50.00	46.08	55.39	50.00	46.08	56.08	50.00	46.10	56.45	50.00	46.10
	GME	64.35	50.00	46.08	64.28	51.33	48.89	69.63	51.04	48.24	70.88	50.38	46.87
	FdGars	47.36	49.19	48.76	47.54	49.40	48.93	47.71	49.52	49.02	47.91	49.42	48.93
	GraphConsis	64.12	64.72	61.3	63.89	64.46	62.93	60.94	61.44	62.73	61.02	61.67	63.03
	CARE-GNN	69.73	65.68	52.86	70.47	66.94	57.55	72.42	67.32	57.39	70.99	66.80	56.47
	FRAUDER	72.21	66.44	55.34	72.51	67.30	58.22	73.72	67.91	59.24	72.22	66.98	59.26
	IDGL	**85.38**	**74.50**	**70.23**	**88.65**	**78.65**	**72.84**	**90.04**	**80.06**	**74.36**	**91.14**	**82.36**	**76.37**

information than the single one, which may provide the chance to make performance improvements. On the other hand, the richer data means a more complex relationship, which means that it is unworkable to directly apply GNNs to fraud detection under the multi-relation graph, and we need to deal with the relationship between the node and its neighbors more carefully. GraphConsis, CARE-GNN, and FRAUDRE have achieved the promising performance by introducing similarity measure and fraud-aware module into the node aggregation process, and IDGL outperforms all other SOTA methods via the learnable high- and low-filter to adaptively learn the difference and similarity commonalities between the node and its neighbors to facilitate the target task.

Second, it has been introduced in Table 1 that node imbalance is widespread in fraud detection. For GNN-based fraud detection methods, CARE-GNN and FRAUDRE take the influence of node imbalance into consideration to eliminate the training bias towards the majority class (i.e., the normal users), and achieve better performance than other methods. However, they haven't taken edge imbalance into consideration. As we discussed in Sect. 4.2, we categorize the edge type into three classes: N-N, F-F, and F-N. For F-N, we can treat it as a guide to learn the difference between the fraudsters and the normal users, and F-F is rare but valuable for us to learn the commonalities between the fraudsters, which helps better fraud detection. Thus, an edge sampling method is proposed to make the model pay more attention to the edge of F-N and F-F. Consequently, IDGL achieves better performance than CARE-GNN and FRAUDRE by taking both node and edge sampling into consideration.

4.4 Ablation Analysis

High- and Low-Filters. To demonstrate the effectiveness of the adaptive filter, we conduct the ablation study on the Amazon dataset by ranging the percentage of the training dataset from 10% to 40%, as shown in Fig. 4 (a), and a similar

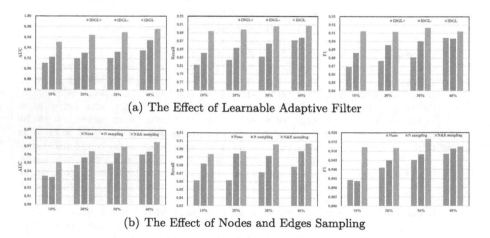

(a) The Effect of Learnable Adaptive Filter

(b) The Effect of Nodes and Edges Sampling

Fig. 4. Ablation Analysis of Learnable Adaptive Filter and Nodes/Edges Sampling on Amazon dataset with AUC, Recall and F1.

result can also be observed on YelpChi dataset. Specifically, we construct two ablation models by replacing the learnable adaptive high- and low-filer with the only low-filer (i.e., $\alpha_{ij,r} = 1$, denoted as IDGL+) and the only high-filter (i.e., $\alpha_{ij,r} = 0$, denoted as IDGL−), respectively. We can observe that both IDGL+ and IDGL− can be applied to fraud detection with competitive performance. Additionally, IDGL− have better performance than IDGL+, because the fraud graph is of great disassortativity as proved above, and IDGL+ only aggregates the low-frequency signals from its neighbors without considering the difference between classes which makes itself submerged with lack of discrimination. IDGL outperforms such two methods by combining the advantages of low- and high-filters adaptively.

Node and Edge Sampling. To demonstrate the effectiveness of node and edge sampling, we construct two ablation models by removing either edge sampling or both of them on the Amazon dataset with ranging the percentage of training dataset from 10% to 40%, as shown in Fig. 4 (b), and the similar result can also be observed on YelpChi dataset. We can observe that compared with the ablation model without any imbalance-oriented sampling, the one with node sampling performs better as it can mitigate the imbalance issue to some extent. By further introducing edge sampling to make the model pay more attention to the valuable edge types (i.e., F-F and F-N), the performance has been further improved, which shows the effectiveness of node and edge sampling.

4.5   Parameter Sensitivity and Running Efficiency

In this section, we investigate the sensitivity and running efficiency.

First, with 40% of the Amazon dataset as the training set, we vary the value of embedding dimensionality in the range of [8,64], and the result is depicted in Fig. 5(a). We can observe that it first makes a slight improvement with embedding size increasing, and it becomes stable after 32. Considering a larger embedding dimensionality requires higher computational complexity, we finally set d as 32 to make the balance between performance and complexity.

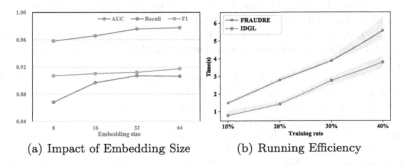

(a) Impact of Embedding Size   (b) Running Efficiency

Fig. 5. Performance of IDGL with varing embedding size and running efficiency on Amazon dataset.

Second, to investigate the running efficiency of IDGL, with different percentages of the training set on the Amazon dataset, we compare the average training time of each epoch with FRAUDRE, which has the most competitive performance among all the baseline methods. To be fair, we set the number of convolution layers to 2, the embedding size to 32, and the batch size to 256 for both of them, and the result is depicted in Fig. 5 (b). We can observe that IDGL runs faster than FRAUDER with more time efficiency.

5   Conclusion

In the paper, we propose an imbalanced disassortative graph learning framework called IDGL to solve the graph disassortativity and imbalance issues. To tackle the graph disassortativity, an adaptive dual-channel convolution filter is further developed to adaptively combine the advantage of dual-channel (i,e., the low- and high-frequency) signals from its neighbors, which helps assimilate the nodes with assortative edges and discriminate the nodes with disassortative edges. For graph imbalance issues, a label-aware nodes sampler and edges sampler are designed with the consideration of nodes' popularity and corresponding label class frequency, which helps the model simultaneously eliminate the bias towards the major classes and pay more attention to the valuable edges (i.e., F-F and F-N). Extensive experiments on two public fraud datasets demonstrate the effectiveness of our method.

Acknowledgments. We first gratefully acknowledge anonymous reviewers who read this draft and make any helpful suggestions. The work is supported by the National Nature Science Foundation of China (No. U22A201181, U1803262, U1736206), National Social Science Fund of China (No. 19ZDA113), and the Application Foundation Frontier Project of Wuhan Science and Technology Bureau (No. 2020010601012288).

References

1. Bo, D., Wang, X., Shi, C., Shen, H.: Beyond low-frequency information in graph convolutional networks. arXiv preprint arXiv:2101.00797 (2021)
2. Cui, G., Zhou, J., Yang, C., Liu, Z.: Adaptive graph encoder for attributed graph embedding. In: KDD, pp. 976–985 (2020)
3. Dou, Y., Liu, Z., Sun, L., Deng, Y., Peng, H., Yu, P.S.: Enhancing graph neural network-based fraud detectors against camouflaged fraudsters. In: CIKM, pp. 315–324 (2020)
4. Dou, Y., Ma, G., Yu, P.S., Xie, S.: Robust spammer detection by nash reinforcement learning. In: KDD, pp. 924–933 (2020)
5. Ge, S., Ma, G., Xie, S., Philip, S.Y.: Securing behavior-based opinion spam detection. In: 2018 IEEE BigData, pp. 112–117. IEEE (2018)
6. Hamilton, W., Ying, Z., Leskovec, J.: Inductive representation learning on large graphs. In: NeurIPS, vol. 30 (2017)
7. Kaghazgaran, P., Alfifi, M., Caverlee, J.: Wide-ranging review manipulation attacks: model, empirical study, and countermeasures. In: CIKM, pp. 981–990 (2019)

8. Kipf, T.N., Welling, M.: Semi-supervised classification with graph convolutional networks. arXiv preprint arXiv:1609.02907 (2016)
9. Li, Q., Wu, X.M., Liu, H., Zhang, X., Guan, Z.: Label efficient semi-supervised learning via graph filtering. In: CVPR, pp. 9582–9591 (2019)
10. Liu, Y., et al.: Pick and choose: a GNN-based imbalanced learning approach for fraud detection. In: WWW, pp. 3168–3177 (2021)
11. Liu, Z., Dou, Y., Yu, P.S., Deng, Y., Peng, H.: Alleviating the inconsistency problem of applying graph neural network to fraud detection. In: SIGIR, pp. 1569–1572 (2020)
12. Liu, Z., Chen, C., Yang, X., Zhou, J., Li, X., Song, L.: Heterogeneous graph neural networks for malicious account detection. In: CIKM, pp. 2077–2085 (2018)
13. McAuley, J.J., Leskovec, J.: From amateurs to connoisseurs: modeling the evolution of user expertise through online reviews. In: WWW, pp. 897–908 (2013)
14. Shi, F., Cao, Y., Shang, Y., Zhou, Y., Zhou, C., Wu, J.: H2-FDetector: a GNN-based fraud detector with homophilic and heterophilic connections. In: WWW, pp. 1486–1494 (2022)
15. Veličković, P., Cucurull, G., Casanova, A., Romero, A., Lio, P., Bengio, Y.: Graph attention networks. arXiv preprint arXiv:1710.10903 (2017)
16. Wang, D., et al.: A semi-supervised graph attentive network for financial fraud detection. In: ICDM, pp. 598–607. IEEE (2019)
17. Wang, J., Wen, R., Wu, C., Huang, Y., Xion, J.: FdGars: fraudster detection via graph convolutional networks in online app review system. In: WWW, pp. 310–316 (2019)
18. Wu, F., Souza, A., Zhang, T., Fifty, C., Yu, T., Weinberger, K.: Simplifying graph convolutional networks. In: ICML, pp. 6861–6871. PMLR (2019)
19. Zhang, G., et al.: FRAUDRE: fraud detection dual-resistant to graph inconsistency and imbalance. In: 2021 ICDM, pp. 867–876. IEEE (2021)
20. Zhong, Q., et al.: Financial defaulter detection on online credit payment via multi-view attributed heterogeneous information network. In: WWW, pp. 785–795 (2020)

Vision Papers

A Challenge for the Next 50 Years of Automated Service Composition

Marco Aiello[⊠][iD]

Department of Service Computing, IAAS, University of Stuttgart, Stuttgart, Germany
marco.aiello@iaas.uni-stuttgart.de

Abstract. Automated Service Composition emerged as a promising area of research at the beginning of the century. After twenty years, it appears to have reached a stagnating state where only little progress is made. In the present vision paper, I propose a challenge for automated service composition to be achieved in the next 50 years. I set a scene in 2052 that service composition should be able to handle by then. Finally, I draw a parallel with autonomous driving to identify the major milestones in the quest to fully autonomous service composition systems.

Keywords: Automated Service Composition · Service-oriented Computing · Maturity Levels · Artificial Intelligence Planning

1 The Promises of Automated Service Composition

Automated service composition refers to systems that utilize distributed, discrete units of software by orderly invoking their execution with the goal of satisfying a set of user-defined specifications. The core idea is as old as the field of software engineering. In fact, as soon as software was complex enough to require artisan talent and engineering techniques, the intuition of using modular designs came about. Instead of writing code for every subtask, one could reuse parts of existing code, possibly resident remotely on a network. To make things simpler for the developer, the input/output syntax of these parts must be precisely specified in order to enable composition. These were the first steps in the direction of manual software composition and, with the subsequent advent of software services as units of invokable functionalities, of service composition.

1.1 A Parallel with the Automotive Industry

A parallel with the automotive industry and the process of driving a car will help understanding automated service composition evolution. Since the first 'ride' of Berta Benz in August 1888, people have been manually steering their vehicles and controlling their detailed motion. With the passing of time, more automation has been introduced to support the driver, such as synchronised gear shifting,

© The Author(s), under exclusive license to Springer Nature Switzerland AG 2022
J. Troya et al. (Eds.): ICSOC 2022, LNCS 13740, pp. 635–643, 2022.
https://doi.org/10.1007/978-3-031-20984-0_45

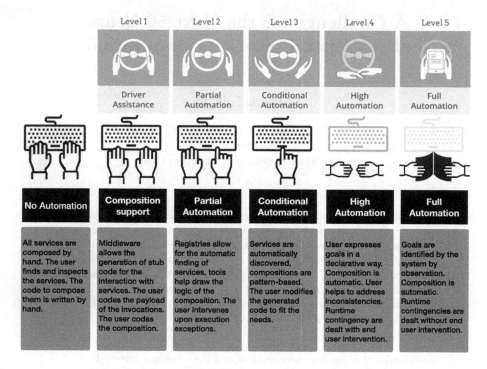

Fig. 1. Maturity levels of Automated Service Composition

automatic shifting, cruise control, adaptive cruise control, lane assistance, and so on. Automation in the past decade has reached a degree that prompted the automotive industry, via the Society of Automotive Engineers, to define levels of automation, also to set an agenda for the progress towards fully autonomous vehicles. The levels are: Level 0 - No Driving Automation; Level 1 - Driver Assistance; Level 2 - Partial Driving Automation; Level 3 - Conditional Driving Automation; Level 4 - High Driving Automation; and Level 5 - Full Driving Automation. Current modern vehicles can exhibit Levels 1 and 2 of automation, with some manufacturers claiming to have reached Level 3 and promising to reach Level 4 very soon. The top part of Fig. 1 shows the levels of automation, going from supporting the driver all the way to completely taking over all driving tasks from him/her.

One could say that the work of the software engineer, from the point of view of software composition, is undergoing a similar process. From the early days of completely manual composition (Level 0), we have now tools and execution environments that support the developer in creating compositions. However, the real goal is that of full automation. Systems that just compose software to satisfy user needs. Yet another job category will be swallowed by automation, that of developers; and perhaps most tasks of software architects will follow suit. Section 4 presents a detailed definition of the levels of automated service composition in comparison of those of automated driving, as shown in Fig. 1.

1.2 Composition Throughout the Years

Attributing a new technique to one specific event or person is difficult; and most often a source of injustice. What I think is fair to say is that with the birth of computing as a science, the increasing complexity in programs and the availability of evermore powerful machines, a need emerged for structured programming. This would then lead to the idea of modularization, reuse, and composition. The sixties and early seventies were fertile times for this kind of innovation. The address "Mass Produced Software Components" of Douglas McIlroy at a NATO event in 1968 made the need explicit as he mentioned the possibility to componentize software so that systems could be built from preexisting components [9]. The movement of creating personal computing experiences was also intertwined with the need of programming tools to go with them. In this spirit languages like SmallTalk could be designed.[1] The idea of orchestrations of agents as the fundamental model of building distributed systems emerged the following years [5]. And the 1980s were fundamental for the establishment of what we call today Object-Oriented Programming: a model in which software is designed as the interaction of formally specified objects and their instances.

The next milestones have to do with the scale of the software components. They went from the microworld of individual objects, to the scale of entire subsystems. This led to the birth of component-based software engineering which established itself as a subfield of software engineering in the 1990s [4]. The final radical innovation that triggered a major shift was the advent of the Web. Even though it was not designed with the goal of creating a computing infrastructure, over time it became one. Additions, extensions, and patches catered for a shift from a Web of information for people to a mixed Web for people and programs [1]. Furthermore, the wide adoption of it made sure that almost any entity would have a Web presence, or better said, an entry point to its information system. Opening up a pletora of opportunities, industry and academia got creative. People started to play with the idea of composing Web pages to add value for users [8]. The industry came up with dedicated protocols for Web service interactions [13] and identifying an added value with respect to component-based software engineering [12]. Soon a new community gathered around the concept of Service-Oriented Computing [10]. As automated service composition was one of the central challenges, proposals to address it were soon made. Artificial Intelligence planning was seen as a promising tool [2] and adopted by several researchers, e.g., [3,7]. Other approaches using Petri Nets, Semantic Web technologies are also part of the early proposals [11].

---

[1] See [6] for a great depiction of those fervent and creative times.

1.3   The First Winter of Automated Service Composition

"Automated service composition is dead!" stated a colleague recently. I was a bit shocked to hear that, but sympathetic. That statement made me reflect about all the promises that were made about automated service composition and the fact that they were mostly unrealized. Admittedly, I was as guilty as anybody else. In the early days of Service-Oriented Computing emerging as a field, I was promising that organizing a trip would be as easy as saying where and when you wanted to go. I was promising that interacting with your home would be as easy as saying that you wanted to go to bed and all would be set for you, or that emergency situations, such as falling or a gas leak would be handled safely and promptly. But why did we promise that and why didn't we really achieve it? I think the "why" has to do with the excitement of seeing service implementation emerge in abundance. The idea of being able to invoke an informational service, or a remote functionality about more or less anything made us high on opportunities. We really thought that creating a system was only about gluing together the various elements, because all the necessary ones would always be available and easy to invoke. We also believed that the world would be so disciplined that everybody would provide enough 'semantic,' trustworthy information about their services that one could really use it for automated service composition. And there was a technical reason too. The advent of the Web had created a unique platform of Web servers. Companies and service providers all had a Web presence at the turn of the millenium and this also meant that port 80 was open for all to go through via HTTP.[2] In other words, there was a privileged, always open door to the information systems, databases and services of all companies that, with a bit of internal collaboration, meant full interoperability and compositionability. These opportunities inebriated us, and made us promise too much, too fast, a bit like that self-driving car automaker.

However, if the promises were too optimistic, I also think that they were not ungrounded. There were a number of technological hurdles that we assumed would be easily overcome and that would empower fully automated service composition. These have to do with the availability of full semantic descriptions of the services, with the actual trust and security that needs to be guaranteed, with clear business models that benefit all participants. These hurdles are still there, but are not insurmountable. *Automated service composition is not dead, it's just waiting for the next big shift in technology to be able to flourish.* It is in a lethargic state which is typical of winters. Yes, automated service composition is in its first winter, very much as the field of Artificial Intelligence, formally born in 1956, fell in its winters in the early 1970s and late 1980s. Machine learning techniques are very promising in this respect. Possibly automated service composition is waiting for machine learning techniques to allow for the automatic description of services and interfaces, so that they can be composed without expert intervention. It is waiting for reliable trust and security models of execution, and other major technical and technological breakthroughs that can drive it towards fulfilling its original promises.

---

[2] For a more detailed treatment, see Chap. 7 of [1].

Taking the view that automated service composition is not dead, but simply in its first winter, I provide next a challenge to be realized in the next 50 years, a possible situation that automated service composition should be able to handle in 30 years, and a roadmap of the crucial milestones that will bring us there. The milestones are presented mimicking the ones of autonomous driving and presented as dividing the planned evolution into five plus one levels.

2   The Challenge

John McCarthy, one of the founding fathers of Artificial Intelligence, challenged his community in the 1950s promising that within 50 years a computer would beat the world chess champion. In May 1997, IBM Deep Blue defeated the human world champion Garry Kasparov in chess. The same year, the RoboCup initiative was started with the following goal: *"By the middle of the 21st century, a team of fully autonomous humanoid robot soccer players shall win a soccer game, complying with the official rules of FIFA, against the winner of the most recent World Cup."* So what is the challenge of automated service composition for the next 50 years? I postulate that the challenge is that **by the year 2075 automated service composition will power the first software based prime minister of a democratic country.** The advantages should be rather obvious. Such Automated Service Composition prime minister will not be susceptible to corruption. It will be efficient in optimizing all software and human based services for the common good of the country. It will work 24/7. It will work on the basis of the given democratic requirements as expressed by the parliament or by explicit people participation in direct democracy forms. If requirements are contradictory or unrealizable (e.g., the majority of the people asking for reducing taxation to zero), it will try to find a composition and, after some time for searching the vast space of possible compositions, it will provide a detailed explanation for its decision which will be: *"No."*

3   An Automated Service Composition Scene in 2052

It is late afternoon of a Summer day of 2052. Bob comes home. The automated service composition home automation system recognizes Bob, his location, and his mood. It then uses a speaker near him to say: *"Bob, welcome home. You seem a bit concerned and maybe sad. Can I organize something for you tonight?"*

Bob, who is fond of astronomy and has named his automated service composition system "Io," replies: *"Not sure I want to do anything, maybe just a pizza and a movie."*

Io: *"How about you invite Alice over? I could organize that for you."*

Bob: *"Yes Io, good idea. I think she is in town and I'd like to spend the evening together."*

Io connects to Europa, the automated service composition system of Alice, to ask about Alice's willingness to spend the evening with Bob and to verify her availability. After a positive reply, Io starts a service composition process. It connects to one of the city drone services. It orders Bob's favourite pizza and negotiates Alice's pizza choices with Europa. It checks the contents of the fridge for drinks and desserts and places an order for automatic delivery of missing favourites. It prepares a music playlist as the intersection of Alice and Bob's most played evening songs. The service composition starts its execution as orchestrated by Io.

Food and drinks are delivered by air. The music list is ready. A taxi drone is sent in front of the building of Alice at the agreed time. Alice is informed by Europa and leaves her home. She hops on the drone and thinks about what movie she would fancy that evening. The drone takes off and goes into one of the platooning lanes that are defined for that city. It joins a platoon of twelve drones going from East to West. After 8 min of flight, the drone lands in front of Bob's home. She leaves the drone and enters the building. Bob is informed of her arrival and goes to the door.

Alice and Bob are happy to see each other and move to the living room. They start chatting about their days. Io recognizes the atmosphere and starts playing the music. In a short pause from talking of the two it intervenes. *"Can I serve you a cocktail? The usual one maybe?"*

Bob looks at Alice: *"Would you like that?"*

Alice acknowledges and Bob adds: *"Thank you Io. I will prepare them myself."*

Bob takes over the task as he knows Alice likes to be treated old school and likes when he does something personal for her. The `making cocktails` goal of Io changes, allowing for the human to take over most of the service composition tasks. Bob finds the glasses and ice ready. The robotic kitchen arms have done the *mise en place,* so he just has to decide on the quantities and order of mixing. He adds some fresh mint from a pot on his balcony. Something Io has not yet learned he likes. He then proudly offers the drinks to Alice, while both sit relaxingly on the couch.

While waiting for the pizzas to be delivered, a list of possible movies to watch appears on the main wall screen of the living room. Alice and Bob ponder the various choices, most likely the hardest service selection problem of the evening.

4   Where Are We Now?

Deepening in the parallel with the automotive industry will help us understand where we are now in automated service composition. Level 0 corresponds with driving an old timer, no automation whatsoever. In automated service composition terms, this is the equivalent of identifying services at design time and writing by hand all the code for the subsequent invocation of services. Level 1 is driver assistant and corresponds to composition support, also depicted in Fig. 1. At this level, we have middleware that manages message exchanges via publish and subscribe or one-to-one infrastructures. Code for the invocation of the selected services is automatically generated, but the content of the messages and the semantic of the interactions is coded by the developer. The logic of the composition is basically coded by the system designer with no support. Level 2 of Partial Driving Automation corresponds to a situation in which service discovery is highly automated. Tools also support the creation of the composition logic. The runtime of the composition is supported by appropriate tools and middleware, but unforeseen exceptions need to be handled by the system owner. Level 3 of Conditional Driving Automation corresponds to the situation in which service discovery is fully automated. This includes automatic service selection, substitution, and quality of service based discovery. Compositions are partially automated and are generated based on patterns. The patterns are both designed by experts and learned by observation of repeated executions. The runtime of the composition is fully supported. Generated compositions are typically inspected by the user who can possibly modify the generated code. The compositions are presented in intuitive graphical or textual forms for domain experts who are not necessarily expert developers. Level 4 of High Driving Automation corresponds to a situation in which service composition becomes almost entirely automated. The user expresses requirements in a declarative form, and the system creates the compositions. Services are provisioned automatically exploring the run-time availabilities and service qualities. User may need to intervene in case of inconsistencies or the unavailability of essential services to satisfy the original requests. The runtime is highly automated and adaptive to varying execution conditions. User intervention may be occasionally needed for boundary cases. Level 5 of Full Driving Automation corresponds with systems fully capable of automated service composition. The end-user does not even need to express goals, as these are automatically mined by the system through learning and the observation of executions, possibly of any other user too. The service discovery, selection and invocation is fully automatic. Composition is equally automatic. It is based on functional, non functional, and instance properties of the services. Contingencies, unavailabilities, changes in service properties are handled by the system at runtime with the objective of satisfying the end-user's goals under the constraints of the moment. The user needs to do nothing. It can provide feedback to the automated service composition system with the goal of improving the overall quality of the compositions and their executions.

The vehicles traveling on a highway today are a mix of mostly Level 0 ones, several Level 1, and some Level 2. Similarly for automated service composition, today most systems are built with Level 0 technologies, especially the smaller scale systems. Though several are using Level 1 and Level 2 technologies. Upper levels are available only as research prototypes often working in very specific domains and controlled environments. Level 5 systems do not exist, to the best of my knowledge, even as research prototypes.

It should be noticed that what we term 'user' in the levels above actually has varying meaning depending on the level. The lower the level, the more the user is a developer with very good technological knowledge. The more we go towards the higher levels, the more the user is the end-user of the system and his/her knowledge of the technology becomes less relevant. Again something similar to the automotive industry. In case of a small random failure, decades ago, the driver was expected to be able to do essential repairs—i.e., on a Level 0 car— while today the best thing a driver can do on a Level 1 or 2 car is to contact a service center. The service center will then initiate remotely the execution of a diagnostic process, after which the driver can be advised on what to do.

5   Outlook

While Alan Kay observed that *"the best way to predict the future is to invent it,"* predictions are deemed very difficult in general, as Niels Bohr noticed, *"especially about the future."* Clearly, the present interpretation of the history of automated service composition, the vision about its future and what is challenging are very personal, but what I consider general is the observation of where we are in the field. The goal of this treatment is to open the discussion within the community, and possibly in the neighbouring communities too, on what are the many milestones to be reached and then surpassed. As Artificial Intelligence has seen its winters, only to subsequently experience sprouting springs, I think that Automated Service Composition is in a similar situation. After its explicit recognition at the beginning of the century and the strong promises of the early days, it is now in a stale position, some would even say comatose, but there is hope for a major technological and scientific paradigm shift that can give new life to it and bring it to higher levels of maturity; making it a building block of a more efficient, sustainable, and reliable society.

Acknowledgements. The inspiration to write this paper came after a discussion of the IFIP Working Group 6.12: Services-Oriented Systems held during SummerSOC 2022, on July 3rd in Crete. I am indebted to all participants of that event for the fruitful discussion. I am also grateful to Heike Aiello, Luigia Carlucci, Ilche Georgievski, and Frank Leymann who have read and commented early drafts. All the opinions and remaining errors can only be ascribed to myself.

Note. The present paper was written following the very same principles of composition at the core of Automated Service Composition. In fact, any central section can be composed with any other central section of the paper without affecting the reading flow. It can also be omitted. So any reading of the sections such as 1,2,3,4,5, or 1,4,3,2,5, or 1,3,2,5 or 1,2,5 and so on are valid ways for going through this material. Try it!

References

1. Aiello, M.: The pervasive future. In: The Web Was Done by Amateurs, pp. 129–140. Springer, Cham (2018). https://doi.org/10.1007/978-3-319-90008-7_10
2. Aiello, M., et al.: A Request Language for Web-Services Based on Planning and Constraint Satisfaction. In: Buchmann, (eds.) TES 2002. LNCS, vol. 2444, pp. 76–85. Springer, Heidelberg (2002). https://doi.org/10.1007/3-540-46121-3_10

3. Berardi, D., Calvanese, D., De Giacomo, G., Lenzerini, M., Mecella, M.: Automatic composition of e-services that export their behavior. In: Orlowska, M.E., Weerawarana, S., Papazoglou, M.P., Yang, J. (eds.) ICSOC 2003. LNCS, vol. 2910, pp. 43–58. Springer, Heidelberg (2003). https://doi.org/10.1007/978-3-540-24593-3_4

4. Heineman, G., Councill, W.: Component-Based Software Engineering. Putting the Pieces Together, Addison-Westley (2001)

5. Hewitt, C., Bishop, P., Steiger, R.: A universal modular actor formalism for Artificial Intelligence. In: Proceedings of the 3rd International Joint Conference on Artificial Intelligence (IJCAI) (1973)

6. Kay, A.C.: The early history of Smalltalk. In: History of programming languages–II, pp. 511–598 (1996)

7. Lazovik, A., Aiello, M., Papazoglou, M.: Planning and monitoring the execution of Web service requests. In: Orlowska, M.E., Weerawarana, S., Papazoglou, M.P., Yang, J. (eds.) ICSOC 2003. LNCS, vol. 2910, pp. 335–350. Springer, Heidelberg (2003). https://doi.org/10.1007/978-3-540-24593-3_23

8. McIlraith, S., Son, T.C.: Adapting Golog for composition of semantic Web-services. In: Fensel, D., Giunchiglia, F., McGuinness, D., Williams, M. (eds.) Proceedings of the 8th International Conference on Principles of Knowledge Representation (KR), pp. 482–496. Morgan Kaufmann (2002)

9. McIlroy, D.: Mass-produced software components. In: Proceedings of the 1st International Conference on Software Engineering, Garmisch Patenkirchen, Germany, pp. 88–98 (1968)

10. Papazoglou, M.: Service-Oriented Computing: Concepts, characteristics and directions. In: Proceedings of the Fourth International Conference on Web Information Systems Engineering, 2003. WISE 200, pp. 3–12. IEEE (2003)

11. Rao, J., Su, X.: A survey of automated Web service composition methods. In: 1st International Workshop on Semantic Web Services and Web Process Composition, pp, 43–54 (2004)

12. Stal, M.: Web services: Beyond component-based computing. Commun. ACM 45(10), 71–76 (Oct 2002). https://doi.org/10.1145/570907.570934

13. Weerawarana, S., Curbera, F., Leymann, F., Storey, T., Ferguson, D.F.: Web Services Platform Architecture: SOAP, WSDL, WS-Policy, WS-Addressing, WS-BPEL, WS-Reliable Messaging, and More. Pearson (2005)

Quality Engineering in AI Services

Fabio Casati[1]([✉]) and Boualem Benatallah[2]

[1] Servicenow, Santa Clara, CA, USA
fabio.casati@servicenow.com
[2] Dublin city University, Dublin, Ireland
boualem.benatallah@dcu.ie

Abstract. This short paper discusses some of the challenges in testing AI systems, proposes some good practices and advocates a shift to a customer-driven approach, driven by problems customers need to solve rather than problems engineers can solve.

1 AI Services and Systems - It's Not Just a Model

Engineering quality in AI systems today - or even understanding what quality means - is still an art. In many ways, the distance between the hopes and the practices of AI providers and the actual outcomes for customers is massive, as it was for the early days of software engineering when software started to be something that serves enterprise customers and consumers rather than being a tool for scientists.

AI systems are designed developed, deployed and operated by a large, cross enterprise team: you have the data scientists, the devops engineers, the product managers (PMs) defining requirements, the legal team, security and privacy, the customers who use/deploy the system and makes it avail to their users, and the list goes on. AI today, and especially enterprise AI, is a fairly delicate machinery that is "touched" by many different people with varying skill levels and discipline.

In the following discussion on engineering quality we assume, as it almost invariably is, that an AI system is a complex entity which is i) built from data, frameworks, processing pipelines that create the "model" served at inference time, and ii) ML models are integrated into a workflow which comprises various safeguards/limitations around the use of AI (e.g., use this model only for requests in English and when the model confidence is high) as well as humans that can consume (or reject) the suggestion/decision coming from AI (Fig. 1).

Notice that we will use the terms AI and ML fairly interchangeably: here we are only concerned with "intelligent" systems where parts of its computation logic is learned from data (Fig. 2).

Finally, we stress that in the following we do not provide a complete discussion of how to engineer quality into AI systems. Rather, we point out some common mistakes and gaps we often see in research and practice, and underline the high level practices that can help reduce the occurrence and mitigate the effects of these flaws.

© The Author(s), under exclusive license to Springer Nature Switzerland AG 2022
J. Troya et al. (Eds.): ICSOC 2022, LNCS 13740, pp. 644–652, 2022.
https://doi.org/10.1007/978-3-031-20984-0_46

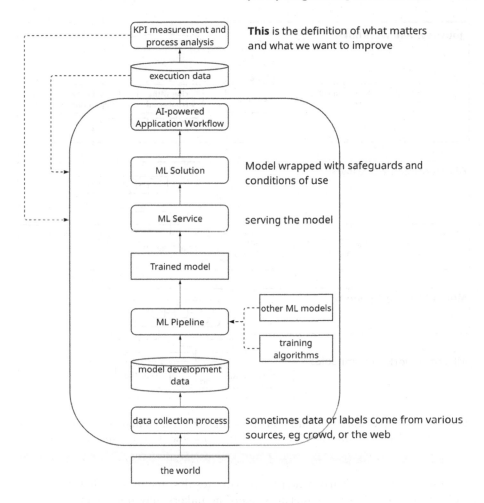

Fig. 1. Developing an AI-powered workflow.

2 Common ML Quality Engineering Mistakes

2.1 Obvious and Widely Known Mistakes - Which We Still Do All the Time

Test Data Leakage. This occurs when the test dataset is used to take decisions on model parameters, hyperparameters, when selecting a model over another, or when deciding if AI is right for the problem at hand. Pretty much everybody is aware that you are not supposed to train on test data. However, very rarely is a test dataset really "held out". Often one tries it, sees that performances are not as expected, and then goes back to change some aspects of the model.

It may be that this is the right thing to do as long as i) one knows that this means that we cannot really trust the test results much, and ii) this is

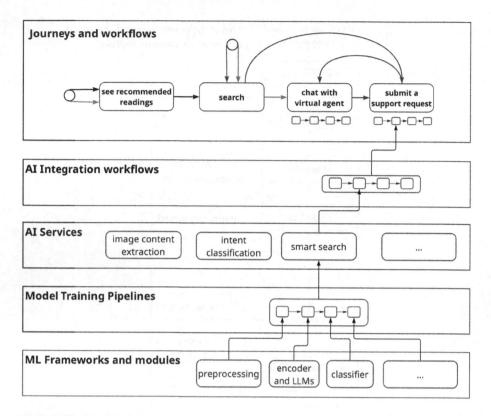

Fig. 2. AI-powered workflows are built from frameworks, composed by ML pipelines to create services that are then integrated into workflows to solve specific use cases.

communicated very clearly when presenting results, including when presenting results to non-experts (as sometimes decision makers may not be aware of these "nuances").

Class Imbalance and Distribution. This problem manifests itself in several ways. First, in ML we should always consider the quality of our model with respect to the simplest baseline: the one that always predict the majority class. This is simply because if the trivial baseline works just as well, we might save us the trouble to put ML in.

In general, being aware of the class distribution gives us a sense for how hard the problem is. More entropy generally means lower accuracy. Furthermore, suppose you have C classes, where each class appears with a certain frequency (or probability, in a frequentist world) $P(c)$. Now, what do we want from our test dataset? If you want to test overall accuracy, then the class distribution in your test dataset should match what you expect to find in production. So, if you have a class c that appears rarely, you may have very few instances of it in the test dataset, so that you will not be able to determine how accurate is your classifier in predicting c. But, since it appears rarely, it does not mess up your overall accuracy metrics. However, if what you care about is how your model behave when the true class is c, then you need a lot of examples of c in the test dataset. For example, you use stratified sampling to create the test dataset or oversample c. When you do that, you cannot report on overall model accuracy any more because your test dataset is different than production.

Train/Test Data Size. The overwhelming majority of train/test data split we have seen are around 80%/20% (scikit-learn has a default of 75/25). It is a mistake that we replicate and that has come to be accepted, but today you rarely come across a case where this makes sense. We do not measure test dataset size in percentage, but in absolute number since that affects and gives us information on the margin of error.

The other very frequent error is making decisions based on test data of, say, 100 samples, and preferring a new model M2 over current production model M1 because it classifies 4% more accurately on the test set. Why is that so bad? Take the "easiest" problem: assume the case of binary classification. Suppose you get an accuracy of .78 for model M1 and .82 for model M2. What can you conclude? Nothing. Should you put M2 into production in place of M1? Absolutely not. In fact, in our experience few people are aware of how massive the 95% confidence interval for 100 samples is: it's almost 20 points. And that difference between M1 and M2 is not significant even when we consider 50% confidence interval (!). Even for 1000 samples, a result of 80% accuracy has a 5 points margin of error.

Again, your customers may not know this. They may not be scientists. If we write that number on the slides after we test with 100 samples, we are misleading our listeners. If classification is not binary, then people tend to report accuracy statistics by class, for which again the number we report is meaningful depending on how many test samples we have for that class. If we report on that, again, we are misleading our audience.

So in the end what should we do? The problem is not that hard actually: we should decide what we care about. "We", here, is the business side. What kind of "guarantees" do we expect from our model? Suppose that the guarantee we want is that we can detect urgent (priority 1) requests with a certain recall. Then in the test dataset we want a large enough sample of such requests (maybe oversampling them), and we will report on the results and how certain or uncertain you are based on that sample.

2.2 Less Obvious but Equally Common Pitfalls

Cross Datasets Data Leakage (Or, Lack of Real Test Datasets). This problem is very frequent when we need to apply the same *ML pipeline* (not the same model) to different datasets. For example, assume we are building an intent classification pipeline to be used for different companies, customers, or domains. Say we have data for customers $Cust_1, Cust_2, .., Cust_K$. One approach we can follow is to assess a variety of ML pipelines by performing train/test on the K customers data we have and pick the one with best overall performance - say, the one that performs reasonably well for all K customers. We then put this pipeline into our product so that every customer (not just these K ones, but any other customer that wants to use our product) can enjoy our ML classifier, now built into our product.

Data scientists and managers are now confident because we followed good practices in terms of test dataset for the K customers. However, what we have done is in fact to use the test datasets to decide on which pipeline to pick, and this is a form of data leakage. If you want to have a sense for how your model will perform, you train/test and pick a model with data from a subset K1 ¡ K of the customers, and then apply the pipeline (train/test) over the remaining customers.

This situation is tricky because K is usually not in the thousands. In fact most likely it can be a hundred, a dozen, or a handful.

In this case you can use all your five datasets to pick the best ML pipeline, but you need to be aware that you do not have many quality guarantees. In other words, you do not know that you have picked the best ML pipeline and you do not know that the quality you are going to get is similar to what you saw during model development and testing. All you have is an informed guess and this is probably your best guess. Again, i) this is important to stress when you present your results, and ii) you should deploy the ML pipeline in production in a trustworthy way: when a new customer uses your product, you train/test on that customer's data, derive your "guarantees" and confidence intervals, and decide if ML should kick in or not. The risk you face is that your decision to go with that pipeline was wrong and you need to update your product, which is painful but doable. Simpler and older, well understood models and more regularized pipelines here may be safer than a super-duper latest hit model.

Metrics That Matter. This is by far the most common and most impactful mistake when measuring quality of AI systems. Science and engineering teams will measure and report on metrics such as F1, accuracy, and recall. These metrics have nothing to do with AI solution quality or success as experienced by customers and users. The use of those metrics is a result of the silos present in nearly every company that separates customers from product managers from data scientists, and by the lack of a design thinking culture. The three most common mistakes here are:

1. Not understanding, and clearly stating for the development team, which are the KPIs we want to help our customers improve with the AI systems we are asking them to use.
2. Forgetting that an AI system is not an AI model: It is a model inserted in a pipeline that goes into a complex systems and interacts with humans, so that the impact In other words, you need to assess if the AI-powered workflows improve KPIs with respect to, for example, when the execution is left to humans without AI intervention, and need to remember that the model is not the only knob you can turn.

An important corollary of the two points above is that accuracy and related metrics are not metrics of interest. In fact, accuracy is the metric you want to use only when you do not care about your model being accurate. More on this in "The Accuracy Paradox" [1].

Another corollary is that you need to be able to measure KPIs and trace how the AI-powered workflows affect the KPI. As a minimum you can "ballpark" it, ideally you can measure it thanks to "observability" and impact analysis tools.

The final corollary is that you need to drive the quality you want based on the KPIs (and on the need for consistency as we will see later), not on a generic desire to make this or that part of the model and system better or faster, or on the wish to use state of the art models because they are impressive or because you can. This seems obvious, but the data scientists tendency is to drive towards the latest and better models, while from a reliability standpoint older and better understood solutions are often preferable.

Regression and Updates. ML systems are never static, they continue to learn, either periodically (via manual or automated retraining with new data every few days or weeks) or continuously. Every time you change the underlying model you change the behavior of a complex system, and if you deploy the new model you are changing the behavior of that complex production system. Most customers are not happy to have a process that serves thousands or hundreds of thousands of users change behavior without any control or guarantee.

The fact that the new system is "better", even in terms of improving the KPIs, does not mean we want to deploy it. There are two reasons for this, and we already saw one: often we are not sure the new system is really better. The second reason is that even if the new model and system is better, most likely it will not be "Pareto-better" (perform equally well or better in *all* cases): there may be some cases for which it now fails, but used to work well before. This is often cause for trouble. You may tell your customers or your users that life is better with the new model, but the ones for whom things got worse will not be happy. Furthermore, when things do not work well people usually may develop a workaround to cope with it, while new failures are harder to digest.

Practically, it is worth collecting the samples for which the new model works worse than the old one and show at least some statistics to decision makers so that they can i) make an informed decision, and ii) alert people of the shortcomings of the new system.

Sleepworthy AI: Engineering for Consistency and Peace of Mind. An aspect that is both rarely understood and hard to test for is checking if an ML model knows when it does not know. In general, you want a model that tells you when it is uncertain, so that you as AI system developer can decide to keep AI out of the way and leave decisions to humans in those cases, and takes more control when it is certain. This is important for two reasons:

1. You want to capture high confidence errors, areas in which the model strongly believes to be correct but is wrong. These are errors of the model from which

your system has no defense, as it will trust the model confidence. If you detect high confidence errors in your model, then you should try to see if you can improve your model's ability to reject its own inferences, as discussed in [2].

2. On the opposite side, you want to identify patters in the samples that your model can classify with both high confidence and accuracy (while accuracy does not mean quality, having both accuracy and high confidence almost always does). For example, you may detect that you do great in requests coming in French. Detecting and explaining (to humans) these patterns is important because even if your model overall does not work that well, you may decide to deploy it only for a subset of cases. This will also help boost the customer's confidence in your AI

Training on the Future. Historical data that you use for training/testing often has a time element to it. You train the system at a given time and you apply to run predictions on future items. In these cases, you should train the model on the oldest samples and test it on the samples closer in time to the go-to-production time, to have a more accurate estimate of how well you will do in prod. For example, you train on user request data from January to August, test on September data, and if you are happy you deploy in October. If you test on January data, i) you are training from the future and testing on the past, and ii) your test data is more far away from current condition and your test is less meaningful.

Another caveat here is that most likely, while you do want to test, you then also want to train the model on the entire dataset. Maybe in September the new iPhone came out and many requests are on that. You want your model to capture those, too, and in general to be trained on the most recent data. Now you are in a pickle: you train model $M1$ on Jan to august data, test on September data, but then train $M2$ on January to September data and push it to production without test data. $M1$ and $M2$ should be not that distant, $M2$ should be better than $M1$, but we do not really know. Should you do that? This is a tough choice with no clear winner. However, there are a few things we can do to mitigate the problem. First, we can test how time-dependent our models are. For example, we can train with data from January to May, test on June and July, and compare that model with one trained on January to June data and tested on July data, to see if we have surprising behaviors. There is no guarantee here but we can pick up on warning signs if we see unexpected behaviors.

The second is that actually we want the test dataset to be as large as we need it, but not larger. The larger the test dataset, the bigger the difference between $M1$ (on which we report statistics to managers and customers) and $M2$, which goes to production. So, we should keep the test dataset as small as we can while giving the statistical properties/intervals we want.

Finally, we go back to sleepworthy AI: we deploy $M2$ "slowly", starting from high confidence cases, and expand as you gain confidence, or use a weighted combination of $M1$ and $M2$ where you progressively shift to M2 as you learn to trust that its predictions are in line with expectations or better.

Trustworthiness, "Fairness" and Appropriateness. This is another big black hole today, too large to discuss here, so we just refer the reader to [3]. The only aspect we underline here is that fairness is not something that is measured with a number between 0 and whatever. It has more to do with a somewhat subjective and biased analysis of the adoption of a specific model and system for a specific purpose, and the path to fairness rests more on the thinking, design and development process followed by all the parties involved than on easily computable metrics. A lot of help here can be provided by checklists and guidelines and are related to following a process that is as transparent and open as possible, to collect perspectives of different groups and individuals. The transparency involves the entire process, including aspects frequently overlooked such as crowdsourced data collection, that require their own reporting specific to the method of collection [4].

3   Building AI Systems We Can Rely on

In Summary, here are some good practices we need to add to our ML devops toolbox and we must adhere to if we want AI systems that customers can rely on.

1. Results presentation and analysis that brings out and emphasizes all uncertainties and limitations so that they are clear for the specific audience. A lot of this can be achieved via i) training in experiment design and analysis, ii) checklists and iii) standardized experiment reporting slides and templates which include an explicit points on limitations and uncertainties.
2. Metrics that matter. Draw (literally) the AI workflow in production and whatever abstraction level you feel appropriate and write down the customer KPIs of interest. Either you know them or at least try to guess them - at least you have a hopefully reasonable goal to achieve. Then from that derive the properties of the model and system that improve KPIs with respect to the as-is.
3. Transparent and trustworthy design/dev process. We singled out experiment design and reporting earlier just because it is ubiquitous and widely misunderstood, but in general the entire design/dev/prod process needs to be made explicit, along with its assumptions and limitations. This is not just for the ML fairness angle but to surface the implicit and explicit assumptions that drive decisions. Indeed, implicit assumptions are always the biggest project killer.
4. "Sleepworthy", consistent, self-limiting AI. Consider consistency and peace of mind as key "implicit" KPIs you want to preserve throughout the AI system lifecycle. Your testing, deployment and production monitoring aims at being as unsurprising as possible. As an old ad used to say, "power is nothing without control". In production AI, excitement and the Wow factor is nothing without peace of mind, consistency and reliability.

It goes without saying that tools may help all of the above, but today they are few and far apart, and rarely designed for customers or project manager.

References

1. Casati, F.: The Accuracy Paradox. Available on Medium at: https://tinyurl.com/theaccuracyparadox
2. Sayin, B., Yang, J., Passerini, A., Casati, F.: The science of rejection: a research area for human computation. In: Proceedings of The 9th AAAI Conference on Human Computation and Crowdsourcing (HCOMP 2021)
3. Barocas, S., Hardt, M., Narayanan, A.: Fairness and Machine Learning. fairmlbook.org (2019)
4. Ramírez, J., et al.: On the state of reporting in crowdsourcing experiments and a checklist to aid current practices. In: Proceedings of CSCW 2021. Available at: https://arxiv.org/abs/2107.13519

Service-Based Wireless Energy Crowdsourcing

Amani Abusafia$^{(\boxtimes)}$, Abdallah Lakhdari, and Athman Bouguettaya

The University of Sydney, Sydney, NSW 2000, Australia
{amani.abusafia,abdallah.lakhdari,athman.bouguettaya}@sydney.edu.au

Abstract. We propose a novel service-based ecosystem to crowdsource wireless energy to charge IoT devices. We leverage the service paradigm to abstract wireless energy crowdsourcing from nearby IoT devices as energy services. The proposed energy services ecosystem offers convenient, ubiquitous, and cost-effective power access to charge IoT devices. We discuss the impact of a crowdsourced wireless energy services ecosystem, the building components of the ecosystem, the energy services composition framework, the challenges, and proposed solutions.

Keywords: Service computing · Energy services · Wireless energy charging · Crowdsourcing · IoT · Wireless power transfer

1 Introduction

Internet of Things (IoT) is a paradigm that enables everyday objects (i.e., *things*) to connect to the internet and exchange data [1]. IoT devices usually have capabilities, such as sensing, networking, and processing [1]. The number of connected IoT devices is expected to reach 125 billion in 2030 [2]. This potential pervasiveness of IoT provides opportunities to *abstract* their capabilities using the *service paradigm* as *IoT services* [3]. IoT services are defined by their functional and non-functional attributes. The functional attributes define the purpose of the service, such as sharing internet access using WiFi. The non-functional attributes are the properties that assess the Quality of Service (QoS), e.g., signal strength, reliability, etc. For example, an IoT device owner may offer their WiFi as a hotspot (i.e., service provider) to other nearby IoT devices (i.e., service consumers). A multitude of novel IoT services may be used to enable intelligent systems in several domains, including smart cities, smart homes, and healthcare [3]. Examples of IoT services are WiFi hotspots [4], environmental sensing [5], and energy services [6]. Of particular interest is the use of energy services.

Energy service, also known as *Energy-as-a-Service (ES)*, refers to the *wireless power transfer* among nearby IoT devices [6]. We consider a particular set of IoT devices named *wearables*. Wearables refer to anything worn or hand-held like smart shirts, smartwatches, and smartphones [7]. Wearables may harvest

J. Troya et al. (Eds.): ICSOC 2022, LNCS 13740, pp. 653–668, 2022.
https://doi.org/10.1007/978-3-031-20984-0_47

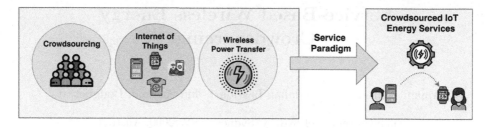

Fig. 1. The components of IoT energy services ecosystem

energy from natural resources such as kinetic activity, solar power, or body heat [8,9]. For instance, a smart shoe using a PowerWalk kinetic energy harvester may produce 10–12 watts on-the-move power[1]. In this respect, wearing a Power-Walk harvester may generate energy to charge up to four smartphones from an hour's walk at a comfortable speed. Energy services may be deployed through the newly developed "Over-the-Air" wireless power transfer technologies [6,10]. Several companies focus on developing the wireless charging technology of IoT devices over a distance, including WiTricity[2], Energous[3], Cota[4], Powercastco[5]. For example, WiTricity started based on the work of [11] where they succeeded in transferring 60 W of power wirelessly to power a light bulb. Another example is Energous which developed a device that can charge up to 3 W power within a 5-meter distance to multiple receivers.

Crowdsourcing is an efficient way to leverage IoT energy services to create a self-sustained environment [3,6]. IoT users may *collaborate* to share their spare energy to charge nearby IoT devices and extend their battery endurance [12,13]. Crowdsourced IoT energy services present a *convenient* and adaptable solution as devices do not need to be tethered to a power point or use charging cords, and power banks [14]. In addition, crowdsourcing energy offers an *ubiquitous* power access for IoT users as they may be charged anytime and anywhere, even while moving [6,14]. Charging IoT devices wirelessly from a central source usually requires a high-frequency magnetic field to transfer the energy over a distance [15]. Studies have shown that a strong magnetic field has a harmful impact on humans [15,16]. On the contracts, crowdsourcing IoT energy services enables charging by aggregating energy from multiple close-by devices. As the devices are near, transferring the energy will require a low-frequency magnetic field. Hence, crowdsourcing energy services offer an alternative solution to charge devices wirelessly without compromising users' health [17,18]. In this paper, we propose to leverage the service paradigm to enable a self-sustained IoT energy services

---

[1] bionic-power.com.

[2] witricity.com.

[3] energous.com.

[4] ossia.com.

[5] powercastco.com.

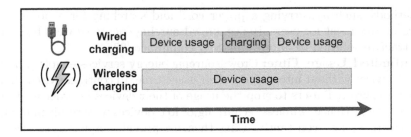

Fig. 2. Usage-time using wire vs wireless charging technologies

ecosystem by utilizing three components, crowdsourcing, IoT, and wireless power transfer technologies (see Fig. 1).

This paper maps out a strategy to leverage the service paradigm to utilize IoT energy services in smart cities. We envision a sustainable ecosystem that allows on-the-go wireless energy crowdsourcing to recharge IoT devices in smart cities. First, we highlight the benefits of the energy services ecosystem. Then, we present a holistic service-based ecosystem to conceptualize the idea and call for future validation. Next, we describe the ecosystem in terms of the environment, service-oriented architecture, and enabling technologies. We also present the envisioned framework and the contemporary approaches for composing IoT-based energy services. Finally, we discuss the uprising challenges to implementing the envisioned ecosystem and highlight the potential future research directions that may address these challenges.

2   Impact of Crowdsourcing Energy Services Ecosystem

Crowdsourcing wireless energy services provides numerous benefits to both the environment and IoT users. Each of the benefits is discussed in depth below.

- **Enabling Sustainable IoT Ecosystem:** The proliferation of IoT devices leads to a significant increase in energy consumption [19,20]. IoT devices' global energy demand is predicted to reach 46TWh by 2025 [20]. This tremendous energy demand accounts for 6% to 8% of the global carbon footprint generated by information and communication technologies [21,22]. Crowdsourcing energy services reduce carbon footprint by reducing dependence on fossil fuels to charge IoT devices. In addition, crowdsourcing energy services rely on renewable or spare energy resources. The renewable energy may be harvested from natural resources such as body heat, solar energy, or kinetic movement [23].
- **Extending Battery Endurance:** IoT devices are constrained by the size of their batteries [24,25]. The small size of the battery results in a limited energy storage capacity. This limited capacity hinders the capabilities of IoT devices. Increasing the battery capacity for IoT devices faces several challenges,including, safety, weight, cost, and recycling [26]. Other charging

methods, such as carrying a power cord and searching for a power outlet, are inconvenient for users. Hence, crowdsourcing energy services becomes an attractive solution to improve battery endurance [27].

- **Unlimited Usage Time:** Crowdsourcing energy services enable recharging IoT devices without interrupting their usage time. In contrast, wired charging may require IoT users to stop the usage of their devices in order for them to be charged. Hence, wireless recharging of IoT devices may result in unlimited usage time, i.e., constantly using them to provide or access services (See Fig. 2). Thus, crowdsourcing energy services prolong the IoT device's usage lifetime, especially when the external energy supply is unavailable.

- **Spatial Freedom:** Crowdsourcing wireless energy services provide spatial independence for IoT users. As previously mentioned, IoT devices are frequently required to be tethered to power points or carry power banks to be charged. The last obstacle for IoT devices to achieve their *spatial freedom* is both charging wires and pads. The prospected environment is expected to enable wireless power transfer delivery up to five meters [28].

- **Flexible Contracts:** Unlike traditional services, crowdsourced energy services environment don't have lock-in contracts [29]. The flexible contracts enable consumers and providers to request or offer full or partial services according to their preferences [29,30]. In addition, providers and consumers may extend their stay-time to offer or receive an energy service [31].

- **Ubiquitous Power Access:** As aforementioned, energy services offer spatial freedom for IoT devices. Therefore, crowdsourcing energy services offer an *ubiquitous* power access to charge IoT devices anytime and anywhere. This *ubiquity* of wireless charging facilitates access to energy for IoT users.

- **Convenience Charging:** The *ubiquity* of wireless charging offers a convenient alternative to charge IoT devices [14]. In addition, as previously discussed, the *flexibility* to participate in crowdsourcing energy services without any long term contract offers convenience for IoT users. IoT users might offer or request energy services without any lock-in contract. They can also move around freely while providing or receiving energy [32]. This convenience ensures that the ecosystem will expand widely.

- **Business Edge:** As previously mentioned, energy services offer a convenient solution to charge IoT devices. Thus, energy services may be used as a complementary service to provide customers with the best quality of experience when visiting a business [17]. For example, energy services, like WiFi, may be used to charge customers' wearables in a cafe. Such a service will increase customers' satisfaction with a business. Customer satisfaction is the main factor in ensuring that customers keep coming back to businesses, i.e., maintaining or increasing foot traffic [33]. For example, a case study showed that "Sacred", a cafe in London, had a noticeable increase in foot traffic after installing wireless charging points[6]. The *foot traffic* in a business has a direct impact on its revenue. [34].

---

[6] air-charge.com.

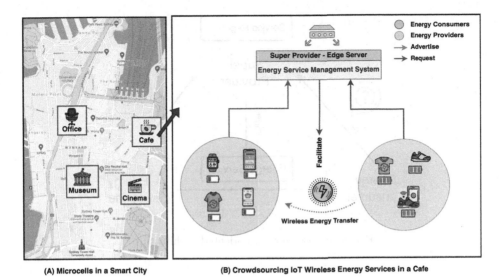

(A) Microcells in a Smart City   (B) Crowdsourcing IoT Wireless Energy Services in a Cafe

Fig. 3. Crowdsourcing IoT energy services scenario

3   Crowdsourcing Energy Services Ecosystem

The energy services ecosystem setup consists of three major components: (1) The context of the envisioned prospective environment, (2) The abstraction of the ecosystem as an energy service-oriented architecture, and (3) The enabling technologies to implement the foreseen ecosystem, In what follows, we discuss each component in detail.

3.1   Prospective Environment

The envisioned crowdsourced IoT energy environment is a *dynamic* environment that consists of IoT users congregating and moving across *microcells* [6,35]. A microcell is any confined area in a smart city where people may gather (e.g., coffee shops, restaurants, museums, libraries) (see Fig. 3 (A)). In this environment, IoT users are assumed to act as energy providers or consumers (see Fig. 3 (B)). Their IoT devices are assumed to be equipped with wireless energy transmitters and receivers. Energy providers may use their wearables to harvest energy [36]. The IoT users might share their spare or harvested energy to fulfill the requirements of nearby IoT devices. Energy Providers advertise services and consumers submit requests to the IoT coordinator. The super provider manages the IoT coordinator. A super provider is typically a microcell's owner who manages the exchange of energy services between providers and consumers. The IoT coordinator is assumed to be deployed one hop away from the energy providers and consumers (e.g., router at the edge) to minimize the communication overhead and latency while advertising energy services and requests. The super provider limits a consumer's requested energy and uses a reward system to encourage providers

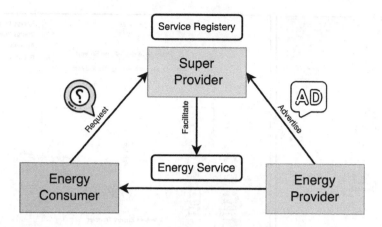

Fig. 4. Energy services oriented architecture

to share energy. Rewards come in the form of stored credits to providers. The collected credits may be used later by the provider to increase the limit on the amount of requested energy when they are in the consumer role. Providers may also be a consumer and vice-versa. Providers receive rewards based on the amount of shared energy.

In the energy services environment, IoT devices may share energy using the energy service model. Note that energy services exhibit *functional* and *non-functional* (Quality of service (QoS)) properties [29]. In this respect, the functional property of energy service is represented by the wireless service delivery of energy to nearby IoT devices. The non-functional (QoS) properties may include the amount of energy, location, duration of sharing, etc.

3.2 Energy Service Oriented Architecture

A key aspect to unlocking the full potential of the energy services ecosystem is to design an *end-to-end* Service Oriented Architecture (SOA) to share crowd-sourced energy services. We identify three key components of the SOA: energy service *provider*, energy service *consumer*, and *super provider*. (see Fig. 4). An *energy provider* refers to an IoT device that may share their energy. An *energy consumer* refers to an IoT device that requires energy. A super provider is typi-cally a microcell's owner who manages the exchange of energy services between providers and consumers.

3.3 Enabling Technologies

The implementation of a crowdsourcing energy services ecosystem strongly depends on the recent technology of wireless charging. Wireless charging tech-nologies are the transmitters and receivers that enable the *wireless* transfer of

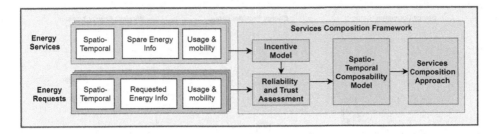

Fig. 5. Crowdsourcing energy services framework

energy [10]. For example, Xiaomi's Mi Air charger transmits energy wirelessly to nearby IoT devices[7].

Energy harvesting technologies are another technology to enable a sustainable crowdsourcing energy services ecosystem. Energy harvesters may enable a green crowdsourcing ecosystem to charge IoT devices [37]. The IoT devices may harvest energy from natural resources, including kinetic movement, solar power, or body heat [8,9]. The harvested energy may be used to charge the device itself or to be shared with nearby devices [38].

4 Crowdsourcing Energy Services Framework

The energy service framework is responsible for composing and managing the received energy services and requests. An energy service is described by the IoT owner's spatio-temporal preferences, available energy, usage, and mobility model (See Fig. 5). Similarly, an energy request is described by the IoT owner's spatio-temporal preferences, amount of requested energy, usage, and mobility model. We envision the composition framework to consist of four components: (1) an incentive model. (2) a reliability and trust assessment, (3) a spatio-temporal composability model, and (4) a service composition approach. In what follows, we discuss each component in detail.

4.1 Incentive Model

Typically, in crowdsourcing environments, users resist sharing their resources [39]. Similarly, IoT users may resist sharing their energy since energy is a scarce resource [30,40]. Hence, an incentive model is needed to encourage providers to share their energy. Designing an incentive model shall consider the context of the environment and the behavior of the IoT users [30,41].

4.2 Reliability and Trust Assessment

The participation of IoT users in the energy crowdsourcing ecosystem is influenced by reliable and trustworthy providers, and consumers [42]. To guarantee

---

[7] mi.com.

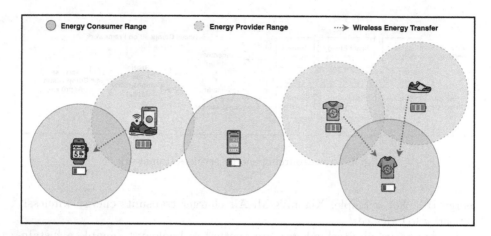

Fig. 6. Energy consumers may be charged from energy providers within the power transfer range

high-quality services, both reliability and trust are required in crowdsourced IoT systems. High-quality services will encourage and maintain users' participation in the energy services ecosystems. Therefore, when managing and composing energy services, it is imperative to assess the reliability and trustworthiness of IoT energy users.

4.3   Spatio-Temporal Composability Model

Energy services and requests may have different times and locations [6, 29]. Successfully delivering energy services requires providers and consumers to be within the power transfer range. For example, if a provider's location is out of the power transfer range from a given consumer, the system shouldn't match them (See Fig. 6). Thus, an effective filtering method is needed in order to efficiently match services to requests. A composability model was proposed to index services nearby a signal request based on time and space [29]. The same model may be used to filter multiple services and multiple requests.

4.4   Services Composition Approach

A single energy request may not be fulfilled by one energy service due to the limited resources of IoT devices [29]. In such cases, the system may utilize the shareable nature of energy by composing multiple nearby energy services to one request or vice versa [17]. Similarly, a single energy service may be used to fulfill one or multiple energy requests [29]. Hence, we may have different modes of composition (See Fig. 7). Additionally, energy service providers and consumers may have different Spatio-temporal preferences. Therefore, the service composition approach should consider these preferences in matching and composing energy services and requests.

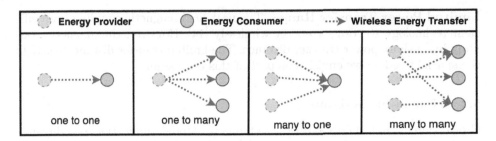

Fig. 7. Modes of energy services composition

5   Challenges in Crowdsourcing Energy Services

To exploit the potential of crowdsourced energy services for charging IoT devices, multiple challenges must be tackled. These challenges can be classified into three main categories enabling technologies, human-in-the-Loop, and system deployment. The following subsections describe the challenges encountered in each category and propose possible solutions.

5.1   Enabling Technologies

The deployment of a crowdsourcing energy services ecosystem highly relies on the current Wireless Power Transfer (WPT) technologies. Although WPT technologies are advancing rapidly, there are technological constraints that impede the ecosystem from being fully deployed [43]. Challenges posed by technology include energy loss, miniature energy delivery, and restricted power transmission range. Each of these constraints is discussed further below.

Energy Loss. Using the recently developed wireless power transfer technologies, consumers may spend more energy to receive the requested energy [44]. The consumed energy may include the energy required for service discovery, energy delivery, and connection establishment between the consumer and the provider [45]. The huge energy loss impedes the energy services ecosystem from fulfilling its purpose of charging nearby IoT devices. Therefore, minimizing energy loss is a challenge yet to be addressed.

Miniature Delivered Energy. Even though there is rapid development in wireless power transfer technologies, the amount of delivered energy is insufficient to what is currently required [14]. The small amount of delivered energy may be justified by the energy loss in delivering the energy service as aforementioned. Hence, Delivering a considerable amount of energy wirelessly over a distance is still a challenge that hinders the full deployment of the energy services ecosystem.

Limited Power Transfer Range. The near-field magnetic coupling is an efficient technology to transfer energy wirelessly [14]. However, the magnetic coupling has a short power transfer distance. The limited transfer distance restricts the spatial freedom we envision as part of this ecosystem.

5.2   Human-in-the-Loop

Crowdsourcing IoT energy services is a human-centered application as it depends on their participation behavior. Modeling human behavior is challenging as it requires modeling complex behavioral, psychological and physiological characteristics of human nature [46]. In our environment, the human factor has several influences on the ecosystem. First, the deployment of the ecosystem depends on the IoT users' willingness to participate in the energy sharing process [30]. Second, the mobility of IoT users in this dynamic environment could impede the delivery of energy services [32]. Third, energy services are offered by IoT devices that are simultaneously in use by their owners. Therefore, the consistent wireless energy delivery from one IoT device to another depends on the device owners' usage frequency. Finally, the spatial and temporal preferences of IoT users differ, which affects the availability of energy services. In what follows, we discuss each of the aforementioned challenges.

Provisioning Resistance. Individuals are likely motivated to engage in the energy services ecosystem since they can easily access nearby energy resources. However, since energy is a scarce resource, they may be reluctant to share it [30]. Service resistance is the reluctance to provide services due to limited resources [47]. In the energy services context, service resistance refers to the unwillingness to provide energy to IoT devices [30]. A provider's resistance is influenced by the provider's available energy and the size of the requested energy. As a result, one of the challenges is to predict providers' resistance to offering their energy service and devise a correct incentive to overcome it. Since humans get impacted differently by different incentives, determining the effective incentive for energy providers is a challenge that still needs to be addressed.

Modelling Human Mobility. IoT devices change their locations regularly according to the mobility of their owners. The mobility of the crowd has multiple impacts on the crowdsourcing ecosystem. First, the mobility of the crowd across microcells determines the availability of energy services and requests. Second, The IoT users' mobility affects the connectivity between IoT devices. Highly moving IoT devices within a microcell may result in disconnecting the wireless energy transfer between them. A disconnection in the delivery of the energy transfer may result in its failure [32,42]. Therefore, the mobility of IoT users should be modeled and analyzed to manage the energy services in the ecosystem better. The mobility model of IoT users should be studied and investigated on a micro level as indoor mobility and a macro level as mobility patterns across microcells. The indoor mobility models should reflect the users' movement within a confined space [48]. Indoor mobility models will enable the ecosystem to filter services and requests from a spatial perspective within the power transfer range. Moreover, it will allow the ecosystem to predict users' movement and their impact on disconnecting a service delivery. On the other side, the outdoor mobility pattern of an IoT user may be used to proactively plan for them when to request energy [35]. Furthermore, it enables us to understand the crowd movement and predict the undersupplied areas [49]. Thus, mobility models are needed to unlock the full potential of the ecosystem.

Modelling Usage Patterns. The energy usage pattern of providers may impact the consistency of provisioning energy services [31]. An energy provider with highly dynamic usage of their device impacts the delivered energy service quality (QoS). Providers may offer their spare energy while simultaneously using it for their devices. If a provider is heavily using their device, they may end up consuming their advertised service while sharing it. Thus, energy services may fluctuate due to the providers' usage. As a result, IoT devices' energy usage behavior must be modeled to ensure consistent provision of energy services [48,49].

Determining Services Availability. Matching energy services and requests in a crowdsourced environment is challenging due to the uncertain availability of energy services and requests [17]. Predicting the availability of energy services is challenging as it relies on detecting the mobility patterns of IoT Users and their energy usage patterns. Defining the mobility patterns mainly focuses on analyzing the spatio-temporal attributes and potential regularities hidden in individual movement trajectories [50]. However, the existing literature to determine mobility patterns has low accuracy due to the *flexible nature* of human movement [49]. Thus, the challenge of detecting human mobility patterns hinders the prediction of service availability.

5.3   Deployment of Energy Services Ecosystem

The deployment of the energy crowdsourcing ecosystem raises several challenges. In what follows, we discuss each challenge and its impact of on the ecosystem.

Balancing Local Provisioning and Demand. Naturally, energy users' preferences to provide or receive energy vary in time and space. The variety in energy users' preferences may severely affect the *balance* between the amount of required and provided energy within a confined area. The *imbalance* between the energy *demand* and the available services may result in *oversupplied* and *undersupplied* areas in a smart city. Under-supplied areas will result in unfulfilled energy requests, which may discourage the participation of IoT users in the ecosystem. Hence, ensuring the availability of energy services to fulfill the requirement of consumers is essential to the sustainability of the ecosystem. A redistribution of energy service across over-supplied and under-supplied areas may achieve better-balanced energy availability. Another possible direction is using an incentive model to increase participation in provisioning energy services [30].

Loose Contracts. As previously mentioned, energy services offer flexibility as they do not require lock-in contracts [31]. For instance, providers may offer full or partial services according to their preferences [29]. However, this flexibility may impact the commitment of IoT users. The uncertain commitment of IoT users may add uncertainty to the energy transfer process and thereby impact the participation of IoT users in the ecosystem.

Reliability. Considering reliability in the energy ecosystem encourages the participation of energy users in crowdsourcing energy services [6,42]. The reliability of an energy provider refers to the probability that an energy service will be successfully delivered with the advertised Quality of Service (QoS) attributes. Similarly, the reliability of an energy consumer refers to the probability that an IoT energy service will be successfully received with the same submitted requirements. The reliability of the energy provider is impacted by their usage pattern and mobility. As aforementioned, a provider that heavily uses their device might consume their advertised energy. Also, a highly mobile provider will cause frequent disconnections in the energy transfer between the devices-similarly, the reliability of an energy consumer is impacted by their mobility patterns. Like providers, a highly mobile consumer will cause frequent disconnections in the energy transfer between the devices. Accordingly, it is vital to consider the reliability of energy users while managing and composings energy services.

Trust. The definition of trust is "the confidence, belief, and expectation regarding the reliability, integrity, and other characteristics of an entity" [51]. To guarantee high-quality services, trust assessment is required in crowdsourced IoT systems [4]. High-quality services will encourage and maintain users' participation in the energy services ecosystems. The trust assessment must evaluate the trustworthiness of energy providers and consumers. The trustworthiness of energy providers may represent the provider's reputation, their service reliability, and their security level [4]. Likewise, energy consumers' trustworthiness may represent their reputation and their security level. Although trust assessment has been studied in other areas, it remains a challenge in IoT ecosystems due to several reasons [52]. First, the dynamic nature of the crowdsourced IoT environment makes it challenging to keep an accurate record of the devices' reputations. For instance, IoT devices are usually moving, and their existence may be temporary. Second, IoT devices typically lack a global identifier, which makes it difficult to maintain a globally accessible profile for these devices. As a result, a novel trust assessment framework is required to assess the reputation of IoT devices [52].

Security. The goal of IoT device security is to prevent and protect against IoT attacks and service failures [53]. Attacks on IoT devices may compromise the privacy and confidentiality of users, infrastructures, data, and IoT devices [54]. Furthermore, IoT attacks such as denial-of-service attacks may impede the delivery of services to IoT Users. Securing IoT systems is a critical challenges because users may not adopt many IoT systems if they are not secure [55]. Existing security architectures and protocols are difficult to integrate in IoT devices due to their limited computing power and storage size [56].

Privacy. The global digital data generated by IoT devices is expected to reach 180 Zettabytes by 2020 [57]. As a result, protecting IoT data and the privacy of users who generate or consume data has become a major concern in research and industry [58]. Privacy refers to "The claim of individuals, groups, or institutions to determine for themselves when, how and to what extent information about them is communicated to others" [59]. Maintaining the privacy in IoT ecosystems is challenging as it conflict with the need to use the IoT data to achieve their functions. The data utilization may invade the privacy of IoT users [52]. For example, IoT Data are required to enhance the energy crowdsourcing process by profiling the energy providers and consumers. The collected IoT data may include the IoT users' mobility behavior and their energy consumption model. Collecting such personal information might violate the privacy of the IoT users. Therefore, maintaining a balance between IoT data protection and use is a continuing challenge.

6   Conclusion

We presented a novel service based framework to crowdsource wireless energy from neighboring IoT devices to charge low-in-battery IoT devices. First, we highlighted the benefits of adopting a crowdsourced wireless energy services ecosystem. We then envisioned and designed an architecture to implement the proposed ecosystem. Lastly, we discussed the open challenges and recommended research directions for possible solutions.

Acknowledgment. This research was partly made possible by LE220100078 and LE180100158 grants from the Australian Research Council. The statements made herein are solely the responsibility of the authors.

References

1. Whitmore, A., Agarwal, A., Da Li, X.: The internet of things-a survey of topics and trends. Inf. Syst. Front. **17**(2), 261–274 (2015)
2. Markit, I.H.S.: The Internet of Things: a Movement, not a Market. IHS Markit, Englewood, CO (2017)
3. Bouguettaya, A., et al.: An internet of things service roadmap. Commun. ACM **64**(9), 86–95 (2021)

4. Ba-hutair, M.N., et al.: Multi-use Trust in Crowdsourced Iot Services. IEEE TSC (2022)
5. Kelly, S.D.T., et al.: Towards the implementation of IoT for environmental condition monitoring in homes. IEEE Sens. J. **13**(10), 3846–3853 (2013)
6. Lakhdari, A., et al.: Composing energy services in a crowdsourced IoT environment. IEEE TSC **15**, 1280–1294 (2020)
7. Seneviratne, S., et al.: A survey of wearable devices and challenges. IEEE Commun. Surv. Tutorials **19**(4), 2573–2620 (2017)
8. Young-Man, C., Lee, M.G., Jeon, Y.: Wearable biomechanical energy harvesting technologies. Energies **10**(10), 1483 (2017)
9. Manjarrés, J., et al.: Enhancing kinetic energy harvesting-based human activity recognition with deep learning and data augmentation. IEEE IoT (2021)
10. Dolcourt, J.: Over-the-air wireless charging will come to smartphones (2019)
11. Kurs, A., et al.: Wireless power transfer via strongly coupled magnetic resonances. Science **317**(5834), 83–86 (2007)
12. Fang, W., et al.: Fair scheduling in resonant beam charging for IoT devices. IEEE IoT **6**(1), 641–653 (2018)
13. Sakai, K., Sun, M.-T., Wei-Shinn, K., Jie, W.: Towards wireless power transfer in mobile social networks. IEEE TNSE **9**(3), 1091–1103 (2021)
14. Feng, H., Tavakoli, R., Onar, O.C., Pantic, Z.: Advances in high-power wireless charging systems: overview and design considerations. Trans. Transp. Electr. **6**(3), 886–919 (2020)
15. Lin, J.C.: Wireless power transfer for mobile applications, and health effect. IEEE APM **55**(2), 250–253 (2013)
16. Baikova, E.N., et al.: Study on electromagnetic emissions from wireless energy transfer. In IEEE PEMC, pp. 492–497. IEEE (2016)
17. Abusafia, A., et al.: Quality of experience optimization in IoT energy services. In: ICWS, IEEE (2022)
18. Abusafia, A., Bouguettaya, A., Lakhdari, A.: Maximizing consumer satisfaction of IoT energy services. In: ICSOC. Springer (2022)
19. Sharma, P.K., Kumar, N., Park, J.H.: Opportunities and challenges. IEEE Network, Blockchain technology toward green IoT (2020)
20. Arshad, R., Zahoor, S., Shah, M.A., Wahid, A., Yu, H.: Green IoT: an investigation on energy saving practices for 2020 and beyond. IEEE Access **5**, 15667–15681 (2017)
21. Shaikh, F.K., Zeadally, S., Exposito, E.: Enabling technologies for green internet of things. IEEE Syst. J. **11**(2), 983–994 (2015)
22. Ali Eslami Varjovi and Shahram Babaie: Green internet of things (GioT): vision, applications and research challenges. Sustain. Comput.: Informat. Syst. **28**, 100448 (2020)
23. Gorlatova, M., Sarik, J., Grebla, G., Cong, M., Kymissis, I., Zussman, G.: Movers and shakers: kinetic energy harvesting for the internet of things. IEEE J. Sel. Areas in Commun. **33**(8), 1624–1639 (2015)
24. Pasricha, S., et al.: A survey on energy management for mobile and IoT devices. IEEE Design & Test (2020)
25. Raptis, P.T.: When wireless crowd charging meets online social networks: a vision for socially motivated energy sharing. Online Soc. Netw. Media **16**, 100069 (2020)
26. Scrosati, B., Garche, J.: Lithium batteries: status, prospects and future. J. Power Sources **195**(9), 2419–2430 (2010)
27. Dhungana, A., Bulut, E.: Peer-to-peer energy sharing in mobile networks: applications, challenges, and open problems. Ad Hoc Networks (2020)

28. Lakhdari, A., et al.: Crowdsharing wireless energy services. In: CIC, pp, 18–24. IEEE (2020)
29. Lakhdari, A., Bouguettaya, A., Neiat, A.G.: Crowdsourcing energy as a service. In: Pahl, C., Vukovic, M., Yin, J., Yu, Q. (eds.) ICSOC 2018. LNCS, vol. 11236, pp. 342–351. Springer, Cham (2018). https://doi.org/10.1007/978-3-030-03596-9_24
30. Abusafia, A., Bouguettaya, A., Mistry, S.: Incentive-based selection and composition of IoT energy services. In: IEEE SCC, pp. 304–311. IEEE (2020)
31. Lakhdari, A., et al.: Elastic composition of crowdsourced IoT energy services. In: MobiQuitous, pp. 308–317 (2020)
32. Lakhdari A., Bouguettaya, A.: Fluid composition of intermittent IoT energy services. In: SCC, pp. 329–336. IEEE (2020)
33. Chao, T., et al.: C-Flow: visualizing foot traffic and profit data to make informative decisions. Technical Report, University of Maryland (2013)
34. Muller C.C., Woods, R.H.: An expanded restaurant typology. Cornell Hotel Restaurant Adm. Q. 35(3), 27–37 (1994)
35. Lakhdari A., Bouguettaya A.: Proactive composition of mobile IoT energy services. In: ICWS, pp. 192–197. IEEE (2021)
36. Tran, V.H., Misra, A., Xiong, J., Balan, R.K.:. WiWear: wearable sensing via directional WiFi energy harvesting. In: PerCom, March 11–15, 2019, pp. 1–10 (2019)
37. Lakhdari, A., Bouguettaya, A.: Fairness-aware crowdsourcing of IoT energy services. In: Hacid, H., Kao, O., Mecella, M., Moha, N., Paik, H. (eds.) ICSOC 2021. LNCS, vol. 13121, pp. 351–367. Springer, Cham (2021). https://doi.org/10.1007/978-3-030-91431-8_22
38. Worgan, P., Knibbe, J., Fraser, M., Plasencia, D.M.: Mobile energy sharing futures. In: MobileHCI, pp. 1134–1137 (2016)
39. Egger-Lampl, S., et al.: Crowdsourcing quality of experience experiments. In: Archambault, D., Purchase, H., Hoßfeld, T. (eds.) Evaluation in the Crowd. Crowdsourcing and Human-Centered Experiments. LNCS, vol. 10264, pp. 154–190. Springer, Cham (2017). https://doi.org/10.1007/978-3-319-66435-4_7
40. Bulut, E., Raptis, T.P., Dai, H., Liang, W.: Special issue on pervasive mobile energy sharing (2022)
41. Wang, R., et al.: The nudging effect on tracking activity. In: Adjunct Proceedings of the 2021 ACM International Joint Conference on Pervasive and Ubiquitous Computing and Proceedings of the 2021 ACM International Symposium on Wearable Computers (2022)
42. Abusafia, A., Bouguettaya, A.: Reliability model for incentive-driven IoT energy services. In: MobiQuitous, pp. 196–205 (2020)
43. Wireless charging market size, share and growth: analysis - 2027
44. Yao, J., et al.: Wireless IoT energy sharing platform. In: PerCom Workshops, pp. 118–120. IEEE (2022)
45. Na, W., Park, J., Lee, C., Park, K., Kim, J., Cho, S.: Energy-efficient mobile charging for wireless power transfer in internet of things networks. IEEE Internet Things J. 5(1), 79–92 (2017)
46. Delicato, F.C., Pires, P.F.: Challenges in developing collaborative IoT systems. In: CIC, pp. 25–33. IEEE (2020)
47. Shuiguang andothers Deng: Toward mobile service computing: opportunities and challenges. Cloud Comput. 3(4), 32–41 (2016)
48. Menon, R., et al.: DIY-IPS: Towards an off-the-shelf accurate indoor positioning system. In: Mobicom (2022)

49. Zheng, Y.A., et al. IMAP: Individual human mobility patterns visualizing platform. In: Mobicom (2022)
50. Wang, J., Kong, X., Xia, F., Sun, L.: Urban human mobility: data-driven modeling and prediction. ACM SIGKDD Explor. Newsl. **21**(1), 1–19 (2019)
51. Yan, Z., Zhang, P., Vasilakos, A.V.: A survey on trust management for internet of things. J. Netw. Comput. Appl. **42**, 120–134 (2014)
52. Sha, K., et al.: On security challenges and open issues in internet of things. Future Gener. Comput. Syst. **83**, 326–337 (2018)
53. Yang, L., Da Li, X.: Internet of things (IoT) cybersecurity research: a review of current research topics. IEEE Internet Things J. **6**(2), 2103–2115 (2018)
54. Hassan, W.H., et al.: Current research on internet of things (IoT) security: a survey. Comput. Netw. **148**, 283–294 (2019)
55. Liyanage, M., Braeken, A., Kumar, P., Ylianttila, M.: Advances in Authentication. John Wiley & Sons, IoT Security (2020)
56. Payton, J., Du, X., He, X., Wu, J.: Envisioning an information assurance and performance infrastructure for the internet of things. In: CIC, pp. 266–271. IEEE (2018)
57. Kanellos, M.: 152,000 smart devices every minute in 2025: IDC outlines the future of smart things (2016)
58. Mena, D.M., Papapanagiotou, I., Yang, B.: Internet of things: survey on security. Inf. Secur. J.: A Global Perspect. **27**(3), 162–182 (2018)
59. Westin, F.A.: Privacy and freedom atheneum. N. Y. **7**, 431–453 (1967)

Training and Serving Machine Learning Models at Scale

Luciano Baresi and Giovanni Quattrocchi[✉]

Dipartimento di Elettronica, Informazione e Bioingegneria, Politecnico di Milano,
Milan, Italy
{luciano.baresi,giovanni.quattrocchi}@polimi.it

Abstract. In recent years, Web services are becoming more and more intelligent (e.g., in understanding user preferences) thanks to the integration of components that rely on Machine Learning (ML). Before users can interact (inference phase) with an ML-based service (ML-Service), the underlying ML model must learn (training phase) from existing data, a process that requires long-lasting batch computations. The management of these two, diverse phases is complex and meeting time and quality requirements can hardly be done with manual approaches.

This paper highlights some of the major issues in managing ML-services in both training and inference modes and presents some initial solutions that are able to meet set requirements with minimum user inputs. A preliminary evaluation demonstrates that our solutions allow these systems to become more efficient and predictable with respect to their response time and accuracy.

Keywords: Machine learning · Runtime management · Service orchestration

1 Introduction

In recent years, Web services have been enriched with components based on Machine Learning (ML) that allow for new types of interactions (e.g., vocal assistants, chatbots), more customized experiences (e.g., recommender systems), and novel features (e.g., object detection in images, smart auto-completion) [13]. ML-based services (ML-Services) exploit models that, created in a preliminary *training* phase, are then used at runtime to provide required results as predictions on new inputs (*inference* phase) [21].

The training phase is a long-lasting —from several minutes to days— batch computation. Given the inputs of this phase are usually large datasets (e.g., thousands of images), the computation is executed by using dedicated frameworks (e.g., Spark [33], TensorFlow [1]) that run on a highly distributed cluster of virtual or physical machines. The inference phase exploits the generated model in an interactive way and each computation (e.g., a prediction based on a single image as input) lasts a significantly shorter amount of time compared to training (e.g., milliseconds or seconds).

© The Author(s), under exclusive license to Springer Nature Switzerland AG 2022
J. Troya et al. (Eds.): ICSOC 2022, LNCS 13740, pp. 669–683, 2022.
https://doi.org/10.1007/978-3-031-20984-0_48

The quality of these "new" web services is not only stated in terms of constraints on provided performance. For example, traditional Service Level Agreements (SLA) or Service Level Objectives (SLO) [25] usually constrain the maximum allowed response time. An ML-service must also be accurate. It is not a matter of functional correctness (and performance) anymore; an ML-service must offer predictions with a given accuracy and precision [15].

In the training phase, requirements on the response time are specified as *deadlines* [11], which is the maximum allowed time to complete a single training process. In the inference phase, the response time of multiple requests (e.g., the ones received in the last 10 min) is aggregated and constrained by a threshold [17]. In the training phase, requirements on quality can be easily defined through thresholds (e.g., the accuracy should be greater than 90%) since this metric can be measured during the computation using a validation or a testing dataset [28]. However, in inference mode, the quality of the predictions cannot be easily computed since, by definition, the correct output is unknown (if it were not, there would not have been any need for the ML model). Thus, different "indirect" metrics can be considered to estimate the quality of predictions at runtime [29].

The management of ML-services is thus a complex task since multiple interdependent factors affect their overall performance. For example, the response time is affected, among other aspects, by resource allocation. ML computations can be executed on CPUs, but also on dedicated hardware (e.g., GPUs) given their highly parallelizable programming model. However, increasing the computational power is not useful if the data or the model itself are not properly partitioned to allow for a sufficient degree of parallelism. Model quality depends on a number of factors including the parameters of the learning algorithm (i.e., hyperparameters) and the characteristics of the input dataset. Moreover, response time and quality are often correlated. For example, fewer learning iterations allow for faster results but produce, in general, less accurate models.

Some initial approaches have already been presented to tackle single aspects of ML-service management. For example, Nguyen et al. [23] present a solution to predict the time required to train a model using Spark given a user-defined configuration. Li et al. [20] describe a solution for the automated configuration of hyperparameters, while Morabito et al. [22] propose a solution for the automated resource provisioning of ML models in inference mode. However, there is no solution or study that provides a multi-faceted view of the problem.

This paper describes the main aspects and issues of managing ML-services in both training and inference modes. Based on our work in the field, we also illustrate a set of solutions, along with their evaluation, that we have developed during the last few years and that can be used as a starting point to design a fully integrated solution for the management of ML-based systems.

The rest of this paper is organized as follows. Section 2 presents the most important challenges of ML-services. Section 3 describes our solutions and reports their initial evaluation. Finally, Sect. 4 concludes the paper.

2   ML-service Management

This section highlights the main aspects and issues related to ML-service management. It mainly focuses on time and quality constraints during both training and inference phases.

2.1   Training

Training computations require executing highly iterative algorithms that exploit large datasets as inputs. These datasets contain known input-output pairs that are used to generate models that can predict the correct outputs for new, never-seen inputs (inference).

The structure of the model (e.g., the layers of a neural network) is defined by the users beforehand along with a set of *model parameters* whose optimal values are computed as a result of the training process. To do so, the training phase minimizes a *loss* function that compares the outputs generated by the model under construction and the known answers.

During the optimization process, the model parameters are updated multiple times. The execution is organized in *batches*. A batch is the amount of data (i.e., the number of input-output pairs) that is used to update the model parameters. An *epoch* is the amount of batches required to process the whole dataset. Each training process executes multiple epochs, up until a certain model quality or a timeout are reached.

Available Frameworks.   Given that these computations are resource-demanding and require processing large amounts of data that cannot easily fit on a single machine, the training phase of ML models is usually executed through special purpose frameworks that allow for highly distributed and parallelized executions.

The reference programming model for batch computations is *map-reduce* [7], popularized by Google and the Hadoop framework [19]. The computation is organized in two phases: map and reduce. In the former, the input dataset (e.g., a set of user posts) is split into a set of partitions that are processed in parallel by multiple executors that transform each partition into a new set of data (e.g., a list of words occurrences). The latter aggregates the transformed data and produces a result (e.g., the top ten words used by users in their posts) that is usually written into a database or disk.

DAG-based frameworks, such as Spark, are an evolution of this programming model and they allow one to create *direct acyclic graphs* (DAGs) of data transformations and aggregations (not only a sequence of map-reduce computations). As in map-reduce, multiple executors process single partitions of data in parallel. These computations are organized in stages, that is, the execution of a set of operations that do not require data transmission among executors. When a stage is concluded, each executor sends the results of its local computation to another executor (data shuffling), and a new stage (the next in the DAG) is scheduled for execution. In these frameworks, computations and data transfers are executed in-memory without requiring to store intermediate results on (slower) external storage systems.

The aforementioned approaches are general-purpose and not specifically designed for ML training. In recent years, new frameworks, such as Tensor-Flow [1] and PyTorch [24], have been developed as highly optimized frameworks for ML training. They introduce a programming model called *all-reduce* where the executors work on a single batch in parallel with the others. The computed results are then aggregated (*reduce*) and the model update is transmitted to all the other executors (*all*) so that they can use it as a starting point for the next batch. This way, all-reduce allows for the efficient propagation of the results of an aggregation to all the available executors (broadcast), whereas in DAG-based computations a single executor only communicates with another one and broadcast communication is less efficient and more difficult to implement.

All these frameworks do not provide explicit means to set time or quality requirements. Therefore, users must rely on manual solutions and they have to use experience and "guess" the proper configuration that meets expected thresholds.

> Available frameworks provide different programming models. All of them organize the computation in phases (e.g., one phase for each epoch or each batch) to orchestrate multiple distributed executors that work in parallel. None of these frameworks allows one to specify quality and time constrains on carried out activities.

Hyperparameters. While parameters usually refer to the variables optimized during the training process (model parameters), hyperparameters are the variables used to configure the training algorithm beforehand. These parameters deeply affect both the quality of the output and the time required to complete the training process.

The architecture of the model employed for training can be seen as a hyperparameter. In general terms, the more sophisticated the architecture is, the more time is needed to train the model. In terms of accuracy, complex architectures may be able to learn more patterns and subtleties from the data but they may fail in generalizing to new inputs (by assuming that the subtle patterns found in the input dataset characterize any inputs).

Any configuration parameter of the training algorithm is a hyperparameter. For example, the batch size regulates the frequency of updates. Frequent model updates may generate more accurate models but also increase the required synchronization among the executors (e.g., higher response times). The number of epochs regulates the amount of iterations on the entire dataset. The more epochs one can afford, the more optimized model parameters will be. This produces high-quality models at the cost of longer executions.

> Hyperparameters are defined at design time and they impact the quality of the model and the execution time of the training phase. They must be carefully tuned to train the model efficiently and precisely.

Parallelism. To allow multiple executors to cooperate in training models, one can adopt two main strategies to maximize the degree of parallelism of the computations [12]: *data parallelism* and *model parallelism.*

Data parallelism allows one to split the input dataset onto multiple executors, which store a full copy of the model each. This way, the executors can work in parallel on different partitions and the results of the local computations are aggregated in a subsequent phase. This technique is valuable when the input dataset exceeds the memory (and/or storage) of a single executor and allows us to speed up the computation by increasing the number of executors (up to the number of batches). This strategy is available in most of the existing frameworks and it is the easiest to implement.

Model parallelism partitions the model architecture into different parts that are independently stored onto different executors. This strategy is used when the model itself exceeds the capacity of the executor. Moreover, the model architecture may allow for an "intrinsic" parallelism so that some of the model parameters can be optimized in parallel with others. In this case, it is very important to understand the best way to partition the model given the executors available. Recent studies show that model parallelism may also slightly decrease model accuracy [6].

Data and model parallelism can be combined so that both the model and data are partitioned into multiple parts. Each model partition is then replicated onto multiple executors so that they can optimize a subset of model parameters on independent partitions of data.

Data and model parallelisms allow for highly distributed computations. By partitioning datasets and/or models one can accelerate the computation at the cost of more synchronization among executors.

Resource Allocation. To speed up (or slow down) the training phase and meet set deadlines, users can tune the amount of resources allocated to the system. The computations to train ML models are mostly based on matrix operations that can be highly parallelized. For this reason, GPUs and dedicated hardware devices (e.g., TPUs [14]) can be exploited to further accelerate the processing. Resource allocation can be handled at both design time (before training) and runtime (during training).

At design time the number of executors and the resources allocated to them must be configured by considering set requirements, the hyperparameters (e.g., number of epochs), and the characteristics of the input dataset. More sophisticated approaches allow for dynamic resource allocation (e.g., as in Spark[1]. This means that the amount of executors and their resource allocation can be reconfigured over time according to the state of the computation. For example, when the set deadline is approaching, the system may spawn a new executor or increase the amount of computational power allocated to an existing one. Similarly, one can realize that the computation could require more iterations than

---

[1] https://spark.apache.org/docs/latest/job-scheduling.html.

expected to reach a set model quality and more resources could help finish the training process in time.

Memory is also extremely important since slow read/write on the disk can quickly become the bottleneck. The memory allocation of each executor should be adequate to fit both data and model (partitions). Unlike computational power, which can be increased to speed up the processing up to the maximum degree of parallelism, memory is either sufficient or insufficient.

> Resource allocation is key to fulfill time-based requirements. Resource allocation can be tuned at either design time or runtime and executors may be equipped with heterogeneous hardware.

2.2 Inference

Once training activities have generated a model, it is deployed and used to compute predictions on new inputs. These computations are interactive and they are much faster than training: users can submit requests and get a response in the order of seconds or milliseconds.

Unlike training where requirements are defined for the complete process (deadline), during inference, they constrain a set of requests received by the system during a given time window. Requirements can be both related to time (e.g., the 95th percentile of the response time should be less than one second) or to quality.

Available Frameworks. While map-reduce and DAG-based frameworks were designed to host batch computations only, ML frameworks provide some tools to serve models in inference mode. For example, TensorFlow provides *TensorFlow serving*[2], a tool that eases the deployment of models onto web servers to let them be invoked by using a REST API.

When the incoming workload cannot be handled by a single executor, multiple replicas of the same model must be used concurrently (*distributed inference*). Ideally, a framework should allow one to submit requests to a unified API that forwards them to available replicas. Frameworks should also support multiple models running in parallel on a shared infrastructure, since a single ML-service may exploit multiple ML-based components. Unfortunately, in the available frameworks, the support for distributed inference is, at the time of writing, very limited. Moreover, none of the frameworks support time or quality requirements, and users must handle them with external or manual solutions.

> ML frameworks allow one to use models in inference mode but the means to deploy and manage them are limited. Existing frameworks lack support for the specification of quality and time requirements.

---

[2] https://www.tensorflow.org/tfx/guide/serving.

Resource Allocation. In inference, resource allocation is key to be able to keep the ML-service always responsive. Static resource allocation makes only sense when the workload is constant, a scenario that is usually not realistic. When the incoming workload fluctuates, resources must be dynamically provisioned to handle the traffic. Executors can be replicated or reconfigured through CPUs, GPUs, or dedicated hardware allocations.

When a new request is submitted, it must be processed by an available executor. The selection of this executor may be decided according to multiple factors, including the equipped hardware and the amount of requests that it is already handling (queue length). If an ML-based component is close to violating a requirement (e.g., the response time is increasing), faster executors must be selected (e.g., ones equipped with GPUs). If the ML-service is stable, one can leave faster executors to other components.

Memory must be large enough to contain the model, whereas input data are usually much smaller (e.g., a single image) than the ones used in training and they are usually not difficult to handle. If the model is too large to fit onto a single executor, model partitioning can be used to further split the computation.

> Dynamic resource allocation allows for keeping ML-service always responsive when the incoming workload fluctuates. At runtime, requests must be scheduled to proper executors according to their hardware capabilities and the state of the system.

Monitoring. Monitoring the quality of the model in inference mode is a complex task since evaluating predictions on new inputs would require knowing the correct outputs (ground truth).

Since quality cannot be directly computed, alternative metrics must be taken into account. *Uncertainty* is a widespread metric used in the literature to estimate the quality of a trained models [16]. Intuitively, when the uncertainty in predictions is high, it is more likely to produce incorrect outputs. For example, one can use a set of similar ML models (e.g., DeepEnsemble [18]) to compute multiple predictions for each input. If the outputs are similar (low variance), the outputs are probably correct. If the outputs are different (high variance), the uncertainty is high and the prediction quality may have dropped.

In this context, users may set a requirement on the maximum allowed uncertainty and when this threshold is violated, the ML model must be re-trained. This may require the manual collection of a new training dataset or the generation of a new one automatically (e.g., using data augmentation [26]).

> The quality of ML models at runtime cannot be directly monitored for the lack of ground truth. Uncertainty can help estimate the quality of the model and understand when it must be re-trained.

3   What We Have Done so Far

This section describes three solutions we developed for managing some aspects of ML-services: *dynaSpark*, *hyperFL*, and *ROMA*. *dynaSpark* extends Spark by allowing one to associate time requirements with batch computations, and by means of a sophisticated dynamic resource allocation mechanism. *hyperFL* extends Tensorflow and it is also dedicated to the training phase. It exploits heuristics to set hyperparameters values so that quality constraints are met. Finally, *ROMA* is dedicated to the inference phase. It also extends TensorFlow and allows one to set response time requirements that are met through the allocation of both CPUs and GPUs.

3.1   *dynaSpark*

dynaSpark [2,3] extends Spark by introducing advanced and automated resource management. *dynaSpark* allows users to define deadlines that are considered as the desired response time for a single batch execution (e.g., a training process). The goal of *dynaSpark* is to control the resources allocated to the computation so that its execution time is as close as possible to the user-defined deadline. The rationale behind it is that the closer the response time is to the deadline the more efficient the usage of resources is: finishing before the deadline would mean allocating more resources than needed, while terminating afterward implies violating the deadline because of too scarce resource allocation. Moreover, *dynaSpark* can manage multiple Spark computations at the same time (e.g., the training phase of different ML models that run concurrently) and keep their execution time under control.

dynaSpark requires a profiling phase to retrieve the DAG of the computation and performance data of each stage. During the execution, *dynaSpark* exploits dynamic vertical scalability of resources. This means that the resources allocated to executors is continuously reconfigured without the need for restarting them or creating new ones. The framework wraps executors in lightweight containers (e.g., Docker[3]) and control-theoretical planners are used to compute resource allocation in a fast and fine-grained fashion.

dynaSpark exploits a hierarchical control loop. At the top of the hierarchy, a *memory controller* is in charge of dynamically resizing the amount of memory allocated to each running executor. This controller distributes available memory fairly to all running computations and it is only activated when the user submits a new computation or when one finishes. When a new stage of a computation starts, a *stage controller* exploits the deadline submitted by the user and the profiling data retrieved beforehand. As a result, this controller computes a local deadline for the stage along with the number of executors needed to fulfill it. Each executor in *dynaSpark* is equipped with an *executor level controller* based on control theory in charge of keeping the execution time as close as possible to the deadline computed for the stage. By exploiting a feedback loop, it monitors

---

[3] https://docker.com.

the progress of the stage (i.e., how many data samples are processed over the total assigned ones) and allocates processing power (i.e., fractions of CPUs) accordingly. Multiple executors work in parallel on a single stage to fulfill the same local deadline, and data are fairly partitioned among them. This way, the controllers can operate without synchronization and independently from one another.

Since multiple executors can be run on the same node, *dynaSpark* exploits a *node level controller* to manage resource contention. This controller collects all the resource allocations computed by the executor level controllers that are running on the same node. If their sum exceeds the capacity of the node, allocations are scaled down according to different strategies such as Earliest Deadline First [31] (EDF) or proportionally.

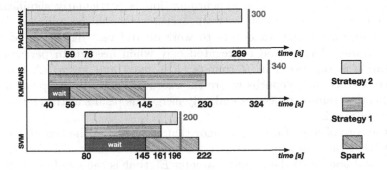

Fig. 1. Concurrent computations in *dynaSpark*.

Evaluation. The evaluation of *dynaSpark* was executed on Microsoft Azure using a cluster of 5 *Standard_D14_v2* virtual machines (VMs) equipped with 16 CPUs, 112 GB of memory, and 800 GB of local SSD storage. Here we only report a single significant experiment that clearly demonstrates the benefits of *dynaSpark*, while [3] comprises a larger and comprehensive set of experiments.

For this experiment, we compared Spark and *dynaSpark*. Spark was configured to use its default allocation mechanism that allocates all the resources to the first computation it receives (FIFO). *dynaSpark* was configured with both a resource contention strategy based on EDF (*Strategy 1*) and a proportional one (*Strategy 2*). The first strategy aims to avoid violations and it is more conservative. The second one tends to let the different application progress simultaneously at a similar pace to minimize resources but with more risk of violating the deadlines.

We executed three well-known ML algorithms in parallel: *PageRank*, *KMeans* and *SVM*. As shown in Fig. 1 we submitted for execution *PageRank* first at instant 0 with a deadline of 300 s, then *KMeans* at instant 40 with a deadline of 300 s and, finally, *SVM* at instant 80 with deadline 120 s. Results show that Spark violated the deadline of SVM while the executions of PageRank and KMeans finished way before expected. This inefficient behavior is caused by the limited resource allocation mechanism built in Spark, its simple FIFO-based strategy for managing resource contention, and the lack of support for deadlines.

In contrast, *dynaSpark* did not violate the deadlines both with *Strategy 1* and *2*. The former always finished significantly ahead of the time given its conservative policy (more resources are allocated). *Strategy 2* resulted, in this case, in a highly efficient resource usage since the three computations were completed just a few seconds before their respective deadlines.

3.2   *hyperFL*

hyperFL [4] is an extension of TensorFlow to allow a set of federated nodes (i.e., Federated ML [32]) to cooperatively train an ML model under quality constraints. Since executors are geographically distributed (e.g., running on a set of edge nodes), the cost of synchronization is particularly significant and the amount of communication between executors should be minimal. For this reason, *hyperFL* assumes executors to work on different datasets and models that are trained locally and aggregated only when needed. In particular, the computation is organized in R rounds (R is fixed and given). A round is a sequence of consecutive epochs where the executors perform independently and in parallel the training processes and only merge the results at the end (similarly to stages in Spark).

At the core of *hyperFL* lays an algorithm, executed at the beginning of each round r, that takes as input a constraint on model accuracy (AC) (e.g., $AC > AC_{SLA}$) and computes the hyperparameter E^r that is the number of epochs to be processed on each executor during r to obtained the desired quality at the end of R rounds.

The algorithm exploits two alternative heuristics: linear and quadratic interpolation, and works in a black-box way since it does not require any prior information om the model: it only exploits monitored data (e.g., the accuracy of the model after each round). To be properly initialized the algorithm needs two rounds in which the computation is executed using a fixed configuration. As a first step, *hyperFL* computes the accuracy to be reached at the end of round r (AC^r). To do so it assumes either a linear progress towards AC_{SLA} from round 0 to R, or a smoother quadratic one. In the second step, *hyperFL* computes E^r as a function of AC^r, the cumulative sums of the epochs computed in rounds $r-1$ and $r-2$, and the accuracy obtained at the same previous rounds.

Evaluation. We evaluated *hyperFL* on a bare-metal single-user server equipped with an AMD Ryzen 5 2600 @ 3.40 GHz (6 Cores/12 Threads) CPU and 32 GB DDR4 @3200 MHz of RAM running Ubuntu 19.10. We used two real-world ML-services: *MNIST* [8] and *Fashion-MNIST* [30]. The former takes as input an image with a handwritten digit and outputs the corresponding number. The latter receives a gray-scale image of a fashion item and outputs the corresponding class (e.g., t-shirt, bag).

Table 1. *hyperFL* results.

	MNIST				Fashion-MNIST			
	Linear		Quadratic		Linear		Quadratic	
r	E^r	AC^r	E^r	AC^r	E^r	AC^r	E^r	AC^r
1	1	0.25	1	0.16	1	0.22	1	0.14
2	1	0.30	1	0.19	1	0.30	1	0.32
3	1	0.36	7	0.51	1	0.38	1	0.42
4	1	0.39	1	0.54	1	0.45	1	0.46
5	2	0.47	3	0.62	1	0.51	2	0.53
6	2	0.52	3	0.68	1	0.57	2	0.58
7	4	0.58	3	0.73	1	0.60	3	0.62
8	6	0.67	4	0.75	1	0.62	4	0.65
9	8	0.75	11	0.79	4	0.67	6	0.67
10	4	0.77	1	0.80	2	0.68	11	0.71

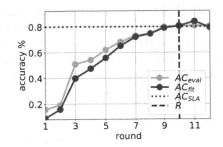

Fig. 2. *hyperFL* accuracy with MNIST.

In the sample of the experiments reported here, we set for *MNIST* $R = 10$ and $AC_{SLA} = 0.80$, while $R = 10$ and $AC_{SLA} = 0.70$ for *Fashion-MNIST*. Table 1 shows the computed epoch E^r along with the obtained accuracy AC^r for each round r for both the services and *hyperFL* interpolation algorithms. *hyperFL* with linear interpolation obtained a steady increment of the accuracy with only one epoch computed for rounds 1–4 (*MNIST*) and 1–8 (*Fashion-MNIST*). As final results in both the services, *hyperFL* with linear interpolation terminated the training with an accuracy that is very close to the threshold but slightly lower.

In contrast, *hyperFL* with quadratic interpolation was able in both cases to reach the target AC_{SLA} by computing higher values of E^r in the first rounds. This can be better visualized in Fig. 2 that reports the result of the experiments with *MNIST* and quadratic interpolation. The chart shows both the accuracy computed on the validation set (AC_{fit}) and the one on the testing set (AC_{eval}). AC_{SLA} was reached exactly at round R, with a peak increment of epochs (11) at round 9. This larger value of E^r corresponds to a small increment in the accuracy (0.01) and shows that a quadratic curve better captures the intrinsically asymptotic behavior of the accuracy compared to a linear approximation.

3.3   *ROMA*

ROMA [5] is a comprehensive resource management solution for ML models in inference mode. In particular, it facilitates the deployment and operations of multiple interactive ML services on shared infrastructures. It extends TensorFlow (and TensorFlow serving) by allowing users to set requirements on the response time. Unlike TensorFlow, *ROMA* provides means for distributed inference and efficiently allocates CPU and GPU resources by considering the state of all served ML-services.

ROMA features a master-slave architecture. The master allows users to submit requests to deployed models and schedules them on the executors that are running on the slaves. Each slave is assumed to be equipped with at least one CPU and zero or more GPUs. The framework wraps each executor in a container, and multiple replicas of the same model can be deployed when the workload increases. We also exploit Kubernetes[4] to orchestrate and configure containers. The master comprises a *gateway* that store requests—received through a REST API—in a dedicated queue (one per ML-service). Two schedulers based on heuristics remove requests from the queues and assign them for execution on a selected executor. A scheduler is dedicated to GPU executions and, as soon a GPU is idle, it extracts a request from the queue of the ML-service that is more likely to violate the set response time. The other scheduler submits requests in a round-robin fashion to available CPUs.

Each slave can host multiple executors that are controlled by control-theoretical planners. As in *dynaSpark*, these controllers vertically scale the CPU resources of each container/executor according to the needs of the ML-service. To avoid unpredictable behaviors, control-theoretical planners are aware of GPU executions that can rapidly decrease the response time of the ML-service under control. A supervisor on each slave is in charge of collecting all computed allocations and resizing them if they exceed the capacity of the node.

ROMA expects executors to be created manually or automatically using external solutions (e.g. Horizontal Pod Autoscaler[5]) and only manages existing resources. Each executor/container is bound to a specific hardware device. In particular, given m ML-services to be deployed onto a slave node, *ROMA* provisions i) m executors containing one model each, and binds them to the CPUs of the node, and ii) one executor, containing all the models, for each GPU.

Evaluation. To evaluate *ROMA*, we used a cluster of three VMs on Microsoft Azure: one VM of type $HB60rs$ with a CPU with 60 cores and 240 GB of memory for the *master*, and two VMs, as *slave* nodes, of type $NV6$ equipped with an NVIDIA Tesla $M60$ GPU and a CPU with 6 cores and 56 GB of memory. We also used an additional $HB60rs$ VM to generate the workloads. We exploited four existing ML-services: *Skyline Extraction* [9], *ResNet* [10], *GoogLeNet* [27], and *VGG16* [34]. The first service uses computer-vision algorithms to extract the skyline horizon from an input image. The other services perform classification task: *ResNet* uses a residual neural network, while *GoogLeNet* and *VGG16* exploit two deep convolutional neural networks.

In the experiments, we run different combinations of these services in parallel under different workloads and we compared the performance of *ROMA* against competitors based on rules or heuristics. The results show that, overall, *ROMA* reduces by 75% on average the number of violations while decreasing by 24% the resources used.

---

[4] https://kubernetes.io.

[5] https://kubernetes.io/docs/tasks/run-application/horizontal-pod-autoscale/.

Figure 3 shows the most complex experiment we run when all the services are executed in parallel in our cluster. In particular, Fig. 3a shows the performance obtained by our framework, while Fig. 3b depicts the results obtained by a competitor. *ROMA* was able to keep the response time of all the ML-services under the set SLAs (maximum response time equal to 0.4 s) thanks to its efficient usage of GPUs and vertical scaling of CPUs. The competitor solution frequently violated the SLAs of services *VGG16* and *ResNet* with a maximum response time of 1.9 s and an average resource allocation that is slightly higher compared to the one consumed by *ROMA*.

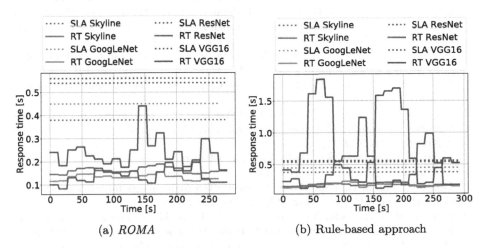

(a) *ROMA*   (b) Rule-based approach

Fig. 3. *ROMA*: performance and comparison.

4   Conclusions

The management of web services that use ML to provide intelligent features poses new complex challenges. ML-services require a training phase (batch) to generate a model that can be used in inference mode to compute predictions on new inputs (interactive). Time and quality requirements are needed to obtain predictable performance and accurate predictions.

This paper describes a set of critical aspects that characterize the management of ML-services in both the training and inference phases. As a base for a future, integrated framework that can handle all these aspects simultaneously, we also describe some initial partial solutions that we developed recently. A preliminary evaluation of them shows the benefits of our approaches that can efficiently and automatically fulfill identified requirements.

Acknowledgments. This work has been partially supported by the SISMA (MIUR, PRIN 2017, Contract 201752ENYB) and EMELIOT (MUR, PRIN 2020, Contract 2020W3A5FY) national research projects.

References

1. Abadi, M., et al.: TensorFlow: a system for large-scale machine learning. In: Proceedings of the Symposium on Operating Systems Design and Implementation, pp. 265–283. USENIX (2016)
2. Baresi, L., Denaro, G., Quattrocchi, G.: Symbolic execution-driven extraction of the parallel execution plans of spark applications. In: Proceedings of the Joint Meeting on European Software Engineering Conference and Symposium on the Foundations of Software Engineering, pp. 246–256. ACM (2019)
3. Baresi, L., Leva, A., Quattrocchi, G.: Fine-grained dynamic resource allocation for big-data applications. IEEE Trans. Software Eng. **47**(8), 1668–1682 (2021)
4. Baresi, L., Quattrocchi, G., Rasi, N.: Federated machine learning as a self-adaptive problem. In: Proceedings of the International Symposium on Software Engineering for Adaptive and Self-Managing Systems, pp. 41–47 (2021)
5. Baresi, L., Quattrocchi, G., Rasi, N.: Resource management for TensorFlow inference. In: Hacid, H., Kao, O., Mecella, M., Moha, N., Paik, H. (eds.) ICSOC 2021. LNCS, vol. 13121, pp. 238–253. Springer, Cham (2021). https://doi.org/10.1007/978-3-030-91431-8_15
6. Chen, C.-C., Yang, C.-L., Cheng, H.-Y.: Efficient and robust parallel DNN training through model parallelism on multi-GPU platform. arXiv preprint arXiv:1809.02839 (2018)
7. Dean, J., Ghemawat, S.: MapReduce: simplified data processing on large clusters. Commun. ACM **51**(1), 107–113 (2008)
8. Deng, L.: The MNIST database of handwritten digit images for machine learning research. Signal Process. Mag. **29**(6), 141–142 (2012)
9. Fedorov, R., Camerada, A., Fraternali, P., Tagliasacchi, M.: Estimating snow cover from publicly available images. IEEE Trans. Multimedia **18**(6), 1187–1200 (2016)
10. He, K., Zhang, X., Ren, S., Sun, J.: Deep residual learning for image recognition. In: Proceedings of the IEEE Conference on Computer Vision and Pattern Recognition, pp. 770–778. IEEE (2016)
11. Islam, M.T., Srirama, S.N., Karunasekera, S., Buyya, R.: Cost-efficient dynamic scheduling of big data applications in apache spark on cloud. J. Syst. Softw. **162**, 110515 (2020)
12. Jia, Z., Zaharia, M., Aiken, A.: Beyond data and model parallelism for deep neural networks. Proc. Mach. Learn. Syst. **1**, 1–13 (2019)
13. Jordan, M.I., Mitchell, T.M.: Machine learning: trends, perspectives, and prospects. Science **349**(6245), 255–260 (2015)
14. Jouppi, N.P., Young, C., Patil, N., Patterson, D.: A domain-specific architecture for deep neural networks. Commun. ACM **61**(9), 50–59 (2018)
15. Juba, B., Le, H.S.: Precision-recall versus accuracy and the role of large data sets. In: Proceedings of the AAAI Conference on Artificial Intelligence, vol. 33, pp. 4039–4048 (2019)
16. Dipu Kabir, H.M., Khosravi, A., Hosen, M.A., Nahavandi, S.: Neural network-based uncertainty quantification: a survey of methodologies and applications. IEEE Access **6**, 36218–36234 (2018)
17. Labidi, T., Mtibaa, A., Gaaloul, W., Tata, S., Gargouri, F.: Cloud SLA modeling and monitoring. In: Proceedings of the International Conference on Services Computing, pp. 338–345. IEEE (2017)

18. Lakshminarayanan, B., Pritzel, A., Blundell, C.: Simple and scalable predictive uncertainty estimation using deep ensembles. In: Advances in Neural Information Processing Systems. Annual Conference on Neural Information Processing Systems, vol. 30, pp. 6402–6413 (2017)

19. Lam, C.: Hadoop in Action. Simon and Schuster (2010)

20. Li, L., et al.: A system for massively parallel hyperparameter tuning. Proc. Mach. Learn. Syst. **2**, 230–246 (2020)

21. Mohri, M., Rostamizadeh, A., Talwalkar, A.. Foundations of Machine Learning. MIT Press (2018)

22. Morabito, R., Chiang, M.: Discover, provision, and orchestration of machine learning inference services in heterogeneous edge. In: 41st International Conference on Distributed Computing Systems, pp. 1116–1119. IEEE (2021)

23. Nguyen, N., Khan, M.M.H., Wang, K.: Towards automatic tuning of apache spark configuration. In: IEEE International Conference on Cloud Computing, pp. 417–425 (2018)

24. Paszke, A., et al.: Pytorch: an imperative style, high-performance deep learning library. In: Advances in Neural Information Processing Systems, Annual Conference on Neural Information Processing Systems, vol. 32, pp. 8024–8035 (2019)

25. Sahai, A., Durante, A., Machiraju, V.: Towards Automated SLA Management for Web Services. Hewlett-Packard Research Report HPL-2001-310 (R. 1) (2002)

26. Shorten, C., Khoshgoftaar, T.M.: A survey on image data augmentation for deep learning. J. Big Data **6**(1), 1–48 (2019)

27. Szegedy, C., et al.: Going deeper with convolutions. In: Proceedings of the International Conference on Computer Vision and Pattern Recognition, pp. 1–9 (2015)

28. Vabalas, A., Gowen, E., Poliakoff, E., Casson, A.J.: Machine learning algorithm validation with a limited sample size. PloS ONE **14**(11), e0224365 (2019)

29. Weiss, M., Tonella, P.: Uncertainty-wizard: fast and user-friendly neural network uncertainty quantification. In: Proceedings of the International Conference on Software Testing, Verification and Validation, pp. 436–441. IEEE (2021)

30. Xiao, H., Rasul, K., Vollgraf, R.: Fashion-MNIST: a novel image dataset for benchmarking machine learning algorithms. arXiv preprint arXiv:1708.07747 (2017)

31. Jia Xu and David Lorge Parnas: Scheduling processes with release times, deadlines, precedence and exclusion relations. IEEE Trans. Softw. Eng. **16**(3), 360–369 (1990)

32. Yang, Q., Liu, Y., Chen, T., Tong, Y.: Federated machine learning: concept and applications. ACM Trans. Intell. Syst. Technol. **10**(2), 1–19 (2019)

33. Zaharia, M., et al.: Spark: cluster computing with working sets. In: Proceedings of the International Conference on Hot Topics in Cloud Computing. USENIX (2010)

34. Zhang, X., Zou, J., He, K., Sun, J.: Accelerating very deep convolutional networks for classification and detection. IEEE Trans. Pattern Anal. Mach. Intell. **38**(10), 1943–1955 (2015)

Author Index